Prepublication praise for MANAGING GLOBAL CHAOS

The end of the Cold War has brought a major gain for world peace, but has also brought into focus new challenges to security throughout the world as societies and regions adapt to rapid change. Our policy-makers are having to think in new ways: about the environment, about religious and ethnic tensions, about migration, population, and access to resources, about new technologies and global communications, as well as about traditional sources of conflict at the governmental level. This has brought new players onto the stage, as diplomats are joined by nongovernmental bodies in the search for better ways to prevent, manage, or diffuse conflict. I welcome this study by the United States Institute of Peace as an impressive and important contribution to this crucial debate.

—*Malcolm Rifkind*
British foreign secretary

The sweep, insight, and ideas presented in this important book make for genuinely rewarding reading: informative, provocative, stimulating, thoughtful.

—*George Shultz*
former U.S. secretary of state

This thoughtful collection of essays makes an important contribution toward understanding and identifying approaches to the prevention, management, and solution of present-day conflicts. A positive development in recent years is the growing attention being given to the "security of people" in addition to the "security of states." The book pays considerable attention to humanitarian intervention and the needs of the twenty-six million people of concern to my office. Despite the apparent chaos in some parts of the world, experience has demonstrated that long-standing refugee problems can be solved, as in Cambodia, Mozambique, and Namibia. I welcome the support for humanitarian action to deal with the consequences of conflict. But what is needed most is political action.

—*Sadako Ogata*
UN High Commissioner for Refugees

This collection distills into clear, accessible readings most of the social-science findings that bear on the resolution of today's ethnic and civil conflicts. Especially comprehensive in its treatment of conflict prevention and management, this volume is a unique resource for classroom use and a timely handbook for thoughtful practitioners in the front lines of the struggle against global chaos.

—*Jack Snyder*
Columbia University

The Institute of Peace has done well in presenting a rich diversity of analyses, of actors, processes, and entry points into the turbulence of the international system. While "realism" and "idealism" alternate in the analyses, the butterfly-wings metaphor that opens the book leaves room for the longer-term vision—that wiser policy choices at every level of human interaction may lead us past ages of warfare to more temperate ways of dealing with human diversity.

—*Elise Boulding*
International Peace Research Association

The C  ict is not. The Institute of Peace lives up to its name by illu-
mina   and the broad range of options that lie between doing noth-
ing a

—*Joseph Nye*
Harvard University

MANAGING GLOBAL CHAOS

CHAOS

SOURCES OF AND RESPONSES TO INTERNATIONAL CONFLICT

edited by **Chester A. Crocker** & **Fen Osler Hampson** with **Pamela Aall**

**United States
Institute of Peace Press**
Washington, D.C.

United States Institute of Peace
1550 M Street NW, Suite 700
Washington, DC 20005-1708

First published 1996
Second printing 1997
Third printing 1998

Printed in the United States of America

The paper used in this publication meets the minimum requirements of American National Standard for Information Sciences—Permanence of Paper for Printed Library Materials, ANSI Z39.48-1984.

For information on prior publication of several chapters in this book, see "Credits," p. 641.

Library of Congress Cataloging-in-Publication Data
Managing global chaos : sources of and responses to international conflict / edited by Chester A. Crocker and Fen Osler Hampson with Pamela Aall.
     p.   cm.
    Includes bibliographical references.
    ISBN 1-878379-59-3 (hard : alk. paper). — ISBN 1-878379-58-5 (pbk. : alk. paper)
    1. Pacific settlement of international disputes. 2. Peace. 3. Security, International. 4. Intervention (International law). 5. Conflict management. 6. World politics—1989– I. Crocker, Chester A. II. Hampson, Fen Osler. III. Aall, Pamela R.
    JX4473.M35 1996
    341.5—dc20   96-31858
                                             CIP

Contents

Foreword

RICHARD H. SOLOMON

Constructing a road to peace has been an "engineering" challenge for centuries of policymakers and scholars alike, and the literature is alive with appropriate images: charting paths, using stepping-stones, laying foundations, paving the way, building bridges. Even negotiations have been characterized by the transportation metaphor, with "track one" referring to the official public process and "track two" to the nonofficial, private one. These images capture the dynamic nature of the exercise as well as the understanding that each stage in the process is connected to the stages that both precede and follow. Constructing a road to peace is therefore not simply a matter of agreeing to a cease-fire and separating military forces, although such steps may be necessary elements of the process. It is also a matter of identifying the sources of conflict, developing a system of early warning about deteriorating conditions that might lead to conflict, and motivating the right people to act on the warnings. It is the challenge of encouraging antagonists to desist from laying land mines and begin creating ground rules

for negotiation. It is also a matter of establishing and nurturing, once peace is achieved, those elements of reconciliation and reconstruction—political, social, cultural, legal, and economic—that allow peace to take root and flourish.

In 1994, the Institute of Peace embarked on a major project to gather some of the best material that had been produced under its auspices on topics of conflict management and peacemaking. The effort was motivated, in part, by uncertainty about the conceptual groundwork and direction of U.S. foreign policy following the collapse of the Soviet Union and the end of the Cold War, with its well-established policy guidelines of containment and deterrence. The project also drew inspiration from the Institute's December 1994 conference, "Managing Chaos," which sought to develop new perspectives on the challenges of dealing with the ethno-religious strife and humanitarian crises that have come to characterize the post–Cold War world.[1]

Originally intended to bring together Institute authors, the project eventually expanded to include contributions from other authors whose expertise provided essential insights into the sources of conflict and approaches to conflict management or resolution. The resulting volume, *Managing Global Chaos: Sources of and Responses to International Conflict,* is comprehensive in its reach. Its many chapters look at both interstate and intrastate sources of conflict, and illustrate not only the wide range of choices available to peacemakers but how these choices are related.

The breadth and depth of this book reflect the Institute's mission of strengthening the nation's capacity to promote the peaceful resolution of international conflict. The Institute pursues this mission by sponsoring policy-relevant research through grants and fellowships, bringing fresh perspectives to bear on complicated problems through working groups and symposia, and disseminating the results to policymakers, practitioners, academics, and more general audiences through conferences, publications, and other public programs. A key and distinguishing feature of the Institute is its Education and Training Program, designed to transmit directly to educators and practitioners the best that the Institute has to offer in the way of insights, analysis, and practical skills for understanding, managing, and resolving conflict.

This book, along with a companion volume, *Peacemaking in International Conflict: Methods and Techniques,* edited by Bill Zartman and Lewis Rasmussen, is the latest addition to the Institute's efforts to fulfill its educational mandate. An earlier volume, *Approaches to Peace: An Intellectual Map,* edited by Scott Thompson and Kenneth Jensen with Richard Smith and Kimber Schraub, charted the different conceptual traditions concerning the pursuit of peace. *Managing Global Chaos* takes a different tack. By combining scholarly and practical perspectives, it allows readers to draw their own conclusions about which peacemaking efforts work under which circumstances, and what other elements are necessary to promote the chances of an enduring settlement to a given conflict.

Facilitating a back-and-forth exchange between scholar and practitioner is one of the Institute's most valuable contributions to meeting the obligations mandated by its congressional charter. The press of policymaking and implementing programs allows those in positions of official responsibility too little time for absorbing and drawing lessons from experience. Scholars, whose training and circumstance give them the time and analytical skills needed to extract these lessons, rarely have the occasion to work under the unforgiving deadlines and imperfect access to information that characterize the policymaking world. *Managing Global Chaos* bridges the gap between these two worlds, and as a result, gives students both inside and outside of government the analytical perspectives and insights needed to map and build many roads to peace.[2]

A project of this scope and magnitude required determined effort by many individuals—above all, of course, the editors of this volume. The Institute is indeed fortunate to have had three experienced and dedicated individuals who shepherded this book from its gestation to its birth. Board chairman Chet Crocker, former peace fellow Fen Hampson, and Deputy Director of Education and Training Pamela Aall brought very different perspectives to the project, based on their varied experiences in the policymaking, academic, nongovernmental, and international educational worlds. The resulting book has profited immensely from that diversity and the interaction of their different professional experiences.

The volume editors were aided by an informal advisory committee of eminent scholars and policymakers: Hans Binnendijk,

National Defense University; Herschelle Challenor, Clark Atlanta University; Louis Goodman, American University; Louis Kriesberg, Syracuse University; Christopher Maule, Carleton University; Barry Posen, Massachusetts Institute of Technology; Robert Rubinstein, Syracuse University; Paul Schroeder, University of Illinois; and Gregory Treverton, RAND Corporation. A number of contributors to the volume also served on the advisory committee, including Eliot Cohen, Alexander George, James Goodby, Richard Haass, Herbert Kelman, Geoffrey Kemp, Samuel Lewis, David Little, Michael Lund, Denis McLean, Janice Gross Stein, and Astri Suhrke, as did several Institute staff members, including Harriet Hentges, Joseph Klaits, and David Smock. Particular recognition is due to Frederick Williams, who served as the research assistant for this project, and to the publication department's Joan Engelhardt, Kay Hechler, and especially Dan Snodderly, whose hard work and commitment to quality are reflected in every page of this book. The Institute is indebted to this creative collaboration of colleagues for the timely production of a volume that I believe substantially advances our education and training mission.

NOTES

1. For an overview of the "Managing Chaos" conference, see the February 1995 issue of the Institute's newsletter, *Peace Watch*. For highlights from the conference, see *Keynote Addresses by Les Aspin and Ted Koppel* (Peaceworks No. 3), *Sources of Conflict: G. M. Tamás and Samuel Huntington on "Identity and Conflict,"* and *Robert Kaplan and Jessica Tuchman Mathews on "'The Coming Anarchy' and the Nation-State under Siege"* (Peaceworks No. 4), and *NGOs and Conflict Management* by Pamela R. Aall (Peaceworks No. 5, reprinted here as chapter 29), all published by the United States Institute of Peace.

2. See Alexander George's important work on this issue, *Bridging the Gap: Theory and Practice in Foreign Policy* (United States Institute of Peace Press, 1993).

Introduction

CHESTER A. CROCKER AND FEN OSLER HAMPSON WITH PAMELA AALL

The idea that chaos can be managed may sound like a contradiction in terms. A chaotic situation is, after all, one that defies any attempt to impose order or define rules of behavior. To describe contemporary international relations as chaotic may suggest that we view the world as hopelessly intractable. That is not our intention. The term is used here as a metaphor for what modern physics calls "chaos"—a world in which seemingly small, local events can provoke systemwide disruptions.

Modern communications technology and the media have indeed turned the world into the global village described by the late Marshall McLuhan. It is increasingly difficult for the public and politicians to ignore events taking place halfway around the globe, whether it is refugees suffering in Rwanda, millions starving in Somalia, a bomb exploding in the marketplace in Sarajevo, or a political leader being gunned down after a peace rally in the Middle East. In chaos theory, a tiny butterfly flapping its wings in Beijing can set forces in motion that can blow thunderstorms into Washington and New York. In contemporary international politics, it seems that the simple act of placing images of starving children on the television screen can rouse presidents to send thousands of troops in a massive humanitarian relief mission to some far-off land. When people talk about the "CNN effect," they are, in fact, referring to the magnifying impact of television on politics and the political hurricanes that may be set in motion when the television camera is turned on.

The butterfly effect is not confined to modern communications. The metaphor also applies to the international repercussions of communal or intrastate conflicts, which increasingly display a capacity to spill across borders through arms transfers, refugees, and the spread of disease. The repercussions can even be felt globally: Ethnic conflict in Chechnya, Georgia, or Azerbaijan, for example, can become a matter of global concern, particularly if Russia decides to intervene. Worsening economic and social conditions in a small Caribbean country like Haiti have consequences that go well beyond that small country's shores, particularly if fleeing refugees end up in the United States or other Caribbean nations. If a radical religious group decides to publicize its grievances by placing a bomb in the basement of a large, downtown office complex in a major city, innocent people get hurt and what was hitherto a "domestic" problem suddenly escalates into a major international one.

Another facet of chaos is complexity. Chaos theory tries to understand complexity and the interactions that lie behind the movement of complex biological and physical systems. That is, it tries to make sense of seemingly random and sometimes catastrophic events. In international politics today, we are increasingly confronted by similar kinds of complexity. That does not mean that the world cannot be understood. But it does mean that traditional concepts like sovereignty and the "nation-state" have developed new layers of meaning. Traditional concepts, like balance of power or ideology, are also not as useful as they once were in explaining the sources of international conflict, particularly when conflicts are rooted in a complex and rich brew of ethnonationalism, religion, socioeconomic grievances, environmental degradation, collapsed states, globalized markets, and geopolitical shifts.

WHY A BOOK ON MANAGING CHAOS?

This book explores the chaotic complexity of international politics in the aftermath of the Cold War. It examines both abiding and changing sources of international conflict, as well as the increasingly intricate patterns of interactions among the different sources and actors. But we have not stopped the inquiry at this point. Too often in the social sciences, description and analysis are not followed up by discussion of practical implications and policy choices. There is, of course, a place for detailed historical analysis of a given case, such as the Balkan conflict. But teachers, research scholars, policymakers, relief workers, and other nongovernmental practitioners also need to address ways to resolve present conflicts or prevent future conflicts from erupting. We entitled this book *Managing Global Chaos* because it discusses what should be done to prevent, manage, defuse, contain, settle, and resolve violent conflicts, whether they occur at the interstate or intrastate level.

That is a tall order. A book of such scope springs from many sources. From its earliest days in 1985, the United States Institute of Peace has supported work engaging both scholars and practitioners in analyzing the many facets of violent international conflict and its management. This reflects the Institute's core mission as stated in its founding congressional mandate: to "advance the history, science, art, and practice of international peace and the resolution of conflicts among nations without the use of violence." As an independent, publicly funded federal institution, the Institute has worked to integrate the theoretical and the practical. It has used its unique convening power and close linkages to the worlds of both research and action to test important conceptual conclusions against actual experience and to broaden the perspective of both those who conduct research and those who negotiate and practice peacemaking.

This substantial accumulation of Institute work provides much of the bedrock of this volume. The contributors—political scientists, historians, psychologists, lawyers, economists, sociologists, journalists, security and peace studies specialists, and practitioners from governmental and nongovernmental sectors—represent some of the very best minds in conflict analysis and resolution and related fields of inquiry. Much of this work has been sponsored or directly supported by the Institute of Peace. Inspired by an earlier Institute volume, *Approaches to Peace*, edited by Scott Thompson and Kenneth Jensen with Richard Smith and Kimber Schraub, which helped define the intellectual map for the peacemaker in 1988, this book is a fresh, "state-of-the-art" assessment of the field, as well as a capstone of the Institute's recent work. We have tried to be as inclusive as possible in the range of topics and disciplinary perspectives covered by the volume, but obviously there are important topics and perspectives that could not be contained in the pages of a single volume in this burgeoning field.

From its beginnings, the United States Institute of Peace has used its programs of education and training to explore the most effective ways to teach about conflict, security, and peace issues. Its growing outreach to the teaching community, especially through its summer faculty seminar program, has underscored the need for a comprehensive and contemporary collection of readings on the sources of and potential responses to global conflict. As teachers in this field ourselves, we know firsthand about the time and effort devoted to gathering material for course readers, which is matched only by the inconvenience and expense to students in obtaining a state-of-the-art collection of readings.

Another source of the theme for this volume is the Institute's extensive experience in training and in relating to various types of practitioners: military officers in peace operations, staff members of humanitarian nongovernmental organizations, official negotiators or mediators, and nonofficial religious and lay groups engaged in making or building dialogue in polarized communal or interstate conflicts. This body of continuing experience led the Institute to organize a highly successful, three-day conference entitled "Managing Chaos" to mark its tenth anniversary in December 1994. Some of those discussions are also reflected in these pages.

In addition, to help the editors in their efforts to make this a unique and comprehensive volume, the Institute brought together an advisory committee of eminent scholars and policymakers to discuss the overall structure and themes of the book, as well as its specific contents; the book has benefited greatly from their counsel.

As editors, we have also designed this volume to reflect our personal conviction about the need to remain engaged in a complex and seemingly chaotic world. It is unsettling to hear from fellow educators about a turning away from the study of international issues. The disappearance of Cold War certainties has stunned students, the general public, and political leaders alike, as they are asked to comprehend the new complexity. Ethnic cleansing in Bosnia, internecine slaughter in Cambodia, and religious warfare in Sudan all appear both intolerable and intractable. If it becomes conventional wisdom that there is nothing to be done about such scenarios (by the U.S. government, the United Nations, or the international community), students and the public may turn away from the subject. That would accelerate and compound the chaos, producing its own sets of butterfly wings affecting the choices of leaders in lands great and small.

This volume hopes to underscore that the real choices in many cases (perhaps most cases) are not between doing nothing or sending in combat forces. Who should intervene, where, and why are among the thorniest issues facing policymakers and attentive electorates. Seeking answers to the question of *how* they should intervene helps to untangle the thicket as it becomes clear that many choices exist in the search to diminish both interstate and intrastate violence. Possible strategies include a range of responses from early warning of impending crisis by humanitarian groups, through collective regional attempts to mediate a conflict, to concerted international actions to make a peace settlement hold. Strategies may also involve many actors from private individuals and groups to international organizations. Returning to the metaphor of chaos, small actions and events can have major system-wide consequences. Just as there are many instances when the combined weight of several governments and international organizations is necessary to bring about peace, there are also various critical points at which intervention by individuals, either as private citizens or as policymakers and practitioners, can make a difference.

That there are many strategies available to meet the challenge of conflict does not mean that the choices are easy. Sometimes the alternative strategies are all unpalatable to various degrees, and often the choices are very hard. Through the thoughtful analysis of lessons learned from cases such as Nagorno-Karabakh and El Salvador, this book attempts to clarify not only what the choices are but also what makes them effective.

STRUCTURE OF THIS VOLUME

This volume is divided into four sections. The first section of the volume, the sources of conflict in a changing world, looks at those factors that are of increasing importance in international conflict processes. The second section addresses the "intervention dilemma" and the instruments that are available to bring military power, coercive diplomacy, collective security, peacekeeping, and humanitarian intervention to bear at different stages in the conflict cycle. The third part explores a wide range of other actors and methods for managing, preventing, and resolving conflicts. The fourth part of the book addresses the increasingly important question of how third parties can help to consolidate the peace once warring parties have reached a negotiated settlement.

At the systemic level, it is worth remembering that much international conflict has structural roots. The existence of anarchy—that is, the lack of an overarching political authority—is the main reason violent conflicts occur. However, in the aftermath of the Cold War the concept of international anarchy has special new meaning. First, the collapse of communism and the Soviet Union has created a multiplicity of new states in Europe and Asia, states that are struggling to define their security interests in an unfamiliar and uncertain regional and international environment. What was once a clear border between East and West has become a buffer and a vacuum. Russia's increasingly assertive policies toward its former colonies pose a challenge to the West that we are only now coming to grips with. Traditional security institutions, like the North Atlantic Treaty Organization (NATO), and emerging ones, like the Organization for Security and Cooperation in Europe (OSCE), are having to adapt to the new security challenges that are emerging along the periphery of the former Soviet Union.

International anarchy also has an increasingly important domestic dimension. Declining state authority and capacities for governance in many countries around the world have unleashed many social and political forces, some of which have taken on violent forms of expression. Domestic instability and violence have a pronounced tendency to reverberate regionally, and even internationally, as refugees of communal and interethnic warfare flood across borders into neighboring states and territories.

We are also beginning to recognize that international conflict processes are driven by the seemingly uncontrolled movement of not just peoples, but also ideas, technology, and communications across borders. These are systemic forces operating at the subsystemic level, which nonetheless have the capacity to induce system-wide change.

Religion is one such force. Governments in some countries, together with various religious movements, have used religious and other cultural symbols to confront the West. Whether we are on the verge of what political scientist Samuel P. Huntington has referred to as a new "clash of civilizations" remains to be seen, but there is little doubt that forces like religion and cultural nationalism have achieved new salience in international politics with the end of the Cold War.

How should we view these different factors and forces as they reshape the international landscape? In the first chapter of this book, "Contending Theories of International Conflict," Jack Levy places many of the factors discussed above in a larger theoretical framework. Reviewing the leading theories of international conflict, Levy concludes that there are different causal paths to war and peace. He argues that, in an age when the locus of conflict has shifted to various regions of the globe, conventional "realist" theories of international politics appear increasingly limited, both geographically and theoretically, to previous eras of European-centered great-power struggles. He suggests that societal-level variables are going to be increasingly important in the future, not only in shaping foreign policy, but also in contributing to domestic instability and international tensions. At the same time, resource scarcities and rising expectations brought on by the processes of democratization are likely to increase pressures on domestic political systems and contribute to tensions among neighboring states.

The rest of Part I of this volume explores some of these new sources of conflict in international politics. Whereas chapters 2 and 3 focus on the "structural" sources of international conflict brought on by the collapse of the Soviet Union and state "failure" in many Third World countries, chapters 4 through 6 deal with social and psychological explanations of conflict, including the rela-

tionships between ethnonationalism and conflict, religion and religious militancy, and identity and conflict. Chapters 7 through 10 address the transborder and transnational aspects of conflict, including such factors as population movement and refugees, arms transfers, and the trade and investment dimensions of international conflict.

Part II of this volume is devoted to stimulating a dialogue between scholars and practitioners on the subject of statecraft, intervention, and international order. Aside from the question about whether to intervene, there are related questions of how and when to intervene. The choice of instruments and the timing of an intervention often exercise a profound influence on the success of an intervention; using the wrong instrument at the wrong moment can make a problem worse, not better. The essence of statecraft is not only making strategic choices about intervention that are consistent with the national interest as well as the interests of the international community, but also ensuring that the appropriate instruments are used at the right moment.

In his lead chapter in Part II, Henry Kissinger discusses the new challenges for diplomacy that confront U.S. policymakers with the end of the Cold War. He argues that the international system in the twenty-first century will be marked by two conflicting tendencies: the fragmentation of power, with the rise of regional coalitions and great powers like China and Japan; and the increasing globalization of world politics, with the growing integration of the world economy and the emergence of problems that can only be dealt with on a worldwide basis, like nuclear proliferation, population growth, and environmental degradation. Reconciling competing values and different historical experiences will pose a major challenge for decision makers in the next century, and the United States will find its foreign policy even more constrained than before, because it will not be able to withdraw from the world or to dominate it.

In view of these constraints, it is critical to consider the full range of tools and methods available to U.S. policymakers and other actors for addressing the many different conflict situations they are likely to face well into the next century. These options range from the direct use of force, to diplomatic threats, to preventive diplomacy, to negotiation, mediation, and other instruments that involve governmental and nongovernmental actors. Part II of this volume examines the different forms that intervention can take and also attempts to draw lessons from previous instances of intervention.

In interventions involving the use of force, the United States finds itself in a stronger position than it was in during the Cold War. The risks of escalation have diminished with the collapse of the Soviet Union, the decline of Russia's military capabilities, and the change in Russia's political stance. Technological developments have created a new generation of conventional weaponry that can be used with great accuracy and lethality against adversaries, demonstrated in the Persian Gulf War. The vulnerability of communications systems has grown with recent advances in electronic warfare. However, the potential for effective military intervention diminishes in civil conflict situations, where it is difficult to distinguish friend from foe in congested urban areas, and in environments where terrorist tactics can wreak havoc against outside peacekeeping forces. American public opinion is also wary of interventions that risk large-scale casualties, especially if vital U.S. interests are not are stake.

Chapters 13 through 18 examine the changing uses of military power, coercive diplomacy, and collective security at the end of the Cold War. Together, they illustrate both the continuing importance of military power in settling disputes and the continu-

ing need for the United States to maintain a strong defense capability. At the same time, they point to the constraints—both domestic and international—on the use of the force and the growing need to develop other instruments of intervention that can complement, and sometimes substitute for, direct military intervention.

In chapters 19 through 25, this volume focuses on the broader question of peacekeeping and humanitarian intervention. There is a lively debate in these chapters between those who believe that peacekeeping is in a state of crisis and those who believe that such operations can continue to make a positive contribution to maintaining international order. Because nongovernmental actors are playing an increasingly important role in situations of conflict, we include several chapters that discuss the role of professional groups, media, and nongovernmental organizations in conflict management and resolution.

The general intractability of today's conflicts does not mean that the United States should allow the fires of regional and intrastate wars to continue until they burn themselves out or one side achieves victory. Large-scale humanitarian disasters—as we have witnessed in Rwanda, Afghanistan, and the Horn of Africa—cry out for solutions to alleviate the suffering. Although the U.S. experience in Vietnam demonstrates that military entanglements in national liberation struggles can be enormously costly, the record in other conflicts suggests that intervention can work under the right conditions and the right set of circumstances.

Chapter 12, along with chapters 26 through 35 of Part III, examines the different diplomatic and political instruments that are available to outsiders for preventing, managing, and settling today's conflicts. These chapters discuss a range of options, including preventive diplomacy, engagement, mediation, and second-track diplomacy, showing how these different intervention techniques have been applied in a variety of different circumstances. The discussion is complemented by several historical case studies that explain why certain techniques worked or failed.

The end of the Cold War has witnessed many negotiated settlements to end regional and intercommunal conflicts; the Dayton Accords are just the latest chapter. Many of these settlements were negotiated and implemented with the assistance of outsiders. Part IV of this volume addresses the larger questions of why some peace settlements succeed while others fail, and what outsiders can do to help prevent failure.

A peace agreement is usually defined by a cease-fire, a rigorously defined timetable for deploying (and subsequently withdrawing) international peacekeeping forces, partial demobilization of forces of the warring parties, and a schedule for elections and other political and economic measures. But the agreement may not fully reflect reality on the ground. For example, demobilizing thirteen-year-old soldiers (as in Mozambique) presents challenges that involve educating, relocating, and finding jobs for young men who have no families and who have spent their entire lives in guerrilla camps.

At the psychological level, expectations are high at the beginning of the peace process. People are usually willing to participate in the transition and to take risks that will help carry the peace process forward immediately after a settlement has been signed. However, the window of opportunity for peace can close if the political and military timetables of the agreement are upset by violations that go unpunished, and if the economic, social, and political situation fails to improve. Individuals and groups lose hope and return to the coping patterns of behavior they developed during the conflict.

Chapters 36 through 41 discuss the measures and approaches that are necessary to consolidate the peace so that a political settlement takes root. These activities include preparing for and monitoring elections, demining, demobilizing, resettling refugees, providing humanitarian assistance, reintegrating displaced populations, repairing and restoring key infrastructure (such as transportation and communications), maintaining law and order, restoring human rights and the rule of law, and engaging in economic reconstruction through investments in the national, local, and household economies.

PURPOSE OF THIS VOLUME

This book is aimed at a variety of audiences and constituencies: civilian and military officials of governmental and intergovernmental bodies; staff of nongovernmental organizations in the fields of humanitarian aid, human rights, rule of law, and conflict resolution; personnel of research institutions and policy-oriented think tanks; and students in security studies and conflict and peace studies at the advanced undergraduate and graduate levels. In the interests of accessibility and space, the editors urged contributors to prepare concise and provocative essays rather than definitive research papers. Accordingly, they have generally confined themselves to selective bibliographic references, even though many of the topics considered here could be the subject of book-length bibliographies. We hope that the material presented in the following pages will whet the appetites of current and prospective peacemakers in the United States and other countries and, in a small way, will contribute to the ongoing process of defining the field of post–Cold War security and peace studies.

Contributors

Chester A. Crocker is research professor of diplomacy at the School of Foreign Service, Georgetown University, and chairman of the board of directors of the United States Institute of Peace. From 1981 to 1989, he was assistant secretary of state for African affairs; as such, he was the principal diplomatic architect and mediator in the prolonged negotiations among Angola, Cuba, and South Africa that led to Namibia's transition to democratic governance and independence, and to the withdrawal of Cuban forces from Angola. He was a distinguished fellow at the Institute in 1989–1990. He is the author of *High Noon in Southern Africa: Making Peace in a Rough Neighborhood*, and is an adviser on strategy and negotiation to U.S. and European firms.

Fen Osler Hampson is professor of international affairs and associate director of the Norman Paterson School of International Affairs, Carleton University, Ottawa, Canada. He is the author of *Nurturing Peace: Why Peace Settlements Succeed or Fail* (United States Institute of Peace Press, 1996); *Multilateral Negotiations: Lessons from Arms Control, Trade, and the Environment; Unguided Missiles: How America Buys Its Weapons;* and *Forming Economic Policy: The Case of Energy in Canada and Mexico,* and the editor or co-editor of eleven volumes, including *Earthly Goods: Environmental Change and Social Justice.* Hampson

was a peace fellow at the United States Institute of Peace in 1993–1994.

Pamela Aall is deputy director of the Education and Training Program at the United States Institute of Peace. Prior to joining the Institute, she was a consultant to the President's Committee on the Arts and the Humanities and to the Institute of International Education. She held a number of positions at the Rockefeller Foundation and managed its International Relations Fellowship Program. In addition, she has worked for the European Cultural Foundation and the International Council for Educational Development. Her research has focused on nongovernmental organizations, Scandinavia, and European institutions.

* * *

Mary B. Anderson, a development economist, is president of the Collaborative for Development Action, Cambridge, Mass.

Mohammed Ayoob is professor and chair of international relations at James Madison College, Michigan State University.

Eileen F. Babbitt is director of the Education and Training Program at the United States Institute of Peace. She was an Institute peace scholar in 1989–1990 and a grantee in 1992.

Pauline H. Baker is president of the Fund for Peace and professorial lecturer at the School of Foreign Service, Georgetown University.

Nicole Ball is a fellow at the Overseas Development Council, Washington, D.C.

Richard K. Betts is professor of political science at Columbia University. He was an Institute grantee in 1992.

Richard E. Bissell is a member of the Inspection Panel of the World Bank and research fellow at the School of International Service, American University. He was an Institute grantee in 1993.

Barry M. Blechman is co-founder and chairman of the Henry L. Stimson Center, Washington, D.C.

Eliot A. Cohen is professor of strategic studies at the Paul H. Nitze School of Advanced International Studies, Johns Hopkins University, Washington, D.C.

Raymond Cohen is professor of international relations at the Hebrew University of Jerusalem. He was a fellow at the United States Institute of Peace in 1988–1989 and in 1996.

Tamra Pearson d'Estrée is assistant professor of psychology at the University of Arizona.

Alexander L. George is professor emeritus of international relations at Stanford University. He was a distinguished fellow at the United States Institute of Peace in 1990–1992.

James Goodby is distinguished research professor of international peace and security at Carnegie Mellon University and has served as principal negotiator and special representative of the president for nuclear security and dismantlement during the Clinton administration. He was a distinguished fellow at the United States Institute of Peace in 1992–1993.

Ted Robert Gurr is distinguished university professor at the University of Maryland and director of the Minorities at Risk Project. He was a peace fellow at the United States Institute of Peace in 1988–1989 and an Institute grantee in 1988, 1989, and 1994.

Richard N. Haass is director of the Foreign Studies Program at the Brookings Institution.

Mark N. Katz is associate professor of government and politics at George Mason University. He was a peace fellow at the United States Institute of Peace in 1989–1990 and an Institute grantee in 1994.

Herbert C. Kelman is Richard Clarke Cabot professor of social ethics at Harvard University and director of the Program on International Conflict Analysis and Resolution at Harvard's Center for International Affairs. He was a distinguished fellow at the United States Institute of Peace in 1988–1989 and an Institute grantee in 1987 and 1992.

Geoffrey Kemp is director for regional strategic programs at the Nixon Center for Peace and Freedom, Washington, D.C. He was an Institute grantee in 1988, 1993, and 1994.

Henry Kissinger was U.S. secretary of state from 1973 to 1977 and is currently chairman of Kissinger Associates in New York.

Ted Koppel is anchor and managing editor of *Nightline.*

Neil J. Kritz is senior scholar on the rule of law at the United States Institute of Peace.

Jack S. Levy is professor of political science at Rutgers University.

Samuel W. Lewis was U.S. ambassador to Israel from 1977 to 1985 and president of the United States Institute of Peace from 1987 to 1993.

David Little is senior scholar on religion, ethics, and human rights at the United States Institute of Peace. He was a distinguished fellow at the United States Institute of Peace in 1987-1988.

Michael S. Lund is senior associate at Creative Associates International, Washington, D.C. He was formerly senior scholar at the United States Institute of Peace and before that director of the Institute's fellowship program.

John J. Maresca is an independent consultant in Geneva. He was formerly special U.S. negotiator for Nagorno-Karabakh and before that was U.S. ambassador to the Conference on Security and Cooperation in Europe. He was a guest scholar at the United States Institute of Peace in 1994 and an Institute grantee in 1994.

Denis McLean is Warburg professor in international relations at Simmons College, Boston. He was New Zealand's secretary of defense from 1979 to 1988 and its ambassador to the United States from 1991 to 1994. He was a distinguished fellow at the United States Institute of Peace in 1994–1995.

Theodore H. Moran is Karl F. Landegger professor of international business diplomacy and director of the Pew Economic Freedom Fellows Program, Georgetown University. He was senior adviser for economics for the Policy Planning Staff, U.S. Department of State, in 1993–1994.

Joshua Muravchik is senior fellow at the American Enterprise Institute for Public Policy Research, Washington, D.C. He was an Institute grantee in 1989.

Adam Roberts is Montague Burton professor of international relations at Oxford University and a fellow of Balliol College.

Donald Rothchild is professor of political science at the University of California, Davis. He was a fellow at the United States Institute of Peace in 1994–1995.

Harold H. Saunders is director of international affairs at the Charles F. Kettering Foundation, Washington, D.C. He was formerly assistant secretary of state for Near Eastern and South Asian affairs. He was an Institute grantee in 1986 and 1996.

Caesar Sereseres is professor of political science and associate dean of the School of Social Sciences at the University of California, Irvine. He was an Institute grantee in 1992.

Richard H. Solomon is president of the United States Institute of Peace. He was formerly assistant secretary of state for East Asian and Pacific affairs and U.S. ambassador to the Philippines.

Janice Gross Stein is Harrowston professor of conflict management and negotiation at the University of Toronto. She was an Institute grantee in 1988.

Kenneth W. Stein is professor of Middle Eastern history and political science and director of the Middle East Research Program at Emory University. He was an Institute grantee in 1989.

Warren P. Strobel is White House correspondent at the *Washington Times*. He was a fellow at the United States Institute of Peace in 1994–1995.

Astri Suhrke is senior fellow at the Chr. Michelsen Institute, Bergen, Norway, and resident associate with the International Migration Project, Carnegie Endowment for International Peace, Washington, D.C. She was an Institute grantee in 1995.

Saadia Touval teaches at the Paul H. Nitze School of Advanced International Studies, Johns Hopkins University, Washington, D.C. He was formerly professor of political science and dean of the Faculty of Social Sciences at Tel Aviv University. He was a fellow at the United States Institute of Peace in 1993–1994.

Ruth Wedgwood is professor of law at Yale University Law School and senior fellow and director of the Project on International Organizations and Law at the Council on Foreign Relations.

I. William Zartman is the Jacob Blaustein professor of international organization and conflict resolution and director of the African Studies and Conflict Management programs at the Paul H. Nitze School of Advanced International Studies, Johns Hopkins University, Washington, D.C. He was a visiting fellow at the United States Institute of Peace in 1992–1993 and an Institute grantee in 1988 and 1996.

PART I

THE SOURCES OF CONFLICT IN A CHANGING WORLD

I

Contending Theories of International Conflict

A Levels-of-Analysis Approach

JACK S. LEVY

A glance through the table of contents of this volume reveals how dramatically our perceptions of international conflict have changed since the end of the Cold War. Conventional concerns about the balance of power, alliances, arms races, deterrence, and superpower confrontation have given way to new concerns about ethnonationalism, religious militancy, environmental degradation, resource scarcity, preventive diplomacy, peacekeeping, humanitarian intervention, and small-state conflict. The perception that the end of the Cold War has changed "all the answers and all the questions"[1] goes too far, however, and the theme of change must be tempered by that of continuity. Many of the factors that play a central role in contemporary international conflicts would have been quite familiar to Thucydides over two millennia ago, and many of the "nontraditional" causes of war discussed in this volume exert their influence through causal

paths that occupy a central place in the mainstream conflict literature.

My aim in this essay is to put many of the factors discussed in the individual chapters in this volume into a larger theoretical context, which I organize around a "levels-of-analysis" framework. I select some of the leading theories of international conflict, identify their key variables, specify the causal paths by which they affect decisions for war and peace, highlight some of the key interaction effects among variables at different levels of analysis, and suggest which of these theories are likely to be most useful for understanding global conflict as we enter a new millennium. I include both traditional models of international war and new theories about ethnonationalism, population movements, and environmental change. I aim to provide an overview of contending theories rather than detailed evidence, examples, or analytical critiques. I begin by discussing

3

the levels-of-analysis framework, which I then use to organize a survey of theories of conflict and war.[2]

THE LEVELS-OF-ANALYSIS FRAMEWORK

The levels-of-analysis concept was first systematized by Kenneth Waltz, who suggested that the causes of war can be found at the levels of the individual, the nation-state, and the international system.[3] The individual level focuses primarily on human nature and instinct theories and on individual political leaders and their belief systems, personalities, and psychological processes. The national level includes both governmental variables (such as the structure of the political system and the nature of the policy-making process) and societal factors (such as the structure of the economic system, the role of public opinion, economic and non-economic interest groups, ethnicity and nationalism, and political culture and ideology). Systemic-level causes include the anarchic structure of the international system, the number of major powers in the system, the distribution of military and economic power among them, patterns of military alliances and international trade, and other factors that constitute the external environment common to all states.

Some scholars have modified Waltz's framework by collapsing the individual and nation-state levels to create a simplified dichotomy of nation (or unit) level and system level.[4] Others have created four or five levels by disaggregating the nation-state level into distinct governmental and societal factors, a practice that I follow here.[5] At the systemic level, it is sometimes useful to distinguish among system characteristics common to all states, dyadic relationships between pairs of states, and the external environment of individual states, although these distinctions are often blurred in the literature. There is no single correct number of levels in the real world, for these alternative schemes are simply analytic constructions, which should be evaluated in terms of their usefulness in generating theoretically important and empirically valid hypotheses to help us understand the dynamics of global politics.

Scholars generally use the levels-of-analysis concept as a framework for classifying independent variables that explain state foreign policy behaviors and international outcomes. This framework helps us ask such questions as whether the causes of war are found primarily at the level of the international system, the nation-state, or the individual, and how variables from different levels interact in the foreign policy process. But the levels-of-analysis concept is sometimes used in a different way, to refer not to the independent causal variables but instead to the dependent variable—that is, to the type of entity (individual, organization, state, or system) whose behavior is to be explained.

In this second sense, the systemic level of analysis refers to explanations of patterns and outcomes in the international system, the dyadic level to explanations of the strategic interactions between two states, the national level to explanations of state foreign policy behavior, and the individual level to explanations of the preferences, beliefs, or choices of individuals. In this usage, the statement that democracies go to war less frequently than do other states is a national-level hypothesis, whereas the statement that democracies rarely if ever fight each other is a dyadic-level hypothesis. The frequent failure of scholars to be explicit about exactly how they are using the levels-of-analysis concept is a source of considerable confusion in the field.

It is logically possible, and in fact often desirable, to combine variables from different levels of analysis in causal explanations. Independent variables from one level can be used to explain dependent variables at another level, and variables from several levels can be combined in an explanation of a single dependent variable. Systemic or dyadic-level security threats can shape individual-level foreign policy preferences (in the direction of hard-line policies to deal with those threats, for example) and also national-level structures (toward an increasing concentration of political power in state institutions, for example).

In addition, national- or individual-level variables can be the primary causes of systemic- or dyadic-level outcomes. Domestic political pressures, bureaucratic conflicts and compromises, or the belief systems of individual leaders can be the main causes of some wars. A logically complete explanation of such cases, however, requires the analyst to go beyond the individual level to explain how individual beliefs and preferences get translated into state decisions and actions, and beyond the state level to explain how the actions of two or more states interact to lead to war as a dyadic or systemic outcome. To the extent that most wars generally involve the mutual and interactive decisions of two or more adversaries, an explanation for the outbreak of war logically requires including dyadic- or systemic-level variables.[6]

SYSTEMIC-LEVEL SOURCES OF INTERNATIONAL CONFLICT

The traditional literature on the causes of war has been dominated by the realist paradigm, a broad systemic-level framework that incorporates several distinct theories. Each of these theories assumes that the key actors are sovereign states that act rationally to advance their security, power, and wealth in an anarchic and threatening international system.[7] They also share the core hypothesis that international outcomes are determined by the distribution of power between two or more states, but different conceptions of power and of the nature of the system lead to different theories and different predictions about what those specific outcomes are.

In the realist world view, assumptions of an inherently conflictual world and uncertainties regarding the present and future intentions of the adversary lead political leaders to focus on short-term security needs and on their relative position in the system, to adopt worst-case thinking, to engage in a struggle for power, and to use coercive threats to advance their interests, influence the adversary, and maintain their reputations. Wars occur not only because some states prefer war to peace; they also occur because of the unintended consequences of actions by those states that prefer peace to war and that are more interested in minimizing their losses than in maximizing their gains, but that are willing to take considerable risks to avoid losses.[8] Even defensively motivated efforts by states to provide for their own security through armaments, alliances, and deterrent threats are often perceived as threatening by others (the "security dilemma"), which leads to counteractions and conflict spirals that become difficult to reverse.[9]

The leading realist theory is balance of power theory, which posits the avoidance of hegemony as the primary goal of states and the maintenance of an equilibrium of power in the system as the primary instrumental goal. The theory predicts that states, in particular great powers, will balance against those who constitute the primary threats to their interests and particularly against any state that threatens to secure a hegemonic position. Balance of power theorists argue that the balancing mechanism almost always works successfully to avoid hegemony, either because potential hegemons are deterred by their anticipation of a military coalition against them or because they are defeated in war after deterrence fails. There is a division and unresolved debate between "classical realists," who argue that stability (defined as the absence of a major war) is further supported by the presence of a "balancer" state, the absence of permanent alliances or a polarized alliance system, and especially by a multipolar distribution of power; and "neorealists," who argue that bipolarity is more stable than multipolarity.[10] Balance of power politics often generates a "checkerboard" pattern of alliances, based on the old realpolitik idea that "the enemy of my enemy is my friend."[11]

An important alternative to balance of power theory is "power transition theory," a form of hegemonic theory that shares realist assumptions but that emphasizes the existence of order within a nominally anarchic system.[12] Hegemons commonly arise and use their strength to create a set of political and economic structures and norms of behavior that enhance the stability of the system at the same time that these structures and norms advance the security of the hegemon. Differential rates of growth lead to the rise and fall of hegemons, however, and the probability of a major war is greatest at the point when the declining leader is being overtaken by the rising challenger. Either the challenger initiates a war to bring its benefits from the system into line with its rising military power or the declining leader initiates a "preventive war" to block the rising challenger while the chance is still available.[13] Hegemonic theory includes the dyadic-level "power preponderance" hypothesis, widely confirmed in the empirical literature: War is least likely when one state has a preponderance of power over another and most likely when there is an equality of power.[14]

An interesting combination of balance of power and power transition theories is "hierarchical equilibrium theory," in which peace is most likely under conditions of equality of power between two major blocs, but with hierarchical dominance within each bloc by a hegemon.[15] Hegemonic theories and hierarchical equilibrium theory each suggest that the erosion or collapse of hierarchical authority within an empire or bloc system will increase the probability of violent conflict between political entities or communal groups in that system, especially if they have a tradition of rivalry. In fact, the very exercise of imperial authority may contribute to postimperial conflicts among its constituent units. Imperial authorities going back to Caesar have exploited divisions or historic rivalries among weaker units within the empire in order to facilitate their own imperial control, and these rivalries can escalate to war once the imperial power is no longer able or willing to control such conflicts.[16]

Another theory in which national growth is an important variable is Choucri and North's "lateral pressure theory." Growing population and advancing technology generate increasing demands for resources that cannot be satisfied by the state's domestic resource endowments or by existing levels of foreign trade. These demands generate "lateral pressure" for access to external raw materials and markets and often for political control through colonial expansion to guarantee such access. Expansions by several states intersect, leading to pressures for states to defend their expanding interests through increased military expenditures and alliances, reciprocal actions by adversaries, conflict spirals, and an increasing probability of war.[17] Although lateral pressure theory has not received as much attention as balance of power theory or power transition theory, its emphasis on population pressures and resource scarcities increases its relevance for the contemporary era.

One variable that affects each of these theories is military technology, particularly the presence or absence of nuclear weapons. The development of nuclear weapons, intercontinental delivery systems, and invulnerable retaliatory forces was a major stabilizing factor during the Cold War because it substantially raised the expected costs of war for all states, the stronger as well as the weaker, the initiator as well as the target. By facilitating direct "countervalue" strikes against enemy populations independent of the military outcome on the battlefield, the new technology allowed both weak and strong nuclear powers to inflict unacceptable damage against the other. As Charles De Gaulle noted, after a nuclear war both sides would have "neither powers, nor laws, nor cities, nor cultures, nor cradles, nor tombs."[18]

This prospect of "mutual assured destruction" made it virtually inconceivable that any state could conclude that it would be better off after an all-out nuclear war than before, blurred the distinction between winners and losers, and strongly reinforced deterrence. In addition, although misperceptions in the form of military overconfidence have driven many wars in the past by erroneously convincing political leaders that war would bring military victory with tolerable costs, the certainty of destruction associated with nuclear weapons leaves little room for such misperceptions on the part of the nuclear powers in the contemporary era.[19] As U.S. President Reagan and USSR General Secretary Gorbachev affirmed, "A nuclear war cannot be won and must never be fought."[20]

Balance of power hypotheses about balancing against primary security threats, power transition hypotheses about the consequences of uneven growth, and lateral pressure hypotheses about resource demands and intersecting interests were developed with the great powers (and the European experience) in mind, but they can be applied to other states in regional systems as well. This must be done cautiously, however, for the central realist assumption of anarchy is not fully satisfied in regional systems, where—unlike great power systems—outside powers can play a significant role. Consequently,

some key propositions of certain realist theories need to be modified for regional systems, which are nested within the larger global system and which are significantly influenced by the distribution of power and influence in that broader system.[21]

The impact of systemic structures on state behavior is not always obvious, however, for those structures may exert their influence by establishing "permissive conditions" for certain types of behavior as well as by creating the conditions that more directly encourage behavior.[22] Many analyses of the 1990–1991 Persian Gulf War, for example, neglect the causal impact of the end of the Cold War and the collapse of bipolarity, which created conditions that facilitated the American and allied responses. Had the Iraqi invasion of Kuwait occurred a few years earlier, the risk of Soviet intervention on behalf of its Iraqi ally would have made it much less likely that an Arab coalition would have formed against Iraq or that the United States would have risked military intervention.

Although it is likely that conflicts involving economic interests, religion, and ethnic identity will play an increasingly important role in world politics now that the Cold War is over, hypotheses about the effects of these variables usually assume American global dominance and the absence of serious military threats to the leading powers in the system. A change in the current distribution of power in the system (the rise of China or the resurgence of Russia, for example) would give rise to a rather different set of political dynamics on the global and regional level. Any analysis of the possible impact of ethnonationalism, international migrations, and environmental change must acknowledge the larger systemic structures within which these variables influence governmental policies and external responses.

Another systemic-level theory, one that derives from a liberal rather than realist paradigm and that also includes a substantial domestic component, is the liberal economic theory of war. The basic argument, which goes back to Smith and Ricardo, is that free trade within an international market economy is the best guarantor of peace. A number of theoretical arguments are advanced to support this proposition. One is the idea that trade promotes prosperity, following the law of comparative advantage, and that prosperity promotes peace, in part because "people are too busy growing rich to have time for war."[23] Tariffs, quotas, and any other restrictions on the natural operation of market mechanisms have the opposite effect.

A related argument emphasizes the intervening role of interdependence rather than prosperity: Because trade increases interdependence and creates mutual vulnerabilities to any interference with free trade, the fear of the loss of the welfare gains from trade deters political leaders from initiating militarized conflict.[24] This assumes, of course, that trade is more efficient than military coercion in promoting state wealth. As the foundations of wealth and power have shifted from territory to industrialization and now to knowledge-based forms of production, the value of territorial conquest has diminished, at least for the advanced industrial states. At the same time, the costs of territorial conquest have increased, with growing cultural self-assertiveness and nationalist opposition to political control, the incompatibility of political control with the liberal foundations of postindustrial economic innovation and productivity, the growth of antiwar attitudes in the West, the increasingly powerful military capabilities of many medium-size states, and the development of nuclear weapons. Liberals conclude, therefore, that trade is economically efficient and that it promotes peace among the advanced industrial states in the contemporary era.[25]

Realists and economic nationalists, on the other hand, argue that because trade and interdependence are usually asymmetrical

they frequently promote war. One trading partner may be tempted to engage in economic coercion to exploit the adversary's vulnerabilities and influence its behavior relating to security as well as economic issues, which can lead to retaliatory actions, conflict spirals, and war. These tendencies are reinforced by demands for protectionist pressures from domestic economic groups that are especially vulnerable to external developments, particularly in bad economic times. Whether the incentives for the gains from trade dominate the incentives for coercion or protection based on economic asymmetries, and whether the latter escalate to trade wars and militarized conflicts, is an empirical question that analysts have only recently begun to analyze systematically, and the results are rather inconclusive.[26]

These economic relationships are likely to become increasingly important sources of international conflicts in the future, particularly for developing states that face serious economic scarcities, but also for the advanced industrial states. As military security threats to these states have diminished significantly with the end of the Cold War, economic competition among them has become more and more salient, particularly as some states have come to define economic primacy as a vital national interest.[27]

It is conceivable that economic rivalries, fueled by parochial domestic interests and by hard-line publics sympathetic to the appeals of economic nationalism, could escalate into strategic rivalries and then possibly into crises or military confrontations. Although the militarization of commercial rivalries was an important path to war between great powers in earlier times, particularly in the seventeenth century, this pattern is much less likely to repeat itself in the future, at least among the leading industrial states. The increasing destructiveness of military technology has weakened the link between economic strength and military power, and the decline of mercantilist economic philosophies and the growth of complex interdependence further undermine the traditional belief that military force might be a useful instrument of state policy to advance the economic interests of society. Still, contemporary economic rivalries are sufficiently intense and the consequences of their possible militarization sufficiently profound that this issue remains a vital area for future research.[28]

The sources of state behavior and international patterns in balance of power theory, power transition theory, lateral pressure theory, and liberal economic theories of trade and war are found primarily at the system level, although domestic demographic and economic variables clearly shape the differential rates of national growth that determine the distribution of power in the system, and liberal theories do recognize the domestic factors that affect the terms of trade between states, the ideologies that help shape state interests, and parochial domestic interests that constrain state behavior. With the exception of some die-hard realists, however, scholars have increasingly recognized that systemic structures fail to explain a significant amount of the variance in the outbreak or expansion of international conflict. This conclusion has led to increasing challenges to realism and other systemic-level theories from theoretical perspectives linked to the societal, bureaucratic-organizational, and individual levels. The argument is not only that these other levels of analysis will become increasingly important in the future, but also that their influence on international behavior in the past has been seriously underestimated.

SOCIETAL-LEVEL SOURCES OF INTERNATIONAL CONFLICT

There has been an enormous surge of research on domestic sources of international conflict after decades of neglect by political scientists, although at this point we have collections of hypotheses rather than well-developed and integrated theories. While interest in Marxist-Leninist theories has waned, scholars have given enormous attention to the relationship between democracy and war and to the ways in which political leaders resort to external military force as a means of bolstering their domestic political support. In addition, many of the newly emphasized causes of war—including ethnonationalism, environmental scarcity and degradation, and population movements—either fit into the societal level of analysis or include that level as a major step in the hypothesized causal chain leading to war.[29]

Marxist-Leninist theory focuses on the domestic economic structure of capitalist societies and posits that the inequitable distribution of wealth generates underconsumption, inadequate domestic investment, and stagnant economies. This leads to expansionist and imperialist foreign policies to secure external markets for surplus products, external investment opportunities for surplus capital, outlets for surplus population, and access to raw materials at stable prices, each of which can result in colonial wars and an escalation in the conflict between capitalist states.[30] Capitalist states also require high military spending to stabilize and stimulate the economy, and this can lead to arms races, conflict spirals, and war.[31]

There have been numerous critiques of the logical consistency and empirical validity of the Marxist-Leninist theory of foreign policy and imperialism, and these have led to alternative theories based on the interests of great powers (regardless of economic system) or of parochial military elites.[32] One common criticism focuses on economic determinism and the absence of political variables to explain the linkages between underlying social and economic conditions and the state policies that result. One theory of imperial expansion that better integrates political and economic variables is Snyder's model of coalition formation and strategic mythmaking.[33]

Snyder observes that states often expand beyond the point at which their imperial interests can be supported by available resources. He rejects attempts to explain this in terms of the interests of a single class or elite and focuses instead on a coalition of elites, each of which prefers a different form of limited expansion, military buildup, or economic autarky. These groups create logrolled coalitions that secure power at the cost of a more expansionist foreign policy than is desired by any single group or that can be supported by available resources. The coalitions reinforce their positions of power and rationalize their policies by propagating self-serving strategic myths that masquerade as lessons of history. These dynamics of overexpansion are most likely to arise in cartelized political systems and least likely to occur in democratic systems, where diffuse interests and the absence of information monopolies work against strategic mythmaking. Snyder applies his model to the great powers in the industrial era (the coalition of iron and rye in Germany in the late nineteenth century, for example). The theory can also be applied to other states in other contexts, however, and it continues to be quite relevant for the future.

Individuals and groups support expansionist policies both because it is in their parochial interests to do so and because of the "rally 'round the flag" effect created by symbolic politics and the images of the enemy fostered by political leaders. Under some conditions this tempts political leaders to undertake risky foreign ventures in an attempt to distract attention from domestic problems and bolster their political support. This is the age-old "scapegoat hypothesis" or "diversionary theory of war." Four centuries

ago, for example, Bodin argued that "the best way of preserving a state, and guaranteeing it against sedition, rebellion, and civil war is to...find an enemy against whom [the subjects] can make common cause."[34] This hypothesis is theoretically grounded in social identity theory and the in-group/out-group hypothesis, which suggests that conflict with an out-group increases the cohesion of a well-defined in-group.

Although the diversionary theory of war appears to fit a number of historical cases,[35] internal political insecurity does not always lead to external scapegoating, which raises the question of the conditions under which this is most likely to occur. Recent studies have begun to specify theoretical models that link domestic politics and the external use of force and to identify empirically the internal conditions under which the use of force is most likely. Among these conditions are low to moderate levels of domestic political support and legitimacy, poor economic performance, and the perception that a diplomatic or military victory is feasible with minimal costs. Another possible variable is regime type, and some have suggested that because of their electoral accountability, democratic leaders may have greater incentives for scapegoating than do authoritarian leaders. The incentives for scapegoating must be balanced against its potential costs, however, and recent evidence suggests that democratic leaders who initiate wars, particularly losing wars, are thrown out of power much more frequently than are nondemocratic leaders.[36]

In fact, one can fact find many examples of democracies engaging in the diversionary use of force against other states. What we do not find, however, is external scapegoating by one democracy against another democracy that escalates to war. A striking finding of recent research, consistent with Kant's "pacific union" among democracies, is that democracies rarely if ever go to war with each other.[37] Elsewhere, I describe this absence of war between democracies as coming "as close as anything we have to an empirical law in international relations."[38] It is contrary to realist theory, which posits that the effect of systemic structures does not vary with regime type and implies that democratic dyads will go to war as often (proportionately) as any other pairs of states.

It is true that democracies occasionally get involved in crises and use limited amounts of force against each other, fight imperial wars, and once in war adopt a crusading spirit and fight particularly destructive wars, as Kant predicted. The evidence suggests that democracies tend to get involved in wars as frequently as do nondemocratic states. But they rarely if ever fight each other, and there are few (if any) unambiguous cases of actual wars between democracies. It has also been demonstrated, at least for the period since 1945, that the absence of war between democracies is not the spurious result of economic or geopolitical factors correlated with democracy.[39]

Scholars have proposed two types of models to explain the dual finding that democracies engage in frequent wars but that they rarely, if ever, fight each other. In the cultural or normative model, the norms of peaceful conflict resolution that have evolved within democratic political cultures are extended to relations between democratic states. In the structural or institutional model, checks and balances, the dispersion of power, and the need for public debate make it more difficult for democratic states to use force against each other. In both models, there are fewer constraints on the use of force by authoritarian regimes, which often attempt to exploit the conciliatory tendencies of democracies. This undermines democratic political leaders' expectations that their peaceful conflict resolution strategies will be reciprocated, reduces their internal constraints on the use of force, and

provides additional incentives for democratic regimes to use force against authoritarian regimes to eliminate their violent tendencies.

The democratic peace has important policy implications, for it suggests that by promoting the development of democracies around the world, the United States can contribute to the elimination of war as well as to the establishment of liberal institutions and political freedom. One recent study questions this prescription, however, arguing that although well-established democratic dyads are peaceful, the process of transition to democracy is a particularly war-prone time for states and that democratizing states occasionally go to war against each other.[40]

Although the empirical validity of this study has been challenged,[41] its theoretical argument is certainly plausible: The democratization process brings new social groups with widely divergent interests into the political process at a time when the state lacks the institutional capacity to integrate conflicting interests and respond to popular demands, which creates enormous social conflict. This is exacerbated if democratization is coupled with the introduction of market forces into nonmarket economies, which leads to popular pressures for state protection against the pain of economic adjustment. Elites competing for mass political support are tempted to make nationalist appeals and engage in external scapegoating in order to bolster their internal support. This scapegoating is particularly appealing to those elites whose interests are threatened by the democratization process and who believe that the symbol of an external enemy might allow political leaders to reverse that process and further centralize political power. Given the intensity of the emotions associated with ethnic loyalties, which are exacerbated by the process of democratization, ethnic rivals make particularly good targets for scapegoating by political elites.[42]

Although scholars began to devote more attention to the sources of ethnonationalism during the 1980s, they said relatively little about its effects on international politics and on its possible linkages to international war in particular. With the explosion of ethnic conflicts after the end of the Cold War, scholars are now beginning to examine how different types of ethnic and communal conflict can lead to intranational and international warfare and the conditions under which each is most likely to occur.[43] In fact, some suggest that the primary sources of conflict in the future will be cultural, rather than ideological or geopolitical, and that a "clash of civilizations" between ethnically and religiously defined peoples will be the primary source of international conflict in the future. Cultural self-awareness is increasing, and conflicts over culturally defined identities are more difficult to resolve through compromise than are conflicts over tangible strategic or economic interests.[44]

Although "ancient hatreds" explanations for ethnonational conflicts—in which the collapse of authoritarian rule in Eastern Europe, the former Soviet Union, and elsewhere removed the "lid" on ancient rivalries and allowed peoples to attempt to settle long-suppressed grievances—are still popular among journalists, many scholars have been skeptical. The "ancient hatreds" hypothesis fails to explain why violent ethnic conflicts have broken out among some ethnic communities but not others, when those violent conflicts occur, and how intensely they are fought.[45] Concern has now shifted toward identifying the conditions that explain the variation in the incidence and the intensity of ethnic conflict.[46]

Ethnonational communities, like states in the world system, are driven by concerns for security against physical and economic threats in an anarchic world.[47] As Snyder argues, nationalism reflects the desire of a group to create a state capable of dealing with such threats, so that nationalism is most likely to arise when state structures have weakened or collapsed entirely, as in the case of Eastern Europe and the former Soviet Union.[48] A number of other factors also affect the security of various national groups and therefore the intensity of nationalism and the likelihood of ethnic conflict.

One factor is ethnic demography and geography. The greater the congruence between state territorial borders and communal boundaries, the fewer the number of stateless nations seeking statehood, the greater the legitimacy of existing states, and the lower the likelihood of ethnic conflict. This is facilitated by large, compact ethnic groupings, for the larger the size of an ethnic community, the greater its security against outside threats. Dense ethnic intermingling creates potentially unstable multi-ethnic states and leaves many ethnic minorities outside of the boundaries of their nation-states. This increases the likelihood of secessionist wars by captive nations seeking to withdraw from the territory of a larger state and create their own state, and of irredentist wars by ethnic groups in one state seeking to retrieve ethnically kindred people and their territory from another state.[49]

The likelihood of the internationalization and expansion of wars of secession and national unification increases if they threaten to alter the balance of power at the regional or global level. This creates incentives for external states to intervene to ensure the further weakening of a potential enemy, block the further disintegration of an important ally, or exploit the window of opportunity to make gains while its enemy is divided. Thus systemic- and societal-level variables can combine to make ethnonational conflict particularly destabilizing for the international system.

In addition to these structural considerations, political leaders may deliberately provoke nationalist fervor. They may invoke the symbols of the nation and engage in ethnic-bashing scapegoating because it facilitates the mobilization of mass armies, adds to the military power of the state, and helps to justify the economic sacrifices necessary to support costly defense efforts.[50] Or, they may be more concerned with domestic challenges to their leadership positions and gamble that scapegoating will help rally the public and bolster their domestic support.[51]

In either case, ethnic scapegoating and the use of self-glorifying and other-depreciating myths further intensify nationalist passions. Chauvinist mythmaking is fueled further by past legacies of suffering at the hands of others, because memories of past genocides, murders, and population expulsions acquire great symbolic value, create incentives for revenge, and block opportunities for conflict resolution.[52] Once political leaders appeal to the symbols of nationalism and use nationalist myths to help sell policies domestically, they can become entrapped by their own rhetoric—entrapped politically by over-selling their policies to the public and creating new domestic coalitions in support of those policies, and entrapped psychologically by coming to internalize the beliefs that they advocate. Once established, enemy images are highly resistant to change, which further undercuts the possibilities of compromise with external adversaries. As Morgenthau notes with respect to the rise of ideologies in the twentieth century: "Compromise, the virtue of the old diplomacy, becomes the treason for the new."[53]

Ethnonational conflict may also contribute to international migration, which has increased significantly since the end of the Cold War and which is now defined by numerous scholars as a possible issue of high politics and source of conflict within and between states.[54] Communal conflicts, violent secessionist movements, and the political and economic oppression from which they derive create incentives for ethnic minorities to migrate in search of security or to join their national homelands. Large-scale population movements may be the deliberate aim of governmental policy as well as the unintended consequence of communal conflict, as demonstrated by the recent history of ethnic cleansing in the Balkans. Governments sometimes adopt forced emigration as a strategy of achieving cultural homogeneity or the dominance of one ethnic community over another, eliminating political dissidents, colonizing areas beyond borders, scapegoating against a prosperous but unpopular ethnic minority, or destabilizing or influencing another state.[55]

There are also economic and environmental sources of international migration. Substantial differentials in income and employment opportunities create economic incentives for people to migrate in search of economic security. In the contemporary era, the collapse of authoritarian regimes has removed some of the political barriers to population movements across borders, and expanding global communication and transportation networks have created new opportunities for international migration. In addition, environmental degradation, droughts, floods, and famines generate large numbers of "environmental refugees."

Population movements can contribute to conflict within and between states through a number of different causal paths.[56] Migration can: (1) put added strain on scarce resources in the host (receiving) country, particularly in large urban areas; (2) change land distribution, economic relations, and the balance of political power among ethnic, religious, or other social groups; (3) undermine state capacity to create markets and other institutions that facilitate adaptation to environmental change; (4) generate a perceived threat to the host country's cultural identity; (5) trigger a social backlash by indigenous people in response to perceived threats to economic security or social identity from migrants; and (6) generally increase communal conflict, political instability, and the likelihood of civil strife.

Migrations may also contribute to international conflict by serving as a focal point for relations between home and host countries. Host countries that cannot easily assimilate the new immigrants or deal with the consequent economic problems and social instability may attempt to influence the home government to stop or slow the flow of refugees or to eliminate the conditions that gave rise to them. If cooperative efforts fail, host countries may resort to coercive threats to achieve these goals, and in the last resort to military intervention to block the flow of refugees. Hard-line actions against the migrants' home country can also serve as a useful scapegoating strategy for political leaders who want to bolster their internal political support. In addition, efforts by home governments to stop unwanted emigrations can contribute to conflict with the host state.[57]

Environmental change is one of several sources of large-scale population movements, but it can also contribute to international conflict through other causal paths; in fact, the implications of environmental change for national security and international conflict have recently attracted considerable attention in the literature. A new neo-Malthusian perspective suggests that rapidly growing and increasingly urbanized populations competing for scarce resources—and the depletion of those resources by land degradation, desertification, deforestation, rising sea levels, and pollution—will generate economic and social problems, environmental refugees, political instability, and serious domestic and international crises.[58] This situation is most likely to arise in developing countries, which generally lack the wealth and institutional capacity to respond to environmental disruptions.[59]

The combination of population growth, uneven resource distribution, and the environmental degradation of scarce resources leads to scarcities that can contribute to violent conflict through a number of different causal paths.[60] The most direct path is through "simple-scarcity" conflicts or "resource wars" between states.[61] This hypothesis is intuitively plausible and is consistent with mercantilist theories of economic power, with Choucri and North's lateral pressure theory, and with Marxist-Leninist theories of imperialism. It also derives empirical support from a number of individual historical cases, including the 1979 "Soccer War" between El Salvador and Honduras, the 1941 Pacific War between Japan and the United States, the 1990–1991 Persian Gulf War, and the seventeenth-century Anglo-Dutch "herring wars," among others.

It is true that a number of factors combine to reduce the likelihood of resource wars in the future.[62] The growing interdependence of the world economy makes it easier for states to satisfy their external needs for resources without political or territorial control over those resources, and changing technology has increased the range of domestic substitutes for key natural resources. Also, as noted before, the strong incur growing military, diplomatic, and domestic political costs if they forcefully expropriate resources from the weak. These factors may be less compelling for nonwestern states that do not share the liberal internationalist view, and far more research is necessary before we can conclude that resource wars are an unlikely path to war in the future.

Although Homer-Dixon may go too far in concluding that the resource war scenario has been relatively rare in the past, he may be correct that the primary impact of environmental scarcity is through its social effects.[63] Scarcity often leads to declining standards of living, increasing perceptions of a zero-sum game among different social groups, and attempts by these groups to pass the costs of economic decline onto others. This can result in increasing class conflict and social discontent, challenges to the legitimacy of the regime, pressures on democratic political institutions and free-market systems, and an increasing probability of civil strife or external scapegoating.

BUREAUCRATIC-ORGANIZATIONAL SOURCES OF INTERNATIONAL CONFLICT

The bureaucratic politics and organizational processes models of foreign policy decision making retain the rationality assumption of realist theory but reject its unitary actor assumption. They assume that different actors in different bureaucratic roles within the executive branch of the government have different interests and different degrees of political power. The policy preferences of each of these actors are often influenced more by the parochial interests of their organization than by the national interests of the state, and foreign policymaking is fundamentally a political process that involves pulling, hauling, and political compromise among these key actors.[64]

Bureaucratic politics and organizational processes can contribute to war through a variety of causal paths. In spite of the popular argument that politically powerful military organizations shift the internal balance of power toward more hawkish policies, most of the evidence suggests that military organizations in most states are generally no more hawkish than their civilian counterparts in decisions for war but are more hawkish with respect to the escalation of war.[65] The real impact of the military on decisions for war is likely to be less direct. Military organizations have an interest in enhancing their size, budget, autonomy, and prestige, and they support those interests by propagating myths or ideologies regarding the severity of external threats and the necessity of enhanced military preparedness.[66] This often leads to arms buildups that go beyond what is required by real security concerns, and these can trigger arms races, conflict spirals, and war. The dangers of escalation are increased by the standard operating procedures of military organizations, which increase the rigidity of policy and deprive political leaders of the flexibility they need to manage a crisis in a way that avoids a war while preserving vital interests.[67]

In addition, military organizations generally have a preference for offensive doctrines, which help rationalize larger military budgets, enhance military morale and prestige, and facilitate seizing the initiative, structuring the battle, and hence reducing uncertainty. Offensive doctrines contribute to war by increasing incentives for territorial conquest, preemptive strikes, and preventive war, by fueling arms races and conflict spirals because they increase the threat to adversary security, and by increasing the destructiveness of war.[68] Although these hypotheses are quite plausible, the central concept of an offensive advantage is extraordinarily difficult to define conceptually, and the magnitude of its impact has never been established by systemic empirical analysis. Moreover, whatever the impact of this factor in previous eras, that impact has probably declined since World War II as a result of the nuclear revolution, the evolution of postindustrial economies, and the growth of democracy and an open press.[69]

INDIVIDUAL-LEVEL SOURCES OF INTERNATIONAL CONFLICT

Individual-level theories trace international conflict to individual political leaders, the content of their beliefs, the psychological processes through which they acquire information and make decisions, and their personalities and emotional states. Unlike theories at other levels, these theories assume that key decision makers often vary in their preferences for foreign policy goals, their images of the adversary, or their beliefs about the optimum strategies to achieve their goals and meet those threats.[70] As a result, different decision makers with different belief systems or "operational codes" about world politics will respond differently under similar situations, so that individuals make a difference in state foreign policy behavior.[71] These beliefs arise from differences in political socialization, personality, education, formative experiences, the lessons people learn from historical experience, and a host of other variables.[72]

The beliefs of political leaders cannot alone explain foreign policy behavior, however, for beliefs have little impact unless those holding beliefs are in a political position to implement them. Theories of foreign policy and international conflict that recognize the importance of individual beliefs must incorporate not only the beliefs themselves, but also an explanation of how the policy preferences of different individuals in different roles and positions of power get aggregated into foreign policy decisions for the state. This facilitates the construction of richer and more descriptively accurate theories of international conflict, but these theories are more complex, less elegant or parsimonious, more demanding in terms of the types of data that are necessary to test them, and less powerful in terms of their generalizability across different states in different situations at different times.

Foreign policy behavior can be affected by the psychological processes involved in individual judgment and decision making, as well as by the content of their belief systems. There has been more and more evidence from social psychology to demonstrate that people are limited in their cognitive abilities to process information, that their perceptions of their environment are shaped by their prior beliefs as much as by the objective evidence, that they utilize heuristics or cognitive shortcuts in lieu of more normatively rational decision rules, and that these heuristics can produce some rather serious discrepancies between the perceptions of individuals and the "real world."[73] I focus here on the consequences of misperceptions for international conflict behavior, but not on the psychological processes that generate these misperceptions.

Misperception-based explanations are often seen as necessary causes of wars, on the assumption that if both sides had correctly assessed the adversary's intentions and the likely outcome of the war, they could have agreed to a settlement commensurate with that outcome while avoiding the costs of fighting.[74] The concept of misperception is extremely difficult to define analytically or measure empirically, however, and there are a plethora of types of misperceptions, but the ones most likely to have a major impact on the processes leading to war are misperceptions of the capabilities and intentions of adversaries and third states.[75]

Exaggeration of the hostility of the adversary's intentions is particularly important. In the short term it can induce one to take counteractions (in the extreme case, a preemptive strike) that trigger a conflict spiral and unnecessary war, and in the long term they can lead to an arms race or system of alliances and counteralliances. Underestimation of the adversary's hostility by a status quo state can contribute to war by undercutting the need to build up military capabilities in the long term or to demonstrate resolve in the short term, either of which undermines deterrence. Alternatively, the underestimation of the adversary's resolve by an aggressive state may lead it to make more coercive military threats in the expectation that the adversary will back down, which results in a conflict spiral. Misperceptions of the adversary's intentions may derive from secondary misperceptions of the adversary's value structure, its definition of its vital interests, its definition of the situation, its expectations about the future, and the domestic or bureaucratic constraints on its freedom of action.

Misperceptions of adversary capabilities can also be critical. The underestimation of adversary capabilities relative to one's own generates military overconfidence and the common belief that a rapid military victory involving minimal costs is quite likely. The overestimation of adversary capabilities may lead one to overreact and initiate an arms buildup that is followed by an arms race and conflict spiral. Alternatively, it can lead to excessive passivity that undermines deterrence. Misperceptions of the intentions and capabilities of third states can have a similar effect. The most common tendency is to exaggerate the likelihood than one's potential friends will intervene on one's behalf and the likelihood that one's potential enemies will stay neutral, and either of these beliefs reinforces military overconfidence. Misperceptions of third-state capabilities, and hence the impact of third states on the course of the war should they choose to intervene, have similar effects.

There is little reason to believe that the role of individual belief systems or psychological processes has been significantly influenced by the nuclear revolution or by the end of the Cold War. We might hypothesize, however, that the recent decline of authoritarian regimes has somewhat decreased the importance of the beliefs or psychology of any single decision maker by bringing more people into the decision making process. On the other hand, we might hypothesize that the end of the Cold War, by destroying the relative simplicity of the bipolar order and increasing the complexity of world politics, has increased the importance of leaders' perceptions of their external environment and of their definitions of the situation. In addition, the greater the complexity, the greater the variation in beliefs, images, and perceptions across individuals, and thus the greater the importance of the processes through which preferences are aggregated at the small-group and organizational level.

CONCLUSION

I have reviewed some of the leading theories of international conflict, specified key variables and the causal paths that lead to war or peace, identified some of the interaction effects between variables at different levels of analysis, and commented on the relevance of various theories as we move into the next century. It is more difficult to reach definitive conclusions regarding the likely causal importance of different levels of analysis for international conflict in the coming decades. First of all, assessing the relative impact of different variables at different levels is an empirical as well as a theoretical question, and such a task is beyond the scope of this chapter. A more important conceptual problem is that theories of international conflict have increasingly begun to incorporate variables from several different levels of analysis, so that an evaluation of the validity of a particular theory is not necessarily congruent with the evaluation of the importance of a particular level of analysis.[76] In addition, although the levels-of-analysis framework serves as a useful organizing framework, we must not apply it so rigidly that it distracts attention from the important task of understanding how variables at different levels of analysis interact in the processes contributing to international conflict.

We must also recognize that the "importance" of various levels of analysis is itself a somewhat ambiguous concept. Theories serve multiple purposes, and variables at different levels of analysis may be more useful for some theoretical purposes than for others. The trade-off between the analytic power, generalizability, and predictive value of parsimonious theories and the descriptive richness of more complex theories is particularly salient. If we want a general theory that can provide maximum explanatory power across different temporal and spatial contexts and generate predictions about unobserved events, then variables based on individual-level beliefs and personalities or governmental-level decision processes are unlikely to be very helpful, because they are so difficult to operationalize and measure for a large number of cases. On the other hand, if we want a theory that can guide a more detailed interpretation of a small number of key historical cases, decision-making variables (in conjunction with others) are likely to be extremely useful.

A few more substantive comments are in order. Although systemic distributions of power will continue to be important in providing the context within which regional systems and dyadic rivalries operate, and although balancing against primary threats and adjusting to changing power differentials through alliances and armaments will continue to be central themes in international relations, realist theories are probably too limited theoretically and too tied to the great-power experience of the past to provide an adequate explanation of international conflict over the next several decades. The locus of conflict has clearly begun to shift away from the great powers and away from the West. Although realist theories help to explain the origins of this shift, they need to be broadened if they are to explain the dynamics of conflict in a changing world.

In terms of levels of analysis, far more attention needs to be directed to societal-level variables. These have been important but neglected in the past, and in all probability they will become increasingly important in the future in shaping the preferences of state leaders and the constraints on their actions. Ethnonational and other identity-based conflicts will be particularly important in influencing the political agendas of states and in contributing to domestic instability and international tensions. The importance of economic variables is also likely to increase, for several reasons. The collapse of the Soviet Union has significantly reduced a major source of military threat to the leading economic powers in the system, and this, along with the declining utility of military power, has increased the importance of economic competition among advanced industrial states.[77]

In addition, resource scarcities—exacerbated by environmental degradation and resulting population migrations—will likely threaten the economic welfare of many developing societies, while processes of democratization will increase popular expectations of a minimum level of economic prosperity and also the influence of parochial economic groups. The combination will put enormous pressure on domestic political systems, many of which have only recently begun to develop the institutions to aggregate demands from different groups in society. In addition, the erosion of the order and certainty of the Cold War will increase internal conflicts over foreign policy goals and the means to achieve them and will therefore increase the importance of individual belief systems and the political processes through which individual policy preferences are aggregated into state foreign policy decisions.

Much of this is speculation, of course. Scholars had enough trouble predicting the end of the Cold War, which some now see in retrospect as overdetermined. Forecasting the future in a more complex and chaotic world is an even more daunting task. But this makes it all the more important that our attempts to understand world politics be guided by well-developed theoretical frameworks that help to illuminate and structure this complexity.

NOTES

I thank Lori Gronich for helpful comments on an earlier draft of this chapter.

1. Charles W. Kegley, Jr., "The Neoidealist Moment in International Studies: Realist Myths and the New International Studies," *International Studies Quarterly* 37, no. 2 (June 1993): 141.

2. This survey builds on my longer review essay, "The Causes of War: A Review of Theories and Evidence," in *Behavior, Society, and Nuclear War,* vol. 1, ed. Philip E. Tetlock, Jo L. Husbands, Robert Jervis, Paul C. Stern, and Charles Tilly (New York: Oxford University Press, 1989), pp. 209–333.

3. Kenneth N. Waltz, *Man, the State, and War* (New York: Columbia University Press, 1959).

4. J. David Singer, "The Levels-of-Analysis Problem in International Relations," in *International Politics and Foreign Policy,* rev. ed., ed. James N. Rosenau (New York, 1969), pp. 20–29; and Kenneth N. Waltz, *Theory of International Politics* (Reading, Mass.: Addison-Wesley, 1979).

5. Robert Jervis, *Perception and Misperception in International Politics* (Princeton, N.J.: Princeton University Press, 1976), chap. 1; and James N. Rosenau, *The Scientific Study of Foreign Policy* (New York: Nichols, 1980), chap. 6.

6. This does not necessarily mean that these variables have a greater causal influence than do individual or domestic variables.

7. Waltz, *Theory of International Politics;* and Robert O. Keohane, ed., *Neorealism and Its Critics* (New York: Columbia University Press, 1986).

8. On taking risks to avoid losses, see Jack S. Levy, "An Introduction to Prospect Theory," *Political Psychology* 13, no. 2 (1992): 171–186; Barbara Farnham, *Taking Risks/Avoiding Losses* (Ann Arbor: University of Michigan Press, 1995).

9. Jervis, *Perception and Misperception,* chap. 3; and John A. Vasquez, *The War Puzzle* (New York: Cambridge University Press, 1993), chap. 5.

10. Hans J. Morgenthau, *Politics Among Nations,* 4th ed. (New York: Knopf, 1967); Edward V. Gulick, *Europe's Classical Balance of Power* (Ithaca, N.Y.: Cornell University Press, 1955); Waltz, *Theory of International Politics,* chap. 6; John Mearsheimer, "Back to the Future: Instability in Europe After the Cold War," *International Security* 15, no. 1 (Summer 1990): 5–56; and Levy, "Causes of War," pp. 228–242.

11. Stephen M. Walt, *The Origins of Alliances* (Ithaca, N.Y.: Cornell University Press, 1987). Thus Churchill commented, "If Hitler invaded Hell, I would make at least a favorable reference to the Devil in the House of Commons." Winston Churchill, *The Second World War,* vol. 3: *The Grand Alliance* (Boston: Houghton Mifflin, 1950), p. 370.

12. A. F. K. Organski and Jacek Kugler, *The War Ledger* (Chicago: University of Chicago Press, 1980), chap. 1; and Robert Gilpin, *War and Change in World Politics* (New York: Cambridge University Press, 1981).

13. The Israeli strike against the Iraqi nuclear reactor in 1981 is the classic preventive strike. Jack S. Levy, "Declining Power and the Preventive Motivation for War," *World Politics* 40, no. 1 (October 1987): 82–107.

14. Daniel S. Geller, "Power Differentials and War in Rival Dyads," *International Studies Quarterly* 37, no. 2 (June 1993): 173–193. The logic is that under preponderance the strong are satisfied and do not have the incentives for war, and the weak, though dissatisfied, lack the capability for war. Note that the stabilizing effects of power preponderance at the dyadic level do not necessarily imply that imbalances of power at the systemic level are stabilizing.

15. Manus I. Midlarsky, *The Onset of World War* (Boston: Unwin Hyman, 1988).

16. These phenomena are illustrated in the case of the former Soviet empire and in Yugoslavia and are discussed in Mark Katz's essay on collapsed empires (chapter 2 of this volume).

17. The authors apply the model to the pre-1914 period and to Japan before and after World War II (to answer the question of why resource demands led to military expansion in the 1930s but to foreign trade after World War II). Nazli

C. Choucri and Robert C. North, *Nations in Conflict* (San Francisco: W. H. Freeman, 1975); and Choucri, North, and Susumu Yamakage, *The Challenge of Japan Before World War II and After* (London: Routledge, 1992).

18. Cited in Robert Jervis, *The Meaning of the Nuclear Revolution* (Ithaca, N.Y.: Cornell University Press, 1989). See also Thomas C. Schelling, *Arms and Influence* (New Haven, Conn.: Yale University Press, 1966).

19. Geoffrey Blainey, *The Causes of War,* 3rd ed. (New York: Free Press, 1973), chap. 3.

20. *New York Times,* November, 22, 1985. These arguments are less compelling, however, for new nuclear states with retaliatory forces that are smaller, less redundant, more vulnerable, and backed by less sophisticated command and control systems. Consequently, we cannot necessarily generalize from the stability of superpower deterrence to stability among newer nuclear states in an era of proliferation.

21. The usefulness of the balance of power or power transition theories for understanding the power dynamics of regional systems in the future depends in part on whether the restraining influence of the great powers continues to diminish after the end of the Cold War and collapse of bipolar bloc systems, on whether economic sanctions provide an effective tool of restraint in an increasingly globalized and integrated world economy, and on whether the great powers, alone or in conjunction with the United Nations, are able to cooperate to establish effective collective security and peacekeeping systems.

22. That is, systemic structure may serve as necessary as well as sufficient conditions for behavior.

23. Blainey, *Causes of War,* p. 10. This relationship is complex, however, for peace may also create the conditions for prosperity.

24. The assumption that increased economic interdependence between the United States and the Soviet Union would increase Soviet incentives to cooperate on security issues and help deter uncooperative behavior was a cornerstone of U.S. detente policy in the 1970s. The economic interdependence of the great powers in 1914, however, did not deter them from getting involved in an enormously destructive general war.

25. Richard Rosecrance, *The Rise of the Trading State* (New York: Basic Books, 1986).

26. Soloman W. Polachek, "Conflict and Trade," *Journal of Conflict Resolution* 24, no. 1 (March 1980): 55–78; John R. Oneal, Frances Oneal, Zeev Maoz, and Bruce Russett, "The Liberal Peace: Interdependence, Democracy, and International Conflict, 1950–86," *Journal of Peace Research* 33, no. 1 (February 1996): 11–29; and Katherine Barbieri, "Economic Interdependence: A Path to Peace or Source of Interstate Conflict?" *Journal of Peace Research* 33, no. 1 (February 1996): 29–49.

27. Samuel P. Huntington, "Why International Primacy Matters," *International Security* 17 (Spring 1993): 68–83.

28. Perhaps the classic case of the militarization of a commercial rivalry involved England and the Netherlands in the seventeenth century. For a analysis of its historical evolution and theoretical implications, see Jack S. Levy and Salvatore Ali, "From Commercial Competition to Strategic Rivalry to War: The Rise of the Anglo-Dutch Rivalry, 1609–1652," in *The Dynamics of Enduring Rivalries,* ed. Paul F. Diehl (Champaign: University of Illinois Press, forthcoming). For a hypothetical account of the militarization of the current Japanese-American rivalry, one in which the causal dynamics are strikingly similar to those of the Anglo-Dutch rivalry nearly four centuries ago, see George Friedman and Meridith Lebard, *The Coming War with Japan* (New York: St. Martin's, 1991).

29. Admittedly, these factors do not fit neatly into a levels-of-analysis framework, which implicitly assumes that states are the primary actors and that there is a clear distinction between the domestic and the international realms. Both the actors whose behavior we want to explain (ethnic and other forms of communal groups) and the independent variables that influence them cut across state lines. Although this does complicate the applicability of a levels-of-analysis framework, to the extent that these groups are politically organized we can still ask whether the factors that influence group behavior derive primarily from factors external to the group, from leaders' concerns for their political support within the group, or from the belief systems or idiosyncracies of the leaders themselves. Politically unorganized groups are both more difficult to analyze and generally less influential in international politics.

30. Imperialist policies help shape the structure of the international capitalist economy, which creates further opportunities for capitalist states and imposes serious constraints on the more dependent states in the world system. Thus there are important connections between the societal and systemic levels of analysis in some neo-Marxist theories. See Immanuel Wallerstein, *The Politics of the World Economy* (Cambridge, U.K.: Cambridge University Press, 1984).

31. V. I. Lenin, *Imperialism* (New York: International Publishers, 1939); Bernard Semmel, ed., *Marxism and the Science of War* (New York: Oxford University Press, 1981).

32. Waltz, *Theory of International Politics,* pp. 18–29; Joseph A. Schumpeter, *Imperialism and Social Classes,* trans. Heinz Norden (New York: Augustus M. Kelley, 1951); Anthony Brewer, *Marxist Theories of Imperialism* (London: Routledge and Kegan Paul, 1980).

33. Jack Snyder, *Myths of Empire* (Ithaca, N.Y.: Cornell University Press, 1991).

34. Cited in Jack S. Levy, "The Diversionary Theory of War," in *Handbook of War Studies,* ed. Manus I. Midlarsky (Boston: Unwin Hyman, 1989), p. 259.

35. These cases include the decisions of both British and Argentine leaders to go to war over the Falklands/Malvinas in 1982, Reagan's decision to invade Grenada, Saddam Hussein's decision to stand firm in the face of U.S. coercive threats, and Serbian policy in Bosnia.

36. Bruce Bueno de Mesquita and Randolph M. Siverson, "War and the Survival of Political Leaders: Regime Types and Political Accountability," *American Political Science Review* 89, no. 4 (December 1995): 841–855.

37. Immanuel Kant, "Eternal Peace," in *The Philosophy of Kant,* ed. C. J. Frederich (New York: Modern Library, 1949), pp. 430–476.

38. Jack S. Levy, "Domestic Politics and War," *Journal of Interdisciplinary History* 18, no. 4 (Spring 1988): 662.

39. Criteria for war include a military conflict involving at least 1,000 battle deaths, and criteria for democracy include regular elections, tolerance of opposition parties, and a parliament that at least shares powers with the executive. Possible exceptions to this "law" might include the American Civil War and the Spanish-American War. Bruce Russett, *Grasping the Democratic Peace* (Princeton, N.J.: Princeton University Press, 1993). Note that it is democratic regime type, not similarity of regimes, that makes a difference, for authoritarian regimes often fight each other.

40. Edward D. Mansfield and Jack Snyder, "Democratization and the Danger of War," *International Security* 20, no. 1 (Summer 1995): 5–38.

41. Andrew J. Enterline, "Driving While Democratizing," *International Security* 20, no. 4 (Spring 1996): 183–193.

42. Renee de Nevers, "Democratization and Ethnic Conflict," in *Ethnic Conflict and International Security,* ed. Michael E. Brown (Princeton, N.J.: Princeton University Press, 1993), pp. 61–78.

43. An ethnic community is "a named human population with a myth of common ancestry, shared memories, and cultural elements; a link with a historic territory or homeland; and a measure of solidarity." Donald Horowitz, *Ethnic Groups in Conflict* (Berkeley: University of California Press, 1985), pp. 55–92. Nationalism involves the devotion of the primary loyalties of group members to the ethnic or national community and the desire for their own independent state. Stephen Van Evera, "Hypotheses on Nationalism and War," *International Security* 18, no. 4 (Spring 1994): 6; Ted Robert Gurr, *Minorities at Risk* (Washington, D.C.: United States Institute of Peace Press, 1993); and Manus I. Midlarsky, ed., *The Internationalization of Communal Strife* (London: Routledge, 1992).

44. Samuel P. Huntington, "The Clash of Civilizations," *Foreign Affairs* 72, no. 3 (Summer 1993): 22–49. Huntington argues that the clash of civilizations will replace the clash of princes that began with the Treaty of Westphalia in 1648, the clash of nations that began with the French Revolution 1789–1792, and the clash of ideologies that began after World War I and the Russian Revolution. This provocative argument underestimates the importance of nationalism and other sources of division within broadly defined Islamic, Confucian, and western civilizations, but it highlights the importance of previously neglected variables. For a critique see David Little's essay on religious militancy (chapter 5 in this volume) and *The Clash of Civilizations? The Debate: A* Foreign Affairs *Reader* (New York: Foreign Affairs, 1993).

45. Serbs and Croats fought each other very little before this century, for example.

46. Michael E. Brown, "Causes and Implications of Ethnic Conflict," in *Ethnic Conflict and International Security,* ed. Michael E. Brown (Princeton, N.J.: Princeton University Press, 1993), p. 6; and Jack Snyder, "Nationalism and the Crisis of the Post-Soviet State," *Survival* 35, no. 1 (Spring 1993): 5–6.

47. Barry R. Posen, "The Security Dilemma and Ethnic Conflict," *Survival* 35, no. 1 (Spring 1993): 27–47.

48. Snyder, "Nationalism," pp. 7–11.

49. This is especially likely if these groups have been oppressed by national majorities or if other ethnic groups are growing in power. Van Evera, "Hypotheses on Nationalism and War," pp. 10–22; and Donald Horowitz, "Irredentas and Secessions," in *Irredentism and International Politics,* ed. Naomi Chazan (Boulder, Colo.: Lynne Rienner, 1991), pp. 9–22.

50. Barry R. Posen, "Nationalism, the Mass Army, and Military Power," *International Security* 18, no. 2 (Fall 1993): 80–124.

51. In the case of the disintegration of Yugoslavia and the war in Bosnia, for example, it is not clear whether Serbian political leaders promoted nationalist fervor primarily to mobilize the country for dealing with external security threats and opportunities, or for dealing with internal challenges to their privileged political positions from forces more sympathetic to pluralist politics. V. P. Gagnon, Jr., "Ethnic Nationalism and International Conflict," *Inter-national Security* 19, no. 3 (Winter 1994–95): 331–367.

52. Van Evera, "Hypotheses on Nationalism and War," pp. 23–30.

53. Hans Morgenthau, *Politics Among Nations,* 5th ed. (New York: Knopf, 1973), p. 253. On the persistence of images see Janice Gross Stein's essay in this volume (chapter 6).

54. F. Stephen Larrabee, "Down and Out in Warsaw and Budapest: Eastern Europe and East-West Migration," *International Security* 16, no. 4 (Spring 1992): 5–33. Note that the framing of environmental issues in terms of "high politics" and national security may also serve a political strategy. The symbolism of national security increases the prospects that these issues may be put on the policy agenda and that research on these topics might gain funding from the government or foundations. See Marc A. Levy, "Is the Environment a National Security Issue?" *International Security* 20 (Fall 1995): 35–62; and Daniel Deudney, "The Case Against Linking Environmental Degradation and National Security," *Millennium* 19, no. 3 (Winter 1990): 469. See also Astri Suhrke's essay in this volume (chapter 7).

55. Myron Weiner, "Security, Stability, and International Migration," *International Security* 17, no. 3 (Winter 1992–93): 91–126.

56. As Suhrke argues in chapter 7 of this volume, however, international migration does not always lead to social conflict. Under some conditions, migrants are assimilated into the host country, particularly when they provide needed labor and skills and when population movement takes the form of gradual migration (often in response to gradual changes in demography and economic incentives), rather than sudden displacement arising from ethnic conflict or environmental disaster.

57. For example, the construction of the Berlin Wall in an attempt to stop the flood of refugees from East Germany led to the Soviet-American Berlin Crisis in 1961.

58. Paul Kennedy, *Preparing for the Twenty-First Century* (New York: Random House, 1993); and Robert Kaplan, "The Coming Anarchy," *Atlantic Monthly,* February 1994, pp. 44–76.

One of the major research projects on these questions concludes that the environmental concerns most likely to lead to international conflict include the depletion and degradation of forests, good agricultural land, fresh water, and fish stocks, whereas atmospheric changes such as greenhouse-induced global warming and stratospheric ozone depletion will not have a major effect for several decades and then only in conjunction with these other scarcities. Thomas F. Homer-Dixon, "On the Threshold: Environmental Changes as Causes of Acute Conflict" and "Environmental Scarcities and Violent Conflict: Evidence from Cases," in *Global Dangers,* ed. Sean M. Lynn-Jones and Steven E. Miller (Cambridge, Mass.: MIT Press, 1995), pp. 43–83, 145–147.

Another path through which environmental degradation might contribute to international conflict involves pollution across state boundaries, the possibility of coercive state responses to reduce that pollution, and a conflict spiral that escalates to war. But the magnitude of such conflicts is likely to be small in relation to those over economic or identity issues. See Deudney, "Environmental Degradation and National Security," p. 473; and Suhrke's essay in this volume (chapter 7).

59. Note that the question of whether environmental change is a security issue, which has attracted considerable attention in the literature, is much broader than our more specific question of whether environmental change contributes to international conflict. Environmental change can threaten core values and individual security without involving international conflict. For discussions of environmental change as part of new conceptions of security see Richard Ullman, "Redefining Security," *International Security* 8, no. 1 (Summer 1983): 129–153; for critics of this connection see Deudney, "Environmental Degradation and National Security"; and M. Levy, "Is the Environment a National Security Issue?"

60. Environmental change can also affect conflict indirectly by influencing regime type. Some argue that the social need to manage irrigation waters in arid zones led to the rise of autocracies in earlier societies, that ample rainfall contributed to the rise of democracy, and

that the latter is more peaceful than the former. Karl A. Wittfogel, *Oriental Despotism* (New Haven, Conn.: Yale University Press, 1957); and Manus I. Midlarsky, "Environmental Influences on Democracy," *Journal of Conflict Resolution* 39, no. 2 (June 1995): 224–262.

61. Homer-Dixon argues that conflicts over nonrenewable resources tend to be more destabilizing than disputes over renewable resources and that disputes over river water tend to be particularly serious ("Environmental Scarcities," pp. 157–159). On the seriousness of conflicts over water, see Peter H. Gleick, "Water and Conflict: Fresh Water Resources and International Security," in *Global Dangers,* ed. Lynn-Jones and Miller, pp. 84–117; and Miriam R. Lowi, "Bridging the Divide: Transboundary Resource Disputes and the Case of West Bank Water," in *Global Dangers,* pp. 118–143.

62. Deudney, "Environmental Degradation and National Security," pp. 470–471.

63. Homer-Dixon, "Environmental Scarcities," pp. 157–159; and Deudney, "Environmental Degradation and National Security," p. 471.

64. Graham T. Allison, *The Essence of Decision* (Boston: Little, Brown, 1971).

65. Richard K. Betts, *Soldiers, Statesmen, and Cold War Crises* (Cambridge, Mass.: Harvard University Press, 1977). Admittedly, there have been few systematic comparative studies of this relationship.

66. Stephen Van Evera, "Primed for Peace: Europe After the Cold War," *International Security* 15, no. 3 (Winter 1990–91): 18–23.

67. In addition, the unpredictability of bureaucratic compromises can increase adversary uncertainty regarding one's intentions, thereby enhancing the misperceptions that contribute to war under certain conditions. For an application of the organizational process model to the July 1914 crisis, see Jack S. Levy, "Organizational Routines and the Causes of War," *International Studies Quarterly* 30, no. 2 (June 1986): 193–222.

68. Stephen Van Evera, "The Cult of the Offensive and the Origins of the First World War," *International Security* 9 (1984): 58–107; and Jack S. Levy, "The Offensive/Defensive

Balance of Military Technology," *International Studies Quarterly* 28, no. 2 (June 1984): 219–238.

69. Van Evera, "Primed for Peace," pp. 12–16.

70. On images of the enemy, see Ole R. Holsti, "Cognitive Dynamics and Images of the Enemy," in *Image and Reality in World Politics,* ed. John Farrell and Asa Smith (New York: Columbia University Press, 1967), pp. 16–39; and Richard Ned Lebow, *Between Peace and War* (Baltimore, Md.: Johns Hopkins University Press, 1981).

71. Alexander L. George, "The 'Operational Code': A Neglected Approach to the Study of Political Leaders and Decision Making," *International Studies Quarterly* (June 1969): 190–222.

72. On experiential learning, see Jack S. Levy, "Learning and Foreign Policy: Sweeping a Conceptual Minefield," *International Organization* 48, no. 2 (Spring 1994): 279–312; see also Janice Gross Stein's essay in this volume (chapter 6).

73. Daniel Kahneman, Paul Slovic, and Amos Tversky, *Judgment Under Uncertainty: Heuristics and Biases* (Cambridge, U.K.: Cambridge University Press, 1982); Richard Nisbett and Lee Ross, *Human Inference: Strategies and Shortcomings of Social Judgment* (Englewood Cliffs, N.J.: Prentice-Hall, 1980); and Jervis, *Perception and Misperception.*

74. James D. Fearon, "Rationalist Explanations for War," *International Organization* 49, no. 3: 379–414.

75. This builds on Jack S. Levy, "Misperception and the Causes of War: Theoretical Linkages and Analytical Problems," *World Politics* 36, no. 1 (October 1983): 76–99. See also Robert Jervis, "War and Misperception," *Journal of Interdisciplinary History* 18, no. 4 (Spring 1988): 675–700. Note that each of these forms of misperceptions can also contribute to peace, although through different causal paths. Exaggeration of adversary capabilities, for example, may lead a state to reject a decision for a preventive or preemptive war that would have been rational with complete information. Note also that misperceptions are not necessarily nonrational. Given the extent of complexity and uncertainty in the world, rational information processing sometimes leads to incorrect predictions.

76. Liberal economic theories, for example, incorporate the structure of the global economy, internal economic sources of economic expansion and contraction, domestic pressure groups, and economic ideologies. Snyder's coalition model incorporates stages of economic development, coalitions among parochial interests at both the domestic and governmental level, the impact of systemic outcomes on the balance of power between competing domestic elites, and the psychological impact of self-serving strategic myths. Hypotheses on environmental scarcity and degradation recognize that the most significant impact of systemically induced environmental change on international conflict may be through intervening societal-level variables.

77. On the declining utility of military power since the end of the Cold War, see John Lewis Gaddis, *The United States and the End of the Cold War* (New York: Oxford University Press, 1992); Michael J. Hogan, ed., *The End of the Cold War* (New York: Cambridge University Press, 1992).

2

Collapsed Empires

MARK N. KATZ

The collapse of the Soviet empire occurred with astonishing speed, beginning in the latter part of 1989 when the Marxist-Leninist regimes of Eastern Europe were overthrown and culminating in the latter part of 1991 when the USSR disintegrated. In the short period of time that has elapsed since then, this extraordinary event has had a dual impact on international relations. On the one hand, the Soviet military withdrawal from Eastern Europe and the Third World brought an end to the Cold War, allowed democratization to proceed in many states previously ruled by Marxist dictatorships, and led to significant progress in resolving several Third World conflicts that had become prolonged and exacerbated during the Cold War. On the other hand, the collapse of the Soviet empire has been followed by the emergence, or re-emergence, of conflict in several areas that had been relatively quiescent during the Cold War. Many of these new conflicts (such as the civil war in Tajikistan, the war between Armenia and Azerbaijan over Nagorno-Karabakh, and the fighting in Chechnya) are taking place within the former Soviet empire. But conflicts have also erupted or intensified since the collapse of the Soviet empire in several countries outside of it, including former Yugoslavia, Somalia, Yemen, and Rwanda. In addition, several Third World conflicts in which the superpowers were not deeply involved during the Cold War have persisted after it, including secessionist struggles in India, Sri Lanka, Turkey, and Sudan.

The reduction in East-West tension and the threat of nuclear war that resulted from the collapse of the Soviet empire is obviously a welcome development. The outbreak of new regional conflicts since then and the persistence of others, however, are not. Is this regional instability likely to be a temporary or permanent feature of post–Cold War international relations? It is obviously impossible to provide a definitive answer to this question: The collapse of the Soviet empire has occurred too recently to determine its lasting effects.

As extraordinary an event as this has been, however, it is not unique. Many other empires have collapsed in the past. A brief examination of how the collapse of other empires has affected international relations in the past can help put in perspective how the demise of the Soviet empire may affect contemporary international relations. First, however, something needs to be said about what an empire is, or more precisely, the various forms empires have taken.

Basically, an empire is an agglomeration of nations over which (usually) one nation has acquired control. Many empires have been territorially contiguous, but they need not be so, as the overseas empires of the European colonial powers demonstrated. Empires have often been outright dictatorships for both the predominant nation and the subordinate ones within them. Sometimes, however, democratic states, such as Britain and France, have ruled far-flung empires.

Often, the dominant nation within an empire has directly ruled the subordinate nations without any pretense about the latter possessing sovereignty or any degree of independence. Sometimes, however, the subordinate nations have formally been independent, as with the many "protectorates" of the British empire and the East European "people's republics" of the Soviet empire. The reality of their subordination, though, has often been made clear by the occupation of these states by soldiers from the imperial power and their inability to pursue foreign or even domestic policies without approval of the imperial power. In other instances, however, there has been a degree of ambiguity as to whether or to what extent one nation was in fact part of an empire. During the periods when an empire rises and falls, this issue is often actively contested.

There has been great variety, then, in the structure of empires throughout history. But whatever their form, the dominant nations in them have faced the common problem of retaining control over the subordinate nations over the long term.[1] How they have done this is less the focus of attention here than what happens when the dominant nations ultimately become unable or unwilling to continue this difficult task and their empires collapse. Nevertheless, something must be said about how empires are held together, since this can have a significant impact on what transpires after they fall apart.

Empires are built through conquest. Yet even the conquest of one nation by another can involve more than just the successful application of force. In his classic account of the Roman conquest of France, Julius Caesar described how he took advantage of the many divisions among the Gauls, allying with weaker tribes in order to defeat stronger ones.[2] Cortez conquered Mexico with a tiny number of Spaniards by successfully building an alliance with the many tribes who sought to throw off the oppressive rule of the Aztecs.[3] The expansion of British influence in India often occurred through British forces siding with weaker princely states against stronger ones.[4] The expansion of the Russian empire was facilitated through local rivalries which St. Petersburg was able to exploit in some areas, such as the Caucasus.[5] Similarly, the expansion of Soviet power into the non-Russian regions of the collapsed tsarist empire was actively supported by non-Russian communists in them.[6] Once it achieved a "beachhead" with the assistance of these local allies, the imperial power was in a position to undercut those allies and solidify its own rule.

Whether empires expand through exploiting divisions in other countries or through outright conquest, dominant nations have sought to retain their empires through more economical means than the constant application of force against subordinate nations. It is especially difficult, and hence undesirable, for a dominant nation to use force when the population of the subordinate nations it seeks to rule is equal to or greater than its own. So successful empires have resorted to other means.

One method has been to send settlers from the dominant nation to colonize subordinate ones within the empire. Sometimes, this colonization has occurred on such a large scale that settlers from the dominant nation have become the majority within the subordinate nation, as with British colonization of the eastern seaboard of what is now the United States, as well as of Canada, Australia, and New Zealand. But even where the settlers from the dominant nation only form a sizable minority, they may be able to control the subordinate nation long after the retreat or collapse of the empire that had initially sponsored their colonization, as with the whites in South Africa and the Spanish in Latin American countries, who ruled over much larger indigenous populations. Colonization of Kazakstan by Russians occurred in such large numbers under both the tsarist and Soviet empires that the Russians may be able to determine the future of this republic despite its having gained independence.[7]

Another method a dominant nation uses to retain control of a large multi-ethnic empire is to import troops from some subordinate nations under its control to keep other subordinate nations pacified. The British empire, for example, successfully used troops from nations that had been subordinate to it for a relatively long period of time, such as Ireland and India, to pacify nations that became subordinate to it later.[8] The Soviet armed forces pursued a deliberate policy of stationing non-Russian troops outside their home republic and in other republics instead. Moscow apparently judged that while non-Russian troops could not be relied upon to use force against their own ethnic group, they would not be at all reluctant to do so against others.[9]

A third method of retaining control over subordinate nations is to co-opt minorities within them. Such minorities often eagerly cooperate with the imperial power since its protection allows them to become far more powerful than they would be otherwise. Minorities that have played this role include the Christians in French-ruled Lebanon, the Alawites in French-ruled Syria, and the Sunnis in British-ruled Iraq.[10]

A fourth method a dominant nation uses to retain control over subordinate ones is to exploit rivalries between them. Even if subordinate nations oppose being ruled by the dominant nation within an empire, interethnic rivalry often induces different groups to see the imperial power as an ally against their local opponents. The British were particularly successful at employing this method. In some cases where strong local rivalries did not exist, the British helped to create them by allowing or overseeing the immigration of a nonindigenous ethnic group into a colony, as in Northern Ireland, Palestine, Fiji, Guyana, and elsewhere.[11] The Soviets also employed this technique among the non-Russian nations of the USSR. There is increasing evidence that Stalin deliberately drew contentious borders in order to exacerbate or even create tensions among non-Russians.[12] He succeeded in doing just this in several instances, such as between Armenians and Azeris, Uzbeks and Tajiks, and Georgians and Abkhaz.

What is noteworthy about these methods is that they have often worked, at least for a time. To the extent that a dominant nation can maintain order relatively peacefully, an empire performs a positive function in the Hobbesian sense. In *Leviathan*, Hobbes wrote that the function of the state is to remove individuals from the "state of nature" in which conflict prevails by providing order within its borders. A well-run empire serves to remove the subordinate nations within it from the state of nature by placing a higher authority—the dominant nation—above them. States, however, continue to live in the state of nature since there is no higher authority above them.[13]

As unjust as the subordinate nations may consider the imperial order to be, in a well-run empire the dominant nation does in fact protect the subordinate ones against external threats and against one another. When an empire collapses, of course, the once-dominant nation no longer provides this service to the once-subordinate nations. What is more, the way an empire was constructed and held together can affect not only how it collapses, but also the internal and external politics of its components long after the empire has collapsed.

As was mentioned already, settlers from the once-dominant nation within an empire often continue to rule over a subordinate nation long after it has ceased to be part of the empire. Similarly, indigenous minorities that assisted the dominant nation in retaining control over a subordinate one often dominate it themselves long after the empire collapses. In instances where a dominant nation acted to hold in check subordinate nations at odds with each other, there is no such restraint on their rivalry after the collapse of the empire. And while dominant nations protected subordinate nations from opponents outside the empire when the empire was powerful, this protection either diminishes substantially or is completely eliminated after the empire collapses. As a result of these problems, the collapse of empires can give rise to prolonged periods of conflict and disorder—a phenomenon observed by St. Augustine as the Roman empire was collapsing.[14]

A recurrent theme in the literature about the collapse of empires from earliest times to the present is how the collapse of one empire can lead to the rise of other empires. Thucydides, for example, described how the overextension of the Athenian empire led both to its own decline and to the increasing power of its opponents.[15] Paul Kennedy described a historical cycle in which empires expand, but then come to grief as a result of "imperial overstretch" and are subsequently replaced by other empires which are, in turn, subject to the same cycle.[16]

For much of history, the rise and fall of empires took place in a world where empires were the norm. With the introduction and spread of democratization, though, this norm came to be increasingly challenged not only in subordinate nations, but even in the dominant nations within empires. At the time when President Woodrow Wilson enunciated his Fourteen Points at the end of World War I, the delegitimation of empires as a norm in international relations had become widespread.[17]

The end of World War I began a highly unstable period resulting from the collapse of several empires (the Ottoman, Austro-Hungarian, German, and Russian) and the increasing vulnerability of others (all the remaining West European ones). This period became unstable in part due to the forceful attempts by Germany, Japan, and Italy to create empires rapidly. It also became unstable, however, due to the great popularity but extreme lack of clarity in the concept of national self-determination—the organizing principle for world politics that Woodrow Wilson offered as an alternative to empire.[18] Although it took an enormous effort, the challenge to the existing system of international relations posed by the imperial ambitions of the three Axis powers was utterly defeated in 1945. The popularity of the principle of national self-determination, however, has proved to be disruptive to international relations ever since Woodrow Wilson enunciated it at the end of World War I—especially after the collapse of first the West European empires and, more recently, the Soviet/Russian empire.

Francis Fukuyama has written that democracy within a state represents the triumph of the principle of equality.[19] On the international scale, this quest for equality finds its expression in the desire for national self-determination—the desire for one's own nation to be recognized by others as equal to them in the sense of possessing sovereignty and not being subordinate to other nations. Serious problems, however, often arise in attempting to apply this principle of national self-determination. "Nations" do not necessarily live in neatly segregated groups, but mixed up together. This can often lead to different nations claiming the same territory. Despite his optimism about the eventual triumph of democracy worldwide, Fukuyama himself acknowledged that rival national identities within a given state can seriously hamper the ability of democracy to function within it.[20]

This situation has been exacerbated, however, by the continuing legacy of the imperial past on the very large number of new states that became independent after the collapse of so many empires during the course of the twentieth century. Over a hundred new nations were born during this process of decolonization. Most of these new nations, however, were "unnatural" in important respects. Often, they had not existed at all as nations before colonization, or they had not existed within their postcolonial borders. Some of those that had existed in the past were large or small empires themselves, in which one ethnic group dominated others. The modern borders between most new states were established either through conquest, negotiation between empires, or simply by administrative fiat within an empire. This process took little or no account of whether or not the groups living within these new borders considered themselves to be part of a single nation coterminous with the borders.

When these colonies became independent, the governments that came to power in these postcolonial states were often fiercely "anti-imperialist," but they sought to uphold the legacy of empire that they inherited in two important respects. First, virtually none of them has been willing to cede any territory to neighboring states or to allow regional secession, despite the arbitrary nature of the borders they inherited from the colonial powers. Some postcolonial governments, of course, have challenged the inherited imperial order by demanding territory from their neighbors, but even these revisionist states (indeed, they in particular) have been unwilling to acknowledge that others' claims to their territory may be as legitimate as their claims to the territory of others.

Second, in many instances, the postcolonial governments were or became replicas of the old imperial order in the sense that one ethnic or other group came to dominate the entire country. Instead of that group coming from outside the country, as during the colonial era, it came from within the county after independence. This could occur when a leader came to power (often via a coup d'etat) who was insecure and, hence, mainly appointed people from his own region, tribe, or even family to important posts, believing that they would be more loyal allies. But this phenomenon of one group dominating a country could also be directly inherited from the colonial era. In some instances, the European settler population was able to maintain control of a postcolonial regime even though it formed a minority, as occurred most notoriously in South Africa. In other instances, the minority group with which the European power had formed an alliance in order to maintain its rule over a colony managed to remain in control after independence, as occurred in Lebanon, Syria, Rwanda, and Burundi.

Thus, while almost all of the countries that were colonies at the beginning of the twentieth century are now independent, the legacy of empire was maintained in them through the preservation of artificial borders or the dominance of one ethnic or other group over the armed forces and the government. This legacy, however, has been seriously challenged in many countries through attempts to alter borders between nations, to secede from an established state and create a new one, or to end the monopoly on power within a state held by one ethnic or other group. With the collapse of the Soviet Union, the end of the Cold War, and growing demands for democracy, these challenges to the legacy of empire have increased dramatically throughout the world.[21]

Of course, challenges to the legacy of empire in most parts of the world existed before the end of the Cold War—some even since well before the beginning of it. The main difference between the Cold War and the post–Cold War era may simply be that now there is one less empire: the Russian/Soviet one. Why is there any reason to think that challenges to the legacy of empire in the post–Cold War era will be any more a problem for international relations than before?

Although the West European colonial empires virtually disappeared during the Cold War era, the legacy of empire they left behind remained quite strong during it. While newly independent states, as well as others, experienced attempts by regions to secede from them, almost none of these attempts succeeded. Bangladesh was the only significant exception during the Cold War era, and it was unique: Unlike most regions where attempts at secession have occurred, Bangladesh was geographically discontiguous from the rest of the country from which it seceded.[22]

In addition, there were relatively few territorial shifts during the Cold War era. Most of those that took place were small-scale exchanges of territory negotiated peacefully. Some territorial shifts did occur through force, but these were generally viewed as illegitimate, both by the state losing the territory and by the international community as a whole.[23]

Finally, while there were numerous coups d'etat and other changes in government throughout the world during the Cold War era, very few destroyed the imperial legacy of a small, authoritarian group ruling over a large population without its consent where this existed. There were cases, of course, when a pro-western government was ousted and replaced by a pro-Soviet one and vice versa. Sometimes these changes also involved the political authority of one ethnic group being destroyed and replaced by another one. What this usually represented, though, was simply a state shifting from the sphere of influence of one superpower to the other. The new regime was no more sympathetic to attempts at secession, demands for democratization, or attempts by non-ruling ethnic groups to share power than the previous regime.

The relative stability of the legacy of empire during the Cold War, however, did not occur simply because the local forces challenging it were weak and the local forces defending it were strong (though this was often the case). The United States and the Soviet Union also played an instrumental role in upholding the legacy of empire during this period.

The United States generally supported the process of European decolonization after World War II. Fear of communist expansion, however, soon became the primary concern of U.S. foreign policy. This fear led American foreign policy to oppose European decolonization in some instances, most notably with regard to the Portuguese empire. Washington also supported a number of pro-American dictatorships, many of which served to uphold the dominance of one ethnic or other group over others in many countries. Despite American support for democracy in general, Washington's foreign policymakers feared that democratization could not succeed in a country that had lit-tle or no experience with it. Washington also feared that the attempt to achieve democracy could result in Moscow's allies coming to power. The certainty of keeping an unsavory but reliable ally in power was usually preferred to a process that would definitely unseat that ally and might also result in a complete loss of American influence.

In addition, American foreign policy during the Cold War generally opposed secession. This was partly due to the fear of communism: Movements seeking regional secession from states allied with Washington were often, in the Cold War context, seen as probable allies of Moscow. This, however, was not the only motivation for America's position on this issue. The United States also opposed secession when most other governments in the surrounding area opposed it. For example, the United States opposed secession in Africa for fear of alienating the antisecessionist governments of the Organization of African Unity (OAU), virtually all of which were firmly committed to maintaining the legacy of empire in Africa.[24]

The Soviet Union portrayed itself as, and many in the West and elsewhere saw it as, a revolutionary power dedicated to bringing change to the rest of the world. The Soviet Union certainly did work to bring change to the Third World by promoting Marxist revolution in many countries; but the Soviet Union was also a status quo power in two important respects. First, Moscow was unwilling to allow political change in the USSR, Eastern Europe, or those Third World countries where pro-Soviet Marxist regimes had come to power. Second, although Moscow did seek to change governmental policy or to change the government itself in many states, the Soviets for the most part did not support demands for altering borders or for secession. Moscow sought change, but only change within the existing pattern of states created by the legacy of empire.

Moscow's preference for co-opting the legacy of empire to its purposes instead of challenging it was especially evident in Soviet policy toward secessionist movements in the Third World. Galia Golan has shown that while Moscow gave significant assistance to anticolonial or other movements seeking to "liberate" an entire country, it gave little or no support to groups seeking secession. Indeed, Moscow not only indicated its political opposition to many of these movements, but actually gave military assistance to governments (including non-Marxist ones) in order to suppress some of them. Moscow did give some support to Kurdish rebels seeking secession from Iraq and to Eritrean rebels seeking secession from Ethiopia, but in both cases Moscow switched to helping suppress these movements after pro-Soviet regimes came to power in Baghdad and Addis Ababa. In these two cases, Moscow's aid for secessionists was not designed to help them achieve their goals, but merely to weaken the anti-Soviet regimes they were fighting against.[25]

During the Cold War era, then, both superpowers generally opposed challenges to the legacy of empire, especially with regard to the question of secession. The typical situation that secessionists faced was that one superpower gave military assistance to the regime trying to suppress them while the other gave little or, more likely, nothing to the secessionists. Secessionists were sometimes able to obtain external support from regional powers. Often, however, the only arms they obtained were the ones they captured from the government they were fighting. It should not be surprising, then, that attempts at secession were so unsuccessful during the Cold War era.

The collapse of the Soviet Union in 1991 led to the independence of the fifteen "union republics" of the former USSR. This huge burst of secession—along with its recognition by Moscow and the international community—has had two important effects. First, it has provided successful "role models" to others, leading them to initiate or reinvigorate secessionist efforts elsewhere. Second, the fact that the independence of the non-Russian republics of the former USSR was recognized both by Moscow and the international community in general has provided a legitimacy to secession in the post–Cold War era that it did not have previously; this legitimacy has encouraged secessionists elsewhere that their cause too might be recognized. The secessions of Slovakia and Eritrea were recognized both by the countries they seceded from and by the international community in general. The secessions of Slovenia, Croatia, Bosnia, and Macedonia from Yugoslavia have been generally recognized by the international community, though not by Serbia until the U.S.-brokered peace agreement of November 1995. The international community has played an important role in establishing the de facto, though unrecognized, secession of the Kurdish regions of northern Iraq. The secession of the "Somaliland Republic" (former British Somaliland) from the rest of Somalia has not been recognized, but it is not being actively contested either.

However much of a demonstration effect these examples of secession in the post–Cold War era might have, their occurrence provides no guarantee that attempts at secession will succeed elsewhere (including elsewhere in the former USSR). There are, however, other important changes in the post–Cold War era that may increase the prospects for secessionists and others challenging the legacy of empire to achieve their goals.

One important change is that with the decline in power that it has suffered, Russia is no longer willing to defend the legacy of empire in the Third World. Russia has,

however, signaled its support for the legacy of empire closer to home—such as in former Yugoslavia through its support for Serbia—and has demonstrated its unwillingness to allow secession from the Russian Federation. But both the ineffectuality and unpopularity of Boris Yeltsin's military efforts to defeat secessionism in Chechnya during 1994–1995 have raised doubts about Russia's ability or willingness to do even this.[26]

Another important change is that the United States no longer fears that secession or other challenges to the legacy of empire will, if successful, redound to the benefit of a hostile USSR, since the latter no longer exists. Challenges to the legacy of empire are now seen as having only local or, at most, regional effects. Although the United States may not support secession or other challenges to the legacy of empire, it is unlikely to have a compelling reason to oppose them either. As congressional opposition even to peacekeeping missions in the post–Cold War era has shown, the executive branch is likely to find it extremely difficult to convince Congress and the public to support American military involvement to protect the legacy of empire in different parts of the world. Absent a global or a strong regional threat to U.S. interests in the post–Cold War era, the American public is unlikely to see defending the legacy of empire as vital or even important to American interests.[27] For similar reasons, America's principal Western allies are also unlikely to undertake vigorous efforts to defend the legacy of empire.

This means that secessionists and others challenging the legacy of empire face a very different set of circumstances in the post–Cold War era than they did during the Cold War. These challengers may be no more likely to receive outside military assistance now than they were previously. But the defenders of the legacy are now far less likely to obtain military assistance from the great powers—unless they can afford to purchase it with hard currency.[28] This means that the military balance between challengers and defenders is likely to be much less unequal in the post–Cold War era than during the Cold War. Although it will still be difficult for challengers to achieve victory, it may become increasingly difficult for defenders to defeat them.

The future of international relations after the collapse of the Soviet empire cannot be foretold with any certainty. There appear, however, to be three possible trends that could emerge.

First, the collapse of this last major European empire may indeed presage the fragmentation of multi-ethnic states generally. Other large multi-ethnic states in which sizable minorities form the majority in one or more sections of the country—such as India, China, and Indonesia—might become increasingly vulnerable to secession or even collapse. The world may see a greater number of smaller, more ethnically homogenous states come into existence—many of which may become involved in protracted, bitter conflicts over tiny bits of territory, as have Armenia and Azerbaijan. In such a world, fragmentation itself, rather than any one aggressive state or expanding empire, would be the greatest threat to stability.

Second, the post–Cold War era may come to resemble the post–World War I era, in which the fragmentation resulting from the collapse of old empires merely served as a prelude to the rise of new ones. It is difficult to envision from the perspective of the mid-1990s that one or more vigorous empires might arise in ten to twenty years to pose a serious threat to the rest of the world. But in 1919, it may have appeared highly improbable that Germany, Italy, and Japan would be in a position to pursue aggressive imperial ambitions in the 1930s and 1940s, or that Russia would be able to do so later. Just as occurred in the post–World War I

era, fragmentation in international relations may eventually serve to facilitate the rise of new empires in the post–Cold War era.

Third, and more optimistically, frustration with the inability to achieve narrowly nationalist goals, combined with an increasing desire for democratization, may lead to the construction or reconstruction both of federal systems that seek to balance the interests of the majority and regionally dominant minorities in multi-ethnic states and of regional organizations that seek to harmonize the interests of member states in areas where neighboring countries have become exhausted by chronic conflict.

Of course, these three possible trends are not mutually exclusive: Different ones may prevail in different regions. Nor does the appearance of either or both the first two trends, which may involve conflict in a region, preclude the eventual emergence of the third, more pacific one, in that region. Although Europe experienced fragmentation after the collapse of several empires in World War I, a vigorous attempt to unite the continent in a single empire by military means in World War II, and the rise of another empire that dominated Eastern Europe for over forty years, a regional organization serving to harmonize the interests of several countries—including ones that had recently been at war with one another—managed to grow and thrive in Western Europe. Not only has what became the European Union outlasted the Soviet empire, but many states that had been part of the latter are now actively seeking to join the former, partly to avoid the ill effects of fragmentation, effects they experienced after the collapse of empires at the end of World War I and as a result of inclusion within another empire as subordinate nations following World War II.

However, while the European Union offers a hopeful example of how the legacy of empire can be overcome, other regions have not been able to resolve many of the problems they inherited from the collapse of the Ottoman, Austro-Hungarian, British, French, and other empires decades ago. Even the noteworthy progress that has taken place in Western Europe only occurred after two world wars engulfed the region. It is not foreordained that other regions must experience similarly cataclysmic conflict in order to overcome the legacy of empire and achieve peaceful integration. But the experience of other states struggling with the legacy they inherited from various empires decades after their collapse indicates that the legacy of the Soviet empire will not be quickly or easily overcome.

NOTES

1. With the passage of time, dominant nations have sometimes adopted different strategies for retaining control over subordinate nations within an empire. For a discussion of the different methods employed by the Romans to address this problem, see Edward N. Luttwak, *The Grand Strategy of the Roman Empire: From the First Century A.D. to the Third* (Baltimore, Md.: Johns Hopkins University Press, 1976).

2. Julius Caesar, *The Conquest of Gaul*, trans. S. A. Handford (Harmondsworth, Middlesex, U.K.: Penguin Books, 1951).

3. Bernal Diaz, *The Conquest of New Spain*, trans. J. M. Cohen (Harmondsworth, Middlesex, U.K.: Penguin Books, 1963).

4. Percival Spear, *India: A Modern History* (Ann Arbor: University of Michigan Press, 1961), chaps. 16–19.

5. Lesley Blanch, *The Sabres of Paradise* (New York: Carroll and Graf, 1960), especially chap. 19.

6. Bohdan Nahaylo and Victor Swoboda, *Soviet Disunion: A History of the Nationalities Problem in the USSR* (New York: Free Press, 1990), chaps. 2–6.

7. Philip S. Gillette, "Ethnic Balance and Imbalance in Kazakhstan's Regions," *Central Asia Monitor* no. 3 (1993): 17–23.

8. Byron Farwell, *Queen Victoria's Little Wars* (New York: W. W. Norton, 1972).

9. Teresa Rakowska-Harmstone, "Nationalities and the Soviet Military," in *The Nationalities Factor in Soviet Politics and Society*, ed. Lubomyr Hajda and Mark Beissinger (Boulder, Colo.: Westview Press, 1990), pp. 82–83.

10. George Lenczowski, *The Middle East in World Affairs*, 4th ed. (Ithaca, N.Y.: Cornell University Press, 1980), pp. 263–267, 314–318.

11. Fred J. Khouri, *The Arab-Israeli Dilemma* (Syracuse, N.Y.: Syracuse University Press, 1968), pp. 18–21; D. A. Low, *Eclipse of Empire* (Cambridge, U.K.: Cambridge University Press, 1991), pp. 287–288, 305; and Brian Hunter, ed., *The Statesman's Year Book, 1991–92*, 128th ed. (New York: St. Martin's Press, 1991), p. 591.

12. Paul A. Goble, "Stalin Draws the Borders," *Central Asia Monitor* no. 2 (1995): 12–14.

13. Torbjorn L. Knutsen, *A History of International Relations Theory* (Manchester, U.K.: Manchester University Press, 1992), pp. 88–91.

14. Ibid., pp. 14–19.

15. Thucydides, *The History of the Peloponnesian War*, ed. Sir Richard Livingstone (London: Oxford University Press, 1978).

16. Paul Kennedy, *The Rise and Fall of the Great Powers: Economic Change and Military Conflict from 1500 to 2000* (New York: Vintage Books, 1989), pp. xv–xxv, 438–446.

17. Knutsen, *History of International Relations Theory*, pp. 188–191, 208–212.

18. "In 1918, when the Versailles Conference was inundated by petitions for sovereignty and statehood, Wilson was taken aback. In 1919, he confessed that he had no idea there existed so many nationalities" (ibid., p. 256).

19. Francis Fukuyama, *The End of History and the Last Man* (New York: Free Press, 1992), chap. 19.

20. Ibid., chap. 20.

21. For listings of these challenges to the legacy of empire, see Morton H. Halperin and David J. Scheffer with Patricia L. Small, *Self-Determination in the New World Order* (Washington, D.C.: Carnegie Endowment for International Peace, 1992), pp. 123–160; and Mark

N. Katz, "The Legacy of Empire in International Relations," *Comparative Strategy* 12, no. 4 (October–December 1993): 367–373.

22. Gary Goertz and Paul F. Diehl, *Territorial Changes and International Conflict* (London: Routledge, 1992), p. 137.

23. Ibid., p. 87.

24. For a succinct discussion of American foreign policy regarding secession during the Cold War, see Halperin et al., *Self-Determination in the New World Order,* pp. 11–12.

25. Galia Golan, *The Soviet Union and National Liberation Movements in the Third World* (Boston: Unwin Hyman, 1988), pp. 262–265, 275–286.

26. Benjamin S. Lambeth, "Russia's Wounded Military," *Foreign Affairs* 74, no. 2 (March–April 1995): 86–98; and John Colarusso, "Chechnya: The War without Winners," *Current History* 94, no. 594 (October 1995): 329–336.

27. Bruce W. Jentleson, "The Pretty Prudent Public: Post Post-Vietnam American Opinion on the Use of Military Force," *International Studies Quarterly* 36, no. 1 (March 1992): 49–74.

28. According to U.S. government sources, total arms exports by all countries fell by 70 percent from 1987 until 1993 (the latest year for which figures are available at the time of writing). U.S. arms exports fell by approximately one-third between 1989 and 1993. Moscow's arms exports fell from a level of about $23 billion per year during the 1980s to only $2.5 billion per year in 1992 and 1993. U.S. Arms Control and Disarmament Agency, *World Military Expenditures and Arms Transfers, 1993–1994* (Washington, D.C., February 1995), pp. 14–18.

3

State Making, State Breaking, and State Failure

MOHAMMED AYOOB

Two significant realities of the current international scene must form the backdrop to any discussion of the failure and disintegration of states and the problem of international order and governance in the last decade of the twentieth century. The first is the incontrovertible fact that the overwhelming majority of conflicts since the end of World War II have been located in the Third World. The second is the equally unassailable fact that most conflicts in the Third World either have been primarily intrastate in character or have possessed a substantial intrastate dimension, even if they appear to the outside observer to be interstate conflicts. This means that problems of international and domestic order have become inextricably intertwined during the current era and are likely to remain enmeshed well into the foreseeable future.

The validity of both these assertions is borne out by tabulations of wars and conflicts made by several scholars, including K. J. Holsti and Evan Luard.[1] That these two trends—concentration of conflicts in the Third World and the primacy of domestic sources of conflict—have continued into the 1990s is confirmed by the figures presented in the *SIPRI Yearbook 1993*, which demonstrate that of the major armed conflicts that were waged in thirty locations around the world in 1992, all but one were intrastate in character. Almost all of these conflicts were located in the old or new Third World.[2] The new Third World refers to states in Central Asia, the Caucasus, and the Balkans that have emerged out of the disintegration of the Soviet Union and the dismemberment of Yugoslavia. There are abundant data, therefore, to support the conclusion that the overwhelming majority of conflicts in the international system since 1945 have been "a ubiquitous corollary of the birth, formation, and fracturing of Third World states."[3]

The end of the Cold War has led not to the irrelevance of the Third World as an explanatory category, but to its expansion as new states have emerged following the breakup of the Soviet Union and of Yugo-slavia and as ethnic antagonisms that had been forced underground by the twin forces of Russian imperialism and Leninist ideology have resurfaced with a vengeance. In terms of their colonial background, the arbitrary construction of their boundaries by external powers, the lack of societal cohesion, their recent emergence into juridical statehood, and their stage of development, the states of the Caucasus and Central Asia and of the Balkans demonstrate political, economic, and social characteristics that are in many ways akin to the Asian, African, and Latin American states that have been traditionally considered as constituting the Third World.

STATE MAKING IN THE THIRD WORLD

The events of the last few years, by removing the Second World from the international equation, have helped present the dichotomy between the global core and the global periphery—the First World and the Third World—in very stark terms.[4] By removing the Cold War overlay from Third World conflicts and thus exposing their fundamental local dynamics, the end of bipolarity has also demonstrated the close linkage between these conflicts and the dynamics of state making (and its obverse, state breaking and state failure) currently underway in the global periphery.

However, the dichotomous representation of the First and the Third Worlds that is currently fashionable hides the essential similarity in their process of state making, which has been (and is) crucial in determining the political trajectories of states. This point becomes clear if one compares the current situation in the Third World not with that prevailing within and among the industrial democracies today, but with the situation from the sixteenth to eighteenth centuries in Western Europe, when the ear-liest of the modern sovereign states were at a stage of state making that corresponded with the stage where most Third World states find themselves today.[5]

The process of state making has been most succinctly defined by Cohen and colleagues as "primitive central state power accumulation."[6] Thus defined, state making must include the following:

- the expansion and consolidation of the territorial and demographic domain under a political authority, including the imposition of order on contested territorial and demographic space (war);

- the maintenance of order in the territory where, and over the population on whom, such order has been already imposed (policing); and

- the extraction of resources from the territory and the population under the control of the state, resources essential not only to support the war-making and policing activities undertaken by the state but also to maintain the apparatuses of state necessary to carry on routine administration, deepen the state's penetration of society, and serve symbolic purposes (taxation).[7]

All three broad categories of activities outlined above, however, depend on the state's success in monopolizing and concentrating the means of coercion in its own hands in the territory and among the population it controls. That is why the accumulation of power becomes so crucial to the state-making enterprise; the more primitive the stage of state building the more primitive and, therefore, the more coercive the strategies employed to accumulate and concentrate power in the hands of the agents of the state. Cohen and colleagues stated in a seminal article published in 1981: "The extent to which an expansion of state power will generate collective violence depends on the *level* of state power prior to that expansion. . . . The lower the initial level of state power, the stronger the relationship between the *rate* of state expansion and collective violence."[8] One needs to be reminded that the violence generated during the process of state making is the result of actions undertaken both by the state and by recalcitrant elements within the population that forcefully resist the state's attempt to impose order.

The inherent similarity in the logic of the state-building process provides us explanations for the current replication by Third World states of several dimensions of the early modern European experience of state making. Simultaneously, the difference in the pace at which state building has to be undertaken and completed in the Third World and the dramatically changed international environment in which Third World state making has to proceed explain the divergence in other dimensions from the earlier European model of state building. The similarities and the differences are equally important, as is the bearing they have on problems of authority and governance with Third World states.

It should be noted that in most of Europe, state making usually antedated the emergence of nations and nation-states by a couple of centuries. This is why it is essential not to confuse the building of modern sovereign states with the emergence of nation-states in the nineteenth and twentieth centuries. The distinction between modern sovereign (or, as Charles Tilly would call them, "national") states and nation-states has been highlighted by Tilly, who has defined the former as "relatively centralized, differentiated, and autonomous organizations successfully claiming priority in the use of force within large, contiguous, and clearly bounded territories." Nation-states, on the other hand, are those "whose peoples share a strong linguistic, religious, and sym-

bolic identity."[9] Nationalism, the necessary condition for the establishment of nation-states, although not of sovereign states, has been defined by Ernest Gellner as "primarily a principle which holds that the political and the national unit should be congruent."[10]

Sovereign and relatively centralized states that have performed successfully over a long period of time—and have therefore knit their people together in terms of historical memories, legal codes, language, religion, and so forth—may evolve into nation-states or at least provide the necessary conditions for the emergence of nation-states, but they are not synonymous with the latter. Historical evidence has convincingly demonstrated that in almost all cases in Europe, with the exception of the Balkans (an exception that may provide the clue to the current violence and strife in that region), the emergence of the modern sovereign state was the precondition for the formation of the nation.[11]

This generalization applied as much to latecomers such as Germany as it did to the earliest examples of modern states such as England and France. Without the central role performed by the Prussian state, Germany would probably have remained nothing more than a geographic or cultural expression. The similarity between the German experience on the one hand and the French experience on the other has been summed up well by Cornelia Navari: "When Hegel insisted that it was the state that created the nation, he was looking backwards to the history of France, not forward to the history of Germany. When Germany was unified 'from above' in 1870 and the Reich was formed, this way of proceeding did not appear to most Germans to be at variance with the experience of their Western neighbors—a substitution of Union 'by force' for the 'organic growth' of France and England. It appeared to be a repetition of it, differing only in that it was less bloody. Here, as there, the state was moving outwards into diverse feudal remnants of the old order, dissolving them, making all obedient to the same law."[12]

The chronological sequence of the establishment of the sovereign state and the evolution of nationalism in the Third World bears very close resemblance to that of modern Europe, with the state taking clear historical precedence over the nation. As Anthony Smith has put it very succinctly, "the western model is essentially a 'state system' rather than a 'nation system'; and this has been its fateful legacy to Africa and Asia." Smith goes on to point out that despite the differences in geopolitical and cultural terms between Europe and the Third World, "the central point ... of the western experience for contemporary African and Asian social and political change has been the primacy and dominance of the specialized, territorially defined, and coercively monopolistic state, operating within a broader system of similar states bent on fulfilling their dual functions of internal regulation and external defence (or aggression)."[13]

In this context, it is instructive to note Tilly's point that "the building of states in Western Europe cost tremendously in death, suffering, loss of rights, and unwilling surrender of land, goods, or labor.... The fundamental reason for the high cost of European state building was its beginning in the midst of a decentralized, largely peasant social structure. Building differentiated, autonomous, centralized organizations with effective control of territories entailed eliminating or subordinating thousands of semi-autonomous authorities.... Most of the European population resisted each phase of the creation of strong states."[14] Tilly's description of conditions in Europe at the birth of modern sovereign states has an uncanny resemblance to present conditions in many Third World societies. It thus helps to explain why if one arranges the current state-building strategies employed in the Third World on a continuum ranging from coercion to persuasion (with the two ends representing ideal types), even those states like India that fall relatively close to the persuasive end of the continuum are forced to rely on significant amounts of coercion—as witnessed in Punjab, Kashmir, and the northeastern states—to entrench and consolidate the authority of the state in regions where it faces, or has faced, major challenges.

In order to replicate the process by which relatively centralized modern states are created, Third World state makers need above all two things: lots of time and a relatively free hand to persuade, cajole, and coerce the disparate populations under their nominal rule to accept the legitimacy of state boundaries and institutions, to accept the right of the state to extract resources from them, and to let the state regulate the more important aspects of their lives. Unfortunately for Third World state elites, neither of these two commodities is available to them in adequate measure.

Our point regarding the availability of time becomes clear if we examine the amount of time it took for the states of Western Europe to emerge as full-fledged sovereign states, enjoying the habitual obedience of their populations, basically secure in the legitimacy of their borders and institutions, and, therefore, in a position where they could respond positively to societal demands, since these demands no longer ran counter to the logic of state building and the accumulation of power in the hands of the state.

It was not until the beginning of the twentieth century that the states of Western Europe and its offshoots in North America emerged as the responsive and representative modern states that we know them to be today—the end products of the state-making process that had unfolded for at least three or four hundred years. Although leading historians of state building in Europe differ about the exact dating of the origins, in the sense of beginnings, of the modern sovereign state, there is little argument about the fact that "it took four to five centuries for European states to overcome their weaknesses, to remedy their administrative deficiencies, and to bring lukewarm loyalty up to the white heat of nationalism."[15]

Unfortunately for Third World state makers, their states cannot afford the luxury of prolonging the traumatic and costly experience of state making over hundreds of years *à la* Europe. The demands of competition with established modern states and the demonstration effect of the existence of socially cohesive, politically responsive, and administratively effective states in the industrialized world make it almost obligatory for Third World states to reach their goal within the shortest time possible or risk international ridicule and permanent peripherality within the system of states. In this context, it is valuable to point out that there was no dearth of "Somalias" and "Liberias" in seventeenth- and eighteenth-century Europe.

The pioneers of European state making (although not the latecomers like Germany and Italy) were remarkably free from systemic pressures and demonstration effects, because all the leading contenders for statehood—England, France, Spain, Holland—were basically in the same boat, trying to navigate the same uncharted sea. Where European states did not have this opportunity and had to telescope some of the sequential phases that together constituted the process of state building into each other, they suffered from a "cumulation of crises."[16] This applied particularly to the states of Germany and Italy, which emerged as unified sovereign entities only in the closing decades of the nineteenth century and were immediately faced with the pressures of mass politics. In fact, it can be argued that the emergence of Italian fascism and German nazism was a result of the Italian and German state elites' inability in the first two decades of the twentieth century to respond successfully, in a context of mass politics, to the accumulated crises threatening their respective states.[17]

If this was the case with Germany, which had the well-established Prussian state at its core, one can well imagine the enormity of the challenge faced by the postcolonial states of the Third World. The latters' problems have been compounded by the fact that they are under pressure to demonstrate adequate statehood quickly, to perform the task of state making in a humane, civilized, and consensual fashion, and to do all this in an era of mass politics. The inadequacy of the time element and the consequent fact that several sequential phases involved in the state-making process have had to be collapsed or telescoped together into one mammoth state-building enterprise go a long way toward explaining the problems of authority and governance faced by the Third World states today.[18] Furthermore, the demand for humane treatment of subject populations during the early stages of state building has made that task in the Third World enormously difficult and complicated.

Given the short time at the disposal of state makers in the Third World and the consequent acceleration in their state-making efforts necessary to demonstrate that they are moving speedily toward effective statehood, crises erupt simultaneously, become unmanageable as the load they put on the political system outruns the political and military capabilities of the state, and lead to a cumulation of crises, which further erodes the legitimacy of the already fragile postcolonial state.

INTERNATIONAL NORMS OF STATEHOOD AND HUMAN RIGHTS

In addition to these internal factors, the workings of the international system, especially the policies adopted by the superpowers during the Cold War era, have also complicated the process of state making in the Third World. By exporting superpower rivalry to the Third World in the form of proxy wars, both interstate and intrastate, and by transferring weapons to governments and insurgents in fragile polities in volatile regional environments, the bipolar global balance during the Cold War era greatly accentuated the insecurities and instabilities in the Third World.[19]

Even more important, certain international norms that have crystallized relatively recently have also had mixed effects on the security and stability of Third World states. Some of these new norms were actually adopted as a result of the entry of the postcolonial states into the international system and because of the pressure generated by the Third World majority, both within international forums like the United Nations General Assembly and outside.

The first of these norms relates to the inalienability of juridical sovereignty or statehood once conferred by international law and symbolized by membership of the United Nations. The sanctity of the borders of postcolonial states forms the logical corollary of this norm. While this international norm has done much to preserve the existence of several Third World states that may have otherwise been inviable, it has also, paradoxically, added to the security predicament of the Third World state. This point can best be understood by recalling that the elimination of states considered inviable, either because of their internal contradictions or because their existence did not suit great power aspirations, was perfectly acceptable to the European international community virtually through the end of the First World War.

The international consensus on the alienability of juridical statehood began to change during the interwar period and crystallized after the Second World War in the context of the decolonization of Asia and Africa. Colonies, once granted independence, acquired the right to exist as sovereign entities, even if many of them (especially in Africa) did not possess "much in the way of empirical statehood, disclosed by a capacity for effective and civil government."[20] This change has meant that while this international norm, which crystallized after World War II, has protected the legal existence of postcolonial states without regard to their internal cohesiveness or the effectiveness of their domestic control, it has been unable to solve the security problems that such states face as a result of the contradictions present within their boundaries and inherent in their state-making process.

It is worth noting here that this guarantee encompassing juridical statehood and territorial integrity seems to have begun to weaken in the post–Cold War era. However, this change in international norms, if consolidated, is unlikely to alleviate the Third World's security predicament. In fact, it is likely to worsen that situation considerably and to add to the prevalent instability and disorder in the Third World, because it has become linked to the issue of the right of ethnic groups to self-determination. It appears, therefore, that the Third World is caught in a no-win situation as far as this set of international norms is concerned.

A second set of international norms that has affected the security of the Third World is related to the issue of human rights, with primary emphasis on civil and political rights. While the modern conception of human rights can be traced to the natural law approach developed in eighteenth-century Europe, the recent normative force that human rights have acquired in the international arena is the result of the acceptance by the vast majority of states of the existence and the validity of such rights for all human beings, irrespective of their status as citizens of particular states.[21]

The changing attitude toward human rights as a legitimate concern of the international community has meant that they needed to be brought within the ambit of international law and rescued from their status as the exclusive preserve of sovereign states in relation to their own citizens. This led to their inclusion in the Preamble and Article 1 of the United Nations Charter and to their codification in the Universal Declaration of Human Rights adopted in 1948 and the two International Covenants on Human Rights that were opened for signature and ratification in 1966 and became operative in 1976.

This was a major development in the evolution of norms that govern the international system, for it acknowledged more clearly than ever before that individuals, as well as states, could now be considered subjects of international law. It also signified the international acceptance of the principle that individuals and groups have rights that are independent of their membership of individual states and that derive not from their national status but from their status as members of the human species.

The major problem with the implementation of human rights in the Third World is the fact that the concept of human rights owes its empirical validity to the existence and successful functioning of the industrialized, representative, and responsive states of Western Europe and North America. These states set the standards for effective statehood, as well as for the humane and civilized treatment of their citizens. They do so by their demonstrated success in simultaneously meeting the basic needs of the large majority of their populations, protecting their human rights, and promoting and guaranteeing political participation. But these states have, by and large, successfully completed their state-building process, are politically satiated and economically affluent, and possess unconditional legitimacy in

the eyes of the overwhelming majority of their populations. They can therefore afford to adopt liberal standards of state behavior in relation to their populations, because they are reasonably secure in the knowledge that societal demands will not run counter to state interests and will not put state structures and institutions in any grave jeopardy.

What are currently considered in the West to be norms of civilized state behavior —including those pertaining to human rights of individuals and groups—are, in the Third World, often in contradiction with the imperatives of state making. These imperatives, as has been pointed out more than once, not only sanction but frequently require the use of violent means against recalcitrant domestic groups and individual citizens. Furthermore, the international norm upholding human rights runs directly counter to the norm which prescribes the inalienability of juridical statehood for Third World states.[22] While the latter is uncompromising in upholding the legality of the existence of Third World states within their colonially constructed boundaries, the former undermines the political legitimacy of these same states by prescribing standards and yardsticks in terms that most Third World states, struggling to perform the minimum tasks of maintaining political order, will be incapable of meeting for many decades to come.

Moreover, the simultaneous but contradictory operation of the two norms contributes to the creation and augmentation of internal discontent within Third World states. It does so by, on the one hand, forcing all the diverse and dissatisfied elements within Third World states to remain within their postcolonial boundaries and, on the other, encouraging these very elements to make political, administrative, and economic demands on the states that these states cannot respond to. The states cannot respond either because they lack the capabilities to do so or because doing so could seriously jeopardize their territorial integrity.

One can make the argument on behalf of Third World states, still struggling to translate their juridical statehood into empirical statehood, that the case for human rights (whether of individuals or groups) and against the state's use of violent means to impose order is not as morally unassailable as it may appear at first sight. This point can be made most effectively in the context of the failed states phenomenon, where state structures have completely collapsed.[23] In these cases, it can be demonstrated that in the absence of even rudimentarily effective states to provide a minimum degree of political order—as in Lebanon for the fifteen years of civil war, or as currently in Somalia, Afghanistan, Rwanda, Burundi, and Liberia, to mention just a few examples—the concept of human rights remains nothing more than a pure abstraction. In such a context, the human rights ideal is impossible to implement even minimally, because in the absence of the sovereign a truly Hobbesian state of nature prevails, and the very survival of large segments of populations cannot be assured.

These comments should not be taken as an apologia for authoritarian regimes in the Third World that ostensibly emphasize order at the expense of both justice and political participation. Authoritarian regimes quite often contribute a great deal to the creation and augmentation of disorder in Third World states despite paying lip service to the objective of maintaining and promoting order. Iran under the shah, the Philippines under Marcos, Zaire under Mobutu, and Nicaragua under Somoza—to quote but a few instances—all provide good examples of this tendency.

It is also true that most regimes in the Third World—especially authoritarian ones, but not excluding such democratic governments as that in India under Indira Gandhi—attempt to portray threats to their regimes as threats to the state. Discerning analysts must, therefore, carefully distinguish between issues of regime security and those of state security. However, in many cases, given the lack of unconditional legitimacy both of the regime and of the state structure in the Third World and the close perceptual connection between regime and state as far as the majority of the state's population is concerned, the line between regime security and state security becomes so thin, and the interplay between the two so dense, that it is virtually impossible to disentangle one from the other. As one perceptive scholar pointed out in connection with the Middle East, "those who rule must attempt to encourage loyalty to the state, of which they hope themselves to be the chief beneficiaries, while at the same time seeking to disguise the fact that their system of power, and thus the identity of the political structure itself, frequently owes more to the old ties of sectarian and tribal loyalty."[24] In many such countries the fall of the regime is likely to signal the failure of the state as well; any student of Tudor England or Bourbon France will find this phenomenon very familiar.

ETHNONATIONAL SELF-DETERMINATION

The human rights issue raises a further problem. Given the multi-ethnic nature of most Third World states, if human rights are interpreted as group rights and, therefore, are seen to include the right to ethnonational self-determination, they are likely to pose grave threats to the territorial integrity and juridical statehood of postcolonial states, once again pitting one set of international norms against another. The renewed legitimation of the notion of ethnonational self-determination following the end of the Cold War—especially in Europe, symbolized by the prompt recognition accorded to the successor states to the Soviet Union and Yugoslavia and the separation of Slovakia from the Czech Republic—is likely to give a fillip to demands for ethnic separatism in the Third World.

Given the latent tensions between ethnicity and state-defined nationalism even in functioning federal polities like India and the clear contradiction between ethnonationalism and state-defined nationalism in much of the Third World, any development anywhere in the international arena that may encourage ethnic separatist demands in the context of state and regime fragilities prevalent in the Third World is bound to add to the great strains already existing within these polities.[25] The veracity of this assertion is borne out by the fact that "under the banner of self-determination, there are active movements in more than sixty countries —one-third of the total roster of nations— to achieve full sovereignty or some lesser degree of 'minority' rights. A number of these movements have developed into ongoing civil wars."[26]

In this context, the international community's (and especially the major powers') endorsement of the doctrine of ethnonational self-determination—even if limited to exceptional cases as in the Balkans, the former Soviet Union, and the former Czechoslovakia—is bound to augment the challenge to the legitimacy of the principle that postcolonial states in their present form are territorially inviolable. The effects of such a contagion spreading have been summed up in a recent Council on Foreign Relations study that concluded that "while the creation of some new states may be necessary or inevitable, the fragmentation of international society into hundreds of independent territorial entities is a recipe for an even more dangerous and anarchic world."[27]

A major problem with ethnonational self-determination relates to the definition of the ethnic self seeking to determine its future. The self-perception and self-definition of ethnicity is usually subject to change, depending on the context in which it operates at any point in time. This is what Crawford Young has referred to as "the dynamic and changing character of contemporary ethnicity: Far from representing a fixed and immutable set of static social facts, cultural pluralism is itself evolving in crucial ways and is in major respects contextual, situational, and circumstantial."[28] Therefore, to link such a potent ideology as that of self-determination to a malleable idea like that of ethnicity—and then to legitimize this combination by reference to the principle of human rights of groups—is bound to introduce even greater disorder in the Third World than is already present, because it endows the demands of every disgruntled ethnic group with the legitimacy of the ideal of national self-determination. The danger is that this is exactly what the renewed popularity of the idea of ethnonational self-determination may end up achieving to the great detriment of both order and justice in the Third World.

The problem is further confounded by the fact that given the ethnic mixtures of populations in most countries, hardly any pure ethnic homelands still exist. This fact contradicts the ethnonationalists' assumption that "the earth's entire population, or most of it, divides into a finite number of distinct, homogeneous peoples. It follows that the world's ideal condition consists of that finite number of nation-states."[29] Attempts at ethnonational self-determination are, therefore, bound to run into resistance from ethnic minorities in presumed ethnic homelands. As William Pfaff has succinctly put it: "The ethnic state is a product of the political imagination; it does not exist in reality. . . . The idea of the ethnic nation thus is a permanent provocation to war."[30] Such conflict is expected to result either in virulent forms of ethnic cleansing or in the carving out of microstates from the mini-states established on the basis of ethnic nationalism, or both.

Quasi-States and Failed States

Related to the issue of ethnonational self-determination is the failed states phenomenon. Jack Snyder has succinctly described the link between the two by describing ethnic nationalism as "the default option." According to Snyder, ethnic nationalism "predominates when institutions collapse, when existing institutions are not fulfilling people's basic needs, and when satisfactory alternative structures are not readily available."[31] While this may not provide the total explanation for the revival of ethno-nationalism, it does capture a very major ingredient that has contributed to the recent popularity of the ethnonationalist ideology, namely the lack of effective statehood. This is true not only in the case of the components of the former Soviet Union and of the former Yugoslavia, but also in many parts of the Third World. The lack of effective statehood was responsible for the emergence of what Robert Jackson has termed "quasi-states" in the Third World.[32] These quasi-states can now clearly be seen as precursors of failed states in the global South.

The end of the Cold War has had an important impact on the transformation of some of these quasi-states into failed states. This is especially true in the case of those states that had witnessed high levels of superpower involvement in the military sphere, including the arena of arms transfers, during the Cold War era. At the height of the Cold War, the superpowers attempted to strengthen client governments in internally fragmented states, often seeking to maintain a semblance of stability within countries that were allied with one superpower or the other. One major instrument of such support was the transfer of large quantities of relatively sophisticated arms to friendly regimes. In several instances, such arms transfers led to countervailing transfers of weaponry by the rival superpower to forces opposed to the central authorities. Afghanistan during the 1980s came to epitomize this action-reaction phenomenon.[33]

Past superpower policies of pouring in arms into fragmented polities have, however, become a major source of instability and disorder in the post–Cold War period. The presence of large quantities of relatively sophisticated weaponry (ranging from AK-47s to Stinger missiles) and the withdrawal of superpower support to weak and vulnerable regimes—support that was essential to prevent the central authorities from being overwhelmed by domestic rivals who, in turn, were divided among themselves—have created near-total anarchy in countries like Afghanistan and Somalia, where central authority has completely collapsed thereby turning these quasi-states into failed states.

Democratization in the Third World

Many state elites in the Third World seem to have realized that the only way to prevent state making from being transformed into state failure is to grant greater political participation to those sectors of society—whether ethnic or socioeconomic—that were heretofore excluded from the exercise of political power. The recent wave of democratization in the Third World is in substantial part the result of the realization among the ruling elites in the developing countries that the survival of their states and regimes is crucially dependent upon defusing the severe crisis of legitimacy that they face in the last decade of the twentieth century.

It would be too naive to suggest, however, that democratization—defined in terms of increasing guarantees for the exercise of civil and political liberties and in terms of political participation through the medium of competitive electoral politics—by itself, and in all contexts, will succeed in neutralizing ethnic separatism.[34] The success of the democratic experiment in defusing ethnic tensions will, therefore, depend on a number of factors, identified by de Nevers as including "the speed with which ethnic issues are recognized; the level of ethnic tension when the democratization process begins; the size and power of different ethnic groups within the state; the ethnic composition of the previous regime and its opposition; the political positions of the leaders of the main ethnic groups; the presence or absence of external ethnic allies; and the ethnic composition of the military."[35]

There is, however, another side to the democratization coin. The demands of state building and democratization can only be reconciled if the democratizing state in the Third World is credibly able to monopolize the instruments of violence within its territories, thus preventing dissident groups from attempting to change the state's boundaries when political controls are relaxed. This monopoly over instruments of violence is essential because "often the first act of forces liberated by the introduction of democracy is to seek some permanent escape from the state they see as having oppressed them."[36]

This is where the most severe problems are likely to arise, even if democratic political systems become the norm rather than the exception in the Third World. Democratic and (even more important) democratizing regimes cannot afford to be seen as weak when confronted by separatist challenges and cannot, in the final analysis, give up their right to lay down and enforce the rules (even if some of these have been negotiated with the opponents of the state) by which the game of politics is to be played within the boundaries of states over which they preside. Otherwise, the "democratic center may be questioned for its inefficiency in creating or its weakness in handling the secessionist crisis, opening the way for military intervention."[37]

This point is inadequately understood by most proponents of democratization in the Third World, who tend to equate democratic states with weak states on the assumption that strong states are bound to be autocratic by nature.[38] By making this assumption they fail to learn from the European experience that democracy emerged as the final stage of the state-building process and not at the expense of state building. Even in today's context, when democratization cannot wait until state building is completed, it cannot thrive in the absence of the political order that only a strongly entrenched state can provide.

Democratization, therefore, must complement rather than contradict the process of state making; without the political order that can be provided only by effective states, the gains of democratization cannot be sustained. Anarchies—as the examples of Lebanon, Somalia, Liberia, and Afghanistan clearly demonstrate—are no respecters of democratic values.

However, the reconciliation of the two imperatives of the consolidation of state power and democratization is not, and will not be, an easy task even if tremendous good will is present on all sides. Major tensions are bound to arise between state elites and their ethnic and political opponents who would like to put significant curbs on the power of the central state. In addition, where separatist insurgencies are already under way, major problems between separatists and democratizing central governments are likely to center around two basic questions: What is the guarantee that groups espousing separatism will indeed surrender all arms and reconcile themselves to autonomous or semi-autonomous status that will continue to be essentially dependent upon the good faith and the continuing political sagacity of the central government?

What is the guarantee that central authorities after persuading separatist ethnic groups to lay down their arms and thus having overcome immediate internal security crises, will continue to abide by their commitment to popular political participation, the constitutional protection of minority rights, and regional autonomy?

The answers provided by the Third World's historical record to both these questions do not leave much room for optimism. Furthermore, if one goes by the earlier European experience, one is likely to conclude that the historical juncture at which most Third World states find themselves today is unlikely to permit a great deal of ethnic accommodation and political participation. These two processes usually run counter to the overriding imperative of consolidating state power and fashioning a state that is sovereign, not merely juridically but also empirically. However, one can make an effective argument that the late-twentieth-century context is so dramatically different from the late-eighteenth- or even the late-nineteenth-century contexts that radically new solutions must be found for this dilemma.

In other words, the problem of reconciling the demands of state making with those of democratization and human rights—as well as with demands for regional autonomy, devolution of powers, and protection of minority group rights—will have to be addressed much more creatively, and mutually acceptable solutions will have to be found, if the twin specters of failed states and destructive ethnonationalism are to be kept at bay. Above all, this means that the trajectories of democratization (including the preservation of group rights and local autonomy for substate units) on the one hand and of the consolidation of coercive power and concentration of legitimate authority in the hands of the state on the other must not diverge radically. In fact, they

should ideally become mutually legitimizing agents, with democratization legitimizing the greater concentration of authority in the hands of the state and the concentration of centralized power legitimizing and facilitating the loosening of political controls and the guaranteeing of political and civil rights to the citizenry.

Most important, the two processes should not be allowed to become the polar opposites of each other. Faced with a stark choice between the territorial integrity of the state and democratization, state elites are invariably bound to opt for territorial integrity over democratization. Where the processes of territorial integrity and democracy collide, democratization cannot prevail without the disintegration of the state. Therefore, in order for the strategy of democratization to work successfully without threatening the disintegration of states, the state elites' decision to democratize must be firmly linked to the negotiated surrender of separatist groups where they exist. The disarming of such groups should proceed in tandem with the implementation of any plans for autonomy or devolution of powers that may have been negotiated between the parties.

THE ROLE OF THE INTERNATIONAL COMMUNITY IN DEMOCRATIZATION

The international community, working through the United Nations, can play a constructive role in encouraging reconciliation between state building and democratization. It can do so if it adopts a restrictive approach toward recognizing new political entities that attempt to break away from established states in the Third World. A too-permissive approach to state breaking, as witnessed in the case of the former Yugoslavia, will add to conflict and anarchy rather than preserve international order. Colonially imposed state boundaries may be an iniquitous way of delineating the borders of Third World states, but every other alternative appears to be infinitely worse.

The United Nations must not fall into the trap of giving legitimacy to demands for secession from member-states, unless the terms have been peacefully negotiated with the parent state. Exceptions like the Eritrean case must not influence, let alone determine, the norms of international behavior. Eritrea was a special case because its separation was negotiated with the new regime in Ethiopia. Furthermore, Eritrea regained the colonially crafted political identity within the colonial boundaries that had been compromised in 1952 by the internationally sponsored merger of the former Italian colony with the Ethiopian empire and the subsequent flagrant violation by Addis Ababa of Eritrean autonomy that had formed an integral part of the merger agreement.

International norms and the policies of international actors—primarily great powers and international institutions—can play a crucial role in persuading domestic protagonists to make deals without violating the sovereignty of existing states. Above all, the international community can strengthen the juridical status and bolster the political authority of Third World states by refusing to countenance secessionist demands, while trying to persuade all parties to accept the notion that self-determination must be de-linked from secession and should be defined in terms of empowering those segments of the population that have been denied access to political and economic power. In other words, self-determination should be perceived as synonymous with democratization (and its attendant power-sharing arrangements), rather than with the breakup of existing states.

This attitude will send clear signals to all concerned that the sovereign existence of postcolonial states is an essential prerequisite for the creation and maintenance of both domestic and international order. It will also signal that regimes that do not demonstrate a willingness to democratize must be ready to face international opprobrium, pariah status, and even sanctions. Such a stance on the part of the international community is necessary to prevent the Third World from sliding into greater anarchy. For, above all, it must be recognized that the problem of order in the Third World cannot be tackled by trying to transcend the Westphalian model (a world made up of sovereign states), but by attempting to strengthen it. The root cause of disorder in the Third World is linked to the inadequacy of state authority and not to the excessive use of state power. The augmentation of authority usually leads to a decrease in the reliance on force by the state because, as Robert Jackman has argued, power without force is the true measure of the political capacity of states.[39]

NOTES

1. Kalevi J. Holsti, *Peace and War: Armed Conflicts and International Order, 1648–1989* (Cambridge, U.K.: Cambridge University Press, 1991), table 11.1, pp. 274–278; and Evan Luard, *War in International Society: A Study in International Sociology* (London: I. B. Tauris, 1986), app. 5, pp. 442–446.

2. Ramses Amer, Birger Heldt, Signe Landgren, Kjell Magnusson, Erik Melander, Kjell-Ake Nordquist, Thomas Ohlson, and Peter Wallensteen, "Major Armed Conflicts," in *SIPRI [Stockholm International Peace Research Institute] Yearbook 1993: World Armaments and Disarmament* (Oxford, U.K.: Oxford University Press, 1993), p. 81.

3. K. J. Holsti, "International Theory and War in the Third World," in *The Insecurity Dilemma: National Security of Third World States*, ed. Brian L. Job (Boulder, Colo.: Lynne Rienner, 1992), p. 38.

4. Shahram Chubin has made a similar argument forcefully in "The South and the New

World Order," *Washington Quarterly* 16, no. 4 (Autumn 1993): 87–107.

5. For greater detail on this argument, see Mohammed Ayoob, "The Security Predicament of the Third World State: Reflections on State Making in a Comparative Perspective," in *The Insecurity Dilemma,* ed. Job, pp. 63–80.

6. Youssef Cohen, Brian R. Brown, and A. F. K. Organski, "The Paradoxical Nature of State Making: The Violent Creation of Order," *American Political Science Review* 75, no. 4 (1981): 902.

7. For expanded discussions of the process of state making and its relationship to organized violence, see Keith Jaggers, "War and the Three Faces of Power: War Making and State Making in Europe and the Americas," *Comparative Political Studies* 25, no. 1 (April 1992): 26–62; and Charles Tilly, "War Making and State Making as Organized Crime," in *Bringing the State Back In,* ed. Peter B. Evans, Dietrich Rueschemeyer, and Theda Skocpol (New York: Cambridge University Press, 1985), pp. 169–191.

8. Cohen et al., "The Paradoxical Nature of State Making," p. 905 (emphasis in the original).

9. Charles Tilly, *Coercion, Capital, and European States, AD 990–1990,* (Cambridge, Mass.: Basil Blackwell, 1990), p. 43.

10. Ernest Gellner, *Nations and Nationalism,* (Ithaca, N.Y.: Cornell University Press, 1983), p. 1.

11. For details of this argument and the data on which it is based, see Charles Tilly, ed., *The Formation of National States in Western Europe* (Princeton, N.J.: Princeton University Press, 1975). See also Cornelia Navari, "The Origins of the Nation-State," in *The Nation-State: The Formation of Modern Politics,* ed. Leonard Tivey (Oxford, U.K.: Martin Robertson, 1981), pp. 13–38.

12. Navari, "Origins of the Nation-State," p. 34.

13. Anthony D. Smith, *State and Nation in the Third World* (New York: St. Martin's Press, 1983), pp. 11, 17.

14. Charles Tilly, "Reflections on the History of European State Making," in *The Formation of National States in Western Europe,* ed. Tilly, p. 71.

15. Joseph R. Strayer, *On the Medieval Origins of the Modern State* (Princeton, N.J.: Princeton University Press, 1970), p. 57.

16. Stein Rokkan, "Dimensions of State Formation and Nation Building: A Possible Paradigm for Research on Variations within Europe," in *The Formation of National States in Western Europe,* ed. Tilly, p. 586.

17. For theoretically informed accounts of the "cumulation of crises" in Italy and Germany, see the chapters on Italy and Germany by Raymond Grew and John R. Gillis, respectively, in *Crises of Political Development in Europe and the United States,* ed. Grew (Princeton, N.J.: Princeton University Press, 1978).

18. The earliest modern states of Western Europe were able to complete their state-making process in three near-distinct phases: (1) establishing the centralized, "absolutist" state at the expense of a feudal order that had begun to lose much of its economic and political utility; (2) welding together the subjects of the centralized monarchy into a people with a common history, legal system, language, and, quite often, religion (in the sense of Christian schisms), thus leading to the evolution of a national identity and the transformation of the centralized monarchical state into a nation-state; and (3) gradually extending representative institutions (dictated by the necessity to co-opt into the power structure new and powerful social forces that emerged as a result of the industrial revolution), over decades if not centuries. Above all, as Stein Rokkan has pointed out, "what is important is that the western nation-states were given a chance to solve some of the worst problems of state building before they had to face the ordeals of mass politics" ("Dimensions of State Formation and Nation Building," in *The Formation of National States in Western Europe,* ed. Tilly, p. 598).

19. For details of this argument, see Mohammed Ayoob, *The Third World Security Predicament: State Making, Regional Conflict, and the International System* (Boulder, Colo.: Lynne Rienner, 1995), chap. 5.

20. Robert H. Jackson, "Quasi-States, Dual Regimes, and Neoclassical Theory: International Jurisprudence and the Third World,"

International Organization 41, no. 4 (Autumn 1987): 529.

21. R. J. Vincent, *Human Rights and International Relations* (Cambridge, U.K.: Cambridge University Press, 1986), pp. 19–36.

22. As Seyom Brown has pointed out, the intellectual position that "servicing . . . basic human rights is the principal task of human polities—and that the worth of any polity is a function of how well it performs this task—has put the legitimacy of all extant polities up for grabs, so to speak. Whether particular nation-states, and the prevailing territorial demarcations, do indeed merit the badge of political legitimacy is, according to this view, subject to continuing assessment; accordingly, neither today's governments nor today's borders are sacrosanct." *International Relations in a Changing Global System: Toward a Theory of the World Polity* (Boulder, Colo.: Westview Press, 1992), p. 126.

23. For a discussion of failed states, see I. William Zartman, *Collapsed States: The Disintegration and Restoration of Legitimate Authority* (Boulder, Colo.: Lynne Rienner, 1995).

24. Charles Tripp, "Near East," in *Superpower Competition and Security in the Third World,* ed. Robert S. Litwak and Samuel F. Wells, Jr. (Cambridge, Mass.: Ballinger, 1988), p. 113.

25. For an incisive discussion of the difference between ethnicity and ethnonationalism, see Ashutosh Varshney, "Contested Meanings: India's National Identity, Hindu Nationalism, and the Politics of Anxiety," *Daedalus* 122, no. 3 (Summer 1993): 230.

26. Lloyd N. Cutler, "Foreword," in Morton H. Halperin and David J. Scheffer with Patricia L. Small, *Self-Determination in the New World Order* (Washington, D.C.: Carnegie Endowment for International Peace, 1992), p. xi.

27. Gidon Gottlieb, *Nation Against State: A New Approach to Ethnic Conflicts and the Decline of Sovereignty* (New York: Council on Foreign Relations, 1993), p. 2.

28. Crawford Young, "The Temple of Ethnicity," *World Politics* 35, no. 4 (July 1983): 659.

29. Charles Tilly, "National Self-Determination as a Problem for All of Us," *Daedalus* 122, no. 3 (Summer 1993): 30.

30. William Pfaff, "Invitation to War," *Foreign Affairs* 72, no. 3 (Summer 1993): 99, 101.

31. Jack Snyder, "Nationalism and the Crisis of the Post-Soviet State," *Survival* 35, no. 1 (Spring 1993): 12.

32. Robert H. Jackson, *Quasi-States: Sovereignty, International Relations and the Third World* (Cambridge, U.K.: Cambridge University Press, 1990).

33. For details of the situation in Afghanistan in the 1980s during the height of superpower involvement in that country's civil war, see Olivier Roy, *Islam and Resistance in Afghanistan,* 2nd ed. (Cambridge, U.K.: Cambridge University Press, 1990).

34. Democratization is used in the sense of movement toward democracy; the latter is perceived as the desired goal, while the former is the process through which this goal is achieved or at least approximated.

35. Renee de Nevers, "Democratization and Ethnic Conflict," *Survival* 35, no. 2 (Summer 1993): 31–32.

36. John Chipman, "Managing the Politics of Parochialism," *Survival* 35, no. 1 (Spring 1993): 168.

37. Larry Diamond, Juan J. Linz, and Seymour Martin Lipset, "Introduction: Comparing Experiences with Democracy," in Larry Diamond, Juan J. Linz, and Seymour Martin Lipset, *Politics in Developing Countries: Comparing Experiences with Democracy* (Boulder, Colo.: Lynne Rienner, 1990), p. 29.

38. For example, Rajni Kothari, *State Against Democracy: In Search of Humane Governance* (Delhi, India: Ajanta Publications, 1988).

39. Robert W. Jackman, *Power Without Force: The Political Capacity of Nation-States* (Ann Arbor: University of Michigan Press, 1993).

4

Minorities, Nationalists, and Ethnopolitical Conflict

TED ROBERT GURR

Effective management of ethnopolitical conflict by civil or international authorities presupposes an understanding of its nature and causes. This chapter attempts to give order to some of the current evidence and explanations about ethnopolitical conflicts. These are conflicts in which groups that define themselves using ethnic or national criteria —like the Mayans of Chiapas and the Bosnian Serbs—make claims on behalf of their collective interests against the state, or against other political actors. The following general points need to be kept in mind.

- The "ethnic criteria" used by these groups to define themselves may include common descent, shared historical experiences, and valued cultural traits. There is no warrant for assuming that any one basis for ethnic or cultural identity (such as religion, language, race, or a common homeland) is inherently more important than any other.

- The claims made by ethnopolitical groups include material and political demands, as well as claims arising from their cultural and religious concerns. One cannot explain away the significance of cultural identity by arguing that what "really" motivates such groups is the quest for well-being or power. The important factor is that ethnopolitical groups organize around their shared identity and seek gains for members of their group. It is seriously misleading to interpret the Zapatistas as just a peasants' movement or the Bosnian Serbs as the equivalent of a political party: They draw their strength from cultural bonds, not associational ones.

- Ethnopolitical groups are highly diverse. National peoples are territorially concentrated cultural groups, usually with a history of separate political existence, who seek political independence from or greater autonomy within the states that govern them. The Mayans of Chiapas and the Bosnian Serbs illustrate two different types: The Mayans are indigenous peoples, the Bosnian Serbs are ethnonationalists. Minority peoples are culturally distinct groups in plural societies who seek equal rights, opportunities, and access to power within existing political communities. The Shiites of southern Iraq are one example, African Americans in the United States and Brazil are another.

- The claims and political strategies of ethnopolitical groups vary according to their type and circumstances. National peoples usually seek "exit," a goal that often leads to ethnonational rebellion and state repression. Minority peoples want "access," a goal that is usually pursued by conventional political action and protest campaigns. In political systems that are open and responsive to ethnopolitical claims, leaders of ethnopolitical groups usually choose to pursue both kinds of objectives by nonviolent strategies. In states that suppress or ignore such claims, leaders are likely to follow strategies of violence that often escalate into protracted communal warfare.

HOW SERIOUS IS THE ETHNOPOLITICAL CHALLENGE TO GLOBAL SECURITY?

Ethnopolitical conflict has been the world's most common source of warfare, insecurity, and loss of life for several decades. The evidence cited below comes mainly from the Minorities at Risk project, an ongoing global study of the status, grievances, and conflicts of politically active ethnic groups.[1]

- Nearly 100 national and minority peoples took part in serious, violent conflict at some time between 1945 and 1990. Sixty of these conflicts were fought over issues of group autonomy and lasted at least a decade.

- At the beginning of 1996, there were more than forty violent ethnopolitical conflicts under way, at least one of them in every world region. In our judgment, about half of them are at risk of escalation and repression: They are likely sources of future humanitarian crises.

- Since 1945, according to research by Barbara Harff, there have been nearly fifty episodes of genocide and mass political murder targeted at more than seventy different ethnic and religious minorities and causing a total of at least 9 million and as many as 20 million civilian fatalities.[2]

- At the beginning of 1995, there were about 23 million internationally recognized refugees; another 27 million were internally displaced. The great majority of these people were fleeing from civil wars, interethnic rivalries, and campaigns of mass murder and ethnic cleansing.[3]

The alarmist interpretation of these kinds of data is that the world is on the downward slope to anarchy within and among states and to polarization of the world along lines of cleavage among civilizations.[4] Other evidence suggests a somewhat more optimistic outlook.

- Of the fifty most serious ethnopolitical conflicts being fought in 1994, ten were escalating and fifteen were stable; the others were deescalating, either because of military defeats (ten conflicts) or because of negotiations and government-initiated reforms (fifteen conflicts).[5] The latter include several supposedly long-term and "intractable" conflicts that are on the verge of enduring settlement, for example, the Phillipine Moro, Palestinian-Israeli, and Northern Ireland conflicts.

- One-sixth, at most, of the world's population identifies with politically active cultural groups. More precisely, a survey

Table 4.1. Minorities at Risk in 1995, by Region.

World Region	Number of Countries with Minorities at Risk	Number of Minorities at Risk	Population of Minorities at Risk (1995 est.)
Western democracies and Japan (21)	15	30	90,789,000 (10.8%)
Eastern Europe and Soviet successor states (27)	24	59	53,704,000 (12.3%)
East, Southeast, and South Asia (21)	19	57	441,732,000 (14.4%)
North Africa and the Middle East (19)	11	26	94,263,000 (27.3%)
Africa south of the Sahara (38)	28	66	226,695,000 (36.9%)
Latin America and the Caribbean (23)	17	30	112,320,000 (23.3%)
TOTAL (149)	114	268	1,019,503,000 (17.7%)

Note: Politically significant national and minority peoples of 100,000 or more in countries with 1995 populations greater than one million, based on current research by the Minorities at Risk Project, Center for International Development and Conflict Management, University of Maryland. Changing political circumstances and new information lead to periodic updates in the inclusion or exclusion of groups under observation. Numbers of countries above the one-million population threshold are shown in parentheses in the "World Region" column. Most population figures for national and minority peoples are estimates, although some are conjectural. Percentages of regional population are shown in parentheses in the "Population of Minorities at Risk" column and are calculated from UN estimates for all countries in each region.

just completed by the Minorities at Risk project has identified 268 politically significant national and minority peoples in the larger countries of the world. The outer bound of potential supporters for these ethnopolitical movements is slightly more than one billion, or 17.7 percent of the global population. These groups are much more numerous in some regions than others, as shown in table 4.1. The proportions in the western democracies, the post-Communist states, and Asia are below the world mean; and two-thirds of these peoples are minorities who seek recognition and rights within existing societies, not a redrawing of international boundaries. (For maps showing minority proportions in the Americas, Europe, Africa, Middle East and West Asia, Soviet successor states, and Asia, see pp. 56–61. Note that these geographic regions do not correspond exactly with the world regions listed in table 4.1.)

MODERNIZATION AND ETHNOPOLITICAL CONFLICT

The upward trend in ethnopolitical conflict that has captured world attention in the 1990s began in the 1960s, as we showed in the Minorities at Risk study.[6] The end of the Cold War made such conflicts more visible. Some were provoked by contention for power in post-Communist states. But neither the Cold War nor its passing created the cultural identities, animosities, or aspirations that spark these conflicts. Rather, the trend is best understood as an indirect consequence of global processes of modernization.

Modernization refers to three large and interdependent changes that have reshaped

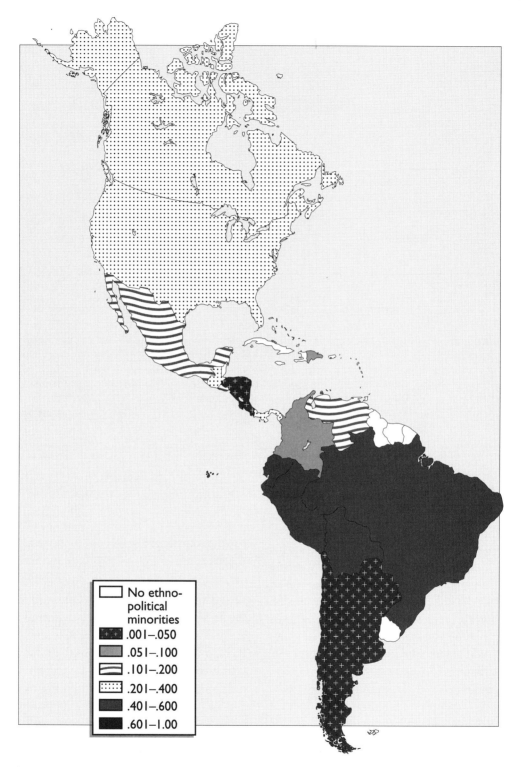

The Americas: Minority Proportions of Country Population

Legend:
- No ethno-political minorities
- .001–.050
- .051–.100
- .101–.200
- .201–.400
- .401–.600
- .601–1.00

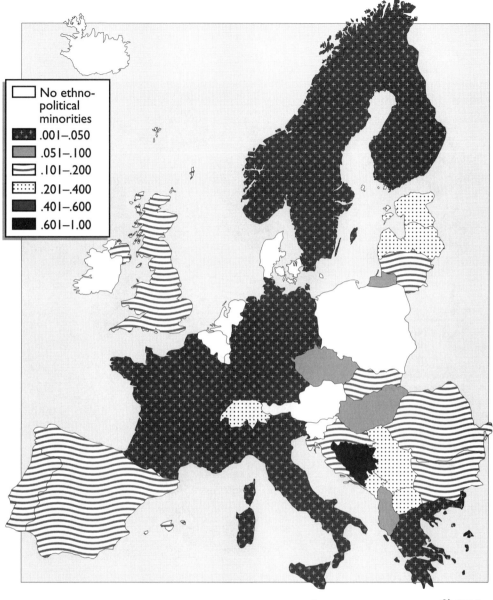

Europe: Minority Proportions of Country Population

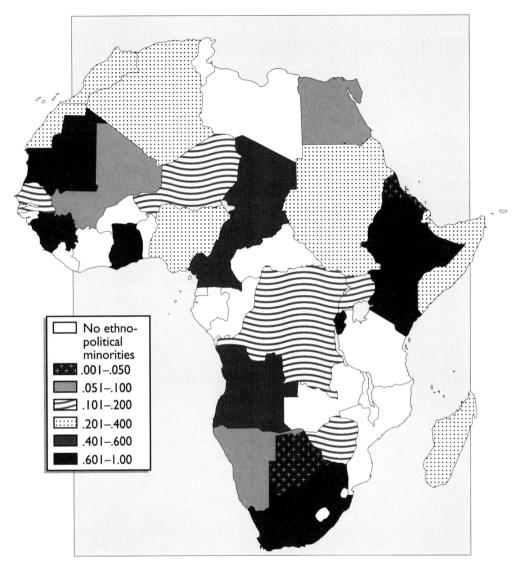

Africa: Minority Proportions of Country Population

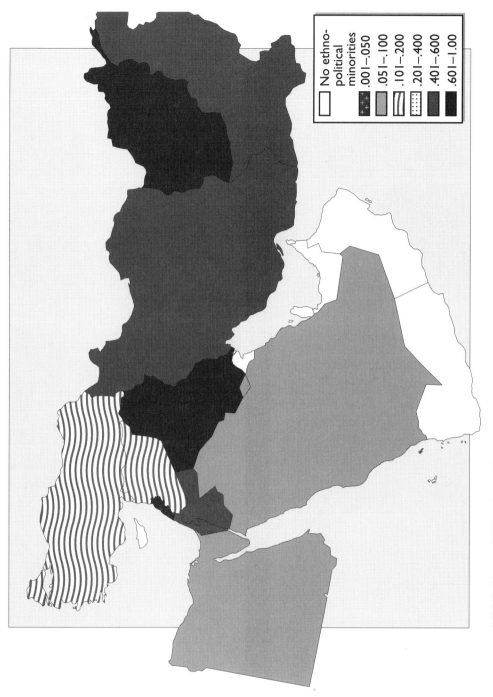

Middle East and West Asia: Minority Proportions of Country Population

No ethno-
political
minorities
.001–.050
.051–.100
.101–.200
.201–.400
.401–.600
.601–1.00

Soviet Successor States: Minority Proportions of Country Population

Legend:
- No ethno-political minorities
- .001–.050
- .051–.100
- .101–.200
- .201–.400
- .401–.600
- .601–1.00

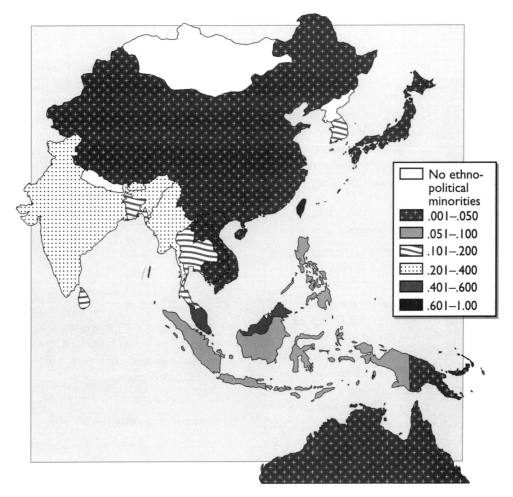

Asia: Minority Proportions of Country Population

the world in the last half-century: the growth of the modern state and the state system, economic development, and the communications revolution.[7] The processes of modernization are not new, but their pace and reach since 1950 have no historical precedent. In combination they have vastly increased interaction and competition among cultural groups, as well as contention between cultural groups and the state.

Expansion of State Powers

Virtually all new and postrevolutionary states of the last half-century have been committed to consolidating and expanding their powers, emulating the precedents established by the successful states of the industrial North. This objective dictates, among other things, that states subordinate the special interests and relative autonomy of hundreds of ethnic groups to state elites' conception of national identity and interest. State building almost everywhere in the Third World has meant policies aimed at assimilating national and minority peoples, restraining their historical autonomy, and extracting their resources, revenues, and labor for the use of the state. The building of new Communist states in Eastern Europe after 1945 had the same implications and consequences.

Some minority peoples, including most of the overseas Chinese of Southeast Asia, for example, have been able to share power and prosperity at the center of new states. Others—especially in Africa, where the reach of state power is limited—have been able to hold on to de facto local autonomy. But the net effect of state building in most parts of the world has been to substantially increase the grievances of most culturally distinct groups, those who have either not been strong enough to protect their autonomy or not been allowed to participate meaningfully in power at the center.

The Development of a Global Economic System

The worldwide impetus to industrialize and to exploit underutilized human and natural resources has benefited some cultural groups and harmed others. Ethnoclasses in developing societies have often gained from expanding economic opportunities; some also have mobilized in efforts to overcome discriminatory barriers that restricted their access to new wealth. Indigenous peoples have been most adversely affected. Like it or not, their resources and labor are being absorbed into national and international networks of economic activity. They are almost always disadvantaged by the terms of their incorporation. Their reactions have been especially sharp in response to the alienation of the lands, forests, and natural resources on which they are both culturally and materially dependent.[8]

The Communications Revolution

The spread of the mass media and the ready availability of electronic forms of communication facilitate or enhance every stage in the conflict process. Rapid and dense communication networks make cultural groups more aware of their identities and shared interests, bringing them into close contact with supporters and sources of inspiration elsewhere. They also give leaders powerful means to mobilize mass followings and coordinate their political actions. Virtually every new communication technique has been adapted by ethnopolitical groups for their own purposes. Islamic activists have used audio cassettes to spread their gospel of revival and revolution since the 1970s. The Miskito Indians of Nicaragua used the radiophones of Moravian churches to coordinate their resistance to the Sandinistas in the early 1980s. A great many ethnic activist organizations now are on the Internet; the GreenNet is especially favored by activists.

WHY MINORITIES REBEL: POLITICAL MOBILIZATION OF ETHNIC GRIEVANCES

The central question of this chapter is why and how culturally distinct groups become engaged in protest and rebellion against the state. Modernization sets the larger context. The specifics of each group's situation determine how it acts within that context.

The first assumption of the explanation sketched below is that cultural identities—those based on common descent, language, and belief—are stronger and more enduring than most other collective identities. The second assumption is that cultural identity is most likely to provide the basis for political mobilization and conflict when it provides the basis for invidious distinctions among peoples. By "invidious distinctions" we mean inequalities among cultural groups in status, economic well-being, and access to political power that are deliberately maintained through public policy and social practice.

The explanation proposed here thus incorporates two kinds of theoretical assumptions that are usually treated as antithetical. In conflict analysis, the competing theoretical perspectives are relative deprivation and group mobilization: The former contends that peoples' discontent about unjust deprivation is the primary motivation for political action, whereas the latter emphasizes leaders' calculated mobilization of group resources in response to changing political opportunities.[9] In studies of ethnonationalism, the competing viewpoints are primordialist and instrumentalist: The former regards ethnic nationalism as a manifestation of persisting and primordial cultural traditions, whereas the latter interprets ethnicity as "an exercise in boundary maintenance" and assumes that ethnopolitical movements are an instrumental response to unequal treatment.[10]

The argument, in brief, is that a cultural group's shared grievances about unequal treatment and its desire to protect a valued identity provide the essential bases for mobilization and shape the kinds of claims made by the group's leaders. If peoples' grievances and cultural identity are both weak, they seldom can be mobilized by any leaders in response to any external threat or opportunity. On the other hand, the conjunction of shared grievances with a strong sense of group identity and common interest —as among black opponents of apartheid in South Africa, and Shiites and Kurds in Iraq after the Gulf War—provides highly combustible material that fuels spontaneous action whenever external control weakens. The combination animates powerful political movements and protracted conflict whenever it can be organized and focused by group leaders who give plausible expression to national and minority peoples' grievances and aspirations.

The details of this explanation are worked out in the next three sections. First, we consider the traits of the group and its interactions with others; then, the domestic political environment in which the group is situated; finally, the international political environment. Factors at all three levels shape the grievances of cultural groups, their degree of mobilization, and their strategic choices between protest and rebellion. Figure 4.1 provides a graphic summary of these elements and some of their interactions.

GROUP HISTORY AND STATUS

Four background factors shape disadvantaged cultural groups' sense of grievance and their potential for acting on it. Most of these factors are the residues of long-term social and political processes and are relatively slow to change.[11] They are shown at the top of figure 4.1.

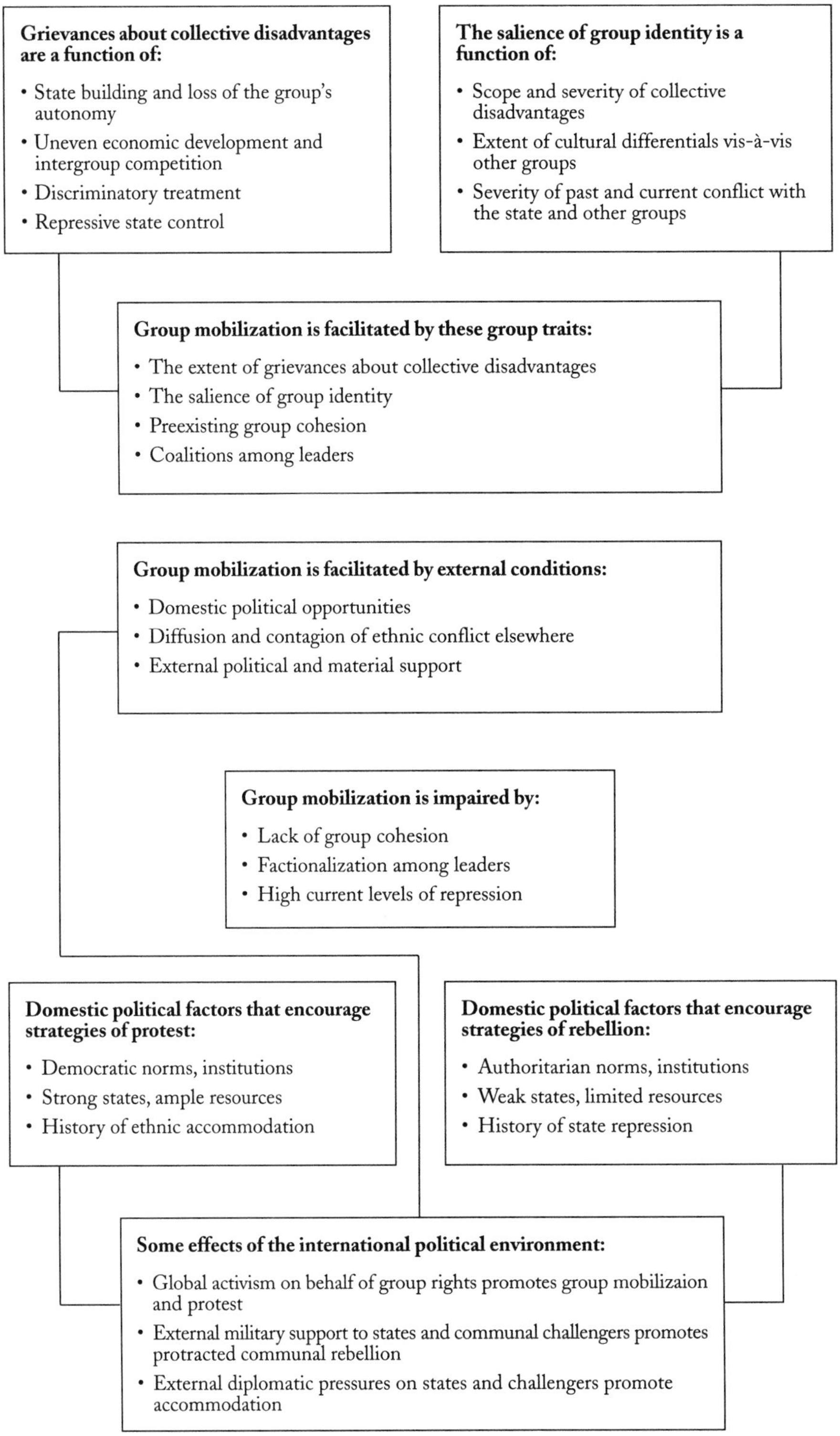

Figure 4.1. Sources of Mobilization for Ethnopolitical Protest and Rebellion.

Extent of Collective Disadvantages

The extent of a cultural group's collective disadvantages vis-à-vis others is the main source of its members' grievances and perceptions that they have a common interest in collective action. "Disadvantage" means socially derived inequalities in material well-being or political access in comparison with other social groups. The Minorities at Risk project gathered information for the 1980s on the political and economic inequalities and discrimination affecting some 220 politically active ethnic groups. The results illustrate the seriousness and pervasiveness of interethnic inequalities.

To determine political differences between each ethnopolitical group and the majority, we rated group members' political disadvantages relative to the majority (or typical) group on six dimensions: access to national or regional political positions; access to civil service positions; recruitment into the military and police; voting rights; rights to organize political activity on behalf of the group's interests; and rights to equal levels of protection. The results showed the following:

- 16 groups (7%) had political advantages relative to the majority.
- 32 groups (14%) were no different from the majority.
- 57 groups (25%) were slightly disadvantaged compared to the majority.
- 59 groups (26%) were substantially disadvantaged compared to the majority.
- 60 groups (27%) were extremely disadvantaged compared to the majority.

Four-fifths of the groups were thus found to be politically disadvantaged. We then examined whether these differences were due to active policies of discrimination. Discrimination was rated on a five-point scale based on whether group members were limited, by social practice or government policy, in their enjoyment of political rights or access to political positions in comparison with other groups in their society. The findings were that three-fourths of the groups experienced political disadvantages as a consequence of discrimination, past or present.[12]

- 61 groups (27%) experienced no political discrimination.
- 38 groups (17%) had experienced past neglect but benefited from current remedial policies.
- 24 groups (10%) experienced past neglect with no remedial policies.
- 49 groups (21%) experienced political discrimination as a prevailing social practice.
- 45 groups (20%) experienced formal political exclusion or recurring repression or both.

These indicators of political differentials and discrimination were then correlated with 1980s data on each group's political grievances and its participation in protest and rebellion. The results suggest that there is a direct, causal path from political inequalities and discrimination to the intensity of grievances expressed by group leaders; the more intense the expressed grievances, the greater the extent of political action. The same kind of analysis was done of economic differentials and discrimination. This analysis also showed a close link between the extent of discrimination and the intensity of demands for economic rights, but a somewhat weaker link from economic demands to group protest and rebellion.[13]

These analyses demonstrate conclusively the connections between persisting group disadvantages and the kinds of political, economic, and social grievances that cultural groups articulated in the 1980s. Their grievances are the combustible materials around which political leaders mobilize groups for political action.

The Salience of Group Identity

Group identity is usually valued in and of itself, but it varies considerably in salience, that is, in how important it is to group members at any given time. If a group is disadvantaged and subject to active discrimination, its sense of collective identity and common interest tends to be high. Among national peoples who are already engaged in conflict, the salience of group identity is also high: Conflict with out-groups builds solidarity. Among minority peoples, group identity often is weakened by assimilation and cross-cutting membership in plural associations. In groups of all types, identity may be diluted by cleavages within the group. Group leaders confront the issue of whether the sense of common identity is strong enough to overcome more narrow loyalties to clans, classes, and communities within the group.

Many of the appeals used by ethnopolitical leaders aim at increasing the salience of group identity by invoking historical memories and cultural symbols. Serious episodes of conflict leave persistent residue in peoples' memories and for a long time after can be invoked by leaders to justify political action. Serbian nationalists, for example, made effective use of fifty-year-old memories about atrocities committed by the Croatian Ustashi to mobilize Serbian support for their 1991–1992 war with breakaway Croatia.

The salience of peoples' cultural identity at a given point in time is due mainly to three factors: the severity of their collective disadvantages vis-à-vis other groups, the extent of cultural differences between them and other groups with whom they interact, and the intensity of their past and ongoing conflict with other groups and the state.

Extent of Group Cohesion and Mobilization

A strong sense of collective grievance and group identity are both necessary conditions for sustained mobilization, as was proposed earlier in this chapter. They are not sufficient conditions, however. Some degree of group cohesion is needed to convert common grievances and identity into purposeful action. Cohesive groups are those held together by dense networks of communication and interaction. Mobilization refers to the extent to which group members are prepared to commit their energies and resources to collective action in pursuit of their common interests. Cohesion, like collective identity, is impaired in groups that have competing leaders and political movements. Thus, effective mobilization in divided groups often depends on the formation of coalitions among diverse segments and contending leaders.[14] Failure to form coalitions reduces the scope and political impact of collective action and makes it easier for states to co-opt or ignore ethnopolitical challengers.

A group's cohesion is shaped by its social, political, and economic organization, past and present. Cohesion tends to be greater among groups that are concentrated in a single region (like the Tamils of northern Sri Lanka) rather than dispersed (for example, the Chinese of Malaysia). Groups whose traditional authorities still command respect, like the Issaq clan in northern Somalia, are relatively cohesive; so are those in command of an autonomous regional government, like the Kurds of Iraq since 1992. Religious movements can provide strong networks that form the basis for political mobilization, as the traditionally black churches did for the U.S. civil rights movement of the 1950s. Economic associations may play the same role: Trade unions are the main vehicle for political activism by the Indian Tamil plantation workers of central Sri Lanka. Modern political movements and parties are the most common agencies of ethnic mobilization, but it is rare for one political organization to incorporate most or all members of a cultural group.

In summary, at a given level of collective grievance and identity, a cultural group's potential for political mobilization is determined by the scope and strength of its pre-existing organizational networks and by the success of its potential leaders in forming coalitions. This general proposition, like the preceding one, is shown schematically in the top portion of figure 4.1.

Repressive Control by Dominant Groups

As a general principle, force directed against people who think it is unjust provokes both anger and caution. Cultural groups whose subordinate status is maintained through repression usually nurture deep grievances against dominant groups but are hesitant to act on them. The apparent apathy and acquiescence of Southern blacks to white dominance in the United States before the 1950s and of native peoples until the 1970s was based on a hard-learned, culturally transmitted belief that open resistance to discrimination was very risky. Cultural norms of caution and myriad day-to-day calculations based on fear of consequences were a heavy drag on their leaders' efforts at mobilizing action on behalf of civil rights and tribal autonomy. Figure 4.1 incorporates this double-edged proposition: To the extent that a group's disadvantages have been established and maintained by force, its grievances are intensified but its potential for mobilization is reduced.

OPPORTUNITIES FOR POLITICAL ACTION

The ways in which grievances, identity, and mobilization are translated into protest and

rebellion are complex and depend on context, too much so to be summarized in general propositions. Some episodes are reactive, such as the Los Angeles riots of 1965 and 1992, each of which was provoked directly or indirectly when police used force against individuals resisting arrest. But most ethnopolitical conflicts, including all sustained campaigns of protest and rebellion, are shaped by the strategic assessments and tactical decisions of the leaders and activists of politically mobilized cultural groups.

The concept of political opportunity is useful for analyzing this central issue, because it directs attention to the factors that influence the decisions made by leaders of ethnopolitical groups. Some opportunity factors are internal to the group: the extent of common grievances, the salience of group identity, and networks among its members.

These are the elements from which leaders build political movements. Large structural factors outside the group also shape its opportunities, including the character of the state and its resources and whether the group has transnational kindred; these factors are considered in the next two sections. More immediate factors are changes in the group's political environment, such as shifts in state power and policy, the prospects of attracting political allies, and the availability of international political and logistic support. These immediate factors influence the timing of political events, the kinds of claims made, and the choice of particular tactics.[15]

An example gives some substance to these bare-bones generalities. On Australia Day (January 26) in 1972 several young urban Aboriginal activists pitched a tiny tent on the lawn of Parliament House in Canberra, proclaiming it an Aboriginal "embassy" to the federal government. This event followed nearly a decade of episodic protest over land rights and civil rights issues by local groups. What precipitated the "embassy" declaration was an announcement by the

Liberal party prime minister that Aborigines would not be granted freehold rights to their large reserves in the Northern Territory. The Aboriginal embassy proved to be a brilliant tactical stroke, because it took advantage of two shifts in political opportunity. First, it immediately preceded the campaign for national elections, and second, it coincided with a Southeast Asia Treaty Organization conference in Canberra that was closely covered by the international press. The federal government inadvertently added to the publicity given the Aboriginal demands by staging a six-month-long comic opera of police, political, and legal machinations to get rid of the tent embassy. Aboriginal land rights were taken up as an issue by the Labor party, which won the 1972 elections and instituted major changes in policy toward Aborigines.[16]

It is not clear from their accounts just how carefully activists Kevin Gilbert and Tony Corey calculated the opportunities facing them when they decided to pitch a tent on Australia Day. They acted initially from a strong sense of collective grievance; but there is no doubt that once they saw the possibilities inherent in the situation, they and their supporters played it for full political effect. The case suggests in microcosm just how complex are the processes that lead from grievances to mobilization to protest.

THE STATE CONTEXT OF POLITICAL ACTION: EFFECTS OF STATE POWER AND DEMOCRACY

The political context of communal action is set by the state's political institutions and capabilities. Political systems shape the opportunity structures that guide ethnopolitical leaders' choices among exit, loyalty, and voice. If the choice is voice, then the openness and resources of the state influence what groups demand and their strategic choices about protest or rebellion. Our observations in the Minorities at Risk study point to the special significance of three factors: the scope of state power, the political values and practices of institutionalized democracy, and the destabilizing effects of democratization.

Uses of State Power

Strong states are those that have ample resources and the organizational capacity to control or regulate most economic, social, and political activity. The strongest states in the late twentieth century have included most of the advanced industrial democracies, China, and, until the 1980s, some Soviet-bloc states. As we observed above, the postcolonial and postrevolutionary states of the twentieth century usually have sought to build strong states on the western or Soviet models. Since almost all new states govern ethnically plural societies, state building has usually meant policies aimed at assimilating individual members of cultural groups, restraining their collective autonomy, and extracting their resources and labor for the state's use. The expansion of state power is likely to have cross-cutting effects on national and minority peoples: increased grievances, increased costs of acting on them, and increased payoffs for cooperating with and assimilating into dominant groups. In one analysis of the Minorities at Risk data, we developed an indicator of the growth of state power during the 1960s and 1970s. The states whose powers expanded most rapidly in these decades were mainly in the South. Some sought to establish state socialism: Burma, Laos, Algeria, Guinea, Ethiopia, and Nicaragua. Others included the Philippines, Sri Lanka, Mali, Sudan, and Zambia.[17] In almost all these states, the policies aimed at controlling resources and socioeconomic activity more or less directly provoked resistance by adversely affected cultural groups. Since most minorities were concentrated in peripheral regions, rebellion was a more feasible and promising strategy of resistance than urban-based protest. Examples include the Karen and Shan in Burma, Tibetans in the People's Republic of China, and the Miskito in Nicaragua under Sandinista rule.

The outcomes of minority peoples' resistance to state building are problematic. Strong, resource-rich states have the capacity either to accommodate or to suppress national peoples and minorities at relatively low cost, depending on the preferences of state elites. Rulers of weaker states face starker, zero-sum choices. They can expand the governing coalition at risk to their own positions, or they can devote scarce resources to all-out warfare against communal rebels. A third alternative is to negotiate independence or autonomy with ethnonationalists. The example provided by the deconstruction of the Soviet Union, a strong but declining state, was not a historical fluke; at least ten intact multinational states face serious separatist challes that may lead to future break-ups.[18] As is suggested below, the choices that state elites make in such situations depend not only on how strong the state is but on political institutions and values: Democratic elites are inclined to accommodation, while nationalist-authoritarian elites are more likely to fight.

In summary, the general proposition is that ethnopolitical action in the most powerful states is likely to be limited in scope and to take the form of protest, whereas protracted communal conflict will typify weak states that are attempting to extend their reach.

Institutionalized Democracies

The resolution of ethnopolitical conflicts in institutionalized democracies depends most fundamentally on the implementation of universalistic norms of equal rights and opportunities for all citizens, including ethnoclasses, and on pluralistic accommodation of indigenous and regional peoples' desires for separate collective status.[19] Detailed comparisons made in the Minorities at Risk study show that national and minority peoples in contemporary industrial democracies face few political barriers and are more likely to use the tactics of protest than rebellion.[20] The reasons are inherent in the political cultures and policies of modern democratic societies. In the past half-century the political leaders of these societies have become relatively responsive to the interests of politicized ethnic groups, in particular to groups able to mobilize large constituencies and allies in persistent campaigns of protest. Groups using violent protest and terrorism, on the other hand, have risked backlash and loss of public support. Thus, the calculus of ethnopolitical action in democracies favors protest over rebellion.

The advanced industrial democracies also score high among the activist and powerful states, which means that they have the resources to respond favorably to grievances expressed within the democratic framework. On this count again, the opportunity structure for cultural groups in democracies provides incentives for protest and disincentives for rebellion.

Transitions to Democracy

Democratization is the process whereby many formerly autocratic states in the Second World and Third World seek to establish more participatory and responsive political systems. The success of democratization in general and its effects on ethnopolitical conflict are problematic.[21] The Soviet and Eastern European regimes relaxed coercive restraints on nationalism and interethnic rivalries at a time when the institutionalized means for their expression and accommodation either did not yet exist or were fragile and distrusted. The successor republics of the USSR face the same uncertainties. The result has been a resurgence of communal activism, both protest and rebellion.[22] Similar consequences can be expected to follow from democratization in multi-ethnic Third World autocracies. The most dubious expectation of all is that authoritarian states such as Sudan, Iraq, and Burma might be able to defuse ethnopolitical wars by moving toward democracy.

Two general propositions about the effects of state institutions and power on political action by ethnopolitical groups are incorporated in figure 4.1. In established democracies, the opportunities for ethnic mobilization are substantial and the potential payoffs are significant for cohesive groups that rely largely on nonviolent tactics. The proposition is that institutionalized democracy facilitates nonviolent communal protest and inhibits communal rebellion. This tendency is reinforced in strong states, those that have ample power and resources to respond to pluralist interests. The fact that the tendency is lessened in weak states is one reason why democracy in a divided state such as Lebanon had little staying power.

In democratizing autocracies, by contrast, the opportunities for national and minority peoples to mobilize are substantial, but states usually lack the resources or institutional means to reach the kinds of accommodations that typify established democracies. In these states, democratization is likely to facilitate ethnically based protest and rebellion. The serious risk is that the rejection of accommodation by one or all contenders will lead to civil war and the reimposition of coercive rule. Both the USSR and the Federal Republic of Yugoslavia faced this situation in 1990–1991. The majority of Soviet and Russian leaders chose democracy and decentralization; Serbian nationalists chose to fight rather than switch, with devastating short-term consequences.

Ethiopia is a state that reached the same choice point by a different path: Protracted regional rebellions culminated early in 1991 in the seizure of power in Addis Ababa by a coalition of contending groups. In the short run, the revolutionaries acted on the principles that brought them victory. They governed by a transitional constitution that recognized ethnic units as constituent parts of the Ethiopian state and gave them the right, in principle, to self-determination. When Eritreans overwhelmingly voted to act on the principle, Ethiopia's new leaders accepted the independence of Eritrea. But they have been more recalcitrant about responding to claims of other communal groups (Oromos, Somalis, Afars) for some combination of greater regional autonomy and shared power in Addis Ababa. In Ethiopia, as in the post-Communist world, there will be a long-lasting risk that those who inherit the wreckage of multinational empires will attempt to recreate them.

THE INTERNATIONAL CONTEXT OF ETHNOPOLITICAL ACTION

Myriad international factors help shape the aspirations, opportunities, and strategies of ethnopolitical groups. They also affect state policies toward minorities. The nature of international engagement is a major determinant of whether ethnopolitical conflicts are of short duration or long and of whether they end in negotiated settlements or humanitarian disasters. Some of these connections are discussed below and summarized in figure 4.1.

Foreign Support for Contenders

Foreign sympathizers can contribute substantially to a cultural group's cohesion and political mobilization by providing material, political, and moral support. Indigenous rights organizations such as the American

Indian Movement (in the 1970s) and the World Council of Indigenous Peoples (in the 1980s and 1990s) have promoted the establishment of numerous indigenous peoples' movements. The Palestine Liberation Organization (PLO) has directly organized and supported oppositional activity by Palestinians in Jordan, Lebanon, and Israel's Occupied Territories. Rebellious Iraqi Kurds have at various times had the diplomatic and material support of the shah of Iran, the Iranian revolutionary regime, Israel, and the United States (1972–1975 and since 1991). The general proposition is that this external support usually enhances group cohesion and contributes directly to its mobilization for ethnopolitical action.

External support for ethnonational groups is frequently countered by external support for Third World regimes facing ethnopolitical challengers. In many instances, bilateral military and developmental assistance and political support enhances a state's capacity to counter such challenges. United States military, economic, and diplomatic support was for a long time essential for Israel to maintain continued control over the Palestinians of the West Bank and Gaza. Less well known are the decades of tacit U.S. support for Indonesian campaigns to subdue and incorporate the Papuans of Irian Jaya and the people of East Timor.[23] In many other instances, the support for embattled states has come from Third World regimes. Examples include Cuban support for Marxist regimes fighting communal wars in Ethiopia (1977–1990) and Angola (1975–1990) and India's intervention in the Sri Lankan government's war with Tamil rebels (1987–1990).[24]

The most tragic and destructive consequences occur when competing powers support different sides in ethnopolitical wars. Such proxy wars are usually protracted, very deadly, and not likely to end in negotiated settlements unless and until it is in the interest of the external powers. When external support is withdrawn, possibilities for settlement may open up, as has happened in Angola. In Afghanistan, however, the cessation of Russian and U.S. support in 1991 led to a new phase of civil war, fought this time not between Marxists and Islamists but among communal rivals for power. The country has been devastated by conflict among political movements that represent the Tajiks, Uzbeks, and other minorities who oppose efforts by the historically dominant Pushtuns to regain political control.

Proxy wars were particularly common during the Cold War, but by no means were limited to superpower rivalries. In their 1980s war Iran and Iraq both encouraged Kurdish minorities on their enemy's terrain to fight from within. Internationally the Iran-Iraq war ended in a stalemate; within both countries the Kurds lost. In Iraq the retribution took the horrific form of a genocidal campaign in 1988 called Al-Anfal.[25]

International Diffusion and Contagion of Ethnopolitical Conflict

Group mobilization is also prompted by the occurrence of ethnopolitical conflict elsewhere—more precisely, by the processes of diffusion and contagion.

Diffusion. Diffusion refers to the direct "spillover" of conflict from one region to another, either within or across international boundaries. For example, nearly twenty national peoples in the Caucasus have been caught up in ethnopolitical tumult in the 1990s through the diffusion (and contagion) of proactive and reactive nationalism—first by Armenians and Georgians, then by Ossetians, Abkhaz, Azeris, Chechens, Ingush, Lezghins, and nearly a dozen others.

The most intense and complex spillover effects in ethnopolitical conflict happen among groups that straddle international boundaries—intense and complex, because they draw in a multiplicity of ethnic and state actors. Political activists in one country often find sanctuary with and get support from their transnational kindred. Generations of Kurdish leaders and fighters in Turkey, Syria, Iraq, and Iran have sustained one another's political movements in this way. In 1995–1996 Chechens outside Russia, descended from the exiles and political refugees of an earlier era, gave open support to their rebellious cousins in the Caucasus. If a disadvantaged group's kindred are a favored or dominant group in a neighboring state, they often can count on their diplomatic, political, and sometimes military support: The Republic of Armenia's support for Armenians in Nagorno-Karabakh is a case in point. The ethnonationalist Moros in the Philippines had the political and material support of the Malaysian government during the early phase of their 1970s civil war against the Marcos regime, partly because Malaysians sympathized with their Muslim coreligionists, partly because Malaysia wanted a counter to Philippine claims to the Malaysian province of Sabah.

National peoples may also be able to take risky advantage of interstate warfare to pursue their own interests. At the end of World War II, help from the USSR enabled the Kurds to establish the Mahabad Republic in northwestern Iran; it was soon suppressed by the Iranian government. Various Kurdish factions continued to pursue autonomy during the Iran-Iraq War, as noted above, and in the aftermath of the 1991 Gulf War. In this and most other examples we have identified, spillover effects contribute to communal rebellion, not protest. Of the groups identified in the Minorities at Risk study, nearly two-thirds have kindred in one or more adjacent countries.

As a rule, a disadvantaged group's potential for mobilization and rebellion is increased by the number of segments of the group in adjoining countries, by the extent to which those segments are mobilized (whether as disadvantaged minorities or as a dominant group in control of the state), and by their involvement in open conflict (including civil and interstate war).

Contagion. Contagion refers to the processes by which one group's actions provide inspiration and guidance, both strategic and tactical, for groups elsewhere: The diffusion of conflict is direct, contagion is indirect. While some evidence suggests that internal conflict is in general contagious, we think the strongest force of communal contagion occurs within networks of similar groups.[26] Informal connections have developed among communal groups, especially since the 1960s, so that, for example, New South Wales Aborigines in the early 1960s organized freedom rides, and Dayaks in northern Borneo in the 1980s resisted commercial logging of their forests with rhetoric and tactics remarkably like those used by native Canadian peoples in the early 1990s.

More precisely, networks of communication, political support, and material assistance have developed among similar groups that face similar circumstances. The two densest and most well-organized networks, discussed below, link Islamic minorities and indigenous peoples. Groups that are tied into these networks acquire better techniques for effective mobilization: plausible appeals, good leadership, and organizational skills. Equally or more important, they benefit from the inspiration of successful movements elsewhere, successes that provide the images and moral incentives that motivate activists.

Around the periphery of the Islamic world are three fault lines—in Africa, Central Asia, and Southeast Asia—across which Islamic and non-Islamic peoples confront one another. The reassertion of traditional religious and political values throughout the Islamic world has encouraged self-assertion by Islamic minorities among states straddling the fault lines that are governed by Christian, Marxist, and Buddhist majorities. In a number of instances, moral encouragement for Muslim minorities has been accompanied by material and diplomatic support. Malaysian support for the Moros, cited above, was a relatively early example. Libya also provided assistance for the Moros, as it has for politically radical Muslim movements in a number of other countries. Since 1979 Iran's revolutionary Islamic government has encouraged resistance by Shiites in Lebanon and in countries throughout the Gulf. Meetings of the Organization of the Islamic Conference provide a forum for the exchange of ideas and encouragement among activists and officials of Islamic states.[27]

The global indigenous rights movement stems from the coalescence in the 1970s of regional groups like the American Indian Movement and the Circumpolar Arctic People's Conference. They soon established contact with indigenous peoples throughout the world. Since the early 1980s the World Council of Indigenous Peoples has provided one of several global foci for discussions, publicity, and joint action. Conferences, newsletters, personal visits, and representations to United Nations bodies have communicated a common vocabulary of grievances and demands, rationales for action, models of political organization, and examples of successful strategies and tactics for the defense of group interests.[28]

International Conflict Management

Since the end of the Cold War there has been a distinct shift in international orientations toward ethnopolitical conflict, away from sponsoring proxy wars and toward promoting the accommodation of contending interests. Efforts at international management of ethnopolitical conflict take myriad

forms, some of them analyzed in detail elsewhere in this volume. The United Nations and regional organizations like the Organization for Security and Cooperation in Europe actively encourage member-states to curb human rights abuses against minorities. More than half of the United Nations' current peacekeeping operations aim at separating the contenders in ethnopolitical conflicts.[29] International interventions are complemented by bilateral efforts. For example, the countries of origin of Europe's immigrant workers are acutely concerned about the workers' status in the host society. There is ongoing nonconflictual diplomacy between France and the countries of the Maghreb over these issues, as there has been between the governments of Germany and Turkey.

International pressures also can be effective in promoting negotiated solutions to protracted communal conflicts. The Organization of the Islamic Conference played a decisive role in promoting negotiations from the 1970s to the 1990s that have largely ended hostilities between Moro nationalists and the Philippines government. The United States used diplomatic and economic levers in the 1990s to prompt the Israeli government and the PLO to engage in meaningful and ultimately successful negotiations. The United States also participated in the 1980s international embargo on military and other assistance to apartheid South Africa that contributed to the peace process.[30] These examples illustrate the expanding scope of international activities aimed at reducing ethnopolitical conflict.

CONCLUDING OBSERVATIONS

Well-intentioned outsiders who hope to encourage peaceful solutions to ethnopolitical conflict can draw a few general lessons from this overview.

- The origins and dynamics of ethnopolitical conflict are highly complex. Theories that emphasize the supposedly crucial role of a single factor, such as historical animosities or religious differences, should be avoided. Such factors usually become significant because they are invoked by contemporary ethnopolitical leaders seeking to mobilize support among threatened and disadvantaged peoples, not because religious or historical differences generate a primordial urge to conflict.

- Conflict management strategies that fail to recognize the importance of peoples' cultural identities or that fail to address the grievances that animate their political movements, will also fail to reduce conflict. For example, attempts by many European governments to improve the status of Roma (Gypsies) by emphasizing protection of their civil and political rights have had little practical effect because of pronounced cultural differences between dominant groups and the Roma that justify discrimination by the former and resistance and predation by the latter. The Roma are without doubt the most despised and unequally treated people of modern Europe, east or west, and their status is unlikely to change unless the issue of cultural difference is confronted, not by policies of assimilation but of pluralistic coexistence. In a very different setting, the state-building strategy of assimilating minorities has failed to curb rebellions by Kurds in Iraq or Turkey, because it does not address the desire of many Kurds to give political form to the expression of their cultural identity.

- Ethnopolitical conflict is virtually always a two- or *n*-party game. Concentrating conflict-management efforts on one party to the exclusion of others is a no-win strategy. The principle is widely recognized by those concerned with managing interstate conflict, but not necessarily by those dealing with intrastate conflict. The government of Burundi has been under great international pressure since 1994 to check the escalation of potentially genocidal conflict between the dominant Tutsi and Hutus. Yet sporadic massacres continue, not because the government is recalcitrant but because Hutu and Tutsi militants are beyond the reach of international influence. It is difficult to conceive of strategies that would engage militants who seek to eliminate their opponents in efforts at conflict management. But if militants cannot be checked by state power—and Burundi is a weak state—violent conflict will continue until international efforts are brought directly to bear on them.

- Efforts at conflict management that neglect the international context are equally problematic. Transnational support and inspiration are vital to most ethnopolitical movements, and their leaders are susceptible to overtures from a wide range of international actors—the United Nations and regional organizations, of course, but also individual states that bring resources and political credibility to negotiations. International encouragement and diplomatic pressures aimed at the governments of multi-ethnic states are essential instruments for redirecting their policies toward national and minority peoples. The chances of success for preventive diplomacy will be enhanced if it engages representatives of ethnopolitical movements as well as state elites.

- It is important to recognize and encourage the participation of regional and international nongovernmental organizations (NGOs) as intermediaries and mediators in situations of ethnic conflict. The World Council of Churches played a crucial role in brokering the 1972 agreement that ended the first phase of Sudan's civil war. Former President Jimmy Carter, working from The Carter Center at Emory University, was instrumental in bringing about a successful conclusion to the 1988–1989 negotiations that ended eight years of warfare in Nicaragua between the Miskito Indians and the Nicaraguan government. In the 1990s International Alert, a London-based NGO, has played a significant behind-the-scenes role in reducing tensions in a half-dozen ethnic and political conflicts in the global South. These NGOs function effectively in part because they are trusted by parties to conflict, and they are trusted because they are seen to operate independently of big-power political interests.

NOTES

1. The project was begun by the author in 1986 and since 1988 has been based at the University of Maryland's Center for International Development and Conflict Management. Funding for the current phase has been provided by the United States Institute of Peace, the National Science Foundation, and the Korea Foundation. Reports on its findings include T. R. Gurr, *Minorities at Risk: A Global View of Ethnopolitical Conflicts* (Washington, D.C.: United States Institute of Peace Press, 1993); Gurr, "Peoples Against States: Ethnopolitical Conflict and the Changing World System," *International Studies Quarterly* 38, no. 3 (September 1994): 347–377; and Gurr, "Communal Conflicts and Global Security," *Current History* 94, no. 592 (May 1995): 212–217.

2. Data on past humanitarian crises and initial risk assessments of future cases are reported in Barbara Harff and T. R. Gurr, "Victims of the State: Genocides, Politicides, and Group Repression from 1945 to 1995," in *PIOOM Newsletter and Progress Report* (PIOOM Foundation, Leiden University, The Netherlands) 7, no. 1 (Winter 1995): 24–38.

3. Hal Kane, *The Hour of Departure: Forces that Create Refugees and Migrants* (Washington, D.C.: Worldwatch Paper 125, June 1995), p. 9.

4. For an overview of these debates, see *Sources of Conflict: Highlights from the* Managing Chaos *Conference,* Peaceworks No. 4 (Washington, D.C.: United States Institute of Peace, August 1995).

5. Analysis of cases listed in the appendix to Gurr, "Peoples Against States," pp. 369–375.

6. Gurr, *Minorities at Risk,* chap. 4. The trend peaked in the early 1990s and by 1995 ethnopolitical conflict in most world regions was declining, according to unpublished analyses of new data from the Minorities at Risk project.

7. The foundation of modernization theory was laid down by Karl Deutsch, *Nationalism and Social Communication* (Cambridge, Mass.: MIT Press, 1953). An early reappraisal of what modernization means for ethnic identities is Walker Connor, "Nation-Building or Nation-Destroying?" *World Politics* 26, no. 3 (April 1972): 319–355. A more recent assessment is Saul Newman, "Does Modernization Breed Ethnic Political Conflict?" *World Politics* 43, no. 3 (April 1991): 451–478.

8. An important comparative analysis is George Psacharopoulos and Harry Anthony Patrinos, eds., *Indigenous People and Poverty in Latin America: An Empirical Analysis* (Washington, D.C.: World Bank, 1994).

9. The relative deprivation and mobilization approaches are summarized and contrasted by James B. Rule, *Theories of Civil Violence* (Berkeley: University of California Press, 1988), chaps. 6 and 7.

10. One of many discussions of the two approaches is George M. Scott, Jr., "A Resynthesis of the Primordial and Circumstantial Approaches to Ethnic Group Solidarity: Towards an Explanatory Model," *Ethnic and Racial Studies* 13, no. 2 (April 1990): 147–171. The quotation is from William A. Douglass, "A Critique of Recent Trends in the Analysis of Ethnonationalism," *Ethnic and Racial Studies* 11, no. 2 (April 1988): 192.

11. The arguments that follow are specific to disadvantaged groups but are potentially

applicable to advantaged minorities whenever they feel threatened by groups who challenge their position. The essential difference is that advantaged groups ordinarily have more resources, sometimes all the powers of the state, for the organized defense of their interests. Thus, they usually use state coercion to defend their positions, sometimes in the extreme form of genocide.

12. The study included advantaged minorities as well as disadvantaged ones. Moreover, some groups that were not politically disadvantaged were subject to economic discrimination, or vice versa.

13. The analyses of group differentials and discrimination and their correlations with grievances and group conflict are described in greater detail in Gurr, *Minorities at Risk,* chaps. 2 and 3, and in Gurr, "Why Minorities Rebel: A Global Analysis of Communal Mobilization and Conflict since 1945," *International Political Science Review* 14, no. 2 (April 1993): 161–201. This presentation follows the presentation of results used by Connie Peck, *The UN as a Dispute Settlement System: Improving Mechanisms for the Prevention and Resolution of Conflict* (The Hague: Kluwer, 1996), chap. 4.

14. Coalition formation can be as important for successful ethnopolitical movements as it is for revolutionary movements; see the comparative analysis in Jack A. Goldstone, T. R. Gurr, and Farrokh Moshiri, eds., *Revolutions of the Late Twentieth Century* (Boulder, Colo.: Westview Press, 1991), chap. 14.

15. The concept of political opportunity is commonly used in analyses of the origins and dynamics of social movements, for example by Charles Tilly, *From Mobilization to Revolution* (Reading, Mass.: Addison-Wesley, 1978); and Sidney Tarrow, *Power in Movement: Social Movements, Collective Action, and Politics* (New York and Cambridge: Cambridge University Press, 1995). Milton J. Esman gives it a prominent role in his comparative analysis of ethnic political movements in *Ethnic Politics* (Ithaca, N.Y.: Cornell University Press, 1994).

16. This summary account is from T. R. Gurr, "Outcomes of Public Protest Among Australia's Aborigines," *American Behavioral Scientist* 26, no. 3 (January–February 1983): 360.

For more detail, see M. A. Franklin, *Black and White Australians* (Melbourne, Australia: Heinemann Educational, 1976), pp. 209–212.

17. As reported in Gurr, "Why Minorities Rebel," based on data for 227 groups. The scope of state power was measured as of 1986, the rate of change in state power was measured across the period 1960–1986.

18. A number of contemporary states besides the USSR and Yugoslavia are candidates for some kind of political deconstruction. In 1993 Czechoslovakia fissioned peacefully into two independent republics. Those at risk in 1996 include Ethiopia, Sudan, Zaire, South Africa, Iraq, Sri Lanka, India, Burma, Pakistan, Canada, and Belgium. In Canada and Belgium, and possibly South Africa, devolution—if it occurs—is likely to be peaceful. All the others are or have been racked by protracted communal wars.

19. Until very recently, Israel and South Africa were best characterized as restricted democracies because large communal groups under each country's control were denied political and economic rights. The generalizations in the text are applicable to them now but not in the recent past.

20. See Gurr, *Minorities at Risk,* chaps. 2 and 6.

21. As a general rule, protest is more common than rebellion in democracies; for evidence and interpretation see T. R. Gurr, "Protest and Rebellion in the 1960s: The United States in World Perspective," in *Violence in America, Vol. 2: Protest, Rebellion, Reform,* ed. Gurr (Newbury Park, Calif.: Sage Publications, 1989), pp. 111–115. On the problematic consequences of the recent wave of democratization see Samuel P. Huntington, "Democracy's Third Wave," *Journal of Democracy* 2 (Spring 1991): 12–34.

22. The breakup of the USSR has transformed some communal conflicts—such as the one between Armenia and Azerbaijan—into interstate conflicts and has intensified hostilities between newly dominant groups and Russian and other nonnational minorities in most of the new states. See Ian Bremmer, ed., *Understanding Nationalism: Nation Building and Ethnic Minorities in the Post-Communist States* (Ithaca, N.Y.: Cornell University Press, 1996).

23. President Kennedy played a key role in prompting the Dutch withdrawal from Western New Guinea, now Irian Jaya, in 1962, which paved the way for the Indonesian takeover in 1963 that provoked a series of harshly repressed rebellions. Neither in this case nor in the Indonesian invasion of East Timor in 1975, which also prompted a protracted but unsuccessful war of independence, did the United States openly oppose Indonesian policies. Instead, development and military assistance continued, including provision of military equipment used against regional rebels.

24. The Angolan civil war of 1975–1991 was a left-right struggle superimposed on an underlying communal struggle for control of the newly independent state. The southern Ovimbundu people, represented by the National Union for the Total Independence of Angola (UNITA in Portuguese), relied on U.S. and South African assistance in a protracted conflict with the Soviet- and Cuban-supported government in Luanda, which was controlled by the Mbundu. The Indian government initially intervened in the war between Sri Lanka and Tamil rebels as a peacekeeping force, with the reluctant agreement of the Sri Lankan government. Failing in their effort to disarm the Tamil rebels, the Indian troops became combatants but were no more successful at suppressing the insurgency than the Sri Lankan government, and they withdrew at that government's request.

25. For an overview see Kanan Makiya, "The Anfal: Uncovering an Iraqi Campaign to Exterminate the Kurds," *Harper's Magazine,* May 1992, pp. 53–61.

26. A conceptual analysis of diffusion, contagion, and other international effects on internal conflicts is William Foltz, "External Causes," in *Revolution and Political Change in the Third World,* ed. Barry M. Schutz and Robert O. Slater (Boulder, Colo.: Lynne Rienner, 1990). Stephen Saideman makes a persuasive argument that contagion is only likely to affect groups in similar economic and political circumstances to those that initiate a successful movement, in "Is Pandora's Box Half Empty or Half Full? The Limited Virulence of Secessionism and the Domestic Sources of Disintegration," paper presented to the Annual Meeting of the American Political Science Association, Chicago, 1995.

27. Despite these examples, analysis of the issues and intensity of serious ethnopolitical conflicts that began before and after the end of the Cold War provide no general support for Huntington's "clash of civilizations" thesis. See Gurr, "Peoples Against States," pp. 356–358.

28. See Franke Wilmer, *The Indigenous Voice in World Politics: Since Time Immemorial* (Newbury Park, Calif.: Sage Publications, 1993).

29. An important recent study of this topic is Milton J. Esman and Shibley Telhami, eds., *International Organizations and Ethnic Conflict* (Ithaca, N.Y.: Cornell University Press, 1995).

30. Preventive diplomacy is the generic term for these and other international means for managing ethnopolitical conflict. See Michael Lund, *Preventing Violent Conflicts: A Strategy for Preventive Diplomacy* (Washington, D.C.: United States Institute of Peace Press, 1996); and Lori Fisler Damrosch, ed., *Enforcing Restraint: Collective Intervention in Internal Conflicts* (New York: Council on Foreign Relations, 1993). A recent study of peacekeeping is Paul F. Diehl, *International Peacekeeping* (Baltimore, Md.: Johns Hopkins University Press, 1993). For theory and case studies of international conflict reduction, see I. William Zartman and Victor A. Kremenyuk, eds., *Cooperative Security: Reducing Third World Wars* (Syracuse, N.Y.: Syracuse University Press, 1995).

5

Religious Militancy

DAVID LITTLE

Has religious militancy replaced the ideological zeal of the Cold War as a serious source of national and international conflict? Some analysts contend that it is now "cultural" rather than "iron" curtains that divide the world, and that religion fuels the conflict in a special way by inspiring intolerant and irreconcilable images of "identity and commitment" among competing civilizations.

"Even more than ethnicity," Samuel P. Huntington argues, "religion discriminates sharply and exclusively among people. . . . As people define their identity in ethnic and religious terms, they are likely to see an 'us' versus 'them' relation existing between themselves and people of different ethnicity and religion." Huntington posits that a belief in universal human rights, including a sharply restricted public role for religion, has "little resonance" in nonwestern cultures. In particular, he foresees the strong likelihood of a "Confucian-Islamic connection," with potentially adverse implications for the West.[1]

Huntington's thesis is a provocative one and has attracted much attention in the media and popular press. In its support, one can point to governments in countries like Iran and Sudan and to Islamic movements throughout the Middle East and elsewhere, which readily resort to the language of cultural confrontation. In many of these places a spirit of religious militancy, sometimes called "fundamentalism,"[2] prevails, and it often includes support for violence against the manifestations of sacrilege and oppression seen to be imposed upon Muslim peoples by the West and its sympathizers.

Although relations between Asia and the West have not been expressed in such violent terms, grave "civilizational tension" is frequently reported. Economic independence has been accompanied by a new sense of cultural self-assertion. Asian countries are now less inclined than they once were to acquiesce to western cultural preferences, as, for example, in the interpretation of human rights or the development of certain political and social institutions. Conversely, the West, forced of late to compete on less favorable terms and more constrained by strictly economic interests, finds itself culturally on the defensive. Asian leaders like

Lee Kuan Yew of Singapore have begun lecturing the West on its manifold deficiencies and the need for some reverse readjustments of its own.

While the new spirit of cultural aggressiveness is not usually associated with religious militancy, especially in East Asia, there is some interesting counterevidence. The "Confucian revival" in places like Taiwan, Japan, South Korea, and China, while lacking some of the more obvious features of militancy, represents a self-conscious attempt to reconstitute Asian identity on the basis of classical texts and traditional symbolic resources. In that endeavor, Confucian revivalists have become "forceful critics of modern Western culture" in a way reminiscent of Islamic activism.[3]

Religious militancy is unambiguously present in non-Confucian Asian countries, such as India and Sri Lanka. Once again, there is a strong reaction against "western secularism," and particularly against the alleged failure of the West to appreciate the importance of a distinctive cultural and religious heritage in providing the foundations of national purpose and unity.

The destruction of the Babri Mosque by a Hindu mob in the Indian town of Ayodhya on December 6, 1992, marked a radical rejection of the secular tradition in Indian political life, a tradition that had been based on a commitment to religious impartiality. The new Hindu militants think that one religion—Hinduism—is better than all others and should therefore be dominant in public life. The Ayodhya incident illustrated the deep tensions over religious identity between Hindus and Muslims in India, and it called to mind comparable tensions between Sinhala Buddhists and Tamil Hindus in neighboring Sri Lanka.[4]

Not all religious movements are militant in the same way, and it would be a grave mistake to ignore the internal diversity and complexity that is present within cultures and civilizations. If there is official antagonism toward the West concerning the interpretation of human rights and the character of political and economic responsibility in countries like Sudan, Saudi Arabia, South Korea, or China, by no means does every religious militant in those countries share the same view. In many places, significant constituencies exist, frequently religiously oriented, that resolutely oppose the official perspective on human rights and related issues and actually express views that are compatible with concerns voiced in the West. Frequently, this consensus includes commitment to the principles of religious and ethnic tolerance and nondiscrimination.[5] Some dissidents, in fact, are in their own way quite "militant" about these principles. The idea that the members of a nation, including the religiously active, all share a unified cultural or civilizational outlook is a myth often invented by governments in their own interest, perhaps playing on reaction to the "excesses" of western societies.

Furthermore, the various states and societies that make up "Islamic" or "Confucian" or other "civilizations" exhibit important national differences among them. For a variety of reasons, including deep religious divisions, Islamic states like Iran, Sudan, and Saudi Arabia represent anything but a common front in their domestic or foreign policies, and there is no prospect of overcoming those differences anytime soon. Nor is it the case that Islamic activists who constitute much of the political opposition in places like Pakistan, Algeria, Jordan, and the new Palestinian territory are part of a unified movement.[6] In each instance, the focus is predominantly national rather than international. By the same token, there are significant divergences of national interest among the Confucian countries in Asia, as there are among the inhabitants of those countries.

In the case of India and Sri Lanka, religious militancy is not primarily tied to broad civilizational objectives and values that transcend state boundaries. On the contrary, militants in those countries are consumed with the organization and control of national life: Religious and ethnic identity is strongly linked to political self-determination.[7]

> From its very beginning in the nineteenth century nationalism in India has fed upon religious identifications. This is true not only for the two most important religious communities in India, the Hindus and the Muslims, but also for groups like the Sikhs and, in Sri Lanka, the Buddhists. In all these cases nation building is directly dependent on religious antagonism, between Hindus and Muslims, between Sikhs and Hindus, [and in Sri Lanka] between [Sinhala] Buddhists and [Tamil] Hindus.[8]

In examining religious militancy, then, it is important to look carefully at the diversity of outlooks and ideals that exist among religious militants in a given culture or civilization, including their propensity for violence, and their attitudes toward human rights and the principles of religion and ethnic tolerance and nondiscrimination. In addition, it is necessary to study religious militancy in relation to nationalism, the impulse to achieve political, ethnic, and cultural autonomy by means of taking control of an independent nation-state, sometimes coercively.[9]

FOUR TYPES OF RELIGIOUS MILITANCY

Loose talk about religious militancy suggests the need for greater precision. Religious militancy can, in fact, take quite different forms. Though some militants do resort to direct violent action, by no means do all of them, contrary to what is popularly believed. Moreover, while some militants are ethnically and religiously exclusive and intolerant, others are not. Some versions of militancy entail and support the human rights principles of religious and ethnic tolerance and nondiscrimination. Others deny or seriously compromise them.

A significant segment of religious people throughout the world—whether Christian, Muslim, Jewish, Hindu, Buddhist, or other—uses much of the language of militancy, that is, the language of warfare and combativeness. Such groups typically represent themselves as in a fighting mode.[10] They are "fighting back" or "fighting against" the enemies of what is true and right; they are "fighting under" a sacred mandate, "fighting for" the implementation of righteous beliefs and actions, and "fighting with" instruments and weapons they consider appropriate to the task.

However, there are at least four different positions concerning what the battle is exactly about and how it should be fought, as well as who the enemy is and how that enemy should be treated. We shall designate the four positions as follows: violent intolerance, civic intolerance, nonviolent tolerance, and civic tolerance.

Two preliminary points are important. To be tolerant is, at a minimum, to respond to a set of beliefs and practices initially regarded as deviant or objectionable without forcible interference.[11] Conversely, to be intolerant is not to practice such forbearance under the same circumstances. ⌐ four types of militancy will be un⌐ accordingly. Second, these desi⌐ only types, and as such are i⌐ While real-world positio⌐ toward one type or ⌐ considerable over⌐ ious position⌐ may in fa⌐ of the⌐ sic⌐ the⌐

Violent Intolerance

Some religious militants are strongly committed and disposed to the direct use of violence (defined simply as "forcible action") in pursuing their mission. There have been numerous recent and widely publicized examples: Ayodhya, the bombing of the New York Trade Center by Islamic militants, the massacre by a Jewish zealot of two dozen Muslim worshippers in Hebron, the attacks in Algeria against civilians by the Armed Islamic Group, and the explicit blessing of violence by both Serbian Orthodox and Croatian Catholic Christians in the conflict in the former Yugoslavia.

For some religious believers, the direct use of violence is obligatory. According to a member of the Kach and Kahane Chai parties in Israel, "We're in a war, and in a war there are no innocent people. . . . [Palestinians are all] guilty by association."[12] An Egyptian organization known as Islamic Jihad, responsible for the assassination of Anwar Sadat in 1981, expressed related sentiments in a document entitled *The Neglected Duty*, published in the early 1980s:

> The "duty" that has been profoundly "neglected" is jihad, and it calls for "fighting, which means confrontation and blood." . . . Anyone who deviates from the moral and social requirements of Islamic law [is] a fit target for jihad; these targets include apostates within the Muslim community as well as the more expected enemies from without. Perhaps the most chilling aspect . . . is [the] conclusion that peaceful and legal means for fighting apos[tates] are inadequate. The true soldier of [Islam] is [within some limits] allowed to [use virtu]ally any means available to achieve [it].[13]

[. . . proponen]ts of Serbian Orthodoxy [espouse a v]iolent and highly intoler[ant religious] nationalism in the [same way whic]h the Serbs are not [alone. . . . Ce]rtain parts of the

Catholic church have played a similar role in Croatia.

> The Serbian Orthodox Church has been a self-conscious contributor to the development of a [Serbian] nationalistic ideology. . . . "One who is not Orthodox is not Serb," [was a statement] adopted by the patriarchate in the 1920s. . . . When this war finally erupted, the use of religious symbols and targets, and even religious leaders, in the war effort indicated that a form of religious identification had accompanied nationalism into the souls of even those who were avowedly nonreligious. Religious symbols appeared in many forms—on military weapons and vehicles, in the use of the three-finger Chetnik sign (symbolizing the Trinity), and in cross marks carved or burned into the bodies of Muslims. . . . Finally, there have been cases of priests blessing weapons and soldiers on the front lines of battle.[14]

Violent intolerance—a position so recurrent in various traditions it appears to be generic—involves a kind of sacred application of the notion of "necessity" or "public emergency." The idea is that a given group or "people," who are taken to be specially chosen representatives of the divine order, believe themselves and all they stand for to be catastrophically threatened by a particularly sinister enemy. A good example is found in the world view of the Deuteronomic tradition as recorded in Hebrew scripture: "'[That] world . . . is fragile and fraught with danger, and Israel's survival is perceived to be in jeopardy. . . . Chaotic social forces—enemies, criminals, and indigenous outsiders—threaten to undermine its social and cosmic order. . . .' Defining the 'Other' [as] deserving of destruction is a means of asserting and of creating a self [and a people] worthy of preservation."[15]

According to the terms of the "necessity defense" or the "right to survival," extreme conditions, involving a threat to the very foundations of social and cosmic survival, warrant an extreme response against an enemy whose very existence constitutes continuing danger. Thus, violence and intolerance become interwoven.

> [This] ideology actually motivates and encourages war, implying that wars of extermination are desirable in order to purify the body politic of one's own group, to eradicate evil in the world beyond one's group, and to actualize divine judgment.... [A] sharp line is drawn between us and them, between clean and unclean, between those worthy of salvation and those deserving elimination. The enemy is thus not a mere human ... but a monster, unclean, and diseased.... [In this way,] people ... accept the notion of killing other humans by dehumanizing them.[16]

According to Islamic Jihad and *The Neglected Duty,* cited earlier, wherever they turn, Muslims, and the faith they espouse, are desperately imperiled: "With regard to the lands of Islam, the enemy lives right in the middle of them. The enemy even has got hold of the reins of power, for this enemy is (none other than) these rulers who have (illegally) seized the Leadership of the Muslims. Therefore, waging jihad against them is an individual duty, in addition to the fact that Islamic jihad today requires a drop of sweat from every Muslim."[17]

Although some mention is made of respecting restrictions on the use of force, such as the immunity of noncombatants, militants of this sort are inclined to consider themselves finally exempt from such restrictions because of the uniquely sacred character of the emergency they believe themselves to face. To describe the enemy as they do—as apostate, the enemy of God—is to have an especially weighty reason to disregard or minimize the ordinary forms of forbearance expected under conditions of armed conflict. Similarly, the Palestinian organization, Hamas, gives no sustained

attention in its charter to limits on the use of force because the conditions of "sacred emergency" in which they find themselves require that the traditional limits "must be stretched."[18]

Those committed to violent intolerance, like some of the Serbian Orthodox, often combine religion and ethnicity in the strongest "us-versus-them" terms, although, again, such attitudes are by no means limited to the Serbs in the Balkan conflict.

> The aim of the "theology of the nation" was to provide a sense of belonging for Serbs, especially for those living in other parts of Yugoslavia. Leading theologians focused on the sufferings of the Serbs,... stressing the uniqueness of the genocide of the Serbs. In 1991, this perspective was authorized by the Serbian Orthodox bishops when they referred to the suffering of the Serbian nation during World War II ... as the sin of all sins and equated it with the suffering of Christ.... There has been ecclesiastical sanction for quite astounding conspiracy theories regarding currently perceived dangers, ... [including an alleged] Vatican/Tehran/fundamentalist plot against the Serbian people.[19]

Civic Intolerance

Religious people may express their militancy and intolerance not only on the battlefield, but also in the voting booth. In preferring ballots to bullets, religious activists forswear taking violence into their own hands, relying instead on "legitimate violence" or the processes of civic enforcement associated with an established legal and political system as the appropriate way to implement their objectives.[20]

A good example is the Pakistan political party, Jama'at-i-Islami, founded in 1941 by Abu'l A 'la Maududi, the influential theologian of Sunni Islam. On the one hand, the Jama'at-i-Islami is a reformist party that has employed constitutional and legal methods to achieve its goals. Maududi has consistently rejected violence and advocates "the ultimate triumph of Islamic forces through democratic elections," based on a process of balanced change that evolves over time.[21] Accordingly, the Jama'at has played an important role in the political life of Pakistan over the years, even though it has never been particularly successful at the polls. It has often shaped the public debate and has served to confer religious legitimacy upon the state, and to reinforce the Islamic identity of Pakistan.[22]

On the other hand, the militant rhetoric of Maududi and that of his followers has a strongly intolerant cast to it.

> Maududi [has] advocated discrimination against non-Muslims.... He [has] favored the reimposition of the *jizya* tax traditionally imposed on [non-Muslims], excluding them from military service, and eliminating them from high positions in government. He [has] asserted that Islam "does not permit them to meddle with the affairs of State."[23]

> [According to Maududi, the] constitution should contain [as it does] an unequivocal provision ... that *shari'a* is the supreme law of Pakistan.... [Above all,] the penal law must ... be "Islamized".... It is Maududi's Jama'at-i-Islami [party] which has been agitating for the implementation of such punishments as hand amputation for theft, etc.[24]

In general, Sri Lankan Buddhist nationalism serves as another example of civic intolerance. On occasion, the Sinhala majority, who are mostly Buddhist, have asserted their claims to cultural and political preeminence over the Tamil, and mainly Hindu, minority by means of violence. But for the most part, these claims have been pursued politically, according to the system instituted by the British before they relinquished

colonial control in 1948. The problem has been that while democratically designed, the system was unable to prevent the Sinhala Buddhists from achieving majoritarian domination. It thus failed to produce a genuinely pluralistic, multi-ethnic society in Sri Lanka, one committed to civic tolerance and nondiscrimination, and the result has been continuing ethnic strife and civil war.[25]

The Sinhala Buddhist "revivalists" of the late nineteenth and twentieth centuries—playing on resentments born of colonialism, the perception of a "Tamil threat," the imperatives of nationalism, and social and economic uncertainties—artfully manipulated ancient legends concerning Buddha's alleged associations with Sri Lanka, as well as certain preferential relations traditionally established between the government and the Buddhist monastery. The nationalists thereby reinforced a cultural fact of the greatest significance: "In the Sinhala language, the words for nation, race, and people are practically synonymous, and a multiethnic or multicommunal nation or state is incomprehensible to the popular mind. The emphasis on Sri Lanka as the land of the Sinhala Buddhists carried an emotional popular appeal, compared with which the concept of a multiethnic polity was a meaningless abstraction."[26]

Nonviolent Tolerance

To complicate things further, the word "militant" is not limited to the two types considered so far. It also applies to other, more sublime, expressions of religious commitment that have radically different implications for the treatment of outsiders.

One author, for example, speaks of the "militancy" of Jesus's nonviolent message. Jesus is said to reject passivity and acquiescence in the face of wrongdoing every bit as much as he rejects violence. He "articulates

. . . a way by which evil can be opposed without being mirrored, the oppressor resisted without being emulated, and the enemy neutralized without being destroyed."[27] Jesus's teachings are filled with the language of battle and of combativeness, but the preferable means for prosecuting the battle are nonviolent.

The same may be said of more contemporary advocates of nonviolence. Life for Gandhi is one continuing spiritual battle: Enemies exist and they must be militantly and courageously opposed.[28] It is only that violent means are not effective instruments of warfare. "I do believe," he once said, "that where there is only a choice between cowardice and violence, I would advise violence. . . . But I believe that nonviolence is infinitely superior to violence."[29] Martin Luther King, Jr., placed a similar emphasis upon the existence of evil and injustice and on the need to combat them unrelentingly. The very terms he adopted for what he regarded as the acceptable means of doing battle— "nonviolent resistance" and "noncooperation with evil"—themselves convey a spirit as militant as it is nonviolent.

The Buddhist leader of the Tibetan government in exile, the Dalai Lama, is still another example. He believes that certain attitudes and ways of acting are the "enemy" of enlightenment and right living, but the appropriate way to fight them is through nonviolence. He has no doubt that these destructive attributes are clearly manifest in "the cruelty and degradation" perpetrated against the Tibetan people by the Chinese government from the time China occupied Tibet in 1949–1950. He affirms his great admiration and respect for the courage of the Tibetans in resisting such oppression, even when it is violently expressed. At the same time, he considers nonviolence the nobler and more effective way to continue the struggle against the Chinese, a way that,

in his view, actually requires more resolution and self-discipline—more militancy—than the way of violence.[30]

The effect of nonviolent militancy is to sublimate violence. The ultimate enemy is not external, not outside oneself or one's group; rather, it lies within. Fighting others obscures the fight within oneself. Primary attention is thus directed inwardly, not outwardly. For Gandhi, the ultimate battle is waged in the heart of every human being.[31] Jesus instructs his followers to consider the log in their own eye before they address the speck in the eye of their neighbor.[32] The Dalai Lama teaches that an enemy may not truly be subdued by retaliating in kind, for then one simply reproduces within oneself the hostility, fear, anger, and resentment the enemy represents. Genuine victory occurs only when those emotions are subdued and are replaced with love and compassion. The fundamental problem with violence is that it stimulates in the human heart negative, disruptive emotions, rather than positive, peaceful ones.

To sublimate violence, after the fashion of the nonviolent militant, is to create the conditions of tolerance. The idea of "tolerant militancy" is by no means as self-contradictory as it might at first seem. Militancy of this sort is tolerant because it finds strong reasons for "bearing with" apparent enemies in the name of waging war against the real ones that lie within each person. The Dalai Lama goes so far as to welcome, rather than evade, his enemies— to be grateful for the threat and conflict they represent—because their presence provides the occasion to practice the self-restraint essential to final self-conquest. As he puts it, "tolerance can be learned only from an enemy; it cannot be learned from your guru."[33]

There is a striking convergence between the outlook of the nonviolent militant and the idea of tolerance expressed in international human rights documents like the Declaration on the Elimination of All Forms of Intolerance and Discrimination Based on Religion or Belief. As the declaration assumes, intolerance involves the use of violence, whether direct or "legitimate," to impose religious belief or to favor one religion or belief system over others by persecuting or discriminating against dissenters and outsiders or by putting them at a disadvantage. Such behavior has "brought, directly or indirectly, wars and great suffering to [human]kind," and its elimination is likely to "contribute to the attainment of the goals of world peace, social justice, and friendship among peoples."[34]

It follows from these assumptions that the optimum way for religions to convey their message—to exercise their militancy—is through nonviolent communication, through persuasion and appeal, rather than through the use of official or unofficial violence. Practicing self-restraint in the face of beliefs considered threatening—learning to "bear with" such beliefs rather than forcibly suppressing or punishing them—produces peace and friendship. These are, of course, exactly the fundamental tenets of nonviolent militancy.

Civic Tolerance

One important difference, however, exists between the assumptions of nonviolent militancy and those underlying the human rights norms. The nonviolent militant inclines to favor the absolute renunciation of violence, including "legitimate violence," as practiced by the established civil authority.[35] The human rights norms, by contrast, assume that it is permissible to adopt laws in accord with the norms of tolerance and nondiscrimination and to enforce those laws by means of "legitimate violence" when necessary. Thus, in distinction from

"nonviolent tolerance," human rights norms imply what might be called "enforced" or "civic" tolerance.

A classic example of religious militancy committed to civic tolerance is the seventeenth-century English Puritan sect known as the Levellers, who fought on Parliament's side against Charles I in the Puritan Revolution (1642–1648). The Levellers were the radical contingent of the so-called New Model Army, and one of their leaders, John Lilburne, is properly known both as a "militant Christian" and as "the first English democrat."[36]

Although many of their ideas did not gain acceptance until a half-century later, the Levellers proposed radical political and legal reform, which set them at odds with more conservative Puritans like Oliver Cromwell.[37] They favored nothing less than a constitutional democracy based on "universal assent . . . from all and every one of the People."[38] Their proposals included equality before the law, division of powers, judicial reform, and, of greatest interest here, a revolutionary doctrine of religious freedom and tolerance. According to *The Case of the Army Truly Stated*,

> All Statutes, for the Common Prayer Book, and for enforcing all to come to Church, whereby many religious and conscientious people are daily vexed and oppressed, be forthwith repealed and nulled. As also that all Statutes against [religious gatherings], under the pretense of which, religious people are vexed for private meetings about the worship of God, may be likewise repealed and nulled. . . . [And that] all oppressive Statutes, enforcing all persons though against their consciences to pay Tithes . . . may be forthwith repealed and nulled.[39]

Elsewhere, the Levellers sought to exclude all religious tests for public office. As they put it, laws "shall not disable any person from bearing any office in the commonwealth for any opinion or practice in religion, though contrary to the public way."[40]

Such demands rested on religious convictions of the following sort: "The inward man is God's prerogative; the outward man is man's prerogative. . . . [The inward government is directed] only by the Word, not by the sword. For the sword pierceth but the flesh; it toucheth but the outward man; it cannot touch the inward. Therefore where by the Word . . . a conversion is not, nor cannot be, obtained, there no human compulsive power or force is to be used."[41]

The same general spirit that combines religious militancy with a commitment to enforce freedom of conscience, religious nondiscrimination, and civic impartiality toward religion continues to find contemporary expression. An example is the large number of committed Christians who condone using force in the present civil war in Sudan in order to overturn the existing government. From their point of view, the government favors a particular interpretation of Islam, and thereby places all nonadherents at a serious disadvantage. They advocate establishing a "secular" government dedicated to equal treatment for all religious and ethnic communities, according to the international norms of tolerance and nondiscrimination.[42]

CONCLUSION

Assuming these four types of religious militancy, the crucial empirical question is why religious groups in given circumstances conform to one type rather than another. The beginning of an answer, it seems, has to do with the varying conditions under which religious identity is related to violence.

Religion yields an image of individual and group identity by providing "cosmic orientation." Believers acquire ways of responding to and interpreting profound "existential perplexities," such as the origins and destiny of the universe and of humanity, the reality of suffering and death, and the challenge of living righteously. The sacred scriptures, doctrines, rituals, institutions, and traditions that serve to resolve those perplexities, and with which the believer comes to identify, offer a "metaphysical home," in which the believer finds comfort and security. Like a temporal home, religions are seen to stand in need of protection against alien forces that would destroy them and thus rob their adherents of the sense of security they provide. For a believer, protecting religion is the same as protecting the fundamental habitat of oneself and one's group.

This is where violence, or "forcible action," comes in. Religions appear invariably to make room for violence as a legitimate means of defense. Hebrew scripture (whether interpreted by Jews or Christians), the Koran, the Bhagavad Gita and other Hindu writings, and some influential Buddhist texts, for example, all supply the foundation and inspiration for enlisting political and military power in the cause of securing certain sacred values and ways of life.

So long as a religious group assumes that forcible action is capable of protecting its basic identity, the group will be inclined to employ force under what it considers to be conditions of severe threat. As we have seen, particularly in the case of violent intolerance, the perceived emergency is pictured in external terms: The enemy is some alien group that must, at all costs, be subdued and controlled by physical force. Violence is, by definition, a last resort, and may have to be used with minimal restraint, for all other means of dealing with the threat are taken to have been exhausted. Moreover, there are, no doubt, certain attendant frustrations and resentments that heighten the attitudes of the violently intolerant religious militant, such as the ineffectiveness or inaccessibility of political institutions and the sense of being beleaguered by antagonistic cultural forces or of being subject to an unfair or deteriorating economic environment.[43] The above examples of violent intolerance all conform to such indications.

The same general assumptions about the positive relation between religious identity and violence apply both to violent and civic intolerance. The crucial difference is that groups that are civically intolerant encounter a social, political, and legal setting more amenable to securing and implementing the preferred way of life, as in Pakistan or, in part, Sri Lanka.

But if religions are drawn toward the use of violence as a way of protecting themselves and all they stand for, they are, at the same time, recurringly distressed by violence and its effects. The theme of nonviolent tolerance that emerges and reemerges persistently in several religious traditions testifies to that. At bottom, it is concluded that violence is in reality not militant enough. It simply does not effectively protect or secure religious identity, but, on the contrary, destroys it. By contrast, nonviolent tolerance is deemed to be the most acceptable expression of religious militancy.

It is likely that special conditions encourage nonviolent tolerance. The futility of fighting against overwhelming force, as in the case of present-day Tibet, may be one of those conditions. On the other hand, the use of violence to protect and advance religious identity does appear, in case after case, to produce highly negative consequences.[44]

Civic tolerance, and the system of human rights norms compatible with it, represents a kind of compromise between nonviolent tolerance and the two types of intolerance. It assumes that tying religious identity to violence is ineffective and self-contradictory. Accordingly, it distinguishes between the "inward" and the "external," between the "law of the spirit" and the "law of the sword," and embraces the provisions for freedom of conscience, belief, and exercise that follow from

that distinction. At the same time, civic tolerance allows the use of violence, both as a way to establish a system of law and government consonant with the norms of religious freedom and as a way to enforce such a system once it is established. It is obvious that civic tolerance can only exist where the political, economic, and cultural conditions favor such a system.

NOTES

1. "The Clash of Civilizations?" *Foreign Affairs* 72, no. 3 (Summer 1993): 27, 29, 40, 45ff.

2. "Fundamentalism" may not be the correct term for classifying the religious attitudes and practices under consideration. Those who favor its use argue that the central attributes of the fundamentalist movement in America in the 1920s (when the term first gained currency) are currently found worldwide. Appropriately adjusted for cultural and regional variations, the attributes include a militant reaction to the secularizing and morally permissive tendencies associated with "modernity," absolute commitment to an inflexible interpretation of scriptural or doctrinal foundations, and rigid and exclusive classification of people according to whether or not they adhere to the prescribed fundamentals. The series of volumes published by the University of Chicago under the title "The Fundamentalism Project" (edited by Martin E. Marty and R. Scott Appleby) is committed to the comparative study of "fundamentalism," even though it displays considerable open-mindedness concerning the use of the term.

Those opposing such use of the term believe it to be pejorative and note that it requires so much adaptation and interpretation in accounting for cultural and regional differences as to reduce its usefulness as a term of comparison. (For example, see Mark Juergensmeyer, *The New Cold War? Religious Nationalism Confronts the Secular State* [Berkeley: University of California Press, 1993], pp. 4–6.)

While an interesting case can be made for using the term, it seems advisable to choose other words. "Religious militancy"—the term used in this essay—appears to be less offensive

Two preliminary points are important. To be tolerant is, at a minimum, to respond to a set of beliefs and practices initially regarded as deviant or objectionable without forcible interference.[11] Conversely, to be intolerant is not to practice such forbearance under the same circumstances. The four types of militancy will be understood accordingly. Second, these designations are only types, and as such are ideal or artificial. While real-world positions tend to gravitate toward one type or the other, there can be considerable overlap or tension. Often, various positions present in a given movement may in fact divide in reference to some or all of the four types. That kind of internal tension and diversity is particularly apparent in the case of entire religious traditions.

Some segments of Serbian Orthodoxy have reinforced a violent and highly intolerant form of Serbian nationalism in the Balkan conflict, although the Serbs are not unique in that respect. Certain parts of the Catholic church have played a similar role in Croatia.

and less culturally and historically conditioned than the word "fundamentalism." In addition, it has the advantage of being appropriately equivocal, capable of communicating considerable nuance and variation.

3. Tu Wei-ming, "The Search for Roots in Industrial East Asia: The Case of the Confucian Revival," in *Fundamentalisms Observed*, ed. Martin E. Marty and R. Scott Appleby (Chicago: University of Chicago Press, 1991), p. 773. This essay is a good example of both the appeal and the difficulties of employing the word "fundamentalism" in comparative study. The author points out that the "fundamentalism problematic" is relevant to East Asia, especially in respect to the critique of modernity as embodied in western culture. On the other hand, the Confucian revival is not committed to an absolutist, literalist interpretation of classical texts, nor does it appear to define the world in the highly exclusivist way that fundamentalists characteristically do.

4. Peter van der Meer, *Religious Nationalism: Hindus and Muslims in India* (Berkeley: University of California Press, 1994), pp. 10–11. It is sometimes asserted that the Sri Lankan conflict is solely ethnic or linguistic, and "has nothing to do with religion." It is true that the Tamil minority have not been discriminated against because of their religious beliefs, but because they have a different language and ethnic identity. However, it is also true that Buddhism has been actively invoked by the Sinhala majority as a basis for legitimizing Sinhala cultural and political preeminence in Sri Lanka. Ethnic identity, particularly in the Sinhala case, is thus deeply infused with religion. As a matter of fact, it is not unusual in cases of ethnic conflict for religion to function as a warrant for discriminating against groups designated not by their religion, but by their race, language, or gender. See David Little, *Sri Lanka: The Invention of Enmity* (Washington, D.C.: United States Institute of Peace Press, 1994).

5. In China, for example, groups of Catholics, Protestants, Buddhists, and Muslims have attempted to practice their religion freely against strong government opposition and have resisted discriminatory and repressive measures. See *Continuing Religious Repression in China* (New York: Human Rights Watch/Asia, 1993); and David Little and Scott W. Hibbard, *Sino-Tibetan Coexistence: Creating Space for Tibetan Self-Direction* (Washington, D.C.: United States Institute of Peace Press, 1994). The same is true in Saudi Arabia. During the 1990s, an increasing number of Christian worshippers have been arrested simply because they have sought to express their religious beliefs. Similarly, Shiite Muslims in Saudi Arabia "have been arrested, detained, and tortured for advocating freedom of religion and equal rights for members of their community." *Saudi Arabia: Religious Intolerance* (New York: Amnesty International, 1993), p. 1. For reference to religious dissent against the government of Sudan, see page 87 in this chapter. See also Ann Elizabeth Mayer, *Islam and Human Rights* (Boulder, Colo.: Westview Press, 1995), pp. 14–15.

6. See Scott W. Hibbard and David Little, *Islamic Activism and United States Foreign Policy* (Washington, D.C.: United States Institute of Peace, forthcoming).

7. The contacts between Tamil Nadu in southern India and the Sri Lankan Tamil movement have been deeply conditioned by the dynamics of national politics in both India and Sri Lanka. Indira Gandhi initiated military and other forms of assistance to the Tamil insurgents in the early 1980s, largely in response to domestic political concerns. Moreover, the ethnonational objectives of the Sri Lankan Tamil insurgency movement are very much a product of Sri Lankan experience, and Tamil expatriate support for the insurgents, which is considerable, is similarly strongly nationalistic in character.

8. Hibbard and Little, *Islamic Activism and United States Foreign Policy*, p. 2. Also, see Van der Meer's book for a compelling account of the role of religion in the political and cultural conflicts that currently afflict India. For a discussion of the rise of religious nationalism in Sri Lanka, see Little, *Sri Lanka: The Invention of Enmity*.

9. In light of the considerable attention currently being paid to the importance of "religious nationalism," it is rather remarkable that Huntington pays little attention to this phenomenon. The words "nationalism" and "nationalist" appear

only four times in his article (pp. 31, 35, 37, 44), and then only incidentally.

10. "The Fundamentalism Project: A User's Guide," in Marty and Appleby, *Fundamentalisms Observed,* pp. ix–x.

11. "At a minimum," because tolerance is a complex notion, involving attitudes as well as actions. Moreover, the word is ordinarily used in several different ways. See David Little, "The Indivisibility of Tolerance: Human Rights and Peace" (forthcoming) for an examination of some of the complexities. *Webster's New International Dictionary* (1928) states: "Tolerance implies an attitude of (esp. intellectual) forbearance with reference to views, opinions, or actions with which one is not one's self fully in sympathy."

12. Cited in John Kelsay, "Religion and the Roots of Conflict," *Religion and Human Rights* (New York: Project on Religion and Human Rights, 1994), p. 1.

13. Juergensmeyer, *The New Cold War?* p. 60.

14. Gerald Shenk, *God With Us? The Roles of Religion in Conflicts in the Former Yugoslavia* (Uppsala, Sweden: Life and Peace Institute, 1993), pp. 37–40. See pp. 40–43 for a similar description of Croatian Catholicism. See also Srdjan Vrcan, "The War in Former Yugoslavia and Religion," *Religion in Eastern Europe* 15, no. 2 (April 1995), for a supplementary discussion of the role of religion in the Balkan conflict; and Paul Mojzes, *Yugoslavian Inferno: Ethnoreligious Warfare in the Balkans* (New York: Continuum, 1994), especially chap. 7, "The Religious Component in the Wars."

15. Susan Niditch, *War in the Hebrew Bible* (New York: Oxford University Press, 1993), p. 75. The citation is from Louis Stulman, "Encroachment in Deuteronomy: An Analysis of the Social World of the D Code," *Journal of Biblical Literature* 109 (1990): 613–632.

16. Ibid., p. 77.

17. Cited in John Kelsay, *Islam and War* (Louisville, Ky.: John Knox/Westminster Press, 1993), p. 106.

18. Ibid., p. 107.

19. Schenk, *God With Us?* pp. 38–39. See Mojzes, *Yugoslavian Inferno,* pp. 129–135, for a discussion of the Roman Catholic contribution to Croatian chauvinism.

20. Max Weber introduces the phrase "legitimate violence" in his famous definition of the modern state: "The state is an association that claims the monopoly of the *legitimate use of violence*" (my emphasis). Weber, "Religious Rejections of the World and Their Directions," in H. H. Gerth and C. Wright Mills, *From Max Weber: Essays in Sociology* (New York: Oxford University Press, 1958), p. 334.

21. Mumtaz Ahmad, "Islamic Fundamentalism in South Asia: The Jama'at-i-Islami and the Taglighi Jama'at of South Asia," in Marty and Appleby, *Fundamentalisms Observed,* p. 500.

22. See Hibbard and Little, *Islamic Activism and United States Foreign Policy,* pp. 68–69.

23. Mayer, *Islam and Human Rights,* p. 136.

24. Mohammed Khalil, "Islam and Human Rights" (unpublished paper), p. 30.

25. See Little, *Sri Lanka: The Invention of Enmity.*

26. K. M. de Silva, *Religion, Nationalism, and the State,* USF Monographs in Religion and Public Policy, no. 1 (Tampa: University of South Florida, 1986), p. 31.

27. Walter Wink, *Engaging the Powers* (Minneapolis, Minn.: Fortress Press, 1992), pp. 189–190.

28. Rein Fernhout, "Combating the Enemy: The Use of Scripture in Gandhi and Godse," in *Human Rights and Religious Values,* ed. An-Na'im, Gort, Jansen, and Vroom (Grand Rapids, Mich.: Eerdmans, 1995), p. 128.

29. Wink, *Engaging the Powers,* p. 190.

30. Tenzin Gyatso (the Dalai Lama), *Freedom in Exile* (Camp Hill, Pa.: A Cornelia and Michael Bessie Book, 1990), pp. 229–237, 261.

31. Fernhout, "Combating the Enemy," p. 124.

32. Luke 6: 41–42.

33. Tenzin Gyatso, *The Dalai Lama at Harvard,* ed. and trans. Jeffrey Hopkins (Ithaca, N.Y.: Snow Lion Publications, 1988), p. 185.

34. Preamble of the Declaration against Intolerance, Resolution Adopted by the General Assembly 36/55, November 25, 1981.

35. Advocates of nonviolence are not always entirely consistent on this question. For example, Martin Luther King, Jr., claimed he was absolutely committed to nonviolence, while at the same time reminding the government of its responsibility *to enforce* the law of the land against segregation. See David Little, "Civil Rights and Peace: Martin Luther King, Jr., and the World Struggle for Justice and Peace" (forthcoming).

36. Pauline Gregg, *Free-Born John: A Biography of John Lilburne* (London: J. M. Dent and Sons, 1986), p. 359.

37. See Richard Ashcraft, *Revolutionary Politics and Locke's Two Treatises of Government* (Princeton, N.J.: Princeton University Press, 1986), pp. 149–165, for a discussion of the connection between the Levellers and the thought of John Locke.

38. "A Manifestation from Lt. Col. John Lilburne, et al.," in *The Puritan Revolution: A Documentary History*, ed. Stuart E. Prall (Garden City, N.Y.: Anchor Books, 1968), p. 167.

39. Ibid., pp. 143–144. This document was principally composed by the Levellers.

40. "The Second Agreement of the People" (1648), from John Lilburne, *Foundations of Freedom*, in A. S. P. Woodhouse, *Puritanism and Liberty* (Chicago: University of Chicago Press, 1974), p. 365.

41. Richard Overton, "An Appeal to the People" (1647), ibid., p. 332.

42. There is, to my knowledge, little literature on this subject. This conclusion is drawn from direct conversations with Sudanese Christians and confirmed by expert observers of the situation there. Other examples of civically tolerant religious militancy would be certain "Third World theologians [including people like Bishop Desmond Tutu of South Africa] who are actively engaged in the struggle against poverty, racism, and political repression" and who explicitly reject an "absolute commitment to nonviolence" in pursuing that struggle. See James Cone, "Martin Luther King and the Third World," in *We Shall Overcome: Martin Luther King, Jr., and the Black Freedom Struggle*, ed. Peter J. Albert and Ronald Hoffman (Washington, D.C.: Pantheon Books, 1990), p. 214.

43. See Donald Rothchild and Alexander J. Groth, "Pathological Dimensions of Ethnicity," *Political Science Quarterly* 110, no. 1 (Spring 1995): 73–75.

44. See David Little, "Belief, Ethnicity, and Nationalism," *Nationalism and Ethnic Politics* 1, no. 2 (Summer 1995), especially pp. 286–287.

6

Image, Identity, and Conflict Resolution

JANICE GROSS STEIN

Embedded enemy images are a serious obstacle to conflict management, routinization, reduction, or resolution. Once formed, enemy images tend to become deeply rooted and resistant to change, even when one adversary attempts to signal a change in intent to another. The images themselves then perpetuate and intensify the conflict.

Structural explanations of conflict generally give little attention to the processes that mediate between attributes of the environment and behavior. Rather, they assume that conflict can be explained independently of the images of its participants and their perceptions of threat. However, modern psychology has demonstrated repeatedly that stimulus-response models are inaccurate representations of human behavior. Insofar as the same stimulus is interpreted differently by different individuals or groups, beliefs matter.

The identity of individuals and groups in part shapes how they see the world; the way people see the world shapes how and when they perceive threat, as well as how they formulate their goals, assess constraints, process information, and choose strategies. Individuals are not passive receptors of environmental stimuli, but they actively construct representations of their environment. The extent of individual and group variation in interpretation suggests that structural explanations of political behavior are rarely determining.

Images of an enemy can form as a response to the persistently aggressive actions of another state or group. These kinds of individual and group images are not the subject of this chapter. A conflict generated by aggressive or militant leaders with vested interests in escalating conflict is generally not amenable to reduction unless intentions change. Therefore, I focus on conflict generated by images that form when the intent of the other is not hostile, when action is ambiguous in an unstructured environment;

I also examine conflict generated by images that were once accurate, but that no longer reflect the intentions of one or more parties. Under these conditions, social-psychological analysis is important both to explain the conflict and to generate prescriptions to reduce its intensity.

The analysis focuses on the images of leaders, but it also examines the roles of elites and publics to analyze the still ill-understood social-psychological processes of the creation, retention, and revision of enemy images by individuals and by groups. In this connection, I pay particular attention to the impact of group identity. I first examine the psychological, social, and political processes that create and reinforce hostile images. In the second part of the chapter, I explore the conditions under which adversarial images are likely to change. To explain the changes in enemy images that facilitate conflict management, routinization, reduction, and resolution, I draw on propositions from social psychology to develop a concept of "trial-and-error learning" from failure, looking particularly at the strategies one adversary can use to promote change of image by another.

IDENTITY AND THE CREATION OF ENEMY IMAGES

An image refers to a set of beliefs or to the hypotheses and theories that an individual or group is convinced are valid. An image includes both experience-based knowledge, and values or beliefs about desirable behavior.[1] When these individual images are shared within a group, they become stereotyped.[2] A stereotyped image is a group belief about another individual, group, or state that includes descriptive, affective, and normative components. Stereotyped enemy images, generally simple in structure, set the political context in which action takes place

and decisions are made. Converging streams of evidence from social psychology, cultural anthropology, international relations, and comparative politics suggest that individuals and groups are motivated to form and maintain images of an enemy even in the absence of solid evidence confirming hostile intentions.

Enemy images can be a product of the need for identity and the dynamics of group behavior. Social psychologists have identified a fundamental human need for identity. Identity is the way in which a person is, or wishes to be, known by others; it is a conception of self in relation to others. An effective identity includes beliefs and scripts for action in relation to others. An individual almost always holds more than one identity and generally moves freely among these identities, depending on the situation. I, for example, am a mother when I am with my sons, a wife when we visit my in-laws, a teacher with my students, and a scholar with my university colleagues. Individual identity is highly situational and relational.

One important component of individual identity is social identity, or the part of an individual's self-concept that derives from knowledge of his or her membership in a social group or groups, together with the value attached to that membership.[3] Social psychologists suggest that people satisfy their need for positive self-identity, status, or reduction of uncertainty by identifying with a group.[4] These needs then require bolstering and favorable comparison of the "in-group" with "out-groups."[5] Membership in a group leads to systematic comparison, differentiation, and derogation of other groups.

The most striking finding of social psychologists is that social differentiation occurs even in the absence of material bases for conflict. This need for collective as well as individual identity leads people to differentiate between "we" and "they," to distinguish between "insiders" and "outsiders," even when scarcity or gain is not an issue. In an effort to establish or defend group identity, groups and their leaders identify their distinctive attributes as virtues and label the distinctiveness of others as vices. This labeling responds to deep social-psychological needs, can lead to the creation of enemy stereotypes, and can culminate in conflict.

A study of massive state repression leading to group extinction, for example, concluded that genocides and politicides are extreme attempts to maintain the security of one identity group at the expense of other groups.[6] Ethnocentrism, or strong feelings of self-group centrality and superiority, does not necessarily culminate in extreme or violent behavior. It does, however, draw on myths that are central to group or national culture and breeds stereotyping and a misplaced suspicion of others' intentions.[7]

Social identity and differentiation do not, however, inevitably lead to violent conflict.[8] If they did, conflict would occur at all times, under all conditions. Several important qualifications are necessary before we can address the relationship between identity and violence. First, personal and social identity are often in tension with one another. By identifying strongly with a group, people inevitably deemphasize their individual identity, and those with a strong sense of individual identity give less weight to their group identities. Human rights activists, for example, characteristically identify less with a particular group and more with norms of individual responsibility. People also generally identify with several groups. I am a Torontonian at home, an Ontarian when I travel in Canada, and a Canadian when I travel abroad. People typically identify with a group whose importance is salient in a given situation.[9]

The critical question is under what conditions identity and violent conflict are related. Why are relationships among some groups so much more competitive and violent than among others?[10] Hutus and Tutsis have engaged in violent conflict six times since 1962, while Québecois and Anglophones in Canada—despite important and deep differences between the two groups—have not fought for over two hundred years. Moreover, substantial numbers of Québecois also share multiple identities, including strong and positive identification with Canada. What explains why strong group identity precipitates violent conflict only in some situations?

At least part of the answer lies in the variability of identity. Social identity is not given; it can be chosen freely by an individual, imposed by others who have the authority and resources to do so, or socially constructed through interaction with others.[11] Ethnic or national identity intensifies, for example, during periods of social, economic, or political crisis, when it is brokered by leaders who create or reinterpret histories and traditions.[12] Serbian leaders quite deliberately sharpened ethnic differentiation in the period following Marshal Tito's death and the weakening of the state structure.

Conflict does not develop when the sources of identities or the identities themselves are compatible. I experience no conflict, for example, among my multiple identities as a Torontonian, an Ontarian, and a Canadian. When the identity an individual chooses is incompatible with the identity imposed by others or the social context in which identity is constantly being re-created, conflict can develop. Muslims living in Bosnia-Herzegovina, for example, defined themselves as Serbs or Croats until the 1970s, when the Serb and Croat identities began to be re-created to exclude Muslims. Only then did they begin to define themselves as Bosnian Muslims with a distinct political identity. Even then, however, incompatible political identities may not be sufficient to create violent conflict. To return again to the Canadian example, some Québecois see fundamental incompatibilities with being a Quebecker and a Canadian, but do not consider resorting to force. They do not because they are committed to norms of fairness and due process, and they expect these commitments to be reciprocated by their counterparts in English-speaking Canada.[13]

Conflict can trigger violence among groups under conditions of scarcity. Some evidence suggests that culturally and physically similar groups can generate hostility and aggression toward one another when in competition for scarce resources.[14] Analyses of civil violence also conclude that relative deprivation is the most important condition for participants in collective violence.[15] As the gap grows between material expectations and assets, aggression toward those perceived as the cause of relative deprivation will grow and intensify. Relative deprivation is a useful starting point in explaining the growth of hostile imagery and stereotypes in a state where the economy is declining. Loss aversion is likely to intensify stereotyping: When expectations remain stable, but capabilities decline, people who are experiencing a decline in their assets are especially likely to become angry and to provide fertile ground for imagery that is hostile to another group.[16]

Conflicts of identity are particularly acute when group members believe that recognizing another's identity can compromise their own, when they perceive that granting rights to the other is an abdication of their own identity. Throughout much of its history, the Israeli-Palestinian conflict has been this kind of existential conflict: Because both identities are tied to the same territory, leaders on both sides long felt that acknowledging the other's identity would funda-

mentally compromise their own.[17] In these kinds of existential conflicts over identity, enemy images are easily formed and resistant to change.

COGNITION AND ENEMY IMAGES

Common cognitive biases can also contribute to the creation of enemy images. The egocentric bias leads people to overestimate the extent to which they are the target of others' actions. Leaders are thus likely to see their group or state as the target of the hostility of others even when they are not.

The fundamental attribution error leads people to exaggerate systematically the importance of others' dispositions or fixed attributes in explaining their undesired behavior. Leaders are, therefore, likely to attribute undesirable behavior to the "character" of other groups or states, rather than to the difficulties they face in their environment.[18] Syria's president rarely draws a distinction between Israel's leaders, ignores differences among political parties, explains Israel's behavior as a consequence of its Zionist character, and dismisses the impact of public opinion on the policy of a democratically elected leadership. President Assad consistently exaggerates the "disposition" of Israel's leadership at the expense of the situation it confronts.

Identity and cognitive biases do not always contribute to conflict through stereotyped enemy images. These images are necessary, but insufficient explanations of the formation of enemy images. If they were sufficient, individuals, groups, and states would have strong enemy images all the time. This is clearly not the case. The critical variables are the kinds of environments in which individuals and groups seek to satisfy their needs and the norms that they generate and accept. Certain kinds of international and domestic conditions facilitate the formation of enemy images.[19]

THE INTERNATIONAL AND DOMESTIC CONTEXT

The international environment of states can create conditions in which identity or cognitive biases trigger the creation of enemy images, even in the absence of aggressive behavior by others. The distinguishing characteristic of a "security dilemma" is that behavior perceived by one group or state as threatening and aggressive is actually a defensive response to an inhospitable strategic environment. To enhance their own security, leaders take measures that simultaneously diminish the security of others.[20] For forty years, leaders in the Soviet Union and the United States saw their own behavior as a defensive response to the aggressive intentions and actions of the other.[21] Interpreting a defensive action as offensive can feed and fuel an image of an enemy that is then reinforced over time in a spiraling process of interaction.

The formation of enemy images can also be triggered by domestic factors. Identity conflict is often a competition for ownership of the state and control of its resources. States can stand above and attempt to mediate conflict—for example, by giving representation to different groups as in Belgium —or can be the creature and the instrument of one exclusive group, as in Nigeria where the Hausa Fulani dominate the military regime.[22] The expropriation of the identity, symbols, and resources of the state by one group to the exclusion of others is a strong predictor of the likelihood of stereotyping.

Groups and coalitions whose interests are served by conflict abroad or ongoing hostility can capture the political process and propagate enemy images designed to intensify hostility. Entrepreneurial leaders or elites whose domestic support is uncertain or threatened can manipulate identities to bolster political loyalty.[23] To gain public support, parochial interest groups that benefit from militarist or imperialist policies create strategic rationalizations or "myths." Over time, some elites come to believe the myths that they have learned, making these images extraordinarily resistant to change. A process of mythmaking that perpetuates hostile imagery is most likely in countries, like the former Soviet Union, with concentrated interest groups that trade and logroll.[24]

Differences in domestic political conditions make some kinds of populations more receptive to elite manipulation than others.[25] In controlled political regimes, leaders and elites who dominate the instruments of communication can more easily manipulate identities and mass images. Both the kind of regime and the organization of society affect the creation of hostile imagery. The hallmark of a deeply divided society, one that is likely to sustain significant hostile imagery and experience violent conflict, is the presence of separate structures organized on the basis of identity, structures that infuse every aspect of society. In Lebanon, for example, political offices—from the highest level to the local levels—have traditionally been allocated on the basis of religious identity. In this kind of society, creating and maintaining ethnic stereotypes and enemy images is easy.

Political, economic, and psychocultural factors are relevant to the growth of hostile imagery. The salience and intensity of identity, especially ethnic identity, as social differentiators are critical predictors of stereotyping. Salience and intensity are themselves tied closely to the perceived stakes of ethnic relations.[26] The greater the gap between expectations and capabilities, the more important the values that are endangered by declining capabilities, and the smaller the range of other satisfactions that can compensate for the loss in assets, the more receptive populations are to elite attempts to stereotype others.[27]

This analysis suggests that identity itself is not a cause of stereotyping and violent conflict. Even when competitive identities are present, stereotyping is likely only when it is triggered by the exclusionary acts of leaders, either by monopolizing the resources of the state against groups within their own societies or by pressing claims against those within others. Leaders and elites evoke threats to political identity that then provoke stereotyping and contribute to violence.

THE PERSISTENCE OF ENEMY IMAGES

Once stereotyped images are in place, they are extraordinarily difficult to change. Because enemy images contain an emotional dimension of strong dislike, there is a strong desire to maintain the existing image and little incentive to seek new information about a foe.[28] Stereotyped images also generate behavior that is hostile and confrontational, increasing the likelihood that an adversary will respond with hostile action. A cycle of reciprocal behavior then reinforces adversary images by providing allegedly confirming evidence of hostile intentions. Enemy images tend to become self-fulfilling and self-reinforcing.[29]

Enemy images are also the product of deeply rooted social and psychological needs and frequently serve the interests of important groups and elites. Consequently they become central and well-embedded within larger belief systems. Research has established at least three different schemas of enemies: imperials, barbarians, and degenerates.[30] For example, throughout the Cold War, the Soviet leadership saw the United States as an "imperial" enemy; Chinese leaders have at times stereotyped others as "barbarians"; and the Ayatollah Khomeini in Iran described western leaders as "degenerates." Many other examples could be cited.

Theories of cognitive consistency expect that the least central parts of a belief system—that is, those with the fewest interdependent cognitions—will change first. Central beliefs are generally most resistant to change; people tend to modify at the margin and to change peripheral beliefs first.[31] In the process of making inferences, people seek to maintain their beliefs by reducing the challenge of discrepant information. The well-established tendency to discount inconsistent information contributes significantly to the persistence of stereotypes.[32] When people receive discrepant information, they generally make the smallest possible change in their beliefs; they will change their beliefs incrementally, allowing a large number of exceptions and special cases and making superficial alterations, rather than changing their central beliefs. Indeed, exposure to contradictory information frequently results in the strengthening of beliefs.[33] When the Soviet leadership cut defense spending, for example, John Foster Dulles explained that they did so out of weakness rather than from any intention to prevent a spiraling arms race. People also tend to actively seek and interpret information that confirms the negative image.[34]

Cognitive psychology has identified a number of heuristics, or mental rules of thumb, that can make enemy images resistant to change even in the face of discrepant information.[35] They describe how individuals process information, using convenient shortcuts. Two of the best-documented heuristics are availability and representativeness.[36] The availability heuristic posits that people tend to interpret new information in terms of what is most easily available in their cognitive repertoire, that is, in light of what they already know.[37] An enemy image is usually easily available and salient. The heuristic of representativeness suggests that people are likely to exaggerate similarities between one event and a prior class of events.[38] When action is ambiguous, people tend to treat it as representative of earlier hostile behavior.

IMAGE CHANGE

Stability in enemy images is the default and change the exception. Yet conservatism does not hold unconditionally. Belief systems and schemata, the active reconstruction of experience at a higher level of abstraction, also change, at times dramatically. Psychological, social, and political variables affect the propensity of change in enemy images.

Change in images is partly a function of the rate at which discrepant information occurs. Cognitive psychologists identify several factors that facilitate change. They suggest that important beliefs can change dramatically when there is no other way to account for "large" amounts of contradictory data.[39] Greater change will occur when information arrives in large batches, rather than bit by bit. President Bush, for example, did not change his image of Gorbachev even though the Soviet leader made a series of unilateral gestures to the United States. Only when information about large changes arrived in a rush, did he finally alter his well-established image of the Soviet leader.

Significant change in beliefs about others also occurs when people are exposed to inconsistent information and are persuaded that the behavior is not an arbitrary response to their environment but reflects the "nature" of the others.[40] Croatian and Muslim leaders are unlikely, for example, to change their image of Serbians if they attribute change in Serbian policy to their military setback by the Croatian forces in Krajina. The social and political conditions that promote uncharacteristic attributions to dispositional rather than situational factors have not been satisfactorily identified.[41]

Images can also change incrementally over time. As people consider information about an adversary inconsistent with their previous knowledge, they incorporate into their belief the conditions under which the image does not hold. This kind of process permits gradual change and adjustment.[42] When controlled political systems become more open or as leaders and elites receive new information about their rival, their image of the "other" can change incrementally.

Cognitive explanations of image change pay insufficient attention to the emotional factors that can motivate—or inhibit—change. Not only "cold" cognition but also "hot" emotions affect the likelihood of image change. The lower the intensity of an emotional commitment to an identity and its associated images, the less resistant these images are to change in the face of contradictory information.[43]

Most theories of social cognition do not adequately specify the external conditions or mediating causes of any of these changes.[44] Critics rightly contend that the neglect of context is disturbing; the social in "social" cognition research is largely absent.[45] Theories of social cognition do not explicitly model the processes that link changes in the environment to cognitive constructs or explain how images change. They do not examine the political and social interests with a stake in change, nor do they explore the social configurations that promote change in group images. Until they do, theories of social cognition will remain an inadequate theoretical tool in the analysis of change in enemy images.

POLITICAL LEARNING

To explain the changes in enemy images that facilitate conflict management, routinization, reduction, and resolution, I draw on propositions from social psychology to develop a concept of trial-and-error learning from failure. Learning is a subset of cognitive change; not all change is learning, but all learning is change. Learning is an explicitly normative concept: It measures cognitive change against some set of explicit criteria.

There is as yet no unified theory of learning, and psychology has not identified the conditions or thresholds that predict when different forms of learning are likely to occur. Furthermore, most psychological theories of learning are not very useful in specifying the dynamics of learning, in large part because they analyze learning within highly structured environments. Learning theories in educational and experimental psychology are associationist. They treat learning as a change in the probability of a specified response in the face of changing reward contingencies.[46] This concept of learning is not helpful in social and political environments where appropriate responses are unknown or disputed.

Political psychologists distinguish between simple and complex learning. Learning is simple when means are better adjusted to ends. Complex learning occurs when people develop more differentiated images and when these images are integrated into higher order structures that highlight difficult trade-offs.[47] Complex learning, at its highest level, may lead to a reordering or a redefinition of goals. From this perspective, learning must include the development of more complex structures as well as changes in content.[48]

These concepts of learning are a useful approach to explaining changes in hostile images that then shape or permit new directions in policy, but they fail to distinguish change from learning. Without some evaluative criteria, any cognitive change can be considered learning, and the concept of learning becomes redundant. Change in cognitive content or structure does not always constitute the "learning" that is necessary for conflict reduction. Saddam Hussein, for example, in the year preceding his decision to invade Kuwait, simplified his schema and concluded that the United States was engaged in a conspiracy to undermine his regime. Since the United States had no intention of undermining his regime and took no action to do so, this cognitive change is more accurately characterized as paranoid thinking that led to escalation of conflict.[49] Although these changes in Saddam's schema do provide a powerful explanation of his foreign policy behavior, they cannot, however, be considered learning.[50] Inescapably built into the concept of political learning is an evaluation of the structure and content of cognitive change.[51] These kinds of evaluative judgments inevitably are and will be contested.

More helpful are several strands of social-psychological theory and research that examine the liabilities of success and the benefits of failure in promoting organizational learning.[52] When failure challenges the status quo, it can draw attention to problems and stimulate the search for solutions. Only certain kinds of failure promote learning—highly predictable failures provide no new information, but unanticipated failures that challenge old ways of representing problems are more likely to stimulate new formulations. When Bosnian Serb forces suffered an unexpected and humiliating military defeat at the hands of Croatia, Slobodan Milosevic moved vigorously to push a reformulated policy in Bosnia-Herzegovina. Responding to failure, leaders "learn through experimentation" rather than through more traditional patterns of avoidance.[53]

Learning through failure can provoke a series of sequential experiments that generate quick feedback and allow a new round of trial-and-error experimentation.[54] This trial-and-error model of learning captures the dynamics of social cognition far more effectively than cognitive theories in which the perceiver is a "passive onlooker, who doesn't *do* anything—doesn't mix it up with the folks he's watching, never tests his judgments in action or interaction."[55] It does not represent learning as a neat linear process with clear causal antecedents, but as a messy, dynamic, interactive social, organizational, and political process.

In the text below, I first examine the internal conditions that can promote learning by one adversary. For present purposes, I define learning as changes in enemy images that promote conflict management, routinization, reduction, and resolution. I then explore the strategies that leaders or groups can use to promote the kinds of changes in their adversary's image of themselves that can lead to a reduction in conflict. The distinction between internal and external stimuli to learning and change in enemy image is artificial, since the process is usually highly interactive, but it is convenient for analytic purposes.

Former presidents Anwar Sadat of Egypt and Mikhail Gorbachev of the Soviet Union are two outstanding examples of political learning. Both developed far more complex and differentiated images of their adversary and initiated a series of actions that triggered a process of conflict reduction.[56] Changes in the images of their adversary led to changes in behavior that in turn provoked further changes in their enemy images. Learning accelerated in the doing.

To develop a satisfactory explanation of image change through political learning, we need to identify the conditions and strategies that promote learning. One obvious explanation is the change in the international distribution of capabilities—the relative decline in Egyptian and Soviet capabilities as compared to Israel and the United States, respectively. If changes in Egyptian and Soviet enemy images are a straightforward response to structural changes in the international system, then the analysis of political dynamics and image

change is unnecessary. If, on the other hand, there were important divisions within the Egyptian and Soviet leadership, and interpretations of the environment were contested, then structural factors alone cannot provide a sufficient explanation of the change in Egyptian and Soviet concepts. In both Egypt in the mid-1970s and the Soviet Union in the mid-1980s, there were deep divisions within the leadership. New interpretations of their environments were bitterly contested. It is therefore unsatisfying to explain the changes in Egyptian and Soviet images of their adversaries as rational adaptation to unambiguous feedback from their environments.[57]

Social and political factors can also be important triggers of image change and political learning.[58] Shifting political coalitions can be a powerful explanation of image change if new leaders are chosen primarily because of the content of their beliefs. In these two cases, however, both Sadat and Gorbachev struggled to shape coalitions to support policies that flowed from their changed images; new coalitions did not demand changes toward their adversary from their leader.

Generational change and political succession can also explain a fundamental change in leaders' images; the source of change is not individual learning but a change in elites. Generational change is helpful but not entirely satisfactory as an explanation of image change in the Soviet Union, and it is irrelevant in Egypt. Gorbachev was a generation younger than Brezhnev and many of his colleagues, but many in Gorbachev's generation did not change.[59] In Egypt, Sadat was of the same generation as Gamal Abdel Nasser, and Sadat learned after he had been president for several years.

Political succession and domestic politics are helpful in explaining whose images prevail under what set of political conditions. Shifts in social structure and political power determine whether leaders can implement policies based on changed images. However, they do not and cannot address the important question of why Gorbachev and Sadat began to "think" differently about conflict and how and why they changed their images and developed new concepts to organize their thinking about foreign and defense policy.

Why Leaders Learn

The changes in Gorbachev's and Sadat's images of their adversary suggest two conditions that motivated political learning.[60] The first condition was the importance of domestic reform to both men. Gorbachev came to office committed to domestic restructuring of a largely stalemated economic and political system. Gorbachev quickly learned that future resource commitments implicit in the standing threat assessments of the Soviet military would seriously constrain economic restructuring at home.[61]

Anwar Sadat similarly was motivated by his domestic agenda. After the October war in 1973, Sadat gave new importance to the role of the private and the foreign sectors, which were expected to provide both finance and technology. The new economic strategy of quasi-liberal experimentation was consistent with Sadat's strategy of conflict reduction: Stabilizing of Egypt's security environment was essential if the capital and investment necessary to push the economy forward were to flow into Egypt.

A second factor common to both leaders was their prior experience of the failure of alternatives to accommodation. Even before he became general-secretary, Gorbachev invited experts from the Foreign Ministry and the Academy of Sciences to private discussions of Soviet policy in Afghanistan. He was told of the growing costs of the Soviet intervention and its poor prospects; Afghanistan was the Soviet "Vietnam."[62]

Many also argued that NATO's deployment of Pershing II missiles had been provoked by Moscow's deployment of highly accurate intermediate range nuclear systems.[63] Stimulated by the failures in the Soviet economy, in policy in Afghanistan, and in arms control, Gorbachev learned through extensive consultation with specialists and experts and through trial-and-error experimentation.[64]

Sadat also learned from failure. Both he and Egyptian generals recognized that Egypt had fought the war in 1973 under optimal conditions: A military alliance with Syria had permitted a coordinated two-front attack for the first time, Arab oil producers had joined in the accompanying diplomatic offensive, and Egypt had the strategic advantage of surprise. Yet even under those conditions, Egypt had come perilously close to a serious military defeat after important initial military successes in crossing the Suez Canal. In the years following that war, Sadat had expanded the gains he had made through a process of phased disengagement with Israel. In this context, he was reluctant to risk the limited gains he had achieved in renewed warfare.

In both cases, failure of earlier policies underlined asymmetric capabilities and unfavorable trends. The evidence suggests that both leaders were motivated to learn and to change their images of their adversary. Both searched for new information: Gorbachev from experts in academic institutes and government and from American interlocutors, and Sadat through intermediaries and then through secret meetings between high-level Egyptian and Israeli leaders. Both leaders were receptive to the information that they received, largely because they were motivated to change existing images and policies. Both began with a small change in image, moved tentatively to small actions, accepted feedback, learned, and initiated a new series of actions that generated further feedback and change.[65] Gorbachev and

Sadat ultimately became confident that their adversaries would reciprocate their acts of reassurance. Learning was not orderly and linear, but experimental, through trial and error. In both cases, enemy images changed as a result of a complex interactive relationship between political learning and action that provided quick feedback.

Gorbachev and Sadat were motivated to change their images of their adversaries by their interest in freeing resources for domestic reform and by the earlier failure of alternatives to accommodation. These two stimuli to learning are not easily manipulated by others from the outside. They were the cumulative result of long-standing trends in Soviet and Egyptian domestic and foreign policy. Although this kind of fundamental learning is not necessary for crisis management or the routinization of conflict, it is an essential precondition of conflict reduction and resolution. Fundamental learning encouraged both Gorbachev and Sadat to use strategies of reassurance to initiate a process of conflict reduction.

STRATEGIES OF CONFLICT MANAGEMENT AND REDUCTION

Hostile imagery must change if conflict is to be reduced and resolved. Interstate conflict has been managed and routinized without modification in elite, much less public images, but neither civil violence nor interstate conflict can be resolved unless images change and leaders and publics learn. The process must also be reciprocated: Once leaders or groups begin to change their image of their adversary and are interested in attempting to resolve their conflict, they must change the image their adversary has of them if conflict reduction is to make any progress.

When leaders recognize that misperception and stereotyping govern their adversary's judgments as well as their own, they can try, by making an irrevocable commit-ment, to reassure their adversary of their benign intentions and to create incentives for conflict reduction.[66] This is precisely the strategy adopted by President Sadat in 1977.[67] Dissatisfied with the progress of negotiations in the autumn of 1977, yet unprepared to accept the status quo, Sadat searched for a dramatic move that would both reduce the tension and distrust between Egypt and Israel and induce Israel to make major concessions to reduce the conflict. It was the distrust built up over decades, he argued, that constrained the attempt to negotiate the issues at stake and fueled the cycle of wars. Sadat began secret negotiations between Egypt's deputy prime minister and Israel's foreign minister in Morocco; each agreed to make a critical concession—Israel indicated its willingness to return most of the Sinai peninsula to Egyptian sovereignty, and Egypt agreed to peace and the establishment of diplomatic relations with Israel.[68] Although these proposals were not fully satisfactory to either party, both sides were assured that their concessions would be reciprocated rather than exploited. Shortly thereafter, Sadat went to Jerusalem and spoke to the Knesset of the Egyptian terms for peace. Egyptian demands were unchanged, but Israel's leaders and public paid attention to the irreversible deed rather than to the content of the words. Through this single, dramatic act of reassurance, Sadat changed the trajectory of the conflict by changing his image both among the elite and the public in Israel.

Sadat's arrival in Jerusalem challenged the most important set of beliefs about Arab goals among Israel's leadership and public. His visit provided the dramatic evidence that was needed to overcome deeply entrenched enemy images. A broad spectrum of Israelis had assumed that Arab leaders were unrelentingly hostile, so much so that they were unprepared to meet Israel's leaders face-to-face. Once these core beliefs were shaken and Israel's identity was acknowledged, it became easier for Israelis to begin to revise associated assumptions and expectations.

President Sadat spoke over the heads of Israel's leadership directly to Israel's public. With his flair for the dramatic, he created the psychological and political symbols that would mobilize public opinion to press their more cautious and restrained leaders. In so doing, he removed a constraint on Israel's leaders and created a political inducement to action. Public learning, far more than elite learning, seems to require a dramatic and irrevocable demonstration of an adversary's benign intentions. Elites are more likely to learn incrementally, as they focus their attention on changing information over time. The public only selectively focuses its attention and is likely to be more resistant to gradual learning. Public opinion did change in Israel in response to a highly visible, unexpected, dramatic action.

Under this very special set of conditions, reassurance through irrevocable commitment succeeded brilliantly. The two critical components that make an irrevocable commitment reassuring to an adversary are its obviously high cost to the leaders who issue the commitment and its irreversibility. The strategy has been used so infrequently because it is often very difficult and very risky to design a commitment that is both high in cost and irreversible.[69] Leaders frequently have neither the resources nor the information necessary to make irrevocable commitments. In attempting to change an adversary's image through a self-binding commitment, leaders face a difficult trade-off; they are more likely to make offers that are reversible and less costly, but reversible low-cost offers are far less likely to lead to fundamental change in an adversary's image.

Reassurance through irrevocable commitment also requires a degree of freedom from domestic political and bureaucratic constraints. In Egypt after the 1973 War, Sadat had great autonomy in decision making and, indeed, could withstand the resignation of his foreign minister. Even so, making an irrevocable commitment to leaders long identified as antagonists can be difficult to justify to the public. Yet it is the public nature of the commitment that contributes to its irreversibility and credibility.[70] For all these reasons, the making of self-binding commitments to jolt an adversary to change its image and learn is likely to be difficult.

When a strategy of irrevocable commitment is impossible, one strategy that builds in some opportunity for learning is an adapted version of graduated reduction in international tension (GRIT).[71] The initiator announces in advance that it is beginning a series of conciliatory actions designed to reduce conflict and then implements these actions whether or not the other side reciprocates. Such actions should be easily verifiable. As each step is implemented, the initiator invites its adversary to reciprocate, but does not specify the appropriate response. Furthermore, a reciprocal response by an adversary is rewarded by a somewhat more conciliatory action. These actions, however, should not impair the defensive capacity of the initiator. If the other side attempts to exploit the concession, the initiator should respond with an appropriate action, but only to the degree necessary to restore the status quo.

Experimental studies concur that strategies like GRIT, which build in a series of conciliatory initiatives taken independently of the other's actions, are more effective than strategies that reciprocate directly and immediately.[72] Moreover, they were as effective among players who were judged generally competitive by their previous actions as among those who were generally cooperative. A second effective approach is a reciprocal strategy that is slow to retaliate and slow to return to conciliation; this variant of reciprocity makes allowances for initial misperception and modest learning.[73]

The experimental evidence may be overly optimistic when action occurs outside the laboratory. Gorbachev went far beyond a graduated strategy of reciprocity as he attempted to change American images of the Soviet Union. In 1985, he initiated a series of unilateral conciliatory actions and persisted even when they were not reciprocated.[74] Despite this series of unilateral Soviet actions, many in Washington resisted changing their images of the Soviet Union and remained skeptical of Gorbachev's intentions.[75] Paradoxically, it was Gorbachev who "learned by doing" in a complex interactive relationship between beliefs and behavior—action led to further changes in his beliefs as he made inferences from his behavior about his convictions.[76] Large and significant amounts of discrepant information were necessary before American leaders changed their image of the Soviet Union. It took Soviet tolerance of the destruction of the Berlin Wall, a dramatic and irreversible signal, to change American images and provoke fundamental learning.

CONCLUSION

Analysis of Gorbachev's and Sadat's policies suggests that strategies of conflict resolution that focus only on competing interests are likely to be insufficient to stimulate the learning that is fundamental to changing hostile imagery. In both enduring interstate rivalries and bitter ethnic conflict, interests are shaped by images, which are in turn partially shaped by identity. What we see as a threat is a function in large part of the way we see the world and who we think we are. Serbian memories of Croatian attacks during World War II and "betrayal" by the great powers—their identity as victims in a hostile world—shape the way leaders define their interests and help explain the continu-

ing support by Croatians for leaders and policies that impose terrible costs.

If threatened identities facilitate the creation of hostile imagery and contribute to violent conflict, then securing these identities must be a fundamental component of conflict resolution. If they are to be effective, peacemakers who confront bitter civil wars or enduring interstate rivalries must address interests in the broader context of images and identity. In the former Yugoslavia, the conflict can be managed temporarily by territorial partition and safe havens, but only temporarily. The conflict can be resolved only if all the parties recognize the legitimacy and the permanence of the others' identities. President Sadat's recognition of Israel's legitimacy was the critical key that unlocked the long and difficult peace process that culminated in mutual recognition by Israel and the Palestinians of the legitimacy of the other's identity.

In conflicts between states, reciprocal recognition of legitimacy and renunciation of the use of force can most directly secure threatened identities and reshape interests. In civil conflicts, the challenge is the same but the strategies must be somewhat different. Fractured states can be reconstructed through political separation and mutual recognition of competing identities, through a consociational or group building-block approach (where elite leaders accommodate and groups remain distinct), or through an integrative approach that seeks to forge multi-ethnic coalitions with cross-cutting ties.[77]

Prime Minister Yitzhak Rabin recognized in the last years of his life that there could be no military solution to the conflict between Israelis and Palestinians, and he made the fundamental decision to recognize the political identity of Palestinians. He began by negotiating with Palestinian leaders from the West Bank and Gaza, but he concluded that they did not have sufficient authority to make peace. He was reluctant to negotiate with Yasser Arafat, the chairman of the Palestine Liberation Organization (PLO), because he was pessimistic that the two could find an acceptable settlement. Rabin nevertheless allowed his foreign minister, Shimon Peres, to explore through a private channel the possibility that Arafat would agree to a gradual, incremental process that would allow Israel to test the intentions of the PLO in exchange for recognition of the political identity of the Palestinians and the creation of the Palestine National Authority. Critical to the process was mutual recognition of identity and political separation of the two peoples. Over time, secured identities should reshape images and interests as the two peoples disengage and redefine their political, economic, and national frontiers.

Mutual recognition and political separation is the most far-reaching strategy of conflict reduction. In 1989, after a brutal civil war that lasted over a decade, leaders of Lebanese religious groups modified the fundamentals of their prewar consociational bargain. Instead of privileging the Maronite Christian community, Muslims and Christians now share power equally. The arrangement still provides for a Maronite Christian president, a Sunni Muslim prime minister, and a Shiite president of the National Assembly; political decisions are still made by leaders at the top while their communities remain distinct.

The forging of multi-ethnic coalitions with cross-cutting ties is yet another strategy. This has been the traditional strategy in India and Canada, for example, and it was the principal demand of the Muslim leadership of Bosnia-Herzegovina. The agreement reached in Dayton honors a multi-ethnic Bosnia in principle, but its political arrangements provide for de facto separation of Bosnian Serbs from Muslims and Croats. In Canada, an intense political debate now rages between those who argue that a multicultural and multi-ethnic coalition is the only approach that recognizes the plurality of identities in Canada and those who insist that formal recognition of the distinctiveness of Québecois identity and political restructuring of Canada is essential.

In all these cases, conflict reduction required more than reciprocating small concessions in a gradually building process. The core of the solution lies in the often-difficult decision by senior leaders to acknowledge, respect, and accommodate different identities and to share political power. Informal track-two diplomacy (privately mediated diplomacy among elites closely connected to political leaders) can facilitate the discussion of deep identity issues in parallel with the more formal negotiation of interests that are gradually redefined after identities are recognized. The international community can facilitate power-sharing arrangements by tying progress in conflict resolution to the broader range of issues associated with membership in good standing in the global community.

All these strategies assume that identities are fixed and that they must be accommodated as they are. Such a pessimistic assumption is unwarranted. I have argued that identity is not given, but that it is socially reconstructed as interactions develop and contexts evolve. In his brilliant analysis, Benedict Anderson observed that nations, unlike families and clans where individuals can know the others, are "imagined communities," whose past, tradition, and connections are interpreted and reinterpreted through time.[78] Political identities similarly depend on imagined communities whose traditions are constructed and reinterpreted. Identities can therefore be reshaped and reconfigured as leaders and communities restructure their relationships.

Identities are complex structures, with components that emphasize shared communitarian traditions and norms that usually emphasize protection of the weak, social responsibility, generosity, fairness, and reciprocity as well as honor, reputation, and vengeance. The emphasis given to these different norms varies with the situation. Skilled mediators can emphasize the positive values of responsibility, fairness, and compassion as important elements of honor and reputation. Appeal to the "best" in the tradition of an identity may shift the emphasis within an "imagined community" to create the space for fairness and reciprocity that can ultimately change images, reshape interests, and culminate in tolerance and recognition of others' identities.

Threatened identities are conducive to hostile imagery, incompatible definitions of interest, and violent conflict. Often, violent conflict escalates to a painful level of destruction before serious attempts at conflict management (much less conflict resolution) begin. Yet defeat and destruction are extraordinarily expensive teaching tools. In their wake, deep enmity can preclude the fundamental learning that is necessary for image change and tolerance of the identities of others. Only after repeated failures do the parties begin to negotiate the issues, and then usually at only a superficial level. The challenge for peacemaking in the twenty-first century is to engage the parties earlier and at a deeper level so that the identities of some can be stretched to tolerate the identities of others.

NOTES

1. Milton Rokeach, *The Nature of Human Values* (New York: Free Press, 1973), p. 5; and Yaacov Vertzberger, *The World in Their Minds: Information Processing, Cognition, and Perception in Foreign Policy Decision Making* (Stanford, Calif.: Stanford University Press, 1990), pp. 114–127.

2. Daniel Druckman, "Nationalism, Patriotism, and Group Loyalty: A Social Psychological Perspective," *Mershon International Studies Review* (1994): 38, 43–68.

3. Henri Tajfel, *Human Groups and Social Categories* (Cambridge, U.K.: Cambridge University Press, 1981), p. 255.

4. Michael Hogg and Dominic Abrams, "Toward a Single-Process Uncertainty-Reduction Model of Social Motivation in Groups," in *Group Motivation: Social Psychological Perspectives*, ed. Michael Hogg and Dominic Abrams (London: Harvester Wheatsheaf, 1993), pp. 173–190.

5. Henri Tajfel, *Social Identity and Intergroup Relations* (New York: Cambridge University Press, 1982); Henri Tajfel and John C. Turner, "The Social Identity Theory of Intergroup Behavior," in *Psychology of Intergroup Relations*, 2nd ed., ed. Stephen Worchel and William G. Austin (Chicago: Nelson-Hall, 1986), pp. 7–24; Michael Hogg, *The Social Psychology of Group Cohesiveness: From Attraction to Social Identity* (New York: New York University Press, 1992); Marilynn B. Brewer and Sherry K. Schneider, "Social Identity and Social Dilemmas: A Double-Edged Sword," in *Social Identity Theory: Constructive and Critical Advances*, ed. Michael Hogg and Dominic Abrams (London: Harvester Wheatsheaf, 1990), pp. 169–184; and David Messick and Diane Mackie, "Intergroup Relations," *Annual Review of Psychology* 40 (1989): 45–81.

6. Barbara Harff and Ted Robert Gurr, "Toward Empirical Theory of Genocides and Politicides: Identification and Measurement of Cases Since 1945," *International Studies Quarterly* 32, no. 3 (September 1988): 359–371.

7. K. Booth, *Strategy and Ethnocentrism* (London: Croom Helm, 1979).

8. Jonathan Mercer, "Anarchy and Identity," *International Organization* 49 (Spring 1995): 229–252, argues that social identity theory confirms the neorealist argument that an anarchic international environment produces self-help behavior. Mercer does acknowledge, however, that the impact of differentiation on military conflict will depend on political, economic, and historical factors.

9. John C. Turner, Michael A. Hogg, Penelope J. Oakes, Stephen D. Reicher, and

Margaret S. Wetherwell, *Rediscovering the Social Group: A Self-Categorization Theory* (Oxford, U.K.: Basil Blackwell, 1987).

10. For an excellent discussion of this issue, see James M. Goldgeier, "The Role of Political Psychology in Rethinking Security Studies," unpublished paper.

11. Ted Hopf, "Russian Identity and Foreign Policy in Estonia and Uzbekistan," unpublished paper.

12. T. Ranger, *The Invention of Tradition* (Cambridge, U.K.: Cambridge University Press, 1983).

13. For a discussion of how moral norms and obligations that prevail in primary groups are reinterpreted at the national level, see Paul Stern, "Why Do People Sacrifice for Their Nations?" *Political Psychology* 16, no. 2 (1995): 217–235.

14. Muzafer Sherif, *In Common Predicament: Social Psychology of Intergroup Conflict and Cooperation* (Boston: Houghton Mifflin, 1966). The impact of "relative deprivation," or a context in which all groups stand to lose but some groups stand to lose more than others, is disputed.

15. Ted Robert Gurr, *Why Men Rebel* (Princeton, N.J.: Princeton University Press, 1970), pp. 12–13.

16. Gurr, *Why Men Rebel*, pp. 46–50. For a discussion of loss aversion and its impact on cooperation, see Janice Gross Stein and Louis Pauly, eds., *Choosing to Cooperate: How States Avoid Loss* (Baltimore, Md.: Johns Hopkins University Press, 1989).

17. Herbert C. Kelman, "Creating the Conditions for Israeli-Palestinian Negotiations," *Journal of Conflict Resolution* 26, no. 1 (March 1982): 39–76.

18. Susan T. Fiske and Shelley E. Taylor, *Social Cognition* (Reading, Mass.: Addison-Wesley, 1984), pp. 72–99.

19. D. M. Taylor and F. M. Moghaddam, *Theories of Intergroup Relations: International and Social Psychological Perspectives* (New York: Praeger, 1987).

20. They are likely to do so when geography is harsh and provides no buffer zone or margin for error; when offensive and defensive technology are difficult to distinguish; and when the relative power balance between adversaries is changing so that for at least one of the two, the advantages of striking first are substantial. See Robert Jervis, "Cooperation under the Security Dilemma," *World Politics* 30 (1978): 167–214.

21. Richard Ned Lebow and Janice Gross Stein, *We All Lost the Cold War* (Princeton, N.J.: Princeton University Press, 1994).

22. Paul Brass, ed., *Ethnic Groups and the State* (Towota, N.J.: Barnes and Noble Books, 1995); and Ted Robert Gurr, *Minorities at Risk: A Global View of Ethnopolitical Conflicts* (Washington, D.C.: United States Institute of Peace Press, 1993).

23. Human Rights Watch, in a report issued in 1995, concluded that "time after time, a proximate cause of violence is governmental exploitation of communal differences. . . . The 'communal card' is frequently played, for example, when a government is losing popularity or legitimacy and finds it convenient to wrap itself in the cloak of ethnic, racial, or religious rhetoric." *Playing the Communal Card: Communal Violence and Human Rights* (New York: Human Rights Watch, 1995), p. viii.

24. Jack Snyder, *Myths of Empire: Domestic Politics and International Ambition* (Ithaca, N.Y.: Cornell University Press, 1991), pp. 2–6, 31–49.

25. Goldgeier, "The Role of Political Psychology in Rethinking Security Studies," incisively reviews the social psychological literature on this question.

26. Milton J. Esman, *Ethnic Politics* (Ithaca, N.Y.: Cornell University Press, 1994) and "Ethnic Politics and Economic Power," *Comparative Politics* 19, no. 4 (1986): 395–418.

27. Gurr, *Why Men Rebel*, p. 59.

28. Druckman, "Nationalism, Patriotism, and Group Loyalty," p. 63.

29. Dean G. Pruitt and Jeffrey Z. Rubin, *Social Conflict* (New York: McGraw-Hill, 1986), pp. 117–118.

30. Richard W. Cottam, *Foreign Policy Motivations: A General Theory and a Case Study* (Pittsburgh, Pa.: University of Pittsburgh Press, 1977); Richard Herrmann, *Perceptions and Behavior in Soviet Foreign Policy* (Pittsburgh, Pa.: University of Pittsburgh Press, 1985); Herrmann,

"The Empirical Challenge of the Cognitive Revolution: A Strategy for Drawing Inferences about Perceptions," *International Studies Quarterly* 32 (1988): 175–203; and Herrmann and Michael P. Fischerkeller, "Beyond the Enemy Image and Spiral Model: Cognitive-Strategic Research after the Cold War," *International Organization* 49, no. 3 (Summer 1995): 415–450.

31. J. R. Anderson, *The Architecture of Cognition* (Cambridge, Mass.: Harvard University Press, 1982).

32. L. Ross, M. R. Lepper, and M. Hubbard, "Perseverance in Self-Perception and Social Perception: Biased Attributional Processes in the Debriefing Paradigm," *Journal of Personality and Social Psychology* 32 (1975): 880–892.

33. E. R. Hirt and S. J. Sherman, "The Role of Prior Knowledge in Explaining Hypothetical Events," *Journal of Experimental and Social Psychology* 21 (1985): 519–543.

34. Pruitt and Rubin, *Social Conflict*, pp. 112–119.

35. Heuristics refer to the rules leaders use to test the propositions embedded in their beliefs. D. von Winterfeldt and E. Edwards, *Decision Analysis and Behavioral Research* (New York: Cambridge University Press, 1986).

36. When people "anchor," they estimate the magnitude or degree of a phenomenon by picking an "available" initial value as a reference point and making a comparison. Fiske and Taylor, *Social Cognition*, pp. 250–256, 268–275.

37. Michael Ross and Fiore Sicoly, "Egocentric Biases in Availability and Attribution," *Journal of Personality and Social Psychology* 37 (1979): 322–336.

38. Daniel Kahneman and Amos Tversky, "On the Psychology of Prediction," *Psychological Review* 80 (1973): 237–251.

39. Robert Jervis, *Perception and Misperception in International Politics* (Princeton, N.J.: Princeton University Press, 1976), pp. 288–318.

40. Jennifer Crocker, Darlene B. Hannah, and Renee Weber, "Person Memory and Causal Attributions," *Journal of Personality and Social Psychology* 44, no. 1 (1983): 55–66.

41. Lee Ross, "The Intuitive Psychologist and His Shortcomings: Distortions in the Attri-bution Process," in *Advances in Experimental and Social Psychology* 10, ed. L. Berkowitz (New York: Academic Press, 1977), pp. 174–220.

42. E. T. Higgins and J. A. Bargh, "Social Cognition and Social Perception," in *Annual Review of Psychology* 38, ed. M. R. Rosenzweig and L. W. Porter (Palo Alto, Calif.: Annual Reviews, 1987): 369–425.

43. Vertzberger, *The World in Their Minds*, p. 136.

44. An exception is Ralph Erber and Susan T. Fiske, "Outcome Dependency and Attention to Inconsistent Information," *Journal of Personality and Social Psychology* 47 (1984): 709–726.

45. James H. Kuklinski, Robert C. Luskin, and John Bolland, "Where is the Schema? Going Beyond the 'S' Word in Political Psychology," *American Political Science Review* 85, no. 4 (December 1991): 1341–1380.

46. T. L. Good and J. E. Brophy, *Educational Psychology: A Realistic Approach* (New York: Longman, 1990).

47. Ernest Haas, *When Knowledge Is Power: Three Models of Change in International Organizations* (Berkeley: University of California Press, 1990), p. 84.

48. See, for example, Haas, *When Knowledge Is Power*.

49. In an effort to deal with the problem of evaluation, analysts refer to pathological learning, or changes that impede future cognitive growth. See James Clay Moltz, "Divergent Learning and the Failed Politics of Soviet Economic Reform," *World Politics* 45, no. 2 (January 1993): 301–325.

50. See Janice Gross Stein, "Deterrence and Compellence in the Gulf: A Failed or Impossible Task?" *International Security* 17, no. 2 (Fall 1992): 147–179.

51. For a similar argument, see George W. Breslauer, "What Have We Learned About Learning?" in *Learning in U.S. and Soviet Foreign Policy*, ed. George W. Breslauer and Philip E. Tetlock (Boulder, Colo.: Westview Press, 1991), p. 825–856.

52. Sim B. Sitkin, "Learning Through Failure: The Strategy of Small Losses," *Research in Organizational Behavior* 14 (1992): 231–266.

53. D. T. Campbell, "Reform as Experiments," *American Psychologist* 24 (1969): 409–429.

54. See C. Argyis and D. A. Schon, *Organizational Learning* (Reading, Mass.: Addison-Wesley, 1978).

55. Ulric Neisser, "On 'Social Knowing,'" *Personality and Social Psychology Bulletin* 6 (1980): 603–604, cited in Kuklinski et al., "Where is the Schema?" p. 1346.

56. The scope of their learning is detailed in Janice Gross Stein, "Political Learning by Doing: Gorbachev as an Uncommitted Thinker and Motivated Learner," in *International Relations Theory and the Transformation of the International System*, ed. Richard Ned Lebow and Thomas Risse-Kappen (New York: Columbia University Press, 1995), pp. 223–258, and "The Political Economy of Strategic Agreements: The Linked Costs of Failure at Camp David," in *Double-Edged Diplomacy: International Bargaining and Domestic Politics*, ed. Peter Evans, Harold Jacobsen, and Robert Putnam (Berkeley: University of California Press, 1993), pp. 77–103.

57. Steven Weber, "Interactive Learning in U.S.-Soviet Arms Control," in *Learning in U.S. and Soviet Foreign Policy*, ed. Breslauer and Tetlock, pp. 784–824.

58. Haas, *When Knowledge Is Power*.

59. For evidence of how politically contested much of Gorbachev's "new thinking" was, see Stephen M. Meyer, "Sources and Prospects of Gorbachev's New Political Thinking on Security," *International Security* 13, no. 2 (Fall 1988): 124–163.

60. Richard Ned Lebow, "When Does Conciliation Succeed?" in *International Relations Theory and the Transformation of the International System*, ed. Lebow and Risse-Kappen, pp. 167–186.

61. Meyer, "Sources and Prospects of Gorbachev's New Political Thinking on Security."

62. Interview of Vadim Zagladin, Moscow, May 18, 1989, and Anatoliy Gromyko, Moscow, May 19, 1989.

63. See Robert Herman, "Soviet New Thinking: Ideas, Interests, and the Definition of Security" (doctoral dissertation, Cornell University, 1995).

64. Stein, "Political Learning by Doing."

65. See Stein, "The Political Economy of Strategic Agreements," and "Political Learning by Doing."

66. Dean G. Pruitt and Peter J. Carnevale, *Negotiation in Social Conflict* (London: Open University Press, 1992), p. 146, term this kind of strategy "unilateral conciliatory initiatives."

67. Z. Maoz and D. S. Felsenthal, "Self-Binding Commitments: The Inducement of Trust, Social Choice, and the Theory of International Cooperation," *International Studies Quarterly* 31 (1987): 177–200.

68. Moshe Dayan, *Breakthrough: A Personal Account of the Egypt-Israel Peace Negotiations* (New York: Knopf, 1981), pp. 44–52.

69. Maoz and Felsenthal, "Self-Binding Commitments," p. 198.

70. Ibid., pp. 191–192.

71. Charles Osgood, *An Alternative to War or Surrender* (Urbana: University of Illinois Press, 1962).

72. S. Lindskold, P. S. Walters, and H. Koutsourais, "Cooperators, Competitors, and Response to GRIT," *Journal of Conflict Resolution* 27 (1983): 521–532.

73. D. G. Pruitt and M. J. Kimmel, "Twenty Years of Experimental Gaming," *Annual Review of Psychology* 28 (1977): 363–392.

74. In 1985, Gorbachev announced the suspension of Soviet countermeasures in response to the deployment of intermediate-range nuclear forces (INF) by NATO and a moratorium on further deployments of SS-20s. That same year, he proclaimed a unilateral moratorium on nuclear testing. The Soviet Union also paid its back dues to the United Nations for peacekeeping, began to cooperate with the International Atomic Energy Agency, and reworked its position in the Strategic Arms Reduction Talks (START) in October 1985. In January 1986, Gorbachev urged a program of complete nuclear disarmament to be achieved in three stages by the year 2000. In 1987, the Soviet Union agreed to intrusive on-site verification inspections as part of the INF agreement and announced its decision to withdraw from Afghanistan. In December 1988, at the UN General Assembly,

Gorbachev also announced the unilateral reduction of active Soviet military forces by 15 percent and the withdrawal of more than 40 percent of Soviet tank divisions from Eastern Europe, together with 50 percent of Soviet tanks.

75. Interviews, Policy Planning Staff and National Security Council Staff, Washington, February 1989.

76. M. P. Zanna, J. M. Olson, and R. H. Fazio, "Attitude-Behavior Consistency: An Individual Difference Perspective," *Journal of Personality and Social Psychology* 38 (1980): 432–440.

77. Timothy D. Sisk, *Power Sharing and International Mediation in Ethnic Conflicts* (Washington, D.C.: United States Institute of Peace Press, 1996).

78. Benedict Anderson, *Imagined Communities*, 2nd ed. (London: Verso, 1991).

7

Environmental Change, Migration, and Conflict
A Lethal Feedback Dynamic?

ASTRI SUHRKE

Increasing concern in the early 1990s over the negative impact of climate change strengthened fears that environmental degradation and demographic pressures would displace millions of destitute people in the developing world and create a wake of social upheaval. The idea of the "environmental refugee" as both a victim and a source of conflict was widely accepted by the media, and it soon emerged in the scholarly literature as well. "The masses of forcefully uprooted persons . . . might become a key element in the lethal feedback dynamics between environmental degradation and violent conflict," wrote the political scientist Nazli Choucri in 1992 (p. 101).

The purpose of this chapter is to examine these concepts more closely. I will argue that the empirical basis for current concepts of conflict-generating "environmental refugees" is weak and that other paradigms are more appropriate for creating policy-relevant theory. In particular, I move away from a paradigm that assumes close links between environmental change and national security and, in a related dimension, postulates that contemporary social developments will lead to severe—indeed, catastrophic—resource restraints and hence fundamental insecurity in the twenty-first century.

ENVIRONMENT AND SECURITY: THE DEBATE

When the Cold War ended, analysts and activists dealing with a broad spectrum of issues pried the concept of national security loose from its conventional military bedrock. In the developing world, reformers argued that achieving development goals was the essence of security, an idea that also was promoted by the United Nations Development Program (UNDP) in the concept of "human security" (1994). Following similar logic, protecting the environment was presented as a security issue by a school of analysts in the North and to some extent also in the South. An important argument in this perspective held that those conflicts among groups and states that reflected competition for scarce environmental resources would increase as resources deteriorated or were rapidly depleted. Environmental issues thus became a security matter. Movements of refugees and illegal migrants were also subsumed under the new security paradigm by appearing as threats to established cultures, wealth, and power and because in at least one well-known instance, the prospect of unwanted illegal migration brought on a military intervention (the United States in Haiti in 1994).

In part, the "extended security" concept was an analytical innovation arising from attempts to make sense of the post–Cold War world. Other reasons for the emerging paradigm were embedded in the multifaceted linkages between a scholarly discourse and the sociopolitical context of its time. As the end of the superpower rivalry weakened the rationale for maintaining the massive military establishments built up by western states during the Cold War, activists and analysts dealing with the environment, humanitarian crises, and migration saw an opportunity to move their issues onto the policy agenda. They were supported by mounting evidence of the gravity of the issues. In the ensuing debate about what constituted "security," an underlying competition for resources and determination of policy priorities was clearly evident. By elevating matters of environment, migration, and development to the domain of "high politics" reserved for traditional national security matters, reformers hoped to mobilize political attention, support, and funds, as Marc Levy has pointed out (1995). If social conflict, for instance, were found to be rooted in environmental degradation, environmen-

tal rather than political and military factors would need to be studied and addressed. Vested interests and other political actors responded accordingly. One reaction, for instance, was to develop new functions for the military by deploying armed forces in humanitarian emergencies and exploring their role in protecting the environment.[1]

A parallel public policy debate related to long-term trends of social development. Focusing on demographic trends, patterns of resource use, and state structures, one school of thought painted a near-catastrophic picture as the twentieth century draws to a close. In this neo-Malthusian perspective, the world—especially the South—is beset by increasing crises and conflict generated by fast-growing populations competing for declining resources, as well as by massive urbanization, uncontrollable migration pressures, and reduced state capacity to regulate conflict where it was most needed (that is, in the poorest areas of the world). The historian Paul Kennedy developed the argument in a comprehensive treatise, *Preparing for the 21st Century* (1993); in the United States, the same perspective was popularized by Robert Kaplan (1994) and, from an environmental perspective, Norman Myers (1993).

For analysts, this political landscape represented both dangers and opportunities. Fundamental changes in international relations had created space and receptivity to conceptual innovation and unorthodoxy. There was more mobility between "high" and "low" politics. More problematic, since concepts of "security" and "crisis" had traditionally attracted political attention and funding—and now had acquired additional paradigmatic legitimacy from catastrophe treatises—there were implicit incentives to define a subject of inquiry in those terms. A systematic bias favoring the conflict-and-crisis perspective developed.[2] The consequences were not only analytical. In a field where the subject areas—population, environment, migration—were all emotionally and politically charged, the political implications of paradigmatic choice were significant. By subsuming migrants under the rubric of "security," analysts established primary connotations with "enemy" and "defense": Migrants (and refugees) thus *prima facie* became threats rather than victims or assets, which in many cases they surely were. In this way the security paradigm reinforced popular stereotypes of migrants as undesirable, even if the analysis itself differentiated between types of "threats" and actual versus perceived danger (Weiner 1993, 1995). This does not necessarily mean that the security paradigm is inappropriate for migration and environment issues, only that its applicability in relation to the empirical material must be assessed with great care.

THE ENVIRONMENT, MIGRATION, AND CONFLICT: THE DEBATE

The collective claim of the literature on security and the environment is that pressures on the environment have increased to the point where the security of states is affected in four principal ways: (1) environmental degradation can cause health hazards or jeopardize the economic livelihood of a significant part of the population; (2) intensified competition for declining or degraded resources can create conflicts within or among states; these in turn can generate regional instabilities that affect nations further afield; (3) environmental degradation may force people to migrate, thereby creating conflict over scarce resources in the receiving areas; and (4) the existentialist argument advanced by a school of environmentalists and "ecological economists" to the effect that an environmental resource has an intrinsic value regardless of its being consumed (even in the form of being seen), and hence its loss is a matter of security. All the claims are controversial and have been

criticized. The criticism concerns methodology as broadly understood to mean unclear definitions, unsubstantiated claims, generalizations from single cases, and paradigmatic confusion.[3]

The fullest elaboration to date of the links between environmental degradation, migration, and conflict comes from a three-year Canadian-led international research project on "environmental scarcities" and "violent conflict." Project leader Thomas Homer-Dixon hypothesized at the outset that "large population movements caused by environmental stress would induce 'group identity' conflicts, especially ethnic clashes" (1994, p. 7) and that "waves of environmental refugees [would] spill across borders with destabilizing effects" (1991, p. 77). Similarly, Nazli Choucri (1992) claimed that "environmental degradation forces people to move, sometimes across borders, and most assuredly to impinge on and ultimately challenge those [host] populations," thus becoming a key element of conflict (p. 101). Choucri does not offer any empirical support for this statement, however. Homer-Dixon cites only one case affirming the migration thesis, and the substudy on migration in the project found no systematic links to support the hypothesis (Suhrke 1993). Homer-Dixon, a principal proponent of the paradigmatic links between security and environment issues, nevertheless argues (1994) that the single affirmative case disproves the null hypothesis that there are no links whatsoever between environmentally induced migration and conflict. Formulated in this way, the null hypothesis is indeed disproved, but that conclusion comes as no surprise and is hardly very interesting. The more challenging task is to understand the nature of the various links between migration and conflict and the conditions under which they operate.

To address these questions, it is first necessary to deal with some general theoretical perspectives that affect the inquiry. One concerns the impact of demographic growth on migration. In the Homer-Dixon model, population increase generates pressures on the environment and thereby increases out-migration. More conventionally, but in the same direction, demographic growth appears in migration models as a cause of out-migration through pressures on the employment sector. However, one of the few recent studies that systematically examines the relationship between population growth and international migration counsels caution. Using aggregate data analysis of migration to the United States from sending countries with four different demographic characteristics in the 1989–1993 period, Mary Kritz (1995) found that rates of natural increase and fertility were not directly related to migration.[4] To what extent we can generalize from this case to other migration patterns is unclear; the point is that we cannot assume that population growth is both a necessary and sufficient cause of migration.

A second, common misconception concerns what happens when people are displaced. Both Homer-Dixon and Choucri suppose that conflict ensues. But the literature clearly has an alternative paradigm: Migration does not "most assuredly" lead the migrants to "impinge upon and challenge the host population," as Choucri writes. That happens only under conditions of zero-sum interaction—whether actual or perceived. The alternative is a value-added model, where migrants are incorporated into the host society without collective strife, typically by providing needed labor and skills. Nor does ethnic differentiation between host population(s) and newcomers necessarily make the incorporation process conflictual. Ethnic studies have documented numerous cases of an alternative model based on the principle of ethnic division of labor. Because of different modernization rates and traditional skills, ethnic groups position them-

selves differently in the market and the society; the result is interdependence and cooperation in the manner of a Durkheimian "mechanical solidarity" (Horowitz 1985).

A third notion often encountered in the conflict perspective is that rural out-migration, induced by environmental stress and economic stagnation, feeds the urban conglomerations of the developing world, which become centers of social unrest. While this clearly has some validity, the process certainly does not explain all urban growth nor even a great deal of social conflict in the developing world. During the past fifteen years, less than half of the urban growth in the developing world as a whole is estimated to have resulted from migration (Findley 1994).[5] Moreover, the most prolonged and devastating conflicts in the developing world in this period were not urban in origin, but stemmed from broader struggles over the social order and interlocking international rivalries (for example, in Central America, southern Africa, the Horn of Africa, and Indochina).

Increasingly, the extent of the pathology of the megacities in the Third World has been challenged in numerous microlevel studies, leading to a new "accommodationist" school of thought about the functionality of large cities (Perlman 1976; Richardson 1993). The main reasons advanced by Samuel Huntington in the late 1960s to explain the low level of collective urban violence relative to the rapid pace of urbanization apparently remain relevant. Despite the evident misery and tension in the cities, urban centers represent upward mobility for the migrants (which is why they continue to come), and the migrants tend to be cautious and conservative, focusing more on immediate ways to improve their livelihood than on broader political struggles (Huntington 1968).

While this suggests which generalizations do not apply in an unqualified manner to the environment-migration-conflict equation, are there any that do?

First, it is evident that similar migrations can create conflict in one receiving area, but not in another. For instance, migration from Bangladesh to the neighboring state of Assam in India has created significant conflict (and constitutes the evidence cited by Homer-Dixon), but this is not the case with Bangladeshi migration to the Middle East, or even to other parts of India. Hence, a host of intervening variables must be analyzed and categorized to determine the different outcomes.

Second, an environmental factor can often be identified as a cause of migration, especially if the "environment" is broadly defined to mean resource scarcity.[6] How, then, does one distinguish between economic and environmental migrants? Take, for example, a Mexican peasant whose land has deteriorated due to adverse climate change and whose product has been squeezed out of the market due to increasing price competition brought on by the North American Free Trade Agreement: Is his migration to the United States economically or environmentally induced? Obviously, it is both. In such cases, only microlevel studies can determine the relative weight of each and the corresponding policy implications.[7]

With these benchmarks of caution established, we can rephrase the central question posed at the outset: Under what conditions does environmentally related migration cause conflict?

ENVIRONMENTAL CHANGE AND MIGRATION

Does Environmental Degradation Cause Population Flows?

The puzzle has several parts. The first concerns the role of environmental degradation as a cause of out-migration. To facilitate the analysis, it is useful to narrow the concept of environmental change to processes that are presumed to be accelerating and to be having significant "push" effects on potential migrants. These are desertification, land degradation, deforestation, and rising sea levels induced by global warming. Recognizing the importance of these processes, the 1992 United Nations Conference on Environment and Development identified four fragile ecosystems: regions with severe deforestation, regions with severe desertification, low-lying coastal areas, and "vanishing" islands in the Indian and Pacific oceans.

The scholarly literature on this topic is meager. Conventional migration studies did not treat the environment as a separate factor. Yet common sense—as well as catastrophes such as the recurrent drought in the Sahel in the 1970s and mid-1980s—tells us that environmental change can be an underlying cause of mass migration by affecting structural socioeconomic conditions. Environmental change can also be the proximate cause of displacement as most obviously demonstrated by the flooding of habitat in low-lying river deltas (for example, Bangladesh). Analysts differ, however, on the relative importance of environmental variables and how to measure them.[8] Migration experts tend to see environmental change as a contributory factor, but one that is difficult to isolate and assess (Bilsborrow 1991; Hugo 1995; Kritz 1990). Analysts who come to migration from environmental or developmental concerns assign greater weight to the environmental factor, whether as an underlying or proximate cause. Indeed, the term "environmental refugee" came from this literature (El-Hinnawi 1985; Jacobson 1988).

Does Environmental Degradation Cause Distress Migrations?

An unstated assumption in the migration-conflict sequence is that forceful or sudden displacement, particularly of large numbers of people, is more likely to produce instability or conflict in the receiving areas than gradual movements and migrations that respond, at least in part, to demands for skills and labor. But are population movements caused by environmental change actually distress migrations of this kind? Is there something about the nature of environmental degradation that tends to produce refugee-like movements rather than more ordinary migration flows?

The environmentalists writing about migration tend to argue that this is so. For instance, Norman Myers (1992) emphasizes that several forms of environmental degradation are "slow-onset," often hidden processes that suddenly reach a threshold at which the damage is irreparable. A forest has been exploited for centuries, but the depletion and damage have gone unnoticed until the self-renewing capacity of the trees is exhausted. "Quite suddenly . . . the tree stock starts to decline" (p. 6). The migration consequences of this scenario fall in the distress category: Forced and possibly large-scale population movements would take place if the calamity suddenly struck all members of the community at once.

This dynamic may be characteristic of some degradation process, but forest depletion is rarely a hidden process that suddenly bursts into view only when well advanced. Deforestation is a gradual and visible process, certainly visible to the local people who register the consequences in concrete terms. Every year they experience diminishing returns: There is a longer walk to the forest's edge and less wood to collect, as Fernandes and colleagues (1988) observed among India's "scheduled" tribes in Orissa. In this case, some responded by migrating in search of work and becoming indistinguishable from the massive flows of migrant labor in the subcontinent. Others lacked the resources or will to get out and waited for the

end of the process, a refugee-like situation with likely outcomes being complete social marginalization, starvation, bonded labor, or early death.

This example suggests a dual migration consequence, equivalent to the sociological distinction between migrants and refugees. The duality seems to operate with respect to common forms of environmental degradation, including deforestation, rising sea levels, desertification, and drought. The implications for social conflict must be modified accordingly. Much of the migration caused by environmental degradation suggests a gradual movement that spreads the impact and gives both migrants and receiving areas some room to adapt.

The assumption that distress migrations —which do occur—are likely to produce instability or conflict in the receiving areas requires critical examination as well. A more differentiated model can easily be suggested: Flood and famine victims are so powerless and marginalized as to be unable to make effective demands of any kind on the receiving area. In a real sense, they cannot constitute a "threat," at least not in the early phase of displacement. Furthermore, international relief agencies typically act to mitigate a large-scale humanitarian disaster by providing resources to both the refugees and the host populations. Tension and conflict may occur in a second phase, when and if displacement becomes long term and the victims acquire some autonomy to make demands on their hosts. The scenario is familiar from numerous refugee situations throughout the developing world (United Nations High Commission on Refugees 1993).

The dual migration dynamic in environmentally related displacement can be illustrated briefly.

Deforestation. Deforestation has various negative economic effects, including loss of topsoil; sedimentation of rivers, lakes, and coastal areas, which affects fisheries; and loss of water for industrial, agricultural, and domestic use. Land degradation and soil erosion are major problems, reducing the return from the land and exacerbating cycles of flood and drought (as, arguably, upstream deforestation in the Himalayas increases downstream flooding of the densely populated Ganges delta plain). In a typical coping response, family members migrate, often seasonally, as exemplified by Thailand's mostly seasonal rural-to-urban migration (Hurst 1990).[9] These people are typically incorporated in the burgeoning urban economy of Bangkok without causing collective social conflict. Here, migration appears as a solution rather than a problem.

Indigenous forest dwellers are affected in a more fundamental way. Being bound to the forest culturally, socially, and economically, tribal people are highly vulnerable to the loss of forest. Loss usually entails victimization and disintegration, as the community is destroyed and its members dispersed (for example, in Central America, the Amazon basin, and India).

Deforestation that affects agricultural communities "downstream" is common and could greatly inflate existing migrations. The other category of potential migrants is quite small, since the world's indigenous forest population has already been severely reduced. As future "environmental refugees," they would have minimal impact on the receiving areas. Their efforts to resist change have caused conflict in the place of origin, although the inequality of power between the protagonists has limited the scope of conflict.

Rising sea levels. A rising sea level is expected to affect coastal populations, notably in China, Vietnam, Bangladesh, and Egypt, as well as in the South Pacific atolls and the Maldives. Urban concentrations on delta plains will be exposed, and the number of potentially displaced persons could be many millions.

By all accounts, however, a rising sea level is a slow process. According to the 1990 report of the International Panel on Climate Change (IPCC), sea levels might rise by 30 to 110 centimeters by the year 2100, affecting 360,000 kilometers of coastline.[10] In a worst-case scenario for Bangladesh, other researchers have estimated that 13 percent to 15 percent of its population could be displaced in the next sixty years (Fairclough 1991, p. 88; Jacobson 1988, p. 34). If the displacement occurred at a steady rate, some 200,000 to 300,000 people would be displaced annually. This figure is sizeable, yet it represents fewer than one-quarter of the new arrivals who enter Bangladesh's labor market every year. Moreover, the slow process gives coastal people and the authorities concerned some time to adjust. Many Bangladeshi would try to migrate within the country or to neighboring areas (legally or illegally), thus increasing the pressure on already dense out-migration routes. A sea-level rise can also be expected to inflate existing and well-established migration streams of Pacific Islanders to Australia and New Zealand and of Egyptians to the Persian Gulf states.

In addition, situations of acute displacement will probably increase. The remaining communities will be exposed to more frequent and more destructive floods and tropical storms that cause death and displacement.[11] The situation captures the involuntary and vulnerable nature of a refugee situation; dependence and impoverishment result as the victims congregate, usually in adjacent areas. For instance, those who survive nature's attacks on the Bangladeshi coast lack the means to move much beyond the first relief station. As flood victims, they are both powerless and marginalized; these refugees evidently do not end up in conflict-generating international migration in the region.[12]

Desertification and drought. Desertification is typically a cumulative process, stemming from low rainfall, overgrazing, deforestation, or overuse of common land. The impact is gradual, manifesting itself in declining productivity, diminishing pasture areas, and worsening droughts that gradually deplete human populations and livestock reserves. Households resort to a range of coping strategies, including migration to new grazing land or towns, as observed in the Sudan and Central Sahel (Bilsborrow and DeLargy 1991). Circular migration is common, involving both long-term and short-term cycles. Even under conditions of prolonged drought, this pattern held in Mali in 1983–1985 when a severe drought struck. With migration rates already at high levels, the drought merely had the effect of shifting the movements to less resource-demanding migrations to nearby regions (Findley 1994).

If conditions worsen, herds are killed, seeds are consumed, and the land may be abandoned for long periods. This was the pattern of pastoralist migrations in the Sahel in the 1970s, when cumulative effects of drought and apparent desertification caused famine and mass flows of people to urban areas in search of food (Watts 1983). As with flood victims, the famine victims were largely powerless and marginalized. Congregating around relief stations in provincial towns, families usually split up, as able-bodied men migrated to search for work on plantations or mines in the Sahel or neighboring countries, while women, children, and the old remained as international relief clients (Helland and Vaa 1986; Somerville 1986).

MIGRATION AND SOCIAL CONFLICT

"Environmental refugees," then, primarily constitute victims rather than "threats," a condition reflecting their extreme powerlessness. But what can be said of migrants in general? At first glance, the history of migration and social conflict is too rich and contradictory to be very helpful.

Historically, migration has been both a solution and a problem, a source both of conflict and of mutual enrichment. Ancient migrations and colonial expansion involved conquest of territory and peoples; later, spontaneous or colonially induced migrations in Africa and Asia laid the foundation for ethnic conflict that erupted in the postcolonial state, often with large time lags.[13] Current migrations in the Indian subcontinent suggest the contemporary range: Native peoples and new settlers fight over land (in the northeast hill areas), old and new arrivals clash over political power in urban areas (the *mohajir* and the Sindhi in Karachi), nativist movements turn violent to exclude newcomers (in Bombay and Assam), and established industrial workers fight with displaced tribals over employment (Bihar).

But the history of migration is also a history of new forms of coexistence, of integration and assimilation, and of nonviolent relations. Migrants—including refugees—have historically brought valuable new labor and skills to the receiving area. In nineteenth-century Europe, unprecedented migrations were generated by factors that are also relevant in the developing world today: rapid population growth, economic and revolutionary technological change, and epidemics of plant disease or parasites causing crop failure (Moch 1994). The result was a massive out-migration from rural areas. While a moving frontier in the Americas and Australia made it possible to absorb many migrants readily, substantial intra-European and rural-to-urban movements also took place. The process certainly involved social stress and tensions, thus constituting a form of violence against the unwilling migrants themselves, as Barrington Moore (1966) has argued with respect to the rural-to-urban migration caused by the earlier Enclosure in England. But the migrations did not set off immediate, collective violence. The reasons lie partly in the element of mutual gain and interdependence realized in the receiving areas.

There is no reason to assume that the consequences of contemporary migrations, including those caused in whole or in part by environmental degradation, will be any less complex. To sort out these consequences, a typological analysis can be useful. A preliminary categorization of two major types of migration is set out below.

TOWARD A TYPOLOGY: TWO CASES

The IPCC (1995) concludes that recurrent and more severe drought—like the probable destruction of "some human habitats" due to rising sea levels—will probably cause migrations and place "additional stress on already stressed social and political systems" [4(3)(c)]. More specifically, the IPCC identifies two principal kinds of migration likely to result from the climate change projected in the next 100 years:

- Migrations due to rising sea-levels: Coastal areas will be most affected, especially urban concentrations in delta areas; Bangladesh and China are among the most exposed.
- Migrations due to increasingly frequent and severe drought in arid and semi-arid regions: Populations dependent upon rain-fed agriculture and livestock will be most affected.[14]

These movements represent common and well-researched cases and hence form useful starting points for a typology of environmentally related migration and conflict.

Out-Migration from Bangladesh

The long-standing movement of the Bengali, coastal people into neighboring upland areas (Assam, Tripura, and also the Chittagong Hill Tracts in Bangladesh) is a classic case of conflict-generating migration. Its characteristics can be briefly summarized: The sociopolitical dynamic is conflictual because the numbers of migrants involved are large and because of the direction of migration. The upland people react with the historically conditioned fear that tribal and hill communities have of being taken over by the more numerous and aggressively modern coastal people. In the hill areas, the contest concerns land (which tends to have zero-sum characteristics), and losses incurred by the upland people are magnified by the significance that land has for their survival in both a social and an economic sense. In the case of Assam, this conflict was brought to a head by developments in the 1970s as the political apparatus of the central state aligned itself with the migrants against the indigenous people. The peculiarly competitive structure of Indian politics in this period turned the illegal Bangladeshi migrants into valuable "vote banks" for the all-India Congress party and thereby threatened the local political party. The result was a nativist movement and, in a complicated but related dynamic, large-scale violence. Subsequent political compromises have defused the conflict somewhat, but the underlying source of tension remains.

By contrast, out-migration from Bangladesh did not generate similar violence and social conflict when the migrants moved to urban areas with more flexible economies and a demand for labor and when the migrants did not become tools in the political contest in receiving areas. For instance, the substantial Bangladeshi migration to the Gulf countries is a tightly controlled and managed labor migration. There is also large-scale and partly illegal Bangladeshi migration to Europe and East Asia. These migrations are not associated with collective violence, but, rather, with social tension and occasional violence against individual migrants. Likewise, large-scale, illegal

Bangladeshi migration to the Indian capital of New Delhi has caused considerable social tension, but not collective violence, probably reflecting the capacity of the urban economy and society to absorb the migrants.

Out-Migration from the Sahel

Population movements in and from the Sahel in the 1970s and the mid-1980s typify a pattern of distress migration among agricultural and pastoral peoples in semi-arid regions.

Pressures on the land and severe droughts in the 1970s (and again in the mid-1980s) led to large-scale out-migration (Bennett 1991; Hjort and Salih 1989; Watts 1983). Of the Sahelian region's estimated population of 36 million (1985), uncounted hundreds of thousands of pastoralists and farmers became what today would be considered "environmental refugees." Perhaps 2 million were displaced by the 1984–1985 famine. Many ended up in temporary relief stations in provincial towns, later to be dispersed as casual labor in mines, plantations, and shantytowns in the Sahel region and neighboring coastal states.

The "environmental refugees" from the Sahel were absorbed at least temporarily by the national economies and aided by foreign relief. Subsequently, some returned to their home areas; others were permanently displaced to urban areas, where they represented one of several sources of urban growth, ranging from relatively modest (in the larger cities) to significant (in provincial towns). As in earlier rural-to-urban migrations in Europe, the process involved great personal and social costs for the displaced people, but it was not accompanied by large-scale collective social conflict or violence. The social and political implications in the longer run remain unclear.

Some political tension and overt conflict did occur. Somerville (1986) has identified three types of conflict, all occurring within or between areas affected by the drought. Strain arose between drought-hit states as famine victims moved, often with their herds, from one afflicted region to another (for example, from Mauritania to Mali), and the authorities of the receiving state in at least one case sought to close the border. Second, tension arose in urban areas within drought-affected states as towns and cities swelled with new arrivals. Thus, urban unrest in Senegal in 1971 and 1973 has been attributed to the drought. Third, and by far most common, however, was political tension brought on by intensified competition by major actors within the state or by corrupt use of relief assistance, that is, conflicts that were not related to migration.

Given the catastrophic famine and large-scale movement of people, an occasional border closing and scattered urban unrest may count as modest consequences. The main reasons for such modest effects are the characteristic powerlessness of "environmental refugees," the cushioning effect of traditional ethnic and kinship ties, and the ready availability of foreign relief assistance that mutes the immediate competition for food. Nevertheless, political tensions of this kind are likely to recur, and they may intensify in the event of renewed distress migrations or if climate change creates a more permanent population shift from the northern to the southern Sahel, as the Organization for Economic Cooperation and Development's *Club de Sahel* predicted in 1988.

The Sahelian and the Bangladeshi cases suggest a simple matrix that may be used for developing a further typology (see figure 7.1).

CONCLUSIONS AND POLICY IMPLICATIONS

As for contemporary migrations that are set off in whole or in part by environmental

Migrating Group	Direction and Outcome	
	Rural Areas	Urban Areas
Coastal communities	Social conflict	[Interdependence]
Upland, "tribal," and/or pastoralist communities	[Social conflict]	Individual conflict and suffering

Figure 7.1. Migrations and Social Conflict Matrix. (The group terms resemble the concepts of "advanced" and "backward" communities that Donald Horowitz used in his analysis of the logic of secessionist movements, "Patterns of Ethnic Separatism," *Comparative Studies in Society and History* 23 [April 1981]: 165–195. This matrix is inspired by that article. Note that the bracketed categories are not discussed in the text.)

degradation, the political consequences will be shaped by a systemic bias. The areas most exposed to degradation are likely to have the least economic and technological capacity to cope with change; these are the agricultural and least diversified economies in the developing world. Thus, international resource transfers are necessary to modify the causes and mitigate the consequences. This particularly applies to distress migrations: The impact of "environmental refugees" will mostly be felt locally, often in near-impoverished or also-affected areas, since persons displaced by flood or famine typically lack the resources to move long distances. Beyond this, migration patterns are complex and numerous, as are the sociopolitical consequences in terms of conflict or coexistence. To sort out these complexities, a typology as indicated above can be useful.

When environmentally related migration leads to conflict, the analysis must distinguish between a conflict in which two parties are actively engaged, and the victimization and exploitation that connote a dominant one-way relationship. Both situations can result from population movements, partly

depending upon the type of migration involved (notably refugee versus migrant movements). For this reason alone, the security paradigm with its emphasis on "threat" and "enemy" is inadequate, and can be quite misleading when applied in a migration context.

Considerations of policy must take this dual conflict as a starting point. Sometimes measures to protect the migrants are critical to reduce conflict (in the form of victimization); at other times, the indigenous people must be protected against migrants in order to reduce conflict (in the form of a contest between two parties). For instance, when upland or "tribal" people fear that "advanced" coastal communities are invading their territory and manifest conflict results, issues of nativist rights and regulation of the political process to deal with the newcomers (or control their entry) become central. This point is reinforced by a comprehensive recent study of minority rights and conflicts (Gurr 1993). When the newcomer becomes a victim rather than a threat—as in the Sahelian movements—the needs of the migrants should move to the forefront of policy to reduce both the individual suffering and exploitation and the potential for social unrest sparked by their arrival. Similar considerations apply to the needs and rights of international migrants, whether legal or illegal, as affirmed by the Cairo 1994 International Population Conference.

These policy implications mostly take migration as a given and seek to mitigate its consequences. Similar views have become dominant in much of the specialized migration literature as it applies to both international movements and rural-to-urban migration (Castles and Miller 1993; Kasarda and Parnell 1993; Papademetriou and Hamilton 1995). While a range of policy measures can modify the underlying causes of migration—in this case focusing on environmental variables—the limits of change are indicated by the terminology used by the IPCC. Reflecting the cumulative scientific knowledge on climate change, the IPCC report speaks of "mitigation and adaptation" instead of "prevention" and "solution."

NOTES

This chapter was written when the author was a resident associate with the International Migration Project at the Carnegie Endowment for International Peace. She wishes to thank members of the project, particularly Kathleen Newlands, for their useful comments.

1. In one of several initiatives on the eve of the Rio Conference on the Environment and Development (1992), a Swedish minister formally proposed assigning military units to the United Nations for a wide range of environmental tasks ("Green Berets").

2. It is indicative that the idea of encroaching desertification in the Sahel, which was promoted by the UN Desertification Conference in 1977 and the Brundtland Commission report, relied heavily on the measurements of one study that showed a southward-advancing desert. While a body of contrary scientific data was developing, the UN Environment Program revived the crisis perspective in 1991 by commissioning a technical study that again showed the desert to advance and concluded that a multimillion-dollar ten-year rehabilitation program was required (Bie 1992).

3. For recent criticism see Levy (1995) and Nelson (1995a, 1995b) on the existentialists.

4. Kritz found that countries with low and moderate population growth rates send more migrants to the United States than countries that are growing more rapidly. The single most important factor determining migration was the existence of social networks, as indicated by the statistical relationship between migrant stock in the United States and migration; the second most important variable was population size.

5. Regional variations are important. Urbanization in Asia is largely due to natural population increase; in Africa migration from rural areas is relatively more important; and in Latin America, urban-to-urban migration is an increasingly significant cause of urban growth (Choguill 1994).

6. Thus, Homer-Dixon (1994) includes population pressures on land to substantiate the claim that "environmental scarcity" causes large migration movements (pp. 20–23).

7. One analytical solution, as Bilsborrow (1991) suggests, is to treat the environment as a contextual factor that manifests itself in the decision making of the potential migrant. Environmental change may induce out-migration by reducing income, increasing risk, or making the environment less healthy and pleasant (social effects).

8. In the minimalist view, environmental change is a contextual variable that can contribute to migration, but analytical difficulties and empirical shortcomings make it hazardous to draw firm conclusions. The other perspective sets out a maximalist view, positing that environmental degradation is a direct cause of large-scale displacement of people. For examples of minimalism, see Kritz 1990; National Academy of Sciences 1991; and Bilsborrow 1991. For maximalists, see El-Hinnawi 1985; Jacobson 1988; Mathews 1989; and Myers 1989.

9. Deforestation has also been held responsible for the increasing numbers of flash floods in Southeast Asia, which, apart from numerous

deaths, have caused economic damage and at least temporary displacement.

10. The 1995 report uses scenarios of 10–80 cm and 10–112 cm rise by the year 2100 (IPCC 1995).

11. Some observers claim that the process is already underway, although long-term data sets are hard to obtain and difficult to interpret (Islam 1991).

12. Conflicts arising from illegal Bangladeshi migration into Assam—which is repeatedly held up as a classic case—involved mostly migrants from the Mymensingh border district, not the coastal areas (Hazarika 1993; Weiner 1978).

13. "Clashes between migrants and the indigenous populations," Myron Weiner (1978) writes, "have been a prominent feature of postindependence politics within multiethnic societies" (p. 75). In fact, many of the examples he mentions have a very significant time lag: The Chinese were imported by the British colonial rulers of Malaya in the mid-nineteenth century; the so-called "communal problem" did not arise until the mid-twentieth century, when it took a violent form. Ethnic violence in Sri Lanka in the second half of the twentieth century has its roots in two earlier migrations; one is truly ancient ("Jaffna Tamils"), the other was colonially induced ("Indian Tamils"). The role of migration as a "cause" of such conflict is remote, and its explanatory power is akin to that of original sin. Rather, the critical variables that explain a change from potential to manifest conflict must be sought in the subsequent pattern of incorporation (or not) of the migrants.

14. At issue here is not the complex relationship between climate change and desertification. Scientists have been divided on the impact of global warming on the drylands, depending on the role of rainfall, temperature, and winds (Bie 1992). Some conclusions are counter intuitive; for example, that global warming will actually increase rainfall in the Sahel and hence move the vegetation line further north (cited in OECD 1988).

REFERENCES

Bennet, Olivia, ed. 1991. *Greenwar: Environment and Conflict.* London: Panos Institute.

Bie, Stein W. 1992. "The Degradation of African Drylands: New Evidence." *Forum for Development Studies* 1: 5–10.

Bilsborrow, Richard. 1991. "Rural Poverty, Migration, and the Environment in Developing Countries: Three Case Studies." Background paper prepared for the World Development Report, Chapel Hill, N.C.

Bilsborrow, Richard, and Pamela D. DeLargy. 1991. "Land Use, Migration, and Natural Resource Deterioration: The Experience of Guatemala and the Sudan." Carolina Population Center, University of North Carolina, Chapel Hill.

Castles, Stephen, and Mark M. Miller. 1993. *The Age of Migration.* London: Macmillan Press.

Choguill, C. L. 1994. "Crisis, Chaos, Crunch? Planning for Urban Growth in the Developing World." *Urban Studies* 31, no. 6: 935–945.

Choucri, Nazli. 1992. "Environment, Development and International Assistance: Crucial Linkages." In *Resolving Third World Conflict: Challenges for a New Era*, ed. Sheryl J. Brown and Kimber M. Schraub. Washington, D.C.: United States Institute of Peace Press, pp. 89–118.

El-Hinnawi, Essam. 1985. *Environmental Refugees.* New York: United Nations Development Program.

Fairclough, A. J. 1991. "Global Environment and Natural Resource Problems: Their Economic, Political and Security Implications." *Washington Quarterly* 14, no. 1.

Fernandes, Walter, et al. 1988. *Forests, Environment, and Tribal Economy.* New Delhi: Indian Social Institute.

Findley, Sally E. 1994. "Does Drought Increase Migration? A Study of Migration from Rural Mali during the 1983–1985 Drought." *International Migration Review* 28, no. 3 (Fall): 539–553.

Gurr, Ted Robert. 1993. *Minorities at Risk: A Global View of Ethnopolitical Conflicts.* Washington, D.C.: United States Institute of Peace Press.

Hazarika, Sanjoy. 1993. "Bangladesh and Assam: Land Pressures, Migration, and Ethnic

Conflict." Occasional Paper Series of the Project on Environmental Change and Acute Conflict, no. 3, March. Cambridge, Mass.: American Academy of Arts and Sciences.

Helland, Johan, and Marikken Vaa. 1986. "Mali: Matforsyning og Katastrofebistand." Report to the Norwegian Department for Cooperation, Oslo.

Hjort, Anders af Ornäs, and M. A. Mohamed Salih, eds. 1989. *Ecology and Politics.* Uppsala, Sweden: Scandinavian Institute of African Studies.

Homer-Dixon, Thomas F. 1991. "On the Threshold: Environmental Changes as Causes of Acute Conflict." *International Security* 16(2): 76–116.

———. 1994. "Environmental Scarcities and Violent Conflict." *International Security* 19, no. 1 (Summer): 5–40.

Horowitz, Donald. 1985. *Ethnic Groups and Conflicts.* Berkeley: University of California Press.

Hugo, Graeme. 1995. "Environmental Concerns and International Migration." Paper presented at a conference on migration, Washington, D.C., September. Center for Migration Studies.

Huntington, Samuel. 1968. *Political Order in Changing Societies.* New Haven, Conn.: Yale University Press.

Hurst, Phillip. 1990. *Rainforest Politics.* London: Zed Books.

International Panel on Climate Change. 1995. "Preliminary Report" (Internet).

Islam, Muinul. 1991. "Ecological Catastrophes and Refugees in Bangladesh." Paper presented at the Conference on Worldwide Refugee Movements, New School for Social Research, New York, November 8–9.

Jacobson, Jodi. 1988. *Environmental Refugees: Yardstick of Habitability.* Worldwatch Paper no. 86. Washington, D.C.: Worldwatch.

Kaplan, Robert. 1994. "The Coming Anarchy." *Atlantic Monthly,* February 1994, pp. 44–76.

Kasarda, John D., and Allan M. Parnell, eds. *Third World Cities.* Newbury Park, Calif.: Sage.

Kennedy, Paul. 1993. *Preparing for the 21st Century.* New York: Random House.

Kritz, Mary M. 1990. "Climate Change and Migration Adaptations." Cornell University Working Paper Series 2.16. Ithaca, N.Y.

———. 1995. "Population Growth and International Migration: Is There a Link?" Paper prepared for the Conference on Migration Policy in Global Perspective, New School for Social Research, New York, September 8.

Levy, Marc. 1995. "Is the Environment a National Security Issue?" *International Security* 20, no. 2 (Fall 1995): 35–62.

Mathews, Jessica Tuchman. 1989. "Redefining Security." *Foreign Affairs* 68: 2.

Moch, Leslie Page. 1994. *Moving Europeans: Migration in Western Europe since 1650.* Bloomington: Indiana University Press.

Moore, Barrington. 1966. *Social Origins of Dictatorship and Democracy.* Boston: Beacon Press.

Myers, Norman. 1989. "Environment and Security." *Foreign Policy* 74: 23–41.

———. 1992. "Population-Environment Linkages: Discontinuities Ahead?" UN Expert Group Meeting, New York, January 20–24. IESA/P/AC.34/3.

———. 1993. *Ultimate Security.* New York: W. W. Norton.

National Academy of Sciences. 1991. *Policy Implications of Greenhouse Warming.* Report of the Adaptation Panel. Washington, D.C.: National Academy Press. Prepublication manuscript.

Nelson, Robert H. 1995a. "How Much Is God Worth? The Problems—Economical and Theological—of Existence Values." Paper prepared for the annual meeting of the Southern Economic Association, New Orleans, November 18–20.

———. 1995b. "Sustainability, Efficiency, and God: Economic Values and the Sustainability Debate." *Annual Review of Ecological Systems* 26: 135–154.

Organization for Economic Cooperation and Development. 1988. *The Sahel Facing the Future.* Paris.

Papademetriou, D. G., and K. A. Hamilton. 1995. *Managing Uncertainty.* Washington, D.C.: Carnegie Endowment for International Peace.

Perlman, Janice. 1976. *The Myth of Marginality.* Berkeley: University of California Press.

Richardson, Harry W. 1993. "Efficiency and Welfare in LDC Megacities." In *Third World Cities,* ed. John D. Kasarda and Allan M. Parnell. Newbury Park, Calif.: Sage, pp. 33–57.

Somerville, Carolyn M. 1986. *Drought and Aid in the Sahel.* Boulder, Colo.: Westview Press.

Suhrke, Astri. 1993. "Pressure Points: Environmental Degradation, Migration, and Conflict." Occasional Paper Series of the Project on Environmental Change and Acute Conflict, no. 3, March. Cambridge, Mass.: American Academy of Arts and Sciences.

United Nations Development Program. 1994. *The Human Development Report.* New York.

United Nations High Commissioner for Refugees. 1993. *The State of the World's Refugees.* New York and Geneva.

Watts, M. 1983. *Silent Violence: Food, Famine, and Peasantry in Northern Nigeria.* Berkeley: University of California Press.

Weiner, Myron. 1978. *Sons of the Soil.* Princeton, N.J.: Princeton University Press.

———. 1995. *The Global Migration Crisis: Challenge to States and to Human Rights.* New York: HarperCollins.

———, ed. 1993. *International Migration and Security.* Boulder, Colo.: Westview Press.

8

Military Technology and Conflict

GEOFFREY KEMP

The relationship between military technology and conflict is definitely a chicken-and-egg affair. The existence of military technology in a conflict region reflects the need for countries to defend themselves against adversaries or to redress grievances. Yet arms competition between adversaries can itself become a source of conflict or even a precursor for war. As a result, there are many different hypotheses concerning this relationship. While many believe that arms races result in wars, it is not easy to demonstrate a simple cause and effect. The real issues are the impact of weapons acquisitions on the stability of military balances and the relationship between these balances and other factors that contribute to conflict.

Likewise, it is difficult to identify specific weapons that contribute to an increase or decrease in the potential for armed conflict. Weapons, including weapons of mass destruction, do not cause wars or assure peace by themselves—any more than handguns alone are responsible for murders or reduced crime in American cities. The critical factor is the political-military environment into which the weapons are introduced. If the environment is inherently unstable and adversaries have a record of resolving disputes by force, new weaponry may heighten the perceptions of threat, providing a catalyst for war. However, if the environment is stable and the prevailing climate is one of reconciliation and peaceful dialogue or, alternatively, if both adversaries anticipate unacceptable casualties in a war, the impact of new weapons may be less dangerous and could even contribute to stability. Thus, weapons that may be considered destabilizing in one region may be deemed stabilizing in another.

In this essay I argue that there is no general theory of the relationship between arms and conflict; that cases can be found to fit many hypotheses; and that recent dramatic changes in technology have made it increasingly difficult to predict the effects of those charges.[1] Before confronting some of the future issues, some background is useful.

Throughout history the possession and production of arms has largely been a monopoly of the dominant political authority in a particular country or region. Until recently, most such authorities were oligopolies, if not outright dictatorships; the right of ordinary citizens to manufacture and own arms is not a universal right. Thus, one of the enduring beliefs of the National Rifle Association is that the constitutional rights of American citizens to bear arms is a unique and special right and is the most reliable way to ensure that the citizenry is not left defenseless against authorities who traditionally have a monopoly of organized military force at their disposal. While this prerogative is uniquely American and highly controversial, the sentiments it reflects are shared by many of the subject peoples of the world, ancient and modern, who have been systematically denied access to arms and are inherently suspicious of arms control. For instance, during the nineteenth century an international initiative was launched by the European powers to ban the transfer of breech-loading rifles to subsaharan Africa on the grounds that such arms in the hands of natives would be a source of instability. If the colonial powers had far superior arms to rule over their subjects, small forces of militia could control vast areas of territory. This line of reasoning was summarized by the British satirist Hillaire Belloc: "Whatever happens/We have got/The Maxim gun/And they have not."

So long as military technology is a monopoly of the state or the colonial power, civil unrest and uprisings are controllable. However, once those who wish to change the status quo gain access to modern military technology—by covert purchase, mutiny, or rebellion—a more even distribution of power results, which often leads to civil war and revolution. Therefore, in considering the long-term perspectives on arms and conflict it is worth remembering the origins of the American revolution and the important role that arms, both locally produced and procured from overseas (especially France), had

on the course of the War of Independence. Without this access to arms, American revolutionaries could not have fought against Britain. As it was, they were able to sustain their confrontation and eventually wear down an initially far superior power.

In recent years, a different set of questions has emerged in the context of arms and international relations. Three are especially important: (1) the relationship between developments in nuclear technology and the potential for conflict among the superpowers; (2) the relationship between the transfer of military technology from the great powers, who have traditionally been the major producers of arms, and the propensity of the recipients to engage in armed conflict; and (3) the impact on regional security of recent changes in the international system and new developments in military technology.

THE COLD WAR, THE CENTRAL ARMS RACE, AND THE BREAKUP OF THE SOVIET UNION

Since the early 1950s the debate about the impact of military technology on the international system has focused on two events: the central arms race between NATO and the Warsaw Pact countries and the proliferation of weapons technology to conflict regions in the rest of the world. Throughout the Cold War, there was ongoing controversy concerning the stability of the central arms race.

There were two limiting arguments. Pessimists argued that constant changes in nuclear weapons technology and the momentum of the arms race made the balance of power delicate and therefore inherently unstable and dangerous. This group included many of the advocates of unilateral arms control and arms reductions. The Campaign for Nuclear Disarmament (CND) launched in the 1950s and the nuclear freeze movement that gained momentum in the 1980s are two prominent examples of this line of thinking. Optimists held that the peace in Europe and between the superpowers was secure precisely because the horrors of war were too dreadful to contemplate. This was the view of most western governments that subscribed to the principles of deterrence and supported investments in nuclear force modernization as the best way to ensure stability and a balance of power between NATO and the Warsaw Pact forces. Both schools concurred that one effect of the central balance of power, be it delicate or stable, was to export the Cold War to regional conflict areas, which, in turn, led to an accelerated regional arms buildup. However, there was much disagreement about whether regional arms races themselves made local conflict more or less likely.

Parallel to the arguments concerning the balance of power, a secondary set of issues concerned the economics of the various arms races. Again, pessimists argued that both the central and regional arms races were spurred by the desire of the military-industrial complex in the advanced countries to promote arms sales. Others made a very different case, namely that the spread of weapons of mass destruction to regional conflicts was stimulated by the reluctance of the industrial powers to provide adequate conventional arms. Examples of this reaction would be the decisions made at different times by Israel, South Africa, and Pakistan to develop nuclear weapons after being subject to arms embargoes by the key industrial states. It is also clear that both the Republic of Korea and Taiwan came close to going nuclear for the same reasons and were only persuaded from doing so by extremely vigorous U.S. diplomatic intervention and increased support for their conventional armed forces.

During the Cold War, most modern theories of the arms race evolved. The primary focus was the impact of thermonu-clear weapons on the balance of power and the propensity for conflict. In view of the enormous, quantifiable destruction potential of nuclear weapons, the relatively small number of them in inventories (as compared with conventional weapons), and the assumption that an all-out thermonuclear war would be of short duration, it was possible to articulate mathematical models of nuclear war. These models led most observers to believe that so long as there was proximate symmetry between the parties, a balance of terror would deter any side from risking war.

Although it remains unclear whether nuclear deterrence during this era was inherently stable or unstable, there is no doubt that for the last thirty years the Warsaw Pact and NATO countries enjoyed a nominally stable, but putatively dangerous relationship. This stability resulted from several conditions:

- the awesome destructive capacity of thermonuclear weapons;
- the total integration of nuclear weapons into the force structures and military doctrines of the opposing alliances;
- clearly demarcated and accepted borders separating the forces;
- explicit policies regarding the use of force should either side invade the other;
- virtual consensus that there could be no victor in the event of full-scale war;
- an understanding that escalation to nuclear war would be highly likely if war broke out;
- clear lines of communication between the adversaries;
- clear acceptance of Soviet and American dominance among the Pact and NATO members;
- the ability of the adversaries to contain their competition in regional conflicts outside the central theater and to resist

military intervention in the conflicts within the alliances; and

- stable regimes in both of the opposing camps.

The relationship between military technology and the most spectacular event of modern times—the breakup of the Soviet Union—is less clear. Between 1989 and 1991, the largest and possibly the most authoritarian and tightly controlled empire the world has ever seen collapsed. Comparable in scope to the dissolution of the Austro-Hungarian and Ottoman Empires at the end of World War I and the defeat of the Axis powers in 1945, that collapse will have a profound and lasting impact on the international system for decades to come. However, unlike the situations in 1919 and 1945, when the victorious military powers were able to impose some sort of order on the reemerging political boundaries, the events following the Soviet Union's demise have been anarchic.

The Soviet Union imploded. It was not defeated in a classic military encounter whereby the victors could dictate terms to the vanquished. New countries sprang up so fast that mapmakers could scarcely keep pace with the new names and new boundaries that spread across the Eurasian land mass. The Iron Curtain was shattered, and in its place hundreds of new borders came into being.

Although the breakup did not happen because of war, there is debate about how much the burden of war preparations contributed to the outcome. Some have argued that the United States' decision in the 1980s to deploy the extremely sophisticated Pershing II missile to Europe and to develop a space-based antimissile defense system was the final straw that convinced Mikhail Gorbachev that the Soviet Union had no option but to abandon the arms race with the richer western countries and to reform the Soviet economy. Once this decision was made, a floodgate of change opened that he was unable to control.

There was hope that a new world order would emerge reflecting the basic western ideals that were upheld in the fight against communism. Peace, democracy, and economic development were to be the triumvirate of the future. The cornerstone of the new world order would be a more cooperative security environment, in which the traditional trappings of power politics—with major military alliances armed and prepared to fight each other—would be replaced by a mutually reinforcing defense concept, an expanded NATO without the Warsaw Pact as an enemy. Each participant would contribute to overall security and the body itself would agree on rules of engagement to resist movements of aggressor countries that deviated from the norm. A new emphasis on the United Nations and other international organizations would be paralleled by a new focus on economic competition and cooperation as the key ingredients for global growth and political stability. The close relationship between military technology and security would be a thing of the past. But this hope was not to be fulfilled. The clearest legacy of the Soviet Union's demise has been chaos and regional conflict.

In sum, the breakup of the Soviet Union has undermined one of the key elements of the Cold War balance of power—stable borders and stable regimes—and has encouraged the further proliferation of weapons and the spread of new forms of extremely violent terrorism. The implications of this trend are considered in the last section of this essay.

THE TRANSFER OF MILITARY TECHNOLOGY AND CONFLICT

Since the late nineteenth century, the transfer (either by sale, loan, or gift) of military technology from industrial to less industrial countries has been an important influence on international relations. Today, a revolution in military technology poses a new set of challenges and issues.

Over the decades, most industrial powers have regarded arms transfers as a necessary adjunct of national policy and strategic doctrine. In the case of the United States, it can certainly be argued that, on balance, arms sales and military assistance programs have benefited American strategic interests. American military supplies to allies were instrumental in winning the three critical wars of this century: World War I, World War II, and the Cold War. Other examples can be cited. American arms have been essential to assuring Israel a qualitative edge and denying Arab coalitions any prospect of military victory. American military supplies to Saudi Arabia during the 1970s and 1980s permitted the United States and the Saudis to develop one of the most elaborate and modern logistical bases in the world, which was crucial to allied victory in Operation Desert Storm.

Critics of U.S. arms transfers argue that these policies have often led to disastrous, entangling confrontations, including the Vietnam War and the Iran-Contra scandal. They further argue that peacetime arms sales to undemocratic countries strengthen corrupt dictators, promote aggressive behavior, and siphon off scarce economic resources that could be used more productively and humanely on other endeavors.

In the early 1970s, a new phenomenon occurred, namely the emergence of very rich oil-producing countries of the Middle East that had purchasing power but few skills to produce arms. The rapid buildup of arms in the Middle East and Persian Gulf area strengthened the argument that regional arms races were dangerous and that the recipients would have difficulty in absorbing, maintaining, and operating their advanced

equipment without continued intense support from their suppliers. The classic example of this relationship existed between the United States and Iran from 1971 to 1979 and culminated in the deposition of the Shah and attempts by the Khomeini government to sell military equipment back to the United States.[2]

Arms transfers are important tests of friendship. Nuclear weapons and their related delivery systems are the most sophisticated weapons. The only recipients of U.S. strategic nuclear delivery systems or support systems and technical knowledge have been Great Britain and France, which have also been the closest U.S. allies. Britain, in particular, has had an extremely close nuclear relationship with the United States. Most recipients of U.S. arms have not been permitted the full array of frontline equipment and key subsystems, even when able to pay full market prices. It may therefore be possible to rank the intimacy of relations between states according to the quality of the arms and other military support that have been provided.

American arms sales to close allies such as Britain are rarely criticized, because they are seen to be part of the NATO alliance and the need to integrate military doctrines and force capabilities to serve common goals. Equally relevant, arms transfers carry important messages in relations between major powers and minor powers. U.S.-Soviet rivalry in the Third World was built around competitive arms supply relationships with a long list of countries, large and small. Soviet arms supplies to Egypt in 1955 opened the way for more assertive Soviet diplomacy in the region. Seventeen years later, the United States used arms aid to bring Egypt back into the western fold when President Sadat terminated his military relations with the Russians in 1972. In 1985–1986, when Iraq and Iran were desperately fighting for survival in their brutal war, both relied on supplies from the outside to keep them going. The effectiveness of the American arms embargo against Iran was a key reason the Ayatollah Khomeini gave instructions to obtain American arms, even if it meant doing business with the United States and the hated Israelis. The White House thought it could use the supply of arms to cajole or tempt Iran into a better relationship and at the same time obtain the release of hostages; the Israelis thought that by supplying arms they could protract the war or, alternatively, ingratiate themselves with those members of the regime who might be favorably disposed to have a relationship with Israel once Khomeini left the scene.

The end of the Cold War has had two profound effects on arms transfer activities. First, it has led to a massive reduction in military aid from the superpowers, which has had the most impact on former Soviet clients. Syria's decision to join the Middle East peace process was directly related to Gorbachev's decision to end military aid. Second, the withdrawal of the superpowers from regional rivalries in Africa, Latin America, and South and Southeast Asia has had very different outcomes. In Africa, chaos and conflict continue but with less immediate international interest. South and Southeast Asia are steadily building up their military inventories (India and Pakistan both have nuclear weapons). In Latin America, more democratic regimes have emerged and the arms race is less a burden than it used to be.

THE GULF WAR AND ATTITUDES AND BEHAVIORS TOWARD MILITARY TECHNOLOGY

The Gulf War has had an important effect on thinking about modern warfare and the global demand for advanced arms and related technologies.[3] The war revealed the vulnerability of the infrastructure in modern societies to precision bombardment. High technology improved both the precision and survivability of strike aircraft and cruise missiles. The global positioning system provided precise navigational information that enabled highly accurate artillery placement, logistical resupply, and battlefield mapping. Thermal sensors and night vision equipment on U.S. tanks and helicopters enabled them to target the enemy at night and through the thick smoke of oil well fires. The advanced Joint Surveillance and Attack Radar System (JSTARS) enabled U.S. forces to detect and track slow-moving ground targets against a cluttered background. This system, which is orders of magnitude more powerful than the older Airborne Warning and Control System (AWACS), was used to guide missiles in flight.

The industrial states, especially the ones that already possess a nuclear arsenal, saw the war as further proof of the need to restrict the proliferation of weapons of mass destruction, especially in the nuclear field. Yet some weaker states interpreted the U.S.-led technological onslaught in an entirely different manner. Nuclear weapons (and perhaps other weapons of mass destruction) are the only tools smaller, less technologically equipped countries can hope to acquire and deploy in the face of U.S. stealth aircraft, precision-guided munitions, and advanced command, control, communications, and intelligence (C3I). The war reinforced the notion that weapons of mass destruction may be needed as an equalizer between the high-tech U.S. forces and smaller states resisting U.S. and western directives. While the Gulf War highlighted the impact of such high-tech arms, fiscal realities restrain many states and may force some to consider a short cut, the less expensive option of developing certain types of weapons of mass destruction, especially chemical and biological weapons.

The response of specific countries to the Gulf War has varied. In Russia, which over the years had provided much of Iraq's arms, several schools of thought developed about the Gulf War. Some saw Iraqi ineptness as the cause for the poor performance of Soviet equipment. Others did not see any revolutionary change brought about by the use of advanced technology in the war, but they did think that the war confirmed the Soviet vision of a military-technical revolution. In that sense, the war reaffirmed the importance of developing new and improved military technology. A third approach suggests that the war was the beginning of a different type of conflict, in which the central issue becomes troop control. Through coordinated fire, maneuver, and radio-electronic combat, each side will seek to inhibit enemy troop control (and protect its own). In this scenario, ground troops become less important as new technology is used to destroy enemy C3I and combat systems.

The People's Republic of China (PRC) did not radically alter its view of military technology because of the Gulf War. The PRC was already modernizing, and the war merely reinforced that trend. The local and conventional context of the war also fit with Chinese projections for their own forces. Elements of the Chinese leadership that believed human factors could offset a military-technological edge did suffer a setback in the Gulf War. Overall, however, the Chinese continue to view the improvement of their military equipment as one aspect of the larger drive for economic modernization.

India was credited with one of the larger lessons of the war after a retired Indian army chief of staff said the results of the war suggest that adversaries should not fight the Americans without nuclear weapons. In Israel, the war highlighted a number of continuing security concerns. Iraq's surprise attack on Kuwait, a surprise to most officials around the world, reminded Israelis that even highly advanced intelligence has limits; technical measures do not eliminate the threat of surprise attack. U.S. weaponry reinforced Israel's emphasis on air power, electronic warfare, and precision-guided missiles.

Located next to the theater of operations, Iran recognized the power and speed of allied forces in the defeat of a former military adversary. Iranian leaders, accustomed to such bungled U.S. operations as the hostage rescue attempt in 1980, gained a new respect for U.S. military capabilities. Saudi Arabia moved in two directions as a result of the Gulf War. The Saudis rushed to purchase the latest aircraft, missiles, and other advanced weaponry; yet Saudi Arabia does not intend to develop an autonomous ability to repel aggressors, especially given its small population. Instead, the high-tech hardware is meant to delay a future aggressor until international (or U.S.) help arrives. High-tech weaponry cannot eliminate the need for alliances, especially against Iraq or Iran. Thus, even as Saudi Arabia bolstered its arsenal, it also worked to develop quiet but close military and security relations with the United States and other western powers.

The war has also generated new thinking about the nature of future combat. U.S. attempts to limit Iraqi civilian and even military casualties during the Gulf War have fanned interest in a new class of nonlethal weapons for future warfare. These include chemical agents that cause metal fatigue in enemy machinery, destroy their optical systems, choke engines, or "glue" equipment. Increased global deployment of electronically controlled weapons systems makes military equipment susceptible to high-power jamming and to nonnuclear electromagnetic pulses that destroy and paralyze electronic systems or systems connected to antennas or batteries. Infrasound generators (at very low frequencies) could be tuned to incapacitate humans temporarily, causing disorientation, vomiting, or bowel spasms.

The continuing information and communication revolutions have had a profound effect on how armed forces may wage war. While technological advances have vastly improved the efficiency and effectiveness of modern weapons systems, they have also opened up areas where the military is extremely vulnerable. This has led to the concept of cyberwar, developed by the RAND Corporation, which targets the central information systems of the modern war machine.[4] This novel approach to future warfare advocates conducting (and preparing to conduct) military operations according to information-related principles. Its techniques include destroying enemy information and communications systems, thus winning the "balance of information and knowledge," especially when the enemy has numerical superiority. It prevents the enemy from "knowing itself": who it is, where it is, what can it do when, why it is fighting, which threats to counter first. The Apache helicopter strike against Iraqi air defense controls at the outset of the Gulf War and the deception practiced by a relatively small number of Marines to lead the Iraqi army astray embody some principles of the above approach.

As a result, the most effective weaponry and tactics of today may be outdated as the technological and information revolutions continue. The new emphasis focuses even more attention on intelligence, computers, and information. Meanwhile, while many countries saw the Gulf War as a justification for the purchase of advanced aircraft, missiles, and other high-tech military equipment, it remains to be seen which of these arms will be important in future wars.

New Military Technology and Regional Power Balances

The fact that Saddam Hussein was able to target Tel Aviv with SCUD missiles during

the Gulf War demonstrated in the most vivid way possible the important role that missile technology plays in perceptions of geography and military power in the Middle East. As missile and aircraft ranges become longer and longer, as power can be projected over wider and wider regions, and as there is an increasing possibility that weapons of mass destruction may be developed, the former tight strategic circles that defined the military balance among the various regional enemies in the Middle East will have to be expanded. Israel's strategic reach for both offense and defense now has to include concern about Iran and Iraq and possibly even Pakistan, as they all get missiles and capabilities that could reach Israel. Alternatively, as Israel's reach extends, those countries, too, will be worried about their vulnerability to Israeli power-projection capabilities. Similar types of cross-border strategic threat concerns are growing in other areas.

This phenomenon has important implications for regional security regimes in the Middle East and elsewhere. Participation in such a regime has always been a difficult issue in the context of European arms control and it is even more difficult in the case of the Middle East. Thus, even if Israel reaches a military agreement with Syria, Jordan, Egypt, Lebanon, and the Palestinians, it would not let its guard down so long as the Gulf Cooperation Council (GCC) countries, Iran, and Iraq were outside the process. Since they have to be part of the process, and since there is a close relationship among Pakistan, the GCC countries, Iran, and Iraq, it is inevitable that Pakistan's capabilities will be included in Israeli calculus. The same logic applies to countries like Pakistan that worry about Israel.

In many respects, Desert Storm was a highly misleading military encounter because it was so one-sided. One clear lesson, however, is that modern conventional munitions bear absolutely no resemblance to those used in most previous conventional confrontations. The long range and high accuracy achieved by aircraft and missiles and the new real-time reconnaissance capabilities will revolutionize future warfare.

More accurate lethal weapons and better reconnaissance by themselves constitute a revolution. It is important, however, to juxtapose the new conventional capabilities of modern weapons with the dramatically changing target structures in regions such as the Persian Gulf. If one compares a map of infrastructure in the Gulf from 1970 with one from 1990 and then projects forward to 2010, it is clear that there has been and will continue to be an enormous change in the physical appearance of the region, putting an increased reliance on high-tech systems to assure the wealth and day-to-day operation of these desert countries. The combination of a highly intricate and sophisticated oil infrastructure, an increasing dependence on desalinization and other water-distributing systems, and a very elaborate electrical grid system throughout the region points to a highly vulnerable target profile. One lesson of the Gulf War was that small numbers of munitions, accurately delivered against utility systems (such as the Iraqi electrical grid), can have a devastating impact in a very short period of time. Thus, it is not out of the question that a future Gulf War adversary, equipped with the type of technology the United States had as a monopoly in 1990–1991, would be able to cripple the entire economic-industrial infrastructure of a country like Kuwait or the United Arab Emirates in a matter of hours, and in two or three days do devastating damage to Saudi Arabia's vast facilities.

In the coming decade, the ability of states in the Middle East to upgrade their military forces with some of the technologies used by the allies in 1991 will improve. If Iran and Iraq are able to purchase arms and technologies on the open market with few restrictions, they should be able to procure the types of forces that could pose a major threat to the economic well-being of their neighbors. In particular, they—or any other regional power such as Saudi Arabia or Israel—should be able to target high-value economic installations that have fixed coordinates and thus inflict great damage. However, their capacity to destroy high-value military targets that are either security protected (hardened) or mobile will be far more difficult. It is doubtful, for instance, that they will be able to duplicate the sort of military operation conducted by the allies during the Gulf War. While the strike component of regional powers may improve dramatically if they get access to high technology, the reconnaissance component will, in all likelihood, remain beyond their means. During the Gulf War, the United States relied on an extraordinary array of advanced sensors and early warning systems, including AWACS, JSTARS, and a satellite-based communications system that could relay real-time information to the battlefield.

This suggests that the military balance of power in the region will remain in the hands of the United States as long as it maintains a strong forward presence and continues to upgrade the reconnaissance component of its armed forces. While some regional countries might eventually be able to obtain some of the reconnaissance capabilities presently available only to the United States, it is unlikely that they will be able to match the latest systems that are being developed for the U.S. armed forces. Israel, with its own satellite-launching capability, is likely to come nearest to achieving this level of sophistication, though in theory a new Iraqi regime might have the funds to purchase space systems from China or Russia.

What are the strategic implications of this continuing gap between countervalue and counterforce targeting? It suggests that all sides will have a major stake in developing military forces and installations that are mobile, redundant, and hardened. Fixed, vulnerable targets are likely to become hostage targets in the way that American and Soviet cities were hostage to nuclear blackmail during the Cold War. It also suggests that if both sides have the capability to destroy each other's civilian infrastructure, they will either be deterred from war or be encouraged to seek a preemptive military capability, if they calculate that a surprise attack could destroy the adversary's ability to manage its military forces.

MANAGING PROLIFERATION

It would be a supreme irony if one effect of the improvement of nonnuclear weapons is to make chemical, biological, and nuclear (CBN) weapons the "poor war" alternatives to a high-cost "conventional" force. There is no doubt that both Iran and Iraq regard CBN weapons as force equalizers when considering conflict with the United States. Furthermore, it must be assumed that if the "have nots" cannot gain access to weapons of mass destruction for use in military conflict they will inevitably be driven to more extreme forms of terrorism, which we can legitimately term "megaterrorism."

The World Trade Center bombing on February 26, 1993, was a dramatic portent of things to come. Six people died in this attack, but according to the presiding judge at the trial, the attack was meant to topple one tower onto the other tower in a cloud of cyanide gas; tens of thousands of Americans would have died. The gas crystals were supposed to vaporize in the explosion; instead, the gas burned up.[5] In 1995 in Tokyo, fanatics released the nerve gas sarin in the subway. We now know that their plans, too, went astray. Had the gas attack worked as originally planned, thousands of Tokyo citizens would have died, and it is not difficult to anticipate the chaos and horror that would have followed. In Russia, Chechen rebels have taken thousands of hostages in their struggle for independence against Moscow. They call for greater and more devastating acts against the Russian state, including targeting Moscow itself. Given their determination and success to date, we should not ignore what they say.

Megaterrorism is primarily associated with attempts to kill or take hostage thousands rather than hundreds of people. Yet, it is not the only new form of terrorism of which we must be aware. The growth of the Internet, the development of cyberspace as a means of communicating with people around the world, and the extraordinary sensitivity of world financial markets to derivatives and other highly technical stock speculations raise the possibility of cyberterrorism on a vast scale that could collapse financial institutions and sow chaos throughout military communications systems. What used to be in the realm of science fiction is now becoming, unfortunately, a potential reality.

The vulnerability of modern societies to such terrorist acts may not be new, but the willingness of groups to engage in such acts probably is. While there have been numerous speculations about nuclear terrorists, the control of nuclear weapons has so far proved to be relatively successful. This is not the case with chemical or biological weapons, and certainly not with the Internet and cyberspace. Also, as the Oklahoma terrorist bombing in May 1995 demonstrated, high technology may not be necessary to create devastating results for unwary targets. So far, the radical Palestinian terrorists have killed many Israeli civilians by conducting suicide attacks with conventional explosives strapped to their body. It does not take much imagination to see that if they were strapped to some other device containing biological or chemical weapons the effects on Israeli society could be a thousand times worse.

Fortunately, the most blatant attempts at megaterrorism, the World Trade Center and the Tokyo subway, were failures. But this is not cause for complacency. The United States and the international community need to treat these threats as a high priority. However, advocating a blueprint for greater vigilance is not easy, since the sources of terrorism are so diffuse and the motives of the perpetrators so varied. Clearly, one priority must be to work closely with the countries of the former Soviet Union to prevent the covert export of materials that can be used to fabricate weapons of mass destruction, especially nuclear weapons.

The potential danger of "nuclear leakage" is so great that unless urgent practical steps are taken to help the former Soviet republics, including Russia, get better control of these resources, a disaster is probable. This will require much more engagement by the Clinton administration and the U.S. Congress. Specifically, it means that more money will have to be spent to expand and accelerate the U.S. purchase of Russian highly enriched uranium and excess plutonium and to help the Russians implement enhanced security systems, which must include better inventory control, site protection, and environmental controls. More elaborate proposals for an international plutonium bank and a "nuclear interpol" should be considered immediately.[6]

As for containing the risks of other forms of terrorism, one fundamental step for the United States is to improve the cooperation among U.S. government agencies monitoring the activities of terrorist groups. In the case of the World Trade Center bombing, there was virtually no liaison or followup be-tween the domestic agencies responsible for law enforcement (the FBI and the Department of Justice) and the intelligence agencies with expertise in dealing with state-sponsored terrorism.

CONCLUSION

The next century is likely to witness a continued debate about the relationship between military technology and conflict. While the prospects for nuclear apocalypse involving the superpowers have receded, the probabilities for the use of weapons of mass destruction in regional wars or acts of terror have increased. This trend, together with new advanced conventional munitions and the willingness of radical groups to resort to megaterrorism, suggests that the subject at hand will continue to be a central and highly dangerous element of international relations.

Over the past several hundred years, many dramatic technological changes have directly influenced the conduct of war and peace; at the time of their introduction these were not fully understood. Gunpowder, the steamship, the railway, the internal combustion engine, machine guns, radio, tanks, airplanes, and nuclear weapons all fall into this category. Our generation is struggling with the implications of an information revolution that will change the nature of international relations and the role of force in ways we cannot yet foresee. The one clear lesson from history is that new technology has the capacity to be used both to provoke and to restrain conflict, depending upon the prevailing environment in which it is introduced. Until we have a clearer sense of how the revolution in military affairs relates to the other far-reaching structural and social changes brought about by the semiconductor chips, speculation about the future will be just that.[7]

NOTES

1. Some of the themes developed in this essay are examined in more detail in two recent studies by the author: *The Control of the Middle East Arms Race* (Washington, D.C.: Carnegie Endowment for International Peace, 1991) and "The Continuing Debate Over U.S. Arms Sales: Strategic Needs and the Quest for Arms Limitations," in *The Arms Trade: Problems and Prospects in the Post–Cold War World,* ed. Robert E. Harkavy and Stephanie G. Neumann (Thousand Oaks, Calif.: Annals of the American Academy of Political and Social Science, September 1994).

2. The Khomeini government canceled $10.6 billion worth of outstanding arms orders. In addition, it wanted to sell back to the United States seventy-eight F-14 aircrafts purchased by the Shah. "Proposed Arms Sales for Countries in the Middle East," hearing before the Subcommittee on Europe and the Middle East, 96th Congress, 1st session, August 1, 1979, pp. 32, 34. Cited in Shahram Chubin, *Iran's National Security Policy: Capabilities, Intentions, and Impact* (Washington, D.C.: Carnegie Endowment for International Peace, 1994).

3. For more details see Patrick J. Garrity, *Why the Gulf War Still Matters: Foreign Perspectives on the War and the Future of International Security,* Report No. 16 (Los Alamos, N.M.: Center for National Security Studies, Los Alamos National Laboratory, July 1993).

4. John Arguilla and David Ronfeldt, *Cyberwar Is Coming,* RAND Report P-7791 (Santa Monica, Calif.: RAND Corporation, 1992).

5. See Laurie Mylroie, "The World Trade Center Bomb: Who is Ramzi Yousef? And Why It Matters," *National Interest* (Winter 1995–1996): 3–15.

6. For a comprehensive review of the nuclear leakage problem, see Graham T. Allison, Owen R. Cote, Jr., Richard A. Falkenrath, and Steven E. Miller, *Avoiding Nuclear Anarchy: Containing the Threat of Loose Russian Nuclear Weapons and Fissile Material,* Center for Science and International Affairs Studies in International Security, no. 12 (Cambridge, Mass.: MIT Press, 1996).

7. For more reading on the impact of the information revolution on warfare and conflict, see, among others, Department of Defense, *Conduct of the Persian Gulf War,* Final Report to Congress, Pursuant to Title V of the Persian Gulf Conflict Supplemental Authorization and Personnel Benefits Act of 1991 (Public Law 102-25), Washington, D.C., April 1992; Andrew Krepinevich, "Cavalry to Computer," *National Interest* 37 (Fall 1994): 30–42; Michael J. Mazaar, Jeffrey Shaffer, and Benjamin Ederington, *The Military Technical Revolution: A Structural Framework* (Washington, D.C.: Center for Strategic and International Studies, March 1993); and Alvin Toffler and Heidi Toffler, *War and Anti-War* (Boston: Little, Brown, 1993). See also Winn Schwartau, *Information Warfare* (New York: Thunder's Mouth Press, 1994); Martin C. Libicki, "What Is Information Warfare?" *Strategic Forum* 28 (May 1995): 1–4; William J. Perry, "Desert Storm and Deterrence," *Foreign Affairs* 70, no. 4 (Fall 1991): 66–82; and Eliot A. Cohen, "A Revolution in Warfare," *Foreign Affairs* 75, no. 2 (March–April 1996): 37–54.

9

The Resource Dimension of International Conflict

RICHARD E. BISSELL

Resources have been central to international conflict throughout history, sometimes having a starring role but more frequently being pushed into the background. The modern history of conflict has mostly been written by observers smitten by politics and the human drama. The systemic and impersonal nature of resources, whether precious or mundane, has merited a less dramatic role in analyses of conflict—somehow always present, but too often treated as a passive variable in the pursuit of victory.[1]

The history of resources in conflict divides into three parts: cause, mechanisms, and outcomes. Space does not allow extensive treatment here, but these separate roles for resources have to be kept in mind when considering their future importance.[2] In this chapter, I shall instead organize the discussion around the renewability of three types of resources: nonrenewable, diminishing resources; nonrenewable, but substitutable resources; and resources that are renewable with long-term planning. This

breakdown of resources is important because public policy tends to be formulated (with good reason) from a basic outlook about their particular renewability. Indeed, such a perception has always informed the human view of resources. Resources as a cause of conflict predate human society; aggression associated with the availability of food or shelter is well documented in animals and has long carried over into human society, rather more organized and demanding in the types of resources it will fight over. Resources are also essential as a mechanism in conflict. When Napoleon argued that "an army fights on its stomach," he was addressing much more than the need for food. The material required for warfare was as important in driving new metals technologies centuries ago as it has been for driving nuclear technologies more recently. Finally, the decision to end a conflict (even more than to begin it) is based on the expected outcomes: changes in territory, national and personal wealth, access to future income, and so forth. None of these roles of resources can be ignored, and all will form a backdrop for our discussion of the changes in the resource dimension in this essay. This discussion of renewability will have to be informed by the various roles of resources described in extensive literature in the field.

RESOURCES IN THE POST–COLD WAR WORLD

Conflicts come in all sizes, shapes, and cultures. Because resources affect all aspects of life, it is important to distinguish among wars, political-military conflicts, and the ordinary pursuit of national interests. We shall try to avoid dwelling on the last category, except where it serves as the preliminary phase for escalation into political-military conflict or actual war. The first two categories, however, must be examined carefully for the connection between war and conflict. Escalation to violent conflict and war is not automatic, and the role of resources can have several effects. In some cases, the presence of resources at stake will dampen the tendency to war, for fear of damaging the material interests; at the same time, the potential for gain can bring economic classes into support of war. What must be kept in mind, however, is that resource issues rarely stand on their own as the cause of violent conflict. Saddam Hussein did not invade Kuwait solely for oil, nor did Britain decide to retake the Falkland Islands simply because of potential oil production in that area. It is valuable, however, to be able to recognize the role of resources as one factor in decision making for the management of disagreement and conflict among states (both violent and nonviolent). Any study of this issue, indeed, must distinguish between the actual role played by resources in strategic calculations of governments and the role ascribed in public statements. Thus, any "resource conflict" could potentially become

violent; when it does, however, it nearly always involves other issues (such as national pride) being drawn into play. On their own, resources at stake are often outweighed by other political or economic issues (such as long-term trade and investment) that deter the escalation of a conflict.

As other analysis has shown, wars are quite common today, even though they are primarily fought within national borders with spillover into neighboring countries. The proliferation of effective, relatively inexpensive conventional weaponry feeds a cycle of violence among many countries today. The weakness of many governments in enforcing their writ and obtaining the legitimacy of their citizens ensures fertile ground for the commingling of civil and international wars. The weakening of international law has several effects on the role of resources in conflicts. First, many wars and conflicts occur that are never given that label; political-military conflicts erupt rapidly, move back and forth between violent and nonviolent status, and thus are never brought into the formal Westphalian system of war and peace. There is less to gain in the way of legal protection at the end of the twentieth century from a formal declaration of war. Also, in some cases, political leaders want to avoid the higher stakes involved in escalating a specific dispute into general war. It is well known, for instance, that in the 1960s and 1970s, there were several armed battles between the USSR and the People's Republic of China (PRC) about defining their common border and capturing land resources, but both capitals denied their occurrence to the outside world.

Second, the weakening of international law has made authoritative settlement of resource conflicts more difficult to settle. The last notable resource issue at the International Court of Justice (ICJ), for instance, was the division of the oil and gas reserves in the North Sea. The current weakness of the ICJ is illustrated in Asia. A flashpoint similar to the North Sea has emerged recently in the South China Sea, where the armed forces of four different countries (PRC, Vietnam, Philippines, and Indonesia) merge in a conflicting set of claims over open sea and the oil-rich atolls. Aggressive acts are undertaken periodically by one country or another, sometimes involving fatalities, but the conflict has largely been fought by political means, without escalating into a more dramatic mobilization.

The conflict-laden pursuit of national interests makes it more problematic for analysts to see the precise role of resources. It is no clearer today than it was in 1941 what would cause a country deprived of economic resources to go to war. The predisposing conditions that cause a government to take the path of mobilization vary so much that miscalculation is rife. President Roosevelt appeared not to grasp fully the effect of export embargoes on Japan. Such is not to argue that the scrap steel embargo led to World War II, but rather to say that it catalyzed certain key opinions in Japanese circles and among the public who might have otherwise opted against war.[3] Similarly, Saddam Hussein apparently thought that the West would philosophically accept the loss of oil resources in Kuwait. It is important to remember the measures taken "in pursuit of national interests" that are stability threatening in nature. Some such policy initiatives are taken with the intent of overthrowing a leader, forcing a change of government, or reorienting a foreign policy. That kind of proactive measure needs to be included in this discussion, since it invites escalation or retribution that goes beyond the specific interest in question. The kind of conflict not included is the routine trade dispute that operates within an almost-formal set of rules that keeps it from getting out of hand.

The resource dimension covers a very broad spectrum. Some resources are quite "hard" and traditional; strategic minerals and oil are the twentieth-century exemplars. Other resources are "softer," less restricted in supply, but essential to long-term growth and national strategies of countries (for example, water, food, clean air); even if not traditionally seen as an important dimension of conflict, they are playing an ever-greater role in current conflicts. Soft resources are frequently renewable and, therefore, open to management by groups of countries or international organizations in a less threatening way than the traditional strategic resources.

Defense requirements for resources have changed significantly in recent decades. The decline of the World War II–type force structure—with massive investments in ships, airplanes, and tanks—was gradual at first, with the emergence of unmanned strategic weaponry and tactical mobile forces eroding support. The decline then accelerated with the disintegration of the Soviet Union and the emergence of the "military revolutions" in technology in the United States and elsewhere.[4] The priority now given to electronics, precise weaponry, and battlefield surveillance has replaced the large investments of the past. The requirements for resources can be as expensive as in the past, as in rare earth minerals, but they are not as physically massive. In addition, data from the Arms Control and Disarmament Agency and the International Monetary Fund for the last ten years show that the share of national income going into national defense has declined (from 4 percent of the gross domestic product [GDP] in 1986 to 3 percent in 1992), and this is even true in developing countries—except most notably in the PRC—where the military expenditure ratio to GDP has declined from 3.6 percent in 1984 to the current figure of 2.6 percent.[5]

The requirements of the national economy, on the other hand, remain focused on some strategic materials. Oil and its equivalents for the power sector are even more important for the United States and its developed allies than in the past. With over 50 percent of American oil needs being met abroad, it has become a strategic issue with dimensions different than at any time in the past. Fortunately, many of the major importers have taken measures to prevent damage from future supply interruptions, and the diversification of exporters reduces the likelihood of coordination among producers.[6] The risk remains high, however, for much smaller and poorer countries, where the maldistribution of those essential materials and their benefits can become a source of conflict. For instance, as people in many West African countries turn to neighboring countries for supplies (legal or smuggled), low-level violence breaks out. Where the production distribution in small countries yields unequal benefits, civil wars are common (Zaire, Nigeria), and conflicts among elites over the privileges of natural resource wealth tend to flourish.

Resources: Nonrenewable, Diminishing

Among the most modern and the most traditional sources of conflict is the quest for land. It is nonrenewable, and in some cases it is diminishing in a useful sense (that is, farmers wear out the land and make it worthless). While the modern international system rarely allows the actual transfer of land from one country to another, as happened frequently before the twentieth century, today one sees the conflict over land played out in other ways. One type of conflict occurs when the border moves by itself—as when a river defining the border shifts. Another occurs when people move across a border permanently, and then wish to have themselves and their new land incorporated into their former country; this is a particularly virulent issue where two neighboring countries have divergent population growth rates, and the people in the country with a higher rate see no reason not to use the land resources in the other country. Private decisions made in this way have major political repercussions.

Population growth makes land less available on a per capita basis, and it creates a perceived shortage of land. In that sense, the territory available for people is shrinking. A more important way of measuring the shortage of land, however, is through examining land use. When the vast majority of the population lived on relatively low-yielding farm land, a drop below several acres in farm size created conditions in which a normal farmer could not produce enough food to feed an average-size family. In most countries, several conditions have taken the pressure off such a calculation: the creation of off-farm cash income opportunities, the rapid growth of cities (whether for permanent migration or off-season income), and the creation of government-organized social safety nets when production falls too low. Finally, in some countries, the arrival of high-yield agriculture has allowed greater production of crops, investment of farm profits into education to move into nonfarm businesses, and investment in higher-income cash crop systems. Nevertheless, such changes in the countryside reduce the tendency to conflict over land only when safety valves are available for "surplus" population to move to the cities or abroad. It is in this context of other changes that one needs to understand the migration from Turkey to Germany, Mexico to the United States, or North Africa to France. Such shifts of human resources only postpone the day of conflict unless structural changes occur in the country of emigration.

Certain biological resources are also diminishing with some speed, with virtually no chance of reversibility: These lie in the realm we call biodiversity. The elimination of species is virtually coterminous with the clearing of large tracts of natural forest, especially in tropical areas. The growing value of such species for genetic analysis and manipulation, more evident with each passing year, makes their survival an increasingly political matter. As a purely scientific issue, the preservation of biodiversity raises few political issues; indeed, international institutions have been created to store and foster such biodiversity in various ways. The International Center for Maize and Wheat in Mexico (CIMMYT), for instance, has a distinguished history of preserving for public use the invaluable genetic material (geneplasm) for those two crops. Nevertheless, today this quiet international regime of geneplasm centers is facing pressure from two directions. On the one hand, observers are recognizing the extent to which the pool of geneplasm of essential crops is declining and the related need to store the genetic material in ex situ centers as soon as possible. On the other hand, national governments are deciding to capitalize on the value of that declining geneplasm and refusing to let it cross national borders, considering it a national treasure. Particularly in those tropical areas that are known to harbor the greatest reservoirs of biodiversity, such as Southeast Asia and tropical South and Central America, nationalism is expressing itself in terms of the intellectual property inherent in such biodiversity.

The value placed on genetic material is not entirely new. The well-known stories of pirating plants from their native areas in the sixteenth through nineteenth centuries were associated with the competition between colonial empires. The transfer of natural rubber trees from Brazil to Malaya was not accidental. The spread of coffee and tea bushes from one continent to another was enough to provoke conflicts. The first coffee plants outside Arabia were stolen by Dutch traders in 1616. The rapid rise of commercial value of both crops led to mercantilist conflicts among the Dutch, French, and English to monopolize production and sales.[7] The famous 1773 fight in Boston Harbor, known as the Tea Party, was an outgrowth of British attempts to control what was seen as an essential resource. Today, however, we are not merely talking about the specific varieties with proven commercial value; instead, the issue is increasingly the knowledge that biodiversity as a whole is declining and that the remaining geneplasm may have great potential value. A new international organization, the International Plant Genetic Resources Institute, was created in Rome in 1994 to attempt to resolve global disputes over ownership and management of biodiversity; whether it will be successful is unclear.

Resources: Nonrenewable, Discoverable, or Substitutable

Some nonrenewable resources do not play the kind of fixed role in society that national territory does. For a variety of reasons, a depletable resource will have the political character of nonrenewability for a period of time and then, because of additional discoveries of that resource or because of development of an equal or superior substitute, will no longer have the same value. Indeed, its strategic utility may disappear entirely. During the time of high value, however, these resources can play major political roles. Thus, while these resources may appear to cover an enormous range within the definition of "strategic resources," each is treated similarly in terms of policy response.

Among the most important resources to move countries into combat are those in the power sector. The needs of armies and economies for the fuel to move machines, to heat buildings, and to support a diversified economy make the sources of power into strategic resources. The twentieth-century wars over oil can be matched against the wars over coal in the nineteenth century. Alsace-Lorraine was far more than a cultural crossroads for France and Germany—it was a source of invaluable minerals for expanding industrial economies that needed local coal and iron ore. The interconnection of Prussian industrial policy and its political-military strategy ensured that any resistance to its expanding economic reach could result in war, and of course it did. Power and minerals are described as nonrenewable, discoverable, and substitutable because they are not diminishing resources. These are resources whose role can be played by substitutes (for example, coal for oil) or for which scientists can possibly find significant new sources to make it less scarce. Well into the nineteenth century, oil was used only if it bubbled out of the ground on its own volition; when the technology to drill for and seek out oil resources was developed in Pennsylvania, not only did oil become plentiful, but resource industries that oil replaced (such as whale oil) became suddenly less strategic and eventually disappeared as a significant commodity. Each of the resources in this section shares such characteristics, and while wars have been fought in the past over particular resources, some of them would not even be worth a minor diplomatic flap today.

The balance of strategic value among the various power sources can shift quite rapidly—and for entirely unexpected reasons. The development of nuclear energy in the 1950s was seen by its proponents as giving the United States the potential for energy independence from oil, and virtually free, unlimited energy sources into the future. Sources of uranium were sought and developed at great cost in the 1950s to fuel that vision. Today, it appears likely that the United States will never build another nuclear power plant, and the existing ones are liabilities: The Shoreham plant on Long Island recently sold for one dollar, with its massive long-term debt assumed by its prior owner. Such a development does not preclude the return of uranium-based fuel systems in the future in another guise, but that will not happen until the cost-basis of safe nuclear power has been brought into line with other power sources and the public changes its mind about the broader environmental hazards of nuclear power. Other countries, of course, will have a reason to maintain such programs as an adjunct to a nuclear weapons development program, but that is an altogether different reason for the investment.

Instead, we see today the resurgence of oil and natural gas as strategic fuel commodities in a way that could not have been anticipated thirty years ago. This has been facilitated by the rapid diversification of sources geographically, through deep drilling and more efficient production systems. Other support has come from establishing strategic buffer stocks, the enormous production reserve in the Middle East (and Saudi Arabia's long-term strategy of stabilizing oil markets), and the awareness that even in the midst of the Kuwait-Iraq war (with the shutdown of both production capacities), oil markets continued to function smoothly. In the United States, this has been a significant reversal of planning. In the 1970s, with the realization that the United States was 50 percent dependent on oil imports, most planning went into measures to avoid that strategic dependence (coal conversion, renewable, nuclear, and so forth); today, many alternative programs have been cut from government support. Instead, as President Bush made clear in providing U.S. support to Kuwait and its allies in 1991 against the Iraqi occupation, the United States and its European allies will use armed force to safeguard the supply of oil.

Wars over sources of metals have followed much the same pattern throughout history. Metals became strategic as technology and society gave them a value to store wealth or to engage in more effective warfare. Gold and silver, for instance, have long been measures of personal and national wealth. At other times, however, diamonds and other gems—or on some South Pacific Islands, large carved stones—have played that role. Threats to "demonitize" gold in this century have reverberated through the traditions of centuries that made gold the most strategic of metals, yet its practical uses have steadily declined over time.

The more practical strategic metals have been those useful in warfare: copper, bronze, iron, steel, and others that were essential to building stronger spears, guns, tanks, airplanes, and rockets. Each generation of metallurgical innovation leaves some metals behind and picks up on the unique qualities of others. Among the most strategic of metals in World War II, for instance, was tungsten. An essential alloy for large gun barrels (for instance, on tanks) so that they would not overheat in rapid battles, tungsten had only a few sources, and Spain was one of them. As a result, the behavior of Spain as a "neutral" country in that war was measured less by what the government said and more by where it allowed its tungsten to be shipped. A violent but unacknowledged war was fought in that neutral country to control the shipment of the ore to Germany or to the allies. Today, with the advent of electronic warfare, strategic value is shifting to rare earth metals, used in such fine quantities that a microgram sells for tens of thousands of dollars. These trends will continue to change as technology changes demand.

War itself drives the process of innovation for the use of resources. The aphorism that "war is the mother of invention" applies particularly to the substitutable resources. The German capacity to synthesize oil from coal developed rapidly in World War II, producing technologies that were later adopted by the embargoed South African economy in the 1970s and 1980s and also by the United States when it decided to experiment with independence from imported oil. The development of applications of metal composites for faster, higher-altitude airplanes was pioneered in the military environment and then adopted for civilian air transports.

The value of such resources in conflict has changed considerably since the massed-force attacks of World War II. Some military observers say that the Persian Gulf war was simultaneously the last vestige of massed-armies warfare and the first harbinger of new warfare: remotely controlled, electronically guided munitions, focused on precision rather than heavy destruction. This new approach requires much less power and force than the old strategic design. The advent of miniaturized hardware for conflicts considerably reduces the power requirements, and in the most sophisticated battles, the decisive weapons may not be those that destroy humans, but rather those that destroy communications systems.

A defeat in international conflict also can affect the availability of power and metal resources in the industrial and postindustrial economies. It can reduce a country's investment in infrastructure, in research and technology, and in the skilled people required to find and use the resources in question. The defeat of Germany in 1945 resulted in the dissemination of scientists and technologies in several directions. One striking effect of the end of the Cold War and the dissolution of the Soviet Union has been a scattering of the knowledge base that underlay the emergence of Soviet military power. The military-industrial complex of the USSR had within it world-leading research centers and production units for applying these resources; these are now broken up and the key scientists have dispersed to foreign countries to earn a living.

The Soviet Union had such a remarkable storehouse of virtually all traditional and rare metals that it could covertly and extensively test and experiment with their application, industrial and military, without the world knowing about it.

Today, new forms of conflicts over these resources are emerging—not between armed adversaries, but rather between contestants over their exploitation. Elements of the environmental movement have increasingly focused their opposition to government use of natural resources, especially for defense purposes. For instance, in the dramatic public opposition of Greenpeace to nuclear testing, especially the atmospheric testing of weapons by France in the South Pacific, protesters have been arrested and have even lost their lives. Much of the public opposition to nuclear power has been engendered because the organizations opposed to nuclear weapons have associated the two applications of uranium in public perceptions. Likewise, environmental groups have become so effective in opposing the construction of any more large hydroelectric dams in the United States that the role of hydroelectric power has changed from a desirable, renewable form of power to one that is very limited and certainly diminishing.

This discussion of metals and power as critical resources is meant to illustrate the extent to which policies and perceptions often fail to keep up with strategic realities. Change has been the rule rather than the exception in national requirements for these resources, and the accelerating pace of scientific discovery will require an even nimbler policy framework in the future to ensure that the needs of national and global security are met.

Resources: Renewable

Some resources are truly renewable, and their strategic quality comes from being indispensable for individual and national survival. Traditional analysis of resource issues virtually ignore these commodities. This lack of attention flies in the face of reality: People will always need food, fuel, water, and other renewables and they will fight to obtain them. One reason for the inattention to these resources is their banality. In the twenty-first century, however, we are likely to face far more "ordinary wars and conflicts" than those of the past, which focused on reshaping world politics. Existing policy structures are much more capable of alleviating the distress causing such resource conflicts than of permanently settling them.

The quest for food provokes conflicts. The failure of crops in societies without adequate safety nets causes people to migrate in search of places where they can eat. It usually means they want to move to areas already occupied. Indeed, it may only be a move to achieve greater wealth, and others get in the way—whether other farmers, people of another nationality, or people with different plans for use of the land. From the fifteenth century onward England was increasingly faced, for instance, by the move to "enclosure" of the land by landowners, depriving others of access to pasturage and other common uses of the land. It provoked a violent reaction. In the late nineteenth century in the American West, extended violence was engendered by disputes between grazers and farmers, who wanted to use the land in very different ways. The other struggle in the West, well known by now, was between new settlers and the traditional native American Indian uses of the land—incompatible to the point of provoking two hundred years of wars.

The tension between forest and agriculture has taken on particularly dramatic tones in recent decades. The continued rapid expansion of global population causes ever-rising needs for food supplies. The

World Bank currently estimates that by the year 2025 the demand for food in the developing countries alone will double from today's level and will increase another 50 percent by the year 2050.[8] Global agencies, such as the World Food Program, exist to ensure some redistribution of food to meet emergency requirements and thus avert many potential conflicts. Fortunately, some of the largest potential food deficits areas, most notably in South Asia, have undertaken rapid agricultural modernization and thus achieved self-sufficiency for the time being. As incomes continue to rise, however, the demand for higher-quality food will raise the pressure on the land, and the temptation to convert even more land to agriculture will grow.

This pressure occurs at a time when many are arguing for the need to maintain forests, to avoid cultivating hillsides, and to withdraw from infertile land. The conflict is characteristically acute in the Amazon, where millions of settlers have hoped to open up the region to farming and ranching, only to find themselves in violent conflict with traditional tribes that live there, with people who want the land for other uses, and with international opinion that wants to preserve the Amazon forest for environmental reasons. These conflicts, played out on a grand scale in Brazil, are imitated in lesser forms around the world, from the national forests of the United States to the deforested hills of Nepal. They will not go away: The world uses about 3.5 billion cubic meters of wood each year, which is two-and-a-half times more per capita than in 1950.

The second frontier for conflict over renewable resources is the ocean. What is at stake is not the water, but rather the resources in it. Fish were once considered an inexhaustible resource, and human experience had virtually proven it. The world population now harvests 80 million tons of seafood annually from the oceans. However, with the development of modern floating fish factories, there has been a rapid depletion of fish resources, to a crisis point in some species. For example, the blue whale has declined in numbers from 200,000 to about 2,000. The Peruvian anchovy catch virtually disintegrated over a three-year period, dropping from 12 million tons to 2 million tons. The UN Food and Agriculture Organization believes that all seventeen of the major fishing areas of the world have reached or exceeded the sustainable catch levels. As this has been recognized, conflicts have begun to break out. The armed fight over codfish in the North Atlantic among Iceland, Britain, and Norway was a harbinger. The more recent conflict over fishing rights in the Georges Bank area east of Canada pitted the Canadian Navy against trawlers from Spain. It should not have been surprising, however, given the emergence of coastal navies to enforce the fishing rights of the 200-mile exclusive economic zone negotiated in the 1980s. For two decades, there have been repeated confrontations over those fishing rights and the definition of control over resources that did not stay in one place. Fish, after all, do not recognize the 200-mile boundary.

Fresh water has also become an invaluable resource. Again, the sheer needs of growing populations means that the most available water sources are being depleted faster than they can be renewed. Net reductions of water stocks are increasing 4 to 8 percent each year.[9] The onset of drought has caused massive population shifts and ensuing conflicts in Africa several times in the last decade. In Africa (and Asia) 80 to 90 percent of the fresh water use is for agriculture, and when it fails, people starve. In recent decades, over one-half of the increase in global food production has come from the one-third of the farmland that is irrigated.

Control over water that flows through several arid countries is also contentious.

Repeated threats or actual diversions in the Middle East have been sources of political volatility. Sudan proposes to divert the Nile waters from time to time, and the question of access to water in the Syria-Jordan-Israel area is a matter of high politics. Future problems are emerging with regard to deep aquifers that underlie several countries and that are increasingly accessible through new drilling technologies. Many of those aquifers were laid down thousands of years ago, as under the Sahara, and there is no established rule for ownership of that "minable" water. Other prospects for conflict arise from proposals to tow massive chunks of Arctic and Antarctic glaciers to countries for fresh water—again, who owns it and who would control the pace of utilization?

As with many other resources, water problems can be resolved through innovative substitute sources (as Saudi Arabia has done with desalination plants) or through conserved use that reflects a higher cost structure. Almost all societies, however, have treated water as a renewable, virtually free good that is their birthright. Adapting to a different concept of water will entail additional conflicts, armed or otherwise, before a new understanding is accepted.

Air quality has become a resource issue in recent decades as well, inspired in part by the increasing sophistication of monitoring instruments that inform people of pollutants in the air they breathe. The reaction to the nuclear radiation leaks at Chernobyl is an apt illustration, as monitoring systems across Central and Western Europe detected the rising radiation levels, leading to the dumping of vast quantities of milk and other fresh foods from Finland to Italy. Discussion of how to intervene in the Soviet Union to control the Chernobyl situation was extensive, culminating in an international effort to hermetically seal the toxic shell of the power plant.

Renewable resources often appear to the layman to be less contentious, perhaps owing to a misperception that one can always get more of them. The truth is that they represent, at the individual level, the most essential resources of life; their unavailability at a given time can lead to great loss of life, as centuries of famine and associated civil war testify. Prior to the industrial revolution, governments took great care in defining policies for these renewable resources—the storage of grain by the ancient Egyptian kingdom was a key to sustainable power, and the management of fresh water by the Chinese empires was at the core of maintaining civilization. The emphasis on industrial-focused resources, however, has decreased the ability of governments to anticipate and respond to these basic shortages.

TRENDS IN RESOURCE CONFLICTS

Regions and countries deal with resource issues in very different ways. The need for state-of-the-art application of resources is greatest in North America and western Europe. Both military requirements and pressure from public opinion are pushing for new approaches to resource utilization. They emphasize the need for new kinds of resources, for research in their application, and for a push for reconciling contrasting perspectives on resource use. Out of these contradictions has emerged a growing interest in "sustainability," the use of resources of all kinds in a way that avoids long-term depletion and even a revitalization of the natural resource base. This perspective is being applied to the economies in both developed countries and developing countries, even though the issues are quite different.

Some commentators hope that the paradigm of sustainability can defuse conflicts before they reach a crisis point if properly applied by political leaders.[10] If this new approach to economic planning can be effective, it will first occur with regard to renewable resources. Thus, the literature with the greatest promise can be found in the writings on sustainable development issued by the World Resources Institute, the World Bank, and others. It is not clear whether this approach will be successful; its attractiveness on conceptual grounds does not necessarily lead to a positive outcome in the political marketplace. Executing policies to achieve sustainability of natural resources requires a long-term perspective with legitimacy in political discourse, and it is not clear if American politics is in a condition to invest in a long-term vision.

In the industrialized countries, the purpose of many environmental laws is not to ban the use of resources, but to manage their use so that countries do not become desperately short. In the case of oil, it means searching for and developing alternatives that allow a country to sustain a shortfall relatively easily. Some countries have a difficult time undertaking such planning, since it forces them to manipulate economic incentives in a manner that violates market principles without clear long-term gain. Thus, there was hostility to the original creation of U.S. government stockpiles of materials, whether minerals or oil. It was justified in the United States only by making the stockpiles part of military planning; ironically, attempts in recent decades to sell off unneeded stockpiles have frequently been resisted by current producers in the market.

For other countries, particularly less-developed economies, the sustainability issue may revolve around the question of land use, whether for food, for forest, or for housing and urban sprawl. The management of those land resources is difficult where governments have limited authority, but essential to avoid the violence that attends unplanned conversions of land use. The sprawl of shanty towns around cities consistently generates violence, either locally or more generally across a society as grievances of the landed and landless clash. In other countries, the shortage of land feeds ethnic conflicts, easily expandable into civil wars with all the intensity, bloodshed, and long-term hatred that is thereby engendered.

The presence of extensive power or mineral resources creates a different source of conflict, common to the Middle East, South Africa, and other exporters of valuable resources. The creation of envy between countries and within them is accelerated by the enormous wealth that is generated. Attempts to assert control over the resources generate a constant security threat, no matter who controls the wealth. Pools of oil in the Middle East have not created peace and prosperity—instead they have contributed to a perpetual, expensive armed peace punctuated by periodic outbreaks of war. The Middle East is not alone in this regard. The Argentine-British war over the Falkland Islands may have been motivated in part by national pride; the presence and likely exploitation of oil in the economic zone around the islands was a far more tangible precursor to war. In that sense, resources are not the cause of war, but they are major contributors to long-term hostility that can be driven to conflict by other catalysts.

CONCLUSIONS

Resources are an important dimension of conflict and war today, as they have been in the past, in two ways. Sudden changes in resource needs and endowments will destabilize the international system. Such is the price of new technology: This was true when the United States developed nuclear weapons, and it will be true when and if an electric automobile is produced comparable to and competitive with gasoline-powered cars. When power shifts from one resource-based technology to another, the resulting instability is likely to initiate conflicts. Uranium was of limited value until the onset of the nuclear age; the United States then suddenly developed relatively poor uranium sources in the United States at considerable expense in order to avoid vulnerability. In the fifteenth century, the monopoly on coffee growing made Yemen a strategic crossroads, and the theft of coffee plants for cultivation elsewhere turned Yemen into a backwater. The Spanish seizure of the gold mining areas in colonial America generated repeated challenges to their power in Europe and on the high seas.

The second kind of resource dimension is long term, powerful in the way that resources can endow the strength of a political-military-industrial system. The United States and Russia have a hold on resources that has consistently given them an advantage over the smaller resources of any western European country. Such resource endowments generate both allies and enemies. The point is not that such resource endowments can win wars, but rather that they are a major cause of wars. With the prominence given to the health and prosperity of economies in today's international politics, the attention given to such issues can only grow. Without improvements in bridging such international differences, conflicts will also grow.

In this chapter, we have looked at different varieties of resources, from the irreplaceable to those highly replaceable, from the inessential to those basic to life. Among those resources, some have constant characteristics over time and thus play relatively predictable roles in political-strategic calculations. The national security of countries is a factor that has always been a powerful determinant of resource policies, and it will continue to do so. On the other hand, the growth of private needs for resources and the internationalization of the economy that supplies those needs have created a new calculus for resources. Among those private needs, the expression of priorities is confused: Environmentalists may want to see lower consumption of resources, others may want to increase their consumption, and both may feel highly inflexible about the issue. These confrontations over private needs for resources are growing in the democratic spirit of the 1990s and spreading to more countries. Intervention to resolve these conflicts will require more than a bureaucratic answer; it will require public education and the development of a consensus for solutions in a democratic manner. In that sense, the world of resource conflicts is becoming more complex, may become more impervious to solutions and prevention, and is certainly more intertwined with the policy environment of all countries.

NOTES

1. An example would be the analyses of Martin van Creveld, whose work is recognized among experts as definitive studies of the material aspects of war but has a limited readership among the broader public who read about war and conflicts; see, for instance, *Supplying War: Logistics from Wallenstein to Patton* (London: Cambridge University Press, 1979); "Turning Points in Twentieth Century War," *Washington Quarterly* 4 (Summer 1981): 3–8; and "Mobilization Warfare," in *Strategic Dimensions of Economic Behavior,* ed. Gordon H. McCormick and Richard E. Bissell (New York: Praeger, 1984), pp. 26–43.

2. Useful context for the resource conflict issues can be found in Robert Mandel, *Conflict over the World's Resources: Background, Trends, Case Studies and Considerations for the Future* (New York: Greenwood Press, 1988); Arthur H. Westing, ed., *Global Resources and International Conflict: Environmental Factors in Strategic Policy and Action* (New York: Oxford University Press, 1986); and Edward B. Barbier, *Economics, Natural-Resource Scarcity, and Development: Conventional and Alternative Views* (London: Earthscan Publications, 1989).

3. See, for instance, the discussion in D. Clayton James, "American and Japanese Strategies in the Pacific War," in *Makers of Modern Strategy: From Machiavelli to the Nuclear Age,* ed. Peter Paret (Princeton, N.J.: Princeton University Press, 1986), pp. 705–708.

4. The "Revolution in Military Affairs" has taken off as a topic of military strategic writings since the 1992 war in the Persian Gulf. For examples of the debate, covering everything from electronics to economics, see the publications of the National Defense University, Washington, D.C.

5. See Vivek Arora and Tamim Bayoumi, "Reductions in World Military Expenditure: Who Stands to Gain?" *Finance and Development* (March 1994): 24, cited and analyzed in Richard E. Bissell, "Defense Conversion in Developing Countries," report submitted to the United States Institute of Peace, Washington, D.C., August 1, 1995.

6. Shane S. Streifel, *Review and Outlook for the World Oil Market,* World Bank Discussion Paper 301 (Washington, D.C.: World Bank, 1995).

7. Claudia Roden, *Coffee* (London: Faber and Faber, 1977).

8. The best current projections are provided by the International Food Policy Research Institute, Washington, D.C., particularly in the publications of its Project 2025. Another useful source is the periodic projections published by the Worldwatch Institute, Washington, D.C., where recent publications argue that world grain projection is on a long-term plateau, and could thus pose major problems over the next decade.

9. Useful background for the water issues can be found in Scott Barrett, *Conflict and Cooperation in Managing International Water Resources,* World Bank Policy Research Working Paper 1303 (Washington, D.C.: World Bank, May 1994); and S. S. Kirman, "Water, Peace, and Conflict Management: The Experience of the Indus and Mekong River Basins," *Water International* 15 (1990): 200–205.

10. Among the many books on sustainable development, resource conflicts are addressed most directly in Peter Moll, *From Scarcity to Sustainability: Futures Studies and the Environment—The Role of the Club of Rome* (Frankfurt: Peter Lang, 1991); Michael Carley and Ian Christie, *Managing Sustainable Development* (Minneapolis: University of Minnesota Press, 1993); and Clement A. Tisdell, *Natural Resources, Growth, and Development: Economics, Ecology, and Resource Scarcity* (New York: Praeger, 1990).

10

Trade and Investment Dimensions of International Conflict

THEODORE H. MORAN

The globalization of the world economy is occurring at an extraordinarily rapid pace. Even for countries where the size of the market and the abundance of internal resources have made much of the economy relatively self-contained, like the United States, the proportion of domestic economic activities exposed to transborder flows of goods, services, capital, and technology has been increasing at an extremely rapid pace.

Historically, since the Great Depression of the 1930s, the leaders of the major market economies have endorsed the logic advanced in the United States by Cordell Hull, that lowering economic barriers will promote not only growth and prosperity but also peace and stability among nations.

The predominant presumptions have been that countries increasingly linked to each other by economic ties will be more likely to be at peace with each other than countries separated by economic protection and restriction, that firms and workers whose self-interest is buoyed by greater openness will be more supportive of constructive engagement in the international system than firms and workers striving to insulate themselves from external competition, and that polities enjoying the growth and innovation generated by trade and investment will help to stabilize relations among states.

Accompanying the process of globalization, however, has appeared a trend counter to the benign vision of economic and political harmony from more open borders.

The rising flows of trade and investment impose severe adjustment burdens on particular firms and workers whose self-interest may lead them to oppose the path toward greater liberalization of international economic activity. Polities in which the distribution of wealth and income is becoming increasingly unequal, perhaps because of the exposure to external competition, may be less likely to bear the burdens and uncertainties that come with leadership in the international system. And countries that see the relations with their economic rivals as a

155

zero-sum contest may be prone to abandon the win-win strategies of a multilateral economic orientation in favor of more beggar-thy-neighbor efforts to favor themselves and their own regions or blocs.

The balance between forces favoring greater openness and those opposing it may therefore become increasingly precarious and problematic as the world tries to digest the gains achieved in the decades since Cordell Hull's generation launched the contemporary thrust at opening borders to trade, investment, and technology.

At risk are not only the specific economic outcomes from specific economic policies, but much broader political outcomes as well: Will the major industrial states continue to support the liberalization of trade, investment, and technology flows to accommodate the ever-deeper penetration of China, the former Soviet Union, India, and other parts of the Third World into international markets, or will they adopt policies to slow or inhibit such penetration? Will the major industrial states continue to support the liberalization of trade, investment, and technology flows on a multilateral basis, or will they construct a system of subtle preferences on a regional basis that leads to the solidification of economic blocs?

The answers to questions such as these carry genuine strategic implications, such as the prospects for democratic reform in former socialist economies if integration into global markets is hindered and the prospects for the engagement of the major powers, including the United States, in regional alliances if economic blocs are fostered in Asia, the Western Hemisphere, and Europe.

For both political and economic reasons, therefore, it is important to explore quite carefully how the trends toward the globalization of economic behavior (and the policies adopted to cope with them) might continue to constitute a force for cohesion among nation-states, or, conversely, how such trends (and certain policy reactions) might become sources of conflict.[1]

THE GLOBALIZATION OF ECONOMIC ACTIVITY AS A SOURCE OF BENEFIT AND HARMONY AMONG NATIONS

Since 1950, world merchandise exports have expanded at an average annual rate of approximately 6 percent, compared to a 4.5 percent annual growth in world output.[2] In the past three decades, international trade in services has grown more rapidly than merchandise exports. In 1994, international trade in goods and services approached four trillion dollars per year. Foreign direct investment (FDI) has grown even faster than trade. In the past decade, FDI flows have expanded by 27 percent per year, or seven times faster than the growth in output of the countries from which these flows originated. Technology has also been undergoing a process of globalization. International comparisons of patenting, research and development (R&D) expenditures, and density of scientific and engineering personnel show a dispersion of technical competence and technological resources. The growth of trade in technology-based products has been faster than the growth of trade in resource-based or labor-intensive products.

In the United States, the share of the gross domestic product (GDP) represented by the exports of goods and services has more than doubled since 1965, from less than 5 percent to almost 12 percent, for a total of $460 billion in 1993. Imports have also grown in importance to the U.S. economy, rising to a postwar high of 13 percent of the GDP in 1993. In terms of the global stock of FDI, the United States occupies first place as both an investor (accounting for 25 percent of the global FDI stock) and as a recipient (hosting 22 percent of the global FDI stock). The interaction between foreign direct investment and trade is becoming increasingly apparent. In 1990 (the most recent available data), multinational enterprises were responsible for more than 75 percent of United States merchandise trade, with approximately 40 percent of that trade consisting of intrafirm transactions.

Exports of advanced technology products from the United States have been rising at twice the rate of total merchandise exports. (The ten standard advanced technology product categories are biotechnology, life sciences, optoelectronics, computers and telecommunications, electronics, computer-integrated manufacturing, material design, aerospace, weapons, and nuclear technology.) Over the same period, imports of advanced technology products have been rising three times as fast as total merchandise imports. Furthermore, the postwar historical pattern of predominately one-way flows of technology out of the United States has been significantly altered. The National Science Board has found that transfers of technology into the United States have increased substantially in volume and importance over the past twenty years.[3]

The predominance of the evidence suggests that this internationalization of economic activity has had a positive impact on individual nations, on relationships between nations, and on the international system as a whole.

In terms of national welfare, greater openness to competitive market forces, including competitive market forces from abroad, and greater freedom from artificial market restraints are closely associated with higher economic growth and higher standards of living. This holds true for both advanced industrial states and developing nations.[4] To be sure, the process is not pain-free and firms, workers, and communities must adjust to meet new competition (a challenge that is analyzed below). But the gains from trade in goods and services and from trans-

fers of capital and technology typically outweigh the costs by a large margin.

These large net gains accrue to consumers in the form of cheaper, more diverse, and more advanced products. They also accrue to producers. In the United States, for example, one in six manufacturing jobs is devoted to exports.[5] Over the past five years, four-fifths of the increase in American domestic manufacturing production has been dedicated to exports. Export-related jobs pay approximately 18 percent above the U.S. average in wages. Greater access to imports has also become more important for exports. Over the past decade, the import content of U.S. exports has climbed from 10 percent to 14 percent. Thus, on both the import side and the export side, international trade is becoming increasingly central to U.S. prosperity. As for foreign direct investment, inward investment into the United States has provided 4.7 million jobs for Americans and generated $4.1 billion in new domestic R&D.

For those concerned about realpolitik considerations of national power, the higher rates of productivity growth, technological innovation, and overall economic expansion that come from access to international markets determine which states are better able to influence world events, mold and lead common endeavors, manage risks, resist external pressure, and counter or thwart antagonistic threats from others. Countries that lag in productivity, innovation, and economic growth have fewer resources to deploy in the international arena and fewer capabilities to mobilize in their own defense.[6]

Moreover, the historical record suggests that there is indeed a wholesome interaction between the expansion of economic and political links across borders, a benign integrative function of the sort Cordell Hull's generation fervently wished. A close examination of the data shows that the contention that trade and peace go together has solid statistical support.[7] While there may be individual exceptions throughout history, high levels of trade are generally associated with lower levels of antagonism and hostility of the kind that lead to conflict. Indeed, the higher the levels of economic interaction, the greater the quantitative effect on inhibiting hostilities among the states involved.

There are six areas, however, in which trade and investment issues may generate conflict among nations:

- trade deficits and unfair trade practices,
- high-tech trade rivalry ("strategic trade" rivalry),
- national and regional trade discrimination,
- foreign investment and the acquisition of critical domestic industries by foreigners,
- outward investment and the "hollowing out" of the home country, and
- transborder flows and the distribution of "good jobs" versus "bad jobs."

The remainder of this chapter will delineate the concerns that arise in each area, assess those concerns, and attempt to draw what might be the most appropriate policy implications.

THE INTERNATIONALIZATION OF ECONOMIC ACTIVITY AS A SOURCE OF CONFLICT AMONG NATIONS

Trade Deficits and Unfair Trade Practices

Perhaps the most popular conventional way for a domestic public to judge how well its country is doing in comparison to its economic competitors, and whether other markets are as open as its own to receive its products, is whether or not the nation is running a trade deficit.[8] This indicates how hard the country must work in order not to "lose out" to other contestants; it also pro-

vides a measure of how tough it must be in trade negotiations to achieve market access for its own products abroad. The presence of trade deficits, in particular persistent bilateral trade deficits among rival economic powers, may well produce tension and conflict among the states involved.

Assessment. There is perhaps no other area where the gap between economic analysis and popular conception is greater than in discussions of the causes of and remedies for trade deficits. With rare unanimity, the economics community considers trade balances as macroeconomic phenomena; that is, both deficits and surpluses spring from the discrepancy between what a country earns and what it spends or, conversely, what a country invests and what it saves.

As long as a nation (like the United States) consumes more than it produces or saves less than it invests, the economy will run a trade deficit, in essence buying on credit and piling up obligations to foreigners against home country assets. This leads to the unfashionable conclusion that trade deficits are "made at home." They are not the consequence of trade restrictions or unfair trade practices on the part of others. In the case of the United States, for example, the string of contemporary trade deficits comes from the high rate of consumption and the low rate of savings of Americans. In the case of Japan, the reverse outcome, trade surpluses, comes from the high Japanese savings rate and the low propensity to consume.

Moreover, while aggregate trade balances give notice about potential problems in the savings/consumption ratio of individual countries, bilateral trade balances, in contrast, are largely haphazard outcomes and are not sensible targets for policy preoccupation. The United States could reduce the bilateral trade deficit with Japan by one-third to one-half overnight, for example, by permitting the export of Alaskan and other domestic petroleum to that country, but the aggregate U.S. trade deficit would remain unchanged as increased U.S. oil imports from Venezuela, Mexico, and Saudi Arabia made up the difference.

This does not mean that market access is unimportant, however, or that tough measures against unfair trade practices are unwarranted. Pressure for trade liberalization among rival nations is needed to allow each economy to do most of what it does best (as indicated earlier), thus allowing the workforce to be most productively employed. The struggle over market access is therefore a struggle over the composition of trade flows, not over whether the resulting levels are in balance. As former United States Trade Representative William Brock once quipped, he dreamed that one day Japan eliminated all of its trade barriers, and the U.S. trade deficit still did not change! This outcome, however likely to be true in practice, is far removed from the perceptions that drive popularly elected officials in the major industrial powers.

Trade deficits per se are not "bad"; they may represent a period in which a country is importing capital equipment and the ingredients for infrastructure projects that will generate more than enough output to pay for themselves. Some countries have found it to be a sensible national strategy to run a trade deficit for years in a row. On the other hand, trade deficits can also represent a period of excessive consumption; this deficit does not raise domestic productivity but will nonetheless have to be paid off by future generations.

Over the long term, there are both economic and political reasons for nations to want to keep their trade accounts in approximate equilibrium. This balance avoids having foreigners accumulate claims on the assets of the deficit country, and diffuses the mutual accusations, whether accurate or not, about who is responsible for imbalances (profligate consumers or unfair barriers).

Policy implications. The way to correct persistent imbalances (indeed the only way to correct persistent imbalances) is for each country to adjust its savings/consumption ratio, ensuring that it does not spend more than it earns. This macroeconomic realignment, however difficult, can only be made at home.

As for the serious, but nonetheless distinct, issue of market access and unfair trade practices, the major industrial powers have a common interest in ensuring that the new body they have established to manage commercial disputes and adjudications, the World Trade Organization (WTO), gets launched with maximum support and legitimacy in its formative years. This would suggest that troublesome disputes among the principal members (for example, Japanese automobile sector practices, European agricultural sector practices, U.S. trade-and-environment practices) should be pursued in a manner that enables the WTO to adjudicate them most effectively and that issues or subissues not clearly covered under WTO auspices be brought under WTO disciplines as rapidly as possible.

High-Tech Trade Rivalry ("Strategic Trade" Rivalry)

In contrast to the predominant win-win nature of conventional trade interactions, special concerns have arisen about trade competition in high-tech sectors such as aerospace, telecommunications, advanced materials, computers and supercomputers, semiconductors and microprocessors, and biochemicals. Economies of scale dictate that only a few countries may enjoy the presence of a critical industry that has important economic and defense ramifications. Where such high-tech industries are located, and what measures governments might take to ensure that their nations can field a player in such sectors, can become a source of tension and conflict among the governments.

Assessment. Traditionally, trade theory has been built on the assumption that there is perfect competition in the markets where trade takes place. This assumption plays a central role in assuring that all sides are better off in the expansion of trade and worse off when trade is restricted.

Over the past decade, the "new trade theory," also called "strategic trade theory," has focused on industries where markets do not work perfectly—specifically, those with a limited number of firms because of large economies of scale, high technological barriers to entry, and production processes marked by a substantial level of learning-by-doing.[9] (In this context, "strategic" is an economic term that refers to the oligopolistic character of the industry, not necessarily its military significance, although there may be a good deal of overlap.)

From any country's point of view, strategic trade industries are desirable not only because they incorporate a large proportion of high-wage, high-skill jobs, but also because they are likely to generate economic, social, or defense-related benefits to the country above and beyond their strictly commercial value.

National authorities generally want to ensure the presence of their own country's firms in strategic industries. For example, the United States, Europe, and Japan all want to be major players in aerospace, telecommunications, microelectronics, and advanced materials. Yet the large economies of scale in these sectors mean that global markets will only sustain a few production sites, especially the most cutting-edge production sites. Consequently not every country, not even every major country, can expect to have an extensive presence in every key high-technology sector. This situation can lead to a beggar-thy-neighbor duel of national policies that aim to support one's own

firms in strategic sectors at the expense of competitors.

Policy implications. To grapple with the dilemmas of rivalry in high-tech industries, policy debate needs to be informed both by economic analysis and by the analytic considerations that spring from the "prisoner's dilemma" (a situation where the pursuit of self-interest by each party leads to a poor outcome for all) and the dynamics of mutual escalation.

From an economic point of view, objections to strategic trade intervention arise first of all from practical considerations of implementation. There is the problem, as in all industrial policy debates, of devising criteria for picking winners and losers that work better than the market. In addition, there is the possibility of pork-barrel and special-interest politics contaminating the selection process. As a result, despite an appealingly rigorous justification for public sector support for high-tech industries with large economies of scale and dynamic learning-curve advantages, the prospects for creating an effective national policy in this area may be less than favorable.[10]

But perhaps the biggest obstacle to using strategic trade precepts as a guide to policy is the beggar-thy-neighbor dynamic inherent in the theory itself. A nation that uses market intervention to capture vital industries for its own high-tech industries can expect other nations to follow suit. Cycles of public intervention, matching moves, escalation, and retaliation would be endemic. Thus, a policy shift toward government intervention in strategic trade industries as a new norm for national policy would be certain to generate new tensions among the major powers (as indicated later, it would fail the "Golden Rule" test for public policy).

Under such circumstances, it might be wise to draw on lessons from the prisoner's dilemma, namely to search for multilateral means to establish a stalemate and cease-fire in the otherwise escalatory process, seeking common agreement to limit each country's ability to bolster its own companies through direct and indirect governmental preference and support.

National and Regional Trade Discrimination

Just as countries that are political friends and allies tend to develop intense patterns of trade that serve to bind themselves further together, countries that view each other warily are more likely to discriminate against each other in trade relations.[11] It may be crucial therefore to the future of stability in the international political system whether there are mechanisms to minimize or prevent trade discrimination or, conversely, to allow or even foster the creation of exclusive economics blocs.

Assessment. The completion of the Tokyo Round and the Uruguay Round of trade negotiations over the past two decades— with extraordinary expansion of multilateral disciplines over the treatment of goods, services, and public practices (such as government procurement and the protection of intellectual property rights)—might lead one to conclude that discriminatory trade practices among nations and the propensity to form economic "blocs" are on the wane. The reality is otherwise. In the 1980s, the trend was in fact toward greater regionalism: In each of the three major economic areas of the world, there has been an increase in intraregional trade: from 23 percent to 29 percent in East Asia, from 27 percent to 29 percent in the Western Hemisphere, and from 54 percent to 60 percent in Europe.[12]

Even after factoring out the impact of natural determinants of trade patterns (such as geographic proximity and absolute size of the nations in question), as well as the influence of common languages and cultural affinity, it appears that such patterns do indeed indicate the emergence of significant trade blocs in Europe, the Western Hemisphere, and the Asia-Pacific Economic Cooperation (APEC) region. The greatest intraregional bias is in the APEC region, while the most rapid trend in this direction is in Europe. Since the North American Free Trade Agreement (NAFTA) has only recently come into being, a fresh spurt of bloc-oriented activity in the Western Hemisphere may be seen in the near future. (There has been no attempt to measure the emergence of a ruble-bloc in the former Soviet Union; however, recent attempts by Russia to reintegrate the economies of parts of that region suggest that such a development may be underway.)

Policy implications. For those not attuned to the details of trade regulation, avoiding the creation of closed economic blocs may require a surprising level of subtlety in framing U.S. policy. If the threat sprang from the construction of overt walls of protectionism such as high tariffs, as happened in the 1930s, national leaders might find it easier to call forth concerted action to prevent it. But the policies that are likely to push regional free-trade zones in the direction of exclusive blocs are much more arcane— "rules of origin" specifying the amount of domestic content required for a product to qualify as an internal product, obstructive antidumping regimes, preferential subsidies to particular regions, government rewards for engaging in local R&D, and similar policies. In short, the devil is in the details, far below the horizon of most economists, let alone national security strategists.

Rules of origin first became troublesome in the 1980s as the Europeans required a high level of local content for semiconductors, microelectronics, and automobiles to be given favorable treatment within Europe. In the 1990s the United States, Canada, and Mexico went even further in specifying the domestic content needed for telecommunications equipment, printers, copiers, fax machines, color televisions, automobiles, and textiles to have free access within the NAFTA. The question is whether such requirements will be maintained (or even expanded) as NAFTA membership grows within the hemisphere and as the European Union (EU) implements access agreements with the countries of Eastern Europe.[13] If so, these rules of origin will become not only inefficient restrictions on trade (they prevent companies from sourcing from the least-cost supplier), but also important discriminatory devices to keep out products from other regions that do not meet the local content test. Asia and the former Soviet Union will bear the brunt of the discrimination, as will transatlantic trade in general.

Equally obscure to those who are not trade policy experts, antidumping regulations as currently administered can be used to find foreign exporters guilty of "unfair" pricing, even though they are engaging in exactly the same kind of competitive behavior as their domestic counterparts.[14] This "administrative trade protection" has been growing as a tool to prevent external products from entering a national or regional market. Antidumping protectionism has been particularly harsh on exports from Russia, Central and Eastern Europe, and the rest of the former Soviet Union.[15] Since the major industrial states have an important national interest in seeing that trade and investment supplement (and eventually replace) aid in fostering market-based reform in these countries, discrimination against their products seems particularly hard to justify.

The most straightforward way to counter the drift toward exclusive blocs, based on extensive rules of origin, antidumping protectionism, and other special devices like local and regional subsidies, is through persistent efforts to keep the liberalization of trade, investment, and technology flows on a multilateral track. The most powerful multilat-

eral impetus will come from expanding the mandate of the WTO and using it aggressively to limit such discriminatory practices and to help provide an easy and transparent method of accession into regional trading arrangements. The goal will be to ensure that the growth of regionalism does not serve as an excuse to block the penetration of outsiders, which could easily lead to economic and ultimately political tensions between regions.

Foreign Investment and the Acquisition of Critical Domestic Industries by Foreigners

The developed countries have long urged the developing countries to accept and welcome the presence of foreign direct investment in key sectors of their economies. They have been more cautious, however, about foreign investment, especially foreign takeovers, in crucial sectors of their own. The rapid expansion of foreign direct investment and the predominance of investment through acquisition are likely to generate ongoing tensions among states, especially relative latecomers to this process, like the United States, Japan, and other nations in Asia.

Assessment. As a general proposition, FDI provides inputs of technology, management, and capital to the host economy that helps it become more productive. To be sure, national leaders will want to know whether direct investment by foreigners behaves significantly different from domestic firms with regard to such factors as the skill intensity of the jobs, the amount of R&D, procurement practices, and labor relations. One would want to be satisfied that foreign investors did not keep the best jobs and research activities solely for their home operations, or worse, take over indigenous companies and restructure operations in a way that siphons off the most prized functions for headquarters. The evidence suggests that this does not occur; there are no major, systematic differences in behavior between local firms and affiliates of foreign companies when the type of industry is held constant.[16]

To the extent that foreign investors conduct their operations like domestic companies but generate superior performance, there has been a growing willingness to question the importance of firm nationality, as measured by ownership of the stock or the citizenship of the board of directors or the location of parent headquarters. All that need concern national leaders, according to this line of analysis, is whether any given corporation can improve the effectiveness of the local economy. "Who is us?" has become the popular policy question.[17] The answer, to paraphrase the terms of the debate, is "the home-country workforce, the home-country people, but not particularly the home-country's corporations." This stance would lead to unreserved welcome for any and all foreign contestants in the domestic market.

But a national security threat may come from being dependent on foreign suppliers for critical goods, services, and technologies. That threat may take the form of denial, delay of delivery, blackmail, or conditions placed on access or use.[18] The United States has itself been a prime practitioner of the manipulation of dependence in the past. Today, others may be in a position to exercise similar influence, and that influence is likely to increase as the globalization of international economic activity continues. There have been more than four hundred foreign takeovers in the microelectronics, aerospace, telecommunications, and advanced materials industries in recent years, for example, totaling 46 percent of all takeovers and 79 percent of the total value. As a consequence, whatever benefits may accrue from foreign investment, questions of foreign control and domination of critical U.S. industries do begin to arise.

For a threat of denial, delay, blackmail, or the placement of limitations on access or use to be credible, however, there must be a concentration of external suppliers. Whether for semiconductors or flat-panel displays, the fundamental issues that determine whether the dependence of a country on any particular foreign source may be worrisome are the availability of alternative sources and the ease of substitution.[19] These criteria allow national security strategists to distinguish cases that are legitimately problematic from those that are not and help identify industries of concern for national security.

Policy implications. Focusing on global concentration or global dispersion of sources of supply points to an answer to the dilemma of foreign acquisitions of companies in critical technology sectors. The crucial test is whether the international industry is sufficiently monopolized to make delay or denial of supplies possible, and not, as is commonly supposed, whether the company to be acquired is the sole remaining domestic supplier (or one of a very small number). The policy logic is straightforward: If there is no international concentration, there is no credible threat and thus no reason to be concerned about the acquisition.

Difficulties arise when the international industry of the company to be acquired is a rather tight oligopoly. Here, the national security strategist may have to choose between blocking the foreign acquisition and then perhaps propping up an inferior domestic supplier or allowing the acquisition to proceed, with ownership passing to the hands of outsiders who will then hold quasi-monopolistic control over access. In such circumstances, the emerging consensus is that, at least for civilian companies, it may be preferable to permit the acquisition to take place while imposing performance requirements on the new subsidiary to maintain production and R&D within the home country.[20]

The use of performance requirements as a tool of national policy is not the best policy solution, since performance requirements (like the rules of origin mentioned earlier) interfere with the efficient workings of markets. But in the case of foreign acquisitions in globally concentrated critical industries, the use of an objective measure of market domination as a basis for rejecting or modifying proposed takeovers would still be a substantial improvement over the vague and intuitive national security justifications that are now the norm in many parts of the world. The transparency and objectivity of a concentration test should pass the Golden Rule test for public policy; that is, any one nation that wanted to use this approach to protect its own national security interests should be able to live comfortably when the same approach is adopted by others.

Outward Investment and the "Hollowing Out" of the Home Country

While inward investment can be defended along the lines indicated above as supporting the economic interests of the recipient country, there has been growing concern that outward investment may export jobs and result in the hollowing out of the economy in the home country. Such traditional concerns—in Europe, reincarnated in the United States (especially during the NAFTA debate), and beginning to emerge in Asia—can generate tension between potential exporters and importers of foreign direct investment.

Assessment. An accurate appraisal of the "hollowing out" debate demands more careful analysis than is usually accorded to this controversy. Critics of outward investment point to factories that have been closed in the home market, arguing that if "runaway plants" could be kept from moving abroad, the jobs they had previously provided would

be retained in the domestic economy. Proponents of outward investment point to the dynamism of the internationally oriented sectors of the economy, arguing that if impediments were placed in the way of multinational firms' ability to move freely across borders, their contribution to domestic job creation would be severely diminished.

The key analytic assumption for opponents is that operations moved abroad would survive intact if they were kept at home; the key analytic assumption for proponents is that operations kept at home would simply be lost (and the competitiveness of the parent firm weakened) if they could not move abroad as market forces dictated. Both positions are plausible. To judge which is correct requires comparing the job creation and export performance of firms that do invest abroad with those that do not.

The answer to this question, however, must pass one further analytic hurdle. Outward investment, export performance, and consequent job creation are all closely correlated with firm size, R&D intensity, advertising intensity, and skilled labor intensity (among other variables). Thus any rigorous analysis requires comparing the job and export performance of "big" U.S. firms that do invest abroad with "big" U.S. firms that do not, of "R&D-intensive" U.S. firms that do invest abroad with "R&D-intensive" U.S. firms that do not, and so forth. Simply demonstrating that large, R&D-intensive, advertising-intensive, skilled labor-intensive multinational firms export more and create more jobs than average firms will not suffice.

A series of studies have set the problem up correctly and found remarkably consistent results.[21] These studies cover three decades of data for Europe and the United States (empirical work on outward investment from Asian countries is less advanced).

The results show that most outward investment actually acts as a magnet for exports from the home country, generating more jobs in the domestic economy than would occur if the operations were kept at home. One set of studies, for example, has demonstrated that (after controlling for firm size and industry characteristics) the higher the output of American firms in any given foreign area, the larger their exports from the United States to that area. This complementary relationship between outward investment and domestic exports is strong for intermediate goods shipped for further exports, is strong for intermediate goods shipped for further processing, and is also positively related to the American firm's exports of finished products from the United States. Recent research confirms this finding more generally across home countries: Firms that invest and produce abroad export more than firms that do not—they export more in general, and they export more to the countries where they have invested. Such analysis underscores the significance of opening Japan to foreign direct investment, for example, as a method of penetrating Japanese markets with external exports.

Moreover, there is an equally important finding that most outward investment is defensive, that is, takes place in operations that will simply be lost to competition if those operations are kept at home. In short, the stay-at-home option recommended by those who want to place obstacles in the way of outward investment is not a viable policy alternative.

Bringing the strands of defensive-investment and investment-as-magnet together is the discovery that there is a "threshold effect," in which the initial effort to establish a base in a foreign market through direct investment allows a firm to jump to a higher level of exports (and consequent higher level of job maintenance or job creation) in the home market in comparison to firms with similar characteristics that remained at home.

Policy implications. These findings suggest that companies that are inhibited from engaging in outward investment as the industries they participate in evolve will likely be driven out of the market by their competitors. The appropriate policy in such circumstances for a home country is what is called "capital export neutrality."[22] This means that tax structures and other incentives or disincentives should be designed to be neutral, favoring neither operations that companies keep in the home economy nor operations that they shift abroad.

The result may create, in popular parlance, a modest "sucking sound" in home economies around the world. But the sucking sound will come from exports headed toward the economies where the parent companies establish new operations, not from jobs lost that would otherwise be saved by insisting that the firms keep all activities at home.

Transborder Flows and the Distribution of "Good Jobs" versus "Bad Jobs"

The preceding analysis broadly supports the proposition that the internationalization of a country's economy leads to a higher standard of living than the alternative of restrictions on trade and investment. But the higher standard of living (on average) may be achieved in an unequal fashion, with significantly higher benefits for a relatively small fraction of the population and significantly lower benefits for the remainder. Concern about the impact of open borders on the distribution of income and on the possible replacement of jobs with high wages and benefits by jobs with low wages and benefits may be a source of anxiety and dissatisfaction to domestic polities, a source of tension among the governments involved, and a source of opposition to international economic trends and commitments.

Assessment. The composition of jobs and the distribution of income has become a source of concern in most of the major industrial nations. In the United States, family income growth has stagnated over the past two decades and incomes have become more unequal. The real incomes of the lower 60 percent of American families were actually lower in the early 1990s than for similar families at the end of the 1970s. In the twenty-year period after the end of the Second World War, the real income of the median family in the United States grew by 2.8 percent per year, more than doubling. In the subsequent twenty-year period, in contrast, the income of the median American family was practically unchanged, rising by only 0.1 percent per year in real terms (requiring centuries for the income level to double).[23]

In Europe, wage levels have been maintained more successfully in real terms, but at the price of very little job creation. Concurrently, generous levels of support for those unable to find jobs have created a class of unemployed whose jobless condition is being passed from generation to generation. In Asia (particularly in Japan), there are concerns that traditional patterns of lifelong job tenure may be undermined by exposure to international competition.

While economic analysis is easily able to defend the benefits of open international markets for all the countries involved, there is a genuine theoretical concern that rising levels of trade may depress wages for unskilled labor in the importing country, as that country attempts to compete with economies that use even lower wage labor in their exports. (This is called "factor price equalization" theory, originating with Wolfgang Stolper and Paul Samuelson.[24])

Despite the theoretical suspicion that income inequality might be traced to international trade, however, empirical analysis does not support this hypothesis. The relative prices of goods that use highly skilled labor have not been rising relative to those of

goods that use less highly skilled labor. Moreover, for the United States, most trade in fact takes place with partners who pay approximately 90 percent of U.S. wage rates, and imports from the lowest wage suppliers (like China) have not increased markedly over the last three decades (2.0 percent of U.S. GDP in 1960, 2.7 percent in 1990).[25]

Policy implications. Instead of pointing the finger of blame for rising income inequality at trade and entertaining ideas about restraining the growth of trade, the evidence suggests that the decline in wage growth in recent decades has been the result of a substantial slowdown in the rate of productivity increase. The principal explanation for the widening inequality in wages comes from the increasing demand for workers with skills and education. The ability to work with personal computers, for example, generates a substantial wage premium over those who cannot; this factor alone accounts for as much as half of the gap between the wages of college and high school graduates.

The appropriate policy package to address wage stagnation and wage inequality, therefore, must focus not on changing trade flows but rather on raising productivity and enhancing skills among the workforce. For the United States, this focus implies stronger efforts in the field of vocational education, national certification, and lifelong training opportunities. For Europe, it implies greater flexibility and mobility in labor markets. For all countries, it implies high rates of investment in plant and equipment, in research and development, and in human resources.

Indeed, there is an important complementary effect of investing in all three simultaneously. For example, if governments limit investment incentives to plant and equipment and to research and development, while ignoring human resources, firms may design productive processes around deficiencies in the workforce (this is referred to as "dumbing down" technology, for example, using pictures in the cash registers of fast-food restaurants to compensate for the inability of workers to deal competently with numbers). In such circumstances, simply letting markets work on their own might produce perverse outcomes, with countries settling in to a highly automated low-skill equilibrium. While the resulting aggregate standard of living might appear high, the distribution of benefits throughout the population would be greatly skewed and the resulting enthusiasm for international commitments, both economic and political, would not likely be strong. Thus, for all nations, domestic programs that improve the productivity, mobility, and adjustment of the indigenous workforce have an important role to play in dissipating the appeal of isolationism and in ensuring popular support for positive engagement abroad.

ECONOMIC POLICIES AND STABILITY OR INSTABILITY IN THE INTERNATIONAL POLITICAL SYSTEM

This examination of the sources of potential conflict arising from economic issues highlights the synergy between appropriately disciplined domestic economic policies in the major industrial states, self-confidence and support for constructive involvement in the international system, and reasonable prospects for multilateral solutions to common problems arising from the globalization of economic activity.

Better macroeconomic balance between savings and investment in the major industrial powers would enable them to invest a greater proportion of their wealth in plant and equipment, R&D, and human capital. This would both enhance the productivity of their firms and workers (reinforcing their "competitiveness") and generate resources to assist individuals and communities to adjust to the strains that inevitably accompany the greater exposure to international market forces. It would also strengthen their industrial and technological capabilities to meet external challenges, including military challenges. And, with an automaticity that will almost surely be surprising to conventional modes of thought, it will cause trade accounts to right themselves easily and without strain, restoring the long-term equilibrium between exports and imports without any need to bash others and eliminating the prospect of mortgaging the assets of future generations to outsiders.[26]

Domestic macroeconomic self-discipline will not only augment the ability of individual countries to provide resources to influence international events and to participate together in common international endeavors, enhancing what might be called "hard power"; it is also likely to augment the stature, respect, and emulation of countries that choose this path among their peers, enhancing what has been referred to as "soft power."[27] Finally, the result is sure to eliminate some of the self-doubt and preoccupation with "decline" that has affected the public, particularly in Europe and the United States, where the public has turned more inward, defensive, and even isolationist.

As a consequence, there is quite likely to be a greater propensity for national leaders to look for multilateral solutions to common economic problems, ranging from fair and equal market access, to muting of high-tech rivalries in strategic trade industries, to joint efforts to limit discriminatory regional blocs and the exclusion of outsiders, to equal treatment for foreign investors whose behavior matches (and improves) the performance of domestic firms. Clearly, disputes about unfair trade practices and worries about dependence on externally concentrated or monopolistic sources of goods, services, and technologies will remain to be addressed. But the prospects for collective rules and regulations, rather than unilateral accusations and restrictions, will be improved.

This could have beneficial impacts not only on transpacific relations, as U.S.-Japan disputes and APEC–Western Hemisphere suspicions might recede, but also on transatlantic relations, as U.S.-EU controversies and EU–Asian/former USSR fears subside. The emerging market economies of China, Vietnam, India, the former Soviet Union, and the Third World could continue to be integrated into a world economic system relatively confident of its ability to accommodate and adjust. The spillover effects on democratic reform in the newer market economies and on constructive engagement in international affairs in the older market economies, while hard to predict at any given moment in time, could only be positive over the longer run.

In short, decisions on a whole range of what have traditionally been considered issues of "low politics"—involving the reduction of budget deficits, stimulation of local savings, liberalization of antidumping regulations and rules of origin, harmonization of R&D subsidies, and minimal supervision of foreign acquisitions and outward investment by domestic firms—could be harnessed in the service of the "high politics" of political stability and security in the international system.

However, the chance that in the post–Cold War world such "low politics" could dominate the "high politics" looms as a real possibility.

Of first-order concern is the prospect of vicious cycles and downward spirals in the relations among nations in the absence of a better balance between savings and consumption in the major industrial states, especially the United States. Most troubling would be the possibility that aggressive unilateral actions to secure market access, to preempt high-tech rivals, to secure the most favorable jobs and activities for one's own region (while excluding outsiders), and to prevent foreign acquisitions might substi-

tute for efforts to impose appropriate amounts of discipline on domestic macroeconomic behavior. As long as macroeconomic relationships between savings and investment are out of balance at home, the temptation to blame others can inflame passions and generate resentments across borders, but cannot produce solutions.

Were the major industrial nations to succumb to this temptation, much of what has been gained since the beggar-thy-neighbor policies of the interwar period would be lost, and the possibility of economic conflicts leading to serious political tensions among the members of the international community could not be brushed aside.

NOTES

1. This paper draws on and amplifies arguments previously expressed in the author's chapter "Economics," in *Strategic Assessment 1995: U.S. Security Challenges in Transition* (Washington, D.C.: Institute for National Strategic Studies, 1995), chap. 16.

2. The following data come from the *Economic Report of the President* (Washington, D.C.: Government Printing Office, 1994, 1995).

3. Thomas H. Lee and Proctor P. Reid, eds., *National Interests in an Age of Global Technology* (Washington, D.C.: National Academy of Press for the National Academy of Engineering, 1991).

4. *World Development Report 1995: Workers in an Integrating World* (New York: Oxford University Press for the World Bank, 1995).

5. *Economic Report of the President*, 1994, 1995.

6. Paul Kennedy, *The Rise and Fall of the Great Powers* (New York: Random House, 1987); and Aaron Friedberg, "The Strategic Implications of Relative Economic Decline," *Political Science Quarterly* 104, no. 1 (1989): 401-431.

7. Edward D. Mansfield, *Power, Trade, and War* (Princeton: Princeton University Press, 1994).

8. For a critique of this popular view, see Paul Krugman, *Peddling Prosperity* (New York: W. W. Norton, 1994).

9. Paul Krugman, ed., *Strategic Trade Policy and the New International Economics* (Cambridge, Mass.: MIT Press, 1986); and Paul Krugman and Alasdair Smith, eds., *Empirical Studies of Strategic Trade Policy* (Chicago: University of Chicago Press for the National Bureau of Economic Research, 1994).

10. Awarding protection to strategic trade industries may be particularly costly. Research by David Richardson suggests that, under conditions of imperfect competition, trade liberalization leads to efficiency gains that may even run two to three times greater than those under perfect competition. "Empirical Research on Trade Liberalization with Imperfect Competition: A Survey," *OECD Economic Studies* 12 (Spring 1989): 87–125.

11. Joanne Gowa, *Allies, Adversaries, and International Trade* (Princeton, N.J.: Princeton University Press, 1994).

12. For evidence on trading blocs, see Jeffrey Frankel, Ernesto Stein, and Shang-Jin Wei, "Continental Trading Blocs: Natural or Supernatural?" National Bureau of Economic Research Working Paper No. 4588 (Cambridge, Mass.: December 1993) and *APEC and Regional Trading Arrangements in the Pacific* (Washington, D.C.: Institute for International Economics, 1994).

13. For an assessment of rules of origin and the consequent policy dilemmas, see Jeri Jensen-Moran, "Trade Battles as Investment Wars: The Coming Rules of Origin Debate," *Washington Quarterly* 19, no. 1 (1996): 239–257.

14. Richard Boltuck and Richard E. Litan, *Down in the Dumps: Administration of the Unfair Trade Laws* (Washington, D.C.: Brookings Institution, 1991).

15. For an account of the attempt to liberalize antidumping treatment of products from Eastern Europe and the former Soviet Union, which was defeated in 1994, see Robert E. Cumby and Theodore H. Moran, *Testing Models of the Trade Policy Profess: Do We Need a New Paradigm for the New Issues?* (Chicago: University of Chicago Press for the National Bureau of Economic Research, forthcoming).

16. See Edward M. Graham and Paul R. Krugman, *Foreign Direct Investment in the United States*, 2nd ed. (Washington, D.C.: Institute for International Economics, 1991). There is some concern, however, that Japanese investors in the United States may have a greater propensity to import than domestic firms in the same industry, but this could be explained by the relative newness of the investments.

17. The seminal work is Robert Reich, "Who Is Us?" *Harvard Business Review* 90 (January–February 1990): 53–65.

18. For a broader historical perspective on the manipulation of access to monopolistically controlled goods, services, and technologies (including manipulation on the part of the U.S. government), see Theodore H. Moran, "The Globalization of America's Defense Industries: Managing the Threat of Foreign Dependence," *International Security* 15 (Summer 1990): 57–100.

19. Edward M. Graham and Michael E. Ebert, "Foreign Direct Investment and National Security: Fixing the Exon Florio Process," *World Economy* 14 (September 1991): 245–268.

20. Graham and Krugman, *Foreign Direct Investment in the United States*. For the distinction in policy options between foreign acquisitions in critical technology industries and foreign acquisitions of primary defense contractors, see Theodore H. Moran, *American Economic Policy and National Security* (New York: Council on Foreign Relations, 1993).

21. For a summary, see Robert Lipsey, *Outward Investment and the U.S. Economy* (Cambridge, Mass.: National Bureau of Economic Research, 1994); see also C. Fred Bergsten, Thomas Horst, and Theodore H. Moran, *American Multinationals and American Interests* (Washington, D.C.: Brookings Institution, 1978), chap. 3.

22. See Richard F. Caves, *Multinational Enterprise and Economic Analysis* (Cambridge, U.K.: Cambridge University Press, 1983).

23. *Economic Report of the President* (1994), pp. 114–115.

24. Wolfgang Stolper and Paul Samuelson, "Protection and Real Wages," *Review of Economic Studies* 9 (1941): 58–73.

25. Robert Z. Lawrence and Matthew J. Slaughter, "International Trade and American Wages in the 1980s: Giant Sucking Sound or Small Hiccup?" *Brookings Papers: Microeconomics* 2 (1993): 161–226; and *World Development Report 1995: Workers in an Integrating World* (New York: Oxford University Press for the World Bank, 1995).

26. There would still be flows of foreign direct investment across borders as companies sought to exploit opportunities in external markets.

27. Joseph Nye, *Bound to Lead: The Changing Nature of American Power* (New York: Basic Books, 1990).

PART II

STATECRAFT, INTERVENTION, AND INTERNATIONAL ORDER

II

The New World Order

HENRY KISSINGER

Almost as if according to some natural law, in every century there seems to emerge a country with the power, the will, and the intellectual and moral impetus to shape the entire international system in accordance with its own values. In the seventeenth century, France under Cardinal Richelieu in troduced the modern approach to international relations, based on the nation-state and motivated by national interest as its ultimate purpose. In the eighteenth century, Great Britain elaborated the concept of the balance of power, which dominated European diplomacy for the next 200 years. In the nineteenth century, Metternich's Austria reconstructed the Concert of Europe and Bismarck's Germany dismantled it, reshaping European diplomacy into a cold-blooded game of power politics.

In the twentieth century, no country has influenced international relations as decisively and at the same time as ambivalently as the United States. No society has more firmly insisted on the inadmissibility of intervention in the domestic affairs of other states or has more passionately asserted that its own values were universally applicable. No nation has been more pragmatic in the day-to-day conduct of its diplomacy or more ideological in the pursuit of its historic moral convictions. No country has been more reluctant to engage itself abroad, even while undertaking alliances and commitments of unprecedented reach and scope.

The singularities that America has ascribed to itself throughout its history have produced two contradictory attitudes toward foreign policy. The first is that America serves its values best by perfecting democracy at home, thereby acting as a beacon for the rest of mankind; the second, that America's values impose on it an obligation to crusade for them around the world. Torn between nostalgia for a pristine past and yearning for a perfect future, American thought has oscillated between isolationism and commitment, though, since the end of the Second World War, the realities of interdependence have predominated.

Both schools of thought—America as beacon and America as crusader—envision as normal a global international order based on democracy, free commerce, and international law. Since no such system has ever existed, its evocation often appears to other societies as utopian, if not naive. Still, foreign skepticism never dimmed the idealism of Woodrow Wilson, Franklin Roosevelt, or Ronald Reagan, or indeed of any other twentieth-century American president. If anything, it has spurred America's faith that history can be overcome and that if the world truly wants peace, it needs to apply America's moral prescriptions.

Both schools of thought were products of the American experience. Though other republics have existed, none had been consciously created to vindicate the idea of liberty. No other country's population had chosen to head for a new continent and tame its wilderness in the name of freedom and prosperity for all. Thus the two approaches, the isolationist and the missionary, so contradictory on the surface, reflected a common underlying faith: The United States possessed the world's best system of government, and the rest of mankind could attain peace and prosperity by abandoning traditional diplomacy and adopting America's reverence for international law and democracy.

America's journey through international politics has been a triumph of faith over experience. Since the time America entered the arena of world politics in 1917, it has been so preponderant in strength and so convinced of the rightness of its ideals that this century's major international agreements have been embodiments of American values—from the League of Nations and the Kellogg-Briand Pact to the United Nations Charter and the Helsinki Final Act. The collapse of Soviet communism marked the intellectual vindication of American ideals and, ironically, brought America face to face with the kind of world it had been seeking to escape throughout its history. In the emerging international order, nationalism

has gained a new lease on life. Nations have pursued self-interest more frequently than high-minded principle, and they have competed more than they have cooperated. There is little evidence to suggest that this age-old mode of behavior has changed, or that it is likely to change in the decades ahead.

What is new about the emerging world order is that, for the first time, the United States can neither withdraw from the world nor dominate it. America cannot change the way it has perceived its role throughout its history, nor should it want to. When America entered the international arena, it was young and robust and had the power to make the world conform to its vision of international relations. By the end of the Second World War in 1945, the United States was so powerful (at one point about 35 percent of the world's entire economic production was American) that it seemed as if it was destined to shape the world according to its preferences.

John F. Kennedy declared confidently in 1961 that America was strong enough to "pay any price, bear any burden" to ensure the success of liberty. Three decades later, the United States is in less of a position to insist on the immediate realization of all its desires. Other countries have grown into Great Power status. The United States now faces the challenge of reaching its goals in stages, each of which is an amalgam of American values and geopolitical necessities. One of the new necessities is that a world comprising several states of comparable strength must base its order on some concept of equilibrium—an idea with which the United States has never felt comfortable.

When American thinking on foreign policy and European diplomatic traditions encountered each other at the Paris Peace Conference of 1919, the differences in historical experience became dramatically evident. The European leaders sought to refurbish the existing system according to familiar methods; the American peace-makers believed that the Great War had resulted not from intractable geopolitical conflicts but from flawed European practices. In his famous Fourteen Points, Woodrow Wilson told the Europeans that, henceforth, the international system should be based not on the balance of power but on ethnic self-determination, that their security should depend not on military alliances but on collective security, and that their diplomacy should no longer be conducted secretly by experts but on the basis of "open agreements, openly arrived at." Clearly, Wilson had come not so much to discuss the terms for ending a war or for restoring the existing international order, as he had to recast a whole system of international relations as it had been practiced for nearly three centuries.

For as long as Americans have been reflecting on foreign policy, they have ascribed Europe's travails to the balance-of-power system. And since the time Europe first had to concern itself with American foreign policy, its leaders have looked askance at America's self-appointed mission of global reform. Each side has behaved as if the other had freely chosen its mode of diplomatic behavior and could have, were it wiser or less bellicose, selected some other, more agreeable, method.

In fact, both the American and the European approaches to foreign policy were the products of their own unique circumstances. Americans inhabited a nearly empty continent shielded from predatory powers by two vast oceans and with weak countries as neighbors. Since America confronted no power in need of being balanced, it could hardly have occupied itself with the challenges of equilibrium even if its leaders had been seized by the bizarre notion of replicating European conditions amidst a people who had only recently turned their backs on Europe.

The anguishing dilemmas of security that tormented European nations did not touch America for nearly 150 years. When they did, America twice participated in the world wars that had been started by the nations of Europe. In each instance, by the time America got involved, the balance of power had already failed to operate, producing this paradox: The balance of power, which most Americans disdained, in fact assured American security as long as it functioned as it was designed, and it was the breakdown of the balance of power that drew America into international politics.

The nations of Europe did not choose the balance of power as the means for regulating their relations out of innate quarrelsomeness or an Old World love of intrigue. If the emphasis on democracy and international law was the product of America's unique sense of security, European diplomacy had been forged in the school of hard knocks.

Europe was thrown into balance-of-power politics when its first choice, the medieval dream of universal empire, collapsed and a host of states of more or less equal strength arose from the ashes of that ancient aspiration. When a group of states so constituted are obliged to deal with one another, there are only two possible outcomes: Either one state becomes so strong that it dominates all the others and creates an empire, or no state is ever quite powerful enough to achieve that goal. In the latter case, the pretensions of the most aggressive member of the international community are kept in check by a combination of the others; in other words, by the operation of a balance of power. The balance-of-power system did not purport to avoid crises or even wars. When working properly, it was meant to limit both the ability of states to dominate others and the scope of conflicts. Its goal was not peace so much as stability and moderation. By definition, a balance-of-power arrangement cannot satisfy every member of the international system completely; it works best when it keeps dissatisfaction below the level at which the aggrieved party will seek to overthrow the international order.

Theorists of the balance of power often leave the impression that it is the natural form of international relations. In fact, balance-of-power systems have existed only rarely in human history. The Western Hemisphere has never known one, nor has the territory of contemporary China since the end of the period of the warring states, over 2,000 years ago. For the greatest part of humanity and the longest periods of history, empire has been the typical mode of government. Empires have no interest in operating within an international system; they aspire to be the international system. Empires have no need for a balance of power. That is how the United States has conducted its foreign policy in the Americas, and China through most of its history in Asia.

In the West, the only examples of functioning balance-of-power systems were among the city-states of ancient Greece and Renaissance Italy, and the European state system that arose out of the Peace of Westphalia in 1648. The distinguishing feature of these systems was to elevate a fact of life —the existence of a number of states of substantially equal strength—into a guiding principle of world order.

Intellectually, the concept of the balance of power reflected the convictions of all the major political thinkers of the Enlightenment. In their view, the universe, including the political sphere, operated according to rational principles that balanced one another. Seemingly random acts by reasonable men would, in their totality, tend toward the common good, though the proof of this proposition was elusive in the century of almost constant conflict that followed the Thirty Years' War.

Adam Smith, in *The Wealth of Nations,* maintained that an "invisible hand" would distill general economic well-being out of selfish individual economic actions. In *The Federalist Papers,* Madison argued that, in a large enough republic, the various political "factions" selfishly pursuing their own interests would, by a kind of automatic mechanism, forge a proper domestic harmony. The concepts of the separation of powers and of checks and balances, as conceived by Montesquieu and embodied in the American Constitution, reflected an identical view. The purpose of the separation of powers was to avoid despotism, not to achieve harmonious government; each branch of the government, in the pursuit of its own interests, would restrain excess and thereby serve the common good. The same principles were applied to international affairs. By pursuing its own selfish interests, each state was presumed to contribute to progress, as if some unseen hand were guaranteeing that freedom of choice for each state assured well-being for all.

For over a century, this expectation seemed to be fulfilled. After the dislocations caused by the French Revolution and the Napoleonic Wars, the leaders of Europe restored the balance of power at the Congress of Vienna in 1815 and softened the brutal reliance on power by seeking to moderate international conduct through moral and legal bonds. Yet by the end of the nineteenth century, the European balance-of-power system returned to the principles of power politics, in a far more unforgiving environment. Facing down the adversary became the standard method of diplomacy, leading to one test of strength after another. Finally, in 1914, a crisis arose from which no one shrank. Europe never fully recovered world leadership after the catastrophe of the First World War. The United States emerged as the dominant player and Woodrow Wilson soon made it clear that his country refused to play by European rules.

At no time in its history has America participated in a balance-of-power system. Before the two world wars, America benefited from the operation of the balance of power without being involved in its maneuvers, enjoying the luxury of castigating it at will. During the Cold War, America was engaged in an ideological, political, and strategic struggle with the Soviet Union, in which a two-power world operated according to principles quite different from those of a balance-of-power system. In a two-power world, there can be no pretense that conflict leads to the common good; any gain for one side is a loss for the other. Victory without war was in fact what America achieved in the Cold War, a victory that has now obliged it to confront the dilemma described by George Bernard Shaw: "There are two tragedies in life. One is to lose your heart's desire. The other is to gain it."

American leaders have taken their values so much for granted that they rarely recognize how revolutionary and unsettling these values can appear to others. No other society has asserted that the principles of ethical conduct apply to international conduct in the same way that they do to the individual— a notion that is the exact opposite of Richelieu's *raison d'état*. America has maintained that the prevention of war is as much a legal as a diplomatic challenge, and that what it resists is not change as such but the method of change, especially the use of force. A Bismarck or a Disraeli would have ridiculed the proposition that foreign policy is about method rather than substance, if indeed he had understood it. No nation has ever imposed the moral demands on itself that America has. And no country has so tormented itself over the gap between its moral values, which are by definition absolute, and the imperfection inherent in the concrete situations to which they must be applied.

During the Cold War, the unique American approach to foreign policy was remarkably appropriate to the challenge at hand. There was a deep ideological conflict, and only one country, the United States, possessed the full panoply of means—political, economic, and military—to organize the defense of the noncommunist world. A nation in such a position is able to insist on its views and can often avoid the problems facing the statesmen of less favored societies: Their means oblige them to pursue goals less ambitious than their hopes, and their circumstances require them to approach even those goals in stages.

In the Cold War world, the traditional concepts of power had substantially broken down. Most of history has displayed a synthesis of military, political, and economic strength, which in general has proved to be symmetrical. In the Cold War period, the various elements of power became quite distinct. The former Soviet Union was a military superpower and at the same time an economic dwarf. It was also possible for a country to be an economic giant but to be militarily irrelevant, as was the case with Japan.

In the post–Cold War world, the various elements are likely to grow more congruent and more symmetrical. The relative military power of the United States will gradually decline. The absence of a clear-cut adversary will produce domestic pressure to shift resources from defense to other priorities— a process that has already started. When there is no longer a single threat and each country perceives its perils from its own national perspective, those societies that had nestled under American protection will feel compelled to assume greater responsibility for their own security. Thus, the operation of the new international system will move toward equilibrium even in the military field, though it may take some decades to reach that point. These tendencies will be even more pronounced in economics, where American predominance is already declining, and where it has become safer to challenge the United States.

The international system of the twenty-first century will be marked by a seeming contradiction: on the one hand, fragmentation; on the other, growing globalization. On the level of the relations among states, the new order will be more like the European state system of the eighteenth and nineteenth centuries than the rigid patterns of the Cold War. It will contain at least six major powers—the United States, Europe, China, Japan, Russia, and probably India—as well as a multiplicity of medium-sized and smaller countries. At the same time, international relations have become truly global for the first time. Communications are instantaneous; the world economy operates on all continents simultaneously. A whole set of issues has surfaced that can only be dealt with on a worldwide basis, such as nuclear proliferation, the environment, the population explosion, and economic interdependence.

For America, reconciling differing values and very different historical experiences among countries of comparable significance will be a novel experience and a major departure from either the isolation of the last century or the de facto hegemony of the Cold War. Equally, the other major players are facing difficulties in adjusting to the emerging world order.

Europe, the only part of the modern world ever to operate a multistate system, invented the concepts of the nation-state, sovereignty, and the balance of power. These ideas dominated international affairs for the better part of three centuries. But none of Europe's erstwhile practitioners of *raison d'état* are now strong enough to act as principals in the emerging international order. They are attempting to compensate for this relative weakness by creating a unified Europe, an effort that absorbs much of their energies. But even if they were to succeed, no automatic guidelines for the conduct of a unified Europe on the global stage would be at hand, since such a political entity has never existed before.

Throughout its history, Russia has been a special case. It arrived late on the European scene—well after France and Great Britain had been consolidated—and none of the traditional principles of European diplomacy seemed to apply to it. Bordering on three different cultural spheres—Europe, Asia, and the Muslim world—Russia contained populations of each and hence was never a national state in the European sense. Constantly changing shape as its rulers annexed contiguous territories, Russia was an empire out of scale in comparison with any of the European countries. Moreover, with every new conquest, the character of the state changed as it incorporated another brand-new, restive, non-Russian ethnic group. This was one of the reasons Russia felt obliged to maintain huge armies whose size was unrelated to any plausible threat to its external security.

Torn between obsessive insecurity and proselytizing zeal, between the requirements of Europe and the temptations of Asia, the Russian Empire always had a role in the European equilibrium but was never emotionally a part of it. The requirements of conquest and of security became merged in the minds of Russian leaders. Since the Congress of Vienna, the Russian Empire has placed its military forces on foreign soil more often than any other major power. Analysts frequently explain Russian expansionism as stemming from a sense of insecurity. But Russian writers have far more often justified Russia's outward thrust as a messianic vocation. Russia on the march rarely showed a sense of limits; whenever it was thwarted, it tended to withdraw into sullen resentment. For most of its history, Russia has been a cause looking for opportunity.

Postcommunist Russia finds itself within borders that reflect no historical precedent. Like Europe, it will have to devote much of its energy to redefining its identity. Will it seek to return to its historical rhythm and restore the lost empire? Will it shift its center of gravity eastward and become a more active participant in Asian diplomacy? By what principles and methods will it react to the upheavals around its borders, especially in the volatile Middle East? Russia will always be essential to world order and, in the inevitable turmoil associated with answering these questions, a potential menace to it.

China also faces a world order that is new to it. For 2,000 years, the Chinese Empire had united its world under a single imperial rule. To be sure, that rule had faltered at times. Wars occurred in China no less frequently than they did in Europe. But since they generally took place among contenders for the imperial authority, they were more in the nature of civil rather than international wars and, sooner or later, invariably led to the emergence of some new central power.

Before the nineteenth century, China never had a neighbor capable of contesting its preeminence and never imagined that such a state could arise. Conquerors from abroad overthrew Chinese dynasties, only to be absorbed into Chinese culture to such an extent that they continued traditions of the Middle Kingdom. The notion of the sovereign equality of states did not exist in China; outsiders were considered barbarians and were relegated to a tributary relationship—that was how the first British envoy to Beijing was received in the eighteenth century. China disdained sending ambassadors abroad but was not above using distant barbarians to overcome the ones nearby. Yet this was a strategy for emergencies, not a day-to-day operational system like the European balance of power, and it failed to

produce the sort of permanent diplomatic establishment characteristic of Europe. China became a humiliated subject of European colonialism in the nineteenth century, and it re-emerged only after the Second World War, into a multipolar world unprecedented in its history.

Japan had also cut itself off from all contact with the outside world. For 500 years before it was forcibly opened by Commodore Matthew Perry in 1854, Japan did not even deign to balance the barbarians against one another or to invent tributary relationships, as the Chinese had. Closed off from the outside world, Japan prided itself on its unique customs, gratified its military tradition by civil war, and rested its internal structure on the conviction that its unique culture was impervious to foreign influence, superior to it, and, in the end, would defeat it rather than absorb it.

In the Cold War, when the Soviet Union was the dominant security threat, Japan was able to identify its foreign policy with America, thousands of miles away. The new world order, with its multiplicity of challenges, will almost certainly oblige a country with so proud a past to reexamine its reliance on a single ally. Japan is bound to become more sensitive to the Asian balance of power than is possible for America, in a different hemisphere and facing in three directions—across the Atlantic, across the Pacific, and toward South America. China, Korea, and Southeast Asia will acquire quite a different significance for Japan than for the United States, and they will inaugurate a more autonomous and more self-reliant Japanese foreign policy.

As for India, which is now emerging as the major power in South Asia, its foreign policy is in many ways the last vestige of the heyday of European imperialism, leavened by the traditions of an ancient culture. Before the arrival of the British, the subcontinent had not been ruled as a single political unit for millennia. British colonization was accomplished with small military forces because, at first, the local population saw these as the replacement of one set of conquerors by another. But after it established unified rule, the British Empire was undermined by the very values of popular government and cultural nationalism it had imported into India. Yet, as a nation-state, India is a newcomer. Absorbed by the struggle to feed its vast population, India dabbled in the nonaligned movement during the Cold War, but it has yet to assume a role commensurate with its size on the international political stage.

Thus, in effect, none of the most important countries that must build a new world order have had any experience with the multistate system that is emerging. Never before has a new world order had to be assembled from so many different perceptions, or on so global a scale. Nor has any previous order had to combine the attributes of the historic balance-of-power systems with global democratic opinion and the exploding technology of the contemporary period.

In retrospect, all international systems appear to have an inevitable symmetry. Once they are established, it is difficult to imagine how history might have evolved had other choices been made or, indeed, whether any other choices had been possible. When an international order first comes into being, many choices may be open to it. But each choice constricts the universe of remaining options. Because complexity inhibits flexibility, early choices are especially crucial. Whether an international order is relatively stable, like the one that emerged from the Congress of Vienna, or highly volatile, like those that emerged from the Peace of Westphalia and the Treaty of Versailles, depends on the degree to which they reconcile what makes the constituent societies feel secure with what they consider just.

The two international systems that were the most stable—that of the Congress of Vienna and the one dominated by the United States after the Second World War —had the advantage of uniform perceptions. The statesmen at Vienna were aristocrats who saw intangibles in the same way and agreed on fundamentals; the American leaders who shaped the postwar world emerged from an intellectual tradition of extraordinary coherence and vitality.

The order that is now emerging will have to be built by statesmen who represent vastly different cultures. They run huge bureaucracies of such complexity that, often, their energy is more consumed by serving the administrative machinery than by defining a purpose. They rise to eminence by means of qualities that are not necessarily those needed to govern and that are even less suited to building an international order. And the only available model of a multistate system is one built by western societies, which many of the participants may reject. Yet the rise and fall of previous world orders based on many states—from the Peace of Westphalia to our time—is the only experience on which one can draw in trying to understand the challenges facing contemporary statesmen. The study of history offers no manual of instructions that can be applied automatically; history teaches by analogy, shedding light on the likely consequences of comparable situations. But each generation must determine for itself which circumstances are in fact comparable.

Intellectuals analyze the operations of international systems; statesmen build them. And there is a vast difference between the perspective of an analyst and that of a statesman. The analyst can choose which problem he wishes to study, whereas the statesman's problems are imposed on him. The analyst can allot whatever time is necessary to come to a clear conclusion; the overwhelming challenge to the statesman is the pressure of time. The analyst runs no risk; if his conclusions prove wrong, he can write another treatise. The statesman is permitted only one guess; his mistakes are irretrievable. The analyst has available to him all the facts; he will be judged on his intellectual power. The statesman must act on assessments that cannot be proved at the time that he is making them; he will be judged by history on the basis of how wisely he managed the inevitable change and, above all, by how well he preserves the peace. That is why examining how statesmen have dealt with the problem of world order—what worked or failed and why—is not the end of understanding contemporary diplomacy, though it may be its beginning.

12

The Varieties of Intervention

Conditions for Success

CHESTER A. CROCKER

It is a sign of the times that there is renewed interest in studying the lessons we have learned from intervention in foreign conflicts. Generations of policy elites have been learning and revising lessons about war and peace at least since Thucydides' time. We do this in cycles and spasms when we sense that a historic shift of basic importance requires fresh and profound commentary or—simply—when things are not going very well.

This chapter discusses a variety of conflict types and situations in which third parties intervened. The term "intervention" is intended to convey the full range of methods and tools whereby a variety of external parties—for instance the United States, other major powers, the United Nations, and nongovernmental organizations (NGOs)—may become involved in attempts to cope with conflict. It is important to look at both nonmilitary and military forms of intervention, at the question of timing and preemption, and at the problem of defining success in such matters. Finally, this chapter sug-gests some lessons about the necessary conditions for success. Its purpose is not to advocate or critique intervention as such, but to advance a basis for prudent thinking on the topic.

The question of engagement in the management and resolution of conflicts is not one that can be answered by slogans or simplistic reference to degrees of internationalism, unilateralism, or perceived moral imperatives. It is increasingly apparent that students and practitioners alike have to do their homework case by case, shunning abstract formulas and relearning the value of apparently pedestrian notions such as good judgment, operational competence, and the centrality of leadership. If we can learn from the bittersweet experience of past choices, our current state of strategic disorientation may pass.

VARIETIES OF CONFLICT

The post-1945 period has witnessed a rapid decline in traditional interstate conflict, and a comparable rise in internal strife: civil wars, anticolonial and anti-imperial wars, ethnic-religious conflicts, wars over regime legitimacy, wars to overthrow foreign or minority rule and other repressive systems, and wars of governmental and territorial fragmentation (secession, imperial collapse, or failed states). This trend appears to be holding. It is reflected in the distribution of UN peace operations: Nine of the fourteen operations mounted between 1945 and 1987 involved essentially interstate conflict, whereas only six of the twenty-two operations begun between 1988 and 1994 were at least partially interstate in character (Afghanistan-Pakistan, Iran-Iraq, Cuban withdrawal from Angola, Central America, Chad-Libya, and Iraq-Kuwait).[1] Significantly, none of this latter group involved substantial numbers of UN troops (blue helmets).

As the former USSR and Yugoslavia collapsed, the zone of actual or potential conflict has expanded. Much of this conflict potential is also of the internal variety. In regions where traditional interstate conflicts continue—the Middle East and South Asia—conflict tends to be embedded in regional security complexes reflecting ethnic and sectarian divisions. Pure cases of classic interstate rivalries (China and the Spratlies, Iran-Iraq, Iraq-Kuwait, Peru-Ecuador) are harder to find.

It is tempting to view this shift as the explanation for the difficulties we encounter when we "intervene." After all, it is common knowledge that it is especially difficult for outsiders to manage internal conflicts. Familiarity of the sort acquired in civil wars appears to breed a special contempt for the enemy and a heightened incentive for aggressive brutality. When states and empires fall apart, the lesson learned by affected communities is to strike first or pay the price.

The superficial implication is that outsiders would be well-advised to steer clear of trying to manage such affairs. When

protracted social conflicts or ethnic wars are hot, they are simply too hard to handle. Better to let them ripen, say some observers; wait until the parties reach the point of mutual exhaustion or until one side capitulates. Outsiders, some argue, are best advised to wait until there is a peace to make—or, better yet, to keep—before becoming engaged.

Another argument against intervention in internal wars is our vestigial uneasiness about crossing the sovereignty line and getting into other people's business. Not only are outsiders not necessarily best equipped to do these things; they have no self-evident mandate to do them. Nation building, that optimistic term from the early 1960s, was discredited in Vietnam and has hardly been rehabilitated in Somalia. Americans, one might add, have particular handicaps as intervenors in domestic conflicts abroad: Our moralistic political culture and historic aversion to entanglements with dubious or odorous partners clash with real-world conditions that are so very unlike our ideal vision. For all these reasons, we have learned to recognize that the practical impact of intervening in civil wars and nationalist revolutions can be likened to the impact of walking in front of a moving train.

But when arguments like this are marshaled as reasons the United States or the West can do no better than we have done as of late 1995 in Bosnia or Rwanda or to bolster the contention that we should not have gone into Somalia, it is time to take a closer look. We cannot allow the genuine intractability of some forms of domestic strife to become an all-purpose escape clause, relieving us of the burdens of thought, analysis, and strategic leadership. Was it a mistake for the United Nations and the major powers that supported it to (1) oversee the decolonization of Namibia, (2) supervise the Cambodian settlement and elections, (3) sustain the unity and territorial integrity of the Congo (now Zaire) 30 years ago, or

(4) monitor the Salvadoran settlement of 1991? Would we support such efforts today, in the absence of the Cold War logic of yesterday? What are the major differences among the plethora of current and recent cases, and where should we draw the lines?

We should start by reminding ourselves that there are many kinds and levels of conflict, and we should not be stampeded into a pessimistic, one-dimensional mantra after watching a few bad days of CNN. The payoff and the price of successful intervention depend on what phenomena we are responding to. Yes, we probably should avoid military entanglement in nationalist revolutions and civil wars pitting whole groups and classes against one another—unless there are overarching strategic reasons that demand it, as in the case of the United States in Afghanistan and the United Kingdom in Northern Ireland, but not as in the case of the United States in Vietnam. Equally, the record shows that intervention in some types of internal conflict can be effective when there are important stakes and high confidence in the possibility of shaping an acceptable outcome at a reasonable price. Examples include the United States and United Nations in El Salvador, the United Nations in Mozambique and Namibia, France in Chad and Zaire, the United States in Grenada, and Great Britain during the terminal colonial phase in Malaya, Rhodesia-Zimbabwe, Swaziland, and East Africa.

It may be that internal wars based on seemingly primordial sentiments tend toward zero-sum thinking and the progressive elimination of neutral or common ground. Military intervention in cases of this sort (Tajikistan? Sudan?) may require the intervenor to occupy the country and suppress the fighting. There are few volunteers for open-ended imperial policing today, apart, perhaps, from the self-interested Russians along their southern flanks and the Chinese in Tibet.

Equally important, however, there are few pure cases of ethnic conflict in the sense of a spontaneous mass eruption of ethnic antagonisms. A strong case can be made that an apparently pure case such as Rwanda was in part an ersatz creation of ambitious, ethnic entrepreneurs. Perhaps the purest of such cases are, in fact, nationalist rejections of alien, minority, or foreign rule—as happened in Afghanistan, Dutch East Indies–Indonesia in 1945–1949, South Africa, Namibia, Algeria in 1954–1962, Rhodesia-Zimbabwe, and Vietnam. But even in such ostensibly clear cases, the struggles had a complex history and their outcome was influenced by many local and external factors.

When reviewing contemporary conflicts such as Bosnia, Liberia, Sri Lanka, and Rwanda, great care should be taken with the sweeping label "ethnic conflict."[2] In these cases, as in so many others over the past fifty years, reality is shaped decisively by several factors:

- the actions and inactions of foreigners,
- the case-specific balance of forces and the possibilities of asserting external leverage on the parties,
- the goals and ambitions of individual leaders and the opportunities presented to them for achieving those goals, and
- the availability of military hardware and its relevance to the specific circumstances of local conflict.

Upon close inspection, we will find that the much-advertised syndrome labeled ethnic conflict has its roots in a mix of special situations and concrete local factors: the collapse of central institutions, the holding of ill-prepared elections, the emergence of entrepreneurial politicians who use ethnicity as a platform and tool, the splintering of armies and the rise of warlords, unrestrained arms transfers, and the availability of natural and financial resources (legal or criminal) to fuel the descent into violence. In sum, we should be looking beyond the general notion of ethnicity to draw lessons about the sorts of situations that serve as tinder for the fires we associate with the post–Cold War era.

SOME REFLECTIONS ON PREEMPTIVE ACTION

If there is a general lesson that flows from these cases, it is not self-evident that the world's leading nations should look the other way or define local conflicts out of existence by claiming that they are beyond our reach and our interests. Rather, the lesson is to underscore the benefits of preemptive engagement in promoting negotiated alternatives to continued repression or expanding violence and upheaval. Western third parties played these roles successfully in Indonesia in the 1940s, the Middle East for the past thirty years, and southern Africa in the 1970s and 1980s.

A variant on preemptive engagement is the face-saving exit engineered by incumbents themselves, who prefer to retain a measure of control of the process by acting preemptively to promote political solutions: Examples include Gorbachev in Afghanistan, de Gaulle in Algeria, and de Klerk in South Africa. Farsighted incumbents thereby obviate the need for third-party, external intervention. Sometimes, however, they need a little help to recognize the merits of acting preemptively. When this does not occur spontaneously, outsiders can sometimes play a decisive role in encouraging soft landings that preempt drawn-out bloodshed (Reagan in the Philippines, Clinton in Haiti) or dramatic showdowns (Thatcher in Zimbabwe, Bush in Ethiopia).

Once we recognize the importance of preemption, how do we recognize the potential tinder that fuels intractable internal strife, and what can we do about it? One

answer is to underscore the fundamental importance of the process by which politicized conflicts become militarized. (This may or may not have much to do with ethnicity; more likely, it relates to such variables as arms supplies, local law and order, and the relative strength of governmental institutions compared to their adversaries.) Once domestic political conflict becomes militarized, the task of conflict resolution is immeasurably complicated, since the special character and requirements of military hierarchies must be factored into the settlement. To turn this point around, the price of inaction rises dramatically once the political-military threshold is crossed and constituencies with a vested interest in warfare, weapons procurement, and military resource mobilization become entrenched.

Examples of preemptive action to control the tinder include the following:

- *Deferring elections in societies not yet prepared to hold them and likely to become more polarized and fragile as a result of an election.* A poorly prepared and inadequately supervised election in Angola in 1992 led directly to escalated warfare. Separate elections in the republics of the former Yugoslavia in 1990 empowered ethnic nationalists and paved the way for the wars of disintegration. Outsiders should tread warily in promoting and legitimizing electoral solutions to conflicts. They should also encourage creative thinking about power-sharing formulas to accompany elections and provide a safety net beneath them. To be sure, there is a natural tension between peacemaking and democratization: In a crunch, the former comes first, as the South Africans have shown the world.

- *Getting serious about the requirements of disarming, retraining, and reintegrating former combatants into civil society.* Much more could be done to create tailored, multilateral programs for these purposes, so that political leaders and military commanders can make peace and then can live up to their commitments. Once again, Angola in 1991–1992 showed how not to do it: Inadequate resources were made available for programs to attract soldiers and fighters to the encampment sites and keep them there, a weakness that spawned distrust, cheating, and an early return to battle. Problems with demobilization and reintegration of combatants also helped re-ignite fighting in Afghanistan, Cambodia, and Nicaragua. These issues were handled far more skillfully in the El Salvador settlement and in Mozambique, where soldiers actually protested in hopes of being demobilized more rapidly, owing to the inducements offered when compared to the poor conditions of service. Stopping a war requires preemptive action such as reintegrating, channeling, and supporting marginalized groups that are good at causing mayhem and living by the gun.

- *Resisting calls for secession and territorial fragmentation as "solutions" to internal strife.* It is probably too early to draw sweeping lessons from the three most prominent post–Cold War examples: Ethiopia-Eritrea, USSR–former Soviet Union, and the former Yugoslavia. But, we are entitled at a minimum to note that the Eritreans earned their autonomy on the battlefield over thirty years of struggle and, even so, they negotiated an agreed formula for separation and future relations with the Ethiopians. This is more than a question of procedural niceties, as the Bosnian tragedy illustrates. Warren Zimmermann reminds us that Yugoslavia's breakup was identified as the worst possible case in U.S. embassy analyses of the early 1990s, a forecast supported at the time by Bosnian leader Alija

Izetbekovic, who viewed Yugoslavia's survival in some form as essential to Bosnia's own survival.[3] Western disarray and collapse on the principle of agreed, negotiated separation led directly to war. We should think twice about calling for the breakup of more states. If events seem to be headed that way, we should underscore the central importance of a negotiated outcome (as happened in Czechoslovakia). If violence looms, we may need to intervene with massive diplomatic force (that is, threatening denial of all forms of international status) to insist on appropriate norms and procedures to regularize the transformation.

THE VARIETIES OF INTERVENTION

In serious cases in which preemptive activities fail to avert or resolve violent conflict, it is worth underscoring that there is a vast range of intervention options between doing nothing and sending in the U.S. Army's 10th Mountain Division. The spectrum varies with the different stages in the history of a conflict. Conflict resolution theorists speak of entry points during the "life cycle" of a conflict. (See chapter 26 in this volume, "Early Warning and Preventive Diplomacy," by Michael Lund.) Suffice it to say that how third parties can intervene most effectively depends upon (1) their own capabilities, leverage, and linkage to the conflict; (2) the conflict's status, form, and ripeness; and (3) the character of the parties to the conflict, their accessibility, and their decision-making systems. For the United States (and other leading international powers), the issue is what kind of intervention, if any, is responsive to both the circumstances of the conflict itself (including the nature of the local and regional environment) and to the level of our interest in it. The latter point subsumes, of course, the question of whether strong executive leadership can be mobilized to create and nurture adequate domestic public support for the enterprise at hand.

A crucial step, easily overlooked in popular commentary, is analyzing how the "least bad" form of intervention compares with the price of doing nothing at all. Experience in such places as Afghanistan, the former Yugoslavia, and Liberia suggests that it is too easy for decision makers to adopt a narrow view of the choices before them and thereby overlook the political and economic consequences of inaction. At root, this is a political question: How can we encourage bureaucratic and political structures to measure the known price of sticking their neck out and doing something against the less tangible and measurable costs associated with having to pick up the pieces later—human casualties, loss of political prestige, famine and refugee relief, economic reconstruction, and peacekeeping?

In any event, the range of possible interventions is considerable. An interstate conflict situation may literally demand an immediate military response akin to a police action to uphold the law or maintain collective security, as was the case in Operation Desert Storm. But this is an exceptional rather than a typical case in the current global system. Another case, perhaps more typical, is that of Sri Lanka, where a smoldering internal war moves fitfully through stages of apparent ripening, without attracting and sustaining constructive engagement of any external governmental intervenor. India's experience of direct military and diplomatic intervention there in the 1980s was unrewarding for everyone concerned. On the unofficial side, nongovernmental groups have played minor supportive roles behind a sputtering local "peace process" in Sri Lanka.

Diplomatic intervention for conflict management can take several forms. When it is sustained and becomes a central feature of policy toward a region or country—as in the U.S. mediation initiatives in the Middle East and southern Africa over the past twenty years or so—it makes sense to describe such third-party diplomatic intervention as strategic. Conflict management and resolution have become the essence of U.S. regional strategy, and its requirements affect all other regional policies such as arms transfers, covert action, trade and sanctions, and human rights.

Such strategic engagements have successfully advanced U.S. interests when pursued coherently and consistently over time, using U.S. influence to leverage the parties toward agreements.[4] Where direct U.S. leverage is limited, we have had to borrow that of others, as in southern Africa where American diplomacy has been tightly integrated with British efforts in a series of productive initiatives to settle conflicts in Zimbabwe, Namibia, Angola, Mozambique, and South Africa. Apart from the sustained, decades-long commitment to leading the Middle East peace process, there are few other examples of such strategic engagement in peacemaking today, by the United States or anyone else. The U.S.–European Union initiatives toward Bosnia from the early days of Vance-Owen through mid-1995 barely qualify, for want of coherence and effective linkage to and control over the parallel peacekeeping and peace enforcement operation on the ground.[5]

Episodic diplomatic intervention in stubborn, unripened cases, such as in Cyprus and Kashmir, and crisis-driven intervention when fighting flares up, as conducted by Jordan and Egypt when Yemen's fragile unity was shattered by secessionist moves in 1994, are more common than long-term strategic commitment to peacemaking. Unlike the latter, the episodic and crisis-driven types offer little chance for outsiders to develop substantial leverage apart from the leverage inherent in the balance of forces on the ground. (Sometimes, of course, it may take some changes in the military situation to bolster the arm of the negotiators and create fresh openings for settlement. However, this usually works much better when there already exists an active negotiating framework within which the parties and the intervenor operate.) In the case of crises, formulas for settlement may amount to little more than cease-fires that continue to break down until a fresh military status quo emerges. Such interventions represent limited, but nonetheless vital, efforts to suppress or contain the fighting, but they may have little to do with real settlement or resolution.

Periodic negotiation initiatives of the Cyprus type represent exploratory probes to test the parties' temperature, try out fresh ideas, or convey frustration over the gridlock. Such efforts may move the process along, but actual settlement must await a significant change in the underlying situation affecting the parties. Meanwhile, the de facto division of the local communities may harden attitudes and raise the price of a deal.

Finally, it is worth noting the range of potential intervenors. Military intervention in the modern period has taken the form of unilateral action by individual governments (France in Rwanda and Comoros, the United States in the Dominican Republic); ad hoc coalitions of the willing (Lebanon in the early 1980s); regional peacekeeping or peace enforcement efforts (NATO and the European Union in former Yugoslavia); and UN peace operations. A similarly broad range of governmental and intergovernmental players may intervene in nonmilitary ways (overt, covert, economic, diplomatic, public, or private) to manage and resolve conflict.

Increasingly, NGOs of all sorts, reflecting the vast array of western civil society, are intervening abroad and playing a role in conflict situations. Professional groups, media, specialized civil society and conflict resolution groups, humanitarian relief and development organizations, religious bodies, and human rights advocacy groups all belong on this list. Their actual and potential contributions are difficult to quantify, but they are often underestimated by official governmental bodies, just as they are typically overestimated by the NGO community itself. The International Committee of the Red Cross efforts in Sri Lanka and the lead role of the Sant'Egidio community, a Catholic lay group, in Mozambique and Algeria represent current examples of the nongovernmental sector attempting to fill a void. The Mozambique case exemplifies success, although credit must be shared with several governments, including Italy, Britain, Portugal, the United States, Zimbabwe, Botswana, Kenya, and South Africa, as well as with private individuals and UN officials.

Other chapters in this book illustrate in detail the range of potential interventions and intervenors that third parties may bring to bear at various points in the evolution of a conflict. Some interventions can only be conducted by governments or groups of governments, while others are best left to international economic or humanitarian institutions, creative individuals, nongovernmental agencies, and other actors. The spectrum of intervention includes actions taken before conflicting parties have agreed to negotiate and actions that can only be taken after they have reached agreement: sharing intelligence in support of confidence-building measures; external observing and monitoring of human rights commitments; assisting with demining operations to facilitate deployment of peace operations; helping to retrain and demobilize local forces; helping to strengthen or build local legal and judicial systems and to assist divided societies in coping with past injustice or humanitarian crimes; implementing programs to spread skills in intergroup relations, conflict resolution, and religious reconciliation; and implementing democracy-building assistance programs. In the end, there is an interdependence between the "harder" and "softer" forms of intervention, and an awareness of what they all share is the beginning of wisdom.

CONDITIONS FOR SUCCESSFUL INTERVENTION

The subject of intervention typically generates more heat than light. But with a body of modern experience to draw upon, it is possible to complement the previous discussion with some comments about the conditions for success.[6] Before doing so, it is important to underscore that success in most endeavors, including foreign policy, is an inherently relative notion. Success also depends upon the specific case at hand. As a general matter, however, it can be argued that decision makers in national and international security affairs too easily allow excessive expectations to cloud public debate and media coverage.

In some circumstances, success can legitimately be defined as the avoidance of major setbacks or disasters. In others, success may mean a marginal improvement in stabilizing, containing, and checking the human price and territorial spread of a volatile struggle. Finally, success may entail constructing building blocks for a settlement or even obtaining a fully implemented one, complete with resolution of the underlying issues. The short answer to the question of what connotes success is that it depends. But the important point is that those who decide to intervene (in whatever manner) have an obligation to develop their own definition of success and to keep it firmly in mind while laboring to avoid becoming part of the problem and making things worse. Success is unlikely unless the intervenor is equipped with a commitment to succeed, a willingness to take on critics and chal-

lengers, a readiness to offer cover to the inevitable doubters, and sufficient belief in the project to have a chance of shaping the terms of public debate.

Operational Conditions and Requirements

The intervenor requires the capacity for effective and prompt decision making. Whether intervention is military or nonmilitary (but especially when it is the former), there is simply no excuse for getting involved in other peoples' conflicts and then fooling around. Dual key decision systems, elaborate committees, and multiple vetoes do not work in highly complex, distant, and dangerous situations. If a job is worth doing, it is worth doing well. That means that someone must be placed in charge, held accountable, given the requisite mandate and resources, and steadily supported, or else replaced.

Interventions should be viewed as full-time work for those in charge. They should be run like a task force on an around-the-clock basis. This principle of coherent and clear intervention management is valid on an intergovernmental basis as well as within individual governments; similarly, it is valid for both diplomatic and military interventions. A recent study of the Somalia operation concluded: "The three chains of [military] command running during UNOSOM II [United Nations Operation in Somalia] underline the importance of a lesson that should be adapted from Murphy's Laws of Combat: If it takes more than ten seconds to explain the command arrangements, they probably won't work."[7] What is true at the level of military command and control is compounded when political decision makers and military commanders interact.

Prospective intervenors must be on guard for scenarios that risk converting intervention forces into targets or hostages. No armed forces of any kind (UN blue helmets or national units) should be deployed as tokens, symbols, or tripwires in the absence of either previous political agreements and "a peace to keep" or a firm and clear determination to punish credibly anyone who touches them. When power projection becomes overwhelmed by the rigors of force protection, the balance shifts against the outsiders. This is not a new lesson: The British learned it before agreeing to pull out of the Suez Canal Zone (1954) and before abandoning their facilities in Aden (1968); the French learned it at Dienbienphu (1953–1954) and did not repeat such errors in Algeria; the United States learned it in Lebanon in 1983; UNOSOM II learned it in south Mogadishu (May to October 1993); and the United Nations' Permanent Members relearned it in Bosnia.

Intervenors should never lose the political initiative, allow themselves to give away vetoes, or lose control of the clock. An early lesson in decisive interventionism came from London in late January 1964: With the approval of local civilian leaders, a combined arms force of some 5,000 men intervened at six places in three countries (Tanganyika, Kenya, and Uganda) to reverse mutinies, deter coups, and restore civilian control. The operations succeeded with minimal casualties. As another example, despite certain shortcomings, the United Nations Transitional Authority in Cambodia (UNTAC) achieved some key goals because it retained the united support of the main external actors, side-stepped the Khmer Rouge's noncooperation on military issues, and proceeded with elections despite the Khmer Rouge's boycott. The result: no gratuitous vetoes and a 90 percent voter turnout.

In April 1989, the South West African People's Organization (SWAPO), the Namibian nationalist movement, mounted an incursion from Angola into Namibia in hopes of acquiring by force the internal bases it never obtained at the negotiating table. This gambit was thwarted militarily by the South Africans and politically by the united stand taken by the United Nations' field leadership, the British, Americans, Cubans, Russians, and several neighboring African states. The Namibian independence process was put back on track. During the Unified Task Force (UNITAF) phase of intervention in Somalia (December 1992–April 1993), the U.S. leadership defined the military agenda, preemptively engaged both warlords and civilian constituencies, and jump-started a process of political dialogue. These gains quickly eroded when one warlord seized the initiative a few months later, after UNOSOM II took over from UNITAF. By October of that year, Washington was imposing withdrawal deadlines upon itself, a sure sign of mental fatigue and a collapse of political will.

There is an old saying about not changing horses midstream. It applies well to intervention. It would be difficult to imagine—with hindsight—a more poorly executed and timed "hand-off" than the UNITAF–UNOSOM II transition 1993 in Somalia. Within a mere four months of mounting the initial intervention, that intervention's leadership, doctrine, reporting channels and oversight, available resources, and mission mandate were transformed. Worse, the new mandate was significantly more ambitious, while the military resources available to support it were cut back severely. The collapse of continuity and institutional memory coincided with a shift in the power balance, inviting a test of strength. Somalia, of course, offers many lessons. But the seemingly casual handling of the transition guaranteed a subsequent foreign policy failure, even if the intervention was successful in saving hundreds of thousands of lives. The 1995 U.S.-UN transfer in Haiti has proceeded far better, suggesting that lessons can be learned fast.

It helps to know something about the place in which intervention is to occur. When a great nation decides to engage in the affairs of distant regions, it should first make sure that the necessary homework has been done and that the right people are on the policy team. Former President Bush understood this when he selected the team to plan and lead the U.S. effort in Somalia. Had senior people in key capitals known more about the true circumstances that spawned Rwanda's tragedy of 1994–1995, we might have been less blinded by our Somali backlash and more prepared to take an early stand against the butchery. Had the Russians done their homework on Afghanistan (and Ethiopia and Angola) in the late 1970s, they might have averted what Gorbachev later identified as the "bleeding wound" that forced Moscow to dump its ramshackle Third World empire.

A final operational condition for success relates to the special importance of key people, particular nations, and their military forces. The specific personal, professional, and political qualities of the intervenors can make an enormous difference. At one level, this point appears self-evident. But when analyzing vast and complex subjects, it is easy to slip into generalizations that overlook the most important variables. Just as it is hard to imagine Operation Desert Storm without the U.S. armed forces, it is important to identify the factors that have contributed to success in less overwhelming and dramatic interventions.

UN interventions that have worked are those that have enjoyed steady hands on the tiller and reliable and around-the-clock support in key local embassies and their home capitals. The United Nations Angola Verification Mission (UNAVEM II, 1991–1992) did not have these things. The United Nations Operation in Mozambique (ONUMOZ) benefited from both of them. UNTAC enjoyed solid political support from major powers; this ingredient was lost in UNOSOM II. People make a difference: The Namibian transition unquestionably gained from the leadership of an outstanding team of UN civilian and military people.

It is often said that the United Nations cannot handle peace enforcement and that saving failed states is just beyond the reach and political will of the Security Council's permanent members. These judgments sound sensible enough. But much depends upon the times and the context. To illustrate, it may be worth examining the United Nations Operation in the Congo (ONUC, 1960–1964). This, not Somalia, was the first time the international system decided "to paint a country blue." It did so by deploying nearly 20,000 troops plus a large civilian element to central Africa for four years at a cost of some $2 billion (1991 dollars). The effort succeeded in holding together a vast land facing huge internal and external challenges. It checked the further intrusion of the Cold War into central Africa and warded off unknown scenarios of disorder and instability affecting much of the region. ONUC did these things against great odds: divisions on the Security Council and in Africa and the absence of either a clear and agreed-upon mandate or an agreed-upon political framework. Enforcement was used (though without Chapter 7 blessing). ONUC's success reflects the determined leadership of the key civilian and military people who ran it both in the field and in New York; the consistent availability of major military units from key states, especially India; and the continuous assurance of U.S. logistical and financial backing (Washington paid nearly 50 percent of the military costs and 70 percent of the bill for civilian elements).[8]

Thirty years after ONUC, we may forget how divisive and controversial the operation was at the time—not in the United States where the importance of the UN role was understood, but internationally where its "can-do," improvised operating procedures and purposeful but expensive conduct cost it the support of both Moscow and Paris. ONUC had a chilling impact on peace operations generally and especially in Africa, but it helped stabilize a region and, in this sense, worked.

Strategic Conditions for Success

Turning now to the strategic and policy requirements for successful intervention, it is important to ask, first, whether outside intervention will continue to be necessary in the interests of managing and resolving conflict. The short answer is: Third-party intervention (of whatever form) will remain indispensable in the majority of conflict situations that exist around the globe.

To be sure, there are a few places where an indigenous process of peacemaking and reconciliation may prove successful. But even the South African case illustrates a significant pattern of outside factors supporting the locally led and controlled negotiation that produced the settlement and transition of 1993–1994. Strikingly few conflict-torn societies possess anything approaching the wealth of civil society institutions, mediation and negotiation skills, and leadership depth found in the South Africa of the 1980s and 1990s. These things do not exist in Tajikistan, Bosnia, Yemen, Burundi, Haiti, or most other troubled lands. Such resources for conflict resolution may have only just begun to emerge in Sri Lanka, Northern Ireland, and among Israelis and Palestinians.

But we should have no illusion that the process of acquiring local or indigenous capacity for solving conflict will be quick. Outsiders will be needed for the foreseeable future to move peacemaking forward—by undertaking direct actions and diplomatic initiatives, defining the parameters of toler-

able behavior, and legitimizing principles for settlement and for membership of the global system. Often, as in Mozambique during the 1992–1994 settlement process, they are needed to translate a "ripening" situation into the essential building blocks of the transition from war to peace. Without outsiders to provide much of the pressures, ideas, concepts, resources, deadlines, and inducements, there would have been no settlement. Without outsiders to sustain the settlement through several arduous years of implementation, the underlying agreements would have quickly collapsed.

This is not to advocate intervention by elements of the international community in every conflict. The limits on UN capability for effective intervention have been painfully demonstrated during the 1989–1992 crescendo of new peace operations. We have begun to learn that it does no service to the cause of international security to thrust the United Nations forward in order to be seen as doing something about a conflict, unless there is a basis for potential success. Similarly, the U.S. government must not and cannot play such a role everywhere. Nor can any combination of major powers set themselves up as world policemen. There is a limit to how many conflict situations can be managed or settled successfully, even with the most determined leadership and skillful personnel.

Intervention fatigue and the real price tag for major powers of sustaining military deployments in conflicted societies have encouraged growing attention to the possibilities (and limits) of intervention by regional and subregional actors. Where system overload results in a form of triage, as in Rwanda, the net result is to foster regional initiatives and new thinking about security cooperation and burden-sharing between regions of conflict and regions of peace. But there are no panaceas here, either. We are witnessing a trial-and-error phase, which features no ultimate safety nets and an international security structure that is subject to a range of "market" forces.

This leads to a related point about intervention: The challenges of implementation are central to success. Just as conflicts seldom resolve themselves, peaceful settlements do not implement themselves. The role of foreign intervenors cannot end on the day that agreements are signed. Implementing mechanisms are essential to keep things on track, to sustain the political chemistry that produced the deal, and to continue the linkages and pressures that led to the breakthrough. As in other fields of endeavor (law or business), statecraft illustrates the maxim that the real negotiation only begins after the agreements are signed. Outsiders who orphan the settlements they have helped produce will watch them collapse. (See chapter 36 in this volume, "Why Orphaned Peace Settlements Are More Prone to Failure," by Fen Hampson.)

This observation suggests the need for intervenors to devise an explicit implementation strategy to carry things forward from the point of settlement to that of successfully implemented settlement. While each case differs, some core questions arise in many cases. How will the signatory parties remain in communication after the ink is dry? Who will run the implementation process? Who will define success and declare that the implementation phase has been completed? How will the intervening powers coordinate with one another, with local authorities, and with regional or international organizations? Whose task is it to see that parties carry out their commitments? What mechanisms and safety nets are available to rescue the process if it goes off the rails? What roles can outsiders play to observe, monitor, verify, guarantee, and, if appropriate, enforce compliance? How will the various military, political, humanitarian, and economic tracks of a settlement be coordinated, and who will make certain that this happens? How will external civilian, military, and NGO leaders coordinate their actions with one another and with local counterparts?

In any implementation process, there is a central role for imaginative improvisation and spontaneous solving of problems large and small that are certain to arise. This is why top-flight leadership is essential in complex, political-military undertakings. Similarly, a well-led implementation can have a transforming effect on the climate that develops among the parties, making possible compromises and deals that would have been unthinkable before the settlement. But everything hinges on taking the implementation phase seriously. A good test is to identify who is going to make sure that the whole complex operation works. Unless the buck stops somewhere, implementation will be rocky.

A final strategic lesson from past cases of intervention is that the most successful ones were based on understanding the connection between military power and diplomatic strategy. Diplomatic intervention in the name of peacemaking is seldom effective, unless it either reflects an underlying balance of forces or is backed by certain elements of power and leverage capable of affecting that balance. The Bosnian diplomatic ventures of 1992–1995 are only the most vivid recent example illustrating the point.

Equally important, military interventions have a much higher chance of succeeding when they are linked to either a political settlement or an ongoing political process for obtaining one. In fact, military action without a clear political context is of little use: Pressure requires diplomacy to have an impact, just as diplomacy needs an element of pressure to be effective.

A special word is in order about the particular case of humanitarian interventions.

Success in these undertakings can be measured at two levels: saving lives, and creating a political basis for resolving the issues that put lives at risk in the first place. The absence of strong prospects for the second level of success should not become an excuse for doing nothing to protect people when something can be done at an acceptable cost to the intervenors (even if this requires ongoing effort, as in Iraq). But humanitarian action makes so much more sense when conceived as a bridge to a political process that can provide the best basis for a successful exit. This was one of the missing ingredients that undercut the impact of U.S. and UN intervention in Somalia.

Recent history is replete with examples illustrating this military-political nexus. A clear political context was lacking for the second Lebanon intervention of 1983. The U.S. covert war in Nicaragua in the 1980s lacked a political context until the Central American presidents provided one. The brief resumption of the United States' clandestine support for the National Union for the Total Independence of Angola (UNITA) after 1985 was effective because it was linked to, and supportive of, an ongoing negotiation process. The U.S.-UN intervention in Haiti in 1994 derived essential strength from the Organization of American States– and UN-based political framework surrounding the action. It is not an accident that many of the United Nations' successes in peace operations have occurred in cases involving the implementation of a negotiated settlement plan: for example, El Salvador, Cambodia, Mozambique, and Namibia.

By contrast, the thirty-year-old UN peacekeeping presence on Cyprus has played a useful role of the traditional blue-helmet variety through confidence building, ceasefire monitoring, and reducing violence. But its success in these terms has, if anything, reduced the pressures among the parties and the western powers to push for a real settlement. Viewed another way, the UN operation has helped to stabilize the island's de facto partition, which was not its originally intended purpose.

CONCLUSION

This chapter has underscored the variety of contemporary conflicts and the vast menu of potential responses for dealing with these conflicts. Understanding the global disorders of the 1990s requires looking behind the labels, slogans, and abstractions so commonly used to describe events and define our options. This close, case-by-case inspection permits us to see more clearly the vital importance of timing and preemptive action and to weigh more concretely the possible balance of risk and reward in nonintervention against the various forms of intervention available. This approach also encourages us to appreciate the tremendous range of possible intervening actors in the contemporary global system and to appreciate the potential for selective global engagement by the United States, without automatically falling victim to the dangers of overcommitment.

The historic record makes clear that interventions can succeed as well as fail, and it offers a range of operational and strategic lessons from specific cases. Some of the most interesting examples revolve around seemingly pedestrian notions that have long been at the core of effective statecraft: political will and staying power, continuity of policy management in complex undertakings, operational competence and sound judgment in negotiating and implementing settlements, seizing and keeping the initiative, the mutual interdependence of military power and diplomacy, and the role of topflight leadership. Intervention in the affairs of others is a serious business. It is not an arena for mere posturing or for being seen as "doing something." It should be attempted with the best, most committed, and perseverant people and pursued with a relentless intensity.

NOTES

1. One of the best overviews of trends in UN peace operations is Pamela L. Reed, J. Matthew Vaccaro, and William J. Durch, *Handbook on United Nations Peace Operations* (Washington, D.C.: Henry L. Stimson Center, April 1995).

2. The literature on ethnic conflict is too vast to summarize here. In addition to chapter 4 in this volume, "Minorities, Nationalists, and Ethnopolitical Conflict" by Ted Robert Gurr, and the citations therein, readers may wish to consult the excellent collection in Michael E. Brown, ed., *Ethnic Conflict and International Security* (Princeton, N.J.: Princeton University Press, 1993); Stephen Van Evera, "Hypotheses on Nationalism and War," *International Security* 18, no. 4 (Spring 1994): 5–39; Milton J. Esman, "Political and Psychological Factors in Ethnic Conflict," in *Conflict and Peacemaking in Multiethnic Societies,* ed. Joseph V. Montville (Lexington, Mass.: Lexington Books, 1990); and Anthony D. Smith, *The Ethnic Origins of Nations* (Oxford, U.K.: Basil Blackwell, 1986).

3. Warren Zimmermann, "The Last Ambassador: A Memoir of the Collapse of Yugoslavia," *Foreign Affairs* 74, no. 2 (March–April 1995): 6.

4. For a sustained discussion of the history and potential of such engagements in American policy, see Alan K. Henrikson, "Constructive Containment," *Fletcher Forum of World Affairs* 19, no. 2 (Summer–Fall 1995): 1–17.

5. All this changed, of course, with the political and military decisions of the United States and NATO to capitalize on and reinforce changes in the Bosnian military balance, creating the leverage to drive events toward the Dayton agreement and the replacement of the United Nations Protective Force by NATO itself.

6. One of the best extended discussions of criteria for military intervention is by Richard N. Haass, *Intervention: The Use of American Military Power in the Post–Cold War World* (Washington, D.C.: Carnegie Endowment for International Peace, 1994).

7. Kenneth Allard, *Somalia Operations: Lessons Learned* (Washington, D.C.: National Defense University Press, 1995), p. 92.

8. This discussion draws upon the analysis in William J. Durch, "The UN Operation in the Congo, 1960–1964," in *The Evolution of UN Peacekeeping: Case Studies and Comparative Analysis,* ed. William J. Durch (New York: St. Martin's Press for the Henry L. Stimson Center, 1993), pp. 315–352.

13

Using Force

Lessons and Choices for U.S. Foreign Policy

RICHARD N. HAASS

The question of whether and, if so, how to intervene with military force is always controversial for any political system, if only because of the potential costs—both human and economic—of such a decision. When the United States faces this decision, however, the stakes are different: Because of its status and strength, what the United States chooses to do—and not to do—with the military instrument of foreign policy can have an extraordinary impact on events and on the evolution of international relations in the post–Cold War world.[1]

Intervention can mean different things. Military interventions differ from one another in scale, composition, duration, intensity, authority, and, above all, objective. They need not involve shooting; shooting is actually only one way to use military force. The distinction that is generally not useful is the most common, that is, "offensive versus defensive." Not only is this distinction primarily in the eyes of the beholder, but it also breaks down in the real world. The same weapon system can be used both ways; moreover, one can have tactical offensive operations taking place within an overall defensive strategy, and tactical defensive efforts within the context of an overall offensive strategy.

Military interventions can, however, be usefully classified by other purposes: deterrence (in the sense of prevention), prevention (in the sense of preemption), coercion, punishment (punitive), peacekeeping, war fighting, peacemaking, nation building, interdiction, humanitarian goals, and rescue missions. In addition, there is the indirect option of providing military assistance to a party to a dispute, which some would term an intervention.

It is important to use these terms with precision, not simply for reasons of analysis, but also for communication. Two in particular merit some explanation. *Peacekeeping* is used here to refer to operations carried out in a consensual environment. Such operations are more political than military and

197

are carried out by modestly armed forces interposed between local parties. In some cases, the mission will take on additional tasks, such as monitoring elections or troop withdrawals. But the key is the neutrality of the mission and the readiness of the local parties to accept a foreign role.

Peacemaking, on the other hand, is very different. The term is used here not as it often is, to refer to all efforts meant to promote conciliation, diplomatic and military alike. Used so broadly, it is difficult to distinguish it from foreign policy or diplomacy. Rather, peacemaking refers to those military operations that take place in "uncertain" environments and where (unlike peacekeeping) at least one of the local parties is prepared to use force to implement its aims.[2] At the same time, peacemaking is something less than war fighting, given the military restraint exercised (out of political choice) and the limited strength of the opposition. It is sometimes referred to as "aggravated peacekeeping," a term that should only be used guardedly: Great harm has been done (and great tragedy has ensued) in undertaking peacekeeping missions when the reality proved to be something much more demanding and dangerous.[3]

Another concept, not discussed here, is "peace enforcement." This is a legal term, not a military one. It normally refers to actions undertaken pursuant to Chapter VII of the UN Charter. The fact that such actions can range from naval interdiction in support of sanctions to intense war fighting —Desert Storm was a peace enforcement operation—renders the term too broad to be very useful.

Terminology aside, it is most important to recognize that intervening everywhere is not an option, even for a great or superpower like the United States. There will always be more reasons to intervene than resources available or than the body politic is prepared to support. The need to choose is critical.

The good news is that it is possible to make the policymaking process more manageable by examining past experiences. It is essential to appreciate that interests alone do not solve the question of whether and how to intervene. That something is perceived as vital does not mean that military force provides the best or even a viable alternative for policymakers. At the same time, that an interest is less than vital should not rule out the use of military force as a policy. The United States can sustain high-interest, high-cost interventions as well as low-interest, low-cost efforts. What it cannot sustain are interventions that promise to be (or turn out to be) low interest but high cost.

More generally, any intervention must pass four tests:

- There must be an identifiable interest at stake.
- The intervention must have potential to succeed; that is, it must be possible to see how military force can be employed in a way that will protect or promote the interest in question.
- The likely benefits of intervening should outweigh the likely costs once the projected responses of allies and adversaries are factored in. The likely ratio of benefits to cost should compare favorably with that of other choices, including using other tools of policy (diplomacy, sanctions, covert action, humanitarian or military assistance) or doing nothing at all.

CLASSIC SCENARIOS

How do these principles apply? The two most demanding scenarios for the use of force by the United States in the foreseeable future are also the most straightforward. The first scenario is an imminent or actual North Korean invasion of the Republic of Korea. The second is an imminent or actual attack by Iran or Iraq upon Kuwait, Saudi Arabia, or any of several other Gulf states. In both these situations, the decision to respond with force would be almost automatic, given the mix of stakes and commitments. Not surprisingly, these are two theaters in which the United States has fought major military engagements in the post–World War II era, in both cases with considerable assistance from others and with formal international endorsement.

A third demanding scenario requiring the potential use of force raises greater problems: a resurgent Russia bent on reclaiming or reconstructing parts of the former Soviet empire, especially in the Baltics, Eastern Europe, or Ukraine. Such a scenario would raise fundamental concerns over the balance of power and international order. Fortunately, because of Russia's political evolution and the manifest deterioration of its armed forces, a scenario involving either the Baltics or Eastern Europe appears to be far less likely, at least in the near future, than either the Gulf or Korean scenarios. But if it occurred, a revitalized and expanded NATO would have to deter and, if necessary, defend against such an act of aggression.[4]

All these potential scenarios have a traditional, interstate character. At issue are both specific interests and the basic organizing principle of international society, that is, defending state sovereignty against external aggression. Each of these cases involves borders, clear divisions between the territory of the attacking state and the attacked. There is a status quo that can be restored and maintained. Such conflicts can best be fought with massive force used decisively from the outset to destroy the adversary's ability to project military power; such conflicts can best be deterred (prevented) by maintaining capable forces in the area and by leaving no doubt about U.S. willingness to intervene decisively if its interests were challenged.

Another kind of scenario involves more limited potential interventions that are smaller in scope and shorter in duration, but that nevertheless have a clear and important purpose. They include hostage rescues, limited punitive reprisals against terrorists or states supporting them, and interdiction on behalf of sanctions, narcotics policy, or immigration regulation. These potential military interventions can be readily defined and carried out with high expectations of military success, as well as with domestic and international support. Such interventions are more likely to prove successful if they are kept narrow in purpose, involve ample force, and are conducted decisively.

Far more difficult (yet still easy to foresee) are possible calls for military intervention in complex and controversial circumstances. One set of scenarios involves launching preventive strikes on unconventional military capabilities. A second set involves intervening in the internal affairs of others for either humanitarian or political purposes. Both kinds of situations have already been the subject of considerable debate; both are likely to provide the United States with its most difficult foreign policy choices in the years to come.

PREVENTIVE INTERVENTIONS

Preventive uses of force are reactive in the sense that they respond to developments perceived as threats, but they are—and are likely to be viewed as—proactive in every other sense.[5] The temptation to undertake preventive attacks mounts as an emerging threat materializes and the likelihood of conflict grows. Preventive attacks become more attractive if conflict is seen as increasingly probable on decreasingly favorable terms.

Preventive strikes are most likely against two types of targets. The first is terrorist capabilities. The problem with these is that they are often "soft" and easily moved or re-created. The second and more likely set of targets is those facilities central to the development of unconventional weapons. Here the problems stem from a lack of knowledge—as we learned in Iraq, what we don't know can far exceed what we do know—and from inability to destroy the target because of protective measures. Also, preventive attacks can lead to a larger conflict; for example, a limited attack on North Korean nuclear facilities could trigger a massive Korean conflict, possibly including the use by North Korea of capabilities not eliminated in a preventive strike.

There are also diplomatic problems to consider. The notion of preventive self-defense—"legitimate anticipation" in the words of one legal scholar—is not universally accepted in principle and is difficult to apply in the specific.[6] The international community has long embraced the norm of the right of self-defense and is beginning to recognize a second norm of humanitarian intervention. It is, however, a long way from accepting preventive strikes to destroy the nascent unconventional weapons capabilities of states deemed by some to be rogues as a third norm.

The net result is that the preventive use of force is an attractive option only in rare circumstances. Defensive measures and punitive attacks against state sponsors of terror are more effective responses to terrorists, while proliferation concerns can normally be better addressed by a mix of nonproliferation strategies, deterrence, tactical adjustments, and defensive measures. But preventive attacks may be the best option against the emergence of a militarily significant unconventional capability if diplomacy (or diplomacy buttressed by sanctions) fails to place an acceptable ceiling on the threat, if effective defense is not available, and if war seems likely. Indeed, such circumstances could well arise in both northeast Asia and the Gulf region at any time.

INTERNAL INTERVENTIONS

One of the few clear aspects of the post–Cold War world is the prevalence of strife within countries or between those just made independent. Sometimes the fighting is between groups defined by ethnicity or tribe; in other situations, the government (or the lack thereof) is the main problem. The result is conflict that bears many of the characteristics of civil war: the absence of a clear battlefield, no sharp line between combatant and civilian, multiple parties with uneven discipline, and deep emotions that make ending the fighting nearly impossible.

Too many recent examples come to mind: Somalia, Rwanda, Haiti, and Bosnia. In such situations, the United States will have stakes that are humanitarian and possibly economic and strategic. But generally the size of these stakes will be modest or less than vital. Neither U.S. security nor its prosperity will be undermined if many people die and many more are left homeless. Still, depending on the specific circumstances, U.S. security may be affected; and, regardless of the details, this country's sense of decency and morality is offended by what it sees or knows is going on.[7] The result is pressure to do something, often with military force.

Direct military involvement in the internal affairs of another state tends to be for one of three purposes: nation building (recasting the institutions of the society), humanitarian relief (providing protection and the basic necessities of life, often through the establishment of safe havens), or coercion or peacemaking (bolstering an arrangement in the absence of local consent or tilting the balance in favor of a contending individual or group). The question is when to choose one or another of the above approaches and when to do nothing at all.[8]

Answering the question of whether to intervene will be extremely difficult because of the need for selectivity. The impossibility of responding to all such situations cannot be rationale for inaction—just because the United States cannot intervene everywhere does not mean it ought not intervene anywhere—but it does highlight the need to explain and defend decisions to intervene (as well as not to intervene) if domestic and international support is to be forthcoming. As a rule of thumb, the case for intervention grows stronger the worse the humanitarian disaster, the greater the degree to which other interests are at stake, and the more costs can be kept down, either through the design of the operation or the participation of others.

NATION-BUILDING INTERVENTIONS

Like humanitarian intervention, nation-building intervention can be motivated by how a state treats its own people. It can also be motivated by a desire to transform a state's foreign policy so that it does not again resort to force against neighbors. But nation building is a far more ambitious enterprise than humanitarian intervention, which is limited in means and ends. Interventions designed to make a country secure and stable require replacing the existing political authority (or creating one where none exists), so that local people can lead relatively normal lives. Nation building normally requires defeating and disarming any local opposition and establishing a political authority that enjoys a monopoly or near-monopoly of control over the legitimate use of force.

Successful nation building can involve first going to war, as in the case of both Japan and Germany. In both cases, nation building required years of occupation. To succeed, nation building sometimes must seek to do nothing less than remake a political culture. It is more demanding in the near term than humanitarian intervention, but potentially less so over the very long term. It is highly intrusive, as even the limited nation-building efforts in Panama, Grenada, and Somalia all demonstrate.

Opportunities for successful nation building are rare. Few regimes are that dangerous, and even when they are, not many outsiders will want to pay the price. Also, it is impossible to be confident that the values the United States seeks to promote will take root. Neither the United States nor the world is likely to support for a second time the sort of methods—and the time they require—imposed on Germany and Japan after World War II. North Korea appears to be a prime exception because of its demonstrated aggression and the availability of South Koreans to undertake an occupation.

In recent times, for example, the United States shied away from attempting nation building in Iraq out of concern that it would take years, be opposed by both the American people and the Arab members of the coalition, result in many casualties, lead to Iraq's breakup, and in the end fail because of authoritarian and nationalist traditions in Iraq. In Somalia, nation building was not given a fair chance; it was never preceded by the necessary (and expensive) peacemaking. But even if those measures had been taken, there is no guarantee that nation building would have worked—or would have been worth the cost, since a more limited humanitarian alternative was under way. Where nation building was somewhat successful, in Grenada and Panama, the United States enjoyed conditions not easily replicated. Grenada proved receptive in part because of its modest size and population. Panama was accustomed to an intrusive U.S. presence and already had a democratically elected government supported by the majority of the people (although it was prevented from taking office).

Haiti is perhaps the best test case. The political and military weakness of the existing regime and the absence of civil strife meant that an intervention could gain control of the country with relative ease; the major challenge comes now in nation building, a task that the United States is sharing with others and that will be difficult, take years, and still possibly fail because of Haiti's political culture. Also open to question is the wisdom of the U.S. decision to eschew disarming the local citizenry, an approach that reduced American casualties in the near term but may have complicated the long-run task.

SAFE HAVENS

Safe havens can be created as a magnet for people or they can be established where the endangered people already are, if they happen to be concentrated in one or only a few places. A modest number of ground forces and significant air support are required to protect the humanitarian area or areas, that is, to make the safe haven safe. The area is protected further by enforcing a weapons-exclusion zone around it and a no-fly zone over it. In addition, air forces must be ready to carry out disproportionately large punitive attacks on those who violate the area in any way.

This is essentially what the French did for a time in Rwanda and what the United States did at first in Somalia and is still doing in Northern Iraq. The no-fly zone over Bosnia-Herzegovina and the exclusion zone around Sarajevo and five other designated cities might have been additional examples, but the effectiveness of the policy was undermined by the delay in introducing it and by the absence of will to carry out meaningful punitive action. As a result, all six cities designated "safe" by the United Nations were attacked for years, and two fell to hostile forces. Only with the American and NATO decision in mid-1995 to use decisive force against Bosnian Serb forces was the safe area concept given a fair test, which it passed.

This approach has some obvious costs and drawbacks. Safe havens are open-ended, offering no guaranteed exit date for those who maintain them. Some pilots and ground troops will be lost. Except in situations where an endangered population already is concentrated in one area, establishing such zones can either fail to protect some people or force them to migrate to safety, thereby rewarding the aggressor. Most of all, safe havens are limited in what they can accomplish directly. Humanitarian interventions should not be confused with more ambitious interventions, especially peacemaking and nation building.

Still, safe havens offer an attractive policy option. They are designed to provide a respite from the problem at an affordable cost, not a solution.[9] They are needed until the politics of the situation evolve. Safe havens thus not only keep people safe but also buy time for other approaches to work, such as implementing sanctions, providing arms, and engaging in diplomacy or covert action. The utility of safe havens for future Somalias, Rwandas, or even Bosnias is obvious.

PEACEMAKING AND COERCIVE INTERVENTIONS

Opportunities for successful peacemaking and coercive intervention—that is, the uses of force to affect the course of events directly by turning the United States into a limited protagonist in a struggle—are likely to be rare. Vietnam and Lebanon demonstrated that peacemaking is extremely demanding militarily and difficult to sustain politically, both at home (because of the high costs and uncertain prospects for success) and in the target country (where nationalist pressures, the difficulties of working with disorganized internal forces, and the need to act with great restraint in order not to alienate neutral parties must be considered). It can, however, be carried out successfully, as Grenada and Panama demonstrate. (Haiti was a potential peacemaking effort that proved unnecessary when the overwhelming U.S. force was able to enter without opposition.)

Bosnia has become an example of peacemaking, in that the U.S. and NATO forces are buttressing a set of political arrangements amidst considerable political uncertainty and potential physical resistance. Such a presence could prove necessary for a protracted period unless nation building succeeds or a local military balance that discourages renewed fighting materializes from arms reductions, arms buildups, or a combination of the two.

Still, very few situations will involve interests of sufficient importance to justify the inevitable costs of direct American military participation on the side of one of the local parties. Coercive actions—limited uses of force designed to affect the behavior of the targeted party—are easier to mount than peacemaking operations; the problem is what to do if they do not succeed. The choice then tends to be between escalating to peacemaking or backing away from direct military intervention and choosing some other policy instrument, either arming the favored faction (an indirect military option) or pursuing another realm of policy, such as sanctions, diplomacy, or covert action.

UNILATERALISM VERSUS MULTILATERALISM

Much of the American debate over the use of military force has focused on the choice between acting alone and acting with others. In reality, the choice is less stark, as the opportunities for purely unilateral action will be few. In most situations, intervention will be partly multilateral, involving other countries in addition to the United States. The United States will need one or more forms of assistance, including base rights, over-

flight, intelligence, combat forces, economic help, and political support. Two questions are worth asking: In which situations will the United States want to marginalize or even eliminate the involvement of others? In those situations where the involvement of others is deemed either necessary or desirable, in what form should it come?

These are difficult questions, for multilateralism has both positive and negative aspects. On the positive side, multilateralism is closely tied to international legitimacy. Arab force contributions in the Gulf War were critical, for political more than for military reasons, just as the support of the Organization of Eastern Caribbean States was useful during the Grenada action. Foreign involvement also helps at home, where resentment is all but certain to undermine support for a costly and extended intervention if the United States bears most or all the economic, military, and human burdens of the endeavor.

But multilateralism is not without costs. Such costs transcend the economic price of the United States assuming its share of an operation. Keeping the Gulf coalition intact required going to the United Nations, which in turn slowed down the use of force, most notably early in the crisis when ships entering or leaving Iraqi ports were interdicted. Multilateralism can also translate into a loss of control over the situation on the ground. For example in Somalia, the United States encountered problems over both strategy and operations because it shared responsibility with the United Nations and other countries contributing troops. In Bosnia, European governments cited humanitarian operations to justify opposing the more aggressive policies suggested by the United States. The Bosnia experience also illustrated the problems that can stem from a cumbersome chain of command, which involved political and military officials (both on site and at headquarters) representing the United States, NATO, and the United Nations.

There are a number of approaches to multilateralism: loose collaboration among concerned nations; coalitions of the willing; standing regional organizations; international forces organized by and under the United Nations for specific tasks; or the creation of a standing UN army. A policy based on unilateralism combined with modest forms of multilateralism (informal coalitions) seems best. Such a policy offers flexibility and does not require gaining the support of those opposed to a specific undertaking.

The other approaches appear more problematic. Loose collaborations lack the integration and coordination needed for larger undertakings. Strengthening regional organizations ought to be a goal, but it will require years for it to come to fruition. Such organizations tend to lack the consensus to take on missions removed from their core purpose. NATO is a partial exception here, although Bosnia has revealed the difficulty it has in tackling new missions. The United Nations appears most attractive as a legitimizer for war fighting and as an organizer of peacekeeping. Anything more ambitious seems both impractical and arguably unwise, given the divisions in the Security Council and the organization's lack of military capability.[10]

Despite the need for a degree of multilateralism, the United States needs to maintain a unilateral military option. It cannot plan its forces on the assumption that others will be willing or able to bear the burdens of major military undertakings. Nor does the United States want to give others a veto when it decides to intervene with force. Indeed, in some cases, such as large-scale combat or war, multilateralism will be mostly supportive of the United States. In other cases—such as preventive and punitive actions, rescue efforts, or interventions in places where there are special interests

(such as Panama, the Philippines, or the Middle East)—U.S. leaders may want or need to act alone.

As a rule, interventions calculated to be modest and short-term lend themselves to unilateralism (or modest forms of multilateralism). Unilateral uses of force maximize speed and the secrecy of decision making and implementation, and they also heighten political and military freedom of action. This was the case in the Philippines, Libya, and Panama, as well as with the Iran hostage rescue effort. It was also true in June 1993 when the United States launched cruise missile strikes on Iraq. Unilateralism can also be helpful when deterrence or coercion are called for; it avoids the time-consuming debates of joint efforts and does not require building a broad consensus.

But acting alone has its costs and drawbacks. As already noted, it is hard to execute most interventions without some form of help from others. Acting unilaterally can be expensive; it risks domestic support if Congress and the American people ask why the United States is bearing burdens that no one else is. It can also be controversial internationally, as questions of legality and legitimacy inevitably arise. U.S. unilateralism also runs the risk of triggering unilateral actions by others. In any event, the United States will simply not have adequate forces to come close to meeting all the claims on it. It will have to do some things with others or delegate them entirely. Thus, unilateralism can become unsustainable over time if costs begin to mount.

There is little reason for U.S. involvement in traditional peacekeeping, a mission that many countries can readily undertake, unless it is expressly sought by the protagonists and is in an area where U.S. interests justify the contribution, such as the Middle East. Similarly, the United States normally should stay outside of, or minimize its role in, peacemaking and nation building. These missions do not exploit the unique capabilities of U.S. forces for high-intensity combat. They are time consuming and tie down U.S. troops that could be used elsewhere. They are also inherently costly, whether measured in terms of dollars or casualties and lives. Where appropriate, the United States would be wise to advocate and participate in safe havens as an alternative. If, however, peacemaking or nation building are deemed desirable and feasible (in Bosnia, for example), such missions should almost always be undertaken by coalitions, either recognized regional organizations or less formal arrangements. Furthermore, the United States should insist that in return for its support, the mission be designed with an adequate appreciation of the risks and costs.

U.S. participation in multinational peacemaking and nation building raises special questions. Experiences in Lebanon and Somalia both suggest that direct U.S. involvement can be counterproductive, as it can stimulate opposition and aggressive action against the effort; in many settings, taking on the United States and demonstrating an ability to kill or capture soldiers of the world's only superpower has political value. The comparative advantages of the United States in such situations are in the realms of intelligence, transportation, and logistical support. However, the United States will find it difficult to assume leadership if it is unwilling to share the risks; as a result, in situations that meet U.S. criteria, some combat participation may be required if other countries are to be persuaded to join the effort. In these cases, the United States must be aware of the risks and use sufficient force.

U.S. willingness to operate under the command of others should depend upon the circumstances. As a rule of thumb, the greater the stakes and the greater the U.S. role, the more that U.S. forces should act under U.S. commanders. But where U.S.

forces are only a small part of an overall effort, there is no reason to preclude non-American command, particularly if the operation is designed so that U.S. forces enjoy considerable autonomy within the area or mission they are assigned. Here, the NATO parallel comes to mind: essential self-command of U.S. forces in the field, even if overall direction of the operation is shared or held by others. In addition, UN or non-American command poses little problem if the operation is true peacekeeping (and not something more) in a context that is truly consensual. The bigger issue in such cases is not the command arrangements, but whether U.S. forces ought to be involved at all.

CONCLUSIONS

The prospects for the United States intervening effectively with military force—in particular, in those circumstances involving real or imminent aggression by states against their neighbors—have improved. A number of factors—the emergence of a new generation of advanced conventional weapons, the end of the Cold War risk of escalation to global war, the fact that many adversaries find themselves lacking superpower support—support the ability of the United States to use military force effectively on the battlefield. This potential will only be realized, however, if it uses ample force early and decisively.

Three other developments, however, are less encouraging. First, the United States will see its interests challenged more directly and will face humanitarian problems more often in the future. Second, some of these challenges will probably include unconventional weaponry; if the United States is not to be deterred from acting for fear of large-scale casualties, it must develop tactics, strategies, and weapons that will reduce the chance and costs of escalation to chemical, biological, or nuclear arms. Third, there is declining popular and congressional support for military interventions. The proper response is not to bow to this mood, but to take it into account. Sustaining interventions will require substantial political effort from the most senior levels of government. The greater the costs, the greater the effort that will be required.

The potential for intervening effectively with military means for other purposes, particularly internal conflicts, is less clear-cut. The advantages of modern technology that are useful on the open battlefield are often irrelevant in civil conflicts that take place in heavily congested areas where friend cannot be distinguished from foe. Television pictures may increase our desire to act when we see innocent people suffering because of government policy or inaction, and new ways of thinking may provide a legal basis for intervention; but intervening in internal situations can prove difficult and dangerous for an outsider—even one who possesses great power—if the local protagonists are prepared to fight to the end.

The dangers of a more interventionist bias are manifest. Using military force to intervene on behalf of a people against their government or nongovernmental forces is a complicated undertaking that can place the intervening party squarely in the middle of another nation's politics. Moreover, a norm tolerant of intervention can easily be abused by others looking for a pretext to intervene. Even if there is a real reason to intervene, it can quickly lead to counter-interventions by additional outside parties. Indeed, it is precisely these concerns that helped create the norm in favor of state sovereignty and against outside intervention.

This does not argue for always staying out of such situations. What makes a great power great is, in part, a willingness to intervene militarily on behalf of interests that are less than vital. Military force cannot substitute for political and economic efforts, but it can provide a context in which they are more likely to succeed. Sometimes it is necessary to act—when the need is great and it is possible to use force to improve matters at a cost that is commensurate with the stakes. In such cases, the United States may want to consider options that create safe havens, providing long-term relief at a cost it and others can sustain, rather than taking on the more ambitious enterprises of peacemaking or nation building.

The United States will also want to identify a desirable and sustainable division of labor among itself, regional organizations, and the United Nations. However, the presumption should be in favor of continued U.S. leadership, at times alone, more often in informal coalitions. There is a real question about how much the United States can and should seek to devolve formal responsibility to other organizations and the United Nations in particular.

Generally, multilateralism can be a useful or necessary military or political precondition to U.S. intervention; at the same time, it can prove cumbersome or an obstacle. It is not, however, an alternative to U.S. leadership. Multilateralism is most likely to be effective if the United States takes the lead in making the case for a collective response and contributing to the common effort. The more ambitious the undertaking, the more U.S. leadership and participation will be necessary and the more likely the United States will want to act in a loosely structured fashion. The more uncertain the stakes, or the greater the gap between stakes and likely costs, the more careful the United States ought to be about lending support, much less direct involvement, to an effort.

This chapter argues not only for selectivity, but also for what might be described as tailoring; the "how" of the intervention becomes as important as the "whether." This, in turn, suggests a need to emphasize using air power, arming local protagonists, and, above all, creating safe havens in the sort of internal conflicts that have come to characterize the post–Cold War world. It argues for political leadership, both to make the case to others to work with us and to persuade the American people and Congress to give their support. It also argues for fashioning "coalitions of the willing and able" to undertake these missions. Last, history argues for not ignoring other tools of foreign policy, from economic and military assistance to diplomacy and covert action. This last point is critical: The military is but one policy instrument, and, however important or even decisive it may be in some contexts, it cannot be expected to carry the full burden of America's world role.

NOTES

1. For a discussion of the U.S. debate, see Richard N. Haass, *Intervention: The Use of American Military Force in the Post–Cold War World* (Washington, D.C.: Carnegie Endowment for International Peace, 1994); Richard K. Betts, "The Delusion of Impartial Intervention," *Foreign Affairs* 73, no. 6 (November–December 1994): 21–33; Michael Mandelbaum, "The Reluctance to Intervene," *Foreign Policy* 95 (Summer 1994): 3–18; Fareed Zakaria, "The Core versus the Periphery," *Commentary* 96, no. 6 (December 1993): 25–29; and Richard Falk, "Hard Choices and Tragic Dilemmas," *Nation*, December 20, 1993, pp. 755–764.

2. The Joint Chiefs of Staff define situations as permissive, uncertain, or hostile. Permissive contexts tend to call for peacekeeping; uncertain environments for peacemaking; and hostile conditions for war fighting.

3. For a different approach to terminology, see Boutros Boutros-Ghali, *An Agenda for Peace* (New York: United Nations, 1992). For a broader discussion of these issues, see Laurence Martin, "Peacekeeping as a Growth Industry," *National Interest* 32 (Summer 1993): 7. For another skeptical view of the wisdom of intervening in internal conflicts, at least until they

have burned themselves out, see S. J. Stedman, "The New Interventionists," *Foreign Affairs* 72, no. 1 (Winter 1992–1993), 1–16. Also see Robert Cooper and Mats Berdal, "Outside Intervention in Ethnic Conflicts," *Survival* 35, no. 1 (Spring 1993): 138; William J. Durch, *The Evolution of UN Peacekeeping: Case Studies and Comparative Analysis* (New York: St. Martin's, 1993); *The Blue Helmets: A Review of United Nations Peacekeeping* (New York: United Nations, 1990); Marrack Goulding, "The Evolution of UN Peacekeeping," *International Affairs* 69, no. 3 (July 1993): 451–464; Mats R. Berdal, *Whither U.N. Peacekeeping?* (London: International Institute for Strategic Studies, 1993); and Dick Kirschten, "Missions Impossible," *National Journal*, October 30, 1993, pp. 2576–2580.

4. By contrast, and although it would have major repercussions for the balance of power, a direct military response to Russian use of force against Ukraine would not be advisable. Geography and other factors (including the presence of nuclear weapons on both sides) simply work against U.S. and western ability to engage on attractive terms; as a result, U.S. policy is best served by making such Russian action less likely. This involves promoting Ukraine's viability, encouraging autonomy for and proper treatment of ethnic Russians in Crimea, and making clear to Russia the price it would pay in its relations with the West if it acted aggressively. The same principle applies to potential Russian uses of force elsewhere in its immediate vicinity.

5. Preventive strikes are sometimes described as preemptive. The difference is one of context. Preventive strikes are motivated by concern over the emergence of a capability; preemptive strikes are undertaken in the context of a larger crisis (normally, on the eve or brink of war) in which it is feared that this capability might be introduced. Neither term is to be confused with the use of the term "preventive" to describe a deterrent deployment.

6. See Michael Walzer, *Just and Unjust Wars: A Moral Argument with Historical Illustrations* (New York: Basic Books, 1977), pp. 74–85.

7. See David Fisher, "The Ethics of Intervention," *Survival* 36, no. 1 (Spring 1994): 54. This is an important article that finds in the

just war criteria grounds for using military force in many instances where intervention has been delayed or ruled out.

8. For a sampling of the large literature devoted to this question, see Laura W. Reed and Carl Kayson, eds., *Emerging Norms of Justified Intervention* (Cambridge, Mass.: American Academy of Arts and Sciences, 1993); *Right versus Might: International Law and the Use of Force* (New York: Council on Foreign Relations, 1991); Christopher Greenwood, "Is There a Right of Humanitarian Intervention?" *World Today* 49, no. 2 (February 1993): 34–40; Louis Henkin, "Notes From the President: The Mythology of Sovereignty," *American Society of International Law Newsletter* (March–May 1993): 1, 6–7; Barbara Harff, "Bosnia and Somalia: Strategic, Legal, and Moral Dimensions of Humanitarian Intervention," *Philosophy and Public Policy* 12, no. 3/4 (Summer–Fall 1992): 1–7; and David J. Scheffer, Richard N. Gardner, and Gerald B. Helman, *Three Views on the Issue of Humanitarian Intervention* (Washington, D.C.: United States Institute of Peace, 1992). For more cautionary or skeptical views, see the chapters by Michael Akehurst and Hedley Bull in *Intervention in World Politics,* ed. Hedley Bull (Oxford, U.K.: Clarendon Press, 1984); Joshua Muravchik, "Beyond Self-Defense," *Commentary* 96, no. 6 (December 1993): 19–24; Peter Rodman, "Intervention and Its Discontents," *National Review,* March 29, 1993, pp. 28–29; Dimitri K. Simes, "When Good Deeds Make Bad Policy," *Washington Post,* August 29, 1993, pp. C1–2; and Adam Roberts, "The Road to Hell: A Critique of Humanitarian Intervention,"

Harvard International Review 16, no. 1 (Fall 1993): 10–13, 63. For a brief primer, see Raymond W. Copson, *The Use of Force in Civil Conflicts for Humanitarian Purposes: Prospects for the Post–Cold War Era* (Washington, D.C.: Congressional Research Service, 1992).

9. On the larger issue of the increasing need to design a lower risk approach to intervention, see Edward N. Luttwak, "Toward Post-Heroic Warfare," *Foreign Affairs* 74, no. 3 (May–June 1995): 109–122.

10. A contrary view, one sympathetic to a greater UN role, is Richard N. Gardner, "Collective Security and the 'New World Order': What Role for the United Nations?" in *Two Views on the Issue of Collective Security* (Washington, D.C.: United States Institute of Peace, 1992), pp. 1–17; Gregory Harper, "Creating a U.N. Peace Enforcement Force: A Case for U.S. Leadership," *Fletcher Forum of World Affairs* 18, no. 1 (Winter–Spring 1994): 49–63; and *Defining Purpose: The U.N. and the Health of Nations* (Washington, D.C.: United States Commission on Improving the Effectiveness of the United Nations, September 1993). The latter report also favors creating a 5,000- to 10,000-person standing UN force. Other proposals for a UN legion include Brian Urquhart, "For a U.N. Volunteer Military Force," *New York Review of Books,* June 10, 1993, pp. 3–4; and Edward Luttwak, "Unconventional Force," *New Republic,* January 25, 1993, pp. 22–23. Also see exchanges on the issue (subsequent to the Urquhart piece) in *New York Review of Books,* June 24, 1993, and July 15, 1993. See also Urquhart's "Whose Fight Is It?" *New York Times,* May 22, 1994, p. 15.

14

The Role of Force in Diplomacy

A Continuing Dilemma for U.S. Foreign Policy

ALEXANDER L. GEORGE

The proposition that force and threats of force are at times necessary instruments of diplomacy and have a role to play in foreign policy is part of the conventional wisdom of statecraft. And it is true that history supports the view that efforts to deal with interstate conflicts of interest solely by means of rational persuasion and peaceful diplomacy do not always succeed and may result in substantial damage to one's national interests. On the other hand, one can also find in history many cases in which threats of force or the actual use of force were often not only ineffective but seriously aggravated disputes between states or even triggered wars that might otherwise have been avoided.

Given that historical experience supports both the necessity as well as the risks of resorting to force and threats of force, we are left with a central, difficult question in the theory and practice of foreign policy: Under what conditions and how can mil-itary force and threats of force be used effectively to accomplish different types of foreign policy objectives at an acceptable level of cost and risk?

This question has sharply divided American strategic thinkers; it has been a focal point in many controversies over foreign policy since the early days of the Cold War. More recently, in 1992 and 1993, the debate over whether the United States should intervene in the Bosnian crisis, and if so, how and on behalf of what objectives, demonstrated that this question continues to pose acute dilemmas for American policy in the post–Cold War era. This issue and the controversy surrounding it were exacerbated in the early autumn of 1993 when U.S. military forces suffered casualties in Somalia, a development that led to efforts to redefine and restrict U.S. participation in UN peacekeeping efforts. Thus, although the geopolitical and strategic context has changed dramatically, the dilemma remains and can be expected to emerge in a variety of novel settings.

This issue is of central importance in that it undergirds strategies of deterrence and coercive diplomacy that are often employed in dealing with conflicts of interest with other states. Efforts to deter adversaries from serious encroachments on one's interests and those of friendly states often require the ability to make threats that are sufficiently credible and potent enough to dissuade the adversary. This is especially true when sanctions and other nonviolent measures are expected to be or prove to be an ineffective backup to diplomacy. Not only deterrence strategy but coercive diplomacy as well often depend on an ability to generate credible threats to use force if necessary. As the Bosnian case strikingly demonstrates, however, threats appropriate to a situation are not easily generated. In this case, as in earlier crises, ample military capabilities are available but for various reasons are not usable. When policymakers are confronted by a low-level military conflict, they may face the difficult choice between escalating to higher levels of violence or backing down if they lack appropriate and usable military options.

"MASSIVE RETALIATION" AND ITS CRITICS

American strategic thinking and war planning during the early period of the Cold War operated on the assumption that any military engagement with Soviet forces would likely trigger World War III. Accordingly, to prevent such a development it appeared necessary to deter any Soviet military initiatives, however limited their scope, by threatening that the U.S. response might entail general nuclear war. However, when the Soviet Union began to acquire nuclear weapons of its own, policy planners in the Truman administration saw the need to

focus on strengthening conventional capabilities in order to shore up deterrence and have the option of responding to lesser conflicts without resort to nuclear weapons. On the other hand, the Eisenhower administration did not find this an attractive option.

When John Foster Dulles, newly designated to be Eisenhower's secretary of state, announced in January 1954 that "massive retaliation" would be the new administration's policy, he seemed to imply that the United States would respond to low-level aggression against U.S. allies with a strategic nuclear attack against the homeland of the aggressor—whether it be the Soviet Union or the People's Republic of China. The possibility that the United States might convert local wars into a general nuclear war alarmed U.S. and allied opinion, and this in turn led Dulles into a series of efforts to clarify his meaning in a more specific and moderate direction. He was not entirely successful in this respect, and indeed could not afford to be. For massive retaliation was primarily a declaratory policy intended to deter various kinds of aggression against members of the free world. Dulles and Eisenhower used the threat of massive retaliation as a means of warning a would-be Soviet or Chinese Communist aggressor that the United States would not allow it the choice of conditions for combat. Rather, as Dulles put it, the United States would respond "at places and with means of our own choosing."

Massive retaliation, therefore, threatened substantial escalation of any conflict imposed on the United States or its allies. The administration made such threats during several crises. But, in fact, a striking divergence occurred between the slogan of massive retaliation and the Eisenhower administration's actual response to conflicts in Third World areas. When war threatened over Indochina, Lebanon, the offshore islands of Quemoy and Matsu, and Berlin, the Eisenhower administration either refrained from action or desperately sought the conventional forces with which to manage the situation.

Criticism of massive retaliation by defense intellectuals and members of the opposition party mounted during the Eisenhower era. Massive retaliation and its cornerstone, U.S. strategic superiority, they pointed out, had not prevented the occurrence of many limited conflicts. Deterrence of lesser conflicts had failed and would fail again in the future because the threat of massive retaliation was simply not a credible response to low-level aggression, particularly in conflicts in which Soviet forces were not involved. Massive retaliation would become even less credible in the future, as the Soviet Union acquired larger strategic nuclear forces of its own. Moreover, critics argued that for various reasons the United States could not rely on the Eisenhower administration's proposed use of so-called tactical nuclear weapons. Therefore, most critics of massive retaliation and Eisenhower's overall defense doctrine concluded that to deter and deal with lower-level threats to the security of free world allies, the United States would need much stronger conventional war forces.

For all these reasons the major thrust of Kennedy's defense policies was the acquisition of a fuller array of military capabilities that would provide a larger, more diversified set of military options along the entire spectrum of violence. This was expected to make possible many more discriminating and effective uses of force and, accordingly, provide a stronger backup for U.S. diplomacy and a basis for more effective deterrence of limited aggression. Soon after entering the presidency Kennedy announced a new doctrine of "flexible, controlled response" to guide his administration's defense policies. Response to attacks against any part of the free world, he said, would be "suitable, selective," as well as "swift and effective." The president also stated general guidelines for the design and use of military force: "Our weapons systems must be usable in a manner permitting *deliberation* and *discrimination* as to timing, scope, and targets in *response* to *civilian authority*" (italics added).

Thus, the Kennedy administration attempted to develop a concept of controlled use of force appropriate to particular situations that would enable it to employ force and threats of force as a highly refined instrument of diplomacy. It was expected that force and threats of force would continue to be necessary even in an increasingly dangerous world in which both superpowers possessed large strategic nuclear arsenals; therefore, the new administration intended to give greater emphasis than before to ensuring controlled, discriminating use of force.

In time, however, the Kennedy administration's defense doctrine gave new impetus to a controversy over strategy that had emerged during and after the Korean War. Two quite different "lessons" had been drawn from that war that reflected sharp disagreement over the way in which the Truman administration conducted the war and dissatisfaction with its outcome. It may be recalled that after the Chinese Communists entered the war in late November 1950 and imposed upon General MacArthur's forces what has been called "the longest retreat" in American military history, President Truman decided to abandon the ambitious objective he had been pursuing since the late summer of unifying the two Korean states by force of arms. Instead, Truman now limited the American objective to maintaining South Korea's independence and imposed important limits on military strategy and tactics in order to avoid the possibility of triggering escalation to a larger war that might lead to World War III. It was for this reason that Truman rejected General MacArthur's proposal that the war be expanded against the Chinese mainland in order to achieve a military victory, and when the general argued this case publicly, he was relieved of his command.

THE "NEVER-AGAIN" AND "LIMITED WAR" SCHOOLS

General MacArthur's argument that there is no substitute for victory and that the U.S. military should not be forced to fight with one hand tied behind its back was not forgotten. After the war many military and civilian strategists argued that the United States should never again fight a similar limited, inconclusive war. Either it should stay out of such conflicts altogether or, if it intervened, it should use whatever military force might be required to win a decisive military victory.

Those who subscribed to this lesson of the Korean War quickly came to be known as the Never-Again School. The strategic doctrine they advocated regarding American military intervention was appropriately labeled *all-or-nothing*—that is, either the United States should be prepared to do everything necessary to win or it should not intervene at all.

A quite different lesson from the Korean War experience was drawn by other foreign policy specialists. They argued that in the age of thermonuclear weapons the United States might well have to fight limited wars again. One had to expect that other regional conflicts would occur in which the United States would feel obliged to intervene because important interests were considered to be at stake. If, as in the case of Korea, there was a risk that these new regional conflicts could escalate to high levels of warfare that we wanted to avoid, then the United States would most likely have to limit its objectives and the military means it would employ. Quite appropriately, those who drew this particular lesson from the Korean War came to be known as adherents of the Limited War School.

The disagreement over strategy between adherents of the Never-Again and the Limited War viewpoints was not resolved after the Korean War. These contending views had an impact on American policy-making in subsequent crises.

The Never-Again philosophy played an important role in keeping the Eisenhower administration from intervening in the Indochina crisis of 1954. The prolonged and costly French colonial war in Indochina seemed to be ending in defeat when the French army was surrounded by Vietminh forces at Dienbienphu. Everyone in the Eisenhower administration agreed that the loss of Indochina to the communists would severely damage U.S. interests. They regarded it of the utmost importance to contain the spread of Chinese Communist influence in Asia. Eisenhower himself had coined the phrase "row of dominoes" to highlight concern that the loss of any country, however geographically remote, to communism would trigger further setbacks in adjacent countries. As the French defeat drew closer, some of Eisenhower's advisers favored air strikes to relieve French forces surrounded at Dienbienphu. The leading spokesman of the Never-Again School, General Matthew Ridgway, was Army chief of staff at the time. President Eisenhower himself held views that echoed the all-or-nothing thinking of the Never-Again School. Ridgway and Eisenhower believed that before intervening with air power, which could not be militarily decisive, a careful calculation should be made of the additional forces—ground forces—that would be necessary to defeat the communists in Indochina. Their sober calculation indicated that the United States could probably "win" such a war but that to do so would take an even larger military effort than had been expended in the Korean War. Sobered by this hard-boiled cost-benefit analysis, Eisenhower rejected military intervention altogether and decided to try to deal with the consequences of the now certain French defeat through diplomacy.

In the Offshore Islands crisis off mainland China in 1958, when a Chinese Communist invasion of the island of Quemoy seemed possible, the Joint Chiefs of Staff, reflecting the all-or-nothing point of view, asked President Eisenhower to predelegate to them the authority to use tactical nuclear weapons if they judged it necessary to use them to defeat a Chinese Communist invasion. Eisenhower refused to do so this time, reflecting a view associated with Limited War thinking. He believed, just as Truman had in the Korean War, that the president himself must retain tight control over military options that could trigger unwanted escalation of a limited conflict. What this case illustrates, therefore, is not only the tension between the two strategic concepts but also the fact that when confronted by the possibility of unwanted escalation of a local crisis, even a president who sympathizes with the Never-Again philosophy will recognize the need to keep a limited conflict limited and forgo the all-out use of force to gain a military victory. Which of the two strategic philosophies dominated, therefore, was sensitive to the special character of each crisis.

Several years later in the Laos crisis of 1961–1962, the all-or-nothing preference of the Never-Again School was present in the sweeping war plan prepared by Joint Chiefs of Staff that included possible use of nuclear weapons in response to President Kennedy's request for military options in case his diplomatic efforts to secure the neutralization of Laos failed and Communist forces continued to advance on the battlefield. It is not the case that U.S. military leaders wanted to fight a war over Laos; rather, they wanted to make the point that if we did intervene on a small scale to begin with, the war might escalate into a direct clash with Communist

China and then, in order not to lose or fight an inconclusive war as in Korea, it might be necessary to resort to nuclear weapons.

THE IMPACT OF VIETNAM

Let us turn now to developments in U.S. policy toward Vietnam from 1961, when Kennedy became president, to 1965 when Johnson sent American combat forces into Vietnam. One of the puzzles which historians have not yet adequately clarified is the marked decline during this period of the influence of Never-Again thinking in American policymaking. Neither the new civilian leaders nor the new military chiefs who came into office with President Kennedy subscribed to the all-or-nothing position of the old Never-Againers. Instead, Kennedy gave high priority to developing a strong counterinsurgency capability and tried to use it to help the South Vietnam government in Saigon cope with the increasingly strong effort to overthrow it by the Communist-oriented Vietminh insurgents. Before his first year in office was over, Kennedy had sent U.S. military advisers into South Vietnam. Although he was to increase the number of military advisers and indirect military assistance, Kennedy was assassinated before he had to face the critical decision of whether to send U.S. combat forces or to accept the defeat of the Saigon government. His successor in the presidency, however, was confronted with this choice and, encouraged by all but one of his advisers, George Ball, Johnson crossed the threshold and began direct military intervention.

As events unfolded and more and more forces were sent to Vietnam, it became clear that Johnson had been prepared to do a great deal militarily to prevent the overrunning of South Vietnam. But from the beginning he was deeply worried that the Indochina conflict might escalate uncontrollably, draw us into another major war with China, and also force the Soviet Union into substantial involvement in support of North Vietnam. To avoid unwanted escalation, just as Truman had done in the Korean War, Johnson imposed important limits on the objectives and scope of the U.S. military effort. He ruled out an invasion of North Vietnam, limited the targets of air attacks on North Vietnam, and refused to declare a national emergency and request Congress to authorize calling up the military reserves. In consequence, U.S. strategic options for fighting the war were limited. For various reasons, the seemingly attractive strategy of using major U.S. ground forces to seal off the borders between South Vietnam and North Vietnam and Laos and thereby stop infiltration of large-scale North Vietnamese army units and supplies was rejected. Also rejected was another strategic option: the defense "enclave" strategy to protect major cities and ports in the South. The only remaining strategic option was the questionable and increasingly costly one of fighting a prolonged war of attrition to grind down the North Vietnamese armed forces, a contest in which we expected to prevail. However, in March 1968, after the Tet offensive, when Johnson's advisers told him that the war had reached the point at which it no longer made sense to increase U.S. forces and that he should move toward ending it, the president followed their advice.

After assuming the presidency in 1969, Richard Nixon introduced his "Vietnamization" policy of gradually withdrawing U.S. ground forces while beefing up the capability of the South Vietnamese armed forces and trying to negotiate an acceptable settlement of the war with Hanoi. Nixon's policy was a partial, limited success. He succeeded in ending the war in a way that secured his limited objective (which he and Kissinger never openly acknowledged) of obtaining a "decent interval" of time between the with-

drawal of U.S. forces and the likely overrunning of South Vietnam by North Vietnamese forces. In fact, this outcome was virtually inevitable because to end the war Nixon and Kissinger had to make important concessions in the negotiations with Hanoi that left South Vietnam highly vulnerable whenever Hanoi should decide to resume the fighting.

If the Never-Again philosophy had become too impotent to be able to prevent U.S. military involvement in Vietnam in 1965, the unsatisfactory outcome of that war triggered a very strong revival of the all-or-nothing approach to military intervention that had been emphasized by the Never-Again School. This was coupled with severe criticism of the constraints that Johnson had imposed on military strategy and on the conduct of military operations, constraints that, it was argued, had prevented the United States from winning the war. It must be said that those who advanced these criticisms of Johnson's conduct of the war ignored the reasons, already noted, that led him to judge such constraints to be necessary. But the fact remains that instead of allowing the military chiefs to develop and apply a strategy that they thought might produce a quick decisive victory, Johnson had engaged in micromanagement of military operations and slow, piecemeal military pressure—a policy of "gradualism" that ran counter to professional military doctrine for war-fighting. These specific criticisms of Johnson's conduct of the war generated a strong revival and elaboration of the Never-Again approach in the post-Vietnam era. The new version of that doctrine came to dominate U.S. strategic thinking and was used to discredit the rationale of the Limited War approach. Those who continued to have misgivings over the all-or-nothing aspect of the post-Vietnam doctrine had a hard time gaining a hearing.

THE WEINBERGER-SHULTZ DEBATE

Nowhere was this more evident than in the head-on clash during the first Reagan administration between Secretary of Defense Caspar Weinberger and Secretary of State George Shultz. Their debate, at times impassioned if not also acrimonious, was triggered by a number of difficult and controversial decisions the Reagan administration had to make concerning whether American military forces should intervene in some way in the civil war in El Salvador, whether direct U.S. military action of some kind should be threatened against the Sandinista regime in Nicaragua, what role U.S. forces should play in protecting neutral shipping in the Persian Gulf during the Iran-Iraq war, and finally the pros and cons of placing U.S. forces into Lebanon in 1982, an intervention that ended in the loss of the lives of 241 Marines when terrorists bombed their barracks in Beirut.

In addition to disagreeing on specific policies, Weinberger and Shultz cast their views in general philosophical-strategic terms. Secretary of Defense Weinberger, deeply influenced by the disaster of the Vietnam War and strongly supported by the Joint Chiefs of Staff, argued against direct participation of U.S. military forces in Third World conflicts. To intervene in such conflicts, he argued, could once again, as in Vietnam, draw us into prolonged, increasingly costly, and increasingly unpopular wars of attrition that might end inconclusively or in defeat. If we took the first small step of military intervention we might find ourselves, once again, as in Vietnam, on a "slippery slope" that would eventually lead to large-scale involvement of U.S. forces and prestige.

Weinberger and the military chiefs recognized that important U.S. interests were often at stake in such Third World conflicts, but they argued that we should limit ourselves to giving economic aid, military supplies, and advice and to making greater use of covert operations. Beyond indirect assistance of this kind, we should rely on diplomacy to protect our interests.

To this, Shultz objected, arguing that diplomacy and force could not be completely separated. Diplomatic efforts not backed by credible threats of force and, when necessary, with limited use of force would often prove ineffectual, resulting in damage to U.S. interests. The views attributed here to Shultz should not be misunderstood; he was not stating or supporting the extreme position of hawks who argue for much more ambitious uses of military force. Rather, Shultz was articulating the traditional, conventional view that a great power with global interests must back its diplomacy from time to time with credible threats of force and must be willing to use military force on occasion if threats did not suffice. In effect, Shultz was saying to Weinberger, how can I as secretary of state protect and advance American interests if my diplomatic efforts lack teeth?

Shultz went public with his views in a major address on April 3, 1984. He insisted: "Power and diplomacy always go together. . . . Certainly power must always be guided by purpose, but the hard reality is that diplomacy not backed by strength is ineffectual. Power and diplomacy are not distinctive alternatives. They must go together, or we will accomplish very little in the world."

In his speech, Shultz did not reject the "lessons" of Vietnam to which Weinberger, the military chiefs, and many others had subscribed, but he observed that situations do arise when a "discrete assertion of power" will be needed to support our limited objectives.

This speech and another one Shultz made several months later (October 25, 1984) provoked Secretary of Defense Weinberger to rebut Shultz publicly. In a carefully crafted address to the National Press Club in Washington (November 28, 1984) Weinberger presented his own philosophy on the role of force. In this speech, which he titled "The Uses of Military Power," Weinberger listed what he called "six major tests" that should be made in judging whether the United States should employ its own military forces in Third World conflicts. (He later stated these same preconditions for use of force in an article in *Foreign Affairs,* Spring 1986.)

Four of Weinberger's preconditions are of particular interest in that they have dominated American strategy ever since. (Each of his four conditions will be listed here with an indication how it differs from Shultz's position.) First, Weinberger insisted, the United States should use force only when its truly vital interests were at stake. Shultz, on the other hand, felt this condition was too restrictive. He argued that the United States had many important interests which, though less than "vital," also had to be protected and that these interests could often not be safeguarded unless our diplomatic efforts were backed by military power.

The second precondition Weinberger laid down reflected the all-or-nothing maxim and was equally restrictive: "Should the United States decide to commit its forces to combat, we must commit them in sufficient numbers ... to win. If we are unwilling to commit the forces or resources to achieve our objectives, or if the objective is not important enough so that we must achieve it, [then] we should not commit our forces." In other words, the United States government should not intervene unless it was prepared to do everything necessary to win a quick, decisive military victory.

Shultz did not lack sympathy with this view but he took the position that the vast majority of foreign policy conflicts with which the United States must deal are cases that, unlike World War II, "fall short of an all-out national commitment." In this vein

Shultz went on to argue that when confronted by lesser challenges, the lesson of Vietnam that Weinberger emphasized could not be rigidly employed. Shultz argued as follows: "The need to avoid no-win situations cannot mean that we turn automatically away from hard-to-win situations that call for prudent involvement. These [cases] will always involve risks; we will not always have the luxury to choose the most advantageous circumstances."

Weinberger's third precondition for the use of force was that U.S. military forces should not be committed to combat unless they were given "clearly defined political and military objectives"—a condition that, according to many critics of the conduct of the Vietnam War, was not present in that war and contributed to failure there. Shultz, although not unsympathetic with this view, pointed out that there were many murky, complicated crises in which Weinberger's third precondition could not be easily met. When U.S. interests were sufficiently at stake we would have to adapt military power to the situation as best we could. Our political objectives would have to have priority over establishing clear-cut military objectives, and we would have to accept political constraints on employment of military force that deviated from military doctrine on how to use military power most effectively.

Another of Weinberger's preconditions, again drawn from the Vietnam experience, referred to the importance of domestic political support. Notice the form in which Weinberger stated this caveat: "Before the United States commits combat forces abroad, the U.S. government should have reasonable assurance of the support of the American people and their elected representatives in Congress." Shultz certainly understood the importance of domestic political support for use of American forces abroad, but he could not accept Weinberger's extreme and unqualified position on the matter. Rather, the secretary of state argued, decisions to use force in defense of American interests "cannot be tied to opinion polls." And, in a further barbed reply to his cabinet colleague, Shultz reminded him that "a president who has the courage to lead will win public support if he acts wisely and effectively." (Weinberger's other two preconditions, which are not discussed here, were that the use of U.S. forces for combat should be undertaken only as a last resort after exhausting other means for safeguarding our vital interest, and that the relationship between objectives and means should be continually reassessed and adjusted as necessary.)

Although it was the criticism of Vietnam by U.S. military leaders that provided the impetus for a revival of Never-Again thinking, their views were strongly supported by many civilian leaders and strategists. The sweeping rejection of the Limited War concept put those who tried to make the minimal case for the need to back diplomacy occasionally with threats of force or limited military actions (like Shultz in his debate with Weinberger) on the defensive. In fact, those who rejected Vietnam did not limit the lessons they drew and the prescriptions for the future to questions of military strategy. Not only did they revive the basic all-or-nothing maxim of the old Never-Again School; they broadened it into the assertion of a comprehensive national strategy that held that henceforth any contemplated use of force on behalf of foreign policy should be rejected unless it adhered to sound military doctrine for fighting and winning wars.

Thus, the post-Vietnam doctrine called into question, tacitly rather than explicitly, Clausewitz's famous maxim that war is a continuation of politics by other means and that political considerations necessarily take precedence over military logic. Rather, the new doctrine argued, use of force in support of foreign policy must give way, if necessary, to military requirements for the effective, efficient use of force.

TESTS AND CHALLENGES TO THE POST-VIETNAM STRATEGIC DOCTRINE

There was to be no significant challenge to the new political-military doctrine until the Bosnian war. The imperatives of the new way of thinking about the restricted role of force had been reinforced by the disastrous intervention in Lebanon.

The successful U.S. military actions that followed in Grenada and Panama were held to demonstrate the wisdom of the new doctrine's requirement for use of overwhelming force to achieve a decisive outcome quickly and cheaply. The Bush administration's response to Iraq's aggression against Kuwait was entirely consistent with the new doctrine; it constituted a textbook illustration of the wisdom of committing overwhelming military force and using it in accord with sound military doctrine that military leaders were allowed to implement, without micromanagement of military operations by political leaders and without undue political constraints.

In the case of Somalia, U.S. military leaders initially hesitated to send forces to ensure delivery and distribution of food and medical supplies. Their hesitation was overcome by strictly delimiting the objective to the humanitarian task of eliminating starvation, by employing large enough forces to accomplish that mission, and by establishing in advance the terms for quick withdrawal of most U.S. forces and turning over to the United Nations responsibility for disarming Somali clans and reconstructing state structures.

In this way the Bush administration hoped that U.S. forces could intervene effectively on behalf of the humanitarian objective without risk of being drawn into a "quagmire." The strategy for doing so reflected key principles of the post-Vietnam doctrine of getting in with ample force, achieving the military objective quickly, and getting out once it was accomplished. However, critics of Bush's policy of limited humanitarian intervention warned that withdrawal of U.S. forces without adequate disarmament of the forces of rival Somali "warlords," who could be expected to lie low while U.S. forces were present, would lead to a resumption of violence thereafter in a struggle for power. Among those who voiced these concerns was UN Secretary General Boutros-Ghali, but he failed to obtain a broadened commitment from the Bush administration to participate in the necessary effort to secure substantial disarmament of the forces of the rival Somali clans. In effect, one can criticize the Bush administration for making a questionable effort to separate the achievement of humanitarian objectives from the other problems that had to be dealt with in order to obtain the secure environment needed for establishing a stable political structure in the country. Soon after the departure of the bulk of U.S. forces, the UN command in Somalia found itself unable to make progress in encouraging political reconciliation in the country and increasingly at odds with the strongly armed forces of the Somali factional leader General Mohammed Farah Aidid in Mogadishu, the Somali capital. U.S. forces were drawn into the UN effort to neutralize Aidid's forces and to capture him, a decision by the Clinton administration that subsequently received strong criticism at home. The result, a small but politically significant number of American military casualties, led to a major debate as to whether U.S. forces should remain in Somalia.

The domestic controversy over these developments forced President Clinton to delimit the U.S. military role in Somalia and to set a six-month limit for withdrawal of U.S. forces. In addition, the controversy generated by the setback in Somalia reinforced the already-strong inhibition against any U.S. military involvement in Bosnia, even as part of UN peacekeeping forces. The unsettling experience in Somalia also led the Clinton administration to raise questions openly about the wisdom of UN intervention in so many unstable crisis situations.

Although the threat of violence to U.S. forces in Somalia was so low as to make limited intervention initially acceptable, heavy casualties were deemed possible should U.S. military forces intervene in Bosnia. From the beginning of the Bosnian crisis the post-Vietnam doctrine played a significant role in discouraging U.S. military involvement. Neither the Bush nor the Clinton administrations found it easy to identify usable military options acceptable to domestic and international opinion, for dampening the conflict in ways that would avoid a long-term, costly involvement. The dilemma regarding the use of force was identified very clearly by a *New York Times* journalist:

> From the Pentagon's vantage point, the Balkan war was not an inviting conflict. In Panama and again in the Persian Gulf, the Pentagon demonstrated that its vision of warfare is a short violent conflict in which the United States brings overwhelming force to bear and then quickly withdraws, leaving the local inhabitants to sort things out for themselves. Anything short of that tends to be seen as a quagmire in which each small step deepens the military's involvement and raises the prospect of defeat. It is a dichotomy born out of the military's bitter experience in Vietnam and Lebanon. . . . The plans that Western powers are developing for possible military intervention [in Bosnia] are shaped more by the desire to avoid being entangled in the region's blood feuds than to put an end to fighting.

The new Clinton administration seemed more disposed than its predecessor to use force, but its threat of doing so was limited to use of air power and excluded use of ground combat forces. Unilateral military action by the United States was excluded, and the Clinton administration had great difficulty obtaining substantial support from western allies; indeed, it did not appear to press them very hard. In fact, although not excluding use of force in Bosnia, Secretary of State Warren Christopher echoed some of the criteria for use of force that Weinberger had earlier laid down. Appearing before the Senate Appropriations Committee on April 27, 1993, Christopher stated that any use of force would have to meet "four strict tests: the goal must be stated clearly to the American people, there must be a strong likelihood of success, there must be an 'exit strategy,' and the action must win sustained public support."

As the Bosnian tragedy dragged on and the western powers delayed taking military action, numerous voices, including those of George Shultz and Margaret Thatcher, criticized the unwillingness to use force. The post-Vietnam doctrine, they felt, was dangerously inadequate if used as a guideline for policy in any and all circumstances. Critics complained that the administration and its western allies "have allowed themselves to be paralyzed by the all-or-nothing school of military thinking."

Another critic argued that a "discriminate use of force would . . . be a good precedent. If the only time the United States is going to use force is on the huge scale of Desert Storm, the post–Cold War world is going to see few Saddam-like invasions but much more 'ethnic cleansing.'"

Unable or unwilling to make threats of force that were sufficiently credible and potent, Washington's efforts to use deterrence strategy to deter aggression in the Balkans and to employ coercive diplomacy to persuade the Serbs and Croats to undo or at least halt their actions against the Bosnian

Muslims proved largely ineffectual. Within the United States itself, the Bosnian experience revived the tension between the maxims of the Never-Again philosophy and those of the Limited War School, but this challenge to the post-Vietnam doctrine did not succeed in altering policy. In the end, as of the time of this writing, the most the Clinton administration was able to commit itself to was to provide a substantial U.S. force to help implement a genuine agreement among the Serbs, Croats, and Muslims to end the war. And even this "commitment" was qualified by attaching important conditions.

American leaders will have to develop concepts and general guidance for dealing more effectively with the dilemmas we have noted regarding the role of force and threats of force in post–Cold War diplomacy. It has been suggested, for example, that in Bosnia-type situations, threats of force and, if necessary, limited force may be applied effectively only on behalf of setting clear limits to intolerable behavior. It is questioned whether current U.S. strategic doctrine that counsels the use of force only in the service of vital interests, and only as a last resort, serves American diplomacy well in all instances. Whereas no single one of the many individual conflicts throughout the world threatens vital U.S. national interests, taken together they threaten the stability of the international system and the United States may have no alternative but to consider what it can and is willing to do, together with others, to limit this threat.

In the current international environment there will continue to be occasions where threats of force will not be sufficiently credible or potent to deter resorting to war or to reverse such behavior. This was certainly the case in Bosnia; however, that case also indicates that threats of force and exemplary use of limited force can still be used at least to set limits on unacceptable behavior. This limited objective can be accomplished by clearly delineating what responsible members of the international community will not tolerate.

Presidential Decision Directive (PDD) 25, issued in May 1994, lays down very stringent conditions for U.S. participation in UN peacekeeping, peacemaking, and humanitarian operations in an effort to avoid the worst outcomes of U.S. involvement. However, the directive gives little attention to what might be done to achieve better outcomes when preventive diplomacy fails and major violence occurs within or between states. More attention needs to be given to ways of achieving modest, but still useful objectives in such conflicts. Again Bosnia provides a useful example. Thus, when members of the international community made specific, quite limited demands on the Bosnian Serbs, demonstrated unity in their determination, and generated credible threats of force, the Serbs substantially adhered to the lines that were drawn. These limited successes of coercive diplomacy occurred when the West demanded that the Sarajevo airport be opened for delivery of humanitarian supplies, when it called for a "No-Fly Zone" over Bosnia, when air drops of supplies were initiated, and when ultimata were issued regarding Sarajevo and safe havens.

These were indeed modest, yet useful successes. However, the "lesson" of the Bosnian experience thus far is that threats of force were credible and potent enough only when issued on behalf of quite limited demands. Efforts to employ coercive diplomacy on behalf of more ambitious objectives were quite unsuccessful.

This may be the most that was possible in Bosnia because opportunities for timely preventive diplomacy at an early stage in the breakup of Yugoslavia were passed over. The broader, more fundamental lesson of Bosnia is, therefore, not that the international community did eventually establish that limited force is a legitimate policy instrument under such circumstances but, rather, that it is imperative to improve the international community's ability to engage in timely preventive diplomacy.

If the restrictive guidelines set forth in PDD-25 are taken literally, the result would be to exclude participation of American military forces in most situations requiring peacekeeping, peacemaking, and even intervention for humanitarian purposes in unstable, chaotic situations. However, PDD-25 did not prevent President Clinton in the autumn of 1994 from enlisting Security Council support and then ordering U.S. military forces into Haiti to restore democracy and return President Aristide to power. When Washington's ultimatum to the Haitian military junta to step aside failed, the president felt obliged to order American military forces to intervene. They were on their way to Haiti when a last-minute diplomatic mission by former president Jimmy Carter, General Colin Powell, and Senator Sam Nunn succeeded in arranging a peaceful military occupation of the country. Noteworthy in this case is that the president acted without seeking a congressional mandate; in fact, it seemed likely that if Clinton had waited another day or two before sending U.S. forces into Haiti, Congress would have voted to oppose U.S. military intervention. As of this writing, the occupation of Haiti has been remarkably peaceful, with the loss of life of only one American soldier, and the withdrawal of most U.S. forces has begun. Successful use of military force, however, is not likely to moderate the strong opposition to U.S. involvement in peacemaking, peacekeeping, or humanitarian intervention when there is concern for loss of American lives and fear of prolonged involvement.

In conclusion, this brief history of U.S. efforts to consider when and how force can be used as an instrument of foreign policy indicates a continuing struggle between political and military dimensions of the problem. There is a fundamental conceptual tension between the logic of war as a political act and the "logic of the instrument" of war itself that argues for using ample force to destroy or render impotent an enemy's forces. The possibility that the all-or-nothing maxim and related criteria may inhibit a necessary use of force or threats of force when important interests are at stake must be considered. However, to act imprudently on this belief is fraught with risks for any state, especially one that is so greatly influenced by domestic opinion and when Washington feels it necessary not to act alone but as part of a multilateral coalition.

The role of force in diplomacy will continue to pose a difficult dilemma for American foreign policy. The fundamental tension between relevant political and military considerations permits no easy and definitive resolution. Policymakers can expect to be confronted repeatedly with challenging crises and difficult choices.

BIBLIOGRAPHICAL ESSAY

The first part of this chapter draws on Alexander L. George, David K. Hall, and William E. Simons, *The Limits of Coercive Diplomacy* (Boston, 1971), chap. 1, "The Development of Doctrine and Strategy." An incisive, detailed analysis of the major themes of this chapter is provided by Christopher Gacek, *The Logic of Force: The Dilemma of Limited War in American Policy* (New York, 1994). Richard N. Haass, *Intervention: The Use of American Military Force in the Post–Cold War World* (Washington, D.C., 1994) provides an incisive, well-documented analysis of the dilemmas the United States has faced in deciding whether, when, how, and why to intervene abroad.

A standard discussion of the rationale for the Limited War School is contained in Robert E. Osgood, *Limited War: The Challenge to American Strategy* (Chicago, 1957). An early account of the Never-Again School appears in Joseph Kraft,

Profiles in Power (New York, 1966), chap. 14, "The Never-Again Club."

Clausewitz's concept of the dual nature of war, summarized in Gacek's book, is also discussed by Michael Howard, *Clausewitz* (Oxford, 1983), chaps. 2–4; and by Peter Paret in his chapter on "Clausewitz" in *Makers of Modern Strategy from Machiavelli to the Nuclear Age*, ed. Peter Paret (Princeton, 1986).

The "debate" between Weinberger and Shultz is reflected in Caspar W. Weinberger, "U.S. Defense Strategy," *Foreign Affairs* 64 (Spring 1986); and George P. Schultz, address to New York Synagogue, October 25, 1984 (Department of State Bulletin, 1984), and his address at Yeshiva University, December 9, 1994 (Department of State Bulletin, February 1985).

Of the many critical assessments of U.S. strategy in the Vietnam War, particularly influential was Harry G. Summers, Jr., *On Strategy: A Critical Analysis of the Vietnam War* (Washington, D.C., 1981). A useful general survey is Russell F. Weigley, *The American Way of War: A History of United States Military Strategy and Policy* (Bloomington, Ind., 1973).

For a critical analysis of President Bush's humanitarian intervention in Somalia see, for example, Sidney Blumenthal, *New Yorker,* October 25, 1993. For newspaper comments cited in this chapter on Clinton's Bosnian dilemma, see Michael Gordon, "Limits of U.S. Role: White House is Seeking to Minimize Any Use of Military in Balkan Conflict," *New York Times,* August 11, 1992; Elaine Sciolino, "Christopher Explains Conditions for Use of Force in Bosnia," *New York Times,* April 28, 1993; and Paul A. Gigot, "Foreign-Policy President Finally Acts on Yugoslavia," *Wall Street Journal,* August 7, 1992.

Jane Holl offers suggestions for rethinking the current U.S. doctrine regarding use of force in diplomacy in "We the People Here Don't Want No War: Executive Branch, Perspectives on the Use of Force," a paper presented at the Aspen Conference, August 1994.

For PDD-25, "'The Clinton Administration's Policy on Reforming Multilateral Peace Operations," see Department of State Publication 10161, May 1994.

In recent years, numerous writers and observers have urged greater emphasis on preventive diplomacy as an alternative to international interventions after armed conflict has erupted. An excellent treatment of the subject is provided by Australian Foreign Minister Gareth Evans in *Cooperating for Peace: The Global Agenda for the 1990s and Beyond* (St. Leonards, Australia, 1993).

15

Military Power and International Order

Is Force Finished?

ELIOT A. COHEN

The notion that military power has run its course as a force in international politics is a hardy perennial of serious thought about international relations. It has reappeared in the early 1990s, sturdier than ever. That similar views—most notoriously, those advanced before the First World War by authors like Norman Angell—had been proven abysmally incorrect in the years before World War I has not prevented their reemergence. Indeed, in the dispute between international relations "realists" and their various opponents, the continued centrality of military power has remained a constant point of contention. The case for the obsolescence of military power, however, has never been stronger, nor has it ever had advocates as convincing and authoritative as those who now make the case. Even hard-bitten strategic thinkers such as Edward Luttwak have turned their backs on their hard-won expertise in order to argue

that war, or at least large-scale conventional war, has run its course.

The case for the obsolescence of military force has many sides, but two stand out. There is, first, an empirical argument: No matter what the cause may be, it is a simple fact that military confrontation means less in contemporary international politics than in decades. The central issues of international relations in large parts of the world appear, for the time being at any rate, no longer to center on the prospect of clashes between states or coalitions. Thus, the end of the Cold War and the efflorescence of peace between Arabs and Israelis have turned two great arenas of military confrontation into more normal zones of peaceful trade and diplomacy. Military budgets in almost all major states have decreased, and appear likely to continue to do so; where the contrary is the case (China, for example) one may plausibly turn for an explanation to the natural consequences of economic growth, as well as more traditional great power aspirations. Furthermore, threats of force play no role in the relationships among the truly great powers. French diplomats may mistrust Germans, but they do not believe that German military power poses a threat to French security. Japan and the United States may confront each other over trade, but war between the two states remains unthinkable.

A second set of arguments attempts to explain why this change has occurred, all of which look at changes in domestic politics and popular attitudes and beliefs as the determinants of change. Perhaps the best known was advanced by Francis Fukuyama in a famous article (and subsequent book) on "The End of History," which contended that the gradual spread of democracy, broadly understood, would gradually replace the riven world of the nineteenth and early twentieth centuries with a pacific and beneficent—if, to be sure, rather boring—consumerist and liberal culture. Others, such as John Mueller, have contended that war has survived as an atavism, but one which may nonetheless succumb to the good sense of humanity, much as the age-old practice of dueling eventually gave way to lawsuits.[1] Edward Luttwak and others argue that competitive trade has taken the place of warfare and that modern societies have become too sensitive to the loss of life—"debellated," in Michael Howard's useful phrase—to tolerate the kind of bloodshed that afflicted Europe in World War II.

The various proponents of the view that force plays a decreasing role in international relations concede that in some parts of the world—"the slums of international society," as one writer puts it—organized violence has an effect on the conduct of politics. Even so, they can argue that force has proven fruitless. Saddam Hussein's adventure in Kuwait in 1990 only brought disaster upon his country, if not upon himself, and the fighting in Yugoslavia has, in this view, brought only misery and hardship to its inhabitants. The small change of war—the chronic destruction in the Caucasus, the Chechen uprising, the Algerian civil war, the insurgency in Sri Lanka—does not mean much, because it occurs at the periphery of the international system, and in any case, it shades off into banditry, rather than war as traditionally understood. To be sure, such conflicts, hideous in themselves, spin off refugee flows and international terrorism, but these (one might argue) require policing activities and not military responses. Indeed, more than one distinguished military writer has decreed the end of purposive or Clausewitzean war, that is, war directed at political objectives as opposed to senseless eruptions of violence for its own sake.[2]

THE PERSISTENCE OF CONVENTIONAL MILITARY POWER

What should we make of these arguments? The empirical truths cannot be denied: Defense budgets have declined in many parts of the world, and force is indeed unthinkable as a tool of international relations among the most advanced societies. But the world has known periods of sustained international peace before: The critical question is whether the current great-power peace reflects a fundamental change in human society and nature, or merely a particular international order, constructed around a particular and perhaps temporary configuration of power. The peculiar circumstances of the current period in international relations may explain the relative paucity of conventional warfare, or threat of its outbreak, among the great powers. One might similarly argue that the peace created by Rome in the ancient Mediterranean world stemmed not from a revolution in the attitudes of people toward war, but from an unusual and, for centuries, successful arrangement of international politics dominated by a single supreme military power. The current international system rests on an order dominated by the United States, the victor in the Cold War, which generates a quarter of the world's wealth and has a defense budget five times the size of its next largest competitor. For half a century former rivals and opponents—Japan and Germany, most notably, but in a certain sense some of the other European powers as well—have acquiesced in a largely benign American hegemony and have actually adopted many features of American culture. The former opponents of the United States, most notably the Soviet Union and China, have either collapsed or jettisoned the central features of their ideologies that were hostile to the United States. Other countries have turned to—and received—American military protection. The new American empire may best be seen operating in the Persian Gulf, where the armed forces of the United States have established a semipermanent foothold, and where, in good imperial fashion, the local inhabitants pay (in this case, quite cheerfully) the costs of protection. After decades of turning to other powers (first Britain, then Iran, then Saudi Arabia and the emirates) to protect the Gulf, the United States has now permanently established the 5th Fleet in the region, keeping thousands of pilots deployed at bases from which they keep a watch on Iraq and Iran.

American military power serves a number of critical functions. In some areas—the Persian Gulf most notably—it guarantees weak states against attacks by their neighbors. In Asia, in particular, it serves as a guarantee of a system of international relations. The American treaty and alliance relationships with Japan, South Korea, and Australia help shield those countries, to be sure. More important, the presence of the United States stabilizes a region in which a number of states might otherwise feel compelled to develop much larger military forces than they currently have. America's security relationship with Japan does not simply protect that nation against foreign enemies: It indirectly protects China and other Asian states against the consequences that might flow from a frightened and heavily rearmed Japan. Finally, American military power serves not simply as a guarantor but as an organizer of military coalitions, both permanent (like NATO) and ad hoc (like those in Somalia or the Persian Gulf). American military participation is often indispensable to the logistical and intelligence support and the command and control of coalition operations. Where the Americans are willing to lead (as in Yugoslavia), other countries will often follow, even if reluctantly. None of this means that the American imperium, if it may be called such, implies automatic intervention in every large conflict around the world or suggests the overwhelming dominance of the United States in any conflict. It does mean that almost any country embarking on the use of force beyond its borders must think about the possible reactions of the United States. But will states continue to use force to settle international disputes?

The end of the Cold War—itself the product of the crisis of the Soviet system, and not a fundamental change in international attitudes toward the use of force—meant the end of a massive military confrontation in Europe and, in retrospect, spelled the end of conflict in other parts of the world as well. After 1948, the wars of the Middle East were premised on the existence of a Soviet Union that would rearm the Arab states following their confrontations with Israel and that could shield them from their military inferiority to Israel. With the end of the Cold War, all proxy conflicts between the United States and the Soviet Union lost the oxygen that had kept them alive. Cuban soldiers could not rely on Soviet transports and supplies; Marxist guerrillas could not hope for support from Moscow; and isolated North Korea found itself quite literally starved in the absence of ideologically derived support from Beijing.

To read broader trends from this diminution of war over a period of less than a decade, however, is to extrapolate too much. The new world order, which is indeed one in which the role of conventional force has diminished, rests on a number of assumptions, the most crucial of which are the continued military dominance of the United States, the credibility of its security guarantees, and the willingness of the United States to make good on both its promises and its threats. It also rests on other assumptions, including the persistence of a liberal international trading order, a continued absence of catastrophic events (such as the successful use of weapons of mass destruction for political purposes), and the continued high price of conventional military power. All of these assumptions may weaken or collapse over the long term, say, twenty or thirty years. It is already clear that the United States has low tolerance for casualties in minor military engagements. Both of its political parties wish to cut the defense budget, and both have wings that are isolationist. If one were to imagine a world in which, let us say, the United States reduced its military to a third or a quarter its presence size, or in which it refused to provide security guarantees to Europe or Japan, the possibility of conventional warfare among major powers would look rather different than it does today.

A major disruption of the international trading order is unlikely, but not inconceivable. So, too, is the possibility that the enormous conventional military edge of the United States, which depends partly on high barriers to entry to military power, may be eroded by technological developments. A world dominated by smart networks of cruise missiles and sensors relying on commercially developed information technology may put effective military power within the reach of even small states.

Insofar as many of the arguments for the end of an age of warfare rely on an analysis of deep trends in civilization (and of western civilization more broadly), they must confront the apparent disruption of a trend to comity in Europe by the calamities of the world wars. For the broader interpretations of the end of history the Second World War (and, for that matter, the first) is merely a blip in a long-term trend towards peace; for others, the world wars exercised a definitive effect, inoculating western communities against the bacilli of warfare. Both views, however, should give pause to those who see a secular trend away from military power. If the world wars were mere aberrations, one may reasonably anticipate the possibility of other aberrations ahead; in view of their calamitous effects, one might think that the aberration could prove more important than the trends. As for the second argument, one wonders how to prove that humanity (or at least its more developed societies) has been permanently debarred from the regular resort to warfare. World War I did not prevent Europe from exploding in cataclysmic conflict barely twenty years after its close. Great wars may have profound effects on the societies that wage them, but surely those effects may wear away over time or yield to other changes no less great. The horrors of the Thirty Years War taught Europeans to exclude religion, insofar as possible, from interstate conflict. That did not prevent other sources of conflict from exercising no less baleful an effect in succeeding centuries. The people of Yugoslavia had one of the bitterest experiences of any European state during the Second World War: That has not prevented them from resorting to large-scale violence.

In sum, one may accept the view that for a time—ten years, twenty, a half century or even longer—conventional warfare may look unattractive to large and developed states. But the reasons for this period of peace may have much more to do with contingent events than with deep-seated trends. Moreover, the argument for the obsolescence of military force often turns on a distinction between the political utility of force in the past and its relative uselessness now.[3] But one must remember that the role of military power in the past was often less than proponents of a perpetual peace make it out to be. It has always proven difficult, though hardly impossible, to use war as an instrument of foreign policy. More than one head of state has learned, in Churchill's words, that

> the Statesman who yields to war fever must realize that once the signal is given, he is no longer the master of policy but the slave of unforeseeable and uncontrollable events. Antiquated War Offices, weak, incompetent, or arrogant Commanders, untrustworthy allies, hostile neutrals, malignant Fortune, ugly surprises, awful miscalculations—all take their seats at the Council Board on the morrow of a declaration of war. Always remember, however sure you are that you can easily win, that there would not be a war if the other man did not think he also had a chance.[4]

Those who declare that war has become unthinkable err in believing that in the past nations resorted to it confidently or in a calculated fashion. Indeed, as more than one historian has observed, war is a catalogue of folly, unintended consequences, blunder, and calamity. Those facts have never, of course, prevented nations from resorting to it. The origins of war may be found not merely in the cool calculations of political leaders, but in other, less rational considerations—including, for example, a concern with national honor. That diplomats use the words "national credibility" today as

opposed to "national honor" reflects more a change in the language of political discourse than a change in its fundamental nature.[5]

Robert Tucker has recently written that the fundamental problem of American foreign policy today is the "contradiction between the persisting desire to remain the premier global power and an ever-deepening aversion to bear the costs of this position."[6] This apt observation addresses only half of the question of American global preeminence, which surely rests, at least in part, on the willingness of other actors in the international system to challenge it. The recurring tensions between the United States and China, the world's richest and the world's most populous states, have a significance that goes well beyond clashes over trade, the sale of nuclear-related technologies, and the relationship of Taiwan to the mainland. They represent, rather, the first symptoms of a challenge to American hegemony or, if one prefers, global leadership, by the world's rising power. It is conceivable, furthermore, that over time other states and nonstate actors may join China in challenging the American role in world affairs. For the moment, however, it is safe to say that in the Sino-U.S. relationship lies the key to a future challenge to American dominance of world politics.

What should the American course be? To answer the question, one must ask what the world would look like without American military dominance, a circumstance as difficult for us to imagine as our current posture would have been to our ancestors a century ago. It would be a world in which no major Asian or European power could count on the umbrella of American nuclear deterrence or the support of its conventional power. In all likelihood, it would be a world in which Japan and Germany would feel compelled to become more normal great powers, probably armed with nuclear weapons. Smaller states (Taiwan, most notably, but conceivably others, such as Israel) might also openly acquire, or declare their possession of nuclear weapons. Brushfire wars—the Somalias, Bosnias, and the like—would be left to burn themselves out, to an even greater extent than is already the case.

Such a world might not be catastrophic, but there is little doubt that it would pose far greater risks of large-scale warfare—with attendant human, economic, and environmental destruction—than the current arrangement. The alternative is for the United States to preserve its military superiority over other international actors for a period of several decades or more. Such an effort is particularly important as the international system adjusts to the reconfiguration of power brought about by the rise of China, the collapse of Russia, and the spread of free enterprise throughout the world, but particularly in Asia. During such a period of turbulence, the United States has a special contribution to make in providing structure and order without mere dictation. If one accepts this view, one must explore the issue of feasibility and thus must consider the nature of contemporary military power.

THE AVAILABILITY OF MILITARY POWER

Armed force itself is undergoing a transformation as great as that of the economic forces upon which it ultimately rests. We may divide the world's military powers into five groups: the United States, in a category by itself; the great powers, to include Russia and China, as well as the west European states and Japan; the lesser (but still far from insignificant) powers, including countries as disparate as India and Egypt; substate organizations; and international entities.

The central fact regarding the distribution of military power in today's world is the dominance of the United States of America. The United States today probably spends at

Table 15.1. Defense Expenditures (and Percentages of U.S. Expenditures), 1985 and 1994.

	1985 ($b)	1994 ($b)
United States	339 (100)	279 (100)
Russia/USSR	317 (94)	107 (38)
Japan	28 (8)	44 (16)
China	26 (8)	28 (10)
Germany	46 (14)	35 (13)
Iran	18 (5)	2.2 (1)

Note: The expenditures are in 1993 dollars; the numbers in parentheses show the percentage of U.S. expenditures. These figures are subject to the vagaries of poor statistics and the uncertainties of exchange rates. Thus, the 1994 figures for Russia and Japan are certainly much too high, while those for China and Iran are probably too low.

Source: International Institute for Strategic Studies, *The Military Balance 1995–1996* (London: Oxford University Press, 1995), pp. 264–269.

least three and probably much more like five or six times as much on defense as the next-largest power (see table 15.1).

Indeed, allowing for the anomalies of exchange rates and the efficiency of American defense expenditure—which may be relatively greater than that of countries such as Japan, even if inefficient in some broader sense—the discrepancy may be greater yet. The accumulated decades of high defense spending mean that the United States has at its disposal military capabilities that do not merely exceed those of other countries, but lie altogether beyond their reach. The differences begin with the largest military platforms. Only the United States, for example, has a large stealth bomber like the B-2 or 90,000-ton nuclear-powered aircraft carriers. But this possession of military platforms out of the financial and (in some cases) technological reach of other states is but part of the tale. The United States has a mastery of space-based reconnaissance and communications satellites, the ability to project large amphibious and strike forces half a world away, and air power of an operational and technological sophistication unmatched anywhere. Moreover, the quality of American military organization, sharpened in realistic training environments like those of the Army National Training Center or the Nellis Air Force Base is matched only by very few militaries elsewhere.

Other advanced countries can, in selected areas, deploy forces as sophisticated as those of the United States albeit in much smaller quantity, or with more narrowly focused capabilities. A British mechanized brigade is probably as good as its American equivalent; a Japanese conventional submarine can in some (not all) respects perform as well as its nuclear American counterpart; Israeli fighter pilots can deliver limited air strikes within the Middle East with equal precision and safety for their crews. But none of these countries singly, or even together, can match the full range of American conventional capabilities or their global reach. The deployment by the United States of half a million men and women to the Persian Gulf in 1990, in a move conducted by the least developed and most poorly staffed of its theater commands, and for which previous logistical planning provided very little guide, is testimony to the reach of American power.

Ironically, perhaps, the noncombat uses of American military power in the Gulf may have some of the greatest implications for its future use of force. The ability to transport large forces around the globe, to provide them with up-to-date intelligence, and to coordinate their operations (and those of America's allies) are three qualities of American military power that can have a profound impact on a conflict, even if American troops are not directly engaged. Should the United States decide to supply a state or coalition with weapons, training, and comprehensive intelligence and to coordinate their efforts, it can provide a tre-

mendous increase in military power without its own forces firing a shot. This indirect use of military power may prove more effective than its direct use.

Certainly, only the United States can contemplate the full range of conventional military operations, including large-scale air and sea campaigns. For the lesser military powers, however, the choices are far more limited. In the past, many have attempted to duplicate the style of warfare and armament adopted by the superpowers. Countries like Iraq, with its fleet of thousands of tanks and hundreds of aircraft, or Argentina, with a single proud but ill-equipped aircraft carrier, are examples. Their current choices are to purchase a few, high-quality pieces of military technology and rely heavily on foreign support for such basic military functions as training and maintenance. They can turn to the cheaper military technologies (mines, most notably) as a way of making themselves difficult targets for more sophisticated states to attack.[7] Finally, they can (and in some cases have) seek to increase their military power by developing weapons of mass destruction and acquiring weapons (ballistic missiles, in particular) that may be inefficient, but nonetheless do not require the kind of sophisticated infrastructure available only to the larger states.

If the smaller military powers have seen their military potential diminish over time, substate actors—fringe groups such as Hezbollah, for example—have found an increasing amount of lethal military power at their disposal. Whether using conventional explosives or threatening to use unconventional weapons such as nuclear waste, subnational groups have extended their military reach. Exotic military technology—ultralight gliders and remote-controlled mortars, for example—is not too expensive for such groups, and following the dissolution of the Soviet Union, plenty of expertise exists to enable these groups to use them effectively.

States, of course, may exploit these capabilities as well.[8]

Finally, the aggressive use of military power by the United Nations in Somalia and elsewhere and the operations in Yugoslavia by NATO raise the question of international organizations as military actors. Although hardly as potent as states, international military institutions do exist. Ironically, the most important and durable of these, the North Atlantic Treaty Organization, did not use force until after the Cold War. If nothing else, these organizations constitute large military coalitions, governed by more equal and mutual relations than has ever been the case in the past. Cumbersome procedures and military operations on the basis of consensus rather than a clear national policy are to be expected. National priorities and preferences continue to exert the largest role in determining how military operations would unfold. Nonetheless, international military institutions, however feeble and unsatisfactory, seem destined to grow in importance. Standing military committees and arrangements are indispensable for the effective use of force by groups of states, and the trend appears to be toward greater multilateral rather than unilateral displays of military power.

What does the changing pattern of military power signify? Certainly, it represents a change from the norm of the nineteenth and even the early twentieth centuries, when military power itself was more homogeneous and more proportional to the size of the states involved. It was more homogeneous because armies resembled one another closely: One could count divisions, or even bayonets, and come up with roughly equivalent forms of power. Today, however, large elements of military power rest in platforms and organizations that do not exist in all countries—sophisticated airborne warning and control systems, for example. As a result, a country that has an air force

one eighth the size of the United States (for example) probably has considerably less than one eighth America's air power. The qualitative element of military power has grown enormously over time, and that is not likely to change any time soon. It is as if chess players had moved into a world in which one side's rooks and knights had several times the mobility of their opponents, or in which only one side could see the chessboard clearly. The game itself has been transformed.

THE TRANSFORMATION OF MILITARY POWER

In the late 1970s and through the 1980s, Soviet writers began to discuss what they termed a military-technical revolution, what American experts in the 1990s began referring to as a "revolution in military affairs." Despite different emphases, both agreed that warfare stood on the verge of a substantial change, comparable to that wrought by the advent of nuclear weapons, or, before that, the tank and airplane combination of the late interwar period, or, earlier yet, the advent of the railroad, rifle, and telegraph. At the heart of the current revolution in military affairs lies information technology, which has changed financial, economic, and social institutions at a pace that gives no sign of slowing. Some of the key elements of this change are as follows:

- Precision weapons have spread: In NATO operations over Bosnia in 1995, for example, over two thirds of the munitions used had some form of precision guidance, compared to only 8 percent in the Gulf War of 1991.

- Much greater information acquisition and processing capabilities have been developed, including space-based and air-breathing platforms that allow unprecedented amounts of detailed information about an opponent's situation on the ground.

- The military hierarchy has been flattened (and in some cases, eliminated) as a result of the mass proliferation of secure telephone, data transmission, fax, and electronic mail, as well as the rapid dissemination of information to end users in the field.

- A smaller numbers of soldiers has increasing military potential to control a variety of fires brought to bear from great distances.

- New military platforms can compete with older systems: For example, unmanned aerial vehicles, attack helicopters, long-range cruise missiles, and tactical ballistic missiles now begin to displace the functions of manned fighter aircraft and tanks.

This summary does scant justice to the range of changes in present and future military capability.

In theory, this kind of radical change in the conduct of war should work to the disadvantage of the dominant military power. In practice, however, it seems unlikely to do so. Not only does the United States alone have the combination of material, intellectual, and organizational resources to transform warfare: It also has a culture of military innovation that seems likely to drive change even in the absence of an opponent. To be sure, the United States has no pressing incentive to force a revolution in warfare, having won the Cold War and seeing no major opponent looming on the horizon. Nonetheless, the pressures of a shrinking budget and forebodings about China on the one hand and the pressure of technological innovation (spurred in part by a civil society enamored with the computer) on the other seem likely to push the United States to continue to lead in the development of the new means of warfare. Other countries will pursue, if less vigorously or less comprehen-

sively, the same technologies. To the extent that the dominant technologies (particularly information technology) arise from the civilian sector, all military organizations will find themselves attempting to catch up with the private sectors. Already, for example, simulator technology, long a specialty of the military establishment, is being driven by civilian entertainment and business applications.

The revolution in military affairs has implications for international politics. As suggested above, military power will become more opaque than in the past and, as a result, may introduce greater uncertainty into the calculation of military balances around the world. It is already the case that one cannot merely compare classes of equipment as one could, say, in 1940, when the relative merits of aircraft depended almost exclusively on the visible attributes of the platform (shape, engine horsepower, and the like). Today, however, the quality of modern weapons depends far more on less visible attributes, such as avionics, the kind of precision weapons used by the platform, and the command and control system that links all of these together. The platforms themselves—be they airplanes, tanks, or helicopters—may be twenty or thirty years old, but while such age used to mean obsolescence, today it means nothing of the sort. A 1960s vintage tank with a new gun, modern thermal sights, and a suite of reactive armor may be inferior to the most recent tank to roll off an American production line, but it may well match a 1970s vintage Soviet T-72. Thus, straightforward comparisons of military hardware no longer say a great deal about military power.

Complicating matters still further, military power seems headed on a course toward increasing asymmetry. To some extent, various forms of military power have always been asymmetrical: A fortress in the nineteenth century might delay a force of infantry ten times the number of its defenders for days or weeks. The first modern, profoundly asymmetrical weapon system was the submarine, which allowed an inferior naval power such as Germany to challenge the naval supremacy of Great Britain and the United States not by open battle, but by maritime guerrilla warfare. Such asymmetries will only increase in the future. The mine and naval cruise missile can keep the forces of large naval powers from bringing their weight to bear against modest ground forces, and good naval cruise missiles are relatively cheap and available on the international arms market, even to isolated countries such as Iran. Ballistic missiles—resting on half-century-old technologies that have proliferated around the world—allow countries without conventional air power to strike deep into an enemy's rear areas. Unmanned aerial vehicles will, in the future, allow even a relatively primitive military to see a battlefield in ways that would have been unthinkable in the age dominated by manned aviation. Even among the great powers, military organizations will cease to resemble one another very closely, as countries develop a wider variety of combat formations, including heavy armored units, attack helicopter formations, and special forces. In the past, military analysts could hope to weigh military balances on land by looking at homogeneous measures such as armored division equivalents. Problematic as those measures were then, they are even more so now.

If military power becomes more difficult to measure adequately, such uncertainty may induce caution among states, but it may also lead to errors in the other direction as well. A world in which the quantity and quality of military power has become difficult to assess may prove to be a world in which the cost-benefit ratio of warfare may look far more favorable than the peaceably inclined would wish. The lure of push-button warfare, the seeming omniscience

provided by sophisticated computer simulations and displays, and the very real advantages to be derived from launching preemptive attacks with precision-guided weapons may make throwing the first punch look attractive.

As commonly discussed, the revolution in military affairs refers to a change in conventional military power. There are, however, substantial changes afoot in other forms of military force. The first of these is so-called nonlethal warfare, a term that often raises the hackles of military people, who correctly point out that a nominally nonlethal weapon can have very lethal consequences if, for example, a high-power microwave weapon disables an airplane causing it to crash. Nonlethal warfare is by no means new: Tear gas and electronic warfare are examples of military technologies half a century old that were intended to disable opponents or their weapons, not kill people through the use of high explosives or fast-moving bits of metal.

Nonlethal weapons, however, have taken major steps forward, particularly, but not exclusively, in the West. A variety of systems —sonic generators that nauseate and disorient enemy soldiers, sticky foams or super-slippery substances that immobilize individuals or crowds, supercaustics and coagulating agents that ruin machines by eating away at them or clogging their engines—have become available to disable persons or machines. Some commentators have argued that these weapons may transform warfare, particularly small wars. Hard-headed commanders have trained their men to use them and deployed them to the field. Nor are such weapons confined to use by western countries: China has marketed a field-ready blinding laser.

Nonlethal weapons are often extremely nasty—as will become clear when the first supercaustic lands on human flesh rather than on armor plate. It is unlikely, however, that nonlethal weapons portend as great a change as their proponents suggest. They have yet to be proven as reliable weapons in combat, and until they are, soldiers (who are a conservative lot) will prefer to reach for tried-and-true means of disabling an opponent. In some cases, these weapons will run afoul of conventions banning chemical, biological, or particularly inhumane weapons. Nonetheless, they do point to a general evolution in warfare—an increasing focus on killing or disabling technological complexes and not merely the human beings who operate them.

If the promise of nonlethal weapons is probably overblown, the same cannot be said of information warfare. The information revolution is a cliché, but like most clichés, it became such because it reflects a large truth. The explosion of communication over the Internet, the dependence of seemingly mundane mechanical processes (railroad switching, for example) on commands sent at long distances by electronic means, and the pervasiveness of the computer (now in most middle-class homes in the United States and soon to be as prevalent as the television set) are transforming economics and social relations. Presumably, the information revolution will also alter, in no less profound ways, the nature of conflict.

One must say at the outset that we are only in the early stages of the current information revolution and that some of the early exploitation of information manipulation for profit or malice remains secret— concealed by companies that do not wish to ruin the confidence of their customers and clients or by countries that fear revealing their vulnerabilities. Nonetheless, the following broad observations appear to apply:

- Despite the increased awareness of the problem of computer security since the problem emerged a decade or so ago, the vulnerability of financial systems and of all organizations dependent upon information has increased.

- Information warfare attacks do not require anything like the kind of military infrastructure that conventional operations do: A few hackers can do serious damage.

- Information warfare attacks offer three peculiar advantages: They allow covert attacks (one may be at war without knowing it); they allow a certain amount of precision (one can attack a particular company or sector, in ways either relatively benign or lethal); and they can bypass the conventional defenses of distance or military power that have shielded countries like the United States.

- The organization and conduct of information warfare blurs, and in some respect completely obliterates, the boundaries between military and civil organizations upon which current military organization rests. It also blurs the distinction between piracy or banditry, on the one hand, and politically motivated and directed uses of power on the other.

For the time being, it would appear that information warfare has been used primarily to gain information and perhaps conduct some minor forms of information sabotage. No country or even a substantial substate actor has threatened its use openly or waged a sustained campaign that has inflicted substantial damage.

A conflictual international order in which information warfare plays a large role remains difficult to imagine. Many conventional concepts and organizations will have little use: Arms control agreements cannot cover modems or even software and the training of computer scientists. Conceivably some older military concepts (information blockades, perhaps?) may apply. The most likely prospect is that an age in which information warfare occurs will be one in which many, though not all, of the disparities between the great powers (and particularly the United States) and all others will be reduced, although they will not disappear, and in which formal conflict is replaced by chronic information guerrilla warfare.

The two revolutions discussed thus far— a conventional, high-technology transformation based on precision weapons, and another based on the exploitation of the information technologies—may very well coexist with each other, exercising reciprocal influence, perhaps, but working their effects in parallel, rather than together. There may be other transformations under way, which will also coexist. One is the continued proliferation of weapons of mass destruction. One normally thinks of nuclear weapons, but there are others as well: biological weapons, nuclear waste (as recently planted in Moscow by Chechen rebels), and chemical weapons (as in the case of the Aum Shinrikyu cult in Japan). The nuclear proliferation problem has changed over time. Nuclear weapons from the former Soviet Union may have found or may find their way into the hands of states or substate organizations; the diffusion of nuclear related expertise and the lessons of the artful Iraqi hiding of a substantial nuclear program in the late 1980s until the Gulf War of 1991 suggest a continuing and growing problem.

Nuclear weapons may seem a way of trumping the superior conventional forces of the United States and its allies, not so much defeating high-technology threats as stymieing them. Advances in biotechnology seem to guarantee the spread of weapons that can be developed even by countries with modest scientific infrastructures. Although arms control (particularly the nuclear nonproliferation treaty) has helped restrain the spread of nuclear weapons, it has not stopped it. The revelation of the South African and Iraqi nuclear programs, the progress of the North Korean and Pakistani

programs, and the likelihood of a serious Iranian program all indicate trouble ahead.

A world in which weapons of mass destruction are threatened or even used would be dramatically different from the world of the Cold War, governed by the verities of deterrence between the superpowers. Preemptive military action (perhaps using the capabilities of the two transformations discussed above) may become not a theoretical possibility, but a practical necessity. Retaliation may become a reality and not a vague threat. For half a century, nuclear war (and more broadly, warfare involving weapons of overwhelming strength) existed as an abstract construct—deadly serious, no doubt, but abstract nonetheless. The calculus of international power will change profoundly once the world witnesses the actual use of such weapons and certainly if they are used more than once or twice.

The proliferation problem represents not so much a revolution in military power as a resurgence and intensification of older phenomena. The same may be said of the rise of peacekeeping, peacemaking, and humanitarian intervention, which have now employed nearly three quarters of a million soldiers, cost more than $12 billion, and come at a cost of 1,200 deaths.[9] In large part, the tremendous expansion of such international efforts represents not so much the rise of international consensus as the emergence of intolerable disorder in "failed states." In that respect, the situation may be less different from the nineteenth-century experience of imperial policing than one would like to think. At least one group of historians has made the case that a good deal of late British imperial expansion can be explained by the need to limit anarchy, not to acquire territory. A similar logic would seem to apply to the United States, which has displayed little enthusiasm for adventures of this kind and has embarked upon them nonetheless. Moreover, it is often, though not always, the case that multinational enterprises of this kind merely represent the use by the United States and some of its key allies of the United Nations as a convenient cover for its own operations. Nonetheless, the fact remains that international organizations such as the United Nations or NATO have begun mounting military operations of remarkable size and complexity in countries as different as Cambodia and Yugoslavia. Where previous peacekeeping operations involved no more than a battalion or two of soldiers, by 1995 division- or corps-level military organizations were being assembled and deployed.

The practical obstacles to effective international humanitarian intervention, however, remain substantial. International organizations appear to have neither the staying power nor, in many cases, the capacity for decisive action that the individual great powers have. The United Nations, although it has made movements in the direction of creating an effective military staff, has yet to do so, and it has yet to discover a funding mechanism that will enable it to sustain a large military intervention with any degree of confidence. In almost all cases, national policies persist: Underneath their blue berets, Americans remain Americans, French remain French, and Pakistanis remain Pakistanis. Even in such a well-established alliance as NATO, the procedures of coalition decision making can involve excruciatingly complicated procedures for coordination and action.[10]

Nonetheless, despite all the drawbacks of multinational intervention, it seems likely not merely to continue but to grow. More states find themselves facing unbearable demographic and social pressures, and ethnic, religious, and national hatreds—some ancient and deeply rooted, some recent and deliberately cultivated by political leaders—boil to the surface. Multinational states have failed in all corners of the globe: sometimes peacefully (as in the amicable divorce between the Czech and Slovak republics), sometimes with considerable violence (as in Yugoslavia and Rwanda), and occasionally with lesser, but nonetheless substantial uses of violence (in the repartition of Palestine between Jews and Arabs). Ironically, the civil wars that have ensued have on more than one occasion engendered a multinational response.

From a broader view yet, the world would appear to confront the possibility of a substantial expansion of insurrectionary warfare, comparable in magnitude to (but different in its causes, course, and consequences from) that of the revolutionary struggles against European colonial powers in the middle of this century. In part, revolutionary warfare offers, as it did forty or fifty years ago, a way of counterbalancing the conventional strength of one's opponents—as the Israelis have learned in their confrontation with the Palestinians. In part, it is a response to the crisis of governance in developing states, as in Algeria. But no matter the source, it is a form of struggle that will likely persist and gather force well into the next century.

THE PERSISTENCE OF FORCE

Thus, despite the end of the Cold War, the world is very far from seeing the end of force. It may take different forms than in the past, and it may be used for different purposes, but it will continue to play a role in international politics. Conventional warfare as generals have conceived it for decades—the movement of mass armies across frontiers—may recede, but conventional force will still undergird the international order. Much depends on the course of international politics, particularly in Asia, where the potential exists for conventional clashes among the mistrustful states on China's periphery. Above all, a great deal depends on the role the United States chooses to play in the international system. As a kind of benign Rome, it may use the power of its legions to guarantee a general, if unruly, order around the globe, its current military supremacy serving to deter large-scale warfare of the traditional kind. Were it to decide that the burdens of empire—and they are real burdens—are not worth it, however, more than one state will find that the end of Cold War will lead to the possibility of hot war.

More likely, however, the United States will preside uneasily over an international system in which force remains latent and only partly visible to the participants in the world politics. Much of that influence will be felt in nonevents—the kinds of aggressive uses of force that political or military leaders simply do not contemplate because of the possibility of an American response. The danger will be one of confusing a general peace among states with a broader pacification of humanity. Although such a welcome development has occurred in some parts of the world, it would be extremely unwise to think that it has occurred everywhere, or even in most places. Until such an epochal event occurs, American military power will serve as the indispensable security partner of particular states, the leader of coalitions seeking to thwart or contain particularly aggressive powers, and as the guarantor of the stability of the international system itself.

NOTES

1. See, for example, Francis Fukuyama, "The End of History?" *National Interest* 16 (Summer 1989): 3–18; and John Mueller, *Retreat from Doomsday: The Obsolescence of Major War* (New York: Basic Books, 1988), pp. 217–269.

2. See, in particular, John Keegan, *A History of Warfare* (New York: Alfred A. Knopf, 1993).

3. The anti-Clausewitzian argument is made by Keegan (see note 2 above), but by others as well, including military historians Martin van Creveld, *The Transformation of War* (New York: Free Press, 1991); and Russell Weigley, "Militarized Civilian Leadership," in *Historical Dimensions of National Security,* ed. Klaus Knorr (Lawrence: University Press of Kansas, 1976).

4. Winston S. Churchill, *My Early Life* (New York: Charles Scribner's Sons, 1930), p. 232.

5. See Donald Kagan, *On the Origins of War and the Preservation of Peace* (New York: Doubleday, 1995).

6. Robert W. Tucker, "The Future of a Contradiction," *National Interest* 43 (Spring 1996): 20.

7. See Patrick Clawson, ed., *Iran's Strategic Intentions and Capabilities* (Washington, D.C.: Government Printing Office, 1994).

8. Laurie Mylroie, "The World Trade Center Bomb," *National Interest* 42 (Winter 1995–96): 3–15.

9. See "Background Note: United Nations Peacekeeping Operations," July 1995, http://ralph.gmu.edu/cfpa/peace/toc.html.

10. This becomes clear even in the austere official account of Deliberate Force, the NATO bombing operations in Yugoslavia in 1995. See "AFSOUTH-1995.11.06-Operation Deliberate Force," gopher://marvin.stc.nato.int:70/11/yugo.

16

Can Collective Security Work?

Reflections on the European Case

JAMES GOODBY

We shall see how the counsels of prudence and restraint may become the prime agents of mortal danger; how the middle course adopted from desires for safety and a quiet life may be found to lead direct to the bull's-eye of disaster. We shall see how absolute is the need of a broad path of international action pursued by many states in common across the years, irrespective of the ebb and flow of national politics.

Churchill, *The Gathering Storm*

Classical definitions of collective security in Europe have been too narrowly constructed to be a practical guide to policy analysis, especially when considering the use of military force. A more useful approach would be to define collective security as a policy that commits governments to develop and enforce broadly accepted international rules and to seek to do so through collective action legitimized by representative international organizations. This policy finds particularly congenial the notion that democracies tend not to go to war with one another. It accords considerable weight to the role of power in international relations, but does not regard it as the only consideration that should guide national decisions.

Collective security is a strategic concept and a process, but it is not and never may be a condition. Its advantage as a strategic concept is that it is responsive to many post–Cold War security problems, while other concepts, such as balance-of-power politics, are not. Intrastate conflict is a new challenge for collective security, and the international community has been moving fitfully toward establishing rules that justify intervention with military forces in internal affairs in extreme circumstances. Balance-of-power politics has its place in European security, but it is ill-suited to deal with conflicts that, although internal, threaten international peace and security.

Spheres-of-influence policies, which imply a balance of power, are valid in theory and worked well in Europe during the Cold War. Competition for influence, however, is a natural result of efforts to define and defend the outer limits of a great power's reach. Disputes can be generated by such competition, disputes that have little or nothing to do with intrastate conflict, which is often, but not always, based on ethnic differences. Even in cases of conflict generated by competition for influence, collective security policies pressed vigorously and consistently by the smaller nations of Europe and supported by the United States, Russia, and the European Union could help to head off conflicts in Europe.

YUGOSLAVIA: THE REINTERMENT OF COLLECTIVE SECURITY?

A fresh look at collective security after the Cold War must begin by acknowledging that the concept—especially the notion that military forces should be used to uphold rules of behavior—has been catastrophically damaged in its first major post–Cold War test in Europe. From the beginning, the war in the former Yugoslavia was a classic case for collective action. Indeed, from the beginning of the war there was collective action by the European Community and later by the United Nations. Preventive diplomacy was not exercised when it might have made a difference—long before the armed conflict erupted in 1991. At every step of the way—from the preconflict phase of the crisis until the NATO air campaign of August 30–September 14, 1995—collective action was too little, too late. Until the fall of 1995, the governments that were in a position to lead

a collective approach were not willing to pay the price in the use of military force that a commitment to collective security demanded.

The experience of Yugoslavia shows that the concept of collective security was not applied well in that particular case. The many errors of commission (mainly diplomatic) and of omission (mainly military) underscore the difficulty of using military force collectively in circumstances that can plausibly be labeled as civil war. Major nations concluded early on that the benefits of enforcing international norms did not equal the costs of doing so. They were willing to commit forces for humanitarian purposes, but that is not the same as collective security. Despite this record, the experience cannot be used to invalidate the idea of collective security everywhere and forever, particularly in light of the 1995 Dayton Accords.

There was an element of the Prisoners' Dilemma in the equation. The crisis of the Yugoslav succession failed to generate international cooperation because fears of defection distorted the deliberations of those who were in a position to help. Washington saw itself as the major contributor of forces if it became involved, because European nations would not be able to meet the needs. The Western Europeans saw themselves as the victims of a United States that might provide air power but no ground forces to do the dirty work. Russia saw the West gaining influence in a part of the world it regarded as within its sphere of interest.

Equally salient was the fear, quite frankly expressed on all sides, that Yugoslavia was a quagmire that would demand a high price in lives and money. The expectation that the war could be confined to the territory of the former Yugoslavia produced a cost-benefit analysis that consistently led to decisions that were insufficient to meet the escalating needs for a collective response. The value assigned by governments to collective security was not weighty enough to overcome "the counsels of prudence and restraint."

There was no shortage of warning time for preventive diplomacy: The crisis in Yugoslavia was a long time in coming. By the late 1980s, preventive diplomacy in the form of economic programs should have been tried and, by early 1991, crisis prevention in the form of mediation should have gone into high gear. Neither happened. Proclamations of concern were available for the asking, but no serious effort was made at conciliation or mediation. What followed might not have been inevitable, but in the absence of serious collective efforts prior to the outbreak of war, it was nearly so.

A crucial policy question for any government is to identify thresholds in conflicts that justify collective action, especially if that action might lead to armed intervention. In the case of Yugoslavia, governments concluded in the early stages of the dispute that internationalizing it might only make things worse. Intervention in the form of mediation or conciliation can always be ruled out on those grounds. After an armed conflict has erupted, the level of effort required to stop it becomes another threshold that the major nations find it difficult to contemplate, much less decide to cross. These considerations loomed large throughout the crisis of the Yugoslav succession, biasing governments against intervention at all stages of the dispute.

The wars of the Yugoslav succession showed that the question of intervening for the purpose of upholding international rules against aggression becomes extremely complex if the dispute is an internal matter—a civil war or a struggle brought on by the collapse of the system within which a political entity had previously existed. This has made it more difficult to invoke the principle of collective security as a guide to action in response to the disputes and violence that have accompanied the collapse of the Soviet Union and the transition from a bipolar to a multipolar international system.

The decision to intervene collectively even for mediation purposes is not automatic and still less is the decision to intervene with members of the armed forces. It is essential to distinguish clearly between the use of armed forces for crisis prevention, peacekeeping, protective security, and peace enforcing. Peace enforcement lies at the higher end of the scale of violence in collective security operations and is often perceived through the lens of worst-case analysis. Governments should ask themselves whether engaging in an observer mission or air strikes could lead inexorably to requiring peace enforcement at some stage; peace enforcement could theoretically require suppressing conflict on a very large scale in the territory where fighting is taking place. This nightmare is how worst-case analysis tends to portray force requirements. Nonetheless, there are many uses of military force in protective security and even in peace-enforcement operations that fall far short of that objective, yet that may still be important. Security zones or safe havens are likely to be fairly common requirements in the future, as they were in Bosnia. Isolating a specific territory—that is, cutting it off from access to trade and normal traffic—is a military problem to which solutions short of large-scale ground combat can be found. If it is assumed that all peace-enforcement operations inevitably will rise to the extreme end of the scale of violence, paralysis in decision making will result.

COLLECTIVE SECURITY AFTER THE COLD WAR

The concept of collective security is based on four premises:

- Rules of behavior among nations should be encouraged.

- Those rules should be enforced.
- Enforcement actions should enjoy the legitimacy conferred by broad international agreement.
- Those actions should generally be undertaken by multinational coalitions.

Through the first years of the wars of the Yugoslav succession, the nations that were in a position to act on these premises with military force failed to do so. The humanitarian assistance that was provided could not be regarded as an example of collective security, since it was not essentially aimed at developing or enforcing internationally accepted rules of behavior. The economic sanctions against Serbia, on the other hand, could be thought of as collective security since they were directed at developing and enforcing rules. So, of course, can the efforts to bring accused war criminals to justice.

Before deciding that the military component of collective security has little future, we should think more about this elusive idea and how it might fit current circumstances. Much has been written on the subject. Hans Morgenthau, one of the great theorists of realism in American political science, was one of the many who have analyzed the concepts and shortcomings of collective security and its military implications. In his classic book, *Politics Among Nations*, Morgenthau wrote that "the organizing principle of collective security is the respect for the moral and legal obligation to consider an attack by any nation upon any member of the alliance as an attack upon all members of the alliance." Morgenthau explained that the "alliance" to which he referred was a "universal alliance against potential aggression."[1] The principle of universality is generally cited to distinguish collective security, as manifested by the United Nations system, from a collective defense system like NATO, whose membership is limited and where the presumptive aggressor during the Cold War was also clearly understood to be a particular state.

The conditions necessary to make collective security work, Morgenthau thought, were unlikely to exist in practice. The idea of collective security, as he saw it, came down to a willingness to use military force in quarrels in which most of the "universal alliance" had no easily perceived direct stake. Furthermore, at least in Morgenthau's view, collective security was identified with defense of the status quo, and this view has been accepted by more recent writers.[2] In an era in which the status quo is being challenged at every turn, E. H. Carr's insight still resonates: "Few people do desire a 'world-state' or 'collective security,' and . . . those who think they desire it mean different and incompatible things by it."[3]

Carr was right in perceiving that collective security has many different shades of meaning even considering only its military component. Collective security in the context of ethnic, nationalistic, communal, and internal power struggles—such as those in the former Yugoslavia—present very different diplomatic problems from collective security in the context of great power relations or of aggression by one well-established state upon another. A major difference is that the rights and responsibilities of the nations in an international system, as defined over the centuries, do not convey any authority to intervene in the internal affairs of a sovereign state. Quite the opposite is true, and for good reason. Intervention in internal affairs will have to be considered, however, if the concept of collective security in the post–Cold War period is to be applied to the complex problems attendant upon the collapse of the Soviet Union and of the bipolar system. This is not the only notion that distinguishes present-day thinking about collective security from that of earlier times. The following observations point to a way of thinking about collective security that would be relevant to today's world.

Collective security is not required to neglect or ignore the distribution of military power in an international system. Regional conflicts and their outcomes will affect the evolution of the international regime that ultimately will replace the bipolar order of the Cold War. Hard-headed estimates are needed to predict the results of these developments. Balance-of-power considerations may figure in some of those situations; in others, they may not. Relations among the largest states will continue to be affected by power considerations, although perhaps not with the degree of intensity that prevailed between the United States and the Soviet Union during the Cold War.

Collective security can coexist with national policies aimed at maintaining a power equilibrium, so long as the latter policies do not drive the elements of trust and cooperation completely out of the international system. Collective security should work best in a system of democratic states, which much of Europe is becoming, since power balances among such states arguably are less important in security calculations than their shared system of governance. For the time being, the power balance between Russia and the West suggests that war is unlikely. But in the end, Russia's continuing progress toward democracy is the best guarantee of security in Europe. To encourage that, cooperation between Russia and the West in the security affairs of Europe is essential.

Collective security need not be global or universal in scope. The Organization for Security and Cooperation in Europe (OSCE), the largest European security organization, has over fifty members, more than the League of Nations and about the same as the United Nations in its early years. During the early 1990s, the OSCE was endowed by its participating states with structures and procedures so that it could be used for collective security purposes if they so chose. Its status as a regional agency under Chapter 8 of the UN Charter gives it a claim to universalism; the UN Security Council could call on the OSCE to take necessary actions in the name of the global community of nations. The geographic coverage of the OSCE—from Vancouver to Vladivostok—affords ample scope for collective security. Other ad hoc mechanisms on the same geographic scale as the OSCE have been devised to deal with peacekeeping. One of the most promising was the "contact group" established in the spring of 1994 to handle negotiations concerning the war in Bosnia. Members of this group were the United States, Russia, and the European Union represented by Britain, France, and Germany. This contact group proved to be very effective despite differences among its members. A steering committee like this should be adequate to manage many types of collective security operations on a regional basis.

Collective security need not be dedicated to defending the status quo. Any effort to base policies on the idea of collective security would be doomed if the status quo was perceived to be its main focus. The Helsinki Final Act of 1975, the founding charter of the OSCE, proclaimed the principle of inviolability of frontiers, a major preoccupation of Europeans only too aware of the disasters that tinkering with frontiers could produce. But the Final Act also stated that frontiers could be changed peaceably and by agreement, and it made human rights in each participating state a matter of concern to them all. In the end, the Final Act, as the Magna Carta of dissidents throughout Eastern Europe, contributed to ending the division of Europe and was thus one of the greatest conceptual assaults on the status quo of modern times.

Military operations that have had the hallmarks of collective security in both theory and practice have been used in the post–Cold War period to alter the status quo not to defend it. The UN Security Council's authorization of the use of force in northern Iraq was based on the principle that Iraq's treatment of its Kurdish population was a threat to international peace and security, warranting the establishment of a protected zone. This led to a de facto partition of the country. The same principle was invoked in the Security Council's authorization of force in Somalia in December 1992. Establishing surrogate governments for failed states may require the use of force, as was the case in Somalia. The result has been at least a temporary aberration from the norms of self-determination and noninterference in internal affairs. The internationally sanctioned U.S. intervention in Haiti in 1994 is another case in point.

Collective security need not be limited to relations between states, but may also address internal affairs within a state. In addition to these UN decisions, rules regarding acceptable conduct on the part of member states toward their own citizens have been established by the OSCE. Individual human rights have had a prominent place on the OSCE agenda from the beginning. Ground rules covering the behavior of a nation's troops in dealing with internal conflict were added to the OSCE's compact in 1994.

RECONCILING COLLECTIVE SECURITY WITH COMPETING COLLECTIVE DEFENSE SYSTEMS

The major powers of Europe have a common dislike of out-of-control conflict in their neighborhoods, and collective security policies cannot be easily adopted when these conflicts occur within or between countries directly on the borders of the big powers. Collective security is less able to deal with disputes involving the major powers directly, simply because these powers can safely ignore external pressures and resist any attempt to impose sanctions. If collective security is not seen by the major powers to be a sufficient basis for creating conditions of security for themselves, the most acceptable alternative will be alliance systems that lead to clearly demarcated spheres of influence. The beginnings of this trend can already be seen in Central Europe and along the periphery of Russia. Spheres of influence are not necessarily incompatible with a security regime that also embraces principles of collective security. Given a condition where small countries are able and willing to practice independent policies, collective security can coexist with spheres of influence, blunting the sharp edges of confrontation in Europe.

Naturally, the way that Moscow has pursued "peacekeeping" in territories of the former Soviet Union has raised concerns regarding the intentions of Moscow and of the leadership of the Russian military. As early as 1992, former U.S. secretary of state Henry Kissinger flatly charged that "Russian leaders try—at least tacitly—to keep open the option of repeating the events of 1917–1922, when many of the current group of independent republics attempted to break away only to be forced in the end to return to Moscow's fold." He predicted, furthermore, that "it is so-called ethnic conflicts that will be the most likely pretexts of recentralization."[4] By the end of 1992, Russia's use of its military forces quite independently of a legitimate international mandate had become the subject of public concern in the West. *The Economist* quoted the foreign affairs committee of the Russian parliament as follows: "Russian foreign policy must be based on a doctrine that proclaims the entire political space of the former [Soviet] Union a sphere of vital interests. . . . Russia must secure . . . the role of political and military guarantor of stability in all the territory of the former USSR."[5] *The Economist* declared that this was unacceptable, arguing that neither the Commonwealth of Independent States (CIS) nor Russia met the criteria for peacekeeping in the territory of the former Soviet Union, such criteria being neutrality and adherence to a set of rules.

This type of Russian intervention will become the norm if collective security mechanisms based on the OSCE or the United Nations are unable to operate effectively in countries around the periphery of Russia, as has been the case in Moldova and the Transcaucasus. If the nations of the Euroatlantic system, meaning North America and all the nations of Europe, fail to insist upon exercising a proper collective security role even over Russian objections, Russia's claim to untrammeled freedom of action in its neighbors' territories will be legitimized by default. Recentralizing the former Russian or Soviet empire is an unlikely outcome within the next several years despite election rhetoric in Russia, but George Kennan's view of Soviet thinking is relevant to current Russian thinking. Here is what he wrote on December 16, 1944: "As far as border states are concerned the Soviet government has never ceased to think in terms of spheres of interest. . . . Our people . . . have been allowed to hope that the Soviet government would be prepared to enter into an international security organization with truly universal power to prevent aggression. We are now faced with the prospect of having our people disabused of this illusion."[6] Few now conceive of collective security as a "truly universal power to prevent aggression." Its uses are much more limited; otherwise, the problem Kennan saw is much the same today.

Russia obviously perceives that it has interests in the Transcaucasus (Azerbaijan, Armenia, and Georgia) and in Moldova that justify interventionist policies despite the misgivings of the western powers. The United States, its security interests closely linked to Western and Central Europe for most of the twentieth century, naturally sees much merit in the arguments of Central European nations that their membership in NATO will create conditions of peace and stability in East Central Europe. Russia argues that its security would be damaged by this development. Both Moscow and Washington doubt that their interests can be accommodated through the United Nations or the OSCE, the global and regional security organizations to which they both belong. Thus, the stage may be set for confrontation unless a framework is created that blurs and softens the edges of western and Russian power in Europe. The future of the "new Eastern Europe" in the period following NATO enlargement illustrates the point.

To the east of the Central European nations that are prime candidates for NATO and European Union (EU) membership—Hungary, Poland, and the Czech Republic—lie several other nations whose security will be profoundly affected by the interaction of Russia and the West in the period before and after NATO and EU enlargement. These nations will collectively be identified here as "Eastern Europe," defined as the Baltic States, Belarus, Ukraine, Moldova, Romania, and the Balkans. Some might add the Transcaucasus in view of that region's oil reserves and its strategic location adjacent to Turkey, Iran, and Russia.

Russia historically has seen its security as being closely tied to this "Eastern Europe," and of course it still does, as witnessed by numerous statements by private citizens as well as the government. The United States also has interests in this region, just as it had in the Cold War's version of Eastern Europe, and as it has today in Central Europe. At the most basic level, it is important for the United States and the West in general that norms enshrined in the charter of the OSCE, as well as in the UN Charter, be scrupulously observed. These solemn undertakings are supportive of democratic principles and antithetical to aggression. They need constant and consistent reinforcement if collective security policies are to have any chance of moderating the usual consequences of spheres-of-interest policies. The United States also has more specific interests related to its long-term support for the independence of the westward-leaning Baltic States and to more recent assurances given to Ukraine concerning that nation's sovereignty and territorial integrity.[7]

From the viewpoint of external actors, five distinct outcomes for Eastern Europe can be envisaged as Russia, the United States, and the European Union strive to create conditions of security and stability for themselves and others throughout the continent. Obviously the outcome that finally emerges will depend to a large extent on the actions and policies of the countries within the region. They are hardly as malleable as this analysis might suggest.

- Eastern Europe might be integrated into a Euroatlantic community, including both Russia and the United States, through "a series of mutually supporting institutions and relationships," to quote from a declaration of Presidents Clinton and Yeltsin made in Moscow on May 10, 1995. Examples of such relationships are a treaty between NATO and Russia, a more active and coherent role for cooperative mechanisms related to NATO such as the Partnership for Peace (PFP), the North Atlantic Cooperation Council (NACC), a stronger OSCE, and associate memberships in the EU. The point is to create interpenetrating connections, so that the line of demarcation between the West and Russia is blurred.

- Eastern Europe might become a buffer zone between Russia, on the one hand, and an enlarged NATO and an expanded EU, on the other hand. This outcome presumes that the countries of the region

enjoy good relations both with Russia and with the NATO countries but that they are militarily nonaligned.

- Eastern Europe might become part of a Russian sphere of influence. This could take many forms, some of which could include military alliances.

- Eastern Europe might become an area where Russia and the West compete for influence. Obviously, some of the countries arbitrarily assigned in this analysis to "Eastern Europe" are leaning strongly westward (for example, the Baltic states, Slovenia, Croatia), and links with western countries would be quite natural for them.

- Eastern Europe might become part of the western sphere of influence. In this case, the economic, political, and security ties of the countries in this region would be preponderantly with the EU or other western countries.

An international security regime in Europe dominated by opposing spheres of influence will almost certainly emerge if security for the major nations of the Euroatlantic community cannot be found in a regime that includes Russia in some way satisfactory to all the major powers. The implications of this choice should be well understood. Both collective security and spheres-of-interest regimes require commitments of leadership and resources. Both are difficult for democratic governments to create and implement effectively. It is quite possible that spheres of interest could coexist with a collective security regime if dominant powers practiced restraint and smaller states managed their internal affairs skillfully. But carried to the lengths frequently seen in the past in Europe, spheres-of-interest policies promise a return to division and confrontation. Collective security policies offer a hope, even though forlorn, of attenuating the effects of balance-of-power politics while also offering a means of dealing with intrastate threats to international peace and security.

Collective security cannot nullify the fact that great powers cast large shadows: Power plus proximity equals influence. Nonetheless, collective security is one tool that small nations can use to offset, to an extent, the power wielded by larger nations. This is a different requirement for collective security than that presented by the situation in the former Yugoslavia, where the great powers have at least some common interests in stopping ethnic conflict. In the case of a small nation seeking to escape domination by a larger one, the great powers may have few or no common interests. Their interests, in fact, might run in different directions. In such cases, the best hope for a successful collective security arrangement is derived from the interest that great powers have in perpetuating a pattern of behavior that suits their general requirement for predictability, peace, and stability.

INTERNATIONAL ORGANIZATIONS AND THE MANAGEMENT OF COLLECTIVE SECURITY

For better or worse, international organizations are generally the vehicles through which collective security decisions are made and the management of peacekeeping operations is carried out. The procedures that the major nations use to make decisions about collective security can be as important as the merits of any given case in determining the success or failure of collective security. The smaller nations find their voices in international organizations, but for these multilateral creations to work effectively, great powers—Russia, the United States, and members of the European Union—should also try to concert their policies through bilateral and multilateral channels. Ideally, international organizations should be integrated into "a series of mutually supporting institutions and relationships," as Presidents Clinton and Yeltsin recommended.

Ineffectual decision making and weak management are charges laid at the doorstep of most international organizations, generally with much justification. Nonetheless, the key to improving the performance of collective security operations lies in effectively meshing national and international security machinery. Collective decision making amounts to an integration of national policies, not only on basic policies, but also on day-to-day operational issues. The international organizations that governments have established to support their collective actions are often delegated managerial responsibility for implementing policies. It is here that much of the second-guessing and criticism about collective security arises.

The following summary will show that, unlike other regions of the world, Europe is fortunate in having several well-developed security organizations.

United Nations

Yugoslavia was the first crisis on the European mainland that the United Nations was asked to handle. UN observers continued to monitor events in Cyprus many years after the fighting stopped there, but the United Nations did not generally play much of a role in Europe during the Cold War. In fact, Europeans were rather smug about not needing the United Nations to handle crises, feeling that their own regional institutions could cope quite well. It is not clear how relevant the United Nations will be in the future. The wars of the Yugoslav succession have resulted in more responsibility for the United Nations on the European scene than seemed likely when the Cold War ended, but United Nations peacekeepers have worked under severe handicaps, including an ambivalence about their roles and missions. The model that emerged from the

Dayton negotiations gave NATO management responsibility for military peacekeeping operations under the general authority of the United Nations. Many non-NATO countries contributed troops to the Implementation Force (IFOR), including Russia, an important precedent for the future.

The experience underscores the fact that the United Nations is a valuable legitimizing agent, but not the best vehicle for conducting military operations where peace has not been restored. A resolution adopted by the Security Council can be used to justify military action by individual nations joined in a coalition or by nations joined in an alliance. The former was the situation in the Gulf War; the latter was the case with NATO in the Yugoslav conflict. The approval of the United Nations carries a cachet that no other organization can bestow; collective security operations endorsed by the United Nations can be conducted under circumstances where other organizations would be barred. Chapter 7 of the UN Charter confers major responsibilities on the UN Security Council for peace enforcement. There is nothing comparable at present in the charters of other relevant international organizations.

Unfortunately, the United Nations is stretched thin and has come under increasing fire for alleged mismanagement of peacekeeping. Secretary General Boutros-Ghali's report *An Agenda for Peace* contained many good recommendations for strengthening UN preventive diplomacy and peacekeeping operations. For example, the secretary general proposed that the Security Council begin negotiations under Article 43 of the charter, so that member-states could assign armed forces, on a readily available basis, to the United Nations. Boutros-Ghali also suggested a $1 billion reserve fund for peacekeeping.[8] The hard reality is that political differences and shortages of money and human resources are major obstacles to these ideas; obstacles that will not be easily or quickly overcome. The U.S. Congress and other democratic legislatures, worried about accountability, will need a great deal of convincing to fund the United Nations at the exponential rate of increase that peacekeeping demands imposed during the early 1990s. Economic development programs of the United Nations could also suffer if excessive demands are placed on UN peacekeeping functions.

The Clinton administration, after an initial flirtation with "aggressive multilateralism," laid out stiff conditions for its participation in UN peacekeeping operations. In May 1994 President Clinton signed Presidential Decision Directive (PDD) 25, formalizing the administration's approach to peacekeeping and peace-enforcement actions. The conditions included "the advancement of American interests, the availability of personnel and funds, the need for American participation for an operation's success, the support of Congress, and the presence of clear objectives, a clear ending for American participation, and acceptable command and control arrangements."[9] Under PDD-25, there would have to be a threat to international security coupled with a need for widespread relief aid, sudden interruption of democracy or gross violation of human rights, clear objectives, consent of the warring parties before entering the country, a realistic mandate, and a clear exit strategy, as well as sufficient amounts of money and troops for the mission. PDD-25 declared that the United States would not support a UN standing army, that the United States would not earmark any of its forces for UN peacekeeping in advance, and that U.S. troops would not serve under foreign commanders. The decision was made that the United States was bearing too much of the financial burden for peacekeeping and that Washington would reduce its share of the peacekeeping budget to 25 percent.[10]

Secretary General Boutros-Ghali, also frustrated by the United Nations' experience with peacekeeping, suggested that UN peacekeeping operations should be taken over by the major powers operating under a UN mandate. The approach, called spheres-of-influence peacekeeping by some observers, may come to be the preferred approach to peacekeeping, if the great powers continue to be reluctant to give the United Nations the assets it needs.[11]

Organization for Security and Cooperation in Europe

In 1990 the members of the Conference on Security and Cooperation in Europe (CSCE), as it was known then, decided at a summit meeting in Paris to create for the first time a permanent organizational structure to support activities authorized by the participants.[12] The leaders at the Paris summit meeting were beginning to address the consequences of the end of the Cold War, including the end of Europe's division. At the June 1991 meeting of the CSCE's new Council of Ministers, and especially at the Helsinki CSCE summit meeting of July 1992, the participants strengthened the collective security function of the CSCE.[13] Consensus was no longer required to call emergency meetings. A method to provide early warning of conflict was built into the Helsinki Document by establishing a High Commissioner for National Minorities. Several OSCE mechanisms now encourage early consultations on emerging crises. Fact-finding and rapporteur missions have been created and used in Albania, Armenia, Azerbaijan, Belarus, Chechnya, Georgia, Kazakstan, Kyrgyzstan, Moldova, Tajikistan, Turkmenistan, Ukraine, Uzbekistan, and the former Yugoslavia.[14]

It was agreed at the Helsinki summit meeting that the OSCE would undertake peacekeeping operations as a regional agency of the United Nations, as envisaged in Chapter 6 and Chapter 8 of the UN Charter. OSCE members ruled out anything like Chapter 7 responsibilities, the provisions that give the UN Security Council peace-enforcing responsibilities. The OSCE has been positioned by its members as a useful service agency for those who might wish to call upon it for help, but its use as a military instrument in the kind of circumstances the negotiators in Dayton faced in Bosnia is doubtful.

At their December 1994 Budapest summit meeting, the heads of states and governments of the OSCE made several decisions that could give the OSCE a key role in the preventive diplomacy of Europe, including traditional peacekeeping activities as pioneered by the United Nations under Chapter 6 of the UN Charter. In their decisions on "regional issues" they addressed the conflict in Nagorno-Karabakh in the Transcaucasus and declared their readiness to provide, after an appropriate resolution from the UN Security Council, a multinational OSCE peacekeeping force if an agreement was first reached among the warring parties for cessation of armed conflict.[15] This decision set a precedent that might be repeated in other conflicts in the vicinity of the Russian Federation. The outcome was made possible by U.S.-Russian cooperation, as well as the support of the European participants. If there is follow-through, it could turn out to be the most important post–Cold War achievement of the OSCE. At this writing, however, many significant details of the peacekeeping force remain to be resolved, and a will to go forward has been notably absent.

NATO, the NACC, and the PFP

NATO and its related institutions are highly capable of conducting collective military operations. Supreme Headquarters

Allied Powers Europe, the Military Committee, the International Military Staff at NATO Headquarters, and the several NATO military commands have many of the best planners, military leaders, and logistics experts in the western world. The North Atlantic Council (NAC), the NATO International Staff, and the delegations to the North Atlantic Cooperation Council (NACC) constitute a permanently operating consultative mechanism. The integrated military command of NATO offers a unique advantage: The command arrangements of the national forces committed to the alliance are in place and functioning. The U.S. military, always sensitive to serving under foreign command, operates smoothly and well in NATO's integrated command structure.

From its creation in 1949, the North Atlantic Treaty Organization was a collective defense arrangement. NATO embarked on its collective security vocation only in 1992 in accordance with a mandate of the UN Security Council to uphold economic sanctions.[16] NATO's peacekeeping mandate began in April 1993, when it began to enforce the no-fly zone over Bosnia with regular patrols by NATO aircraft in support of the United Nations' humanitarian operations. In August 1993 the heads of state and government of the NATO nations pledged to carry out airstrikes to prevent the strangulation of Sarajevo; they reaffirmed this pledge on January 11, 1994. Following a Bosnian Serb attack on a Sarajevo marketplace on February 9, 1994, the NAC issued an ultimatum to the warring parties that any heavy weapons found in an exclusion zone of 20 kilometers from the center of Sarajevo (with the exception of a 2-kilometer area around the center of Pale) after February 20 would be subject to NATO airstrikes.[17] On February 28, 1994, NATO engaged in its first military action ever, and two U.S. F-16s downed four aircraft attacking a factory in Bosnia. On April 10, 1994, U.S. aircraft bombed Bosnian Serb positions outside the safe area of Gorazde at the request of the UN commander. This represented NATO's first mission against a ground target. NATO aircraft attacked Serb positions the next day in order to protect UN Protection Force troops in the town.[18]

These developments amounted to a dramatic shift in the raison d'être of NATO. NATO's basic mission throughout the Cold War had been to deter or defend against an attack by the Soviet Union. Forces assigned to NATO had been used in coalitions led by the United States, the Persian Gulf war being the prime example as the Cold War was winding down. The NATO air campaign of August 30 to September 14, 1995 —which some believe led directly to the peace accords at Dayton—was the logical extension of these first steps. It consolidated NATO's new role as the premier peace-enforcement agent for the great powers in European territories outside the area of the former Soviet Union.

The NACC was established at the end of 1991 to provide a link between the NATO countries and the members of the former Warsaw Treaty Organization (WTO). It was not originally envisaged as an all-European organization with membership that would include the neutral and non-aligned nations of Europe. NACC had a special role in helping to manage the allocation of conventional force reductions among the states of the former Soviet Union. It has also become a forum for exchanging information among the NATO and former WTO countries on many types of security issues, including peacekeeping.

The Partnership for Peace (PFP) is not, strictly speaking, a multilateral organization at all. It was created at the NATO summit meeting of January 9–10, 1994, to provide a framework for bilateral cooperation between NATO and other European nations.[19] Twenty-seven states had signed agreements by the end of 1995 to cooperate in military training and other activities, with a considerable emphasis on peacekeeping. Multinational training exercises are held to develop those skills. A "16 + 1" formula in which individual PFP members meet with the NAC provides a consultative mechanism.

There are limits on the extent to which military forces connected even tenuously to NATO can be used for peacekeeping in Europe. One of them is the geographic limit likely to be imposed by Russian sensitivities and western reluctance to challenge those sensitivities. Moscow will not welcome the use of NATO committed forces anywhere in the territories of the former Soviet Union. This attitude would apply as much to Moldova as to Tajikistan. It is likely that, if it becomes necessary at all, NATO-committed forces would be used only in East-Central Europe and the Balkans outside the territory of the former Soviet Union. The experience of Russia and the other European forces in the Implementation Force in Bosnia will have a major bearing on the future of peacekeeping in Europe and of NATO's role in it. If this unique experiment in post–Cold War peacekeeping is a success, the model might be applicable in many places, for it would show that Russia and the West can cooperate in military operations in mutually beneficial ways.

Western European Union

The Western European Union (WEU) was formed in 1954 as a device to facilitate rearming West Germany and to bring it into NATO. In the Maastricht Treaty of 1992, the European Union decided to use the WEU as its nascent military arm. Currently there are ten full members of the WEU: Belgium, France, Germany, Greece, Italy, Luxembourg, the Netherlands, Portugal, Spain, and the United Kingdom. In addition, Iceland, Norway, and Turkey hold

associate status within the WEU, while Denmark and Ireland hold observer status. All these nations, except Ireland, are also members of NATO.

During the early phases of the Yugoslav conflict, France sought to activate the WEU for a collective intervention in the former Yugoslavia. Contingency planning envisaged dispatching up to 30,000 troops. The plan was quashed when the United Kingdom objected, citing its experience in Northern Ireland.[20] The WEU entered the peacekeeping/peace-enforcing field in 1992 with NATO, first through maritime surveillance operations in the Adriatic and later by participating in the UN-mandated blockade against the former Yugoslavia. The latter decision was made unanimously by the defense ministers of the WEU meeting in Rome on November 20, 1992.

One advantage of the WEU is that France usually finds it easier to conduct multilateral military operations within the framework of the WEU rather than in NATO. However, in 1995 President Chirac decided to bring France into a closer association with NATO. This decision, together with French participation in the Implementation Force in Bosnia, has shifted the European Union's military center of gravity towards NATO. The disadvantages of the WEU, compared with NATO, are that it lacks the integrated command structure of NATO and the powerful planning and logistics base that NATO can offer. To the extent that the WEU could operate with NATO, perhaps as a combined joint task force, some of those difficulties could be overcome.

Commonwealth of Independent States

On May 15, 1992, several of the newly independent states of the former Soviet Union met at Tashkent and agreed to create a collective security arrangement. The signatory countries were Armenia, Kazakhstan, Russia,

Tajikistan, Turkmenistan, and Uzbekistan. Later, this role of the CIS was recognized by Helsinki Document 1992 and by President George Bush in a joint U.S.-Russian declaration issued in Washington in June 1992.

Progress was slow in terms of creating truly multilateral machinery. More importantly, CIS peacekeeping forces dominated by Russia lacked the quality of impartiality so necessary to peacekeeping when used in border regions of Russia. The problem was complicated by hesitations in withdrawing Russian troops based in the other states of the former Soviet Union. With no housing, no civilian employment for them, and an inhospitable climate for Russian retirees in some of the new states, the withdrawals proceeded very slowly. In addition, Moscow declared itself the protector of ethnic Russians in the newly independent states, placing a new requirement on the Russian Army. This picture was further complicated by the political tendencies represented by leading Russian politicians Vladimir Zhirinovsky, who advocated reestablishing the Russian empire, and Gennady Zyuganov, who favored the voluntary reconstitution of the Soviet Union.

THE PRIME AGENTS OF MORTAL DANGER

The tragedy in the former Yugoslavia happened mainly because "counsels of prudence and restraint" prevailed. There was no effective leadership within the Euroatlantic community until 1995, when violations of the most basic precepts of civilization became too blatant to ignore and ethnic cleansing had resulted in massive transfers of populations. The experience highlighted the absence of consensus even among like-minded nations on an intellectual and political framework that would help them analyze and understand their stakes in the crises and conflicts that have erupted in or near

Europe. The idea of collective security was evoked, but its military instrument discredited yet again by the failure of the major nations to act decisively early in the wars of the Yugoslav succession. The middle course led direct to the bull's-eye of disaster.

International organizations created by governments to act on their behalf in Europe all have their limits. The OSCE is well positioned to conduct observer and mediation missions and to play a role in long-term conflict resolution efforts. Bosnia will be a test of how well the OSCE can serve as an instrument of cooperation in reconstructing civil institutions in that country. The OSCE's military role in peacekeeping does not appear to be very promising, even though it has many potential uses. The United Nations is likely to have an important validation role in Europe and in the nonmilitary aspects of collective security, of which economic sanctions is one valuable instrument. The utility of the United Nations in either mediating missions or peacekeeping missions in territories of the former Soviet Union is doubtful, and its performance in the former Yugoslavia has damaged its credibility in the use of the military instrument. NATO has already shown that it can be a powerful peacekeeping instrument, but its uses are geographically limited: Russia cannot be expected to accept NATO as a peacekeeping mechanism in the territory of the former Soviet Union. The Western European Union may become a useful military tool for the European Union but the association with the United States in NATO is a strong attraction for the Europeans. The CIS has served as a device for Russian intervention, thus far with little pretense of being a truly impartial international force. These are the organizations available to the major nations. A listing of their strengths and liabilities shows that international organizations cannot act in the absence of leadership by the major powers.

Collective security requires that governments perceive a flouting of broadly accepted international norms—particularly those related to the use of force to change borders—as a direct threat to their national interests. This is the beginning of the conceptual and practical difficulties inherent in collective security: Governments find it difficult to discern long-term dangers and, when they do, to persuade wary publics that action is necessary. Of course, no government can possibly be excused from the responsibility of assessing the costs to the nation of embarking on a collective security response to even the most flagrant violation of international rules. For this reason alone, collective security must be regarded as a strategic concept embracing a certain internal logic, as one approach available to the international community, but by no means a fully realized goal and least of all as a condition of international life.

When combined with strategic interests, international norms should weigh especially heavily in the counsels of the major nations. Judgments about collective intervention in Europe by the western nations, including the United States, should proceed from an assessment that their strategic interests in Europe are different from those that they may have in the rest of the world. Rwanda, Cambodia, and Somalia are three of the most tragic examples of suffering known to human history. Humanitarian intervention by the United Nations in these cases was fully justified. Conflicts in Europe, however, presumptively pose a higher order of security risk for the western nations. *Presumptively* is the operative word, because a commonly held view in the United States was that the war in the former Yugoslavia was a problem for Europeans, forgetting that U.S. involvement in two twentieth-century wars in Europe had in fact established the United States as a major factor in European security affairs.

In democracies, the most fundamental test for collective security is whether public support exists for the enterprise. In the United States, public opinion is wary of long or costly military commitments for the sake of the international community; intervention in Yugoslavia was never a popular course in the United States. Even within Europe—rich in all kinds of links with Yugoslavia at all levels, with publics much affected by the suffering in the former Yugoslavia, and absorbing a massive flow of refugees from Yugoslavia to European countries—governments were deterred from upholding international norms in Yugoslavia because they thought the costs of doing so were too high to win public support. Governments were reluctant to admit that their failure to act might move them closer to another major European war. In addition, for long periods there was no American leadership on this issue. Inaction helps to write the rule book of international behavior as much as action.

The four key precepts of collective security are (1) rules, (2) enforcement of those rules, (3) the legitimacy of such enforcement actions, and (4) multilateral actions. All four precepts are evident in the implementation of the Dayton Accords, and history will reveal whether the Bosnian experience has been a successful test of collective security in Europe. It is likely that the European security regime being created out of the present chaos will be based on both collective security and spheres-of-interest policies. Under current conditions, neither of these two strategies in their pure form is likely to meet all the requirements for security as perceived by the major nations. Collective security is flawed because the great powers find it difficult to believe in cooperation. Balance-of-power and spheres-of-influence policies also have escaped the restraints of those who would try to concert great power policies (even where that has been tried), and competition for a maximum degree of power has ensued precisely in accord with realist political theories. The task of maintaining order, if undertaken as the prerogative of a few great powers, can degenerate very quickly to a policy of aggrandizement and of dividing up European real estate to suit the interests of the big powers. The reasons for insisting that collective security be at least a part of the security equation in Europe and for forecasting dangers ahead if Europe relies exclusively on a spheres-of-interest strategy are evident in the baleful light of European experience with balance-of-power politics.

NOTES

1. Hans J. Morgenthau, *Politics Among Nations* (New York: Alfred A. Knopf, 1953), p. 142.

2. Ibid., p. 332; Josef Joffe, "Collective Security and the Future of Europe," *Survival* 34, no. 1 (Spring 1992): 37.

3. E. H. Carr, *The Twenty Years Crisis, 1919–1939* (New York: Harper and Row, 1964), p. 10.

4. Henry Kissinger, "Charter of Confusion," *Washington Post*, July 5, 1992, p. C7.

5. *The Economist*, November 14–20, 1992, p. 60.

6. George F. Kennan, *Memoirs, 1925–1950* (Boston, Mass.: Little, Brown, 1967), p. 222.

7. In a memorandum provided to Ukraine by the United States, Russia, and the United Kingdom on December 5, 1994, on the occasion of its adherence to the nonproliferation treaty, the three powers "reaffirm their commitment to seek immediate United Nations Security Council action to provide assistance to Ukraine, as a non-nuclear-weapon state party to the Treaty on the Non-Proliferation of Nuclear Weapons, if Ukraine should become a victim of an act of aggression."

8. Boutros Boutros-Ghali, *An Agenda for Peace: Preventive Diplomacy, Peacemaking, and Peacekeeping* (New York: United Nations, 1992), p. 44.

9. Elaine Sciolino, "New U.S. Peacekeeping Policy Deemphasizes Role of the U.N.," *New York Times*, May 6, 1994, p. A1. For discussions of PDD-25, see Daniel Williams, "Clinton Peacekeeping Policy to Set Limits on Use of U.S. Troops," *Washington Post*, February 6, 1994, p. A24.

10. Sciolino, "New U.S. Peacekeeping Policy," p. A1.

11. Daniel Williams, "Powers Assert Influence in Peacekeeping Roles," *Washington Post*, July 30, 1994, p. A12.

12. Founded in 1975, the Conference on Security and Cooperation in Europe changed its name to the Organization for Security and Cooperation in Europe in December 1994.

13. "The Charter of Paris Declaration for a New Europe," November 21, 1990, is reproduced in *SIPRI Yearbook 1991: World Armaments and Disarmament* (Oxford, U.K.: Oxford University Press, 1991), pp. 603–610; see also "Key CSCE documents in 1992," *SIPRI Yearbook 1993*, pp. 190–209, note 2.

14. For a review as of mid-1992, see "CSCE Missions," a summary prepared by the staff of the Commission on Security and Cooperation in Europe of the U.S. Congress (Washington, D.C.: U.S. Government Printing Office, September 1992).

15. The *CSCE Budapest Document 1994: Toward a Genuine Partnership in a New Era*, Budapest, December 6, 1994. *The Budapest Summit Declaration* is reproduced in *SIPRI Yearbook 1995: Armaments, Disarmament, and International Security* (Oxford, U.K.: Oxford University Press, 1995).

16. See E. Schmitt, "A Naval Blockade of Belgrade Seen Within a Few Days," *New York Times*, November 18, 1992, p. A1; and W. Drozdiak, "NATO Agrees to Impose Blockade of Serbia," *Washington Post*, November 19, 1992, p. A31.

17. North Atlantic Treaty Organization, press release (94)15, February 9, 1994.

18. C. Sudetic, "U.S. Planes Bomb Serbian Positions for a Second Day," *New York Times*, April 12, 1994.

19. For the text of the announcement, see "Partnership for Peace: Invitation and Framework Document," *U.S. Department of State Dispatch* 5, no. 1 (January 1994): 5–7.

20. J. E. Goodby, "Peacekeeping in the New Europe," *Washington Quarterly* 15, no. 2 (Spring 1992): 153–171.

17

Resolving the Conflict over Nagorno-Karabakh

Lost Opportunities for International Conflict Resolution

JOHN J. MARESCA

Two principal features make the war over Nagorno-Karabakh unique in comparison with other post–Cold War local conflicts: its historic origins, including the beginning of the current conflict as an internal dispute within the former Soviet Union, and the complex forces that underlie the dispute. These elements merit some preliminary examination, because both have contributed to the loss of opportunities for resolving the conflict since the international community began its efforts to address it in January 1992.

The first part of this chapter analyzes these two special features. The second section tracks a number of opportunities that the international community has missed in its efforts to bring about a peaceful resolution and seeks to identify the specific reasons for these failures. The final part summarizes the principal elements common to all

the missed opportunities, suggesting that a stronger and more concentrated outside leadership role, particularly from Washington, could have helped bring about a negotiated settlement.

HISTORY OF THE CONFLICT

The confrontation between the indigenous Armenians of Eastern Anatolia and the Transcaucasus and the Turkic peoples who began migrating into the region in the thirteenth century is one of history's longest and most troubled sagas. The bloodiest chapter was no doubt the period that Armenians the world over know as "The Genocide," during which hundreds of thousands of ethnic Armenians were forced from their homeland in Eastern Anatolia (many of them killed) as the Ottoman Empire crumbled and modern-day Turkey consolidated its territory. The episode would be called "ethnic cleansing" in the vocabulary of modern conflict, and it profoundly marked the Armenian people, especially the widespread diaspora.

The Azeri Turks were somewhat separate from the principal developments of this bloody period, even though there were riots and pogroms in Baku as well. The Azeris were themselves subjugated—by Russia in the northern half of the area they inhabited, and by Persia in the southern half. The northern part of Azerbaijan (north of the Aras River) was a center of the world's oil industry before the turn of the century and was briefly independent at the beginning of the 1920s. But very little of the resulting wealth went to ethnic Azeris, who mainly provided the labor in the oil fields, and the Azeris, unlike their Turkish cousins, remained under foreign domination.

Nagorno-Karabakh, traditionally called Artsakh by Armenians, has always been dominated by a population of ethnic Armenians. Among fellow Armenians, the natives of this area are reputed to have a distinctive personality, with a reputation for stubborn independence and a long tradition of armed resistance to outsiders. But Karabakh has been included in Islamic-Persian and Islamic-Russian governing entities since at least the early part of the nineteenth century.

In the early 1920s, as the Soviet Union established the internal frontiers that would demarcate the three Transcaucasian Soviet republics of Georgia, Armenia, and Azerbaijan, Nagorno-Karabakh's isolation as an autonomous oblast within Azerbaijan was left unchanged. This decision was evidently influenced by Joseph Stalin himself, quite possibly with divide-and-rule objectives in mind. The decision was contested regularly by the influential Armenian lobby in Moscow, but under the repressive Soviet system efforts to change the status of Karabakh were limited and came to naught.

The modern conflict between Armenians and Azerbaijanis dates from about 1988, but obviously has its roots in the existence of the historic Armenian enclave within the Soviet Republic of Azerbaijan. As the Soviet system relaxed into the era of glasnost and perestroika, the Karabakh issue once again emerged. The concept of uniting Nagorno-Karabakh with the Soviet Republic of Armenia became the rallying cry of Armenian nationalists, a substitute for demanding independence, which was still viewed as an impossible dream. A "Karabakh Committee" was formed in Armenia; it was actually an opposition political party, precursor of the present-day Armenian National Movement, the largest party in the Armenian Parliament. The Karabakh Committee led huge demonstrations, both in Yerevan and Stepanakert, the main city of Nagorno-Karabakh.

Azeri resentment of these developments mounted and focused the nascent Azeri sense of nationalism, which was also growing stronger at that time. Demonstrations turned into riots and pogroms against the large Armenian minorities in Sumgait, an industrial city near Baku, and in Baku itself. These events, in turn, spurred reactions on the Armenian side in a classic spiral of vengeance. Huge numbers of Armenians and Azeris fled each other's republic or were forced to leave.

The Soviet government in Moscow made half-hearted efforts to stem the tide of discontent. Direct rule of Nagorno-Karabakh was tried, but failed. The Soviet Army intervened in Baku, killing some Azeris and provoking long-lasting resentment. In Stepanakert the local legislature declared the autonomous oblast of Nagorno-Karabakh independent, basing this act on a clause in the Soviet constitution, whose applicability in the particular circumstances of Nagorno-Karabakh has been subject to debate ever since. Military confrontations began around

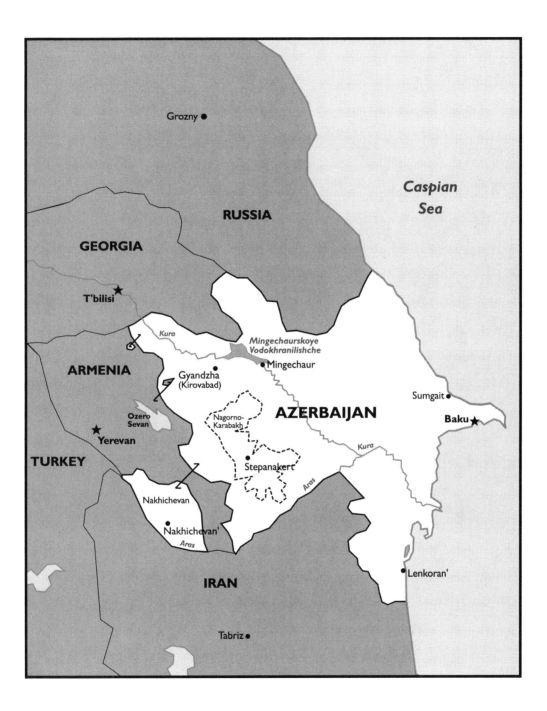

Grozny ●

RUSSIA

GEORGIA

Caspian
Sea

T'bilisi ★

Kura

Mingechaurskoye
Vodokhranilishche

ARMENIA

Gyandzha ●
(Kirovabad)

● Mingechaur

Sumgait ●

Ozero
Sevan

Nagorno-
Karabakh

AZERBAIJAN

Baku ★

★ Yerevan

Kura

TURKEY

● Stepanakert

Aras

Nakhichevan

● Nakhichevan'

Aras

IRAN

● Lenkoran'

Tabriz ●

the frontiers of Nagorno-Karabakh, and the conflict became a war. There were also incidents along the border between Armenia and Azerbaijan, and several smaller enclaves on both sides of this frontier were eventually overrun by the respective countries.

All of this continued as Armenia and Azerbaijan became independent upon the breakup of the USSR in the autumn of 1991. Before that time the conflict, though of some interest to scholars, was considered an internal Soviet problem. It was only when the newly independent states from the former USSR formally joined the Conference on Security and Cooperation in Europe (CSCE) in January 1992 and the United Nations in March of that year that the international community began to consider what its role and responsibility might be with regard to the Azeri-Armenian confrontation over Nagorno-Karabakh.

The first international community effort happened almost as an afterthought before the closing of the meeting of foreign ministers of the CSCE in Prague at the end of January 1992, when the British delegate noted that a conflict existed between two of the new member states and suggested that a CSCE fact-finding mission be sent to the area. By that time, the warring sides and the issues that separated them had been largely defined. The challenge for the international community was thus neither one of foreseeing the conflict nor of preventing it from becoming violent. From the outset of its involvement, the problems facing the international community were those of conflict resolution and reconciliation.

At the same time, the fact that the conflict had for so long been an internal Soviet one, in a region that was little known and of limited interest to the West, meant none of the governments that were in a position to contribute to a solution had a ready store of expertise, specialists, and ideas on the conflict. The West had not watched this problem grow, experienced mistakes in trying to head it off, debated alternative courses of action, or been aware of the special interests in the conflict—all factors that have been important as other conflicts, such as the one in former Yugoslavia, unfolded.

The advantage of this previous ignorance of the conflict was that the West approached this problem with relatively little political baggage, in terms of past positions or engagements. It was thus not under serious suspicion of favoring one side or the other, and it had a relatively high level of credibility with both sides. True, the Azeris believed that the West would automatically favor the Armenian side—many Azeris still believe this. But this suspicion was balanced by a persistent Armenian belief that the West, particularly the United States, would tilt toward the interests of their Turkish allies. Moreover, suspicions on both sides were somewhat allayed at the very outset of western interest in the conflict by an even-handed report from the first CSCE fact-finding mission to the region. In any case, the West generally benefited from its contrast with the Russians (up to then the only power seemingly interested in the problem), who were the subject of deep suspicion and resentment on all sides, even though they were needed and courted by everyone.

A Complex Pattern of Outside Interests and Influences

The other unique feature of the Karabakh conflict is its many-sided asymmetry. The Karabakh Armenians (called Karabakhsis by other Armenians) believe they have exercised their right of self-determination and are fighting their war of independence; the Azeris consider them an armed rebel group and believe the real war is with Armenia. Armenia holds that it is not directly involved in the conflict, but is subject to aggression through blockades by both Azerbaijan and Turkey. Turkey denies that it has a role in the conflict, but asserts that it cannot ignore the suffering of its brothers in Azerbaijan, which is being pressured by Russia. Russia claims that Turkey is encroaching on its sphere of influence and that it alone has the ability and the right to settle disputes in the Transcaucasus. Meanwhile, the Armenian diaspora supports both Armenia and the Karabakhsis, but is split between realists who would like to end the war by acceptable compromise and fanatics who see it as a righteous war to regain lost Armenian lands. Thus, to reach a solution to the conflict there needs to be more than simply an agreement between two opposing sides; there must be at least the acquiescence of all these complex interests.

A Series of Missed Opportunities

Apart from these special features, the conflict over Nagorno-Karabakh has much in common with other local conflicts: long-standing hatreds; ethnic, religious and linguistic differences; the easy availability of weaponry; emerging nationalistic feelings that have long been repressed; weak governments and leaders on all sides; a remote third-world-like setting; an unsophisticated population; exploitation and manipulation from both within and outside the area; and so forth. As is also usually the case, the experience of outside involvement has been one of missed opportunities, each with its specific contributing factors. These missed opportunities are outlined and analyzed below, in rough chronological order.

Fluid Early Period of CSCE Involvement

In many ways, the early period of western involvement in the Karabakh dispute (January–December 1992) was the most opportune moment for a global solution. The credibility of western conflict resolution was at its highest level, since it had not yet been identified with the failures in former Yugoslavia and was not yet understood to be limited by Russian policy to areas outside of the former Soviet Union. Even the CSCE still had credibility, since its capabilities and limitations were unclear. Furthermore, the parties to the conflict were uncertain of their own ability to withstand concerted international pressures.

At the same time, Russian possessiveness about conflict resolution and peacekeeping within the territory of the former Soviet Union had not yet emerged as a major Russian policy thrust. On the contrary, following several failed attempts to resolve the Nagorno-Karabakh conflict, either alone or in partnership with Kazakhstan, Moscow's insistence on managing conflicts within its former empire was at its lowest level. Russian officials were therefore reasonably cooperative with the CSCE's initial efforts to mount a peace process for the Karabakh dispute, although there were some exceptions.

Even the situation on the ground at the time appears in retrospect to have been relatively propitious for a compromise. The Karabakh Armenians were still weak militarily. Their capital, Stepanakert, was under daily bombardment from the neighboring Azeri-controlled town of Shusha, giving the Karabakhsis an apparent incentive to end the fighting; the Azeri army appeared to be the stronger military force and threatened to overrun the Karabakhsis. Also, there was not yet a land corridor from Armenia to Karabakh through which military supplies could be shipped. The situation of the Karabakh Armenians was thus rather precarious, and the government in Yerevan, led by the moderate President Levon ter-Petrossian, still had important influence over them.

In Baku, the regime of Soviet-era holdovers was replaced by a popularly elected government led by the anti-Soviet dissident and nationalist Abulfaz Elchibey, who was seemingly in a somewhat better position to lead the country toward a settlement. Azerbaijan had not yet suffered the subsequent military defeats that revealed its army to be disorganized and incapable of mounting a serious offensive, thus challenging the country's pride. The number of Azeri refugees from Armenian-controlled areas of Karabakh was relatively small and so did not constitute an insuperable political obstacle to territorial compromise.

There was also a degree of high-level western interest in the Karabakh conflict during this period, which would not be seen again for almost two years. Secretary of State Baker personally intervened with the Armenian and Azeri foreign ministers to reach a general agreement on how Nagorno-Karabakh would be represented in the CSCE-sponsored negotiations (by separate representatives of both the Armenian and the Azeri communities of Nagorno-Karabakh), later known in the negotiations as the "Baker rules."

This, in turn, led to U.S. insistence that "preliminary emergency" negotiations begin to prepare for the Minsk Conference on Nagorno-Karabakh, which had been mandated by the CSCE as the peace conference for the Karabakh war. The "Minsk Group" negotiations were the direct result of this high-level American intervention. It is important to note that the informal Minsk Group and its negotiating process were *not* created by the CSCE decision that established the formal "Conference on Nagorno-Karabakh," but by high-level U.S. insistence.

The CSCE negotiating process that emerged from this sequence of events made measurable progress during the summer and fall of 1992. Its first, and still very significant, successes were to gather all the parties to the conflict around a single negotiating table and to create a serious, credible, and sustained negotiating process. These were

not easy tasks, given the asymmetries mentioned above; Azerbaijan was extremely sensitive to giving any implicit status to Nagorno-Karabakh by participating in negotiations with persons purporting to be official representatives of such a place. Each side in its turn either refused to come to the negotiating table or walked away from it and had to be patiently coaxed to participate by the principal western negotiators.

When the process reached a dead end, the U.S. representative revived it by arranging private U.S.-Russian-Turkish talks to agree on a joint proposal to the parties. These smaller discussions became "three plus one" when the Italian Minsk Group chair was added, then "five plus one" after Armenia and Azerbaijan were invited to join, and later led to a reopening of talks of the full Minsk Group.

This early phase of the talks reached useful understandings on the sequence of negotiation and the subjects that would have to be covered in a cease-fire agreement. No less important was acceptance by all sides of the basic pattern and vocabulary of negotiation, procedural points that can stymie peace talks, especially in their early stages.

A full cease-fire agreement was elusive, but was finally pinned down in Stockholm in the "five plus one" group late in the night of December 14, 1992. Those present agreed that it would be presented to the full Minsk Group for endorsement the following morning and subsequently to the meeting of the foreign ministers of the CSCE, in order to receive their stamp of approval and backing. This was as close as the Minsk Group got to a cease-fire during this period, however, because at 8:00 a.m. on the following day the Azeri foreign minister withdrew his country's agreement without explanation, and the whole deal fell apart, concluding the first phase of the Minsk Group's work with a profound disappointment and a very public failure.

The Stockholm meeting was also significant for the Nagorno-Karabakh negotiations in a much broader way, for at this meeting Russian Foreign Minister Andrei Kozyrev gave a hard-line speech that hinted at the direction that Russian policy would follow on issues such as Nagorno-Karabakh in the months to come. He later stated that he was only showing his colleagues what Russian foreign policy would be like if Russian hard-liners should gain power.

Why were the opportunities of this early period missed? The first reason, and the one with the most direct impact, was that both sides of the dispute still harbored ambitions for winning the conflict, either by outright military means or by outwaiting their adversaries. The fatigue of combat had not yet taken its toll, and the famous exhaustion factor had not yet set in. Also, neither side was strong enough politically to risk being accused by its domestic opposition of a sell-out. This was probably why the Azeris backed away from the Stockholm agreement. Also, as appeared later, both sides had plans for military action to advance their cause.

The Karabakh Armenians, with encouragement from elements of the Armenian diaspora, wanted political recognition as a part of any agreement, even if it was only a cease-fire. Such recognition would have provided the basis and rationale for continuing their drive toward independence, whether that effort would be waged by war or through negotiation. The Azeri government, encouraged by Turkey to take a hard line, was determined to avoid any such political recognition, even if it was only implicit. Their attitude was the mirror-image of the Karabakhsis; by refusing to recognize any political status for Karabakh, they justified continued efforts to suppress the uprising. Even details such as whether representatives from Nagorno-Karabakh should have a nameplate at the negotiating table

(and what title might be inscribed on it) were loaded with symbolism and were thus very sensitive. Essentially, neither side was yet ready to find a compromise.

The second major factor that caused the opportunities of this period to be missed was the lack of clear and sustained high-level interest in the issue in the West. This was especially true as the Minsk Group's early success brought it closer to a possible cease-fire agreement on the eve of the Stockholm meeting of CSCE foreign ministers. Concerted efforts by the foreign ministers in the period just before Stockholm, and particularly at Stockholm, could have made the difference and resulted in a cease-fire agreement at that time. But no foreign minister, let alone the group of them, made this a priority for the Stockholm meeting.

The chairman of the Minsk Group did not even attend the Stockholm meeting; his deputy read a statement to the meeting. His absence signaled that no important developments were expected and ensured that the ministers would not focus on this issue. The Russians did not even send their Minsk Group negotiator to Stockholm (it is impossible to know whether this was a deliberate decision presaging the distancing from the Minsk Group's activities that later took place or was really the result of budgetary limitations as the Russians claimed); the Russians were represented in all Karabakh-related discussions by a mid-level official who was informed in only a very general way of the issues and who was not in a position to exert pressure or join in initiatives.

The absence of high-level interest during the Stockholm meeting was the culmination of consistent low-level interest that began with the creation of the Minsk Group. The chairman was an almost unknown second-level Italian politician who had served only as deputy foreign minister and did not speak any of the languages of negotiation (English, Russian, and French). The other representatives sent to the negotiations by the western countries were low-level diplomats, some from their local embassy, or retirees brought back to service.

Despite the fact that the Minsk Group had been created because of a high-level U.S. intervention, the U.S. representative in it received little or no support. In fact, there was no official position of U.S. representative to the Minsk Group, and the incumbent was expected to do this job as a collateral duty while assigned to a full-time position focused on some other task. At Minsk Group meetings, he was accompanied by only one assistant, who changed periodically. The assistant often had to be absent, leaving the U.S. representative entirely alone in the negotiations. This was particularly striking to diplomats who were familiar with the large delegations the United States routinely sends to even the most obscure international meetings.

It was clear to the negotiators who represented the parties to the conflict that the western countries were not very interested in the Karabakh war. This led to another problem: ensuring that the conflicting sides were represented in the negotiations by *interlocuteurs valables*, that is, officials who were open to discussion, prepared to listen to the needs of the other side, authorized to make concessions and agree to compromises, and able to communicate directly with the highest authorities of their regimes when necessary to obtain authorization to agree. People who fit this profile are not numerous in these societies, and it was essential to attract such persons to the negotiating process and to get them committed to pursuing it. Without the presence of serious, responsible representatives from the western countries, attracting such people to the negotiations was impossible. Even worse, it was clear that many of the representatives in the negotiations were sent there only to report to their foreign ministries, thereby compounding the problem of low-level representation. The keen and silent note-taking of these diplomats inhibited the informal exchange of ideas and required the representatives of the parties to the conflict to keep repeating the formal positions of their authorities.

The U.S. representative tried on numerous occasions to upgrade the level and seriousness of the Minsk Group and to create a more productive private inner negotiating group. Although there was some initial success, these efforts ultimately failed because of Russia's determination to play the leading role and Washington's readiness to acquiesce in this matter.

In addition, because the Italian chairman had to have translation into Italian, the French and German representatives also insisted on the equal use of their own languages. This made the Minsk Group an unwieldy and absurdly heavy piece of negotiating machinery, including eleven countries, two noncountries, a chairmanship plus a secretariat, and five interpreting booths. Concessions involving war and peace, life and death, are not made in such a setting.

Moreover, the rules fixed by the CSCE itself at its summit meeting in Helsinki in the summer of 1992 regarding its role in peacekeeping operations created serious doubts as to whether the CSCE could or would actually provide the monitoring force that was an essential element of any cease-fire agreement. There was, of course, no peacekeeping or monitoring force immediately available or credibly in the offing. In addition, the CSCE's rules were so complex and tortured that it was difficult to see how a force could be provided, much less to convince the very suspicious parties to the conflict to trust in such an operation.

The Minsk Group, though informal, was a subsidiary of the CSCE. It therefore operated on the assumption that if the group could arrange a cease-fire, the CSCE would provide the international force to supervise and guarantee it. But the CSCE's Helsinki-agreed procedures resembled a catch-22: Consideration of a possible force by the CSCE could not begin until an operational concept was agreed by the parties. Even if the full CSCE, after its usual laborious debate and the consensus decision of more than fifty countries, approved deploying a force, it could not go to the area until a cease-fire was stable. From decision to deployment would take weeks, possibly months. Yet everyone was aware that without a firm commitment from the CSCE to provide a force promptly, no agreement was possible, because the parties knew a cease-fire would not last unless outsiders were present to supervise it.

The effect of all this was to make the work of the Minsk Group look unrealistic and hollow; the parties had very little faith that any agreement negotiated by such people in such circumstances would hold, and they had little incentive to negotiate in good faith, let alone make serious concessions or join in a compromise. The final failure of this early period, in Stockholm, was the result of all these factors.

Possible Cooperation with Russia

A second period of opportunity began in January 1993 and lasted until the late summer or early fall of that year. It was a period during which the growing insistence of Russia on playing the key role in resolving the Karabakh conflict might have been harnessed in a positive way as part of the CSCE effort.

This period emerged from the failure of the Minsk Group's first phase of work and from a much broader policy change by Russia toward the principle that all conflict resolution and peacekeeping efforts on the territory of the former USSR should be the responsibility of Russia, through the Commonwealth of Independent States (CIS).

This change was heralded by President Yeltsin's assertion in a speech on February 28, 1993:

> Stopping all armed conflicts on the territory of the former USSR is Russia's vital interest. The world community sees more and more clearly Russia's special responsibility in this difficult undertaking. I believe the time has come for distinguished international organizations, including the United Nations, to grant Russia special powers as guarantor of peace and stability in regions of the former USSR [Yeltsin speech at the Civic Union forum, broadcast on Russian television and translated by the Foreign Broadcast Information Service (FBIS), March 1, 1993].

This policy manifested itself through a gradually increasing and more obvious separation of Russia from the work and proposals of the Minsk Group, even when the Russian representative had played a major part in drafting them. At the same time, separate unilateral Russian proposals began to surface, first privately to the parties to the conflict without any information given to the other Minsk Group negotiators, and then more openly in stark contradiction to the joint work of the group. In addition, Russian officials began to ridicule the Minsk Group publicly.

Russia's proposals were invariably based on the concept of a Russian or Russian-controlled CIS "Separation Force," which would be inserted between the warring sides and would be authorized to use force to suppress any violations of an accompanying cease-fire. This, of course, was very different from the international proposals (supposedly also supported by Russia) for an internationally controlled monitoring force not authorized to use force (essentially the same as observers).

Since it was apparent that outside countries, especially the United States, would be extremely reluctant to send personnel to oversee a cease-fire in this remote region of the Caucasus—in conditions that would be expensive, difficult, and dangerous—it seemed logical to try to co-opt Russian interest in the area and to engage the Russians to constitute the bulk of an international force under CSCE control and guidance. The Russians had many assets that would make a major contribution from them virtually essential for the success of any operation around Nagorno-Karabakh: They had considerable military expertise and experience in the area; their people all spoke the only language that is common to both Azeris and Armenians; they were closer to the area than anyone else; and they had indispensable communications and logistics networks at their disposal. Without Russian support, any peacekeeping operation in the Transcaucasus would have a difficult time; with Russian participation, such an operation could have a good chance of success.

The U.S. representative in the Minsk Group and the deputy chairman of the group made concerted efforts during this period to obtain a Russian commitment to support and participate in an international operation. They did this despite a signal lack of backing from Washington, which was in the midst of an overall policy review on peacekeeping and was unable to provide guidance. The U.S. representative was thus left to devise what he thought best, and Washington watched with interest.

At first, prospects were promising. The Russian military appeared extremely reluctant to undertake another intervention in the Karabakh area without a mandate from the CSCE (or preferably from the United Nations, which could authorize the use of force). Also, "sphere-of-influence peacekeeping" had not yet become such a public issue that combined activities were out of the question.

A significant step was made when an agreement was reached among the Minsk Group's "five plus one" at the U.S. Embassy in Rome late in the evening of Sunday, February 28, 1993. This agreement covered the "terms of reference" for deploying a CSCE monitoring force to the conflict and permitted planning for such a force to begin within the full CSCE in Vienna. This was the beginning of the CSCE's tortuous soul searching about whether and how it might provide supervision for a cease-fire in Karabakh; without the agreement in Rome, the CSCE consideration process could have been stopped short.

In the summer and fall of 1993, the U.S. representative offered the Russian representative in the Nagorno-Karabakh negotiations a list of seven conditions for a joint arrangement for supervision of a cease-fire, conditions that could have made a cooperative Russian-international venture possible, under the auspices and control of the CSCE. But the Russians were unresponsive, and their bad faith became increasingly obvious. It was clear that their deliberate intention was not to cooperate, thus ensuring that their own proposal would be recognized by the parties as the only game in town and would ultimately supplant the international negotiating process.

In the fall of 1993, an entirely extraneous factor arose that made it more difficult to pursue private U.S.-Russian negotiations on a cooperative arrangement seriously: a change of the chairmanship of the Minsk Group from Italy to Sweden. The Swedes, who had not participated actively in the earlier work of the Minsk Group, had been influenced decisively by the failure in Stockholm. They were determined to virtually eliminate group meetings of the Minsk Group and to pursue the peace process through shuttle diplomacy of their own in the region. This change was to have the effect of downgrading the U.S. role in the process, even though the United States was the only voice the Russians took seriously.

Several factors led to this lost opportunity. The most important was the policy change in Moscow toward the objective of keeping other countries out of the Russian "sphere of influence." This shift was not generally perceived in Washington or elsewhere in the West until somewhat later, but it became very clear early in 1993 in the Nagorno-Karabakh negotiations. The U.S. representative repeatedly warned both his western negotiating partners and his superiors in Washington of the implications of the shift that was being observed in the Karabakh talks. But Washington and the West had other priorities and preferred to put their faith in the general "assurances" that were being given by the Russians at higher levels.

Another factor in this missed opportunity was the simple inability of the Russians to engage in responsible negotiations on this issue. There were obvious disagreements between the foreign and defense ministries, to the extent that the Russian negotiator on Nagorno-Karabakh, who was supposed to have an interministerial mandate, sometimes learned about the activities of Russia's defense minister in the area when the U.S. representative handed him a copy of the *International Herald Tribune*. Also, when the U.S. representative was finally able to hold direct discussions with a senior member of the Russian Defense Ministry, the Russian Nagorno-Karabakh negotiator was not permitted to attend (nor was anyone else from the Foreign Ministry).

In fact, the strong U.S. leadership role in the early period of the Minsk Group's work may have added to Russian concerns about losing their influence in the region. Moscow was particularly worried about the American effort to engage Turkey as a power that should share responsibility for peaceful settlement of the conflict. The increased Turkish role in the Transcaucasus and Central Asia rang ancient alarm bells for the Rus-

sians and may have encouraged their effort to keep the international community out.

The transfer to a Swedish Minsk Group chairman was perhaps a minor element in this equation, but nonetheless it must be mentioned as a factor. From the beginning of the Minsk Group negotiations, the U.S. representative had been able to balance the weight of the Russians in the talks. But the only basis the U.S. had for playing a role in the Nagorno-Karabakh dispute was as a member of the Minsk Group. For the United States to affect the negotiations, it was therefore essential that the Minsk Group come together. Thus, the U.S. representative consistently tried to give the Minsk Group a stable and self-sustaining existence.

In contrast, the Italian Foreign Ministry saw no national interest in the Nagorno-Karabakh negotiations, which were expensive and politically burdensome. The senior levels of the ministry wanted to be relieved of Italy's Minsk Group chairmanship responsibilities. In the summer of 1993 Italy, which was to succeed Sweden as chair of the CSCE, negotiated a private deal with Sweden under which Sweden would replace Italy as chair of the Minsk Group at the end of November 1993.

The Swedes had a different concept of how they would conduct their chairmanship. They wanted to reduce the number of meetings to almost none, conducting Swedish shuttle diplomacy instead. The U.S. representative warned both Sweden and Washington that this would seriously handicap the ability of the United States to influence the course of the negotiating process, while immeasurably enhancing the Russian role, just when the Russians were seeking to sideline the Minsk Group and establish their exclusive prerogative for sphere-of-influence peacekeeping on the territory of the former USSR. But the Swedes refused to listen, and Washington gave its representative no support in the matter. In fact, officials in Washington seemed relieved that the Swedes would take over at least some of the responsibility for dealing with the growing problem of the Russian role.

To compound the difficulties, these events took place just as the internal U.S. government debate on a new overall approach to peacekeeping was at its most intense stage. This made it even more difficult for Washington to take a forceful position on this specific peacekeeping issue.

High-Level Pressure Point Before Budapest CSCE Summit

The next major missed opportunity came in the fall of 1994, in preparations for the Budapest summit of the CSCE. During this period, the issue of "sphere-of-influence peacekeeping" or "third-country peacekeeping" had come into sharp focus, and arrangements for a future force to oversee the cease-fire around Nagorno-Karabakh were being actively considered. This issue had gradually risen to the top of the international agenda and was even discussed by Presidents Clinton and Yeltsin at their September 1994 meeting in Washington. In a discussion that was reminiscent of the one between the two countries' Nagorno-Karabakh negotiators more than one year earlier, Clinton pressed for Russia to accept a major but less-than-dominant role in a CSCE force, while Yeltsin argued that Russia was the only country willing to take effective action to resolve the dispute and held out for an arrangement that would put Russia in control. The two men could not reach agreement.

As the CSCE summit approached, it became clear that the ability of the CSCE to field a genuinely internationally controlled peacekeeping force for the Karabakh conflict, giving the CSCE a meaningful post–Cold War conflict resolution role, would be a key test of the success of the summit leaders. The Russians also had a stake in this issue, because they had publicly presented their vision of the CSCE as the central international organization for Europe, in which they foresaw a major role for themselves. Had concerted international pressures been applied at the highest level prior to the Budapest meeting, it might have been possible to reach agreement on a structure and guidelines for a CSCE force, including an important but subsidiary Russian contingent.

But such pressure was not applied. On the contrary, President Clinton almost did not go to the Budapest meeting at all. Even though the Budapest summit had been on the international calendar for two years, the White House planned a reception for one of the very same days and then said Clinton could not leave Washington because of a "previous engagement."

The initiative was left to the Russians, who used the occasion for Yeltsin's now-famous warning to Washington not to try to "direct" events in Moscow's "sphere of influence," because such efforts might open up a period of "Cold Peace" between Russia and the West. In hindsight, this was clearly a warning not to try to interfere with Russia's attack on Chechnya, which occurred one week later, as well as a stiff-arm on the Nagorno-Karabakh issue. A general agreement was reached at Budapest on the principle of a joint CSCE-Russian peacekeeping force for Nagorno-Karabakh, but essential "details" such as the chain of command for the force, were left to later negotiations. Moreover the simple equating of the international community, represented here by the CSCE, with one country, Russia, was a step backward.

The events in Chechnya and in Nagorno-Karabakh are closely related—at least in the minds of Russians, who tend to see the problems of the Caucasus as a whole. Any western position on any issue in the Caucasus relates, from the Russian perspective, to other issues in the area. Thus, either strong international opposition to Russian efforts to dominate in the Nagorno-Karabakh conflict or prior agreement on international peacekeeping arrangements for Karabakh might have tempered Russian actions in Chechnya. Similarly, the outcome in Chechnya will affect not only Moscow's ability to field a peacekeeping force for Nagorno-Karabakh, but also its future attitude toward any international peacekeeping operation in the region. Until that outcome is clearer, Russia's decision-making abilities for the whole of the Caucasus will be severely limited.

Also, all the peoples in the region must now view their problems and their relations with Russia in light of the attack on Chechnya; basically they must anticipate that in some set of circumstances "it could happen here." This factor could lead to an increased willingness to accept a compromise.

The reasons for the missed opportunities of Budapest are familiar: lack of high-level western interest and of a high priority for the Karabakh issue, Russian determination to keep outsiders out of what they consider their "sphere of influence," and the lack of an immediately available international peacekeeping force, which permitted the Russians to argue that they were the only ones capable of sending a force to oversee the cease-fire.

DISAGREEMENT OVER WHO WILL PROVIDE A PEACEKEEPING FORCE

From the beginning of Russia's move away from full cooperation with the international community on the Nagorno-Karabakh problem, the possibility of establishing a stable cease-fire has been complicated by disagreement over who would provide and control a peacekeeping force. This would not have been the case if all outside powers had been united in proposing to the conflicting parties a single cease-fire plan, with a single offer

for a peacekeeping force. But the existence of the Russian plan, including a Russian-controlled separation force, gave the warring parties the option of "shopping" for the best offer. Inevitably, this led both sides to choose between the two proposals on the basis of what they saw as their own advantages under each proposal.

The Azeris have steadfastly opposed a Russian-controlled force, or even a large Russian contingent in an internationally controlled force; they have the relatively recent experience of mainly Russian Soviet troops using force to quell rioting in Baku, with numerous casualties. The Azeris tend to see Russia as aligned with Armenia against Turkey and the Islamic world. Upon gaining independence, one of the top Azeri political objectives was to remove all Russian troops from their territory. This was largely accomplished during the government of the pro-Turkish and anti-Russian nationalist President Elchibey. With the prospect of significant revenues from their oil wealth, the Azeris do not believe they need the Russians, and any political figure who advocates or accepts the return of Russian troops risks being overthrown.

Armenia, on the other hand, needs a close relationship with Russia to offset the presence on its frontier of its powerful traditional enemies, the Turks. Armenia therefore did not seek removal of Russian forces from its soil when it became independent, and a Russian army division has continued to be based there. Russian border troops have also continued to guard Armenia's outer frontiers. As Armenia's economic situation has deteriorated because of the war, its dependence on Russia has increased and it has sought a close relationship with Moscow. At the same time, Armenia seeks friendly relations and economic assistance from the West and from the diaspora, so it has kept channels open in this direction as well. This led Armenia to indicate that it would accept a peacekeeping force from any source; the Armenian government's principal objective at this point is to find an acceptable end to the war, so that it can begin to rebuild its economy.

The Karabakhsis are in a somewhat different position than the Armenians of Armenia proper. First, their principal concern in approaching any agreement to end the conflict is their own security. As a small enclave little bigger than Rhode Island, with a population of about 180,000, the Karabakh Armenians cannot afford to relinquish their present favorable position without being absolutely certain of their security. They are also directly dependent on Russia for their military supplies, without which they could not continue the war. They have little contact with the West and no commitment to it, except the Armenian diaspora, which has primarily encouraged them to maintain a hard line. All of this has led them to opt for the Russian offer of a separation force, both because it comes from Moscow and because it would entail a mandate to use force, and therefore it looks more likely to ensure Karabakh's security.

With the concerns of the Karabakhsis in mind, the West, represented by the Minsk Group and the CSCE, upgraded its proposed cease-fire supervision group from a "monitoring" to a "peacekeeping" force. But the difference did not appear great (a peacekeeping force is larger, armed, and plays a more active role in controlling a cease-fire agreement). Nonetheless, the concerns of the Karabakh Armenians about an internationally controlled peacekeeping force persisted, and these concerns mounted as international efforts in Bosnia proved to be weak and indecisive. Moreover, no major countries have made public commitments of important troop formations for an international force; the commitments that have been made tend to be from smaller countries

and to represent small units (for example, the Swiss have offered a medical team). The United States has made it clear that U.S. troops will not be involved, although there might be a few U.S. monitors. There has never been any question of a NATO role, because it is generally recognized that NATO intervention on the territory of the former Soviet Union would provoke Russian nationalists and could be broadly counterproductive. Worst of all, a highly publicized Turkish offer to provide half of the troops in an international force deeply worried all Armenians because it evoked images of "The Genocide."

In these circumstances the Karabakhsis have continued to favor a Russian separation force, while the Azeris continue to oppose it. The episode has added to western concerns about the neo-imperial implications of the overall Russian attitude toward the so-called "near abroad." There has been a growing divergence between the Russians, who are increasingly insistent on recognition of their special responsibilities for peacekeeping in this area, and the West, which is ever more reluctant to accept it. No doubt the brutal Russian attack on Chechnya will make it even more difficult for western governments to accord some form of approval to a Russian peacekeeping force for Nagorno-Karabakh.

The only possible way to bridge the gap is to combine the Russian and international plans, including the cease-fire supervision arrangements; but efforts in this direction have not been successful thus far. Despite the general accord on a combined force reached at the CSCE summit in Budapest in December 1994, final agreement has been blocked by disagreement on two issues: who will control the force and the percentage of the force to be provided by Russia. The Russians want to command this force themselves; the other members of the CSCE want it to be under CSCE command. The Russians want to supply the major portion of the troops, while the other CSCE members want Russian participation to be limited to less than 50 percent. Whether the Azeris would accept a large percentage of Russians, even one less than 50 percent, remains to be seen.

Foreign Minister Kozyrev summarized the Russian view succinctly in an article he published in September 1993:

> Presently we are on the verge of making a similar choice [similar to the choice of a peacekeeping force for Abkhazia] in Nagorno-Karabakh. There is no alternative to a Russian peacekeeping contingent there, which is to acquire the status of UN forces as soon as a settlement mechanism is in place and is to be reinforced by UN units from neutral European countries which are members of the CSCE. Here, both we and the United Nations must perform our historical duty. Shrinking from it would be irresponsible [*Moscow Nezavisimaya Gazeta*, September 22, 1993, translated by FBIS].

The events in Chechnya have already had an effect on this problem, and they are likely to have more. Since December 1994, the attack on Chechnya has made it very difficult for Russia to focus or make decisions on Karabakh issues, resulting in delays and inability to compromise. Over the longer term there is a real question of whether the Russians can staff a peacekeeping force for Nagorno-Karabakh while they remain bogged down in a major military campaign in nearby Chechnya. More ominously, the political effects of Chechnya could bring more hard-line policies across the board in Moscow. That might result in stubborn Russian opposition to any rational solution for Nagorno-Karabakh, with the objective of preventing the international community from gaining any foothold there at all.

THE POSSIBILITY OF PROPOSING A POLITICAL SOLUTION

Another opportunity that has thus far been missed in the Karabakh negotiating process entails a compromise solution for the ultimate political status of Nagorno-Karabakh. This issue was put aside when the Minsk Group first began meeting, because the topic is so delicate that discussing it would have made serious negotiation of a cease-fire much more difficult. The cease-fire was considered the first order of business, while the political solution was left until the convening of the formal Minsk Conference.

However, when a de facto cease-fire came into effect in the spring of 1994 and seemed to hold, an opportune time opened for planning and preparing the ground for a political compromise. Launching a discussion of an ultimate political solution for the status of Nagorno-Karabakh could have bypassed the disagreements over the cease-fire peacekeeping force and created pressure to resolve those disagreements. The United States was well placed to open such consideration because of its unique ability to carry on nuanced discussions through many channels of communication, and because a proposal for a political compromise is most credible if it is identified as coming from the United States.

Such a step could have been associated with the appointment of a senior-level U.S. envoy on the issue, similar to the special envoy the United States has had for years on the Cyprus conflict. In order to stimulate interest in this possibility, the former U.S. negotiator (who by that time had retired) launched a personal proposal for a compromise political solution, publicly urging the administration to appoint a senior special envoy. This personal proposal was widely circulated as a Special Report by the United States Institute of Peace, and it was the subject of a special hearing by the CSCE commission of the U.S. Congress. There was also considerable congressional interest in the appointment of a special envoy; a letter urging this action was sent to President Clinton by thirty-nine members of Congress.

But the administration did not pick up the idea of proposing a political compromise solution, and did not appoint a special envoy. Instead, the Nagorno-Karabakh negotiating function was absorbed into a lower-level position with a broader mandate—watching over relations with all the non-Russian states of the former USSR. This assured that Nagorno-Karabakh would be on a back burner in relation to Russian interests, and it reflected the low priority the administration attached to it in comparison with its interest in maintaining good relations with Moscow.

The reason this opportunity has thus far been lost has been the administration's unwillingness to take a leading position on an issue that Russia plainly considers falls within its "sphere of influence." To do so would be to challenge the Russian claim, while the administration's tendency has been to accept it. This tendency was also demonstrated by the implicit trade-off of U.S. acceptance of a UN Security Council approval of sending a Russian peacekeeping force to Georgia for Russian acceptance of Security Council approval of sending a U.S. force to Haiti.

THE POSSIBILITY OF A PEACE PIPELINE

Another opportunity has existed for some time that could create major and unique incentives for the parties to this conflict to resolve it in the near future. A "peace pipeline" could be built from Baku across Azerbaijan and Armenia to the Turkish Mediterranean coast as a means of exporting the oil resources from Azerbaijan's Caspian Sea shelf. Such a construction project, worth

$2–3 billion, would be an incomparably large investment for the areas through which it would pass. It would also provide Armenia (and through it Nagorno-Karabakh) a sure source of energy for the foreseeable future, which it does not now have. (This might, incidentally, also alleviate the need for Armenia to restart its Chernobyl-type nuclear power reactor at Medzamor, which had to be shut down after it was damaged in the 1988 earthquake; it sits astride one of the earth's major fault lines.)

But most important, a pipeline passing along this route (which is also technically and economically the best available one) would help knit together the countries involved in the Nagorno-Karabakh conflict with a shared interest in maintaining peace and stability in the area in the future. Eventually the pipeline and the oil (and, in parallel, gas) it would carry would bring prosperity to all the countries concerned, reducing the economic causes of resentment that lie behind many disputes.

The decision on a pipeline route has become increasingly urgent with the signing of an $8 billion oil production agreement between Azerbaijan and a consortium of mainly western oil companies in September 1994. An export route will have to be available when the oil begins to flow, about one or two years from now. The decision process is complex, involving the views of the oil consortium companies, specialized construction firms, the major banks and financial institutions that will finance the deal, and the countries in the region that are competing for parts of the route. An important consideration must be how to gain Russian acquiescence, since Russia could undercut a deal if it is not in agreement.

The U.S. government's position on a pipeline route can be decisive, because of its influence on the attitudes of major banks and investors. For example, U.S. opposition to any project that might favor Iran is well known and will likely prevent construction of a pipeline across Iranian territory. The administration has now stated that it favors a pipeline route across Turkey, but it has left options open for the route that would get from Azerbaijan to Turkey. Essentially, this leaves a choice between routes through Georgia or Armenia. If the United States were to take a clear position in favor of a pipeline route across Armenia, it could be a major factor in making such a route credible. The U.S. tendency has been to let the oil companies sort this out; however, left alone, the consortium companies will simply drift toward the path of least difficulty. They are simply unable to take positions based on political considerations, even when such solutions may be in their own best interests.

Obviously, construction of a pipeline across Armenia is impossible unless some major steps are taken toward settling the Karabakh conflict, such as a stable, supervised cease-fire and withdrawal of the Armenian forces that are currently occupying most of southwestern Azerbaijan, where the route (hypothetically along the Aras River through Armenia and Nakhichevan) would pass. Also, there must be a major increase in confidence between Armenia and both Azerbaijan and Turkey, before negotiation could begin. All this could be encouraged by an American government that is prepared to give the matter a high priority.

A real impulse to build this pipeline would have the effect of forcing the negotiations forward. Constituencies would be built on both sides, and these constituencies would favor at least some concessions. Reaching a solution would for the first time carry real, positive incentives for much of the population, helping balance the exclusively negative focus on the need for vengeance for past wrongs.

Once again, the reasons this opportunity is being missed are familiar. The lack of high-level interest and the low level of pri-

ority that the U.S. administration has attached to the issue have meant that it has been left to the bureaucracy to handle. The bureaucracy is unable to take strong, leading positions in the way political leaders can, and the responsible officials have tended to play it safe. Also, the Armenian government and the Armenian diaspora have been woefully slow in perceiving Armenia's interests in this matter, and no one has represented Armenia's interest in the discussions that have already taken place. Armenians have been afraid to broach the issue and risk being accused of "selling Karabakh for Turkish oil money."

CURRENT STALEMATE, STRONGER MANDATES, RUSSIAN OVERLOAD

Currently, there are broad new opportunities for making progress on the negotiating front. For the first time since 1992, Nagorno-Karabakh has an elected leader, its "president," Robert Kocharyan. Azerbaijan's leadership has also been (relatively) stabilized after President Gaidar Aliev repulsed a nascent coup attempt in the fall of 1994 and sidelined his one major potential rival in Baku, Prime Minister Surat Husseinov.

In addition, war weariness has evidently set in, producing a stalemate in the military situation, with the Karabakhsis at the limit of what they can physically control and the Azeris unable to mount an offensive and pinned down with the problems of nearly one million internal refugees. Both Armenia and Azerbaijan desperately need a settlement for economic reasons; Armenia's economy is being destroyed by the continuing blockade by Azerbaijan and Turkey, and Azerbaijan must be able to exploit its oil resources in the near future. Furthermore, both countries, as well as the Karabakh Armenians, have been alarmed by Russia's attack on Chechnya.

But this issue still carries a low priority in Washington, and as long as the approach of policymakers is to subordinate action on a secondary issue to higher-priority issues such as the need for Russia to dismantle its nuclear weapons systems, it will be impossible for issues of this kind to be treated with the active leadership they require. The point is not to question the place of the Nagorno-Karabakh issue among U.S. priorities, but rather to argue that the hierarchical approach to issues is too inflexible. In practice that approach discourages the kind of initiative-taking that would take advantage of opportunities to resolve issues that may be important and dangerous in themselves, even if they are lower down the list from what are deemed to be the issues of top priority. It should be possible to both maintain a sensible order of priorities and seize opportunities.

CONCLUSION

After explaining some of the background features that are unique to the conflict over Nagorno-Karabakh, this study has examined missed opportunities that have occurred over the course of the international community's 1992–1995 effort to mediate a solution to the dispute. The opportunities were missed for numerous reasons, some specific to the particular circumstances surrounding each set of events. But the following broad elements run through all of these episodes and were clearly important reasons for the inability of the international community to arrange a permanent cease-fire, introduce peacekeeping forces, and find a political solution for the status of Nagorno-Karabakh.

Up to now the parties to this conflict have shown little readiness to make the concessions needed for a compromise solution. They have held out for impossible conditions in the hope of winning the conflict, either militarily or by outwaiting their opponents. Each of these parties has a weak government and lacks a sophisticated political establishment that might be able to

consider broader interests rationally. In the emotional political debate that surrounds this bloody war, any government moving toward compromise risks being accused of selling out vital national interests. On both sides, this resistance to compromise has been encouraged by "friends" not directly engaged in the conflict—the Armenian diaspora and Turkey.

Under the hierarchical approach to issues with Russia, the Nagorno-Karabakh conflict has not been considered a top priority by U.S. or other western leaders, because it has not appeared to engage vital western interests. Even when the war has attracted high-level attention, this attention has not been used in a concerted way and has not lasted. The result has been that the readiness of the international community to supply a peacekeeping force and to guarantee a political agreement has been in doubt, and the parties to the conflict have not trusted the West's will to carry through with the actions necessary to ensure the peace.

Growing Russian bad faith culminated in a unilateral Russian proposal to the conflicting parties for a cease-fire to be guaranteed by a Russian/CIS separation force, directly competing with and undercutting the international proposal for a CSCE force. The Russian move permitted the parties to the conflict to "shop around" for the proposal they preferred, thus making agreement impossible. It became apparent that the Russian effort was deliberately designed to make the international proposal look unlikely to succeed, in order to convince the conflicting parties that the Russian offer was the only way to go. This has been part of a broader Russian objective of ensuring that all peacekeeping on the territory of the former USSR would be recognized as Russia's prerogative. Russian unwillingness to accept a reasonable compromise based on a significant, but not controlling, role in an international peacekeeping force has been particularly striking evidence of neoimperialist intentions. One Karabakh Armenian illustrated the negative effects of this effort when he told a western visitor (in March 1995), "We have become the mediators between the Russians and the CSCE."

The Minsk Group negotiation has been too large and too low level for serious negotiation, and the group has had no way to guarantee that the larger CSCE would either agree to or actually produce a peacekeeping force. The CSCE's procedures are so complicated that such a force cannot be provided promptly. The western countries compounded the problem by showing little effort to develop a credible international peacekeeping force. The only U.S. role in mediating the conflict has been within these unwieldy groups, and the United States has excluded any role on the ground, even though it is the only country that can offset Russia's often negative influence. The result has been that the international negotiating effort has appeared ineffectual to the warring parties.

18

Regional and Subregional Organizations in International Conflict Management

RUTH WEDGWOOD

International political theory has recovered from any European naïveté. Early celebration of regionalism as a basis for a new international order testified to the eloquence of Jean Monnet and Konrad Adenauer, but regionalism has not so aptly fit the rest of the globe. The conditions that fueled European regionalism—Europe's Fifty Years' Peace and deepening union—are now recognized as singular; western Europe's interwoven security and economic communities defy political generalization. Among the unique conditions that facilitated European regionalism were a common threat from the Soviet front, Germany's resort to community identity (as part of the European Community) as reassurance to its postwar neighbors, formal American security commitments mooting local balance of power, and the shared fever of postwar economic reconstruction. Europe's effective human rights machinery, rationality of common economic institu-

tions, and quest for cultural reunion beyond the Iron Curtain—even its shared sense of loss in the wake of American preeminence—sustained a regional consciousness that is hard to replicate.

This chapter discusses the evolving role of regional organizations in maintaining international peace and security. It asks whether regional organizations and subregional groups have the potential to play a new and more effective role in international security now that the Cold War is over. The chapter first discusses the strengths and weaknesses of regional organizations, in relation not only to one another but also to the United Nations. It then assesses the recent performance of regional organizations in conflict prevention, crisis diplomacy, and conflict management. Efforts to reform regional organizations are also discussed as part of the general review of regional security response mechanisms in conflict management.

Regional security response mechanisms have evident attractions for conflict management in the post–Cold War world where civil war looms as large as interstate disputes. Preventive diplomacy, peacekeeping, and the declaration of norms can help resolve civil disputes. The secretary general's *Agenda for Peace* proposed in 1992 that the United Nations should look more frequently to regional structures and the possible virtues of a local multilateralism.[1]

Autonomy is the first claim. Regional structures promise a local voice, an alternative to the two-tiered aristocracy of the United Nations. With the retirement of saltwater colonialism, developing countries may not wish to concede the preeminent authority and controlling power of their old masters and may instead seek a mechanism for conflict management in which they play a more central role.

The expanding competence and exclusive membership of the Security Council is a source of friction in the United Nations, with General Assembly budgeteers finding oblique ways to express displeasure.[2] Proposals to restructure the council remain improbable[3]—one may argue this is a good thing, since the council works reasonably well in its present configuration, and there is no agreement on which middle-rank powers deserve a permanent seat beyond Germany and Japan. Even if the council does extend its permanent membership to other second-tier powers, smaller nations will still be left to participate on a rotating and occasional basis. Also, scrutiny by international financial institutions of the domestic conditions for investment creates a new political discipline for developing countries, without even theoretical equality of voice. Challenges to the legitimacy of norm creation and political decision through selective bodies could be side-stepped through regional organizations—at the cost, to be sure, of problems of coordination, lassitude, and

the lack of decisive action often felt in the General Assembly itself.

Regional structures also permit a multilateral voice when the Security Council is hobbled by superpower conflict. This was so during the Cold War, when the United States turned to the Organization of American States (OAS) for authorization in the Cuban missile crisis and, though some would debate its adequacy, to the Organization of Eastern Caribbean States in the Grenada intervention.[4] Even after the thaw of the Cold War, differences of sympathy and interest among the Permanent Five will often stymie effective or decisive action in the Security Council. Vetoes need not be openly cast when council members know one another's preferences and value the pretense of unity; the bridgework and crowns of council dentistry should not be mistaken for effective bite. Regionalism could provide an alternative. It is naive to suppose it would ever displace unilateral action. The ability to act alone will remain the province of major powers. But regional structures can provide broader authority for action and take the edge off neighbors' suspicions.

In peacekeeping, regional action has held out the promise of economy and rapid response. Troops could reach a conflict area quickly, by short-haul air or overland vehicle, and could be sustained locally. Out-of-area intervention is notoriously difficult, requiring resort to American, European, or Russian logistics. In the new era of managing civil war conflicts and humanitarian emergencies, American air power is now as famous for quartermastering as for strategy. Regional action may also enhance and sustain political attention. Refugee flows, rebel sanctuaries, and political mimicry are problems a neighboring country will face if a civil conflict is not quelled, giving a priority to peacekeeping and diplomatic efforts.

So, too, regional action allows ad hoc discretion, a sui generis solution that resists unwanted generalization. Action by the UN Security Council carries the mantle of universalism; council decisions can be avowedly political, but members worry what precedent will be set and how their own ox may be gored. Regional action compartmentalizes the precedent, allowing the argument that it is based on regional customary law or political understanding. Regional action also reduces the visibility of the debate; countries are free to dispense medicines they may not wish to consume in other settings. For example, multilateral intervention in a civil conflict may unavoidably give de facto advantage to one side or another, if only by freezing combat lines; this neglect of the merits for the sake of peace might bring discomfort elsewhere. Leaving intervention to regional organizations and ad hoc "coalitions of the willing" is one way of confining the lawmaking and implicit promises of international practice.

Regional structures build confidence, avoiding unwanted triggers of provocation. In the Yugoslav conflict, a negotiating group of the states most likely to feel drawn into the conflict by traditional sympathies or neighborhood attempted to coordinate policy. The work of the Contact Group—the United States, Germany, France, the United Kingdom, and Russia—prevented surprise and provocation among potential intervenors and confined a local war. Negotiating a common response—within a formal organization or on an ad hoc basis—sustains informal diplomatic and security contacts among interested states that otherwise may incline to unilateral action on an overt or covert basis. Regionalism can create a transparency among jockeying states and prevent misperceptions of intention.

Regional approaches also remain a locus of hope for reconstituting the civic state. All-or-nothing tyranny of the majority— so problematic in new multi-ethnic states lacking the sustaining obbligato of a civil

society—can be leavened if there is some recognition or voice for other ethnic and cultural groups in an international forum; even filtered by nongovernmental organizations, some participation is better than none. The irredentist impulses of neighbors, threatening the stability of international boundaries, may be dampened by providing a regional voice for peoples divided between states. Representation in the United Nations or any large assembly lacks the immediacy of identification; regional structures provide an alternative. One could even imagine, in a revival of the pan-African spirit of Nkrumah and pan-Americanism of Bolivar, that identification with the region could displace the parochial sympathies of tribe or ethnicity, changing the aims and ambitions of political majorities. Though regional organizations have, to date, been archaically statist, providing no immediate voice for indigenous peoples, the new emphasis of the European Union (EU) on regionalism and the human rights work of the European and Inter-American Commissions on Human Rights and Courts of Human Rights show the potential for using regional fora to address civil disputes before they flare into violence.

So, too, the hermetic culture of local militaries and their attitudes towards civilian government can, at times, be changed by involvement in a different mission. In the cases of Argentina, Uruguay, and Ecuador, observers credit participation in peacekeeping operations with a change of view of the military, more cosmopolitan after contacts abroad, charged with a mission besides guarding national honor or private treasure. The involvement of developing militaries in regional peacekeeping forces could help to deepen their understanding of the virtues of stable democratic government.

In preventive diplomacy and conflict termination, the ties of sympathy and familiarity among regional leaders can be persuasive. Neighbors' opportunities for casual and low-key conversations serve as a form of "shuttle diplomacy" and avoid debate on preconditions. The success of a similarly situated neighbor that has resolved a problem of internal governance may carry more weight than the preaching of an out-of-area adviser. Anticipated need for asylum and rescue may also give weight to neighbors. Remonstrances from within the region can avoid some of the freight of history; advice from an outside power may be mistaken for condescension or revived colonialism. Regional neighbors also may have a keener sense of the political structure of a civil conflict; in Somalia, for example, former Organization of African Unity (OAU) undersecretary general Mohamed Sahnoun speculates that appropriate regional mediators could have cobbled together a political settlement.[5]

The weaknesses of regional approaches to conflict management are equally plain. First, regional structures cannot successfully impose the disciplinary measures of economic sanctions, the modern blockade and siege. To chastise an errant state effectively requires a global cordon and economic isolation. A regional grouping can provide moral voice to win broader adherence, as the OAU did in building a sanctions regime against South Africa, but it cannot constrain out-of-area states trading with a captive customer. Even among member-states, the constitutional structure of most regional organizations does not allow mandatory sanctions or embargoes. The OAS recommendation of sanctions against the Cedras regime in Haiti was nonbinding, ignored both by Eastern Hemisphere countries and by some Latin American countries.[6] The efforts to isolate Haiti required Security Council support. Even within a region, making decisions by consensus is often ineffective. Europe's common foreign and security policy, promised under the Maastricht regime, is a case in point—hence the push in the 1996 Inter-Governmental Review Conference for decisions by qualified majority. Regional organizations are not well suited for measures that lack broad political support or require universal implementation to be effective.

A second problem is conservatism, the acknowledged distaste of regional organizations for intervening in domestic conflicts. Developing countries keep a tight grip on the protective shield of sovereignty. Until quite recently, Africa's fragile states and typical one-party regimes were reluctant to criticize their neighbors' methods of enforcing control, for the same temptations might arise at home. As a consortium of heads of state, the Organization of African Unity follows unwritten rules of restraint, a reciprocal deference that inhibits criticism. Fortunately, the list of exceptions to this rule has grown to include the campaign to isolate South Africa; openly expressed OAU disdain for the prolonged military corruption in Nigeria; the creation in 1993 of the OAU's mechanism for conflict prevention, management, and resolution; and subregional efforts to cope with conflict by such bodies as the Southern African Development Community, the Inter-Governmental Authority on Drought and Development, and the Economic Community of West African States (ECOWAS). Still, one rarely forgets that the OAU is an intergovernmental institution, knitting together regimes rather than the other strands of civil society and nation. The rule of *uti possidetis*—accepting all inherited colonial boundaries, even where they divide traditional tribal groups—enjoys general support, just as it has in Latin America. This could be a factor for stability, provided other outlets are available for ethnic reconciliation. Africa's fitful democratization means this process will take time.

In the Organization of American States, the longer national history of member-states, the tradition of the pan-American movement, and the steadier funding and political commitment from the hemispheric superpower have allowed the development of a human rights apparatus that has addressed a number of serious human rights abuses, including disappearances in Argentina and Chile and death squads in Honduras. It is interesting to note that the OAS has not addressed questions concerning Latin African-Americans and indigenous peoples, and the famous 1991 Santiago Declaration on democracy came only after the hemisphere's military regimes had yielded to civilian power in a parallel devolution.[7] Still the Santiago Declaration remains an important landmark event, naming political democracy as a regional concern and pledging to convene an emergency meeting of ministers if any democratic regimes are overthrown. The organization's toothless response to corrupt elections in the Dominican Republic and President Fujimori's suspension of democracy in the Peruvian *autogolpe* ("self-coup") doesn't change the potential importance of this new regional policy. Paired with the Copenhagen Document of the Conference on Security and Cooperation in Europe, the Santiago Declaration internationalizes issues of domestic governance, stating that democracy and human rights are essential to regional identity.[8] OAS evolution has continued in the 1992 "Protocol of Washington"—a proposed amendment to the OAS Charter allowing the OAS General Assembly to suspend from membership any government that comes to power through the overthrow of a democratic regime.[9]

Strong theories of sovereignty are coupled in regional organizations with a reluctance to employ military force abroad. The history of superpower intervention figures again. Diplomats such as Venezuela's Diego Arria have argued that Latin America should value multilateral action in favor of democracy, as a measure quite distinct from the past history of North American intervention, but the OAS has clung to the habit of eschewing military force for any cause.[10] So, too, in Africa, the tenderness of postcolonial boundaries and regimes has left a fear that pro-democratic or humanitarian intervention may mask less generous ambitions. Any African standing force for peacekeeping will be subject to suspicion that it could be misused in interstate relations.

A third problem for conflict resolution at the regional level is lack of resources. Secretary General Salim Salim announced in 1993 that the OAU would establish a new conflict resolution mechanism to mediate and conciliate local disputes. The OAU secretary general has always had a "good offices" capacity, but beyond that the OAU mechanism has gotten off to a slow start. The United States has taken the lead in channeling modest resources to the OAU mechanism (some $5 million since 1994) and is supporting the secretariat's acquisition of necessary data processing and communications equipment, as well as training for observer and monitor missions and the formation of a small cadre of such observers on a standby basis. Such innovation and efforts to strengthen African capabilities are long overdue.

On the purely military side, sustained financial support for regional OAU peacekeeping is simply not available; nor are indigenous logistical capabilities. External financial and logistical help from the United States, European nations, and Japan will be needed if African capabilities are to be strengthened. In the unsuccessful OAU intervention in Chad in 1981–1982, the inability to muster sufficient troops left the peacekeepers hostage between the combatants. During the Rwanda genocide, the OAU's call for troop donations to stem the killing was ignored, and indeed, upon the withdrawal of Belgian logistical support, even the Ghanaian troops in Rwanda under UN auspices were drawn down to a low level. The logistics required to support a subregional deployment—including communications, supply, spare parts, and transportation—exceed the capacity of most developing countries. Some elements for regional peacekeeping could be supplied by commercial contractors. Day-to-day support for troops has been provided in UN peacekeeping, for example, by firms such as Brown and Root, and airlinks can be supplied with leased equipment. The overall capability to plan, coordinate, and sustain a complicated mission is still beyond the experience of most regional militaries. Developing countries are often willing to deploy troops abroad under UN auspices, as a source of training and hard currency, and even to incur casualties, but unevenly trained personnel and the unavailability of basic operating equipment (such as armored personnel carriers in Rwanda) preclude effective operations. The halting attempts to bolster regional peacekeeping, such as the 1995 American pledge of C-130s to facilitate troop transport for an African standing force, only begin to fill the gap in support capability.[11]

Underdeveloped political will is the fourth drawback of relying on regional institutions for conflict resolution. This is not identical to the back-scratching among weak regimes that afflicts the OAU, for the political vacuum exists in Asia as well. The absence of an effective regional organization in Asia, beyond the Association of South East Asian Nations (ASEAN) and the Asia-Pacific Economic Cooperation group (APEC), reflects cultural differences, the political self-sufficiency of local powers, the want of a common threat, persistent local conflicts such as the India-Pakistan dispute, and—during the Cold War—the strong and focused bilateral relationships of major regional powers with superpowers. Unlike Africa and Latin America, Asia has remained a key strategic arena, where the quieter processes of regionalism can easily be deflected. It will bear watching whether

North Korea's nuclear ambitions, China's new restiveness, and the founding of the new ASEAN regional security forum change the political complexion.

Bestowing high hopes on regionalism may have been overwrought when UN Secretary General Boutros-Ghali wrote in the 1992 *Agenda for Peace* that regionalism could "lighten the burden of the [Security] Council" in local conflicts (para. 64). Functionalist logic cannot call effective regional organizations into being. For example, the 1994 inauguration of OAS Secretary General Cesar Gaviria has not brought a new OAS activism in political matters, even though Gaviria has been outspoken in regional economic integration. But Gaviria did act in coordination with other countries in the region to quell a threatened coup in Paraguay in April 1996.

The charter of Dumbarton Oaks and San Francisco provided a root structure for collaboration that may bear fruit in the future. Chapter 8 of the UN Charter looks forward to the "existence of regional arrangements or agencies for dealing with such matters relating to the maintenance of international peace and security as are appropriate for regional action." UN members are obliged to seek a pacific settlement of disputes, and one of the means recognized in the charter, in Articles 33 and 52, is resort to regional agencies. The Security Council can refer controversies to a regional organization for mediation or arbitration under Article 52.

Regional enforcement action is a trickier business. The charter provides that Security Council authorization must be obtained for regional enforcement action—armed intervention or use of military power to enforce sanctions. In lawyers' construction of the UN Charter, this rule of Article 53 has been interpreted flexibly. A "recommendation" by a regional organization for enforcement action by member-states, as in the Cuban missile crisis, has been taken to fall outside the strictures of Security Council preauthorization.[12] And retroactive blessing was given to the military actions of the ECOWAS regional force in Liberia; two years after deployment, the Security Council "commend[ed]" ECOWAS efforts to "restore peace, security, and stability in Liberia," condemned attacks on peacekeeping forces, and provided for the participation of a UN observer force.[13] A peace agreement was produced under the joint auspices of ECOWAS, the OAU, and the United Nations. The normative importance of UN sanction is shown nonetheless by Russia's urgent attempt to secure Chapter 8 standing for the enforcement activities of the Confederation of Independent States (CIS) in the Caucasus and Central Asia.

For low-intensity regional peacekeeping, one can certainly argue that Security Council authorization is not prerequisite. Classical UN peacekeeping was said, in Lester Pearson and Dag Hammarskjöld's drollery, to be authorized by "Chapter 6½" of the UN Charter—deploying troops for lightly armed missions of interposition and separation of forces—distinct from Chapter 7 enforcement action. While bitter experience in the former Yugoslavia leaves doubt that degrees of force can be easily segregated, the United Nations' own practice makes it easy to parry the claim that Security Council authorization is needed for a regional peacekeeping deployment. So, too, the inalienable right of self-defense—individual and collective—falls within a self-help exception recognized by Article 51 of the charter. In the Cold War, NATO stoutly maintained that it was an Article 51 alliance, entitled to act on its own, not a Chapter 8 organization; it will be interesting to see whether NATO's involvement in civil disputes will always be preceded by Security Council authorization, or whether NATO members' treaty commitment to regional peace and security can

be interpreted with the same flexible gloss used in construing threats to international peace under Chapter 7. The Dayton Accords stand as possible precedent that a member-state can give binding consent to the use of force to maintain its internal peace.

In the last five years, there has been a salient pattern of double-teaming among international organizations; major powers with security interests and the UN Security Council have worked effectively with ad hoc regional groupings, formal regional organizations, and specialized subregional groups that adapt their charters for new uses.

In the crisis of Haiti, for example, the OAS attempted to persuade General Cedras to yield power to Aristide's democratically elected government, declined to recognize the Cedras regime, and recommended that all OAS members observe an economic embargo against Haiti, sending a mission of foreign ministers and the OAS secretary general to press Cedras to step down. When these efforts failed, the OAS council of ministers instructed the OAS secretary general to "explore the possibility and convenience" of taking the matter to the UN Security Council; UN sanctions were voted, and Special Envoy Dante Caputo was delegated to represent both the OAS and United Nations in negotiations with the Cedras regime, leading to the Governor's Island Accords. The OAS involvement helped maintain some claim of hemispheric autonomy (throughout the Cold War, it was axiomatic that Western Hemisphere problems did not go to the Security Council) and helped to win the acquiescence and support of Latin American countries that might otherwise have condemned armed intervention. The plan for "forced entry" in September 1994, which induced the Cedras regime to withdraw, was carried out under the authority of a Security Council resolution.[14] The action was spearheaded by U.S. troops, supplemented by multilateral participation that included Caribbean nations. The second-phase transition peacekeeping force deployed in 1995 also had contingents from a number of Caribbean nations, including Trinidad and Tobago, Jamaica, and Guatemala (the irony of the latter's participation, in the face of its own ongoing civil war, escaped public comment). International monitoring of Haiti's 1995 parliamentary and presidential elections, though not fully satisfactory, was placed back in the primary care of OAS election observation teams, with aid from the United Nations. The new model for pro-democratic intervention and reconstructive peacekeeping involves a multifunctional multilateralism, in which national, regional, and global actors seek complementary parts, stepping back when they may have some reservation about the posture or precedent, but ensuring one another a useful and acceptable role.

So, too, in scaling down the Nicaragua conflict, demobilization was supervised by the OAS and the United Nations working in tandem in the International Support and Verification Mission. This cooperative mission facilitated the agreement for democratic elections in 1990, mediating between the armed opposition and the Nicaraguan government, and helped disarm and protect former contras who returned to Nicaragua from cross-border camps. In El Salvador, the United Nations was invited to negotiate an accord between the government and the Faramundo Marti Liberation Front (FMLN), using the good offices of the secretary general's representative Alvaro de Soto, and helped demobilize Salvadoran guerilla; the former president of the OAS Inter-American Court of Human Rights, Professor Thomas Buergenthal, was one of three members of the truth commission of the United Nations Observer Mission in El Salvador, cementing the peace process.[15] The deescalation of the Central American conflict began with the mediation of neigh-

boring states, first in the Contadora group and the Esquipulas process and then through the Friends of the Secretary General, combining American and European states.[16]

In the Cambodia conflict, ASEAN and regional powers such as Indonesia and Australia played key roles in the Paris Peace Conference, and Japan helped to underwrite the peacekeeping mission.[17] The peace process also depended crucially on the willingness of Russia and China to discipline their clients and on U.S. commitment to the negotiations. The peacekeeping mission was conducted under Security Council auspices, with the leadership of Yasushi Akashi; representatives on the ground from each of the major powers enabled Akashi to scale down the mandate when the Khmer Rouge resisted plans for disarmament, conducting elections only in those areas effectively under the control of government forces.

In the former Yugoslavia, UN Secretary General Perez de Cuellar first pronounced the breakup to be a European matter. The European Community's early attempt to stem the conflict was notably unsuccessful. Dispatching observers to Llubjana did not deter the Yugoslav National Army's attack on Slovenia. Many believe that the decision of the European Community on December 16, 1991, to extend diplomatic recognition to the breakaway republics of Croatia and Slovenia provocatively fueled the conflict—convincing Bosnia's president that independence was the only route to avoid engulfment in a Serbian-dominated Yugoslav federation and thwarting attempts to negotiate a looser form of Yugoslav federation. Initially, regionalism frustrated the concerns of the UN community, dramatized in Perez de Cuellar's poignant and unsuccessful plea to German Foreign Minister Genscher to delay recognizing the breakaway republics.[18] Nonetheless, the International Conference on the Former Yugoslavia was convened in London and Geneva under the joint chairmanship of Cyrus Vance as special envoy of the secretary general and Lord Carrington, succeeded by Lord Owen, as representative of the European Community. Later, the Dayton Peace Accord was made possible through the military actions of NATO, responding to the Bosnian Serbs' gross violation of the Srebrenica and Sarajevo safe zones. The Dayton Accord was symbolically signed in Paris, perhaps to represent the future integration of the former Yugoslav republics into a European security structure. The Dayton Accord was authorized both by consent of the parties (with the Federal Republic of Yugoslavia acting for the Bosnian Serbs) and by a Chapter 7 resolution of the Security Council. Though founded on NATO air power, the regional co-paternity of the peace plan is shown most dramatically in Bosnia's new constitution. The European Court of Human Rights will appoint three of the nine judges of Bosnia's Constitutional Court. The Council of Ministers of the Council of Europe will appoint two members of the Human Rights Chamber. The elections for a new national government are to be supervised by the Organization for Security and Cooperation in Europe (OSCE). The full civilian effort is coordinated by the European Union's representative, Carl Bildt. The success of the Bosnian peace process will depend on the vigor of European institutions, as well as on the United States and United Nations. In particular, whether any political center is formed—whether the rule of consensus required by the Bosnian constitution in matters of vital interest and a rotating presidency and ethnically divided House of Peoples can constitute a viable state—will depend on the centripetal force imparted by international institutions, including the regional structures.

A tag-team approach has also been used defensively to discourage regional hegemony. In the internal conflicts in the Cau-

casus and the Central Asian republics of the former Soviet Union, peacekeepers from the Russian Federation and the CIS have intervened in a role that shows, to some, extraordinary restraint and, to others, ambiguous intention. Peacekeeping, like malleable self-defense, can become a mask for ordinary ambitions; a regional peacekeeper may play both sides of the game, instigating insurgency in order to permit a protective intervention. The deployment of observers from the OSCE and the United Nations, though few in numbers, may serve to build greater confidence in CIS peacekeeping and avoid the temptations of Russia's Near Abroad.

Finally, the structure of conflict management in the post–Cold War era must include the effective coalition that won the Gulf War after Iraq's invasion of Kuwait in 1990. The Gulf Cooperation Council (GCC), like the United States, misjudged Saddam Hussein's intentions in 1990 and lacked the military power to push back Iraqi troops. But GCC condemnation of Iraq helped hold together the coalition of UN forces and eased the anxieties of the Saudis in accepting the massive deployment of American and allied forces. Since the Gulf War, the GCC has supported the special UN commission chaired by Swedish diplomat Rolf Ekeus that was assigned to dismantle the nuclear, chemical, and biological weapons capacity of Iraq under the authority of the Security Council as a condition for lifting economic sanctions. To be effective, the commission must establish long-term monitoring to ensure that Iraq does not rebuild these weapons capabilities. This presents the challenge of financing, at a time when the United Nations is undergoing fiscal crisis. The GCC has pledged $100 million in voluntary contributions to finance the Ekeus Commission over the long term, practically enough for a permanent endowment. This model of regional financing against a regional threat is not replicable in poorer areas of the world, but the interweaving of regional and UN political structures is an emerging model for the Middle East, Africa, and Latin America.

Regional security response mechanisms remain attractive options in international relations. However, like partially expressed DNA, the ecology must be right to bring them forward in practice. Recent conflict resolution has combined regional and global actors in ad hoc teams that vary with the political sensibility of the disputants, the preoccupations of the Security Council, and the tasks at hand. Regional and subregional responses are a way of sharing the burden and can strengthen the support necessary for political action. Money, attention, and political culture will determine their use in practice.

Notes

1. Boutros Boutros-Ghali, *An Agenda for Peace: Preventive Diplomacy, Peacemaking and Peace-Keeping* (New York: United Nations, 1992).

2. The practical expansion of Security Council authority includes handling the side effects of civil war (refugee flows and humanitarian needs), attempting to limit civil war conflicts through arms embargoes and sanctions, creating new institutions (the ad hoc tribunals for war crimes in the former Yugoslavia and Rwanda), and articulating new state obligations (mandating the extradition of suspects in state-sponsored terrorism from Libya and the Sudan).

3. See, for example, *The United Nations in Its Second Half-Century: A Report of the Independent Working Group on the Future of the United Nations* (Ford Foundation, 1995); and Erskine Childers and Brian Urquhart, "Renewing the United Nations System," *Development Dialogue* 1 (1994): 1–213.

4. The OAS was asked only to "recommend" member country action in the missile crisis, sashaying around the limits of UN Charter Article 53. See Abram Chayes, *Cuban Missile Crisis* (New York: Oxford University Press, 1974).

5. Mohamed Sahnoun, *Somalia: The Missed Opportunities* (Washington, D.C.: United States Institute of Peace Press, 1994).

6. OAS MRE/RES. 1/91, Doc. OEA/Ser.F/V.1 (October 3, 1991) (demanding "full restoration of the rule of law and of the constitutional regime" and the immediate reinstatement of Aristide, and urging all OAS states to suspend nonhumanitarian economic, financial, and commercial ties with Haiti); and OAS MRE/RES. 3/92 (May 17, 1992) (asking OAS members to deny port access to vessels violating the embargo and to freeze the assets of coup supporters). The Rio Pact allows the imposition of mandatory sanctions, but is designed for interstate aggression, rather than policing civil conflicts. See Inter-American Treaty of Reciprocal Assistance, 62 Stat. 1681 (1948), arts. 8 and 20.

7. "The Santiago Commitment to Democracy and the Renewal of the Inter-American System," OAS General Assembly, OAS Doc. OEA/Ser.P/XXI.O.2 (adopted June 4, 1991); and "Representative Democracy," OAS General Assembly Resolution 1080 (XXI-0/91), OAS Doc. OEA/Ser.P/XXI.O.2 (adopted June 5, 1991).

8. "Document of the Copenhagen Meeting of the Conference on the Human Dimension of the CSCE," June 29, 1990, 29 *International Legal Materials* 1305 (1990).

9. Reprinted in Senate Treaty Doc. No. 22, 103d Cong., 2d Sess. (1994); also 33 *International Legal Materials* 1005 (1994). The protocol has been signed by twenty-nine OAS member-states. In addition, sixteen states have ratified the protocol, including Argentina, Bahamas, Canada, El Salvador, and the United States. It is not yet in force.

10. See OAS Charter, Art. 18, 33 *International Legal Materials* 981 (1994): "No State or group of States has the right to intervene, directly or indirectly, for any reason whatever, in the internal or external affairs of any other State. The foregoing principle prohibits not only armed force, but also any other form of interference or attempted threat against the personality of the State or against its political, economic, and cultural elements." Brazil abstained from the Security Council vote that authorized the "forced

entry" into Haiti in 1994 to restore the constitutional regime of President Jean-Bertrand Aristide.

11. "Pentagon Looks to Military Cooperation with South Africa," Agence France-Presse, August 7, 1995.

12. See "Department of State Memorandum: Legal Basis for the Quarantine of Cuba" (October 23, 1962), in Chayes, *Cuban Missile Crisis,* pp. 141, 146. But see the contrary view of former secretary general U Thant, in *View from the UN* (New York: United Nations, 1978), pp. 160–164, 172–173.

13. UN Security Council Resolution 788 (November 19, 1992).

14. UN Security Council Resolution 940 (July 31, 1994).

15. See Ian Johnstone, *Rights and Reconciliation: UN Strategies in El Salvador* (Boulder, Colo.: Lynne Rienner, 1995); and *Improvising History: A Critical Evaluation of the United Nations Observer Mission in El Salvador* (New York: Lawyers Committee for Human Rights, 1996).

16. See Luis Guillermo Solis, *Collective Mediations in the Caribbean Basin,* in *Collective Responses to Regional Problems: The Case of Latin America and the Caribbean,* ed. Carl Kaysen, Robert Pastor, and Laura Reed (Cambridge, Mass.: American Academy of Arts and Sciences, 1994).

17. See Janet E. Heininger, *Peacekeeping in Transition: The United Nations in Cambodia* (New York: Twentieth Century Fund, 1994), pp. 9–29, 56–57; Michael W. Doyle, *UN Peacekeeping in Cambodia: UNTAC's Civil Mandate* (Boulder, Colo.: Lynne Rienner, 1995), pp. 16–24; and Steven R. Ratner, *The New UN Peacekeeping: Building Peace in Lands of Conflict After the Cold War* (New York: St. Martin's Press and Council on Foreign Relations Press, 1995).

18. David Binder, "UN Fights Bonn's Embrace of Croatia," *New York Times,* December 14, 1991, p. 3.

19

Emerging from the Intervention Dilemma

BARRY M. BLECHMAN

With the end of the Cold War and of the accompanying risk that interventions abroad could result in confrontation, crisis, and even war between the nuclear-armed superpowers, Americans began to rethink the norms governing U.S. involvement in the affairs of other states. Contradictory impulses dominated this debate. The typical American urge to export democratic and humanitarian values encouraged activist policies and involvement in many countries. But the traditional American antipathy toward "overseas entanglements" and particular distaste for military adventures have diminished support for U.S. involvement in many situations that posed a serious risk of American casualties or even significant expenditures.

The resulting policy dilemma caused difficulties for President Bush and bedeviled President Clinton. Both administrations sought to escape from the dilemma by turning to the United Nations, seeking both to legitimate interventions and to spread the burden to a wider group of countries. As a result, the world organization's traditional peacekeeping functions were transformed into more muscular "peace operations." But these UN missions had only mixed results, and the few clear failures led to an adverse political climate in the United States and to specific legislative initiatives that placed tight constraints on U.S. participation in UN peace missions. Consequently, in the most recent situations (Haiti in 1994–1995 and Bosnia in 1995–1996), the United States sought to define new forms of participation in international conflict management, combining UN peace operations with parallel, but separately managed, multilateral interventions.

The success of these new forms of intervention has not yet been determined. At the time of this writing, the end result of the intervention in Haiti is unclear, and the deployment of U.S. troops to Bosnia is just beginning. However, it is evident that neither UN operations nor unilateral activities provide viable instruments for resolving

287

the intervention dilemma. Providing effective means for intervening in conflicts abroad remains a stark challenge for American policymakers.

CONTRADICTORY IMPULSES

The belief that governments have a right, even obligation, to intervene in the affairs of other states seems to have gained great currency in recent years. Modern communications have made people everywhere more aware of situations that seem to cry out for intervention and more familiar with the human tragedies that accompany these horrible calamities. Technology, too, has provided readier means of intervention—whether for diplomats to mediate, for observers to monitor elections, for paramilitary forces to enforce economic sanctions, or for armed forces to carry out military operations—removing many excuses of infeasibility. The governments of the great powers, particularly the United States, have the means to intervene anywhere today, whether they choose to do so or not.

However, far more than the physical means of awareness and intervention has changed. The norms governing interventions themselves have evolved. The sanctity once accorded to state boundaries has eroded considerably; the interdependence and penetrability of states need no elaboration. Serious crises anywhere in the world cause financial markets and currency rates to reverberate, affecting investors' confidence and the business climate overall; companies large and small depend on foreign investors, components, markets, and technologies. Individuals are both more directly affected by turmoil in distant lands and more familiar with foreign countries. Ordinary citizens interact more frequently with people living abroad; people exercise rights to visit and conduct business in foreign countries routinely, almost without

thinking about the legal boundaries that have been crossed.

Most important, however, profound changes have occurred in popular expectations. After decades of little more than formal intonation, the belief that governments can be expected to adhere to certain universal standards of behavior, even within their own borders, seems to have taken hold. This is certainly not to say that all people in all parts of the world have this belief. The view is popular among different populations to different degrees—most strongly in Europe and North America, to a lesser degree in other parts of the world—but the trend is very clear, particularly among the economic and social elites that dominate politics in most countries.

What is the basis for this new view? Apparently, increasing numbers of people are willing to act on what must be an implicit belief that sovereignty does not reside in an abstraction called the state (and certainly not with self-appointed military or civilian dictatorships) but with the people of a country themselves. Even more, the power of all governments, even those popularly elected, is seen as limited: Individuals have inalienable rights that must be observed and protected by all governments. As a result, according to this increasingly powerful view, all governments can be held to certain standards of behavior involving basic human rights and democratic processes. In addition, when a country falls into such disarray that no governing body can end a humanitarian tragedy and guarantee human rights, the world community itself is accountable. When such events occur, people in other countries, and their governments, have not only the right, but the obligation, to intervene on behalf of both oppressed peoples and innocent bystanders.

Historically, when murderous civil wars or large-scale abuses of human rights occurred in a country, powerful outside governments with direct interests in that state sometimes intervened. Today, as a result of the greater currency of the views described above, great powers often feel compelled to intervene in domestic conflicts even when their direct stakes are limited. Sometimes, the officials of a great power hold to the views just described and thus see intervention as a humanitarian responsibility. At other times, if governments hesitate and if the events in question are of sufficient magnitude, various constituencies exert political pressures for action—action to end the slaughter, to feed the refugees, to restore democracy, or, at least, to save the lives of the children. Often, private citizens and organizations become involved in these situations before governments even contemplate acting. Religious charities, humanitarian organizations, and activist political rights groups are involved on the ground in virtually all troubled nations. Their reports and activities reinforce (and sometimes help to create) popular pressure in foreign capitals for some kind of official action.

Thus, in the contemporary world, major powers react when troubles occur in even the most remote parts of the globe. Diplomats are dispatched, good offices tendered, observers placed, and political and economic campaigns of isolation launched. Sometimes, if exercised with persistence and skill, these peaceful means of conflict resolution work. More often, they do not: Dictators stubbornly cling to power, powerful elites continue to oppress the masses, and ethnic factions continue to revenge historic slaughters with the even greater slaughters made possible by modern weapons.

Why do peaceful means fail? Many factors, no doubt, are responsible, but one stands out. In the contemporary age, intervening governments can only rarely credibly threaten military intervention should peaceful means fail. This is the intervention dilemma. Even as the proclivity of major

powers to intervene in domestic conflicts in foreign nations has grown, the natural reluctance of populations to pay the price of such interventions, if challenged, has also gathered steam. This reluctance takes two forms: pressure in many democratic states against the use of public funds for foreign operations and, more pointedly, popular opposition in democratic states to the use of military power in most circumstances.

Thus, increasingly, even while powerful political constituencies demand action by democratic governments to resolve domestic conflicts in foreign nations, even more powerful constituencies resist the use of the one form of intervention that often is the only realistic means of accomplishing the first constituency's demands: the threat or actual use of force. In an international system with no central authority, the absence of credible military threats curtails the effectiveness of all forms of coercive diplomacy and limits the effectiveness of even peaceful means of conflict resolution.

Formally, of course, countless treaties and agreements concluded over the decades have proscribed the use of military force except in self-defense. Such morally based constraints no doubt continue to motivate many in their opposition to the use of force. Even more powerful, however, are more tangible constraints. Increasingly, the citizens of democratic nations appear unwilling to underwrite military interventions with either blood or treasure. Looking at the history of the twentieth century, it is clear that the moral basis for restraint in the use of force has carried only limited weight. The coupling of ethical concerns with the current unwillingness to sacrifice either money or lives for government objectives seems to have turned the tide against military interventions.

In the 1950s, for example, the populations of most European powers clearly expressed their unwillingness to support military operations in most parts of the world, the one possible exception being to defend against a direct attack on themselves. Even the French proved unwilling in 1958 to continue paying the very high price of France's colonialist military intervention in Algeria. (France, of course, continued to intervene in small ways in Africa in the years since, but only on so small a scale that the operations could be managed by highly specialized volunteer units.)

The watershed for the United States came ten years later in Southeast Asia. The popularity of U.S. military operations in Grenada, Panama, and Kuwait may seem to contradict this assertion, but a look at the complete record of U.S. military operations since the withdrawal from Vietnam makes it clear that popular support for military intervention seems to hinge on the plan's brevity, bloodlessness, and immediate—and evident—success. The abrupt U.S. withdrawals from Beirut in 1983–1984 and Somalia in 1993–1994, following isolated, if dramatic, incidents in which U.S. forces suffered casualties clearly demonstrate the American public's opposition to interventions that appear to be either difficult or costly.

Nor is the phenomenon restricted to popular attitudes. Episodes like Beirut and Somalia seem to have impressed both the executive and legislative branches of the U.S. government, as well as both major political parties, profoundly. What else explains the sudden termination of Operation Desert Storm short of its logical strategic objective of deposing the source of the problem, Saddam Hussein? And what else explains the bipartisan hesitancy to undertake even minor military tasks, such as restoring the democratically elected government in Haiti and helping to secure a hard-won peace in Bosnia?

The unpopularity of military operations helps explain why the United States and European governments came to believe in the early 1990s that interventions should be carried out through the United Nations. Trapped between opposing views in the intervention dilemma, the United States and European nations turned decidedly away from unilateral actions and toward multinational activities sanctioned, and often managed, by the United Nations.

The greater cooperation of the Soviet Union that began in the late 1980s made the turn to the United Nations feasible, of course, but it did not cause this major shift in policy. Indeed, as the Soviet military threat receded and the United States increasingly emerged as the world's sole military superpower, one might have thought that the United States would have demonstrated a greater propensity to act unilaterally, or at least in coalition with its traditional allies. All else being equal, it is certainly less complicated to act in one of these modes than under the United Nations' aegis. Just the opposite occurred, however, in the early 1990s, with both the Bush and Clinton administrations turning to the United Nations in virtually every relevant situation.

As a result, the number of peacekeeping and good offices missions carried out each year by or for the United Nations doubled between the mid-1980s and mid-1990s, rising from an average of around ten per year to more than twenty per year (figure 19.1). The increase was largely accounted for by interventions in domestic situations—both civil wars and other kinds of internal conflicts (figure 19.2). Indeed, the annual number of UN missions related to domestic conflicts grew dramatically, rising from less than five per year through the 1980s to an average of roughly eighteen per year in the first half of the 1990s.

Governments turn to the United Nations for several reasons. First, the democracies have shared the goal of creating effective collective means of resolving conflicts since World War II. When the Soviet Union

Figure 19.1. UN Field Missions (Peacekeeping and Good Offices), 1946–1995.

began in the mid-1980s to use its veto power far less frequently, achieving this goal appears to be possible for the first time.

Second, on more practical grounds, acting through the United Nations is a means of sharing the burdens of maintaining international stability—both the tangible burden of money and lives and the political burden of imposing one's will on others. The United States may pay close to one-third the cost of UN peacekeeping operations, but that is still better than the full cost of unilateral actions. Acting through the United Nations, moreover, both legitimates and sanctions military interventions in the eyes of domestic and foreign audiences. As was demonstrated in Kuwait, for example, recourse to the United Nations' formal procedures for the exercise of collective self-defense was essential both

to gain popular support in the United States and to hold together the coalition of nations that actually fought the war.

There is, however, a third reason for the turn to the United Nations, which, even if not perceived by decision makers, also motivates more frequent recourse to the world body. Government officials confronting the intervention dilemma have an additional incentive to turn to the United Nations, because dealing with civil conflicts through the United Nations enables government decision makers to shift the locus of responsibility. Introducing the issue in the Security Council, cajoling action by the world body, is itself a means of satisfying those constituencies demanding intervention. Turning to the United Nations in effect says, "We are acting, we are drawing attention to the

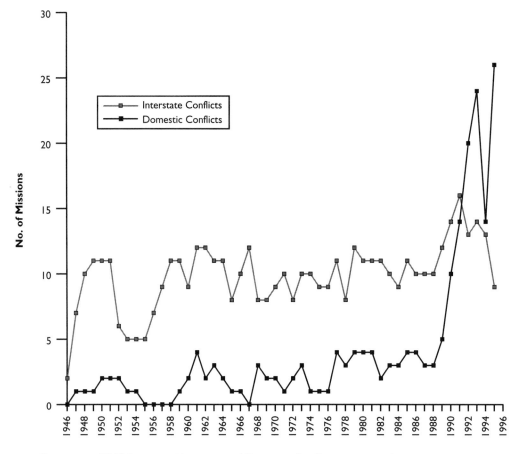

Figure 19.2. UN Missions in Interstate and Domestic Conflicts, 1946–1995.

issue, we are writing resolutions, stepping up pressures, persuading others to join us, etc." At the same time, if UN diplomacy and political pressures prove inadequate and the situation remains unacceptable, it appears not to be the government's failure, but the failure of the world body. Government officials in many countries have been more than willing to practice such scapegoating, as if the United Nations were able to act more effectively or ambitiously than its key members permit.

Naturally, this attempt to sidestep the intervention dilemma by acting through the United Nations fails in many cases. The paper demonstration of action provided by activity in the UN Security Council proves

of only limited value in stanching political pressure for effective intervention in conflicts in foreign nations. At the same time, the cloak of respectability conferred by the United Nations has only limited usefulness in confronting the popular reluctance to undertake military tasks of any substantial difficulty or cost.

In most civil conflict situations, if political constraints make recourse to military force infeasible, the intervenor's leverage is limited. If a civil war is not ripe for resolution, if contending factions are not yet convinced that the price of continued warfare exceeds any potential gain, mediators cannot succeed regardless of their skills. In such cases, only a willingness to separate the combatants forcefully and impose a settlement has even a chance of ending the war, and then only so long as the intervenor is willing to continue sitting on the belligerents.

Similarly, as has been seen repeatedly in recent years, neither political nor economic pressure is typically powerful enough to dislodge dictators who have everything to lose and little to gain by stepping down peacefully. If the use of military power is not a credible instrument of last resort, then the intervenor's objective is often impossible from the outset. In many situations, without a credible threat of effective military action, UN diplomats and mediators are no more effective than national representatives in similarly constrained circumstances.

The United Nations has been a useful vehicle for taking limited military actions to help mitigate the more visible aspects of conflict situations—ensuring the delivery of humanitarian assistance, implementing cease-fires, and so forth—but the use of real force to impose solutions has almost always been ruled out. The prospect of significant financial costs and loss of life has proved just as powerful a deterrent to forceful intervention in foreign nations under the UN flag as under national insignia. As a result, in most UN peace operations, the rules of engagement have carefully specified constraints that both ensured that UN forces remain out of harm's way and made it impossible for them to enforce solutions. In the first case in which such constraints were eased and in which casualties then ensued—Somalia—the haste with which even the world's greatest military power withdrew doomed the mission to failure and proved to many the weaknesses of the United Nations.

EMERGING FROM THE DILEMMA

As a result of these evident problems in UN peace operations, a consensus emerged in Washington in 1993–1994 that the number and scope of military interventions by the United Nations—and the U.S. role in them—should be restrained. A new emphasis was placed on "realism" in deciding when and how to intervene, and this was spelled out in the administration's 1994 peacekeeping policy. In effect, this stress on "realism" was essentially an attempt to break out of the intervention dilemma by mustering pragmatism as the first line of defense against the political impulse to intervene. Rwanda was the first clear demonstration of the new policy. Following the brutal intensification of the civil war in that troubled country in April 1994, the United States worked to maintain "realistic" boundaries on the strengthening of the UN mission there.

A greater emphasis on "realism" in approving UN interventions was clearly appropriate at the time, given the huge expansion in the organization's agenda over the past few years and its clear inability to carry out many of the tasks that were assigned to it. But if the United States continues to define a realistic intervention policy narrowly, it will learn that failure to intervene is not without its own costs. The United States and most other great powers may not have had significant, tangible interests in Rwanda, but they do have economic and political stakes in other places that have been, or might in the future be, rent by civil conflicts. The "realism" that long delayed military intervention in Haiti cost the United States dearly, for example, in terms of financial losses for Americans who did business in Haiti, in terms of the cost of dealing with Haitian refugees on the seas and in the United States, and, most important, in terms of the impact that U.S. timidity had on perceptions around the world of the nation's fitness to lead the world community.

Similarly, the reluctance to take decisive actions in 1992, 1993, and 1994 meant protracted suffering in the former Yugoslavia, as well as serious political strains in Europe and between the United States and its European partners. The reputations of the United States, leading European powers, and the several multinational organizations involved in the former Yugoslavia were tarnished badly, with unknowable effects on related behavior, such as the willingness of the Haitian dictator to stand up to American threats. Throughout this period (and continuing today) the potential for new conflicts in the Balkans and for the broadening of old ones remained high. Such contingencies had the potential to engulf the entire region in war and to trigger even broader and longer-term conflicts among the great powers.

There is also a moral cost of nonintervention that should not be ignored. The impulse for intervention is not some fad, nor is it a plot foisted on innocent populations by a liberal clique, as some have maintained. It reflects the deeply held humanitarian values of democratic populations in the contemporary age. Five hundred thousand people may have died in Rwanda in 1994, many of them children. How do Americans feel about that tragedy? Could it have been prevented or at least restrained in its consequences? How would Americans feel if an investment of a few hundred million dollars could have prevented half of the Rwandan deaths? Every person evaluates such trade-offs, or potential trade-offs, differently. They not only have to judge the cost to Rwandans against the cost to themselves, but they must also reach a judgment about the likely effectiveness of the intervention. There is no single right or wrong answer.

Civil conflicts and humanitarian tragedies affect every American by indicating a failure in fundamental human values. They also affect Americans more tangibly by diminishing business activity, by disrupting financial markets, by stimulating population movements that impose economic burdens and political disruptions on neighboring countries, and by posing risks of broader conflicts that would upset world peace and prosperity in momentous terms. If the United States could prevent such conflicts for free and for certain, citizens would clearly want the government to act. Judging when it is "realistic" to act is a trickier endeavor, requiring hard-headed assessments of options and interests.

The recent failures of the United Nations in a number of interventions—more properly, the failures of the members of the United Nations acting through that body in a number of interventions—should cause Americans to be modest in their estimates of what is realistic. But the United States can and should push the boundaries of realism in the following ways.

By working to make the United Nations a more effective instrument for intervening in conflicts. If the United States had greater confidence in the United Nations' abilities, U.S. leaders would be more ambitious in describing what was realistic. But to become effective, the United Nations needs to be given the means of conducting military operations effectively, including the financial resources to build an infrastructure capable of providing effective command, training, and logistical capabilities and the personnel resources to carry out the mandates of individual missions effectively. Member-states also need to earmark military units for potential use in UN operations and to give them the specialized training and equipment they need to be effective.

By learning from the past to tailor its own intervention missions more effectively. The United States also needs to apply the lessons from past interventions to planning and executing future missions. Judging from the intervention in Haiti, as well as the design of the unfolding NATO intervention in Bosnia, many of these lessons have been taken to heart by American decision makers. Unlike the case in the second Somalia mission, for example, the purposes and objectives of U.S. forces were spelled out clearly in Haiti and Bosnia and circumscribed sharply to avoid unlimited entanglements. Sufficient forces were authorized to attain these goals, as judged by conservative military criteria, and the units were authorized to use force decisively both in support of their own defense and in support of the accomplishment of their missions. Many past failures can clearly be attributed to insufficient forces deployed with unclear mandates and to insufficient license to use force when necessary to achieve the goals of the mission.

Not all the lessons of the past are so widely accepted, however. In Bosnia, for example, some continue to urge that the forces deployed in support of the peace agreement also act to strengthen the military capabilities of the Bosnian government. This is exactly what was done by the U.S. component of the multinational force deployed in Lebanon in 1982, with tragic consequences for both the mission and the troops deployed there. When governments are viewed as only a contending faction by dissident elements, intervenors cannot be both impartial arbiters of a peace accord accepted by all parties and partisan supporters of government authority—not without provoking armed opposition.

Similarly, political pressures have caused the Clinton administration to place a definite one-year time limit on the deployment to Bosnia, although the experience in Lebanon, Somalia, and elsewhere suggest that deadlines are best left vague, with the withdrawal of forces tied, instead, to the achievement of certain established benchmarks. Delays in the planned transition from the U.S. intervention to a UN peace force in

Haiti in 1995 were instrumental in giving the latter a fighting chance for success.

By inducing the executive and legislative branches to work more closely in determining which interventions are in the national interest and how they might best be structured. The executive branch would be in a better position to judge when interventions are realistic—and when they are not—if it worked more closely with the Congress on these issues, long before it reached the point of decision. Legislators necessarily know more than the executive about the beliefs of their constituents, about the balance in any one situation between the intervention impulse and the bias against the use of military force. While executive branch decisions should not be determined by opinion polls, consultations with the Congress can help to reveal not only what the public believes, but also what actions and policies might encourage positive changes in public opinion.

Closer coordination between the branches on these issues also has the potential of building political support either for interventions or for decisions not to intervene, whichever course is chosen. The leadership group and ranking members of key committees should clearly be consulted prior to U.S. approval of new UN missions. When the deployment of U.S. combat forces is contemplated, either as part of the UN mission or alongside it, any administration is well advised, in its own interest and in the interest of sustaining its policy, to seek formal congressional approval of the commitment of U.S. forces. As the branch of government most directly attuned to currents in public opinion, and thus most responsive to them, the Congress can play a special role in helping the executive branch to break out of the intervention dilemma.

20

The Crisis in UN Peacekeeping

ADAM ROBERTS

Despite notable achievements in recent years—including in Namibia, Cambodia, and El Salvador—United Nations (UN) peacekeeping is in crisis. This crisis is both conceptual and substantive: Tried-and-tested principles and practices of UN peacekeeping have had to be modified or abandoned; there have been repeated difficulties in the control and management of peacekeeping operations; and the distinction between peacekeeping and various enforcement activities has become blurred. UN efforts to use peacekeeping forces in ongoing conflicts, as in Bosnia, have exposed the organization to accusations of weakness and of failing to protect fundamental human rights; some peacekeeping operations, as in Angola, have been followed by a resumption of war; and responses to humanitarian crises, as in Somalia in 1992 and Rwanda in 1994, have been extremely slow. The range of conflicts around the world far exceeds the United Nations' capacity to address them; there have been accusations of bias in the choice of which conflicts the UN intervenes in and in the manner in which they are addressed;

and states have imposed numerous conditions on their participation in UN operations. Furthermore, the many proposals to place forces at the general disposal of the UN have failed, and peacekeeping finances are in disarray. There have been a bewildering variety of diagnoses and prescriptions for improvement. This article addresses four main questions:

- What were the essential features of UN peacekeeping up to 1987?
- How has the character of UN peacekeeping changed since 1988, and what are the consequences of the changes?
- In what kinds of crises can UN peacekeeping usefully become involved, and in what kinds is it inappropriate?
- What are the issues that the UN and its member-states need to address?

ESSENTIAL FEATURES OF UN PEACEKEEPING UP TO 1987

Peacekeeping operations, not foreseen in the UN Charter, emerged in response to urgent

297

problems.[1] Indeed, the precise charter basis for many UN peacekeeping operations remained ambiguous for decades. Peacekeeping was often referred to as a "Chapter-6-and-a-half" activity, meaning that it fell uncertainly somewhere between Chapter 6 (on the "Pacific Settlement of Disputes") and Chapter 7 (on "Action with Respect to Threats to the Peace, Breaches of the Peace, and Acts of Aggression"). As long as the fundamental basis of peacekeeping forces remained the consent of the parties involved in the conflict and the Security Council acted according to its own procedures, it did not matter that the precise charter basis for the action floated uncertainly between Chapters 6 and 7.

Up to the end of 1987 there were thirteen UN peacekeeping operations, all but one of which concerned conflicts that had arisen following European decolonization. Many other problems, including East-West conflicts, were addressed through other mechanisms, mainly outside a UN framework.

The traditional tasks of UN peacekeeping operations, as they evolved from the 1950s to the 1970s, included monitoring and enforcing cease-fires; observing frontier lines; and interposing between belligerents. These tasks were generally carried out on the basis of three key principles: the consent of the parties, the impartiality of the peacekeepers, and the non-use of force in most circumstances. These three principles were seen as being interlinked and fundamental to the effectiveness of peacekeeping operations.[2]

Non-use of force, although not an absolute principle, was central to UN peacekeeping for many years. As Marrack Goulding, UN undersecretary general for political affairs, has said:

> More than half the organization's peacekeeping operations before 1988 had consisted only of unarmed military observers. But when operations were armed, it had become an established principle that they

should use force only to the minimum extent necessary and that normally fire should be opened only in self-defense.

However, since 1973 self-defense had been deemed to include situations in which peacekeepers were being prevented by armed persons from fulfilling their mandate. This was a wide definition of "self-defense." In practice, commanders in the field had only very rarely taken advantage of the authority to open fire on, for instance, soldiers at a roadblock who were denying passage to a United Nations convoy. This reluctance was based on sound calculations related to impartiality, to their reliance on the continued cooperation of the parties, and to the fact that their force's level of armament was based on the assumption that the parties would comply with their commitments.[3]

On the basis of the principles established during the first four decades, Goulding went on to define UN peacekeeping as

> field operations established by the United Nations, with the consent of the parties concerned, to help control and resolve conflicts between them, under United Nations command and control, at the expense collectively of the member-states, and with military and other personnel and equipment provided voluntarily by them, acting impartially between the parties and using force to the minimum extent necessary.[4]

In the first decades of UN peacekeeping operations, the need for impartiality and disinterestedness led to the general practice of not using troops from certain countries. In particular, the United Nations, for the most part, avoided using contingents from the five permanent members of the Security Council (especially China and the two superpowers) and forces from neighboring powers. The merits of these practices were obvious: Local conflicts were insulated from Cold War rivalry and regional hegemony. The weaknesses were equally obvious: UN forces sometimes either lacked the authority and strength that a great-power presence could have provided, or they lacked the local knowledge, interest, and staying power that forces from a neighboring power might have had.

There was no shortage of problems in the first thirteen UN peacekeeping operations. The weakness of depending upon the consent of the host state was cruelly exposed by the expulsion of the United Nations Emergency Force (UNEF I) from Egypt in 1967 and the subsequent outbreak of war between Israel and a number of Arab states, including Egypt. Sometimes the performance of the original mandate led to additional tasks that did not sit easily with the three principles outlined above. In the Congo in 1960–1964 the tasks of the UN force came to include assisting in the maintenance of government and public order and using military force to achieve these ends against a variety of challenges. This early case of peacekeeping turning into enforcement succeeded, but at a huge price. In Cyprus in 1974 and in Lebanon in 1982, the presence of UN peacekeeping forces could not prevent the breakdown of order, including major foreign invasions and seizures of territory.

The achievements of UN peacekeeping, although modest, were real: they included the effective freezing (although not the resolution) of certain conflicts; some reduction of the risk, or extent, of competitive interventions by neighboring or major powers; and the isolation of some local conflicts from the East-West struggle, so that the local conflicts did not exacerbate the Cold War. In short, some wars were prevented from spreading and some missions were effectively accomplished. While the development of peacekeeping during the United Nations' first four decades was indeed impressive, it would be wrong, however, to depict it as a golden era.

HOW HAS THE CHARACTER OF UN PEACEKEEPING CHANGED?

Since mid-1988 there has been a dramatic expansion in the number of UN peacekeeping and observer forces. The often-repeated, constantly changing, and ever more impressive litany of statistics shows just how remarkable the expansion has been. From 1948 to 1978, thirteen peacekeeping and observer forces were set up; then, for ten years, no new forces were established. From May 1988 to October 1993, a further twenty forces were created. No fewer than seventeen such forces (five of which had been established before 1979) were still operating in early 1994, involving 70,000 troops, observers, and civilian police.

Reasons for the Expansion of Peacekeeping Activities

A main reason for this expansion in the number of peacekeeping and observer missions has been the increased capacity of the UN Security Council to agree on action in particular crises. The decline in the use of the veto is a symbol of this agreement. From 1945 to May 1990 the members of the Security Council cast the following number of vetoes: China, 3; France, 18; United Kingdom, 30; United States, 69; and the Soviet Union, 114. The last Soviet veto was on February 29, 1984, on a resolution proposing an extension of the last UN peacekeeping force to have been created—the United Nations Interim Force in Lebanon (UNIFIL). Between 1984 and May 31, 1990, the United States vetoed thirty-two Security Council resolutions, in some cases with British or French support, but not one resolution was vetoed by the Soviet Union or China. Then, between June 1990 and May 11, 1993, there was not a single use of the veto, although, of course, its very existence powerfully influenced decisions. On May 11, 1993, Russia broke the record three-year period of not using the veto when it blocked a resolution on financing the long-established peacekeeping force in Cyprus. It is significant that it was on a peacekeeping issue that use of the veto was resumed. Russia had reason to resent being asked to bear the financial burden of UN peacekeeping on the apparently stable island of Cyprus at a time when the United Nations was hardly making a notable contribution to the much more urgent crises facing Russia, both internally and on its borders. Despite this 1993 veto by Russia, the new-found capacity of the Security Council to reach agreement has survived and constitutes a key reason for the increase in the number of peacekeeping operations.

A further reason for the expansion of peacekeeping operations has been a widespread mood of optimism that the United Nations can have a much more central role in international security and that peacekeeping can tackle a wide range of urgent problems. National governments, as well as the United Nations itself, have shared this mood to a surprising degree. The heads of government at the UN Security Council summit at the end of January 1992 and Secretary General Boutros Boutros-Ghali in his *Agenda for Peace,* published in June 1992, reflected and, for a period, reinforced this optimism.[5]

Finally, the end of the Cold War increased the need for international peacekeeping forces. It did so in three distinct ways, each of which presented different problems and opportunities for the United Nations:

- Between 1985 and 1991 a series of regional peace agreements on Afghanistan, Angola, Namibia, Central America, and Cambodia created a demand for impartial international forces to assist in implementing their provisions, such as monitoring cease-fires, troop withdrawals, and elections.

- The decline and collapse of two large communist-cum-federal states—the Soviet Union and Yugoslavia—resulted in new conflicts, leading to strong calls for action under UN auspices.

- Following the end of the Cold War, the major powers were less likely than before to see a conflict in a distant country in geostrategic terms as part of a challenge from their major global adversary that required a unilateral military response. The major powers were, therefore, more willing to see a response (or lack of it) emerge from within a UN framework.

It is not clear, however, that peacekeeping operations are appropriate for each challenge, especially in view of the varied nature of the tasks that have to be performed. Indeed, using the United Nations to tackle some crises may be, as it was sometimes during the Cold War, a substitute rather than a recipe for effective action.

New Types of Tasks for UN Peacekeeping

Since 1988, UN peacekeeping operations have involved a remarkably wide variety of activities, some of which have either been totally new for the United Nations or on a much larger scale than before, such as the following:

- monitoring and even running elections, as in Namibia, El Salvador, Angola, Cambodia, and Mozambique;

- protecting inhabitants of a region, whether the majority or minorities, from the threat or use of force—including by the government of the region or country. This is part of the function of the three United Nations protected areas (UNPAs) in Croatia;

- protecting designated "safe areas," such as certain towns in Bosnia, from attack;

- ensuring the partial demilitarization of particular areas, such as around Sarajevo and Gorazde in Bosnia;

- guarding the weapons surrendered by or taken from parties to a conflict;

- assuring the delivery of humanitarian relief supplies and the performance of a wide range of other humanitarian tasks during conflicts, especially in the former Yugoslavia and Somalia;

- assisting in the reconstruction of governmental or police functions after a civil war, including in El Salvador and Cambodia; and

- reporting violations of the laws of armed conflict (international humanitarian law) by belligerent parties.

There should be no objection in principle to developing and expanding peacekeeping tasks. New circumstances have required new forms of action. These new circumstances have presented problems that have had to be faced and opportunities that have had to be seized. Some of the developments since the mid-1980s are promising. Election monitoring under UN auspices is a good example. Sometimes, as in Nicaragua and Haiti, UN election verification has been conducted on its own and not as part of a peacekeeping mission. In other cases, as in Namibia, Angola, and Cambodia, monitoring or helping to organize elections has been one of the tasks of a peacekeeping force. Although such outside assistance failed to prevent a postelection coup in Haiti in September 1991 or a renewed civil war in Angola in 1992, the picture elsewhere looks more hopeful. Election monitoring is particularly significant for two reasons. First, it associates the UN with multiparty democracy. Second, it enables peacekeeping forces to be involved in something more than merely freezing conflicts: In some countries UN forces can achieve more by assisting in bal-lots than by interposing themselves between belligerents.

Assisting democracy, like other aspects of UN peacekeeping, depends upon local cooperation. When cooperation is denied or withdrawn, problems begin. The nature of postconflict societies can make democracy a distant goal. A United Nations that concerns itself with the type of government operating in member-states may find itself involved in a wide range of complex and dangerous disputes. Sometimes, as in the debacle over Haiti in 1993, the United Nations may be powerless, apart from the use of sanctions, in the face of even a small and weakly armed sovereign state.

Many of the other new or expanded tasks of UN peacekeeping have been more problematic. Humanitarian relief is a case in point. The natural emphasis on such relief has too often been accompanied by a failure to think through the broader questions raised by UN involvement in a crisis. It may be necessary, but it is never enough, to say that the United Nations' role in a crisis is essentially humanitarian. There is also a need for tough analysis of the problems that created the need for aid and of the policies for tackling them.

The establishment of various types of "protected areas" and "safe areas" in the former Yugoslavia has also proved problematic. The UN forces involved frequently do not know exactly what their duties are. To the extent that these include protection against external attack, such areas "soak up" manpower and threaten both the credibility and impartiality of the UN force. These protected and safe areas could easily lead to the United Nations assuming responsibility for horrors and could drag the United Nations into reprisal attacks.

UN peacekeeping forces have become increasingly involved in assisting, or even exercising, certain governmental functions in states that have experienced civil war and, in some cases, have fragmented or collapsed. In varying degrees, this has happened in El Salvador, Cambodia, Somalia, and the UN-protected areas in Croatia.[6] The focus has often been as much on regional administration as on central government. Advising, training, and assisting the police have been a prominent part of such activities. Although success has been limited, the issue of taking on a larger administrative role keeps recurring. For instance, there were some tentative proposals for the possible UN administration of Sarajevo or other parts of Bosnia as part of a peace settlement.

A central difficulty in the expansion of UN peacekeeping tasks has been the blurring of the distinction between peacekeeping and coercive action. This is intimately linked to a tendency to downgrade the requirement of the consent of the parties to a conflict as a condition for establishing and maintaining a peacekeeping operation. There is a much greater interventionist element in peacekeeping today, which is at the heart of the crisis.

Consent as a Basis for Peacekeeping

The downgrading of the consent of the parties to the conflict as a requirement for UN action occurred in three important crises in 1991–1993 and was accompanied by a change in the doctrine of peacekeeping operations.

Crisis in Iraq. The establishment of the Kurd-inhabited "safe havens" in northern Iraq in April 1991 was achieved not by any formal UN peacekeeping force, but by U.S., British, and French forces. These forces were subsequently replaced by a small group of UN guards, who were distinct from peacekeeping forces. This experience did, however, mark a decisive crossing of an important line in the requirements for action under UN auspices. Iraq did not

consent to the initial incursion of coalition forces and, although there were subsequent Iraq-UN agreements under which the UN guards were sent to northern Iraq, Baghdad's later consent was clearly in some measure the outcome of the earlier forcible incursion.[7] The action in northern Iraq, because it both saved large numbers of lives and showed some ability to act against the wishes of a sovereign state, strongly influenced subsequent UN responses to other crises.

Crisis in the former Yugoslavia. Less than a year later, in the exceptionally difficult circumstances of the war in the former Yugoslavia, a second case arose in which the issue of consent was in practice more complex and nuanced than in theory—and this time a UN peacekeeping force was involved. UN Security Council Resolution 743 of February 21, 1992, authorized the United Nations Protection Force (UNPROFOR) in the former Yugoslavia. While the resolution contained evidence of elements of consent, it also specified that the Council was acting under the Security Council's responsibility "for the maintenance of international peace and security"—a coded reference to Chapter 7 of the UN Charter; by referring to Article 25 of the UN Charter, it reminded states of their formal obligation to accept and carry out the decisions of the UN Security Council. Furthermore, this resolution set UNPROFOR up for a definite term of peacekeeping at the discretion of the Security Council.[8] All of this implied, at the very least, that although the operation had begun with a degree of consent of the parties to the conflict, it might continue even without that consent. Subsequent resolutions continued along similar lines.

Within a few months of the establishment of UNPROFOR, the downgrading of consent as an absolute requirement for peacekeeping was also apparent in Boutros-

Ghali's *Agenda for Peace*, where he defines peacekeeping as follows:

> The deployment of a United Nations presence in the field, hitherto with the consent of all the parties concerned, normally involving United Nations military and/or police personnel and frequently civilians as well. Peace-keeping is a technique that expands the possibilities for both the prevention of conflict and the making of peace.[9]

The "hitherto" in this definition became the subject of much comment by individuals and states. There were two main grounds for concern. First, tried-and-tested principles of UN peacekeeping were being changed and perhaps fatally weakened without a full discussion of all the implications. Second, many individuals and states (mainly small or developing nations) feared a new interventionist peacekeeping.

Crisis in Somalia. In Somalia, especially from December 1992 onward, the criterion of consent has been further downgraded. There has been no functioning government to give or refuse consent. Also, as in the former Yugoslavia, the number of parties to the conflict and disputes about the status of the parties make the consent of all hard to obtain and impossible to maintain. The UN Security Council explicitly referred to its powers under Chapter 7 of the UN Charter when it decided to establish the two principal forces in Somalia.

- The Unified Task Force (UNITAF) was a multistate force under U.S. command that operated in Somalia between December 1992 and May 1993.[10] This was not generally regarded as either a UN Force or a pure peacekeeping force, but rather as a UN-authorized force roughly comparable, so far as its legal basis and command system was concerned, to the U.S.-led coalition forces in Korea in 1950–1953 and in Kuwait in 1990–1991.

It had some liaison with the United Nations and the United Nations Operation in Somalia (UNOSOM I)—the UN peacekeeping force that had been set up earlier in 1992 and whose inability to fulfill its mandate had led to the creation of UNITAF.

- UNOSOM II took over responsibilities and personnel from UNITAF in May 1993. Although this is designated as a UN peacekeeping force, it was from the start a most unusual one. Its authorizing resolution departs in a number of ways from the traditional mandate of peacekeeping forces. The resolution explicitly refers to Chapter 7 of the UN Charter and clearly leaves room for a greater use of force than was typical for UN peacekeeping operations.

In the post–Cold War era, therefore, two UN peacekeeping forces—UNPROFOR and UNOSOM II—have been set up largely in the framework of Chapter 7 of the UN Charter, without relying on the consent of the parties to the conflict to the same extent as earlier cases. This marks a significant watershed in the history of the United Nations.

This reduced emphasis on consent has been for good reasons, including a desire to overcome the past weaknesses of peacekeeping, such as in the Middle East in 1967. There has also been a need for a new approach to consent, because in situations of chaos, a peacekeeping force cannot be allowed to have its entire continued existence depend upon the whim of every local leader.

Yet downgrading the consent of the parties as a key criterion for action takes peacekeeping into dangerous territory, involving the United Nations in a series of tasks for which it is hardly ready. The lack of a formal charter framework for all peacekeeping operations may have facilitated a tendency (evident in these cases) to regard peacekeeping as a flexible technique, whose legal basis, purposes, and mode of operating can be radically adapted and to apply it to difficult situations for which it is not necessarily appropriate.

While there has been some downgrading of consent in authorizing resolutions of the UN Security Council, there has not been downgrading of consent in the day-to-day operations of peacekeeping forces on the ground. At this level, whether in Somalia, the former Yugoslavia, or elsewhere, small and exposed UN peacekeeping forces have still had to operate with the agreement of local political and military leaders.

Use of Force

The readiness of the United Nations to use force is directly linked to the issue of consent. In the past, UN forces have been empowered to use force when directly threatened or when their central activities were being openly opposed, but they had seldom resorted to major uses of force. In some peacekeeping operations in recent years, however, there have been unprecedented threats and uses of force. In Namibia in April 1989, UN representatives authorized, or at least tolerated, a South African use of force against infiltrators from the South West Africa People's Organization: This was a necessary condition for the success of the UN peacekeeping and election-monitoring operation.

Events in Bosnia-Herzegovina and Somalia have reinforced the need for peacekeeping to have "teeth," but they have also exposed some of the difficulties involved in peacekeeping operations. There has been proper revulsion over a situation in which parties to a conflict can, at will, stop the distribution of aid, prevent the rotation of UN peacekeeping troops, bombard cities, maintain cruel sieges, and commit war crimes—all with UN forces looking on and seemingly

powerless to act. The calls for action have been made stronger because UN forces frequently assist the passage of journalists, whose reports on what they have seen inevitably lead to demands to put things right.

An increased willingness to use force in support of UN operations was apparent in certain passages of *An Agenda for Peace.* Enforcement was presented as an activity that would be likely to require separate and distinct forces:

> Cease-fires have often been agreed to but not complied with, and the United Nations has sometimes been called upon to send forces to restore and maintain the cease-fire. This task can on occasion exceed the mission of peace keeping forces and the expectations of peacekeeping force contributors. I recommend that the Council consider the utilization of peace-enforcement units in clearly defined circumstances and with their terms of reference specified in advance.[11]

In practice, however, UN "peace-enforcement units" have not been created. Instead, the functions envisaged for these units have been assigned in an ad hoc manner to UN peacekeeping forces themselves (as with certain aspects of the operations in the former Yugoslavia and Somalia); to national forces (as in Namibia and certain U.S. actions in Somalia); and to the North Atlantic Treaty Organization's (NATO) forces (as in the air exclusion zone over Bosnia and in the Sarajevo exclusion zone). UN Security Council Resolution 836 of June 4, 1993, is a landmark in this regard: It authorized member-states, acting nationally or through regional organizations and arrangements, to use air power to support UNPROFOR in and around the UN safe areas in Bosnia.

One form of peacekeeping with a readiness to use force is preventive deployment. Since December 1992, part of UNPROFOR in the former Yugoslavia has been stationed in Macedonia to discourage possible attacks on that former Yugoslav republic. This kind of preventive deployment may have considerable potential and is one of the most interesting new uses of peacekeeping forces. It is a much more direct military function, however, than past peacekeeping operations.

The main practical problems caused by the greater willingness to use force in peacekeeping operations have arisen, not in the context of preventive deployments, but rather in cases of continuing conflict that demand action. When, as in Somalia and Bosnia, local parties defy both existing agreements and the Security Council's pronouncements, the demand for action becomes strong, but the dilemmas involved are difficult.

The first dilemma is that while any strong use of force by or on behalf of peacekeepers may help to restore the credibility of peacekeepers, it may also increase the risks to lightly armed peacekeepers in vulnerable positions. As events in Somalia have suggested, the peacekeepers may be more exposed to attack, robbery, or hostage-taking than they were before. In Bosnia, this fear has led to repeated discussions about whether peacekeepers might have to be withdrawn before any military action was taken, in which case, the much discussed "peacekeeping with muscles" would involve a significant diminution in the range of activities that peacekeepers could undertake.

The second dilemma, closely related to the first, is that the use of force in complex civil wars frequently involves killing and injuring civilians as well as armed adversaries. If this happens, as it did in Somalia in 1993, the United Nations and its leading members risk being accused of acting in a brutal or colonial manner. Military disasters may result from air strikes, naval artillery bombardments, and actions by ground forces. If such dangers are to be minimized, there is a need for local knowledge, first-class intelligence, good decision making, and the skilled performance of military tasks. Not all UN

forces and procedures are strong in all of these respects.

The third dilemma is that some (though not all) uses of force risk undermining perceptions of the impartiality of the peacekeeping force. Such forces often have grave difficulties in maintaining their impartiality anyway, especially if, as in Bosnia, humanitarian aid is needed more by one side than another. A peacekeeping force, like any other force in an alien land, needs local allies and supporters, especially if it is engaged in hostilities. In such circumstances, impartiality must be a casualty. There may even be some risk that the impartiality of UN peacekeeping forces generally, and indeed of the United Nations itself, may be undermined.

The fourth dilemma is that while the UN system of decision making is not well geared to controlling major uses of force, there must be a reluctance to leave the decision to others when the lives of peacekeepers and the reputation of the United Nations are at stake. Hence, the long and complex discussions over the authority to use force in Bosnia, a matter in which national governments, NATO collectively, the UN secretary general, the Security Council, and the commanders of UNPROFOR in the former Yugoslavia and Bosnia all felt entitled to a key role or even a veto. In Resolution 836, the Security Council stated that the use of air power to support UNPROFOR in the safe areas was "subject to close coordination with the secretary general and UNPROFOR." Subsequent correspondence and practice have confirmed the sensitivity of the issue of control over such military activities.[12] There was evidence of U.S. exasperation at certain uses of its armed forces being subject to UN authorization. Some other states, however, including the United Kingdom and France, both of which had troops on the ground in Bosnia, were not opposed to the secretary general's insistence on a degree of UN control.

Despite all these dilemmas, the need for some intelligent means of using force in support of peacekeeping operations remains. If such means cannot be found, those operations will inevitably suffer a decline in credibility. Indeed, this happened in 1993. The travails of the United Nations, and of the western powers generally, in Bosnia and Somalia led to a decline in their credibility in certain other situations, including Haiti. The threats and uses of force in Bosnia in the first half of 1994, while not enough to reverse a fundamentally difficult situation, did restore some of the United Nations' battered credibility.

Some attempts have been made to work out a new strategic role for the United Nations. Kofi Annan, UN undersecretary general for peacekeeping operations, wrote the following in late 1993:

> Today's conflicts in Somalia and Bosnia have fundamentally redrawn the parameters. It is no longer enough to implement agreements or separate antagonists; the international community now wants the United Nations to demarcate boundaries, control and eliminate heavy weapons, quell anarchy, and guarantee the delivery of humanitarian aid in war zones. These are clearly tasks that call for "teeth" and "muscle," in addition to less tangible qualities that we have sought in the past. In other words, there are increasing demands that the United Nations now enforce the peace, as originally envisaged in the charter.[13]

Kofi Annan suggested that NATO could have a key role in the "peacekeeping with teeth" he was advocating. Annan saw the involvement of NATO in peacekeeping operations as a way past the main obstacle to success that he identified in the article: the reluctance of member-states to translate commitment into action by supplying funds and forces. Annan's article foreshadowed the discriminate and effective use of air power in February 1994 in Bosnia, both to enforce the controls on artillery in the Sarajevo exclusion zone and to stop military flights by belligerents. Yet this threat (and reality) of air power, while contributing to decisions to send additional Russian and British troops to Bosnia, did not totally transform the general reluctance of states to commit ground forces to Bosnia. This reluctance was the product of factors that are enduring and not necessarily discreditable: a worry that the aims of a peacekeeping operation may be uncertain, mistaken, or the subject of disagreement between major powers; a nervousness about risking lives in a conflict in which national interests do not seem to be directly engaged; and a fear that major uses of force by peacekeepers could simply drag the United Nations down to the level of the belligerents.

A more far-reaching proposal for a new UN military role has been made by Professor John Ruggie. He has suggested that in civil wars the United Nations needs to adopt a clear strategy "to deter, dissuade and deny," adding that the task is to deny military victory to any one side and "to persuade local combatants that the use of force to resolve disputes will not succeed."[14] The trouble with such a proposal is that in many societies force does have a role that cannot be eliminated entirely. Moreover, it is far from clear whether there is sufficient determination in the international community to teach such lessons to all local wielders of force. The attempt to do so risks creating a situation for the United Nations comparable to that feared by Pentagon planners in the early years of the Cold War, in which the planners worried about having to take on all possible adversaries simultaneously.

Force and the threat of force have a role in the new peacekeeping operations. Any application of force, however, has to be discriminate, both in the choice of situations in which it is brought to bear and in the timing and manner of its application. To rush into generalized advocacy of the use of force, based on a misguided assumption that the United Nations can succeed where so many states and empires have failed, is to invite disaster. The risks in expanding the concept of peacekeeping and in increasing willingness to use force are obvious. Major military activities in the name of peacekeeping may get mired in controversy and tainted by failure. In the process, it is possible that traditional peacekeeping could suffer—with serious effects on both the willingness of states to agree to the presence of such forces and the willingness of donor countries to provide the desperately needed funds and manpower to get peacekeeping operations started.

Involvement of the Permanent Five and Other Powers

Since 1992, peacekeeping operations have included the participation of military units from all five permanent members of the Security Council and some neighboring or near-neighboring states (such as Thailand and China in Cambodia). They have also involved the participation of powers that had hitherto been constitutionally prevented from sending their armed forces into action abroad (such as Japan and Germany). These developments suggest that peacekeeping operations have become a symbol of the determination of the international community to implement its decisions. These developments also constitute additional evidence that peacekeeping is more coercive than before. They also pose problems: Major powers are naturally anxious to keep a degree of control over their forces, and there are inevitable concerns that the forces of the major powers may reflect national military styles and serve national as well as international purposes. The U.S. participation in UNOSOM II in Somalia from May 1993 until the U.S. departure in March 1994 provided a vivid and, at times, tragic illustration of such problems.

The United Nations' need for peacekeeping forces in unprecedented numbers raises a question: Are there still any rules limiting the composition of UN peacekeeping forces? The difficulty in getting contingents to Somalia in 1992 and Rwanda in 1994 suggests that the UN may be forced by circumstances to accept help from wherever it is offered—a conclusion likely to be reinforced by the requirement for a larger number of peacekeepers in Bosnia if there is to be an enduring cease-fire. Boutros-Ghali has indicated that there are still certain limits on which forces can participate in peacekeeping operations. Referring to Bosnia, he said in early 1994 that "we cannot accept troops that might get involved directly or indirectly in the conflict. We don't invite troops with a political commitment, and that's why we don't accept troops from countries bordering on the former Yugoslavia either."[15]

IN WHAT SITUATIONS IS UN PEACEKEEPING USEFUL?

At the heart of the crisis in UN peacekeeping lies the crucial question of selectivity: In which types of situations is peacekeeping appropriate and in which is it not? This question has become pressing for two reasons. First, some UN peacekeeping operations in recent years have proved both unpromising and onerous. Second, the United Nations, due to limits on its resource capabilities, is continuously having to make choices about whether to get involved in particular conflicts and crises.

The United Nations is thus being forced by events to adopt a degree of selectivity that conflicts with the universality of some of its rhetoric. The vision of *An Agenda for Peace* has had to yield to a more mundane reality in which the United Nations can only apply peacekeeping to a limited number of situations. Many recommendations appear on how not to get involved in distant conflicts, yet none is entirely satisfactory.

Civil Wars

It is sometimes suggested that the United Nations should avoid intervening in civil wars. It is argued that the United Nations was not designed to tackle civil wars, its charter does not deal with them, and many involvements in civil wars have been both costly and unrewarding. Internal armed conflicts are notoriously bitter and difficult to resolve.

The use of UN peacekeeping forces in conflicts that are at least partly civil wars is by no means new—for example, Kashmir since 1949, Lebanon since 1958, and Cyprus since 1964. Such use, however, has increased markedly since 1989, including in Angola, Cambodia, El Salvador, Georgia, Mozambique, Rwanda, Somalia, and the former Yugoslavia. This increased use of UN peacekeeping and observer forces in bitter intrastate as well as interstate conflicts has been widely seen as raising serious problems.[16]

In some of these civil wars, the conditions for successful peacekeeping have been notoriously lacking. There has been neither an effective cease-fire nor clear front lines. The bewildering array of nonstate and state entities and regular and guerrilla forces involved makes it unclear which individual leaders actually have the capacity to reach agreements and implement them. Furthermore, the peacekeeping troops dispatched to these countries are in great danger and, in protecting themselves, may well find that they have to lean toward or against particular parties in a dispute, thus jeopardizing their much-valued impartiality. Overall, interventions in such conflicts raise the question of whether the United Nations is justified in taking on problems that it is in fact incapable of solving.

A general rule to save the United Nations from involvement in civil wars could hardly work in practice. The neat distinction between civil and international war often breaks down: Indeed, most conflicts in the world after 1945 have been internationalized civil wars. In any case, there may be extremely strong political pressures for the United Nations to respond to the terrible human catastrophes created by civil wars. Furthermore, the United Nations has had some degree of success in tackling largely internal conflicts, including El Salvador and Cambodia.[17]

Division of the World into Zones

One attempt by American writers to devise a radical rule of thumb for saving the United States from excessive foreign involvement, including UN peacekeeping, has involved the division of the world into "zones of peace" and "zones of turmoil." In this view, 85 percent of the world is assigned to the zones of turmoil and there is relatively little that can be done about it.[18] This pessimistic approach, reminiscent of ancient divisions of the world into "civilized nations" and "barbarians," is hardly a complete description of the world, whose troubles are not neatly parceled into zones. It is too rigid a prescription, making insufficient allowance for the pressure to act in a wide variety of situations. Yet this approach has strengths, including its appeal to an understandably isolationist instinct in the United States following recent heavy overseas involvements and numerous disappointments.

Post-Soviet Conflicts

The United Nations faces a series of difficult choices about whether, and if so how, to become involved in the conflicts in the former Soviet Union. Some of these conflicts are largely internal to a particular new state, while others (such as that between Armenia and Azerbaijan over Nagorno-Karabakh) are more directly interstate in character. There is no reason, apart from prudence and exhaustion, why the United Nations should not intervene in the post-Soviet conflicts. In fact, the United Nations and its leading member-states have been nervous about getting involved. There have been many UN missions to the former Soviet Union, but no serious UN peacekeeping operation has been sent, except the very small and nearly irrelevant UN Observer Mission in Georgia (UNOMIG). This reluctance of both outside powers and the United Nations to get involved in peacekeeping operations in the former Soviet Union poses an awkward problem. Those who advocate a universal and consistent system of UN peacekeeping need to consider the weariness of institutions and states faced with such a daunting array of conflicts. A regional approach may be required.

The Russian government clearly realizes that the international community is not about to launch a series of peacekeeping operations in the former Soviet Union. Instead, Russia has been seeking some kind of international association with actions that may be taken in the "near abroad." On February 4, 1994, Russian Defence Minister Pavel Grachev repeated earlier appeals for a strong UN mandate to undertake peacekeeping missions in the former Soviet republics. He was quoted as saying that "some Western countries reproach us for sending too few peacekeepers to Bosnia, but we have already allocated more than 16,000 servicemen to carry out peacekeeping missions in the former Soviet Union. We carry out an important task and deserve a stronger UN mandate to accomplish it."[19] Needless to say, the governments of many former Soviet republics view such statements as evidence of a sinister attempt to recreate a collapsed empire. Any interventions are bound to have

a different character from any known form of UN peacekeeping. This is not a reason, however, to reject the Russian appeal out of hand: The international community could engage in a serious dialogue with Russia about the circumstances, legal basis, national composition, and functions of future Russian peacekeeping missions in the former Soviet Union.

UN Security Council's Selectivity

Elements of selectivity are inherent in the UN Charter provisions for the Security Council: The veto system prevents action being taken against permanent members of the Security Council; the Security Council's mandatory powers depend on a threat to the peace, breach of the peace, or act of aggression; the Security Council is given considerable discretion; and much space is left for regional arrangements, as well as for individual and collective self-defense.

The UN Security Council has been compelled by events and by increasing caution in many capitals about peacekeeping operations not only to be more selective about involvement in crises, but also to develop criteria for selectivity. A little-noted Security Council presidential statement on peacekeeping, issued on May 3, 1994, listed six factors that must be taken into account when the establishment of a new operation is under consideration:

- the existence of a threat to international peace and security,
- whether regional bodies are ready to assist with peacekeeping,
- the existence of a cease-fire,
- a clear political goal that can be reflected in the mandate,
- a precise mandate, and
- reasonable assurances about the safety of UN personnel.[20]

U.S. Presidential Decision Directive 25

Two days later, on May 5, 1994, the Clinton administration's long-planned Presidential Decision Directive (PDD) 25 on "multilateral peace operations" was unveiled.[21] The directive had been foreshadowed in President Clinton's speech at the United Nations General Assembly on September 27, 1993, in which he had warned against the United Nations' reach exceeding its grasp and had suggested some conditions for U.S. participation in new peacekeeping missions. In some ways, it reflects the U.S. government's post-Somalia disillusionment with UN peacekeeping operations and its perception (whether right or wrong) that much that went wrong in Somalia can be blamed on the United Nations rather than the United States. The directive leaves more scope, however, for U.S. participation in UN peacekeeping than some early press reports had indicated.

The overall approach of PDD-25 is to view peacekeeping and other UN operations as a scarce resource. It strongly affirms that "both U.S. and UN involvement in peacekeeping must be *selective* and more *effective*." It recognizes that certain problems are inherently difficult to tackle. National Security Adviser Anthony Lake said in introducing it that "the reality is that we cannot often solve other people's problems; we can never build their nations for them."

Before there can be U.S. support for multilateral peace operations, says the report, the following factors must be considered: the possibilities of advancing U.S. and international community interests; the existence of a threat to international peace and security; clear objectives; the means to accomplish the mission; consideration of the consequences of inaction; realistic criteria for ending the operation; and, in the case of a traditional peacekeeping operation, the consent of the parties to the conflict and a cease-fire. These are similar to, but slightly more detailed and extensive than, the criteria adopted by the UN Security Council itself two days earlier.

PDD-25 is vulnerable to many criticisms. In particular, the characteristic and understandable U.S. anxiety to work out in advance an end point to an operation, coupled with the equally understandable U.S. worry about casualties, can actually encourage local leaders to be obstinate, knowing that they can outlast an embattled peacekeeping force. In this respect, the report's contents are still part of the mix that proved so troublesome in Somalia.[22]

The Exercise of Judgment

The attempt to develop general criteria for involvement in crises only goes a small way in the direction of effective policymaking. There is no substitute for judgment based not on abstract criteria, but on an understanding of particular countries and crises. This is a limitation of PDD-25 and the 1994 Security Council statement, but it does not undermine the importance of their focus on the problems of selectivity.

The Security Council needs to be discriminating in two ways:

- There is sometimes a case for deciding not to tackle a problem, even if it is serious or constitutes a threat to international peace and security. If there is insufficient will to stay the course, no clear idea of what the United Nations is seeking to achieve, or no adequate local basis for ensuring the implementation of a settlement, it may be best for the United Nations to avoid undertaking a burden that is likely to end with a humiliating exit.
- UN peacekeeping operations need to have a clear overall strategic purpose and to be geared to the particular needs of the country. However, the United Nations is

not always good at long-term strategic thinking. One reason for this is inherent in the whole process of multilateral diplomacy. It is very difficult to get all the members of the UN Security Council to agree on the terms of resolutions dealing with immediate crises without worrying about long-term goals, which can always wait.

WHAT ISSUES NEED TO BE ADDRESSED?

It is possible to conclude that the United Nations must confine its activities to situations in which it can stick to what is seen as the classic approach to peacekeeping. There are, indeed, serious arguments against lightly abandoning tried-and-tested principles. Whether or not there ever was a golden age of peacekeeping, however, a simple return to the old approach seems inadequate. Peacekeeping has been changing because its old incarnations had faults and because the challenges it faces have changed. The need for new approaches is confirmed by the fact that various non-UN peacekeeping operations, especially in Liberia, have faced similar challenges to those confronting the United Nations.

However, new approaches will be redundant if those involved in UN decision making adopt an unimaginative and mechanical approach to their implementation. There is a strong tendency in UN, and also some military, circles to talk of "preventive diplomacy," "preventive deployment," "peacekeeping," "peacemaking," and "peace enforcement," as if these techniques constituted a full set of UN tools for addressing virtually any problem. They do not. There are many problems, of many types, which have eluded the best efforts of statesmen to address them for centuries, and they will continue to do so. If the present opportunities for peacekeeping are to be grasped, there is a need to temper enthusiasm with a sense of

tragedy, an awareness of the sheer difficulty of the problems now being faced, and a recognition that every crisis is unique.

Despite its current difficulties, UN peacekeeping still has some solid qualities that it should not lose in the new era. UN peacekeeping is still, in many parts of the world, acceptable in a way that a purely national or even regional military presence would not be. Furthermore, UN peacekeeping has an impressive record of achievement in isolating conflicts from regional or greatpower rivalry.

The United Nations has been compelled to confront the severe problems of peacekeeping in endemic conflicts, but it is bound to have grave difficulty in coming up with answers. The problem is not just that the United Nations lacks a satisfactory command system that is capable of making quick decisions and effectively coordinating the many different types of force and national contingents deployed. There is as yet little sign of the emergence of a satisfactory doctrine or practice for operations that have an essentially hybrid character, involving elements of both peacekeeping and enforcement. The United Nations faces a situation in which its response to a crisis must be forced into the category of either "enforcement" or "peacekeeping," when neither category quite fits the facts of the crisis.

It is doubtful whether it is right to apply the respected term "peacekeeping" to actions that are not based on the full consent of all the parties to the conflict and that involve the extensive use of force. Is there not something Orwellian about this and other terms, such as "peace enforcement"? Yet what has happened undoubtedly represents an evolution of peacekeeping, has preserved some of its characteristics, and has overcome some of its earlier weaknesses. It would be politically impractical to try to give current UN multinational military operations a new name.

In the face of a baffling range of problems and the undoubted need to restore the credibility of some battered UN peacekeeping operations, it is not surprising that many have come to advocate peacekeeping with "muscles," including more reliance on major military forces and alliances. While events are indeed moving in this direction, the problems that peacekeeping faces are more numerous and complex than such a formulation might suggest. If peacekeeping is to adapt successfully to some of the difficult problems it is asked to tackle, the following issues must be addressed.

Criteria for Involvement in Particular Conflicts

As disappointment with the idea of a universal system of peacekeeping grows, there has been much reconsideration of the criteria to be used by national governments and the United Nations in deciding if peacekeeping forces are an appropriate response to particular conflicts. There are signs that some states are retreating from the idea of universal obligations in the defense of international norms into a reliance on the familiar, and sometimes extremely limited, concept of national interest. While such a reaction is inevitable, other criteria must be considered as well. The most important is whether, in addressing a particular conflict, the United Nations has a real comparative advantage as against other bodies, including states and regional organizations.

Management by the Security Council and Secretariat

The methods of decision making and management of UN peacekeeping operations are odd and are coming under increasing scrutiny.[23] Indeed, the more discriminating the United Nations has to be about its involvements, the more important it will be that the decisions of the UN are seen to be the work of bodies whose composition is regarded as legitimate and whose work is procedurally fair.

Defects in the actual management of peacekeeping forces are commonly attributed to "UN bureaucracy," but that broad-brush accusation often misses the mark. The "bureaucracy" is actually quite small, and among its numerous problems is the need to follow procedural arrangements established by the UN General Assembly and to abide by rules and regulations that are a result of attempts to ensure financial efficiency. The requirements for competitive bidding for materials needed by forces in the field, imposing as they do terrible delays, are a notorious case in point.

One central problem for management is the failure of any one individual or country to accept responsibility for the efficient running of an operation. When things go wrong, the UN system provides far too many possibilities for passing the buck, not only within the organization, but also between member-states and the United Nations. There is a lot wrong with peacekeeping at the moment; so much so that the UN Security Council and the Secretariat may come to be seen as thoroughly fallible bodies. The question of what can realistically be done to prevent the recurrence of mistakes and disasters is bound to arise. Real interest in improving the UN management of peacekeeping forces will arise only if there is also confidence in the judgments of the United Nations. The response from national capitals may well be that states will become more, not less, cautious about contributing money and forces to UN peacekeeping operations.

The Relationship Between UN and National Command

The extent of UN control over peacekeeping operations has become increasingly unclear, especially in cases in which major powers provide large contingents. The experience of peacekeeping operations in several countries, particularly in the former Yugoslavia and Somalia, has exposed the problematic relations between the United Nations and national commands. Both states supplying forces and their commanders in the field have remained independent decision makers, reluctant to defer to UN command, especially over the safety of their troops or the use of air power or other advanced weaponry. Indeed, a simple proposition could be advanced that the greater the military risk in an operation, the more nervous governments will be about handing over control of their forces to the United Nations.

In some instances, there can be a strong case for the UN Security Council authorizing an individual state to take a lead role in a country where there is already a UN peacekeeping presence, but it has been ill-supported and ineffective. This is roughly what happened over Somalia in December 1992 and Rwanda (with the authorization of the French intervention) in June 1994. Such a system of authorization involves an implied reproach to international organizations, yet it may be the only way of addressing certain endemic conflicts and failures of government.

Despite obvious failures, such as those of the United States in Somalia, states may sometimes be better than the United Nations at long-term management of peacekeeping operations. Syria's role in Lebanon has in some respects been more effective than those of either the United Nations or the multinational peacekeeping forces that have also operated there.

Intelligence, Command, and Control

In difficult and dangerous operations, officers naturally want the best systems of intelligence, command, and control. They need quick decisions that they can trust. Inevitably, at present officers tend to fall back on the resources of their own countries. Thus, a multinational peacekeeping force may have different contingents pulling in different directions. Any answer to this problem needs to go well beyond the action taken in 1993 —the creation of the Situation Room at UN Headquarters in New York, which is intended to keep lines open to all ongoing peacekeeping operations simultaneously. A better-equipped directing group should be appointed for each operation, with more resources at its disposal. There is a very strong case for setting up an integrated task force at UN Headquarters for each peacekeeping operation.

Use of Force by or on Behalf of Peacekeeping Forces

In contemporary conflicts in which peacekeeping forces have been involved, there has been intense pressure to threaten or use force for various purposes, including delivering humanitarian relief, punishing attacks on UN personnel, preventing atrocities or flagrant aggression, creating military exclusion zones, and compelling parties to comply with cease-fires or peace settlements. Such pressure to take military action has raised several problems. UN troops may have to choose between losing credibility and losing impartiality. The UN troops risk being perceived simply as one additional belligerent party and may readily become targets for retaliation. In many situations, UN peacekeeping forces must of necessity avoid major uses of force: They may be too small, may lack major armaments, may be restricted by their mandates and the views of their national governments, and may lack popular political support to engage in major offensive operations. It is not surprising that many UN peacekeeping forces seek to apply the old principles of operating with the consent of the parties to the conflict, avoiding the use of force except in immediate self-defense and maintaining impartiality between the belligerents. There is evidence of such thinking in the British Army, including in its recent field manual on peacekeeping.[24]

Yet the costs of military inaction may also be high. As in the former Yugoslavia, UN forces may be formally defined as a protection force, but be unable to protect beleaguered local communities. The UN forces may be unable to prevent or punish visible and continuing atrocities. Peacekeeping forces could even come to be seen as being more concerned with their own safety than with the rights and wrongs of conflicts or with effective action. The situation in Bosnia, until the developments of February 1994, exposed the stark problems of undertaking a peacekeeping operation where there is no peace to keep. The Bosnian Muslims' perception of an ineffectual United Nations was compounded by the UN arms embargo against the former Yugoslavia, which has affected the Muslims heavily. The Bosnian Muslims argue that this arms embargo deprived them of the right to self-defense at a time when the United Nations was unable to provide any other protection.

The UN Security Council will have to be willing to authorize certain uses of force in peacekeeping operations, especially in endemic civil wars. The U.S. use of force in Somalia in 1993 and NATO's use of air power in Bosnia in February 1994 illustrate a significant trend in this direction. Yet ensuring that any use of force is geared to realizable objectives and is under control is astonishingly difficult. There is bound to be a risk of UN forces behaving like a beleaguered colonial garrison. It is very hard to achieve fairness and balance in the use of force within a country, as between the various parties to a conflict; and it is equally hard to achieve anything like fairness and balance in the choice of conflicts in which force is authorized. It is certain that there will be accusations of double standards.

The Question of Privileging UN Forces

With peacekeeping troops in obvious danger in many contemporary conflicts, a peculiarly difficult question is emerging, or rather re-emerging. When UN peacekeeping forces are involved in hostilities, are they to be regarded (at least for the purposes of the laws of armed conflict) simply as belligerents, on an equal footing with other parties? Or are they in some way in a superior position?[25] In recent years there has been a revival of the idea that UN forces are entitled to receive assistance and cooperation from local parties, at least when carrying out such tasks as delivering humanitarian aid. A draft international convention is currently being negotiated under UN auspices to provide a special status for individuals serving in peacekeeping and peace-enforcement operations under a UN mandate. Questions raised by this initiative include the following: Does such a status extend to other international workers, for example those from humanitarian organizations? Are all those who oppose or threaten UN forces in some way "outlaws"? While it is natural to want to give UN forces a privileged status over other parties, there are potential dangers in any such doctrine or practice. Giving UN forces a privileged status could lead to a new kind of colonial mentality, and it could also reduce the incentives for some belligerent parties to observe the rules of war.

UN peacekeeping and observer forces are inevitably involved in other complex issues connected with the laws of war or what is now widely called international humanitarian law. For example, the conflicts in the former Yugoslavia forced the United Nations to confront how to respond to massive violations by belligerents of the most basic rules of war. Insofar as a clear answer has emerged, it appears to be that information on violations may be recorded and passed on, at least by some national contingents through their own national authorities. UN peacekeepers did not arrest suspected war criminals and hold them for possible trial. The establishment of the International Criminal Tribunal for the former Yugoslavia in The Hague in 1993–1994 under UN auspices did not transform this limited UN involvement. The mass slaughter of Tutsis in Rwanda in 1994 has similarly confronted the United Nations and other bodies with the questions of whether and how they can do anything to implement international standards and to punish violations.

Quite apart from such international legal issues, the expansion of UN peacekeeping activities has highlighted a huge range of ethical and disciplinary problems. There have been reports of UN personnel being involved in the illicit sale of diesel oil, use of child prostitutes, and illegal smuggling. As well as better training, such practices point to the need for a stronger and more uniform code of discipline.

The Challenge from Human Rights Organizations

UN peacekeeping operations have come under increasingly strident attack from non-governmental organizations concerned with human rights.[26] In particular, the United Nations is accused of failing to build essential measures for the protection of human rights into its peacekeeping operations. Some of the criticisms are cogent, but others appear to be based on a lack of awareness of the difficult social, political, and military circumstances that UN peacekeepers face. Any peacekeeping operation based on consent requires cooperation with political entities and belligerents whose regard for human rights may be limited, and more forceful

peacekeeping may itself involve violations of rights and even, as in Somalia, lead to civilian deaths.

A related problem is the sharp criticism of UN peacekeepers by humanitarian aid workers in the field, especially in Somalia and Bosnia. The humanitarian aid workers have often complained at being put into a subordinate position, in which urgent humanitarian needs have to wait until a UN military commander has given the approval for an aid convoy to move. The relationship between humanitarian action and peacekeeping is proving much more difficult than anticipated.

The Changing Meaning of Impartiality

In UN peacekeeping, impartiality is no longer interpreted to mean, in every case, impartiality between the parties to a conflict. In some cases, the UN may, and perhaps should, be tougher with one party than another or give more aid to one side than another. In several cases since 1988, economic sanctions have been imposed against a particular state or party; there have also been some arms embargoes. Yet there are important elements in the notion of impartiality that should not be lost, including the idea that the UN represents a set of interests, values, and tasks that are distinct in some respects from those of any one belligerent party. In some peacekeeping operations, "impartiality" may mean not impartiality between the belligerents, but impartiality in carrying out UN Security Council decisions.

The Question of Permanent Armed Forces

The idea of a standing UN force, comprised of professionals recruited voluntarily, has been advanced by Sir Brian Urquhart.[27] There has also been discussion of having UN standing forces on some other basis, such as the hitherto moribund Article 43 of the UN Charter. Such proposals are not limited to peacekeeping. A standing force along one or another of these lines would give the UN secretary general or the Security Council the capacity for a fast military response in certain crises, such as assisting a state threatened by external attack. The proposal to establish a standing force faces problems, however, and is of limited relevance to certain key challenges confronting the United Nations. The sheer variety of tasks tackled by the United Nations makes it improbable that a standing force could be ready for all challenges. Somalia and Bosnia have cast doubt on the capabilities of even quite large professional forces to carry out difficult tasks: In these cases it is more the fact of involvement, the specific mandates of the UN forces, and the decision-making procedures under which they operate that are the main issues for debate. Furthermore, the volunteer force proposal has run up against the familiar problem that governments seem resistant to endow the United Nations with an independent military capacity and to finance it.

Involvement in Administration and Trusteeship

Even in countries in which the United Nations has become involved in peacekeeping because of a general breakdown of government, the organization and its leading members are reluctant to take over responsibility for government. For the most part, the UN role in government has been confined to offering administrative assistance, training, helping to hold or monitor elections, and generally giving advice. In some countries where government scarcely exists, or has failed in its duties, such roles may be inadequate and the issue of a more direct, if hopefully temporary, administration has to be addressed. A major difficulty is that the

historical record of various forms of mandate, trusteeship, and international administration has been mixed. Proposals for such arrangements, however, have continued to appear in international diplomacy, and the concept certainly merits contemporary reconsideration.[28] There has been little sign of willingness on the part of the United Nations or its leading members to accept some kind of trusteeship role in areas where order has broken down. Except in cases of regional hegemony, dominance is out of fashion. No country is rushing to take up the "white man's burden." In some circumstances, there may be good reasons to establish a temporary externally imposed administration, at least when such a proposal has the active support of all the parties to a dispute. The absence of an administrative role may sometimes restrict the options available to UN forces to primarily military ones.

Language

UN forces are often crippled by two kinds of language problems. First, different contingents in the same force may have great difficulty in communicating with one another: There have been much-publicized cases in Bosnia. Second, the contingents may not be able to communicate effectively with the local population: This is particularly crippling when there is a need for intelligence, policing, and administration.

Training

Troops involved in UN peacekeeping forces have been, and are, of extraordinarily uneven quality. Despite the United Nations' urgent need for such forces, there must be a higher basic standard that forces are required to meet before they can be dispatched on a peacekeeping operation. This is one issue that some states and their armed forces are already beginning to address.

Finance

Setting up a UN peacekeeping operation has been aptly called a "financial bungee jump."[29] Peacekeeping is in a continuous state of financial crisis. As of December 31, 1993, peacekeeping operations were in arrears of over U.S.$1 billion, the largest debtors being the Russian Federation ($484 million) and the United States ($193 million). The system of apportioning peacekeeping costs among UN member-states has upset various major powers. The United States has long been expected to bear over 30 percent of the costs of UN peacekeeping operations and wants that figure reduced to 25 percent. Russia is also concerned about the present system, partly because it also has to maintain order in its immediate turbulent environment. By contrast, over 150 states are apportioned for peacekeeping at either one-tenth or one-fifth of their regular UN dues, a situation that requires some modification. An additional problem is that dues for each peacekeeping operation are collected separately, so each UN member-state receives a large number of bills in any given year, sometimes for operations in which it may feel it has little at stake. The questions of apportionment and the effective payment of peacekeeping dues have to be addressed by the UN General Assembly. Whatever the outcome, the ongoing financial crisis is likely to remain a major constraint on the expansion of UN peacekeeping. Uncertainties about payment, which are already making many states reluctant to supply forces, are likely to continue.

CONCLUSION

The problems that peacekeeping now faces confirm that a general and uniform global system of peacekeeping is still not imminent. UN peacekeeping is patchy, ad hoc, contingent upon the interests of major states, and more appropriate in some situations than in others. Indeed, the facts of selectivity may have to be even more openly recognized if a capacity to engage in collective military action under UN auspices is to be maintained. It is vital that the achievements, reputation, and future possibilities of UN peacekeeping operations not be undermined by its involvement in too many conflicts and by a failure to address some of the difficult questions that the United Nations now faces.

NOTES

1. For useful factual surveys of the development of UN peacekeeping, see especially Rosalyn Higgins, *United Nations Peacekeeping*, 4 vols. (Oxford, U.K.: Oxford University Press, 1969–1981); United Nations, *The Blue Helmets: A Review of United Nations Peacekeeping*, 2nd ed. (New York: UN Department of Public Information, 1990); William J. Durch, ed., *The Evolution of UN Peacekeeping: Case Studies and Comparative Analyses* (New York: St. Martin's Press, 1993); and Sally Morphet, "UN Peacekeeping and Election-Monitoring," in *United Nations, Divided World: The United Nations' Roles in International Relations*, rev. ed., ed. Adam Roberts and Benedict Kingsbury (Oxford, U.K.: Oxford University Press, 1993), pp. 183–239. The last book also contains a list of UN peacekeeping and observer forces, pp. 538–542.

2. For a short and clear account of the interrelated character of these principles, see F. T. Liu, *United Nations Peacekeeping and the Non-Use of Force*, International Peace Academy Occasional Paper Series (Boulder, Colo.: Lynne Rienner, 1992).

3. Marrack Goulding, "The Evolution of United Nations Peacekeeping," *International Affairs* 69, no. 3 (July 1993): 455.

4. Ibid.

5. Boutros Boutros-Ghali, *An Agenda for Peace: Preventive Diplomacy, Peacemaking and Peacekeeping* (New York: United Nations, 1992). For a challenging article of the same period, calling for the major powers to give "unconditional subordination of an appropriate element of their

effective military assets to an integrated UN command system," see John Mackinlay and Jarat Chopra, "Second-Generation Multinational Operations," *Washington Quarterly* 15, no. 3 (Summer 1992): 113–131.

6. For an account of the record of the United Nations Protection Force in Croatia, including its failure to demilitarize or control the activities of the Serb forces in the UN-protected areas, see Alan James, "The United Nations in Croatia: An Exercise in Futility?" *World Today* 49, no. 5 (May 1993): 93–96.

7. The texts of the agreements between the United Nations and Iraq are in UN Document S/22663, May 31, 1991. See also Lawrence Freedman and David Boren, "'Safe Havens' for Kurds in Postwar Iraq," in *To Loose the Bands of Wickedness: International Intervention in Defence of Human Rights*, ed. Nigel Rodley (London: Brassey's, 1992), pp. 43–92.

8. Security Council Resolution 743, February 21, 1992, especially the preamble and para. 3.

9. Boutros-Ghali, *An Agenda for Peace*, para. 20. However, in subsequent documents there has been a reversion to a definition of peacekeeping which assumes the consent of the parties. See, for example, the secretary general's report, "Improving the Capacity of the UN for Peacekeeping," UN Documents S/26450 and A/48/403, March 14, 1994, p. 2.

10. UNITAF was authorized by Security Council Resolution 794 on December 3, 1992. This resolution explicitly bases UNITAF on Chapter 7 of the UN Charter.

11. Boutros-Ghali, *An Agenda for Peace*, para. 44.

12. For an outline of the UN secretary general's interpretation of his role in authorizing such uses of force, see Boutros-Ghali's letter to the secretary general of NATO, February 6, 1994, annexed to UN Document S/1994/131, February 7, 1994, and his letter to the president of the Security Council, February 10, 1994.

13. Kofi A. Annan, "UN Peacekeeping Operations and Cooperation with NATO," *NATO Review* 41, no. 5 (October 1993): 4.

14. John Gerard Ruggie, "Wandering in the Void: Charting the United Nations' New Stra-

tegic Role," *Foreign Affairs* 72, no. 5 (November–December 1993): 29–31.

15. Boutros Boutros-Ghali interviewed by Robert L. Kroon, "Q&A: UN Chief Cites a Lack of Political Will Over Bosnia," *International Herald Tribune*, January 24, 1994, p. 2.

16. For thoughtful analyses, see Goulding, "The Evolution of UN Peacekeeping," pp. 451–464; Alan James, "Internal Peacekeeping: A Dead End for the UN?" *Security Dialogue* 24, no. 4 (December 1993): 359–368; and Lori Fisler Damrosch, ed., *Enforcing Restraint: Collective Intervention in Internal Conflicts* (New York: Council on Foreign Relations, 1993).

17. For a balanced discussion of the difficulty of tackling civil wars, see James, "Internal Peacekeeping."

18. Max Singer and Aaron Wildavsky, *The Real World Order: Zones of Peace, Zones of Turmoil* (Chatham, N.J.: Chatham House Publishers, 1993).

19. Reuter report from Moscow, *International Herald Tribune*, February 5–6, 1994, p. 4.

20. Statement by the President of the Security Council, UN Document S/PRST/1994/22, May 3, 1994, discussing the secretary general's report, "Improving the Capacity of the United Nations for Peacekeeping."

21. *The Clinton Administration's Policy on Reforming Multilateral Peace Operations* (Washington, D.C.: U.S. Department of State Publication 10161, May 1994). This is virtually the text of PDD-25, apart from the exclusion of some appendices.

22. For a trenchant critique of inconsistent U.S. attitudes and policies, see Mats R. Berdal, "Fateful Encounter: The United States and UN Peacekeeping," *Survival* 36, no. 1 (Spring 1994): 30–50.

23. For a fine survey, see Mats R. Berdal, *Whither UN Peacekeeping?* Adelphi Paper 281 (London: Brassey's for the International Institute of Strategic Studies, 1993). See also the analysis of the Secretariat's role in managing peacekeeping in the secretary general's report, "Improving the Capacity of the United Nations for Peacekeeping," pp. 8–12.

24. *Wider Peacekeeping,* Army Field Manual, 4th draft (Headquarters Doctrine and Training, Wiltshire, 1994), chaps. 2, 4. See also Charles Dobbie, "A Concept for Post–Cold War Peacekeeping," *Survival* 36, no. 3 (Autumn 1994): 121–148.

25. For earlier discussions, see the Institute of International Law, "Conditions of Application of Humanitarian Rules of Armed Conflict to Hostilities in which United Nations Forces May Be Engaged," 1971 Zagreb Resolution, in *Documents on the Laws of War,* ed. Adam Roberts and Richard Guelff, 2nd ed. (Oxford, U.K.: Oxford University Press, 1989), pp. 371–375.

26. See especially *The Lost Agenda: Human Rights and UN Field Operations* (New York: Human Rights Watch, 1993); and *Peacekeeping and Human Rights* (London: Amnesty International, January 1994).

27. See Brian Urquhart, "For a UN Volunteer Military Force," *New York Review of Books,* June 10, 1993, pp. 3–4, and comments in subsequent issues. Boutros-Ghali now seems to accept that standby arrangements are the best for which he can realistically hope; see "Standby Arrangements for Peacekeeping: Report of the Secretary General," UN Document S/1994/777, June 30, 1994.

28. See Gerald B. Helman and Steven R. Ratner, "Saving Failed States," *Foreign Policy* 89 (Winter 1992–1993): 3–20; and Peter Lyon, "The Rise and Fall and Possible Revival of International Trusteeship," *Journal of Commonwealth and Comparative Politics* 31 (March 1993): 96–110.

29. Dick Thornburgh, Undersecretary General for Administration and Management, "Report to the Secretary General of the United Nations," March 1, 1993, p. 18. This report was written at the end of his one-year appointment to the United Nations, at the request of President Bush, to assess and evaluate the operation of the organization from an "outside" viewpoint.

21

Peace Operations and Common Sense

DENIS McLEAN

*It ain't what a man don't know as makes him a fool,
it's what he does know that ain't so.*—Josh Billings

Where peace operations—in their various manifestations—might fit on the national security canvas (or even whether they have a place there at all) is currently a matter of intense interest in Washington. The conventional wisdom seems to be that "peacekeeping" is a broken reed: ineffective, unrelated to "real soldiering," and with little bearing on U.S. interests. The facts suggest otherwise.

COMPONENTS OF PEACE OPERATIONS

Peace operations cover the broad spectrum of actions intended to forestall, diminish, or end outbreaks of violence on the international scene. They encompass six more or less distinct types of civilian, civilian-military, or just plain military programs designed essentially to give peace a chance in varying circumstances of violence across the broad front of conflict resolution. Each

has defined goals and employs particular techniques; there is much scope for progression from one category to another and a good deal of interaction at each stage. The six forms of peace operations are:

- *peacemaking:* an activist role (military, civilian, or both) involving diplomatic negotiations, conferences, early warning procedures, mediation, conflict resolution, and preventive diplomacy techniques to avoid or resolve a conflict or initiate a peace process;

- *peacekeeping:* the use of international military personnel, either in units or as individual observers, as part of an agreed peace settlement or truce, generally to verify and monitor cease-fire lines;

- *reconstruction:* wide-ranging involvement, by civilians, the military, or both, in providing assistance of a broadly infrastructural nature after the conclusion of hostilities (often incorrectly called peace building);

- *protective engagement or containment:* the use of international military capabilities and the standing of the international community to protect civilian populations, deliver humanitarian relief, or provide a platform for peace negotiations *while strife continues;*

- *deterrence:* the deployment of military forces to dissuade a potential aggressor from pursuing a violent course; and

- *peace enforcement:* the coercive use of military power to impose a solution to a dispute, to punish aggression, or to reverse its consequences.

WHAT IS AND WHAT AIN'T SO

Concerns in the United States about the United Nations in general and peace operations in particular proceed from understandable preoccupation about national roles and responsibilities in the aftermath of the Cold War. Unfortunately, a number of misconceptions and misperceptions have muddled the debate about the nature of peace operations and the value of U.S. involvement in them. What follows is an attempt to put some of the more specious misapprehensions into perspective.

"Peace operations are at best marginal to U.S. interests."

The record shows that this proposition plainly ain't so. As an extension of the traditional U.S. preference for collective action, successive peace operations of all kinds in many places around the globe have served fundamental U.S. security interests well— especially in the Middle East and the Gulf, but also in Central America, Haiti, southern Africa, and Southeast Asia.[1]

For over forty-five years, upholding the security of Israel has been a prime strategic concern of American foreign policy. A range of traditional UN peace operations have helped achieve this goal. The UN Truce Supervision Organization (UNTSO), the United Nations Emergency Force (UNEF) I and II, the United Nations Interim Force in Lebanon (UNIFIL), and the UN Disengagement Observer Force (UNDOF) have all had strong U.S. diplomatic support, but until very recently, few U.S. military personnel have been deployed to these forces. The UN system, in other words, has served fundamental U.S. foreign policy interests. In addition, the Multilateral Force and Observers (MFO) operation created by the United States, Egypt, and Israel under the Camp David Accords ensures that the Sinai region remains demilitarized. An 800-strong U.S. Army battalion is deployed to the force; nine other countries, including New Zealand, contribute.

The problems of Haiti, which directly affect a variety of U.S. national interests, have been addressed by a combination of active multilateral diplomacy channeled through the United Nations and the Organization of American States (OAS) and the deployment of a two-phased peace operation. In August 1994, after three years of inconclusive negotiations, the Security Council authorized member-states to establish a multinational force "under unified command and control . . . to use all necessary means" to facilitate the departure of the military junta that had seized power in September 1991. This gave the United States a clear green light to go ahead with an invasion under its own command to restore the legitimate government of Haiti. Thus the United Nations, taking its authority from Chapter 7 of the UN Charter, legitimized forcible action of a kind that the United States was clearly ready to take. As a consequence, the United States was able to steer clear of unilateralism and its attendant dangers (witness the international reaction to the Russian action in Chechnya); the burdens of intervention were shared by forming a multinational force; and effective provision was made for transition to a second-phase UN peace operation, which has permitted a sharp reduction in the number of U.S. forces engaged.

Somewhat further afield, UN peacemaking, peacekeeping, and reconstruction activities in southern Africa (Namibia, Angola, and Mozambique) have been scarcely less important to the United States, given the extent of U.S. interests in ending South African apartheid and isolation and in developing a coordinated solution to the political and military problems of southern Africa as a whole.

In Southeast Asia, a region in which the United States has invested so much blood and treasure over four decades, negotiations toward a settlement in Cambodia were spearheaded by the United States. But it was the United Nations, working in close consultation with major powers (including Japan and China), that presided over the subsequent successful and broadly based peace process and reconstruction effort, overseeing elections and opening the way to Cambodia's first experiment with representative democracy.

In the Persian Gulf, a region of prime strategic concern to the United States, successive peace operations have served to dampen confrontation and to provide a vehicle for effective international sanctions against Iraq. For example, when the protracted Iran-Iraq war ended in 1988, a UN truce-monitoring force was quickly put into place to verify the cease-fire and monitor troop withdrawals. The UN Observation and Monitoring Force in Kuwait (UNIKOM) is another example of a conspicuously useful, low-cost monitoring operation. The way in which the peacekeeping concept was enlarged after the Gulf War—to provide intrusive inspections and demolition of weapons of mass destruction and their manufacturing capabilities inside Iraq and to create weapons exclusion zones and protected areas for the Kurdish population—was certainly in line with U.S. interests and policies.[2]

Recalling the travails of the United Nations Protection Force (UNPROFOR)—the UN operation in Bosnia which was eventually wound up after the Dayton Peace Accords in favor of the more robust NATO-based Implementation Force (IFOR) operation in 1996—it would be rash to claim that all peace operations are practicable, effective, and invariably supportive of U.S. interests, or indeed of the interests of the international community at large. Furthermore, it is impossible to gauge the exact benefits of each and every mission. By definition, peace operations—being diplomatic rather than military exercises—are more likely to produce an interim than a conclusive result. Their benefits have to be measured either in terms of proving a negative ("We were there, and nothing happened, therefore nothing happened because we were there") or in terms of unquantifiable achievements, such as enhancing trade interests, bolstering regional security, or ameliorating human suffering. Nonetheless, imperfect or imprecise outcomes are by no means necessarily failures; even a temporary cease-fire saves lives and gives time and opportunity for the peace process to take hold.

It is, in short, very difficult to avoid the evidence that peace operations have in general been successful and helpful to U.S. foreign policy interests. Without UN peace operations, the United States would either have to be more directly engaged across the globe[3] or have to accept spreading unrest and its detrimental effects on U.S. national interests and the broader international balance. Peace operations have allowed many of the aims of U.S. foreign policy to be advanced by the community of nations at minimal cost to the United States.

"U.S. interests are best advanced by clear-cut unilateral action, not muddled multilateral efforts."

As we have just seen, the record of multilateral peace operations amply testifies to the advantages to the United States of working with, rather than apart from, the international community. This is not to say that multilateralism is a straightforward and invariably rewarding business; the multilateral approach can be difficult and trying—especially for the United States, of which so much is expected by the international community. Yet responding constructively (not compliantly) to those expectations brings rewards of many kinds. The advantages of collective action in terms of successful coalition building and burden sharing are obvious. Less apparent but no less valuable are the benefits that come from exercising U.S. leadership.

Abstract they might be, but concerns for demonstrating a capacity for global leadership and for eliciting international respect animate all great powers, not least because leadership and esteem can translate into concrete benefits. Although a collective enterprise will, by definition, require shared decision making, the act of putting together a coalition calls for intensive, interactive diplomacy at many levels, integrated military planning and training, and the development of agreed command and control arrangements. These processes in Haiti and Bosnia (especially with the deployment of IFOR under NATO—which means largely U.S.—command) have given the United States the opportunity to exercise leadership of these missions. With its hand thus on the tiller, the United States can turn peace operations into a vehicle to give a new and mutually advantageous sense of purpose to the international community and to the United Nations. Peace operations thus serve U.S. interests in ways that unilateral action could not.

Collective action offers smaller powers an important opportunity to project their national interests and concerns. Joining with others in this way demonstrates an instinct for constructive engagement and sends wider signals about that country's role. Participation in peacekeeping conveys the message to the voters and the world that this is a decent country making a decent contribution.[4]

There is good reason for the United States to foster such instincts and assumptions and to lead other countries into productive partnerships to resolve common problems. A country aspiring to international leadership must engage in coalition building. The alternatives—unilateralism, disengagement, neocolonialism, spheres of influence, or some variant of balance-of-power doctrines—are hardly likely to boost the international prestige and authority of the United States, though they are likely to require considerable U.S. military effort to deal with crises that might have been averted had they been attended to earlier by concerted effort on the part of an engaged coalition.

"Peace operations are expensive and militarily inefficient."

Can we not introduce a sense of proportion into the debate about the efficiency and cost of peacekeeping in general and peace operations in particular? As exercises in diplomacy, the costs of peace operations should properly be balanced against the costs of the war that may follow if diplomacy fails. The UN budget for peacekeeping has certainly risen sharply in the past five years as the concept of peace operations has been developed and applied. But the overall sums involved are still very small when compared with national defense expenditures (or the operations of other national—even local—government agencies).

Whether the costs should come from the foreign policy or the defense budget is a perennial issue in interdepartmental squabbles everywhere. In fact, two separate costs are involved: the national costs of the global allocation to the UN special peacekeeping fund and the costs to the national defense budget of making the necessary military efforts to support peacekeeping operations, whether within or outside of UN programs. In the U.S. Congress, both the House and Senate have introduced legislation that would in effect subsume the two. This would not only eviscerate the U.S. national contribution to UN peacekeeping, it would also undermine the capacity of the United Nations to continue to operate in this field. As such, this proposal would be a gross disservice to the many other countries that maintain their commitments with expenditures under both headings.

At its peak, in 1993–1994, the UN peacekeeping budget was $3.5 billion, which supported seventeen peace operations involving as many as 70,000 personnel in the field and their vehicles, communications, and logistic requirements. Peace operations were in progress or in the course of being established in the former Yugoslavia (the target—never anywhere near attained—was for 39,000 personnel to be deployed in Bosnia and Croatia). In Haiti there were about 6,000 troops, 250 civilians, and 600 police officers; on the Iraq-Kuwait border, approximately 1,100 troops; in Mozambique, 4,000 troops plus 1,100 civilians and police; in Rwanda, the authorized strength was 5,400 troops, plus about 140 military and civilian police; and in Somalia about 15,000 military and police were deployed. Meanwhile, monitoring, verification, and observer teams were deployed in Angola, Cyprus, El Salvador, Georgia, India-Pakistan, Liberia, Tajikistan, and Western Sahara and three around the borders of Israel. This extraordinarily wide-ranging effort cost a sum equal to about half the defense budget of Australia.

The U.S. share of the peacekeeping levy, at about $1 billion, would have been not too much more than the defense budget of New Zealand, and represented about 1/280 of the projected U.S. defense expenditures for the same period. It is true that the U.S. Department of Defense has also paid heavily through the years to provide logistic and airlift support for UN operations in the field. Other troop-contributing countries, however, also pay support costs for the transport, equipment, and allowances of their own forces attached to UN operations, in addition to the peacekeeping levy.

As for military efficiency, one must bear in mind that UN multilateral peace operations are a military arrangement unlike any other. Their purpose is different; their command structure is unique in being obliged to meet often-conflicting separate national interests. Force components, coming from different countries with markedly different military traditions and styles, cannot be expected to cohere in the same fashion as a national force or intensively trained collective security formations as in NATO. Furthermore, governments commit their forces to UN operations for widely differing rationales. Some have a genuine commitment to upholding international order and justice; many have altogether more narrowly material or mercenary considerations; most have broad foreign policy reasons, including bolstering national standing in the world. Participation in peace operations is also widely perceived to bring useful military advantages.

For the most part, the smaller-scale traditional peace operations (peacemaking and peacekeeping) have been well prepared, have kept more or less to schedule, have stayed generally within budget, and have been successful. Where objectives have been limited and clearly defined and the formerly warring parties have been in full agreement about the presence of the force, differences among troop contributors have been relatively easy to accommodate or have not proven fatal to a mission's success. Force commanders have been able to make militarily sound judgments about the caliber of the units available and to deploy them accordingly, secure in the knowledge that the unexpected is unlikely to happen.

The problems began to accumulate with the development of the concept of expanded peace operations, imposing new, poorly conceived, demanding, and wide-ranging tasks on the forces involved. The United Nations did not have the administrative base, the experience, or the military expertise needed to address the operational challenges that arose when the Security Council (and the secretary-general), emboldened by visions of a new world order and the experience of the Gulf War, ventured to build on the concept of classical peacekeeping. Military planning, intelligence, logistics, and communication capabilities were lacking. As is discussed below, much has been done to remedy these deficiencies. The United Nations Secretariat is increasingly able to deploy many of the skills of an operational military headquarters. Some continuing shortcomings are inherent in the organization itself, such as too many lackluster staff and overlaps in the decision-making process. Many of the difficulties encountered nevertheless go with the territory. For instance, much criticism was leveled at the loss of money and supplies during the Somalia operations, yet the critics seemed not to appreciate how complete was the civil breakdown in that country.[5] It is also fair to point out that in almost all cases where United Nations peace operations have been most heavily criticized, member-states themselves had failed to provide the requested troop numbers or to remedy the chronic financial difficulties of the organization.

"The level of direct U.S. involvement in peace operations and the casualties incurred by participating U.S. forces have grown too high."

While this argument is a matter of judgment, a few facts, some of them understandably sensitive in nature, need to be spelled out if the debate on U.S. participation is to reach a reasoned conclusion.

During the Cold War, U.S. forces were, for very good reason, largely absent from peace operations conducted under the auspices of the United Nations. It was widely agreed that the superpowers should not participate. Apart from anything else, their proxies were more than likely to be involved in the fracas that any mission was sent to address; engaging the superpowers would thus have exacerbated Cold War confrontation. This changed in 1989; since then, both U.S. and Russian units and individual observers have become more heavily involved in peace operations.

Furthermore, that level of participation is higher than might seem to be the case at first blush. For example, the United States was generally considered not to be engaged in UNPROFOR, yet a U.S. infantry battalion was deployed for deterrent purposes in Macedonia; U.S. medical personnel were in Croatia; and the U.S. Air Force had a major commitment to air-dropping humanitarian relief supplies inside Bosnia, monitoring the no-fly zone with airborne warning and control system (AWACS) aircraft, and flying up to half of the NATO attack aircraft available to support UN forces on the ground. The U.S. Navy and Marine Corps also made extensive deployments to the Adriatic Sea to support activities in the region.

In fact, such U.S. forces have rarely come under the direct command or control of UN officials. In Somalia, the preliminary deployment—United Nations Operation in

Somalia (UNOSOM I)—proved inadequate and was transformed into the Unified Task Force (UNITAF), an international coalition endorsed by the United Nations but master-minded, commanded, and dominated by the United States. Beginning in March 1993, the U.S. withdrew from this force, which was turned into a specifically UN peace operation, UNOSOM II, under UN command. The United States then deployed 17,700 troops in a joint task force, including a quick reaction force, to support UNOSOM II, but these troops were again under national, not UN, command. The operation in south Mogadishu on October 3, 1993, which precipitated a torrent of criticism of the United Nations and of U.S. support for peace operations when it went awry, was actually under U.S. command.

Loss of life in the military is no easier to accept than in any other circumstances; however, it is inevitable. The United States has very large armed forces (the current strength is about 1.6 million). According to official casualty figures, the total numbers killed on active service worldwide (at home and abroad), including training accidents, have steadily declined over the past two decades. In 1980, 2,391 deaths were reported (equivalent to 117 per 100,000 active duty personnel); in 1994, the figure was 1,105 (69 per 100,000).

From October 1, 1993, to September 30, 1994, 514 service personnel were killed in accidents; 217 committed suicide; 207 died from illness; 80 were listed as "homicides" (presumably murdered); and 19 were killed as a result of hostile action (Somalia). In fiscal year 1991, the year of the Gulf War, 932 died as a result of accidents, 232 committed suicide, 322 died from illness, 108 were murdered, and 143 were killed in action.[6]

Losses sustained in peace operations have plainly been relatively small. Are they nonetheless too high? A large part of the answer must depend on the degree to which peace operations are perceived to advance national interests. Other factors, such as the extent to which participation in peace operations enhances the capabilities of a nation's armed forces, will also come into play. Clearly, judgments about acceptable loss will evolve with changing strategic and political circumstances.

Peace operations—like life itself—can hardly be made proof against all risks and all dangers. Casualties have been incurred in previous operations and can be expected in the future. The forces involved—especially in containment or peace enforcement operations—will have to go "in harm's way." The dangerous and difficult question of how and whether to breach the "Mogadishu line" (between classical peacekeeping roles and taking the offensive to punish assaults on the force or to insist on its ability to carry out its mandate) will not go away. The point is, however, that peace operations are conducted in a casualty-averse fashion; by comparison with other—even normal peacetime—military operations, casualties can be expected to be very light. What is more, the record clearly shows that the casualty burden has been widely shared among participating countries. Once again, multilateral peace operations diminish and diversify the responsibilities that bear on the United States as the sole remaining superpower.

Perhaps some examples will serve to illustrate what is involved. The UN Operation in Mozambique (ONUMOZ) is widely deemed to have been very successful. In just over two years of operations (1992–1995), ONUMOZ helped bring a brutal civil war to an end by presiding over the disarmament and demobilization of contending forces, establishment and training of a new national army, and monitoring of a successful national election. There were 18 fatalities from December 1992 to 1995. UNDOF (the observer force on the Golan Heights), which has monitored a highly unstable cease-fire line since June 1974, had 35 soldiers killed up to January 1995 (17 were Austrians). In UNPROFOR (the protection force in Bosnia), 131 peacekeepers were killed from March 1992 to January 1995. By contrast, the small monitoring operation along Israeli borders (UNTSO) has had 28 killed (including 7 Americans) in over forty-five years of deployment.[7]

"Peace operations are not a job for highly trained military people."

Peace operations these days can be expected at least to brush up against the endemic modern problem of armed violence; in Bosnia, UNPROFOR became deeply enmeshed in it. The military skills required may not lie at the technological end of the spectrum of the profession of arms, but they are of the very essence of soldiering: discipline, effective command and control, good communications, and restraint in the use of force. It is widely accepted in military circles that "good soldiers make good peacekeepers." Nevertheless, no nation is likely to maintain troops solely for peace operations. Effective military training for war and to meet the requirements of national defense will, however, provide troops with the skills required for participation in peace operations. Equally, experience in peace operations can prove valuable preparation for war. For instance, the only active service the British forces sent to retake the Falkland Islands in 1982 had seen was peacekeeping duties in Northern Ireland.

Tasks such as active patrolling, demining, disarming belligerents, separating forces, supervising cantonment of warring armies, guarding weapons depots, and securing passage of relief convoys through hostile territory are all directly related to active-duty soldiering. Often enough, the peacekeepers will find themselves at risk. Worldwide proliferation of weaponry puts them up against heavily armed and, all too often, exceedingly ill-disciplined forces, both regular and irregular. While this territory lies unclearly between peace and war, it is, unquestionably, military territory. From the soldier's point of view, where there is no peace there is war or something dangerously like it.

The key aim of peace operations is to bring order to chaotic circumstances with the minimum use of force. If force has to be used, it must be applied in a limited way to avoid collateral damage and expansion of the conflict. In a world in which conflict between massed armies poses less of a threat than do terrorism, the failure of states, or the outbreak of civil, religious, clan, or ethnic warfare, peace operations challenge conventional military thinking. Most military organizations, including those in the United States, have responded enthusiastically, embracing the need to define and develop the means to meet the new, specialized military requirements of the role.

At the same time, military personnel are not ideally suited to perform all the tasks that peace operations involve. Police officers, for example, with their specialized training in controlling crowds, interacting with the community, defusing tension, and surveilling criminal activity have much to contribute, especially at the early stages of a deteriorating situation. The military is not trained to arbitrate civil or political issues. The police and the military should complement each other, each playing the role for which its training best suits it. Ideally, a peace operations force should be sufficiently diverse to meet all eventualities while preserving its discipline and coherence.

"Resources allocated to peace operations will reduce the overall readiness of the U.S. armed forces."

In operational and training terms, peace operations are a mixed bag. On the positive side, active engagement with a real-life set of problems is likely to be more useful, for both commanders and their subordinates (and across the armed forces as a whole), than participation in any number of contrived exercise scenarios. Modern peace operations can confer good soldiering experience on smaller infantry and specialist units, something of particular value to the Army and Marines. For the individual soldier, participation in a peace operation is an opportunity to render service to others, which many find extremely rewarding.

On the negative side, active duty in a peace operation may not offer the benefits of intensive training in all-arms exercises at home. Much peace operations duty is boring and repetitive, and such work does little to prepare units for the complex, intensive combat roles they may be called to play. Much of the Air Force and Navy involvement in Bosnia, for example, must have been a great deal less rewarding in military terms than comparable effort devoted to battle training. Exercise scenarios can be made much more complex and demanding than routine surveillance patrols on a peace operation. On the other hand, the more decisive intervention by NATO forces clearly offered battle experience to the U.S. Navy and Air Force units involved. Even so, it should be accepted that involvement in the usual run of peace operations is unlikely to enhance national capabilities to fight a major, high-tech war.

Policymakers must listen to military staff who claim that a unit withdrawn from participation in a peace operation needs a period of retraining before it can be redeployed for its primary mission. Policymakers must also recognize that some key support capabilities—for instance, strategic lift aircraft, logistics personnel, and port and terminal services units—may be seriously overstretched if assigned to maintain support for peace operations and for major battlefield

tasks simultaneously. If they are to perform both these functions at the same time, extra resources are needed.

Experience elsewhere suggests it is not impossible to bring the two threads together in coherent training and exercising patterns. The British army, for example, has been obliged for more than twenty-five years to combine wide and active engagement in peace operations in Northern Ireland with readiness to perform the higher-level skills demanded for its NATO role. The French, too, have clearly taken peacekeeping roles seriously, without apparently compromising capabilities at the highest technological and operational levels. It is noteworthy that the British army does not separate out its "second division" units for peace operations, and instead rotates its firstline regiments through peacekeeping training schools and subsequent operational deployment; in due course, those regiments again take their place in the armored or assault infantry divisions in Europe.

The crux of the matter is to make peace operations and overall force development and programming mutually supportive, to use the experience gained in one activity to advantage in performing the other. Focusing exclusively on preparing to fight the "big battle" risks having a magnificent U.S. military instrument rust in its scabbard. Since 1945, U.S. forces have been involved in three major conflicts: in Korea, Vietnam, and the Gulf. But there have been any number of more limited clashes where it has clearly been in the broad international interest to use military skills and training to help contain a problem. General John Shalikashvili, chairman of the Joint Chiefs of Staff, put it this way: "There are some in the Pentagon who'd be very happy if I put outside a sign that read, 'We only do the big ones!' The notion that we exist, first and foremost, to fight our nation's wars I subscribe to. But I also say, 'In this new world we cannot deny our government a very important tool to try to manage crises, bring stability to an area, deal with operations that overwhelm traditional humanitarian organizations.' But you have to be selective—or you could fritter away resources and capabilities."[8]

"Because peace operations can't punish the aggressors or restore order, they are not worth undertaking."

It is difficult not to have some sympathy with such propositions, arising as they do out of frustration at the inability of the international community to summon up the resolve to confront wrongdoers. But the failure to check or punish, for example, the evils of ethnic cleansing in Bosnia should not be blamed on the UNPROFOR troops. If a significant part of the international community wishes to respond to aggression, it can and will do so, especially if there is decisive leadership—as Desert Storm demonstrated. The deployment to Bosnia of NATO and other forces to implement the Dayton Peace Accords is a further demonstration that where there is a will there is a way, in peace operations as in so much else. Where the international will is weak and the strategic interests of the countries concerned less plain, a hesitant international community can hardly take decisive action. If there is the will to punish an aggressor or impose a settlement, it must be expressed in tangible military terms.

Otherwise, the only feasible response may be to launch a peace operation intended to foster a solution without aggressive use of force. Such an operation will be more concerned with protecting refugees, delivering supplies, or promoting the peace process than with inflicting punishment. Completing those tasks may indeed require the intervening force to deter military pressures that could endanger its personnel and undermine its mandate, but that is a different matter from sending a punitive expedition on behalf of the international community.

It is important in this context to remember that the United Nations is its membership. There is little point in blaming the organization for not doing what its members have not given it the resources or the authority to do. Unwillingness on the part of the members to authorize full-scale enforcement missions does not mean, however, that agencies like the United Nations or NATO should—or can—do nothing at all. Clear-cut, decisive, and timely victories in this area will be few. Peace, to misappropriate a phrase of W. B. Yeats, "comes dropping slow."

"All this may be so, but the United Nations itself is ineffective, wasteful, hostile to U.S. interests, and a challenge to U.S. sovereignty."

This kind of complaint against peace operations is strenuously made but poorly supported with facts, as it depends on viewing the commonplace flaws of the United Nations as marks of a unique inadequacy or venality. Again, a sense of perspective is needed. There is no doubt that the United Nations has been, and in many sectors still is, administratively inefficient. Encouragingly, though, far-reaching efforts are now being made to tighten up UN procedures—especially with regard to planning, administering, and conducting peace operations—thanks in no small part to U.S. assistance.

Waste, mismanagement, and fraud are, however, not unknown even within elements of the U.S. federal government and the U.S. Congress; that, of course, does not mean that the entire system is flawed. An altogether more reasonable response is to insist that the agency concerned change its way of doing business. The United States is currently doing just that in respect to the operations of the United Nations. Adopting such a targeted approach is the necessary and constructive way to achieve change. Furthermore, it seems from polls that the American public still wants U.S. foreign policy to continue to make the successful functioning of the United Nations a priority.

In considering the United Nations, it is also important to consider the scale. The United Nations is a small organization in U.S. terms. The central agencies of the United Nations employ 56,000 people— fewer than half the number of civil servants working for the U.S. Department of Agriculture, for example, or slightly more than the permanent employees of the U.S. Congress. Even by the standards of much smaller countries, the United Nations is hardly gigantic. The central UN system has about the same number of employees as the government of New Zealand and an annual budget (including peace operations) about one-quarter that of New Zealand.

The General Assembly of the United Nations will always be dominated by smaller countries, many of which did not share the foreign policy interests of the United States during the Cold War. Again, circumstances have changed and ideological differences have less substance now. The pursuit of favorable relations with the United States is a principal foreign policy aim for almost all countries, except for a handful of pariah states. Moreover, the Security Council, not the General Assembly, is the decisive agency for conducting and authorizing peace operations, and the United States has all the opportunity it needs to be the dominant actor there.

The international system is plainly determined more by inconsistency and disunion than by their opposites. The rise of nationalism—and the profound difficulties of dealing with the ugly consequences of that phenomenon in former Yugoslavia—is hardly consistent with ideas about a new agglomeration of international power that could in any way pose a threat to the sovereignty of the United States. Anyone deluded enough to suppose that there is an international order run by the United Nations has never come up against its inherent weaknesses, its disputatiousness, or its inefficiency when it comes to the business of trying to achieve consensus.

CONCLUSION

The record makes it plain that peace operations have made an extremely positive contribution to the maintenance of international order and to the provision of assistance to those caught up in war. Compared to the alternatives, the costs have been low. In the process, a new spectrum of capabilities to confront challenges to international order and decency has slowly been developed. As Somalia and Bosnia have shown, the international community is reluctant to entertain the idea of putting together comprehensive military capabilities to solve a problem by force—except in those rare cases where clear-cut and widely shared strategic interests are infringed, as they were by the Iraqi invasion of Kuwait. Yet, at the same time, the international community is evidently unwilling to stand idly by while states collapse and civil strife threatens to engulf neighboring countries. Peace operations fill that gap and are here to stay. The aim should be to work together to make collective response as feasible and as effective as possible. The costs of doing so will be only a fraction of the price of forsaking early collective action and resorting to unilateral military action late in the day. Peace operations will not solve all the problems of peace and war. But the range of techniques now available to the international community to head off, or dampen down, conflict and to assist the victims represents a practical and worthwhile new approach to an ancient scourge.

NOTES

1. Although some might argue to the contrary, this preference for collective action is evident in the record of U.S. foreign policy. Despite its occasional popularity, unilateralism has rarely been embraced by U.S. policymakers, who have instead typically opted to work with allies and build coalitions. Isolationism is also out of favor with most policymakers of both U.S. parties, who have noted the consequences of U.S. isolation between the two world wars and have since pursued U.S. interests through engagement with the rest of the world. In short, peace operations represent an approach to international action that accords with a basic strand in U.S. foreign policy, namely, an instinct for collective action in the pursuit of security interests.

2. The cost of UNIKOM in 1994 was $68.6 million, two-thirds of which was paid by the government of Kuwait; the U.S. share was around $6 million.

3. The forces of the British Empire were, for example, almost continuously occupied around the world during the nineteenth century in what were called "Queen Victoria's little wars."

4. In New Zealand, polling following the deployment of an infantry contingent to UNPROFOR in Bosnia in 1993 showed that support for an active role in peacekeeping rose by 5 percent to 75 percent of the population. Those with a favorable or fairly favorable view of the importance of maintaining strong effective armed forces increased in the same period by 2 percent to 69 percent.

5. For a good sense of conditions in Mogadishu at the time, see John L. Hirsch and Robert B. Oakley, *Somalia and Operation Restore Hope: Reflections on Peacemaking and Peacekeeping* (Washington, D.C.: United States Institute of Peace Press, 1995).

6. Figures from Directorate for Information and Reports, U.S. Department of Defense, *Worldwide U.S. Active Duty Military Personnel Casualties, October 1979 through December 1994* (Washington, D.C.: Government Printing Office).

7. Figures from "Background Note," DPI/1634/PKO-January 1995-7M, UN Department of Public Information, New York.

8. Quoted in the *New York Times Magazine*, May 21, 1995.

22

The Delusion of Impartial Intervention

RICHARD K. BETTS

Physicians have a motto that peacemakers would do well to adopt: "First, do no harm." Neither the United States nor the United Nations have quite grasped this. Since the end of the Cold War unleashed them to intervene in civil conflicts around the world, they have done reasonably well in some cases, but in others they have unwittingly prolonged suffering where they meant to relieve it.

How does this happen? By following a principle that sounds like common sense: Intervention should be both limited and impartial, because weighing in on one side of a local struggle undermines the legitimacy and effectiveness of outside involvement. This Olympian presumption resonates with respect for law and international cooperation. It has the ring of prudence, fairness, and restraint. It makes sense in old-fashioned UN peacekeeping operations, where the outsiders' role is not to make peace, but to bless and monitor a cease-fire that all par-

ties have decided to accept. But it becomes a destructive misconception when carried over to the messier realm of "peace enforcement," where the belligerents have yet to decide that they have nothing more to gain by fighting.

Limited intervention may end a war if the intervenor takes sides, tilts the local balance of power, and helps one of the rivals to win—that is, if it is not impartial. Impartial intervention may end a war if the outsiders take complete command of the situation, overawe all the local competitors, and impose a peace settlement—that is, if it is not limited. Trying to have it both ways (limited *and* impartial) usually blocks peace by doing enough to keep either side from defeating the other, but not enough to make them stop trying. And the attempt to have it both ways has brought the United Nations and the United States—and those whom they sought to help—to varying degrees of grief in Bosnia, Somalia, and Haiti.

WHO RULES?

Wars have many causes, and each war is unique and complicated, but the root issue is always the same: Who rules when the fighting stops? In wars between countries, the issue may be sovereignty over disputed territory, or suzerainty over third parties, or influence over international transactions. In wars within countries the issue may be which group will control the government, or how the country should be divided so that adversaries can have separate governments. When political groups resort to war, it is because they cannot agree on who gets to call the tune in peace.

A war will not begin unless both sides in a dispute would rather fight than concede. After all, it is not hard to avert war if either party cares primarily about peace—all it has to do is let the other side have what it claims is its due. A war will not end until both sides agree who will control whatever is in dispute.

Is all this utterly obvious? Not to those enthusiasts for international peace enforcement who are imbued with hope for global governance, unsympathetic to thinking of security in terms of sovereignty, or viscerally sure that war is not a rational political act. They cannot bring themselves to deal forthrightly in the currency of war. They assume instead that outsiders' good offices can pull the scales from the eyes of fighting factions, make them realize that resorting to violence was a blunder, and substitute peaceful negotiation for force. But wars are rarely accidents, and it is no accident that belligerents often continue to kill each other while they negotiate, or that the terms of diplomatic settlements usually reflect results on the battlefield.

Others sometimes proceed from muddled assumptions about what force should be expected to accomplish. In a bizarre sequence of statements in spring 1994, for instance,

President Clinton threatened air strikes against the Bosnian Serbs, then said, "The United States is not, and should not, become involved as a partisan in a war." Next he declared that the United States should lead other western nations in ending ethnic cleansing in Bosnia, only to say a moment later, "That does not mean that the United States or the United Nations can enter a war, in effect, to redraw the lines . . . within what was Yugoslavia."

This profoundly confused policy, promulgated with the best of lawyerly intentions, inevitably cost lives on all sides in Bosnia. For what legitimate purpose can military forces be directed to kill people and break things, if not to take the side of their opponents? If the use of deadly force is to be legitimate killing rather than senseless killing, it must serve the purpose of settling the war—which means determining who rules, which means leaving someone in power at the end of the day.

How is this done without taking someone's side? And how can outside powers pretend to stop ethnic cleansing without allocating territory—that is, drawing lines? Yet Clinton and UN Secretary General Boutros Boutros-Ghali did not make threats in order to protect recognized or viable borders, but to enforce naturally unstable truce lines that made no sense as a permanent territorial arrangement. Such confusion made intervention an accessory to stalemate, punishing either side for advancing too far, but not settling the issue that fuels the war.

Some see a method in the madness. There are two ways to stop a war: Either one side imposes its will after defeating the other on the battlefield, or both sides accept a negotiated compromise. The hope for a compromise solution accounts for a misconceived impartiality.

When is compromise probable? When both sides believe that they have more to lose than to gain from fighting. Because leaders are often sensible, this usually happens before a war starts, which is why most crises are resolved by diplomacy rather than combat. But peaceful compromise has to seem impossible to the opponents for a war to start, and once it begins, compromise becomes even harder. Emotions intensify, sunk costs grow, demands for recompense escalate. If compromise was not tolerable enough to avert war in the first place, it becomes even less attractive once large amounts of blood and treasure have been invested in the cause.

If neither side manages to pound the other into submission and a stalemate emerges, does a compromise peace become more practical? Not for a long time, and not until many more lives have been invested in the contending quests for victory. Stalemates rarely seem solid to those with a strong stake in overcoming them. Belligerents conjure up one set of military stratagems and schemes after another to gain the upper hand, or they hope for shifts in alliances or outside assistance to tilt the balance of power, or they gamble that their adversary will be the first to lose heart and crack. Such developments often do break stalemates. In World War I, for example, trench warfare in France ebbed and flowed inconclusively for four years until the Russian capitulation. This allowed the Germans to move armies from the east and achieve a breakthrough that unglued the Western Front and almost brought them victory in the spring of 1918. Then the Allies rebounded, turned the tables with newly arrived American armies, and won the war six months later.

Stalemate is likely to yield to negotiated compromise only after it lasts so long that a military solution appears hopeless to both sides. In the Iran-Iraq War, where UN mediation was useful, the two sides had fought ferociously but inconclusively for eight years. The United Nations smoothed the way for both sides to lay down their arms, but it is hard to credit that diplomatic intervention with as much effect in bringing peace as the simple exhaustion and despair of war-makers in Tehran and Baghdad. Mediation is useful, but it helps peacemaking most where peacemaking needs help least.

COMPROMISES THAT KILL

If there is any place where peacemaking needs help most, and fails most abjectly, it is Bosnia. There, the West's attempt at limited but impartial involvement abetted slow-motion savagery. The effort wound up doing things that helped one side, and counterbalancing them by actions that helped the other. This alienated both sides and enabled them to keep fighting.

The United Nations tried to prevent the Serbs from consolidating their victory, but without going all the way to provide consistent military support of the Muslims and Croats. The main UN mission was humanitarian delivery of food and medicine to besieged communities, but this amounted to breaking the sieges—a military and political effect. It is hardly surprising that the Serbs interfered when they could get away with it. In line with the humanitarian rationale, the United Nations supported "safe areas"—pockets of Muslims and Croats hanging on in areas conquered by the Serbs. Apart from such limited action to frustrate the last phase of territorial rearrangement by force, UN and U.S. attempts to settle the war were limited to diplomatic mediation, an arms embargo, a "no-fly zone," and economic sanctions on Belgrade.

For over a year, the UN presence inhibited forceful reaction to Bosnian Serb provocations because French, British, and other units on the ground were hostage to retaliation. U.S. and UN threats were not just weak and hesitant; by trying to be both forceful and neutral, they worked at cross-purposes. First, after much dancing around and wringing of hands, the United Nations and the North Atlantic Treaty Organization (NATO) used force on behalf of the Bosnian government, albeit with only a few symbolic "pinprick" air raids against Serb positions. But the outside powers did this while refusing to let those they were defending buy arms to defend themselves. Given the awkward multilateral politics of the arms embargo, this may have been understandable; but as strategy, it was irrational, plain and simple.

Impartiality compounded the absurdity in August 1994, when the UN military commander also threatened the Bosnian government with attack if it violated the weapons exclusion zone around Sarajevo. UN strategy thus bounced between unwillingness to undertake any combat at all and a commitment to fight on two fronts against both belligerents. Such lofty evenhandedness may make sense for a judge in a court that can enforce its writ, but hardly for a general wielding a small stick in a bitter war.

Overall, UN pressures maintained a teetering balance of power between the belligerents; the intervenors refused to let either side win. Economic sanctions worked against the Serbs, while the arms embargo worked against the Muslims. The rationale was that evenhandedness would encourage a negotiated settlement. The result, however, was not peace or an end to the killing, but years of military stalemate, slow bleeding, and delusionary diplomatic haggling.

The desire for impartiality and fairness led outside diplomats to promote territorial compromises that made no strategic sense. The Vance-Owen plan and later proposals mimicked the unrealistic 1947 UN partition plan for Palestine: geographic patchworks of noncontiguous territories, vulnerable corridors and supply lines, exposed communities, and indefensible borders. If ever accepted, such plans would create a territorial tinderbox and a perpetual temptation to renew the conflict. Yet the one case in which Washington said it was willing to thrust tens of thousands of American troops into the Bosnian tangle was to enforce just such an accord.

In Somalia, the United States succeeded laudably in relieving starvation. Then, fearful that food supply would fall apart again after withdrawal, Washington took on the mission of restoring civil order. This was less limited and more ambitious than the outside powers' "strategy" in Bosnia, but it stopped short of taking charge and imposing a settlement on the warring factions.

Incongruously, the international operation in Somalia worked at throwing together a local court and police organization before establishing the other essential elements of government, an executive or a legislature. Then U.S. forces set out to arrest General Mohammed Farah Aidid—who was not just a troublemaker but one of the prime claimants to governing authority—without championing any other contender. The U.S. attempts failed, but killed a large number of Somalis and further roiled the political waters in Mogadishu. Stung by casualties to U.S. forces, Washington pulled out and left UN troops from other countries holding the bag, maintaining an indecisive presence, and taking casualties of their own.

It may have been wise to avoid embroilment in the chaos of conflict among Somali clans. But it was then naive to think that intervention could help to end the local anarchy. As Michael Maren asked in the *New York Times*, "If the peacekeepers aren't keeping the peace, what are they doing?"—especially since the cost of the intervention topped $1.5 billion. The UN operation was not only indecisive, Maren argued, but it fueled the fighting by letting the feuding factions compete for UN jobs, contracts, and cash. In areas where UN forces were absent, the parties reached accommodation in order to reestablish commerce, rather than jockeying for UN resources ("Leave Somalia Alone," July 6, 1994, p. A19).

After early forceful rhetoric by President Clinton had raised expectations about U.S. action, experiences in Bosnia and Somalia helped to brake enthusiasm in New York and Washington for taking on other peace operations. It is indeed wise to be more selective than in the heady days of hope for collective security that followed the end of the Cold War, but it will be unfortunate if the Western powers and the United Nations abandon such missions altogether. If they do not quit completely, the same problem—an attempt to bring peace turning out to postpone peace—can arise again if the misconceptions that produced it are not recognized.

Of course, not all problems are due to impartiality. In Haiti, for example, the United States and United Nations clearly did choose sides, supporting the exiled president, Jean-Bertrand Aristide; eventually the unmistakable U.S. willingness to invade forced the junta in Port-au-Prince to back down. Even there, however, suffering was prolonged by the initially limited character of the intervention.

For over a year after the junta reneged on the Governor's Island agreement, Washington relied on economic sanctions against Haiti, a "trickle-up" strategy of coercion that was bound to hurt the innocent long before it touched the guilty. The blockade gradually devastated the health and welfare of the country's masses, who were powerless to make the policy changes demanded by Washington and on whose behalf the sanctions were supposedly being applied. Yet sanctions offered no incentive to Haiti's kleptocratic elites to cut their own throats, and sanctions were not what made the generals sign the accord brokered by former President Jimmy Carter. Instead, the many months during which sanctions were left

to work were used by the junta to track down and murder Aristide supporters at a steady pace.

Meddling in the tragic saga of Haitian misgovernment is a dubious gamble for the United States, considering the formidable durability of the country's predatory political culture. While the relatively peaceful entry of the occupying U.S. forces was welcome, the fledgling Haitian experiment in democracy may not outlive the departure of U.S. armed forces. The September 1994 agreement did not disband the Haitian military or even completely purge its officer corps, whose corruption and terror tactics have long been most of the problem. Even worse, the accord hinted that—for the first time in the crisis—Washington might have erred on the side of impartiality. American leaders spoke of the generals' "military honor," U.S. troops were ordered to cooperate with the usurpers' security forces, and many of the anti-Aristide gangsters were left free to plot to regain power. Deciding whether to intervene in Haiti was agonizing. Once that was done, however, picking a side was certainly wise. But that choice was weakened by dithering too long with sanctions, then appearing to waver in support for the chosen side when U.S. military force was finally applied.

Impartiality nonetheless remains a norm in many other cases. It has worked in cases that lie beyond traditional peacekeeping, such as the cease-fire mediation between Iran and Iraq or the political receivership of the United Nations Transitional Authority in Cambodia (UNTAC). When looking at the reasons for these successes, however, it becomes apparent that impartiality works best where intervention is needed least, where wars have played themselves out and the fighting factions need only the good offices of mediators to lay down their arms. Impartiality is likely to work against peace in the more challenging cases—where intervention must make the peace, rather than just preside over it—because it reflects deeper confusion over what war is about.

IMPERIAL IMPARTIALITY

If outsiders such as the United States or the United Nations are faced with demands for peace in wars where passions have not burned out, they can avoid the costs and risks that go with entanglement by refusing the mandate—staying aloof and letting the locals fight it out. Or they can jump in and help one of the contenders defeat the other. But can they bring peace sooner than exhaustion from prolonged carnage would, if they remain impartial? Not with a gentle, restrained impartiality but with an active, harsh impartiality that overpowers both sides: an imperial impartiality. This is a tall order, seldom with many supporters, and it is hard to think of cases where it has actually worked.

The best example of imperial impartiality is the UN operation in Cambodia—a grand-scale takeover of much of the administrative authority in the country and a program for establishing a new government through supervised elections and a constituent assembly. Despite great obstacles and tenuous results, UNTAC fulfilled most of its mandate. This success should be given its due. As a model to rescue the ideal of limited and impartial intervention, however, it falls short.

First, the United Nations did not nip a horrible war in the bud; as was the case with Iran and Iraq, it capitalized on fifteen years of exhaustion and bloody stalemate. The outside powers recognized that the main order of business was to determine who rules, but they did not act before the local factions were weary enough to agree on a procedure for doing so.

Second, UN intervention was limited only in one sense: It avoided direct enforcement of the transition agreement when local contenders proved recalcitrant. Luckily, such incidents were manageable, or the whole experiment would have been a fiasco. In other respects, the scale of involvement was too huge to provide a model. Apart from the wars in Korea and Kuwait, UNTAC was the most massive UN intervention in history. It involved thousands of personnel from a host of countries and billions of dollars in expenditures. The Cambodia operation proved so expensive, at a time when other demands on the United Nations were escalating dramatically, that it cannot be repeated more than once in a blue moon.

Third, although UNTAC should count as a success—especially after the election it conducted against all odds in 1993—the operation's results have been unstable. Despite a tremendous UN presence, the terms of the transition agreement were never faithfully followed by all the local combatants and continued to erode after UNTAC's departure. For example, because the Khmer Rouge reneged, none of the Cambodian factions disarmed to the degree stipulated in the agreement; after the election, the constituent assembly never seriously debated a constitution, but more or less rubber-stamped Prince Norodom Sihanouk's demands; and sporadic fighting between the Khmer Rouge and other parties continued before and after UNTAC left.

Fourth, and more to the point, the UN success in Cambodia was linked with impartiality only in principle, not in effect. The real success of the transition overseen by UNTAC was not in fostering a final peaceful compromise among the parties in Cambodia, but in altering the balance of power among them and marginalizing the worst one. The transition did not compel an end to violent strife, but it did facilitate the realignment of parties and military forces that might bring it about. The old Cold War alignment of Sihanouk, Son Sann, and the Khmer Rouge against the Vietnamese-installed government in Phnom Penh was transformed into a new coalition of everyone against the Khmer Rouge. Any peace Cambodia is likely to achieve will come from the new balance of power.

MEDDLING WITHOUT MUDDLING

The "peacekeeping" that has been the United Nations' forte can help fortify peace, but it does not create peace as "peace enforcement" is supposed to do. Since the end of the Cold War, the United States and the United Nations have stumbled into several imbroglios where it was not clear which of the two missions they were pursuing, and there has been much head-scratching about the gray area between operations under Chapters 6 and 7 of the UN Charter. Washington and New York have responded to rough experiences by remaining mired in indecision and hamstrung by half-measures (Bosnia), facing failure and bailing out (Somalia), acting only after a long period of limited and misdirected pressure (Haiti), or holding back from action where more awesome disaster than anywhere else called for it (Rwanda). To do better in picking and choosing, it would help to be clearer about how military means should be marshaled for political ends. The following points should be kept in mind.

Recognize that to make peace is to decide who rules. Making peace means determining how the war ends. If American or UN forces are going to intervene to make peace, they will often have to kill people and break things in the process. If they choose to do this, they should do so only after they have decided who will rule afterward.

If claims or capabilities in the local fracas are not clear enough to make this judgment, then they are not clear enough for intervention to bring peace. By the same token, international forces should not mix in the dangerous business of determining who governs without expecting deadly opposition. An intervention that can be stopped in its tracks by a few dozen fatalities, as the U.S. operation in Somalia was, is one that should never begin.

Avoid half-measures. If the United States or the United Nations wish to bring peace to violent places before tragedy unfolds in full, gruesome detail, they should act decisively by either lending their military weight to one side or forcing both sides to compromise. In either case, leaders or outside powers should avoid what the natural instincts of successful politicians and bureaucrats tell them is sensible: a middle course.

Half-measures often make sense in domestic politics, but that is precisely because peace already exists. Contending interests accept compromises negotiated in legislatures, adjudicated in courts, and enforced by executives because the state has a monopoly on organized force; the question of who rules is settled. That is the premise of politics in peace; in war, that premise is what the fighting is all about. A middle course in intervention—especially a gradual and symbolic use of force—is likely to do little but muddy both sides' calculations, fuel their hopes of victory, or kill people for principles only indirectly related to the purpose of the war. If deadly force is to make a direct contribution to peace, it must engage the purposes most directly related to war—the determination of borders and the distribution of political power.

Do not confuse peace with justice. If outside powers want to do the right thing, but do not want to do it in a big way, they should recognize that they are placing a higher premium on legitimacy than on peace. Most international interventions since the end of the Cold War were not driven by the material interests of the outside powers but by their moral interests: securing peace and justice. Peace and justice, however, are not natural allies, unless right just happens to coincide with might

Outside intervention in a civil war usually becomes an issue when the sides are closely enough matched that neither can defeat the other quickly. When material interests are not directly involved, it is impractical to expect great powers or the United Nations to expend the resources for an overwhelming and decisive military action. So if peace should take precedence, intervention should support the mightiest of the rivals, irrespective of their legitimacy. If the United Nations had weighed in on the side of the Serbs, or had helped Aidid take control in Mogadishu rather than trying to jail him, there might well have been peace in Bosnia and Somalia long ago. If justice takes precedence, however, limited intervention may well lengthen a conflict. Perhaps putting an end to killing should not be the first priority in peacemaking, but interventionists should admit that any intervention involves such a choice.

Tension between peace and justice also arises in assessing territorial divisions like those proposed for Bosnia. If the aim is to reduce violent eruptions, borders should be drawn not to minimize the transfer of populations and property, but to make the borders coherent, congruent with political solidarity, and defensible. This, unfortunately, makes ethnic cleansing the solution to ethnic cleansing. Also, it will not guarantee against later outbreaks of revanchism, but it can make war less constant. Better the model of India and Pakistan than that of Lebanon.

Do not confuse balance with peace or justice. Preventing either side from gaining a military advantage prevents ending the war by military means. Countries that are not losing a war are likely to keep fighting until prolonged indecision makes winning seem hopeless. Outsiders who want to make peace but do not want to take sides or take control themselves try to avoid favoritism by keeping either side from overturning an indecisive balance on the battlefield. This supports the military stalemate, lengthens the war, and costs more lives.

Make humanitarian intervention militarily rational. Sometimes the imperative to stop the slaughter or save the starving should be too much even for the most hard-boiled realists, and intervention may be warranted even if it does not aim to secure peace. This was a motive in Bosnia and Somalia, but intervention there involved presence in battle areas, constant friction with combatants or local political factions, and skirmishes that escalated without any sensible strategic plan. Bad experiences in those cases prevented rapid multilateral intervention in the butchery in Rwanda, intervention which could have saved many more lives.

Operation Provide Comfort, the U.S. humanitarian intervention in northern Iraq, and the recent unilateral French action in Rwanda provide better models. In these cases, the intervening forces carved out lines within which they could take command without fighting, but which they could defend if necessary—areas within which the intervenors themselves would rule temporarily. Then they got on with ministering to the needy populations and protecting them from assault. Such action is a stopgap, not a solution, but it is less likely to make the war worse.

In Bosnia, by contrast, the "safe areas," weapons exclusion zones, and towns supplied by American airdrops were islands surrounded by hostile forces and represented messy territorial anomalies in what was effectively a Serb conquest. It was no surprise that the Serbs would hover, waiting to pounce whenever they thought they might get away with it, probing and testing the resolve of the outsiders to fight, waiting for the international community to tire of the effort to keep the enclaves on life support.

At this writing in the summer of 1996, the Dayton Accords are being implemented. All should hope that they hold, but the fact that they were negotiated successfully does not compromise the lessons suggested here. What made the diplomatic agreement possible was not the cumulative history of indecisive outside intervention, but its reversal. The stalemate was unfrozen in the summer of 1995 by the novel combination of two strong actions that dramatically altered the military balance of power between the Serbs and their adversaries. The main one was the stunning attack by the Croatian army that reconquered the Krajina region, and the other was the massive and prolonged bombing campaign by NATO air forces. The political settlement was reached because force compelled the Serbs to make the crucial concessions. The settlement will hold as long as the Serbs and Croats prefer it to another war (or to collusion to carve up Muslim Bosnia between themselves), or as long as NATO armies remain on the ground and enforce it.

Calling attention to mistakes, confusions, and uncomfortable choices is not intended to discredit intervention altogether. It is meant to argue for caution, because confusion about what is at issue can make such undertakings cause conflict rather than cure it. Doing it right is not impossible. The United States and United Nations have collaborated successfully in peacemaking in the past, most notably in the wars over Korea and Kuwait. Enthusiasm for widespread involvement in local conflicts in the early 1990s was based on expectations that it would require a small proportion of the effort of those two huge enterprises. Unfortunately, this was probably true in some cases where the United Nations held back, as in Rwanda, and untrue in some cases where it jumped in, as in Bosnia. Peacemaking will not always cost as much as it did in Korea and Kuwait. The underlying issues, however, are much the same—who is in charge, and in what pieces of territory, after a war ends. Intervention that proceeds as if the issues are different—and can be settled by action toward the belligerents that is both evenhanded in intent and weak in capability—will more likely prevent peace than enforce it.

23

Humanitarian NGOs in Conflict Intervention

MARY B. ANDERSON

- As the civil war in Tajikistan came to an end, the international community provided assistance to help people rebuild their war-destroyed homes. This was a critical step toward restarting the shattered economy and preparing the way for reconciliation between the two groups that had fought. However, because most of the destroyed homes belonged to people on the losing side of the war, the group that won was suspicious of the motivations of the international aid community, which appeared intent on "strengthening" their "enemies."

- When all warring parties agreed to establish "corridors of tranquility" in Sudan, the United Nations Children's Fund (UNICEF) and the nongovernmental organizations (NGOs) that work with UNICEF were able to reach children on all sides of the conflict, delivering humanitarian supplies and carrying out an inoc-

ulation campaign against deadly childhood diseases. However, some observers note that when warring parties agree to a seemingly humanitarian agenda, they gain public legitimacy, which allows them to continue their warring efforts with less international opprobrium. Their ability to negotiate where and when relief supplies may be delivered also reinforces the power warriors have over the civilians who live in the areas they control.

- As international NGOs moved into postwar Cambodia to prepare for the repatriation of refugees from the Thai border refugee camps, they found that local people resented the "advantages" these returnees had enjoyed in the camps, where NGOs provided health and education training. The intent of the camp-based training had been to support long-term development in Cambodia once the war was over; however, some of the NGOs refused to employ or help the refugees when they returned to their villages, lest they (the NGOs) appeared to be favoring the returnees over the people who had stayed in Cambodia during the war.

Aid agencies that work in conflict areas in the late twentieth century encounter many complex situations. As the vignettes above show, international assistance, provided out of humanitarian concern for the people who live where wars rage, often becomes intertwined with the forces that drive the conflicts that prompted the aid in the first place. As both the numbers of conflicts and the numbers and types of agencies responding to them have risen in recent years, humanitarian NGOs in the United States and abroad have learned to recognize these complexities.

In the following pages, we shall explore the experience of international NGO interventions in recent conflicts. This exploration seeks to increase our understanding of how NGO interventions in conflict settings interact with the forces of conflict. We are especially interested in the impact NGO interventions have in the circumstances of today's intranational, civil, and civilian-based wars, such as those in Somalia, Rwanda, Afghanistan, parts of the former Soviet Union, the former Yugoslavia, and many other areas.

We begin by briefly describing what the international NGOs are, suggesting a categorization of these according to their stated purposes. We then briefly review NGO relations to conflicts in the past and their experiences in recent conflict settings, again suggesting a categorization of NGO approaches as these agencies attempt to cope with the experience of working in conflicts. Finally, we identify some of the changes that have occurred in conflicts in recent years, making the work of humanitarian assistance both more complex and more promising.

What Are the NGOs that Intervene in Conflict Settings?

Nongovernmental organizations are privately organized and privately financed agencies, formed to perform some philanthropic or other worthwhile task in response to a need that the organizers think is not adequately addressed by public, governmental, or United Nations efforts.[1] Churches, civic groups, labor unions, private foundations, and millions of individuals have established organizations that usually operate as tax-free entities to support some group or some cause. While many of these operate within their own borders, a very large number of NGOs have defined their mission as working with people in other countries, as an alternative or adjunct to official foreign aid.

NGOs based in Europe and North America that provide assistance in the international sphere operate from what can be categorized as basically four different mandates:

- the provision of humanitarian relief to people in emergencies,
- the promotion of long-term social and economic development in countries where poverty persists,
- the promulgation and monitoring of basic human rights, and
- the pursuit of peace, including the promotion of the philosophy and techniques of negotiation, conflict resolution, and nonviolence.

Some agencies define themselves in terms of only one of these four mandates; others operate from several and design their programs to make explicit connections among them.

Increasingly, the international NGO community recognizes the interrelationships of these four mandates. Agencies that are primarily committed to providing emergency relief assistance, whether in wars or so-called natural disasters,[2] now recognize that the ways in which they provide such aid have profound effects on the recipients' potential to achieve future sustainable development.[3] Similarly, evidence is growing that development assistance programs that are planned without recognizing their impact on the environment or on aspects of social systems often contribute to the probability of disasters,[4] wars,[5] or both. Recent experiences in the former Yugoslavia and Rwanda seem to indicate that wide publicity about human rights abuses may actually cause some accused groups to harden their positions as "misunderstood" and "maligned" by the international community, thus reinforcing their pursuit of war (and further abuse of human rights). Finally, though the evidence is not yet fully developed, it seems likely that peace-mandated NGOs that promote negotiated solutions to conflicts in developing countries may, in some instances, have a direct impact on the way in which resources are divided and allocated and, thus, on whether and how economic development may—or may not—occur.

Action in any sphere of international assistance is very likely to have repercussions in the recipient society, going beyond those that were foreseen and intended by the NGOs. This may be especially true when the NGO comes from another country and culture and works from values, ideas, and attitudes that are foreign to the recipient community.[6] These sometimes counterintuitive and negative intermandate effects of international NGO programs appear to be heightened in conflict settings. Thus, we need to understand the relationships between NGO humanitarian interventions in conflict settings and the conflicts themselves.

REVIEW OF NGO EXPERIENCES IN CONFLICT INTERVENTIONS

Lives have been saved, postconflict development or redevelopment supported, human rights protected, and conflict-resolution skills attained through the interventions of NGOs in conflict settings over the years. Many recipients of NGO aid can attest to the fact that this assistance kept their families alive under desperate circumstances, helped them escape from imprisonment or exile, provided the extra support needed for them to initiate a self-sustaining enterprise, or supported their pursuit of the values of intergroup harmony. Foreign assistance provided through nongovernmental channels has had a profound impact on the lives of many individuals, has helped spawn the creation of many NGOs in the recipient countries, and has prompted the articulation of operational principles adopted by most donor government and UN agencies. NGOs are valued for their clarity of purpose and the humanitarian basis of their operations; for their encouragement of grass-roots participation in economic, social, and political life; for their innovation and creativity in solving problems; and for their ability to cross national boundaries with a message of interdependence and humanitarian concern wherever people are in need.

However, the NGO record is not without problems and, as noted above, circumstances of violent conflict add complexities to the operating environment of international NGOs that often distort the impact of their interventions. In this section, we briefly examine the historical experience of NGOs in conflict settings and, in more specific terms, the recent experience of NGOs in the wars of the late twentieth century.

NGOs and Conflicts: A Brief Historical Note

Some NGOs had their origins in wars, while others found themselves involved in conflict settings even though they had not been formed to address these circumstances. Examples of the former include the Red

Cross, Catholic Relief Services, and CARE, each of which was formed during or immediately after war, explicitly to provide emergency relief to war victims.[7] Others—such as the American Friends Service Committee, which was started by Quakers in 1917—were formed to provide an alternative to military service for young men whose consciences would neither permit them to carry weapons nor to sit on the sidelines watching the suffering occur. Later, two other "peace churches," the Mennonites (through the Mennonite Central Committee) and the Church of the Brethren (through the Brethren Service Committee) also undertook war-related responses in this same spirit. Even when these three NGOs later began to provide development assistance in Africa, Asia, and Latin America, they made the link between their development efforts and war "prevention," noting that their development motivation was to address some of the economic and social ills that could become seeds of war.

Other NGOs—such as Oxfam, Acción, and Technoserve (to name only a few of the over 100 such agencies in the United States alone)—that were formed in the 1960s and 1970s to provide emergency disaster relief or development assistance in the countries of Africa, Asia, and Latin America subsequently found themselves operating in simmering (and sometimes boiling) conflict settings.[8] For example, many of the agencies that responded to the Guatemalan earthquake of 1976 stayed in that country to work with peasant groups after the emergency was over. Similarly, the Ethiopian famines of the early and mid-1980s prompted emergency responses from NGOs, which continued to provide development assistance to rural communities once the famines ended. In both countries, NGOs that intended to work only on relief or development found themselves operating in an environment where local conflicts affected their staff and their programming. These NGOs soon realized that, in addition to recognizing the impact of these conflicts on their programs, they had to acknowledge the impact of their programs on the conflicts.

Some international NGOs were founded explicitly to support liberation or justice movements in other parts of the world, while others provide humanitarian or development assistance to these movements in direct support of the cause they represent.[9] NGO assistance programs in South Africa, Central America, Eritrea, and Biafra (to name a few of the places where this has occurred) not only provide direct assistance to their "clients," but also assume an advocacy role on behalf of their cause in the political arenas of North America and Europe. The fact that some of these movements are engaged in violent conflict has been accepted by these NGOs as necessary and justified because of the rightness of their cause.

Thus, a great many of the NGOs operating in conflict settings today have had experience in war-related contexts, either because they were formed specifically to provide aid to war victims or because they found themselves operating in such contexts as they pursued their other mandates. This experience shapes the work of NGOs today in two important ways.

First, founded as many of them were under conditions of life-threatening urgency, NGOs have defined themselves as service agencies. They have adopted a purity of motivation that seemed uncomplicated and direct. The suffering of children, who could not in any way be held accountable for the wars that engulfed them, has demanded a humanitarian response from those who could provide it. While subsequent entry by NGOs into longer-term development work has raised other issues, some of the same sense of the purity and urgency of their mission still shapes the work of most NGOs.

Second, except for those that were formed explicitly in solidarity with warring liberation movements, NGOs that entered conflict-ridden settings to provide aid to "innocents" have defined themselves as apolitical. Sometimes claims of nonpartisanship and neutrality are necessary to gain access to needy people in a war setting. More often, NGOs adopt an apolitical stance out of a sense of disdain for politics and the problems it causes. It was, after all, politics that created the wars that caused the suffering the NGOs attempt to relieve. Following the apparent clarity of academe, which divides knowledge into distinct disciplines, NGOs have often acted on the assumption that the realm of politics can be separated from the social, cultural, and economic realms where they work. While NGOs increasingly recognize the naivete of this earlier stance, there is a lingering reluctance to acknowledge fully the political entanglements and implications of their work, which is still essentially driven by the original service motivation.

These two aspects of NGOs' history shape and influence their work today. That is, most NGOs that operate in contexts of violent conflict continue to do so out of a basic commitment to humanitarian service, and while they increasingly acknowledge the political ramifications of their work, they seldom undertake explicit initiatives to address these. In the years since the end of the Cold War, however, evidence has been mounting that in the post–Cold War intrasocietal conflicts that mark a number of societies, NGO interventions—even when they are effective in humanitarian, development, or human rights terms—very often exacerbate the local tensions and suspicions that underlie the violence of the societies they seek to help.[10] We turn now to this evidence.

Although many factors lead to and underlie wars, once the fighting starts, conflict is about power, as each side tries to dominate the other through its war effort. Material resources represent, buttress, and are essential to power. Thus, when NGOs introduce their resources—such as food, cash, and equipment—into settings where people are already in conflict, these resources very often become additional foci for struggle and contention. Externally offered resources play into power struggles in several ways.

Warring factions may demand payment from NGOs (in the forms of "tariffs" or "taxes") for the right to deliver their assistance. These direct payments are then used to support armies and thus subsidize the conflict. Under the chaos of war, NGO resources are often stolen, and these goods may show up in the warehouses of fighting parties, who either organized the theft or bought what was offered by the thieves. In-kind support delivered to civilians, such as food, may be passed on to sons, husbands, brothers, and fathers who are directly engaged in fighting. In the civilian-based wars that prevail today, attempts by NGOs to ensure that only innocent civilians receive aid are confounded as the lines between civilians and armies are blurred. NGO resources, whether used by civilians or by fighters, relieve the burden of governing bodies and army commanders to support the populations or soldiers under their aegis. This then frees internal resources for the war effort.

Sometimes, NGO programs can improve a local resource base in ways that are later used by fighting factions. For example, a road constructed into a remote area of Ethiopia so that NGO staff could deliver needed food during a famine subsequently allowed military vehicles to reach these previously unreachable areas to conscript the young men into the government army. Similarly, an NGO health training program for Cambodian refugees in the Thai border camps resulted in the conscription of some of the trainees as medical personnel to be sent back into Cambodia to care for wounded soldiers on the front lines.[11]

Beyond these direct and indirect ways that NGO resources can be used to underwrite conflict, NGO interventions can reinforce and worsen intergroup tensions in other ways. For example, NGOs must choose to employ some people (and not others), purchase goods from some (and not others), and target their aid toward some people (and not others); these decisions can fuel separate group identities, inequalities, and jealousies. For example, international assistance in Tajikistan logically focused on rebuilding destroyed homes in a postwar setting, which increased the suspicions of the war's "victors," as they saw most of the aid being directed toward the people they had defeated. When development assistance is targeted toward specific groups, it explicitly alters an existing power relationship. While this may be justified to overcome existing discrimination and disadvantage, it may also prompt or reinforce intergroup tensions.

The "message" of some international NGOs as they work in conflict settings, expressed both in the publicity they offer and the modes of their programs, can also reinforce tensions that underlie conflict. We noted above that some observers think that citations of human rights abuses in the former Yugoslavia—certainly called for by every decent standard of humanity—actually had the effect of isolating and hardening the positions of the warring groups, rather than of encouraging their cessation of abuse and participation in a peace process. Similarly, NGOs' use of horror pictures of war atrocities in fundraising for humanitarian work may serve to dehumanize the perpetrators of these atrocities in the minds of the wider public. There is further evidence that NGOs that hire armed guards to protect their resources and staff reinforce prevailing acceptance of the "right" of arms to decide

who gets aid and where and how that aid is delivered.

Although there is evidence that NGO programming interacts with and may exacerbate local intergroup tensions, this does not mean that NGOs create violence or cause wars. The atrocities that NGOs cite in their publicity do, in fact, happen (and are widely reported to the public by the press, whether NGOs cite them or not), and the use of armed guards may appear to be required to distribute needed goods behind the lines controlled by warring factions. The point is that while these messages and these actions are justifiable in relation to moral principles and humanitarian standards, their potential for exacerbating the conflict demands serious reexamination of NGO interventions.

NGO Approaches in Conflict Settings

NGOs adopt different approaches for dealing with the fact that their good works may have negative ramifications in conflict settings. We outline three types of approaches that encompass the ways NGOs carry out their interventions in these circumstances.

The "Mandate Blinders" approach. When blinders are attached to a horse's bridle, its peripheral vision is restricted so that it can see nothing but the road straight ahead. Some agencies work strictly from their specific, original mandates; like the horse with blinders, such agencies focus entirely on the intended purpose of their work. They are committed to the rightness of their primary purpose, and they eschew responsibility for secondary or tertiary impacts of their work. They think that achieving their primary purpose justifies or outweighs any potential negative side effects that may result from their efforts and that, if such side effects do occur, they should be dealt with by someone else. Very often, these agencies operate in emergency settings and cite the urgency of need to justify their approach. They note, for example, that "it is always right to save the life of a child" or "it is always right to deliver food to people who are starving." Moral imperatives and time pressures drive their efforts.

There is growing evidence that such agencies often locate decision making and control in their own hands, thus leaving those whom they help dependent on the techniques and resources of outsiders. Such outcomes inevitably have deleterious long-term effects. While the mandate blinders approach may appear to have advantages in terms of speed and immediate efficiency in saving lives, in many cases it unintentionally disempowers local people to such an extent that the long-term efficacy of their effort is completely compromised. Local people are led to depend entirely on outsiders, both for survival assistance and (perhaps worse) for any efforts to achieve peace.

The "Aid on Our Terms Only" approach. Some agencies (also motivated by their sense of the rightness of their purpose) pursue a specific mandate fully, while monitoring and assuming responsibility for side effects of their efforts. Such groups are particularly aware of the ways in which war can distort and disrupt intended efforts. This approach maintains as its ultimate option the decision to withdraw assistance if the negative side effects of an intervention become too significant to justify its continuation. Agencies that pursue this approach may suspend operations in a given area, notifying local people of their hope to return "when . . ." and spelling out the conditions under which the agency would resume work. Such agencies use both the aid they give and their potential for withdrawing it to affect processes in ways they deem consistent with their mandate.

The "Hippocratic Oath" approach. Some agencies follow an approach that can be likened to the Hippocratic Oath that medi-

cal doctors take as they assume their professional practice. Through this oath, doctors pledge to do whatever is within their power and capability to serve the health of their patients. They recognize that their knowledge—and the knowledge of medical science in general—is imperfect; they assume responsibility for keeping up with current knowledge and using their own experience as the basis for improving their practice of medicine.

In this oath, doctors also pledge that they will "first, do no harm."[12] The phrase, widely quoted by other disciplines, connotes recognition that misapplied medical interventions can do more harm than good. As we have seen, the same holds for NGO interventions in relief, development, human rights, and peace promotion in conflict areas. While no NGO can predict with certainty all the ramifications of its activities in complex settings, recognizing that good intentions can have bad outcomes is a critical step in planning programs, establishing systems for monitoring impacts, and redesigning and altering programs according to experience. Commitment to the Hippocratic Oath approach to conflict intervention means that an NGO takes responsibility for its larger and longer-term impacts and that it continually seeks to learn from both the mistakes and the successes of its own programs and those of other agencies. Such an approach is also deeply attentive to the voices and intentions of the people on whose behalf the NGOs work.

These three approaches constitute the basis for ongoing dialogue and debate both within and among NGOs. In every NGO that intervenes internationally, some staff members advocate one of these approaches while others advocate another. Field operations of the same NGO vary, depending on the favored approach of the particular staff at the site. However, because the evidence is mounting that NGO interventions can have a significant negative impact, the NGO community as a whole is moving toward adopting the Hippocratic Oath approach.

To understand how NGOs may find ways to become more consistently effective in conflict settings, we now briefly explore the changing nature of today's conflicts.

THE CHANGING CONTEXT: NEW COMPLEXITIES AND NEW OPPORTUNITIES

The nature of war seems to have changed significantly in recent years, and these changes pose new complexities and new opportunities for NGO interventions in these settings. As many have noted, few wars in this post–Cold War era are between nations.[13] Instead, most wars are now fought within national borders, between groups who until recently lived and worked side-by-side; in many places, the groups now at war were friends and family members. Power vacuums and power shifts, occasioned by the end of the Cold War and the demise of the Soviet Union, have engendered or exposed political ambitions on the part of putative leaders in location after location. The prevailing mood in many societies seems to be that unless one's own group dominates, it shall become dominated by others. Thus, leaders cite the risks of oppression to take their followers into violent and all-too-durable conflicts with their neighbors. Most wars today are not fought on distant or defined battlefields, but in the living and work spaces of daily life. Civilians are endangered; they are also engaged in the war efforts that surround them. Thus, the lines between the military and civilians have become increasingly blurred.

In these wars, new attitudes seem to be emerging. Press reports and the propaganda of the warring factions cite entrenched and desperate attitudes that reflect a will "to fight to the death." However, private conversations and low-key consultations reveal quite different attitudes among some of the populace in many war-torn societies.[14] These conversations show widespread disaffection with the particular war that people are living in and, even more profoundly, with war in general as a means of solving intergroup problems. Many people living in conflict zones note that the war is "not solving our problems." In fact, they observe that the cycles of action, reaction, revenge, and reprisal are, themselves, causing future conflicts: The problems that prompted the first outbreak of violence are being superseded by even worse, and more intransigent, hatred based on and fueled by the experiences of war.

Citizens in war zones are also privately discussing the ways in which their so-called leaders fail to serve the people's interests. Rather than being excited to patriotic fervor by an ideal, expressed and embodied by a popular and heroic leader, many people are weary of the endlessness of battle for what they perceive as little purpose. Such voices are not openly and widely heard, however. By their own reports, local pressure for pro-war solidarity makes expressing disaffection extremely dangerous.[15] Anyone who questions the war, which has such immediate and terrible impact on the society's daily functioning, is liable to be labeled "disloyal" and "traitorous." The risks of speaking out are great.

Expressions of disaffection with war reflect the changing nature of war today, as compared with wars of the past. Throughout much of history, while people have always decried war as a "last resort," by the time a nation had actually entered a war, most people could be persuaded that it was worthy of their loyalty and sacrifice. When wars were undertaken to fight oppression, to overthrow a colonial or despotic rule, or to redistribute a basic economic resource such as land, many people joined these wars with a commitment to the justice of the cause and pursued war as an effective (if undesirable) mechanism for achieving a just (and desirable) goal. But today, as more and more people in war-torn countries cite the greed of their leaders as the only fuel for continuing battle, they fight (when they must) more for self- and group-preservation than for an ideal world that will be realized through their war.

As the nature of war is changing in these ways, the task of NGOs intervening in conflict settings has become both more complex and more promising.[16]

Intervention is made more complex in three basic ways. First, the international conventions that formerly governed the rules of war between states no longer apply. When wars are fought within countries, fighting factions and their commanders often have little knowledge of or respect for such conventions. Existing international law does not directly apply in these circumstances. Second, when groups within a nation fight over power and the national government is challenged as illegitimate, it is not clear where national sovereignty resides. The international community has few precedents and no clear rules guiding its decisions regarding intervention in such a situation. Third, when wars are driven by political opportunism rather than clear-cut causes of justice, NGOs (and others) do not know with whom to align themselves. Who is right and who is wrong? How can an NGO decide it is justifiable to negotiate with a given regime and lend its aid to support it? When is it important to withhold such support so that local people have the power to choose their leaders without international influence? These issues make intervention by international NGOs (and governments and the United Nations) more complex.

At the same time, the current wars present new opportunities for NGO interventions. We have described the ways in which

NGO interventions can exacerbate conflicts; these had to do both with the introduction and potential misuse of resources and with the moral message associated with NGO interventions. These two areas deserve more attention and exploration by the NGO community as it plans and implements its work in conflict settings.

When there is no clear "right" side in a war and when the acts of war by all sides violate basic humanitarian principles, NGOs have an opportunity to reconsider their apolitical stance. They can (and should) unequivocally denounce war itself as the greatest wrong, even though such a denunciation is a politically charged action. While the moral message of NGO interventions can exacerbate conflict, an explicit moral message against war may also enable local people to articulate their own opposition. This possibility may offer new opportunities for NGOs to ensure that their interventions have a positive impact on conflict.

If a very large number of people in a war setting do not believe that the war in which they are engaged serves any positive purpose, and if they are silenced by the circumstances attendant to such localized wars, then how might NGOs provide assistance in these areas in a way that provides a safe "space" or "voice" for the articulation of war opposition? Safety must be emphasized, because experience shows that naive interventions by external NGOs that implicate local counterparts in unpopular causes can greatly increase the risks these people face in their own political context. NGOs are challenged to find ways to structure their assistance in such a way that allows local people to choose to take up the causes of relief, development, human rights, and peace—and to choose the associated level of risk that they personally find reasonable.

Answers to these challenges lie both in the analysis of how wars are changing and in the ways in which the questions themselves are posed. When large numbers of people are disaffected by war, but have no safe means for expressing their opposition, any program intervention that is not directly beholden to the conflicting parties for its resources and that establishes a space for operations may afford a vehicle for people to disengage from their conflicts. While NGOs are still learning how this can be done, ideas are emerging that both suggest some new directions and, probably even more importantly, suggest that new directions can be found if the right questions are asked and appropriate answers are sought.[17]

Our analysis indicates that there is great potential for externally introduced resources to be diverted to support a conflict. This suggests that it is important to develop programming options that reduce the likelihood of the misuse of resources. Experience shows that resources are most easily "taxed" or stolen when they are amassed in identifiable places and follow predictable routes. Are there ways for agencies to disperse resources to make it more difficult for would-be thieves to realize sufficient gain from any one theft? Are there alternatives for distribution that would be less vulnerable to interception by warriors or thugs? Can fewer resources accomplish defined tasks?

One example illustrates the kinds of options that can reduce the negative impact that occurs when armies use stolen resources. Gender analysis has clearly shown that in many African societies, female farmers are responsible for food crops while male farmers are responsible for cash crops. In spite of this, in many African settings where NGOs and others provide food that is intended for family consumption, they identify male workers to take charge of food distribution. Very often, that food becomes a commodity with value (either for sale, theft, trade, or wielding power over others). External food providers, including NGOs, have accepted this as "inevitable," and perhaps it

is. However, it might also be possible that allocating the weekly food to women and relying on women's distribution patterns to distribute the food might reinstate the notion that food for family consumption belongs in the domain of women and is not a commodity with power and value. The United Nations High Commissioner for Refugees and several NGOs that work in refugee camps in conflict settings are experimenting with this approach to see whether it might prevent some of the abuses of power and increases in conflict that arose from previous distribution systems.

Other ideas for supporting local people's disengagement from conflict through relief and development assistance are being suggested by small experiments in a variety of places. These experiments focus on creating linkages among enterprises managed by different groups in warring societies, thus requiring cooperation if any enterprise is to be economically viable. In one village in Tajikistan, occupied by Garmi people, an NGO helped women develop a wool-production enterprise; in a nearby village of Kulyabi people, it promoted a carpet-weaving enterprise. An arrangement was made for the former to supply the latter with the wool it needed; the guaranteed Kulyabi market for the Garmi products was critical for their mutual survival. Other NGOs are also initiating activities where people from opposing sides may collaborate directly on joint projects in which both have a stake. Still others are exploring the ways in which information can enable people to resist becoming embroiled in battles that will only leave them worse off.

Ending a war requires work at many levels. International forums bring together commanders of warring factions to sign treaties and divide territories. One powerful motivation for these leaders to go to the conference table is the realization that the people on whom they depend for power do not support further war. Increasingly, agencies that implement programs affecting the daily lives of a people have an opportunity (and an obligation) to support these people as they disengage from conflict. To focus on feeding people or on promoting development activities that have long-term prospects is not enough in conflict-ridden societies, because the good that is accomplished can be overbalanced by the inadvertent exacerbation of the forces of conflict. NGOs that undertake interventions to relieve suffering and promote sustainable development and human rights must also accept responsibility for their impact on tensions and suspicions. The most exciting challenges facing international NGOs today are to recognize where things go wrong in order that they "do no harm" and to explore, develop, and implement programs that support local people who seek alternatives to conflict.

NOTES

1. All NGOs receive private contributions or are founded with private funds. Many also rely (sometimes heavily) on funding from their national governments, although a few completely eschew any government funding.

2. The term "natural" disaster usually refers to events that arise from nature such as earthquakes, floods, winds, and fire. However, since disasters occur in relation to human societies and are measured in terms of injury, death, and property loss, we think that there is no such thing as a truly "natural" disaster: Such events only become disasters in relation to human systems and human choices. For example, the organization of an economy may result in the impoverishment of some people, which, in turn, means that they live in high-risk zones such as coastal plains or cannot afford adequate housing that might better withstand earthquakes or high winds.

3. For full discussion of these connections, see Mary B. Anderson and Peter J. Woodrow, *Rising from the Ashes: Development Strategies in Times of Disaster* (Boulder, Colo., and Paris: Westview and UNESCO Presses, 1989).

4. For fuller discussion of this point, see articles in Alcira Kreimer and Mohan Munasinghe, eds., *Managing Natural Disasters and the Environment* (Washington, D.C.: World Bank, 1991).

5. Mary B. Anderson, "International Assistance and Conflict: An Exploration of Negative Impacts," Issues Series No. 1, Local Capacities for Peace Project (Cambridge, Mass.: Collaborative for Development Action, 1994).

6. It is important to remember that all NGOs that come from other countries are not intrinsically "foreign" to the circumstances where they provide assistance. In some instances, solidarity of purpose and philosophy can mean that an international NGO is more of an "insider" than an NGO that is based in a distant part of the country and operates out of a stance that is less sensitive to the circumstances of the people whom it purports to help. This sometimes occurs when urban-based, upper-class, local NGOs attempt to work in remote and rural areas of their countries. Furthermore, some international NGOs (such as the International Federation of Red Cross and Red Crescent Societies and denominational church groups) always work through local counterpart groups. Thus, there is a blurred line between "insider" and "outsider" NGOs operating in any given context.

7. The Red Cross was formed to provide emergency care to the sick, wounded, and other victims of either "manmade" (that is, war) or natural disasters. Catholic Relief Services was founded in 1943 as the War Relief Services to coordinate relief efforts of a variety of Catholic agencies for victims of the Second World War. CARE was started at the close of the post–World War II era and represented a cooperative effort of twenty-two U.S. religious, relief, labor, civic, and service groups focused on providing food packages to needy families in postwar Europe. (It is from this program that the term "CARE packages" originated.) See Landrum R. Bolling, *Private Foreign Aid: U.S. Philanthropy for Relief and Development,* Council on Foundations Report (Boulder, Colo.: Westview Press, 1982) for more on the histories of NGOs in relation to war and to development.

8. See Thomas H. Fox, "NGOs from the United States," in *Development Alternatives: The Challenge for NGOs,* ed. Anne Gordon Drabek, *World Development,* vol. 15, supplement (Oxford, U.K.: Pergamon Press, 1987).

9. The number of NGOs founded explicitly in solidarity with justice movements is relatively small compared to those founded for more general humanitarian reasons. Very often, these NGOs cease to exist when (if) the cause which they support gains its intended aim.

10. We should be clear that we are not suggesting that NGO programs cause conflict or wars; nor can NGO programs, by themselves, end conflicts. But, as they undertake their relief or development activities, NGOs do influence and affect existing tensions within societies; thus, they have either a negative or a positive impact on these societies. It appears unlikely that complete neutrality of impact is possible.

11. For more information about these cases, see Peter J. Woodrow, "Ethiopia Emergency Program: Yifat na Timuga, Ethiopia," and "Promotion of Health Care among Khmer Refugees in Greenhill, Site B, Surin, Thailand," both in *Rising from the Ashes: Development Strategies at Times of Disaster,* ed. Mary B. Anderson and Peter J. Woodrow (Boulder, Colo., and Paris: Westview and UNESCO Presses, 1989).

12. The idea for using this part of the Hippocratic Oath as a pledge for international NGOs working in conflict settings was suggested to me by a participant, himself an M.D., at a conference in Toronto in May 1994, organized and sponsored by the Health Reach program at McMaster University. I regret that I do not know the name of the individual, so I cannot cite him adequately; but the idea he gave those of us who were at that conference has proved extremely useful in my examination of NGO approaches to work in conflict settings.

13. For one discussion of these changes, see the preface in Thomas G. Weiss and Larry Minear, eds., *Humanitarianism Across Borders: Sustaining Civilians in Times of War* (Boulder, Colo.: Lynne Rienner, 1993).

14. The following several paragraphs reflect conversations that I have personally had with people in many parts of the former Yugoslavia, Tajikistan, Afghanistan, Sri Lanka, Pakistan, Lebanon, and elsewhere in the Middle East. As I have discussed these findings with others, many who have experience in other war zones have confirmed that they also hear local people expressing disaffection with both their wars and the so-called leaders who pursue them.

15. Although this idea arises in many settings, two individuals who articulated these dangers most clearly in personal conversations with me were a former mujahideen from Afghanistan and a citizen of a small town in Croatia, both of whom took the risk of initiating important local peace efforts that subsequently engaged a number of their fellow citizens.

16. Obviously, the discussion here is generalized to cover many different circumstances. Still, I believe it accurately reflects realities in many sites including Somalia, Afghanistan (now, not in the anti-Soviet war which preceded the current fighting), Tajikistan, Rwanda, the former Yugoslavia, and perhaps Georgia. In each of these circumstances there are also some real intergroup divisions or histories of inequality that are cited as the root causes of the conflicts. However, many people observe that these root causes serve the purposes of politically motivated leaders to entice fighters to their cause more than the wars serve to solve these root causes.

17. This is the concern of the Local Capacities for Peace Project of the Collaborative for Development Action, Cambridge, Massachusetts. The examples cited are from the case studies being organized through this project.

24

The Perils of Info-Democracy

TED KOPPEL

In journalism as in politics, leadership demands the courage to resist popular opinion if necessary—to set the agenda, rather than always follow the trend or respond to pressure. But mustering that courage is far from easy, not only because the public appetite for serious journalism seems to be diminishing, but also because the news media are so often criticized for doing precisely what they should.

Consider the growing perception that "the news"—television news in particular—is responsible for some of the nation's foreign policy problems. Television brought home the images of starving Somalis, leading to the American-led United Nations rescue operation. That operation, in turn, led to the deaths of U.S. servicemen. The image of one of those men in particular, the dead ranger being dragged through the streets of Mogadishu, created a backlash that led to the withdrawal of most U.S. forces. Television got us in, television got us out.

Are those the conclusions we must draw? And if so, where do they lead? It is often suggested that journalists must consider the consequences of the stories they report. While that has the ring of reasonableness, it is misguided. Journalists must be held responsible for accuracy and fairness, but rarely if ever for consequences.

Suppose the journalists who aired the videotape of those starving Somalis had been able to foresee the consequences—namely, that American servicemen would ultimately lose their lives. Should they have withheld the videotape? Would they not then have been responsible for the consequences of failing to report the story? In this case, withholding the information would arguably have led to the starvation of tens of thousands of people. Every news story, told or untold, has consequences. Since no editor has devised an accurate way of foretelling the future, the safest course is to report the news and risk the consequences.

Similarly, when the news media are accused of "setting the agenda," the solution is not to curtail or inhibit our reporting. It is policymakers who bear the responsibility of setting agendas. If an administration fails to set a clear agenda of its own, it will become

355

the prisoner of somebody else's. Randall Robinson's recent hunger strike is an example. Mr. Robinson, a dedicated and principled man, opposed U.S. policy toward Haiti and was apparently ready to put his own life at risk to force a change. After he had fasted for twenty-seven days, the administration announced significant changes in its Haiti policy.

What Mr. Robinson did was in the finest tradition of citizen protest. But if U.S. policy toward Haiti was right, it should not have been changed because of his fast. And if the policy was wrong, then changing it in response to that kind of pressure amounted to doing the right thing for the wrong reason. (It also raises the disquieting specter of others influencing U.S. foreign policy by martyrdom.) No doubt the Clinton administration will argue that the changes in its Haitian policy had nothing to do with Mr. Robinson's action. But by not having put forward a clear and forceful policy of its own on Haiti, the administration either became hostage to somebody else's policy or left the unmistakable impression that it had done so.

For any administration, the absence of a clearly enunciated policy is the political equivalent of a vacuum. It will be filled by whatever is available. Another telling example is the Korean situation. Senior officials, including the president, have spoken with different voices on how determined the United States is to stop North Korea from making nuclear weapons. But if this could even potentially lead to U.S. military engagement someday, there should be an intensive campaign to explain why nuclear nonproliferation is so important, why the United States is so concerned about North Korean nuclear weapons, and why we would go to war rather than allow them to be built. Without that kind of clarity from the administration, others will fill the void, shape public opinion, and eventually set the agenda.

No administration will ever totally control the agenda, but it can dominate the debate. The failure to engage in a clear, forthright, and timely fashion can cause irreparable damage. The pace of the crisis on the Korean peninsula is not solely in Washington's hands. If it suddenly escalates, the opportunity to prepare public opinion on the importance of this issue may have been squandered. And if U.S. troops are killed, the public will be demoralized—or it may press for an imprudently harsh reaction. Either way, the president's freedom of action will have been inhibited.

Newspapers do not cease publication and television news programs do not go dark simply because policymakers are not ready or willing to share their thoughts. The temptation to defer criticism and debate is understandable but unwise.

Before the House of Commons fifty-three years ago, Prime Minister Winston Churchill pithily summed up the dilemma of leadership in the often-ungrateful arena of a democracy: "I see that a speaker at the weekend said that this was a time when leaders should keep their ears to the ground. All I can say is that the British nation will find it very hard to look up to leaders who are detected in that somewhat ungainly posture."

It was true there, then; it is true here, now.

25

The Media and U.S. Policies Toward Intervention

A Closer Look at the "CNN Effect"

WARREN P. STROBEL

With the rise of "real-time" television in the 1980s, the growth of Ted Turner's 24-hour-a-day Cable News Network (CNN), and the deployment of news media technologies that can transmit video signals to and from virtually anywhere on the planet, government officials, legislators, media professionals, and scholars have voiced growing concern that journalists are exercising an irresistible control over western foreign policy.[1] It is said that dramatic images of starving masses, shelled populations, or dead American soldiers spark ill-considered public demands for action from elected officials. These temporary emotional responses may conflict with the more considered judgment of foreign policy officials, forcing them to take action that will soon have to be reversed or modified.

While the term "CNN effect" has numerous definitions and includes a range of phenomena, at heart it is understood to be a loss of policy control on the part of government policymakers.[2] CNN, it is said, makes, or at least exercises inordinate influence on, policy. Policymakers lose their sovereignty. Thus, George F. Kennan, writing in his diary as U.S. troops landed in Somalia to stop mass starvation, worried that if such decisions are made by popular impulse, "then there is no place, not only for myself, but for what have traditionally been regarded as the responsible deliberative organs of our government, in both executive and legislative branches."[3] During the 1992 presidential election campaign, H. Ross Perot declared that instantaneous worldwide communications have rendered embassies and their inhabitants "relics of the days of sailing ships."[4] More recently, UN Secretary General Boutros Boutros-Ghali has said: "For the past two centuries, it was law that provided the source of authority for democracy. Today, law seems to be replaced by opinion as the source of authority,

357

and the media serve as the arbiter of public opinion."[5]

This essay argues that these concerns, while understandable in the light of recent international changes, are misplaced. The CNN effect is grossly exaggerated, operating in few, if any, of the cases where it is most commonly cited. The media's effect on foreign policy is far more complex than the CNN-effect label would suggest, and far more dependent on the policy actions of government officials themselves than is seen to be the case. It is true that U.S. government policies and actions regarding international conflict are subject to more open public review than previously in history. But policymakers retain great power to frame events and solicit public support—indeed, CNN at times increases this power. Put another way, if officials do not have a firm and well-considered policy or have failed to communicate their views in such a way as to garner the support of the American people, the news media will fill this vacuum (often by giving greater time and attention to the criticisms or policy preferences of its opponents). In this regard, little has changed since Daniel Hallin, studying the reporting of the Vietnam War, an era of much less sophisticated media technology, concluded that the news media's impact is intimately related to the consensus of society as a whole.[6] What *has* changed is the speed with which the news media can expose such gaps.

This analysis will examine the CNN effect as it applies to prospective or actual U.S. interventions in what are now called peace operations or operations other than war.[7] My conclusions are based on more than 100 interviews conducted during 1994–1995 with four main groups: senior policymakers from the Bush and Clinton administrations; military spokespersons and other U.S. officers (primarily from the Army and Marine Corps); print, radio, and television journalists, primarily from U.S. news organizations; and personnel from the United Nations, other international governmental organizations (IGOs), and nongovernmental organizations (NGOs). The findings can be summarized as follows:

- Graphic televised images hold no power to force U.S. policymakers to intervene in a civil conflict where there is no clear national interest.

- There seems to be an inverse relationship between the power of images on policymakers and the presumed costs of intervention. (At the time of the decision, the costs of U.S. action in Somalia appeared to be low.)

- Images do add to the pressures on policymakers to address humanitarian aspects of a crisis, but the news media are not the agenda-setters they are often portrayed to be. Government relief officials, other relief agencies, and U.S. lawmakers play key roles in drawing news media attention to such suffering.

- Because public and media pressures are not specific, policymakers often react with what might be called a minimalist response, attempting to signal more of a policy change than has actually taken place.

- There is evidence that the power of televised images to provoke emotional responses is diminishing as conflict and humanitarian need become ubiquitous features of the post–Cold War era, at least as portrayed on television.

- Media reports have a greater impact when executive branch policy is in flux or is poorly articulated.

- The prevalence of real-time media reports often contracts the policymaking process, giving officials less time before they must respond publicly. But this does not mean the media automatically determine policy outcomes.

In short, the CNN effect does not exist in many places where it is said to be found, and even where its traces can be detected, they are exaggerated, working only in combination with other factors.

The following analysis draws primarily on four cases during the 1990s in which a U.S. administration faced the question of whether and how to intervene with U.S. military forces in foreign crises: the wars in the former Yugoslavia; the famine in Somalia; the ethnic slaughter in Rwanda and the resulting mass movement of refugees; and, finally, the refusal of the coup leaders in Haiti to yield power. First, I examine the broader picture and how the end of the Cold War has given the media greater sway in highlighting foreign policy problems, if not directing solutions. I then examine the case of Somalia, which has received intense popular and policy attention, focusing in particular on the role of relief officials in directing media attention to famine conditions. Next, I examine two cases, Bosnia and Rwanda, where the news media's impact on intervention policy was highly circumscribed. The Sarajevo "market massacres" of 1994 and 1995 provide an opportunity to examine the real-time facet of the CNN effect. Haiti is a case where the news media were actually a negative influence on an administration's desire to dispatch U.S. troops, but the intervention proceeded nonetheless. Finally, I draw some conclusions.

STEPPING BACK

A large body of popular and academic literature points to the notion that the news media have the ability to frame events or affect government policy most powerfully in the presence of a vacuum, created either by the lack of strong communication from elites or by a breakdown in society's consensus. Conversely, a policy that is firm, well-communicated, and has strong prior support is less likely to be affected by media products.[8]

Throughout the forty-five years of the Cold War, it can hardly be said that the press reported *what* the U.S. government wanted regarding foreign affairs. But to a degree that even in 1995 is difficult to comprehend, the American journalistic community largely reported *about* the agenda set by the government—that is, the superpower struggle with the Soviet Union. As *New York Times* Foreign Editor Bernard Gwertzman told his staff in a December 1992 memo: "When one looks back, it is remarkable but not astonishing how much of newspaper coverage since World War II was devoted to foreign affairs, and how much hinged on the Cold War and East-West rivalries. This competition consciously and subconsciously dominated government policies, affecting newspaper coverage as well."[9]

The overarching U.S.-Soviet struggle provided a context within which administration officials could explain their policies to the news media and, in turn, helped the news media explain to readers and viewers the significance of complex and far-off events. The news media were more supportive than is usually remembered of U.S. foreign policy aims during the Cold War. Until the 1968 Tet offensive, the television networks and prestige newspapers such as the *New York Times* largely agreed with the White House's claim of the strategic importance of South Vietnam. Journalists such as the *Times'* David Halberstam criticized the means, not the ends.[10]

The end of the Cold War has deprived American administrations of a ready context in which to explain their policies and created a sort of meta-vacuum. This, the media have filled, using their own professional ideology, which puts a high premium on crisis, drama, and unfilled humanitarian needs.[11] Marine Col. Gary Anderson, who has served on missions in Lebanon,

Bangladesh, and Somalia, said, "The do-something syndrome [is] the big difference between military operations today and military operations as we understood them before the fall of the Berlin Wall." Before, policymakers would say of a humanitarian crisis, "it's the fault of the [expletive] Soviets," he said. "It almost gave you an excuse not to do things you probably didn't want to do anyway."[12]

The purpose of this brief retreat into history is to underscore that while the cameras and other technologies that so concern Kennan are important, so too is the strategic context. That context (or rather, lack of it) is important in understanding the media's expanded role in framing crises and impacting U.S. intervention policy in the 1990s. If governments do not frame the nature of a foreign crisis, the news media are likely to do it for them. This, it can be argued, is what happened following the confused U.S.-European response to the outbreak of civil wars in the former Yugoslavia.

SOMALIA: WHO SET THE AGENDA?

Because it is widely accepted that television images of starving civilians, especially children, forced President Bush to dispatch U.S. military forces to Somalia in the fall of 1992, this is a good place to begin a more detailed examination of the news media's impact on U.S. intervention policy. This analysis challenges that widely held belief on three counts. First, the levels of television coverage were incompatible with the types of pressure usually associated with the CNN effect: Sharp increases in the levels of television reporting tended to *follow* administration actions, rather than precede them. Second, the television coverage (and other media attention) that did take place was almost always a result, not of media initiative and agenda-setting, but of deliberate and successful attempts by others to stir up media

interest in Somalia in order to move policy. These "others" were a loose coalition of U.S. government relief officials, interested members of Congress, and representatives of NGOs and IGOs. Their efforts highlight the growing role in particular of nongovernmental or supragovernmental bodies in international relations.[13] Finally, interviews with numerous Bush administration officials made it clear that they intervened in Somalia largely because they expected it to be an exercise with low costs and high political benefit. Simultaneously, President Bush was wrestling with the question of a potential U.S. intervention in the former Yugoslavia, which senior officials agreed would require tens of thousands of U.S. ground troops. Somalia was chosen partly because it was easier and would relieve pressure for action in the Balkans.

Even a cursory look at patterns of coverage of Somalia by the three U.S. broadcast television networks and by CNN raises questions about the impact of these media on the decision to intervene in Somalia. President Bush's first major decision regarding Somalia, one that "created an activist consensus in the national security bureaucracy where none had existed earlier,"[14] was to begin an airlift of emergency food supplies to drought-affected areas in Somalia and northern Kenya. This decision was announced August 14, 1992, although it had been made two days earlier. Prior to August 14, there were only fifteen network evening news stories in 1992 that mentioned Somalia; six of them were merely fleeting glimpses of Somalia's plight as part of one-minute or forty-second "round-ups" of news from around the world (figures 25.1 and 25.2). CNN coverage patterns were roughly similar, with the exception of a burst of coverage in May stemming from a single correspondent's ten-day visit to Somalia (figure 25.3). Once the airlift decision was announced, television coverage jumped to unprecedented

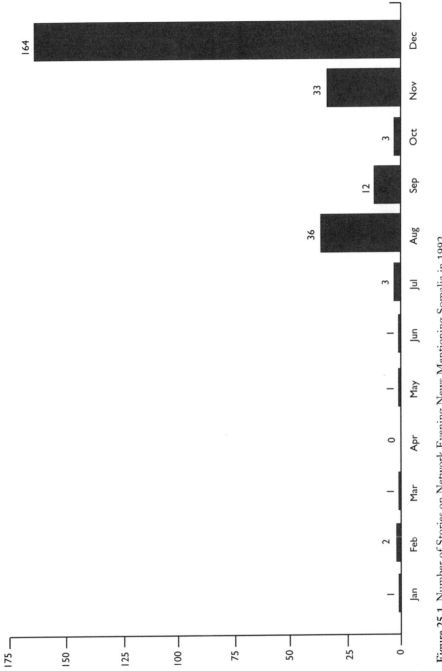

Figure 25.1. Number of Stories on Network Evening News Mentioning Somalia in 1992.

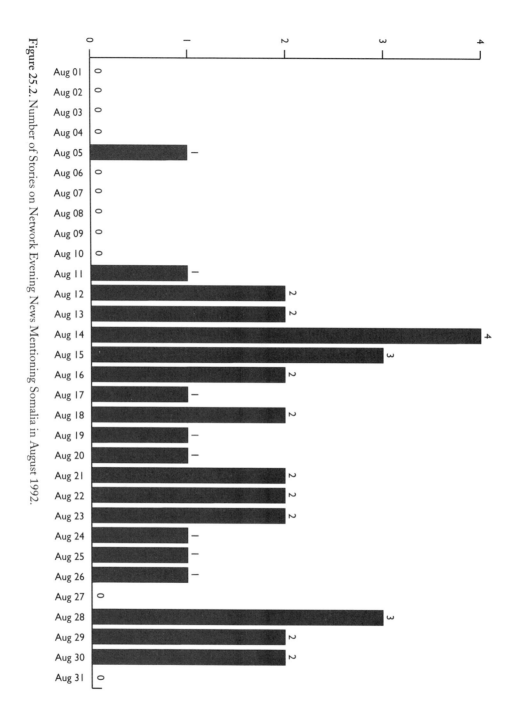

Figure 25.2. Number of Stories on Network Evening News Mentioning Somalia in August 1992.

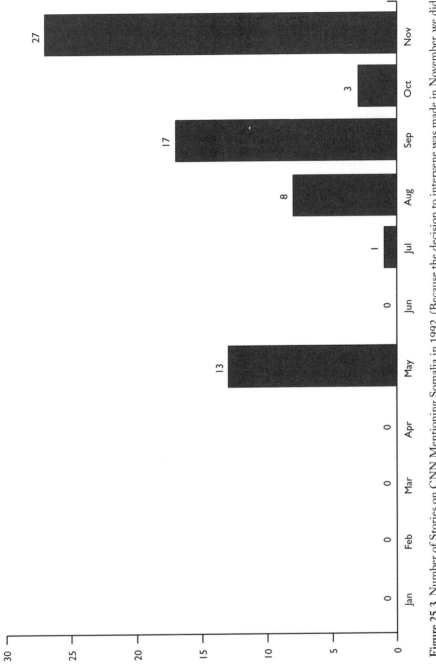

Figure 25.3. Number of Stories on CNN Mentioning Somalia in 1992. (Because the decision to intervene was made in November, we did not include December on the chart.)

levels, remaining relatively high in September, and then almost vanishing in October, no doubt overshadowed by the upcoming 1992 presidential election. Rather than television bringing U.S. troops and airplanes to Somalia in the first place, it was Bush's policy action that attracted increased media attention, with dozens of journalists descending on the country to report on the airlift. Of course, once there, they sent back more reports about the horrible conditions in the countryside. This pattern was repeated in November, prior to Bush's November 25 decision to launch Operation Restore Hope, the dispatch of nearly 30,000 U.S. troops to guard relief supplies. Somalia returned to television's agenda in mid-November, but it was Bush's decision that sparked the most intense media coverage.

Clearly, President Bush himself helped set the news media's agenda regarding Somalia. It remains possible, of course, that a relatively small number of dramatic television news reports moved Bush and his advisors sufficiently to prompt the dispatch of thousands of American combat troops. Indeed, Secretary of State Lawrence Eagleburger, National Security Adviser Brent Scowcroft, and other senior officials spoke of news media pressure as one factor that went into their decision.[15] As we have seen, some of this pressure was self-generated, as a result of the August airlift decision. Where else did it come from? The notion of a CNN effect carries with it the idea that the news media *independently* point out problems and set the government foreign policy agenda, especially regarding crises that call for potential U.S. intervention. But here again, the CNN effect falls short.

If there were times when the news media paid attention to Somalia when Bush and other executive branch policymakers did not have it on their agenda, this was the result of agitation by lesser policy actors, not the Fourth Estate. Activity by interested members of Congress, such as Senators Paul Simon and Nancy Kassebaum (the latter visited Somalia in early July and testified before a House committee on July 22), was directly responsible for the modest increase in television reporting on Somalia in late July and early August 1992.[16]

Equally important were the efforts to attract media attention to the dire crisis in Somalia by U.S. government relief officials and spokespersons for the NGOs, who launched a coordinated effort to inform the world, via the media, of the need for help. Andrew Natsios, the assistant administrator of the U.S. Agency for International Development (AID) with responsibility for disaster relief, was a prime mover in this effort, having long courted the press corps and seen it as a "resource of government." Natsios gave numerous press interviews, and he and other AID officials held a series of briefings for the press in Africa and in Washington. "I deliberately used the news media as a medium for educating policymakers in Washington and in Europe" about how to address the crisis, Natsios said. He also used the media "to drive policy."[17]

Outside the U.S. government, organizations such as the American Committee of the Red Cross and the UN High Commissioner for Refugees (UNHCR), helped journalists to get to Somalia to cover the story. Herman Cohen, the assistant secretary of state for African affairs, observed this process, attending one of the weekly strategy meetings that Natsios held with the NGOs. "They are all in there, planning strategy . . . how do you inform the world?" Cohen recalled. His view of the intervention in Somalia is this: "It started with government manipulating press and then changed to press manipulating the government."[18]

Somalia sheds light on the growing role of nongovernmental and supragovernmental organizations in international affairs. Groups such as the UNHCR, Medecins sans Frontieres (Doctors without Borders), the International Committee for the Red Cross, and dozens of others attempt to affect the intervention policies of the United States and other developed countries by highlighting crises around the world. Their prime source of leverage is the international news media, which both communicate the horrors of a humanitarian crisis and help relief groups raise funds to ameliorate it. "We need the pictures, always the pictures," said one UNHCR official.[19] (Publicity, it should be noted, is a double-edged sword for relief organizations, a power that can be offered one minute and taken away the next. In February 1995, the television cameras were long gone from Rwanda. Dire need remained of course, but donations to UNICEF's orphanage operations had dropped far behind need. "Andy Warhol's 15 minutes of fame are over and Rwanda is no longer flavor of the month," a senior UN official complained.[20])

Relief organizations have helped journalists and their all-important cameras get to the scenes of crises in Somalia, Bosnia, Rwanda, and elsewhere. I am not suggesting there is anything sinister or nefarious about these activities. The cause, of course, is a good one. But that is precisely the point: Relief workers who toil at the scenes of conflict are automatically a good source of information for reporters, and they are assumed, unlike most other policy actors, to have no political interests of their own. Reporters such as Keith Richburg, who covered the Somalia and Rwanda crises for the *Washington Post*, and Roy Gutman, who won a Pulitzer Prize for his reporting from the former Yugoslavia for *Newsday*, both said that relief organizations were important, credible sources of information. In sum, relief organizations and the media depend on and use one another more than they would probably admit, with important implications for U.S. policies toward intervention.

We have established that in Somalia the news media were not independent agenda-setters as is often claimed. The early response to the crisis was framed by the Bush administration itself, through its actions, and by relief officials in and out of government. They cued media interest. Nonetheless, once the images of starvation appeared on American television screens, they did have some further effect. Secretary of State James A. Baker III asked the rhetorical question of whether Bush would have dispatched troops to Somalia in December 1992 absent those images: "We probably wouldn't have," he concluded.[21] The next question is why they had an impact. The answer seems to be that senior Bush administration officials all believed that the Somalia intervention would be low in costs, especially casualties, and high in benefit. One of those benefits was to ease the simultaneous pressure the administration was feeling in the fall of 1992 to engage in a potentially much more costly intervention: the former Yugoslavia. Baker; his successor, Eagleburger; and Scowcroft all used virtually the same words: There was an easy consensus within the administration on doing something about Somalia.[22] In other words, the images from Somalia operated only on a narrow portion of the spectrum of national security concerns: a humanitarian crisis that seemed to be an "easy fix."

While there is no space here for a detailed analysis of Bush administration foreign policy in the latter half of 1992, two anecdotes tell the story. First, Bush, who had fought a war against a Muslim nation, Iraq, was under intense criticism for his refusal to act more forcefully to help the Muslims of Bosnia. Yet at the same time, Boutros-Ghali was criticizing the policy attention being focused on the Balkans, accusing the UN Security Council of "fighting a rich man's war in Yugoslavia while not lifting a finger to save Somalia from disintegration."[23]

Acting in Somalia, according to Scowcroft, was "a way to restore faith" in U.S. foreign policy.[24] Second, and more importantly, senior Bush administration officials assessed the comparative risks they thought were associated with interventions in Bosnia and Somalia—both the subject of gruesome media images—and easily chose the latter. In mid-November 1992, Assistant Secretary of State for Politico-Military Affairs Robert Gallucci presented Eagleburger with two one-and-a-half-page memoranda that argued for forceful U.S. action in both Bosnia and Somalia. In a meeting, Gallucci acknowledged that Bosnia represented a higher risk for U.S. forces and that it might be more difficult to limit the military mission there. Eagleburger told Gallucci: "I don't agree with you on one, but you're right on the other." Recalling the encounter, Eagleburger said, "Gallucci's memo was what decided me." A few days later Eagleburger called Gallucci back following a White House meeting. "He said, 'You're one for two. We're going to do Somalia.'"[25] One of the most important factors in Bush's decision to launch Operation Restore Hope was a surprising, last-minute change of heart by the Pentagon, which dropped its opposition.[26] General Colin Powell, chairman of the Joint Chiefs of Staff, may have predicated his support for Operation Restore Hope on the condition that the United States would attempt no such mission in Bosnia.[27]

In summary, the case most often held up as an example of the CNN effect—Somalia—falls apart under close examination. It was not the media that set the agenda in the fall of 1992, but the Bush administration itself, the Congress, and relief officials in and out of government. The horrible images did have an effect, but a narrow one. Reflecting on the experience, Gallucci said that pictures "don't come anywhere near" forcing an introduction of U.S. ground troops when it is known they will be in harm's way.

"When you're short of that, then the pictures are very useful in getting people to focus on it as a basis for humanitarian support." For anything more than that, "it's gotta answer the question, Why us?" It is to these limits of media power that we now turn our attention.

BOSNIA AND RWANDA: THE LIMITS OF IMAGES' POWER

Georgian leader and former Soviet Foreign Minister Eduard Shevardnadze has eloquently captured one facet of the impact of television on intervention policy: "The dictatorship of the Fourth power, the dictatorship of the TV picture, horrifying millions of peoples with images of mass violence, urges us to adopt humanitarian decisions and to avoid political ones."[28]

There is ample evidence that both parts of Shevardnadze's observation are true; that is, images do not have the power to force policymakers into political-military decisions that they would not otherwise take, but they do pressure those same policymakers to address the more easily solvable humanitarian aspects of a crisis. This can lead to what I call a minimalist response. It might be defined as rhetoric and limited action by government policymakers, designed to suggest a greater change of policy or more activism than has actually taken place. I will examine these phenomena in the cases of the U.S. responses to crises in Bosnia and Rwanda, also referring to another incident—the flight of Kurds to Turkey and Iraq following the Persian Gulf War.

Again, space does not provide for a day-by-day examination of two administrations' responses to the civil wars in the former Yugoslavia. Yet arguably, there were two points at which news media pressures for intervention were at their most intense. The first was in August 1992, with the revelations, first by Gutman in *Newsday* and then on Britain's Independent Television Network (ITN), of the murder and gross mistreatment of Bosnian Muslims in Serb-run concentration camps. The second, the televised bloody aftermath of the February 1994 "marketplace massacre" in Sarajevo, will be examined in a moment.

Gutman's Pulitzer Prize–winning reports in *Newsday* and the vivid ITN images of emaciated men behind barbed wire, recalling as they did the Holocaust, caused an emotional reaction around the world. In the United States, journalists, lawmakers, and other politicians—including presidential candidate Bill Clinton—demanded action to stop the abuses. Yet by this time, the Bush administration had looked at the question of intervention in the former Yugoslavia, and determined it was an abyss that would draw in thousands of U.S. ground troops for an indefinite period (Clinton would later come to this same conclusion). Two factors about this policy decision are important in determining why the media had so little effect: The decision was firmly held, and it was shared by all the senior members of Bush's national security team. As Warren Zimmermann, the last U.S. ambassador to Yugoslavia, put it: "It wouldn't have mattered if television was going 24 hours around the clock with Serb atrocities. Bush wasn't going to get in."[29] Eagleburger used virtually identical language, saying: "Through all the time we were there, you have to understand that we had largely made a decision we were not going to get militarily involved. And nothing, including those stories, pushed us into it. . . . I hated it. Because this was condoning—I won't say genocide—but condoning a hell of a lot of murder. . . . It made us damn uncomfortable. But this was a policy that wasn't going to get changed no matter what the press said."[30]

In other words, while it was difficult for policymakers not to respond to the news media reports and the outcry that they engendered, they decided it would be even more costly to respond. Politically, however, the Bush administration could not afford to be seen as doing nothing or as uncaring. On August 6, 1992, the day the ITN videotape aired, Bush demanded that the Serbs open the camps to international access. A week later, with U.S. support, the UN Security Council passed Resolution 770, demanding outside access to the camps and authorizing member states to use "all measures necessary" (that is, force) to ensure humanitarian relief supplies were delivered. The news media reports also played a role in the establishment of the first war crimes tribunals in Europe since World War II. While some things had changed on the surface, U.S. policy remained largely the same, defined by Bush's August 7 statement that the United States would not intervene with force. Bush recalled Vietnam, saying, "I do not want to see the United States bogged down in any way into some guerilla warfare. We lived through that once." Resolution 770 never was fully implemented.

This lack of real policy change was further confirmed in interviews with officials and reporters. Scowcroft said, "We did some marginal things, but there was a real consensus—and I think probably an unshakable consensus—to make a real difference . . . would require an American or NATO intervention that we did not see justified." Foreign Service officer George Kenney, who on August 25 publicly resigned to protest the lack of substantive U.S. action, said that government concern with the media "only extended to the appearance of maintaining we were behaving responsibly," while in reality refusing further entanglement in the Balkans. I asked journalist Roy Gutman, who actively tried to raise the alarm within the U.S. government once he had confirmed atrocities were taking place, for his assessment of his reports' impact. He curled two fingers in the symbol for a zero. "Really," he said. "What you had is a lot of reaction to reports, but never any policy change."[31] This is the minimalist response.

The U.S. policy response to the wholesale slaughter of ethnic Tutsis and politically moderate Hutus in Rwanda in 1994 provides an even starker example of the limits of images' power to affect U.S. intervention policy when the proposed intervention involves potentially large costs. By this time, the Clinton administration had learned, in Somalia, that interventions undertaken for the best of reasons and involving seemingly low costs can become expensive in terms of lives, money, and prestige. Whether the administration learned the correct lesson from Somalia or whether a small show of force would have halted the slaughter in Rwanda, as administration critics contend, is beside the point here. What is significant, rather, is that in officials' minds, the Somalia experience far outweighed the media pressures to intervene in Rwanda with force while warfare was underway.

Yet, under traditional CNN-effect theory, the pressures were greater in Rwanda than they were in Somalia. On April 6, 1994, the Hutu presidents of Rwanda and Burundi were killed in a mysterious plane crash, which sparked the subsequent slaughter by extremist Hutus. The data in figure 25.4 show that in both April and May, there were forty-three television network evening news stories that mentioned Rwanda. This was more coverage than the networks gave Somalia at any time during 1992, with the exception of December, when U.S. troops already had been dispatched (figure 25.1). Nonetheless, these higher coverage levels did not prompt a significant intervention by the Clinton administration. One senior administration official recalled a particular report that included videotape of corpses of massacre victims floating down a Rwandan river: "None of those provoked or provided the kind of catalyst for a U.S. military inter-

vention. . . . The [later scenes of refugee] camps were a different matter. . . . The mind-numbingness of it all was almost a made-to-order operation for what the U.S. can do and do very quickly. But it was into a basically benign environment."[32]

It was only after the fighting largely had ceased (the Tutsi-led Rwandan Patriotic Front seized control of Kigali in early July), that the administration felt any desire or pressure to intervene. It was at this point that hundreds of thousands of Rwandans, most of them Hutus fearing Tutsi reprisals, fled to and beyond the nation's borders. There was now a clear, quick task that could be performed, one requiring logistics available only to the U.S. military. "'Exit strategy' was the mantra," said a senior Pentagon official. "Everyone felt comfortable enough that that was a specific job that we could perform." Before, during the slaughter, "we didn't see that clear picture."[33]

On July 22, 1994, President Clinton announced a massive U.S. logistics effort in support of the UNHCR and other relief agencies in Rwanda, Operation Support Hope. News media reports, especially television images, contributed to Clinton's decision, officials said. But the actual situation on the ground in Rwanda and the recent history of U.S. intervention in Somalia played a major role in the U.S. response. The media's impact was limited to the humanitarian arena. And the policy response itself was minimalist, inasmuch as Operation Support Hope was tightly circumscribed in its size, duration and scope of activities. Interestingly, the public response to Rwanda—first civil war and then humanitarian tragedy— paralleled that of government policymakers. According to a senior NGO representative, when television was broadcasting images of Rwandans who had been hacked to death, private relief groups "got virtually no money whatsoever" from the viewing public. That did not change until the refugees flooded

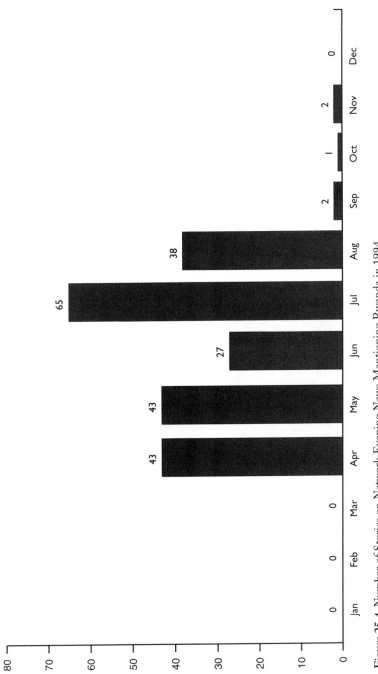

Figure 25.4. Number of Stories on Network Evening News Mentioning Rwanda in 1994.

369

into Zaire and there were "pictures of women and children . . . innocents in need."[34]

The U.S. intervention in northern Iraq following the Persian Gulf War, Operation Provide Comfort, provides another example of what happens when news media reports —images, primarily—collide with administration policy preferences. Bush wanted to end the Gulf War quickly and cleanly, bringing American troops home as rapidly as possible. As the scope of the tragedy of the Kurds following their revolt against, and suppression by, Saddam Hussein became clear in April 1991, Bush repeatedly stated that the United States would not become involved in Iraq's civil war. He again raised the specter of Vietnam. Television and photographic images, meanwhile, showed mileslong lines of refugees snaking up the snowy mountainsides into Turkey, with mothers burying sons and daughters along the way. Senior Bush aides said there is little doubt these images helped propel Bush to act, although the concerns of Turkey, a close ally, and an eyewitness visit to the Iraq-Turkey border by Baker were also key.[35] But here again, the media pressured a U.S. administration to address the humanitarian, not the political, crisis. Bush first authorized an airlift and then a program of U.S.-protected safe havens to draw the Kurds out of the mountains and back to their homes. According to Richard Haass, who oversaw Middle East affairs on Bush's National Security Council staff: "This was an attempt to meet a pressing humanitarian need without getting physically involved on the ground. There was a fear of getting bogged down."[36]

Operation Provide Comfort highlights a point which, although slightly beyond the confines of this paper, is revealing to the topic. Bush felt pressured to act to help the Kurds largely because he had just prosecuted the war with Iraq (and had called on Iraqis to rise up against Hussein). The news media could pin responsibility for the exodus on Bush. In much the same way, media attention and its pressures rose *after* Bush launched the August 1992 airlift into Somalia and *after* Clinton sent U.S. troops into Haiti in September 1994 (cameras captured brutal intra-Haitian violence, to which U.S. troops responded). The cameras follow the troops, not vice-versa. This raises the possibility that the news media's impact is greater once a peace operation is underway than it is on the decision whether or not to intervene. Assuming policymakers know of this potential, the news media can be a negative influence on intervention decisions. Eagleburger described this dread of the media's fleeting nature. If policymakers succumb to media pressures, "those who got you in won't defend you." He said, "They will turn on you. . . . There is no institutional responsibility as to what they've done [compared] to what they were doing. . . . What you're worried about is that you'll orient the United States to a policy and you'll have to reverse it. And that's terrible if you're worried about world stability."[37]

It is now clear that the news media's impact on intervention policy is limited to humanitarian intervention, not political, and even this limited power is not solely its own, but is shared with others who set the agenda. And, as we shall see next, even this impact—the impact of gruesome or tragic images—may decline over time. This does not mean that these images never will shock Western sensibilities again, as they undoubtedly should, just that there is a limit to what the viewing public can absorb. As one viewer told an NBC audience researcher: "If I ever see a child with flies swarming around it one more time, I'm not going to watch that show again."[38]

REAL-TIME INTERVENTION: THE SARAJEVO MARKET MASSACRES

Another facet of the loss of policy control associated with the idea of a CNN effect is the ability of modern news media to transmit graphic images almost instantaneously. This speed, it is said, overwhelms the traditional policymaking structures, forcing decisions that might not otherwise be made, perhaps before all the facts are in.

A good example of the impact of real-time media reports on intervention decisions is the gruesome footage of the February 5, 1994, "marketplace massacre," in which a mortar shell fired by an unknown party (but almost certainly Bosnian Serbs) landed in a crowded marketplace in Sarajevo, killing 68 people and horribly wounding nearly 200 others. In the aftermath of the attack and the public outcry, the United States abandoned its hands-off policy toward the Balkan conflict. It led NATO in issuing an ultimatum to the Bosnian Serbs to remove their heavy weapons from around Bosnia's capital (an extension of this threat would lead to NATO's first use of offensive force in Europe in its history) and established the five-nation "Contact Group," giving new momentum to the search for a diplomatic solution to the conflict. Sarajevens enjoyed a bit of normalcy after nearly two years of siege.

This clearly seems to be a case where videotaped images led the United States into, or at least toward, intervention. But while the images did have an impact, it was not the simple cause-effect one that this glance at events would indicate. At the time of the shelling, the United States already was moving toward a more active role in the Balkans, for reasons that included intense pressure from France and U.S. concern that the inability to affect the conflict was eroding the Atlantic alliance and American leadership. On February 4, the day *before* the shelling, Secretary of State Warren Christopher proposed that the United States lead a new diplomatic effort, combined with the threat of using force.[39] "I am acutely uncomfortable with the passive position we are now in, and believe that now is the time to

undertake a new initiative," he wrote in a letter to Defense Secretary William Perry and National Security Adviser Anthony Lake.[40] "We had a real sense that we didn't have a Bosnia policy that was going anywhere," said a senior State Department official. Before the shelling, "We had already made the psychological determination [about] the direction we wanted to go." This official was in a series of meetings on fashioning a new policy toward Bosnia when the mortar attack occurred—and recalled worrying that the new policy would be seen, incorrectly, as an instant response to the massacre.[41]

This is not to say that the bloody images had no impact; media reports actually had three effects. First, according to White House spokesperson Michael McCurry, they galvanized and accelerated the decision-making process. "The impact of the marketplace bombing . . . was to force there to be a response much quicker than the U.S. government" routinely produces one, McCurry said.[42] Second, it provided ammunition for those, such as Christopher, who had been arguing in administration councils for action. Third, it provided a moment of increased public attention to Bosnia that made it easier for the administration to explain a more robust policy. "It was a short window. We took advantage of it. We moved the policy forward. And it was successful," said McCurry's predecessor, Dee Dee Myers.[43]

In summary, rather than forcing the Clinton administration into doing something (undertaking an intervention) that it did not want to do, the images from Sarajevo helped the administration take a step that some of its senior members were arguing for. The images had an impact because the structure they affected—Clinton administration foreign policy—was itself in flux.

The second Sarajevo marketplace massacre underscores how non-media factors—the strategic and diplomatic environment—determine intervention policy more than the media do. On August 28, 1995, another shell fell in the same market, killing at least thirty-six Sarajevens and horribly wounding dozens more. A UN investigation left no doubt that the Bosnian Serbs had fired the shell. Several weeks before, following the fall of the Srebrenica and Zepa "safe areas" to the Serbs, NATO's defense ministers had gathered in London and pledged to protect the remaining safe areas, including Sarajevo, from attack. The international community's already-reduced credibility was on the line. The only question was "were we going to make good on those commitments?" McCurry said. NATO did, launching a massive air campaign against Bosnian Serb targets. According to McCurry, the equally horrifying images of the marketplace played much less of a role than they had in February 1994—further evidence that over time, the same images lose their power to influence. "Because it's the second time around, it had less shock value," he said.[44]

HAITI

There is one final case of U.S. intervention in the post–Gulf War era that merits a brief look, if for no other reason than that it differs so much from the others. In the cases studied so far, the media (with all the caveats given) were generally a force pushing the United States toward intervention. In Haiti, the media were a force against U.S. intervention. As he prepared to dispatch troops in September 1994 on what he thought would be a full-scale invasion, President Clinton was faced with a news media which reflected the numerous opposing voices in Congress and the foreign policy elite. Prior to former president Jimmy Carter's visit to Port-au-Prince to work out an agreement that allowed U.S. troops peaceful entry into Haiti, 88 percent of network evening news sources voiced criticism of Clinton's policies.[45] Numerous columnists warned against

a U.S. occupation of Haiti. Prestige newspapers such as the *New York Times* and the *Washington Post* editorialized against the administration's course of action, including its decision not to seek congressional authorization for an invasion of Haiti.[46] As Hallin would have predicted, the media reflected the lack of domestic consensus about Haiti's importance.

President Clinton argued that the restoration of stability in Haiti was in the U.S. national interest. He also left himself little choice but to proceed with the dispatch of U.S. troops, having put his credibility on the line by, on numerous occasions, threatening the junta that had stolen power from elected President Jean-Bertrand Aristide. Clinton's Oval Office address of September 15, 1994, boosted support for his policies slightly, but he nonetheless failed to convince the public that U.S. interests were at stake in Haiti.[47] Support for Clinton's handling of the situation rose markedly in the aftermath of the diplomatic agreement reached by Carter on September 18.[48] Once U.S. troops actually landed in Haiti, Congress backed away from its threat to impose a deadline for their withdrawal.

The Haiti case shows that the president retains formidable powers to determine U.S. intervention policies, even without a strategic threat like that posed by the Soviet Union. Clinton defied critics, whose opposition the news media reflected and resonated, and proceeded with an intervention that he felt was necessary. Once he had taken action, criticism remained, but was muted. This was no doubt due in part to a reluctance to undermine U.S. troops once they had been placed in harm's way. It seems likely that, had the Haiti mission encountered serious setbacks, including significant U.S. casualties, this would have restarted the political debate over Haiti, which would have played itself out in the news media. But that, as they say, is another story.

CONCLUSION

This essay has examined the news media's impact on one portion of foreign policy and national security concerns—the decision about whether or not to intervene (in the form of a peace operation) with U.S. military might. There are many other scenarios where the media might have a potential impact. One is an international crisis of great importance to the United States, but where U.S. military intervention is not feasible or realistic. Examples include China's brutal crackdown on student demonstrators in Tiananmen Square in 1989 and the coup attempts in Moscow in 1991 and 1993. Another is when U.S. troops already have intervened and face some setback or change in their mission, as happened with the deaths of eighteen soldiers in Somalia in October 1993. As noted above and expanded upon by this author elsewhere, the news media's potential impact is greater after an intervention is underway. This seems to be true because an intervention elicits the highest levels of media attention, puts U.S. lives and prestige on the line, and prompts significant public attention.

Yet the set of cases examined here make it clear that the CNN effect does not exist regarding intervention policy in the way suggested by Kennan's statements and many others. The cases of Bosnia and Rwanda showed that the power of dramatic news media images to alter policy is limited when that policy is firmly held—in these instances, because the cost of changing policy and intervening significantly would be high. The case of Somalia showed that it was not the media per se that were responsible for setting the agenda. Rather, it was other policy actors. The news media (and television even less than newspapers) rarely "discover" stories on their own. They need a "news peg" to report on—in this case, the statements of members of Congress, the activities of relief

officials, and the actions of President Bush himself. Haiti showed how the executive branch can still lead the nation into intervention, despite resistance from opponents relayed through the news media. Finally, the case of the first Sarajevo "marketplace massacre" showed how what seemed to be a dramatic change of policy was in fact an instance in which the media had an impact when policy was in flux, and thus official commitment to the old policy weak. There are numerous other examples of this phenomenon of media reports filling a vacuum in policy and communication. The most dramatic was the Clinton administration's withdrawal from Somalia following the graphic images of a dead U.S. soldier being dragged down a street in Mogadishu in October 1993. The second mortar attack on the Sarajevo market showed how non-media factors, such as diplomacy and strategy, still play a dominant role in intervention policy.

Perhaps the clearest lesson here is that, in an age of instant, 'round-the-clock television news, foreign policy leadership remains both possible and necessary—perhaps even more necessary than before. Kennan, if we take him at his word, seems to think such leadership a thing of the past. There seems little doubt that CNN and its brethren have made leadership more difficult. Numerous officials spoke of the temptation to respond to dramatic video images and the intense public outcry that often can accompany them. These calls can be resisted, but at a political price. If policy is not well anchored, the temptation to respond to the calculation of the moment can be overwhelming. CNN, in particular, gives opponents of policy—whether in the U.S. Congress or in the streets of Mogadishu—a platform to make their views known instantly, thus complicating the life of today's policymaker. Television feeds on conflict, whether political or physical, emphasizing the challenge to policy. And, as was seen early in this chapter, government officials no longer have the specter of a nuclear-armed Soviet Union with which to temper dissent, build support, or cajole the news media. In late 1995, the Clinton administration was beginning a campaign to persuade the public and the Congress to support the possible dispatch of 20,000 U.S. troops to Bosnia. The White House was told by the television networks that President Clinton could but rarely use their airwaves to make direct appeals to the people.[49]

Nonetheless, while it is neither possible nor advisable to suppress all challenges to policy, this paper has found a clear inverse relationship between leadership and news media impact. When policy is well grounded, it is less likely that the media will be able to shift officials' focus. When policy is clear, reasonably constant, and well communicated, the news media follow officials rather than lead them—by the rules of "objectivity," they can do nothing else.[50] The case of the first Sarajevo market massacre shows how television can be used to advance new policies. Indeed, in the hands of those who understand the role of information in modern governance, CNN can be an extraordinarily powerful—to some, even frightening—tool. It must be noted that each of the cases examined here involved peace operations, where national interests may have been at stake, but these interests were not seen by officials or the public as vital. It seems reasonable to suggest that the power of the executive to frame the debate and present policy options—in short, to use the media, rather than be used by them—increases when the threat to the nation's physical or economic security grows. This, in fact, is what happened during the Persian Gulf War.

Clearly, one area of particular sensitivity for leaders is the media's power to force them to at least focus on cases of humanitarian tragedy. Sometimes, this results in action to address the crisis—if such action is deemed not to involve overly high risks. But many other times, as Shevardnadze saw, policymakers moved to heal the overt wounds while shying away from the much more risky surgery involved in finding a political solution. This finding raises several troublesome questions. Does the public's long-term confidence in U.S. leadership suffer when policymakers, engaging in a minimalist response, promise or suggest more than they can deliver? Are top policymakers and the public spending an inordinate amount of time focused on dramatic crises at the expense of problems that are harder to portray on television? Numerous officials whom I interviewed expressed frustration that more important, but less dramatic problems—the General Agreement on Tariffs and Trade, the future of Russia's reforms, U.S. policy in Asia, to name a few—rarely make the nightly news. Yet this problem may to some extent be self-correcting. Unfortunately for its victims, violence and tragedy, when shown on television, seem to bring diminishing returns in public sympathy and official anxiety. For better or worse, the rude surprise the United States received after intervening in Somalia hastened this self-correction. Whether it is temporary or permanent will become clear over the next few years.

In sum, the awesome powers of communication technology at the news media's disposal have not had as dramatic an impact on this critical aspect of foreign policy as it might seem at first glance. Each of the cases revealed how other, abiding factors played a central role in the decision about whether or not to intervene. These factors included the real potential costs in U.S. blood and treasure; the credibility of the United States on the international scene; the future of important alliances; and the goals and benefits of the proposed mission itself. Journalists have had an impact on the decision about whether or not the United States will send its men and women into combat for a long time, as the case of the Yellow Press, McKinley, and the Spanish-American War shows. They still have an impact—and for the same reasons. What technology per se has changed is the pressures of time. If government officials allow others to dominate the debate, if they fail to communicate their policies and build support, if those policies fail, the news media will reflect all this, and officials will soon find that the impact of the media can be very real—and blindingly swift—indeed.

While the news media have made modern governance more difficult and more risky, Kennan's fears about the obsolescence of official prerogatives are exaggerated at best. Policymakers retain the power to set the agenda, to make policy choices and to lead. To do so, they need a sophisticated understanding, not simplistic descriptions, of the news media's complex role.

NOTES

1. For our purposes, "real-time" means not only images that are broadcast as they are occurring (that is, live) but also those that reach policymakers and other audiences within twenty-four hours of the event. See Nik Gowing, *Real-Time Television Coverage of Armed Conflicts and Diplomatic Crises: Does it Pressure or Distort Foreign Policy Decisions?* Working Paper 94-1, Joan Shorenstein Barone Center on the Press, Politics, and Public Policy, Harvard University, Cambridge, Mass., June 1994.

2. Steven Livingston and Todd Eachus, "Humanitarian Crises and U.S. Foreign Policy: Somalia and the CNN Effect Reconsidered," *Political Communication* 12, no. 4 (October–December 1995): 415–416.

3. George F. Kennan, "Somalia, Through a Glass Darkly," *New York Times*, September 30, 1993, p. A25.

4. Quoted in Johanna Neuman, *Ambassadors: Relics of the Sailing Ships? A Gentle Inquiry into the Diplomatic Trade in the Age of Cyberspace* (Washington, D.C.: Annenberg Washington Program in Communication Policy Studies, Northwestern University, 1995), p. 2.

5. Remarks by Boutros Boutros-Ghali at the Freedom Forum Media Studies Center, New York, March 19, 1995.

6. Daniel Hallin, *The "Uncensored War": The Media and Vietnam* (Berkeley: University of California Press, 1986).

7. "Peace operations" is the term employed by the Clinton administration in its May 1994 policy declaration, where it was defined as "the entire spectrum of activities from traditional peacekeeping to peace enforcement aimed at defusing and resolving international conflicts." "Operations other than war" (OOTWs), as used by the U.S. military, is somewhat broader, encompassing such activities as drug interdiction and relief missions such as those conducted in Bangladesh (Operation Sea Angel) or south Florida (Hurricane Andrew).

8. For example, Hallin, *The "Uncensored War"*; Ted Koppel, remarks at the "Managing Chaos" conference of the United States Institute of Peace, Washington, D.C., December 1, 1994; and testimony of Koppel, Michael Beschloss, and CNN Executive Vice President Ed Turner to the Committee on Foreign Affairs, U.S. House of Representatives, April 26, 1994, Document 79-868 (Washington, D.C.: Government Printing Office, 1994).

9. Bernard Gwertzman, "Memo to the *Times* Foreign Staff," *Media Studies Journal* 7, no. 3 (Fall 1993): 33–34.

10. Hallin, *The "Uncensored War."*

11. *The Media and Foreign Policy in the Post–Cold War World* (New York: Freedom Forum Media Studies Center, 1993).

12. Interview with Col. Anderson, August 1, 1995.

13. Livingston and Eachus, "Humanitarian Crises"; and Eric V. Larson, *U.S. Casualties in Somalia: The Media Response and the Myth of the "CNN Effect"* (draft), RAND, Santa Monica, Calif., March 1995, p. 69.

14. Herman J. Cohen, "Intervention in Somalia," *The Diplomatic Record 1992–1993*

(Boulder, Colo.: Westview Press, 1994), pp. 62–63.

15. Interviews: Eagleburger, February 1, 1995; and Scowcroft, February 27, 1995.

16. For a more detailed examination, see Jonathan Mermin, "Television News and American Intervention in Somalia: The Myth of a Media-Driven Foreign Policy" (paper delivered to the New England Political Science Association Annual Meeting, Portland, Maine, May 5–6, 1995).

17. Interview with Natsios, May 8, 1995.

18. Interview with Cohen, June 1, 1995.

19. Background interview, October 14, 1994.

20. Quoted in Jonathan C. Randal, "Donors Desert Rwandan Orphanage: Contributions for Children Drop When TV Cameras Leave," *Washington Post*, February 20, 1995, p. A20.

21. Telephone interview with Baker, September 11, 1995.

22. Interviews: Baker, September 11, 1995; Eagleburger, February 1, 1995; and Scowcroft, February 27, 1995.

23. Quoted in Cohen, "Intervention in Somalia," p. 54.

24. Scowcroft interview.

25. Interview with Gallucci, May 31, 1995; and Eagleburger interview.

26. Don Oberdorfer, "The Path to Intervention: A Massive Tragedy 'We Could Do Something About,'" *Washington Post*, December 6, 1992, p. A1.

27. "Operation Restore Hope," *U.S. News and World Report*, December 14, 1992, p. 26.

28. Speech to the Royal Institute of International Relations, London, February 16, 1995; translated from *Nezavismaya Gazeta*, March 10, 1995, by Denis Dragounski.

29. Interview with Zimmermann, June 8, 1995.

30. Eagleburger interview.

31. Scowcroft interview; interview with Kenney, January 26, 1995; and interview with Gutman, January 31, 1995.

32. Background interview, November 17, 1994.

33. Background interview, July 10, 1994.

34. Background remarks of senior NGO representative at conference on "Media, Military, and the Humanitarian Crises: New Relations for New Challenges," George Washington University, Washington, D.C., May 5, 1995.

35. Interview with Natsios; and interview with Baker.

36. Quoted in Michael R. Beschloss, *Presidents, Television, and Foreign Crises* (Washington, D.C.: Annenberg Washington Program, 1993).

37. Eagleburger interview.

38. Background interview, November 15, 1994.

39. Elizabeth Drew, *On The Edge: The Clinton Presidency* (New York: Simon and Schuster, 1994).

40. Elaine Sciolino and Douglas Jehl, "As U.S. Sought a Bosnia Policy, the French Offered a Good Idea," *New York Times*, February 14, 1994, p. A1.

41. Background interview, February 3, 1995.

42. Interview with McCurry, May 15, 1995 (at the time of the event, McCurry was State Department spokesperson).

43. Interview with Myers, February 27, 1995.

44. Telephone interview with McCurry, August 30, 1995.

45. "1994: The Year in Review," *Media Monitor* 9, no. 1 (January–February 1995): 3.

46. "Haiti: Consensus and Consent," *Washington Post*, September 14, 1994, p. A20; and "Congress Must Vote on Haiti," *New York Times*, September 13, 1994, p. A22.

47. *ABC News Nightline* poll, September 15, 1994.

48. *ABC News* poll of September 18, 1994; and *CBS News–New York Times* poll of September 19, 1994.

49. Background telephone interview, October 1995.

50. Hallin, *The "Uncensored War."*

PART III

APPROACHES TO CONFLICT MANAGEMENT

Preventive Diplomacy, Mediation, and Multi-Track Initiatives

26

Early Warning and Preventive Diplomacy

MICHAEL S. LUND

The ending of the Cold War clearly increased the willingness of governments to work through the United Nations and other international channels to address conflicts and other problems. Signs of the improved climate include the winding down of regional conflicts, a dramatic reduction of vetoes in the Security Council, a bigger case load in the International Court of Justice, and wider subscription to such governing principles as market economics, democracy, and the rule of law. Despite this more cooperative environment, however, the number of violent conflicts around the world has not declined. From 1989 through 1993, ninety large and small armed conflicts occurred overall. The number in any year remained steady, at about fifty. Previous civil wars and government-minority conflicts persisted or reignited, as in Afghanistan, Sudan, and eastern Turkey. New conflicts erupted, as in Tajikistan, Yugoslavia, and Algeria. The vast majority of these conflicts have been national in nature, dealing with secessionist, ethnic, or ideolog-

ical issues. In 1993, not a single active conflict occurred between states; all forty-seven were internal.[1]

As new conflicts arose, the international community exercised its new-found collective will to try to end them through diplomacy and to alleviate refugee and other humanitarian problems through peacekeeping and relief. Since 1991, peacekeeping missions have increased exponentially. In Mozambique, Namibia, and Haiti, these interventions have gone reasonably well. But in Somalia, Bosnia, and Rwanda, they encountered unexpected frustrations and dangers, while largely failing to stem violence and achieve order. Troubled interventions into perceived quagmires have thus evoked a backlash in some countries that provide troops and financing, including the United States. Many in the U.S. Congress and public question the need for their country's involvement in small-scale conflicts in remote lands and oppose participation in United Nations peacekeeping, arguing for

U.S. engagement only in countries and regions that pose strategic threats to "vital" national interests.

Although eclipsed by the voluble debate and handwringing over failed interventions, a quite different perspective on post–Cold War crisis intervention has also made headway in U.S. foreign policy discussions and international circles. Often appearing under the rubric "preventive diplomacy" or "conflict prevention," this view argues that, rather than trying only to mitigate conflicts when they reach a virtually unmanageable scale, deliberate efforts should be made to keep them from erupting in the first place.

Earlier involvement is likely not only to save lives but to obviate the need for often dangerous, costly, and politically troubled peacekeeping and humanitarian rescue operations. Why can't the United States simply sit out these interventions and hope others will undertake them? Ultimately, it may be unrealistic for major powers to expect to stay withdrawn from regional crises of various kinds, even low-level crises that do not pose immediate threats outside their areas. Countries that at first eschew getting involved— as the United States did regarding Bosnia, Haiti, and Rwanda—find that as these crises unfold, media coverage of atrocities, refugees, and other humanitarian problems and the accumulating political fallout eventually pull them in, directly or indirectly. But this intervention is often at an even higher cost and greater risk, militarily and politically, and more daunting tasks must be faced: containing the bloodshed, alleviating massive suffering, and repairing vast destruction through expensive reconstruction.

Still, if one could assume that the recent civil wars and other national crises were aberrations in a generally pacific era, demanding interventions might not be needed again nor would more cost-effective alternatives be required. But in many observers' judgment, the picture is unlikely to change greatly in the coming years. Even if one does not accept the views of some analysts that virtually the entire developing world is bound for chaos, the destabilizing effects of post–Cold War international trends—increasing economic competition and resulting national dislocations, declining state authority, rising pressures for political participation, spreading arms, and so on—will continue to put many countries and regions at risk of violent conflict.[2] Unstable nations and tense regions present potentially serious future national conflicts or interstate security threats—in Pakistan, Nigeria, Zaire, South Asia, the Korean peninsula, and the Persian Gulf, to mention but a few. Because of the huge costs and other impacts, proponents of this view argue that it is naive for major countries outside these regions to expect that they would be able to turn away from addressing these conflicts. Thus, proactive measures of conflict prevention are preferable to belated mitigation and alleviation of these situations.

BETWEEN IDEA AND POLICY

In recent years, preventive diplomacy has been advocated most prominently by UN Secretary General Boutros Boutros-Ghali in his widely circulated 1992 report *Agenda for Peace*. He urged more deliberate, earlier international involvement in incipient conflicts and called for early warning systems, fact-finding missions, and confidence-building measures between parties to a dispute, as well as preventive deployment of peacekeeping forces and establishment of demilitarized zones. A growing number of world leaders and other observers have echoed the secretary general's call, including leaders in Britain, France, and Germany, as well as Russian President Boris Yeltsin.

Among the most vocal advocates of preventive approaches to conflict have been high-level U.S. officials. Addressing the

UN General Assembly in 1992, President George Bush stated that "monitoring and preventive peacekeeping, putting people on the ground before the fighting starts, may become especially critical in volatile regions."[3] In their 1992 and 1993 *National Security Strategy* reports, respectively, the Bush and Clinton administrations identified both strategic issues and possible national conflicts as threats to U.S. security that require preventive responses.[4]

Despite its reputation of merely reacting to crises, the Clinton administration has been more explicit about the need to head off potential trouble spots than any previous one. In his 1993 confirmation hearings, secretary of state–designate Warren Christopher said, "We cannot careen from crisis to crisis. We must have a new diplomacy that can anticipate and prevent crises, . . . rather than simply manage them."[5] Virtually the whole top echelon of foreign policy officials has since endorsed this idea, using different terms such as "enlargement of democracy," "crisis prevention," and "defense by other means," as befits their respective agency perspectives.[6] In mid-1994, the administration adopted crisis prevention as a major foreign policy theme and started efforts to create an early warning system for the United States.[7]

International forums have also addressed the idea. The UN General Assembly has discussed preventive diplomacy several times; international conferences of professionals and academics have examined it; and special study groups and commissions have been formed.[8]

Conflict prevention is by no means confined to rhetoric and discussion, for it has also prompted concrete actions to ward off particular brewing disputes deemed potentially explosive. A well-known U.S. effort averted a regional nuclear crisis in the Korean peninsula. A less heralded achievement on this scale was the negotiation in 1993 of nuclear arms dismantlement with Ukraine and Russia. Opportunities to prevent national conflicts were missed in Somalia, Rwanda, and Chechnya, and the United States deferred to the European Union's ultimately failed effort to avoid the violent breakup of Yugoslavia in 1991–1992. But a succession of U.S. diplomats has headed the Conference on Security and Cooperation in Europe (CSCE) observer mission in Macedonia since 1992 (the CSCE was renamed the Organization for Security and Cooperation in Europe, OSCE, in 1994), and 550 U.S. troops serve there in the United Nations' only preventive peacekeeping mission to a place where no war has occurred in recent decades. In addition, U.S. emissaries have been dispatched to coax African leaders who are resisting democratization (for example, in Zaire and Nigeria) to turn over the reins of power. Another U.S. initiative seeks to anticipate and avoid further conflicts in the disaster-prone ten-country region of the Greater Horn of Africa. Britain, France, and other states have also launched conflict prevention initiatives in Africa, Central Europe, and Asia. Canada and Indonesia, for example, are sponsoring informal multinational talks concerning the dispute over the South China Sea islands.

Several regional multilateral organizations (RMOs) have not only developed early warning and conflict prevention mechanisms but also applied them in threatened places like Estonia, Macedonia, Congo/Brazzaville, and Guatemala. The leader has been the CSCE/OSCE, which has deployed observer missions or special envoys to over a dozen potential troublespots in Eastern and Central Europe and the former Soviet Union. The Organization of African Unity (OAU) has established and activated a procedure which has "as a primary objective, the anticipation and prevention of conflicts," and the Organization of American States (OAS) has applied new provisions to help consolidate Latin America's many new democracies and protect them from coups. The regional forum of the Association of Southeast Asian Nations (ASEAN) is also examining interstate confidence-building measures.

Less visible but also active in conflict prevention are many nongovernmental organizations (NGOs) that conduct unofficial dialogues and democracy-building and other projects at grass-roots and national levels in areas of high tension, such as Burundi. Other NGOs, think tanks, and foundations have begun research, action, coordination, or lobbying projects, and they are developing computerized networks for early warning and information exchange.

In other words, conflict prevention is an emerging subtext in post–Cold War international discussion, and in several places it has gone beyond wishful thinking. In fact, not since the founding of the United Nations in 1945 or the antinuclear and arms control movements of the 1970s and 1980s has there been so much explicit international interest and effort focused, not just on containing and stopping existing wars, but on preventing them before they occur.

The new interest and activity shows widening recognition that simply ending Cold War hostility is not the same as building a secure post–Cold War peace.[9] But although opportunities for preventive action have been more widely seized, these developments have gone only so far. Whether the inherently appealing idea of conflict prevention can be further developed into an effective, regular international practice will depend on answers to three sets of questions:

- What is preventive diplomacy or conflict prevention? Does it operate differently from other forms of conflict intervention and foreign policy?
- Can preventive diplomacy be effective, and if so, how?

- Can conflict prevention be institutionalized as a more or less regular international function? Who should undertake its early warning and other tasks, and what is the U.S. role?

DEFINITIONS

Confusion arises around such similar terms as preventive diplomacy, preventive action, and preventive engagement, as well as other current phrases like peacemaking, peacekeeping, conflict management, and conflict resolution. These terms are often used interchangeably and loosely. Crisis prevention in particular is often waved like a banner over policy agendas as varied as democracy building, nuclear arms counterproliferation, population control, and sustainable development. However, if policymakers are going to capitalize on the new interest in preventing conflicts in order to develop effective strategies, they need more than slogans. Whether one uses the UN term or its synonyms, preventive diplomacy requires more precise definition.

In *Agenda for Peace,* Boutros-Ghali defines preventive diplomacy as "action to prevent disputes from arising between parties, to prevent existing disputes from escalating into conflicts, and to limit the spread of the latter when they occur."[10] This tripartite definition thus sees preventive diplomacy as acting at several levels of a conflict. It treats the basic causes of disputes (dispute prevention), keeps disputes from becoming violent (violence avoidance), and limits escalation of erupted violence (violence containment). The definition thus spreads preventive diplomacy across almost the entire life cycle of a conflict.

Other observers suggest that defining conflict prevention as actions taken at virtually any conflict stage—from the causes of disagreements through many possible thresholds of bloodshed—is too inclusive and that it blurs important operational distinctions among the interventions made at different stages of conflicts. These differences vitally affect both how conflict prevention is carried out and its prospects for success.[11]

For one thing, the first part of the UN definition—preventive diplomacy as keeping disputes from arising—may miss the mark. Disputes do have sources in basic socioeconomic, political, psychological, and international conditions—for example, poverty, environmental degradation, lack of education, nationalism, and the lust for power. However, although these systemic factors increase the chances that disputes will become violent in the long run, they do not necessarily cause the violence. Not all the areas affected by these conditions are embroiled in wars, even in the developing world. For violent reactions to these factors to emerge, intermediate factors must come into play, such as bellicose actions and ethnocentric demagoguery. But addressing systemic factors will not necessarily confront these proximate sources directly, because policies that address structural conditions in a general way cannot pinpoint where and when particular manifestations of violent conflict will emerge. For example, poor countries like Rwanda received considerable economic aid, but it still experienced bloody slaughters. On the other hand, recent wars also erupted in countries that were not impoverished, such as the former Yugoslavia.

Consequently, preventing conflicts this indirectly by addressing deep-rooted and pervasive conditions requires policies as extensive, intrusive, and often controversial as income redistribution, disarmament, family planning, progressive universal education, and psychotherapy. These may be worthy long-term efforts in their own right, but such an ambitious and comprehensive mandate for conflict prevention in this cost-conscious era would dissipate scarce financial resources and fragment political support.

Furthermore, policies that treat systemic conditions may, in some circumstances, contribute to, rather than prevent, violent conflicts. Rapid socioeconomic reform, development, or democratization, for example, can destroy rather than strengthen the existing channels for regulating social disputes. Fragile societies or brittle regimes may become more susceptible to violence and repression, not less.

Finally, even were it possible, all disputes ought not be prevented, because conflict is not harmful in and of itself. International and societal changes in economics, technology, ideas, communications, and so forth perennially bring the interests of groups and nations into contention over matters such as the control of certain territories, natural resources, or governments. But when these disputes are expressed peacefully—for example, through international negotiations, accepted national politics, economic competition, expressions of cultural and religious diversity, and even nationalism—they can be constructive. It is not disharmony per se that needs remedy; it is rather its resolution through armed force and other forms of coercion that calls for prevention.

In sum, generalized policies aimed at systemic phenomena that generate disputes are not likely to be cost effective in preventing violent conflicts, at least not compared with more focused efforts.

Critics also find the final third of Boutros-Ghali's definition—containment of violent conflicts after they have escalated—unhelpful. True, keeping violence at any level from getting worse is "prevention" in a loose sense. But thinking of preventive diplomacy as controlling the advanced stages of a violent conflict confuses it with crisis management and stopping wars. Labeling a hot line, a cease-fire after a war, or a peacekeeping force to implement a peace agreement "preventive diplomacy" strains meaningful terminology.

Indeed, this approach would include interventions in the middle of the recent civil wars and humanitarian calamities—such as in Somalia and the former Yugoslavia, where belatedness, danger, and cost were the very factors that prompted many to urge a notion of earlier, more proactive involvement. Even relatively small and local, but potentially violent, conflicts should be addressed before they escalate, so Sisyphean salvage efforts can be avoided as much as possible.

This is not merely a semantic distinction. Empirical studies of mediation success and conflict escalation theory appear to confirm the presumption that precrisis and previolence intervention into conflict would generally be easier, be cheaper, and save more lives than reactive responses to manage, contain, or terminate all-out wars. The less violent and enduring the conflict, the greater the ability of third-party mediators to gain access and achieve a peaceful settlement. Issues tend to be simpler and singular, rather than complex and multiple; fatalities, and thus passions, are lower; disputants are less polarized and politically or militarily mobilized behind rigidly opposed causes; communications and institutions may still operate between them; and outside parties are less likely to have joined in on one side or the other. Interventions that act before violence or repression can lead to a spiral of victimization and revenge have a better chance of achieving results.[12] In short, "preventive" efforts that wait until crises or wars materialize are also not likely to be cost effective.

Rather than adhering to the *Agenda for Peace* approach to preventive diplomacy—including the actions taken all the way from the earliest signs of differences to the advanced stages of all-out wars—the most fruitful approach concentrates on the middle part of Boutros-Ghali's definition: preventing low intensity disputes from rising to tense, high-stakes confrontations or the resort to armed force. Conflict prevention operates, conceptually speaking, in between measures for long-term societal and global betterment, on the one hand, and short-term crisis management or war mitigation, on the other.[13]

If conflict prevention thus in essence means preemptive timing of actions at pre-violent stages of particular incipient conflicts, it need not be restricted to this or that technique or method of intervention. Indeed, it might use a variety of intercessory (diplomatic), political, military, economic, judicial-legal, and other methods and policies. These tools include mediation, power sharing, problem-solving workshops, peace commissions, politically conditioned and targeted economic assistance, indigenous dispute resolution procedures, and peace radio, to list just a few. Indeed, many of the policies and methods examined in other chapters of this book—peacekeeping, collective security, track-two diplomacy, rule of law programs, coercive diplomacy, human rights promotion, arms control—are potential tools of conflict prevention. Such tools might be implemented by governments, multilateral organizations, nongovernmental organizations, and individuals, as well as by the disputants themselves. Whether such tools and their implementers actually play a role in preventing conflict depends on whether the parties act deliberately to keep latent or manifest disputes from worsening in those particular instances when tensions are rising and violence is quite possible.

All things considered, a more promising definition of preventive diplomacy, especially for a fiscally tight post–Cold War era, might read as follows:

> Preventive diplomacy, or conflict prevention, consists of governmental or nongovernmental actions, policies, and institutions that are taken deliberately to keep particular states or organized groups within them from threatening or using organized

violence, armed force, or related forms of coercion such as repression as the means to settle interstate or national political disputes, especially in situations where the existing means cannot peacefully manage the destabilizing effects of economic, social, political, and international change.

So defined, preventive diplomacy might be needed either before a new conflict starts or after a violent conflict has abated to avoid relapse.

CONFLICT PREVENTION IN RELATION TO OTHER INTERVENTIONS

This focus for conflict prevention helps to clarify some of the prevalent confusion among terms commonly used for interventions into conflicts—including forms of diplomacy and foreign policy. One illustration of the relationships of these forms of action appears in figure 26.1. The figure depicts the stage in the full life cycle of a typical conflict that preventive diplomacy occupies in relation to actions taken at other points. The conflict in question may be within a state (for example, a civil war), or between states (for example, a border war).

As the figure shows, the course of disputes that become violent can be plotted in terms of two dimensions: the degree of cooperation or hostility that exists between two or more parties or the intensity of the conflict (the vertical axis), and the evolution of the conflict over time (the horizontal axis). The arcing line across the diagram portrays the course of a typical conflict as the intensity of hostility rises and falls over the period of its life.[14]

Arranged down the far left column of the diagram are gradations in the amicability or animosity that can exist among two or more parties, labeled levels of peace and conflict. These gradations differ according to such factors as the parties' degree of awareness of their disputes and separate identity, po-

larization, value congruence or divergence, mutual trust, and hostile behavior.[15] All these levels involve some degree of conflict, but with significantly different levels of hostility, including violence. Examples of recent conflicts at roughly these levels and phases are given in italics inside the arc.

Placed around the outside of the arcing line are several terms used for interventions into conflicts. The figure arranges these terms into two roughly parallel left-to-right sequences: the "P series" (preventive diplomacy, peacemaking, peace enforcement, peacekeeping, and peace building), which is generally used in discussions associated with the United Nations; and the "C series" (conflict prevention, crisis management, conflict management, conflict mitigation, conflict termination, and conflict resolution), generally found in the conflict literature. Which series is used does not matter, as long as it is clear that these terms refer to sequences of different conflict interventions, each applicable to different levels of conflict.[16]

As we can see, preventive diplomacy comes into play in the course of conflicts as tensions in the relationships between parties shift from the status of stable peace to that of unstable peace. Conflict prevention is most operative when ordinary peacetime diplomacy and politics have begun to break down and tensions rise, but before crisis management is necessary. Addressing neither peaceable relationships and conditions of cooperation nor crisis and war, it is activated specifically in troubled, unstable places and times when it is likely that regimes or peoples will take up arms or use other forms of coercion such as repression to "resolve" emerging political differences. The aim is to keep actual disputes from taking the form of confrontation or all-out violence and to return them to the processes of peacetime diplomacy or regular national politics. If conflict prevention fails and the situation deteriorates into a crisis, the notion of

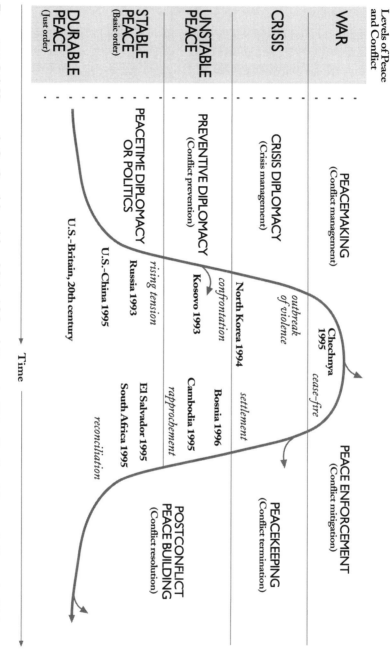

Levels of Peace and Conflict

WAR	
CRISIS	
UNSTABLE PEACE	
STABLE PEACE (Basic order)	
DURABLE PEACE (Just order)	

PEACEMAKING
(Conflict management)

CRISIS DIPLOMACY
(Crisis management)

PREVENTIVE DIPLOMACY
(Conflict prevention)

PEACETIME DIPLOMACY OR POLITICS

outbreak of violence

Chechnya 1995

cease-fire

North Korea 1994

confrontation

Kosovo 1993

rising tension

Russia 1993

U.S.–China 1995

U.S.-Britain, 20th century

settlement

Bosnia 1996

rapprochement

Cambodia 1995

El Salvador 1995
South Africa 1995

reconciliation

PEACE ENFORCEMENT
(Conflict mitigation)

PEACEKEEPING
(Conflict termination)

POSTCONFLICT PEACE BUILDING
(Conflict resolution)

Time

Figure 26.1. Life History of a Conflict. Adapted from Michael S. Lund, *Preventing Violent Conflicts: A Strategy for Preventive Diplomacy* (Washington, D.C.: United States Institute of Peace Press, 1996), p. 38.

preventive diplomacy ceases to apply, at least until the conflict has abated, in which case it is again needed to avoid a renewal of violent conflict.

HISTORICAL DEVELOPMENT

Aware of the various definitions of preventive diplomacy, we can see that it is not simply a recent phenomenon. Like the Molière character who learned he had spoken prose all his life, diplomats and other practitioners have engaged in preventive diplomacy without always using that term. Centuries before Hammerskjold came up with a label (see note 10), city-states, empires, and nation-states used emissaries, treaties, tribunals, and other devices to reduce tension and avert wars.

However, the earlier versions of conflict prevention generally differed from the distinctive post–Cold War notion delineated above because they were shaped by the major powers and statesmen of past eras and the threats they envisioned. A quick review of western practice since the late eighteenth century is instructive, for a gradual transformation is revealed in the "when," the "how," and the "who" of conflict prevention. More specifically, conflict prevention seems to have shifted increasingly from managing crises and containing active wars to earlier involvement to avoid their emergence; from ad hoc, unilateral, and bilateral acts of prudent self-defense to institutionalized multilateral arrangements that apply agreed-on norms and procedures; and from state-to-state relations to a larger array of nongovernmental and governmental prevention tool implementers. We also see the United States moving from being largely a beneficiary of conflict prevention to becoming one of its leaders.

From its founding to the late nineteenth century, the United States was a weak and marginal player in world politics; its foreign policy sought to protect its independence and to advance westward against the encroachments of more powerful Britain, France, and Spain. Its very survival and thriving as a nation was partly due, not to isolationism, but to vigilant diplomacy to avoid wars with the great European powers, a strategy that often took deft advantage of their preoccupation with their own shifting rivalries. The United States negotiated crucial treaties on its own behalf either to avoid or manage escalating crises as early as 1794, when Chief Justice John Jay was dispatched to London after England had seized U.S. vessels bound for England's enemy, revolutionary France. Other war prevention of that period included the deescalation of the *Trent* affair just before the Civil War, after a U.S. captain seized a British ship that had aided the Confederacy.[17]

During much of that century, the United States also benefited to some extent from the Concert of Europe—the first major multilateral agreement to avoid future wars that was adopted among modern states emerging from the Treaty of Westphalia in 1648.

In 1815, on the eve of ending Napoleon's campaign to liberate all Europe from absolutism, his allied opponents England, Russia, Austria, and Prussia met at the Congress of Vienna to set down rules and procedures to govern their own postwar relationships, as well as relationships with defeated France. The resulting arrangements allocated territories, fixed boundaries, reduced militaries, guaranteed security for small states, set up international tribunals, and established periodic consultations among the foreign ministers. The parties also agreed to mutual restraints on their competition in peripheral regions. The goal was not only to avoid direct attacks on one another, but also to remove temptations to seek unilateral aggrandizement from Europe's growing popular unrest.

The concert was a recognition that the great powers' balance of power was necessary but not sufficient to ensure peace; explicit agreements and active management of emerging conflicts were also required. Though hardly perfect, the concert and the less secure Berlin pact of 1871 are regarded as having been key to maintaining a general peace among European powers up to August 1914.

In the late nineteenth century, as the United States was becoming an industrial and military power, it took increasing interest not only in mediating other nations' disputes or conflicts, but also in instituting general procedures for preserving international order. Fearing that the Franco-Prussian War of 1870 would mean further turmoil in Europe, for example, the United States offered its good offices and pushed for prompt, even-handed settlement. Under Nobel Peace Prize–winner President Theodore Roosevelt, the United States mediated the Portsmouth settlement of the Russo-Japanese War in 1905 and helped foster the peaceful Algeciras Conference settlement of the Moroccan Crisis of 1906 between Germany on one side and Britain and France on the other.[18]

The United States' debut as a major sponsor of multilateral institutions to prevent war came when the onset and savagery of World War I abruptly revealed how much the European powers' peace system had degenerated into secret and shifting bilateral pacts, arms increases, and hostile camps. U.S. entry into the war enabled President Woodrow Wilson to play a significant role in designing the League of Nations at the Versailles Conference in 1919, even though Wilson failed to get his own country to join.[19]

Although the league is best known as a symbol of failure in collective security, it made strides in creating and applying procedures to settle disputes peacefully. The League Covenant was the first to define any

war or threat of war as a common threat and to seek to limit arms manufacture. Its provision for regular meetings of a council and assembly, a secretary general and secretariat, and a permanent court exceeded the concert in institutionalizing dispute resolution. The league's provisions for investigating and reporting on threats to international peace, posting observer forces, and imposing sanctions reflected explicit concern with heading off crises before they reached the boiling point. It did manage several disputes successfully, especially in the 1920s, such as those involving the Baltic's Aaland Islands, Bulgaria and Greece, and the Saar region.[20] However, by the 1930s, expedient alliances had displaced the league's hoped-for multilateral enforcement of agreed-on rules for conflict prevention.

The Treaty of Westphalia, the Vienna Congress, and Versailles all saw dominant powers meeting in the wake of major wars to forge multilateral agreements to prevent future ones. This pattern was repeated after World War II, when the victorious Allies created the United Nations in 1945 to save "succeeding generations from the scourge of war." The United States now played the leading role.

The UN Charter went further than previous agreements, committing members to uphold, in the words of Article 2, "effective collective measures for the prevention and removal of threats to the peace ... and settlement of international disputes or situations which might lead to a breach of the peace." The threat or use of force against any state was now outlawed, except for self-defense and peace enforcement by the United Nations itself. A type of early warning procedure allows members or the secretary general to notify the Security Council or General Assembly of any "situation which might lead to international friction or give rise to a dispute ... to determine whether [it] is likely to endanger the maintenance of international peace and security." Technically, this language is not restricted to quarrels between states, but the United Nations' purview originally was understood as interstate disputes, not internal ones; Article 2(7) rules out infringement on members' sovereignty.

Chapter 6 of the charter outlines several ways to handle potentially violent disputes peacefully, first by urging the parties themselves to try a menu of procedures, such as binding decision by the International Court. The Security Council can investigate threatening situations, assist in mediation, and recommend remedies. If such efforts fail to stem an emerging conflict, Chapter 7 authorizes diplomatic sanctions and international military operations. Through economic and social agencies, the United Nations affirms to this day its philosophy that the weeds of war sprout faster in the soil of material want.

From the late 1940s to the 1970s, although occasionally used in minor disputes, these procedures were sidelined by the geopolitical threat to the West posed by the Soviet Union and the ensuing global ideological struggle between opposed blocs. In the 1950s, a U.S. containment policy had set up regional alliances like NATO and the Southeast Asia Treaty Organization (SEATO). The standoff in conventional arms was supplemented by huge buildups of nuclear weapons. Because Security Council action could be blocked by permanent member veto, the United Nations was confined to containing the escalation of regional conflicts that were relatively marginal to superpower interests. Yet, in Hammarskjold's view, the United Nations' good offices, special envoys, and peacekeepers filled regional power vacuums that might otherwise have invited World War III. Larger, more direct confrontations and wars were prevented, however, not primarily by mutual agreements or multilateral mechanisms, but

rather through the tacit forbearance that arose between the United States and Soviet Union as a result of the mutual deterrence of their uneasy balance of power.

The balance of power did not prevent all U.S.-Soviet crises or conflicts, however. As illustrated by the Lebanon crisis of 1958 and the wars in Vietnam and Afghanistan, the bloc leaders vied for regional power through their financial and military support of proxies in the Middle East and other regions. The nearly fatal Cuban missile crisis of 1962 showed the superpowers, however, that when regional rivalries escalated to direct confrontation, their arsenals of fast-acting, potentially devastating intercontinental missiles left precious little time for either early warning or preventive diplomacy —only very high-risk crisis management. As a result, by the mid-1960s, the Americans and the Soviets worked to reduce the possibility of nuclear holocaust by increasing their communications through hot lines and more frequent summit meetings. They began what would become a series of arms control and nonproliferation treaties that gradually limited the testing, building, and dissemination of nuclear and conventional weapons.

Interbloc relations were also mellowing through trade and other commercial relations that increased economic interdependency, as well as through a growing number of educational, cultural, and other exchanges that reduced distrust. In 1975, the two blocs formed the thirty-three-nation CSCE, whose periodic meetings over two decades hammered out common ideals and procedures for military and political confidence building, governance, and scientific and technical cooperation. Because of the increasing nongovernmental links, western antinuclear peace movements pushed their governments toward arms reductions, and Eastern European regimes saw civic organizations sprouting up to press for new freedoms.

This historical retrospective suggests that the bulk of earlier conflict prevention occurred through self-defense and alliances and was at best crisis management. But there were some significant precursors to the emerging post–Cold War notion that preventive measures should be taken at stages of incipient conflicts before crisis management is necessary.

Post–Cold War conflict prevention has moved beyond these predecessors in three ways. First, the notion has spread that despite the prerogatives of sovereignty, internal sources of potential conflicts warrant deliberate monitoring and early responses. More policymakers now accept that national troubles that erupt into violence or repression, causing massive refugee flows or other large-scale loss of life and human suffering, greatly burden the international community and often threaten its security. Thus, preventive diplomacy no longer means only watching for cross-border aggression; increasingly, it looks for such signs of national crises as gross violations of human rights, genocide, ethnic cleansing, collapsing states, and military or executive usurpations of established democratic institutions. University researchers are seeking reliable indicators for such crises as potential civil wars, genocide, and failing states. Rapid communications technologies are opening up more nations' affairs to general view, and databases and information-sharing networks are proliferating, such as "Reliefweb," which puts conflict information on-line worldwide.

The second advance lies in the moves to go beyond particular interventions to institutionalize certain scanning procedures and link them to emerging codes of acceptable international conduct and to possible preventive responses. Back in 1987, for example, Secretary General Perez de Cuellar, reacting to the unexpected onset of the Falklands war earlier that decade, created a UN unit to collect information on incipient

conflicts. Although it was disbanded for lack of wide support, Boutros-Ghali subsequently reorganized the UN Secretariat to create a political affairs branch that could respond to incipient humanitarian crises through linkages with the Secretariat's relief and peacekeeping branches.

A third departure from earlier conflict management is a wider array of intervention tools implemented multilaterally by many global and regional organizations. In addition to the United Nations and regional organizations, these actors include particular states, nongovernmental organizations, and prominent individuals.

EFFECTIVENESS

The next crucial question is whether preventive efforts actually work, and if so, how. Skeptics say the case is based on hope rather than performance. No one can tell exactly when possible conflicts will erupt, and what to do about them. Since prevention is more difficult and costly than claimed by its proponents, it may not be doable at a cost reasonable enough to obtain support.[21]

The critique is misplaced if read to mean that no effective conflict prevention has ever been done. Also, the critics tend to argue from this or that single case of failure and to ignore the cases of apparent success. International organizations and governments have used many measures to avert troubles they believed might occur in their futures—for example, major-power wars and nuclear war. It would be difficult to argue that the number of wars that still occur prove that none of the existing efforts have prevented wars that otherwise might have occurred. Indeed, if conflict prevention procedures of many kinds were not now operating from the remotest village to the UN corridors, more of the world might be engulfed in the legendary war of all against all, or at least be a lot more insecure.

But what past eras considered special new prevention initiatives are today built in and taken for granted in the ordinary workings of international diplomacy and nations' political systems. We rarely hear about the times when these safeguards work, while the news from the unprevented wars is rife. As a result, the case for preventive diplomacy is unfairly hampered as a victim of its own successes.

It is pertinent, however, to question whether conflict prevention can effectively address post–Cold War conflicts in less strategic regions that currently lie outside the protection of the existing "safety nets" or where these nets have unraveled. The tensions in weak African democratizing states, the ethnic nationalisms in the newly independent states of Central Europe, and the security uneasiness among many Asian states represent aspects of this new frontier. In short, the efficacy issue is not whether preventive diplomacy works at all, but rather—where the means of preventing conflicts do not exist or have deteriorated and special efforts have to be made—can they work well, and if so, with what conditions and elements?

SIMILAR CHALLENGES, DIFFERENT OUTCOMES

The post–Cold War years present a natural laboratory for studying this question. Fundamental trends of the era—such as the decline of state socialist ideology, increased political pluralism, the transfer of authority over economic policy decisions and state enterprises to such market processes as private ownership, and the spread of information technology—have simultaneously challenged the economies, societies, polities, and international relations of many nations and societies around the world. By changing the rules of the economic and political game and by redistributing resources and

power, these forces create uncertainty and insecurity, leading to new clashes among competing interests. In several recent instances where turmoil threatened and deliberate preventive efforts were made, crises or violent conflicts still erupted (Somalia, the former Yugoslavia, Haiti, Rwanda); however, in other instances (Estonia, Macedonia, Ukraine, Congo/Brazzaville), the destabilizing changes were handled relatively peacefully. To understand what is effective in prevention requires comparing the apparent successes with the apparent failures.[22]

Many post–Cold War disputes and actual conflicts that have arisen within or across states have involved opposing interests of politically mobilized ethnic and other groups. Some of the same issues arose in all regions, but the following types of conflict tended to characterize one region more than others:

- ethnopolitical "kin-group" disputes or conflicts in Central Europe and the former Soviet Union (involving Croatia, Serbia, and Bosnia; Macedonia, Albania, Greece, and Serbia; Moldova and the "Dniestr Republic"; Estonia and Russia; and Hungary and Slovakia);
- postautocracy "transition" conflicts in subsaharan Africa (Zaire, Congo/Brazzaville, Rwanda, Burundi, Somalia, and Zambia); and
- "new democracy" conflicts in Latin America (Haiti, Guatemala, Peru, and Paraguay).

Across these cases, we can identify at least five factors that seem to be among the most important determinants of violent or nonviolent resolution of emerging political disputes. All five are proximate factors that are more or less amenable to policymakers' manipulation. Three of the factors operate outside the immediate arena of the dispute and pertain to third parties: timing of inducements, breadth and depth of international engagement, and support from regional and other powers. They suggest that preventive involvements will be successful only insofar as certain conditions are met.

First, third parties must be unified in supporting firm, unequivocal pressures behind a process of peaceful settlement—before any one disputant has generated a militant political constituency or actually deployed armed force or coercion on the ground to attempt to resolve the dispute.

For example, in a Hungarian-Slovakian dispute with ethnic overtones concerning the Gabcikov-Nagymaros hydroelectric project on the Danube River, a peaceful settlement was achieved once it became clear to Hungary and Slovakia that their membership in the European Community would be hindered if they continued to balk at settling the issue. Similar inducements were held out to Estonia before it finally passed language and citizenship legislation—the initial drafts of which had provoked its Russian-speaking minority. Russia also had an incentive to remain on schedule with its troop withdrawals from Estonia and the other Baltic states when threatened with the withdrawal of U.S. and other western economic aid.

In contrast, none of the cases that resulted in violence or deadlock shows evidence that substantial third-party mediation efforts were made before significant intercommunal violence or the preemptive use of armed force occurred. In Moldova, for example, no international body took an interest in the growing contention between the Moldovan government and the Dniestr separatist movement on the left bank until the CSCE mediated a cease-fire in 1994 and placed an observer mission in the Dniestr region to monitor it. By that time, the local forces had captured the territory they wanted. In the growing conflict between the Yugoslav federal republics after the breakdown of the Communist Party in early 1990, the outside efforts to pressure the republics to stay together or negotiate their differences were ineffective because the political divisions between the republics had already gone very far, militia preparations were already underway, and violent clashes had already occurred.

Second, multi-tracked intervention strategies must use several policy tools to address the several political, military, and psychological sources of potential violence, such as immediate threats to physical security, intercommunal distrust, and the absence of a workable process to engage the parties in dispute management.

Parties to a conflict often need several carrots for good behavior and sticks for bad conduct. Vulnerable situations—such as Macedonia, Rwanda, and Burundi—require that problems be addressed on several fronts and levels. For example, the key to effective prevention in Macedonia may have been the firm warnings by U.S. Presidents Bush and Clinton to Serbian President Milosevic that armed moves in Kosovo or toward Macedonia would be met with a strong American response and the American presence on the ground (in the United Nations Preventive Deployment Force, UNPREDEP). But more than deterrence was needed to address Macedonia's internal instability, so it was probably the combination of those warnings and the American presence with the CSCE observation mission, the Council of Europe monitoring mission, NGO projects, and the diplomatic recognition of the new Macedonian government that has been responsible for avoiding the spread of the Yugoslavian conflicts. These multiple official and nonofficial actions put the spotlight on Macedonia, signaling a significant international interest and presence.

The situation in Rwanda was a stark contrast. After civil war had waged between the predominantly Hutu government and the predominantly Tutsi Rwandan Patriotic Front since 1990, the OAU and the United Nations arranged a cease-fire and inaugurated a plan for power sharing in the Arusha Accords of August 1993. To monitor the accords' implementation and watch for signs of instability, the OAU and the United Nations dispatched a small military observation force in the fall of 1993. In hindsight, this nominal international presence was insufficient to detect a deliberate effort on the part of the extremist Hutu factions not only to avoid implementing the accords, but also to arm militias that could be ready to retake the country at the first opportunity. That opportunity came when the plane carrying the presidents of Rwanda and Burundi crashed on April 6, 1994, and genocide ensued.

The third condition for successful preventive involvement is measured by the extent to which major global and nearby powers, regional powers, and neighbors actively support (or at least tolerate) preventive efforts, without undermining them by overt or covert political or military backing of one disputant or another. Often, effective local and regional efforts are possible, to the degree that the United States takes an active interest in supporting a resolution of the dispute, although U.S. backing in the past has often been indirect.

U.S. political support of OAS responses to executive usurpations of democratic authority in Guatemala and Peru was clearly important to their effectiveness. In Guatemala, for example, the threat of economic sanctions from the United States added to the pressure that the OAS exerted and was critical to persuading the Guatemalan business community to support the coup's reversal. On the other hand, differences among the United States, Belgium, and France over how to deal with President Mobuto have impeded the chances of defusing the crisis in Zaire. France's wariness of the Tutsi groups in Rwanda and Burundi and its occasional apparent support of Hutu groups have not helped reduce the potential for further violence in those countries.

As an example of the impact of neighbors, it has been crucial for avoiding the spread of war into Macedonia that its neighbors Bulgaria and Albania have recognized the new state and forsworn seeking to change existing borders by force.

The United States' global purview, moral standing, and effective influence as a third party often make it the "first among equals" in supporting particular preventive diplomacy efforts, when it chooses involvement. In the Macedonian case, for example, the U.S. government and American NGOs are often regarded as the most important of the third parties involved. The fact that the three heads of the OSCE mission have been American diplomats reflects the apparent desire local actors have for U.S. involvement and seems to have enhanced the OSCE's local attention and respect. Major and direct U.S. involvement is not always necessary. U.S. actors have proven effective while working under the mantle of international organizations. In the case of the Congo, for example, the U.S. government was in the background as civil war was averted largely because of the efforts of an OAU mediator and local moderates.

The fact that regional organizations were active in the foreground of so many of these cases indicates that they can provide a legitimate vehicle for allowing major powers to participate in a preventive strategy without arousing suspicions of other major powers or other countries in a region. The OAS has acted as a legitimating presence through which the United States could put its power behind initiatives in the Western Hemisphere. The OSCE has acted as a useful meeting ground and focal point for both western and Russian involvement in Estonia, Moldova, and other regions in the former Soviet Union.

Successful preventive action is also fostered by at least two crucial indigenous factors arising in the conflict arena itself: accommodating leaders and the strength of state institutions. These are important variables because they alert third parties to important leverage points for conflict prevention strategies.

The leaders of the parties to a dispute increase the chances of success when they show moderation in their words, actions, and policies; make conciliatory gestures; and seek bilateral or multilateral negotiations with give-and-take bargaining. Failure is likely if they engage in provocative rhetoric, unilateral preemptive hostile acts, uncompromising policies, or coercion and force that worsen tensions.

Despite Estonia's restrictive legislation and an action against a Russian naval base, its behavior was generally tempered by a willingness to accept monitoring and policy suggestions from international bodies, such as the Council of Europe, the CSCE, and a UN human rights delegation. The aliens law and a measure to remove Russian from Estonian schools were submitted to the Council of Europe and the CSCE for comment, and Estonia's President Meri sent their drafts back to Parliament for modification before final enactment. In contrast, Serbian President Milosevic expelled the CSCE observer missions in Kosovo, Sandjak, and Vojvodina.

The peaceful breakup of Czechoslovakia on January 1, 1993, was managed without violence partly because of the clear desire of the leadership of its two parts to keep their negotiations from inflaming ethnic passions in the two communities. But a common tactic of aspiring republican nationalists in Yugoslavia was first to capture control of their parties under the banner of an ethnic group, then push moderates out, and finally unilaterally pass referendums at the most

propitious moments to validate their parties' control. Other cases, too, show that prevention will almost certainly fail where military power is covertly built up, acts of violence are deliberately encouraged, negotiations are preempted by resorting to force or coercion, and international influence and assistance is resisted, except where it consolidates a particular contending faction's own gains. Aware of the Yugoslavian pattern of leaders' whipping up their followers with xenophobic ethnic nationalist rhetoric, both Havel and Meciar made special pleas to their respective constituencies to avoid raising tensions, and the Czech and Slovak elites took pains to keep popular sentiments out of the debate.

Fifth, disputants need to pursue their differences through common governing procedures and institutions, operating on the basis of agreed-on, enforceable rules, such as those of legislatures, regularized election systems, judicial systems, and bureaucracies. Such "strong states" also ensure that the security and armed forces serve the interests of a constitutional order independent of the partisan aims of the political factions in conflict. Preventive diplomacy is less effective if the parties have separate power to set the rules and control their own armies or militias.

Successful dispute management within states is marked by governing institutions that have considerable control over the main political forces in the society and a monopoly of control over security and armed forces (Macedonia, Guatemala, Congo, and the Czech and Slovak republics). Congo/Brazzaville had developed a strong civil service, and its military had become more committed to playing a neutral role in politics. When the OAU mediator arrived, although the army was not ethnically balanced, it had restored order in the center of Brazzaville and was remaining neutral for fear of splitting apart. In Guatemala, military and police forces had been constrained from a political role in recent years; thus they did not automatically support an executive coup before considering the effects that action would have on the economic position of the country as a whole and on its standing in the international community.

In successful dispute settlements between states (Estonia and Russia, Hungary and Slovakia), the main actors have been leaders of established and internationally recognized states. These leaders were constrained in their actions by other states and by international norms, because they stood to lose more (in the form of aid, multilateral memberships, and other inducements from being integrated into the international community) than they could gain politically from promoting ethnic nationalist causes.

Preventive initiatives were much less effective in areas where weak independent governmental institutions had previously existed (Moldova, Yugoslavia), where central state institutions were being torn down (Yugoslavia from the late 1980s to 1991), and where state institutions or their parts were run like a leader's or a group's own property (Somalia, Zaire, Rwanda). In these settings, the main disputants achieved power primarily as the heads of politically mobilized and armed ethnic groups, factions, or political parties; they governed separate political and administrative entities over given territories (that is, "ethnic states"); and they controlled distinct armies and militias that served their aims alone (that is, as warlords).

A major factor making it difficult for mediators to prevent the dissolution of Yugoslavia from erupting into violence, for example, was the disintegration that had been occurring, even before the Communist Party collapsed, since the late 1980s in the collective organs of the state such as the collective presidency and the Yugoslav army.

As early as 1990, republics had stopped sending conscripts to the Yugoslav army; they instead created their own armed republican units within the police. Similarly, the leaders of Moldova and the Dniestr republic shared no common political institutions, and as violence erupted on the left bank, interior ministry forces lined up against a local militia receiving some support from the Russian 14th Army. In Rwanda and Burundi as well, civilian institutions of government (such as cabinet, civil service, and legislature) have been weak in relation to the ethnic group pressures on them. Group leaders have sought to divide up the portions of the state under their respective influences and have had relatively free rein to arm their followers in the countryside.

PROSPECTS

While particular initiatives in preventive diplomacy might be effective to the extent that they incorporate such lessons from recent experience, a final question remains. Can deliberate, comprehensive, and effective international preventive diplomacy advance further than it has? If so, what would it look like?

It is more common now to intervene in an incipient minor conflict because an influential official or government bureau happens to take a special interest. In these instances, however, because of the way large global organizations like the U.S. government and the United Nations operate, early warnings must wend their way up an extensive bureaucratic hierarchy. Even if they reach effective decision-making levels, such situations must compete for the attention of overloaded officials and strained staff. Each time a potentially troublesome dispute emerges, the challenge arises of getting political support for reallocating energy and resources to it, and for taking them away from routine business and other pressing crises. The constraints that such an approach place on effective early warning and prevention might be avoided by emulating the few recent instances in which organizational and staff capacity has been created (such as the OSCE's High Commissioner for National Minorities) to oversee and prevent violent conflict in a given region or country on an ongoing basis. Such efforts designate given officials or units at appropriate levels, earmarking funds for medium-range planning and ensuring that considerations of what should be done now to avoid bigger problems in the future enter the decision-making process.

The few proposals advanced so far for a more institutionalized and coordinated response to post–Cold War conflicts have differed in terms of whether they assume that readiness would be mainly carried out by the UN secretary general and the Security Council, UN regional centers, RMOs in cooperation with the United Nations, or networks of NGOs. The United States and other countries are also experimenting with their separate early warning procedures. Whatever detailed arrangements might emerge, recent experience in the United Nations and in major governments suggests that these efforts should authorize considerable political, financial, and moral support as well as discretion for lower-level decision makers out in the field. The best systems of preventive diplomacy would obviate the need for early warning signals to elbow their way up the ladder to the U.S. National Security Council or the UN Security Council. Preventive measures could then be deployed that are tailored and proportional to the scale of the emerging conflict. In sum, the new mechanisms need to empower embassy officials, aid missions, national governments, subregional and regional organizations, and NGOs as the first lines of defense in conflict prevention.

How likely is such improvement in the ability of the international community to prevent conflict? One factor that will affect whether something like the proposed plans are adopted is the number and types of threats and crises that arise in the next few years. Extant theories see a single feature defining the nature of future world conflicts, such as widespread "chaos" from collapsing nation-states or the clash of regional "civilizations." But the threats and crises in the offing are likely to be more diverse in both type and scale.

Because of their frequency in recent years, the focus in this chapter has been given to incipient national crises, such as the collapse of national economies and states, conflicts between governments and indigenous ethnic or regional minorities, and efforts to reverse newly established constitutional democracies. But a full list of critical situations should include troublemaker regimes, some with nuclear weapons; nuclear or conventional interstate wars over borders and natural resources; and civil wars over the control of states based on clashes between governing ideologies.

Another factor that will shape further development is whether the leaders of the United States and other major powers perceive important stakes in these various conflicts. Individually, only the last three types above might be interpreted as posing compelling threats to the security of many countries and entire regions. The others are smaller, relatively slow to develop, and scattered in locale. Their impacts and costs are highly dispersed and thus would erode international order and resources less perceptibly. Except when they occur in large powerful countries, it is unclear whether U.S. and other policymakers and publics can be persuaded to regard the prospect of the latter national conflicts as serious enough to warrant reallocating some resources to prevention, whether in the form of direct initiatives or support for local, regional, and NGO efforts.

The policy question that government officials need to ask themselves, stated in cost-benefit terms, is whether their government's portion of the shared present costs of launching multilateral preventive responses, plus any undesired side effects, would be far lower than the future costs of business as usual. Ideally, these calculations would factor in the human and material costs of the possible wars, the consequent pricetag for peacekeeping and other attempted remedies, a nation's economic opportunity costs in lost trade and investment, and the political fallout for leaders who would have to handle a series of such quagmires. This comprehensive accounting is rare.[23]

Despite the recent steps in the United Nations, the OSCE, the U.S. government and elsewhere toward more comprehensive early warning and preventive responses, preventive diplomacy is likely in fact to continue to be mostly episodic and half-hearted—except when responding to the large-scale, absolutely compelling dangers. For some time, most potentially violent national disputes could still be left (at least initially) to particular countries' political institutions, and most interstate disputes to whatever devices they initiate. Only occasionally and tangentially will the major powers respond to most national situations at precrisis stages, and then only when they themselves have a keen interest in the region. Thus, the world may see further belated and contentious peacekeeping interventions into local crises.

However, it is also possible that additional advances will be made incrementally toward wider, more regular monitoring of the antecedents of potential crises; promulgating human rights and other international criteria by which to judge nations' behavior; disseminating information about troubling signs; and mobilizing third-party coalitions or multilateral institutions to respond before crises occur. Despite the insularizing domestic forces currently shaping the United States' views of its interests (and that of other influential nations), several domestic constituencies might reasonably be attracted to the notion of paying small premiums for insurance against future disputes becoming deadly, tragic, costly, and risky imbroglios. These latent constituencies include budget-conscious military establishments wishing to avoid further peacekeeping burdens, crisis-exhausted private relief and development organizations, financial investors interested in young markets, and politicians and publics weary of watching moral tragedies unfold and debating potential military quagmires. In sum, astute statesmen, like their forerunners in past eras, might still discern the gains for their nations of collaborating with other governments and international organizations to address incipient violent conflicts sooner, rather than later.

NOTES

1. Peter Wallensteen and Karin Axell, "Conflict Resolution and the End of the Cold War," *Journal of Peace Research* 31, no. 3 (1994): 333–334. The data count armed conflicts over territory or governmental control that involved at least one government and resulted in more than twenty-five battle-related deaths.

2. According to the influential article "The Coming Anarchy" by Robert Kaplan, Sierra Leone and West Africa epitomize "the withering away of central governments, the rise of tribal and regional domains, the unchecked spread of disease, and the growing pervasiveness of war" that is occurring more and more in much of the developing world (*Atlantic Monthly*, February 1994, pp. 46, 48, 54).

3. "Remarks of President Bush to the United Nations General Assembly," New York, September 21, 1992. Transcript provided by United Nations Publications Office, Washington, D.C., p. 2.

4. The White House, *National Security Strategy of the United States,* Washington, D.C., January 1993, July 1994.

5. "Nomination of Warren Christopher to Be Secretary of State, Hearing before the Committee on Foreign Relations," U.S. Senate, 103rd Cong., 1st sess., January 13–14, 1993, p. 21.

6. For example, National Security Adviser Anthony Lake affirmed in 1994 that "in addition to helping solve disputes, we must also help prevent disputes, . . . [placing] greater emphasis on such tools as mediation and preventive diplomacy." Remarks to the Brookings Institution Africa Forum, May 3, 1993. See also Brian Atwood, "Emerging Markets," speech at Wharton Business School, March 5, 1996.

7. Thomas Lippman, "Finding Theme in Foreign Policy," *Washington Post,* June 30, 1994, p. A10.

8. From January 1994 to September 1995, the United States Institute of Peace operated the first known post–Cold War project devoted specifically to analyzing policy issues and methods of preventing conflicts before they become violent. Since then, several other organizations have taken up this subject. See, for example, Carnegie Commission on Preventing Deadly Conflict, *Progress Report,* Washington, D.C., July 1995.

9. An eminent historian not known as a wild-eyed idealist concludes his recent study of major wars, "A persistent and repeated error through the ages has been the failure to understand that the preservation of peace requires active effort, planning, the expenditure of resources, and sacrifice, just as war does. . . . The only choices available to leaders . . . [are] whether to seek to avoid the crisis by working to preserve the peace, to act realistically while there is time, or to avoid the responsibility until there is no choice but war." Donald Kagan, *On the Origins of Wars and the Preservation of Peace* (New York: Doubleday, 1995), pp. 567–573.

10. Boutros Boutros-Ghali, *An Agenda for Peace* (New York: United Nations, 1992), p. 11. The term "preventive diplomacy" was originally coined by UN Secretary General Dag Hammarskjold at the height of the Cold War to describe UN mediation and peacekeeping efforts to keep regional conflicts like the Suez, Lebanon, and Congo from provoking confrontations between the two superpowers. Thus, at its inception, this term referred to containing regional conflicts, not necessarily keeping them from arising—the third aspect of Boutros-Ghali's definition. Note that Hammarskjold and Boutros-Ghali intended preventive diplomacy to refer to both military and nonmilitary methods. See Dag Hammerskjold, "Introduction to the Annual Report of the Secretary General on the Work of the Organization, 16 June 1959–15 June 1960," General Assembly, Official Records, 15th Session, Supplement 1A, in *From Collective Security to Preventive Diplomacy: Readings in International Organization and the Maintenance of Peace,* ed. Joel Larus (New York: John Wiley and Sons, 1965), p. 405.

11. Trevor Findlay, "Multilateral Conflict Prevention, Management, and Resolution," in *SIPRI Yearbook 1994* (Oxford, U.K.: Oxford University Press, 1994), pp. 13–52; Michael Lund, chap. 2 in *Preventing Violent Conflicts: A Strategy for Preventive Diplomacy* (Washington, D.C.: United States Institute of Peace Press, 1996); and Raimo Vayrynen, "Preventing Deadly Conflicts: Global and European Perspectives," paper prepared for the Second Pan-European Conference in International Relations, Paris, September 13–16, 1995 (second draft, January 1996).

12. On the effect of early timing on mediation, see Jacob Bercovitch and Jeffrey Langley, "The Nature of Dispute and the Effectiveness of International Mediation," *Journal of Conflict Resolution* 37 (1993): 670–691. On escalation dynamics, see Connie Peck, "An Integrative Model for Understanding and Managing Conflict," *Interdisciplinary Peace Research* 1, no. 1 (May 1989): 7–36; Louis Kreisberg, *Social Conflict* (Englewood Cliffs, N.J.: Prentice-Hall, 1982), chaps. 1–5; Ronald J. Fisher, *The Social Psychology of Intergroup and International Conflict Resolution* (New York: Springer-Verlag, 1990), chaps. 1, 4; and Dean G. Pruitt and Jeffrey Z. Rubin, *Social Conflict: Escalation, Stalemate, and Settlement* (New York: McGraw-Hill, 1986), chaps. 1, 2, 5, 6.

13. This more focused notion does not imply that the international community should stop

trying to reduce the long-term prospects for future conflicts through appropriate economic development assistance, economic reform, democracy building, education, health, and free trade. But development programs alone cannot substitute for efforts to tackle more manifest causes of violent conflicts in the medium term, which, if left unattended, destroy opportunities for development of any kind. To prevent conflicts, such systemic measures need to be fashioned to "do no harm" and must be attuned more precisely to the conflict conditions and dynamics of particular places and times that are vulnerable to instability and violence. Also, when prevention has failed, the international community must still endeavor to contain or end crises and wars and alleviate the human suffering they cause; but preventing them is even better than trying to stop them and having to rebuild war-torn societies.

14. The smoothly curving bell shape is oversimplified to characterize an "ideal type" conflict. As suggested by the several lines and arrows that deviate from the line, the course of actual conflicts may involve downturns, upturns, or other trajectories at any point. Some relationships may operate almost constantly at crisis levels, violent conflicts that have ceased can reescalate, etc.

15. The stages of peace and conflict can be defined as follows:

War is sustained fighting between organized armed forces. It may vary from low-intensity but continuing conflict or civil anarchy (Somalia, Algeria) to all-out, "hot" war (World War II, Vietnam).

Crisis is tense confrontation between armed forces that are mobilized and ready and that may engage in threats and occasional low-level fights, but that have not exerted any significant amount of force. The probability of the outbreak of war is high (Cuban missile crisis of 1962). In national contexts, this condition might involve a high level of political violence (Colombia; Burundi, 1995 to present).

Unstable peace is a generally high level of tension and suspicion among parties, but only sporadic overt violence, if any. A "negative peace" prevails; parties perceive one another as enemies and maintain armed forces as a deter-

rent against one another (United States–Iran). There is thus some prospect of crisis and war, such as through miscalculations. Government repression of opposition or minority groups is one domestic variety of this level of conflict (Kosovo, Burma).

Stable (or cold) peace is a relationship of wary communication and limited cooperation (for example, trade) for the sake of mutual convenience and benefit and within an overall context of basic order. Value or goal differences exist, but disputes are generally worked out in nonviolent, more or less predictable ways. The prospect of confrontation or war is low (U.S.-Soviet detente, late 1960s; Israel-PLO accommodation, 1995; U.S.-Chinese relations, 1995). Domestic equivalents of this involve national political compacts among competing, sometimes hostile political factions (South Africa, 1994–1995).

Durable (or warm) peace involves a high level of cooperation, including military alliance against common threats. A "positive peace" prevails based on shared values, goals, and institutions (for example, democracy as a political system), economic interdependence, and a sense of community. Peaceful, institutionalized settlement of disputes prevails, so there is no felt need to safeguard one's own security against other parties through maintaining arms. The domestic form of this status ranges from processes of national reconciliation to a functioning, legitimate constitutional democracy with shifting political cleavages. The possibility of conflict or repression is virtually nonexistent (U.S.-Canada; European Union's goal of common economic institutions and foreign policies; unified Germany).

16. The other terms of the "P series" and "C series" can be defined as follows:

Peacemaking involves the uses of various carrots and sticks to deter, suppress, or terminate a violent conflict between parties.

Peace enforcement is the use of armed force, as under Chapter 7 of the UN Charter, to contain or end a violent conflict.

Peacekeeping refers to efforts to maintain a cease-fire and foster a political settlement between the parties to a violent conflict by separating their armed forces, as under Chapter 6 of the UN Charter.

Postconflict peace building is an inclusive term that involves efforts not only to maintain order but also, after a settlement is implemented, to increase cooperation among the parties to a conflict and to deepen their relationship by addressing the conditions that led to the dispute, fostering positive attitudes and allaying distrust, and building or strengthening common institutions and processes through which the parties interact. Postconflict peace building is also called *conflict resolution*. When peace building is used long after an old conflict ceases but when new violence is feared (in an attempt to prevent it), it falls under the term preventive diplomacy.

Crisis diplomacy or *crisis management* refers to efforts to keep situations of high tension and confrontation between conflicting parties from erupting into the use of armed force or violence; it is usually associated with threats of force or violence.

Conflict management involves efforts to contain and reduce the amount of violence used by the parties to a conflict and to engage them in communication that looks toward settling their dispute and ending the violence. It is sometimes called *conflict mitigation*.

Conflict termination is the cessation of armed hostilities between the parties.

17. Further examples would include the negotiations with Russia over U.S. fishing and trading rights below Alaska, as reported in the Monroe Doctrine speech of 1823, and the 1850 Clayton-Bulwer Treaty that reduced rising U.S.-British tensions over Central America. See Eugene Rostow, *A Breakfast for Bonaparte: U.S. National Security Interests from the Heights of Abraham to the Nuclear Age* (Washington, D.C.: National Defense University Press, 1992).

18. Roosevelt also led the United States in managing disputes or crises affecting Venezuela, Guatemala, El Salvador, Nicaragua, and Honduras and in helping to establish an international court in Central America to manage its revolutionary upheaval; he also submitted U.S. disputes to international adjudication by the Hague Court.

19. Yet, from 1920 to 1922, Washington hosted the first major naval arms limitation talks, which produced treaties among the Pacific powers, the United States, Britain, and Japan. The

United States also provided good offices for many inter-American disputes and fostered the precursor to the Organization of American States.

20. Lorna Lloyd, "The League of Nations and the Settlement of Disputes," paper presented at the Woodrow Wilson House Symposium on the Occasion of the 75th Anniversary of the Paris Peace Conference, March 4–5, 1994, Washington, D.C.

21. Stephen Stedman, "Alchemy for a New World Order: Overselling 'Preventive Diplomacy,'" *Foreign Affairs* 73, no. 3 (May–June 1995): 14–20. A reply is offered in Michael S. Lund, "Underrating Preventive Diplomacy," *Foreign Affairs* 73, no. 4 (July–August 1995): 160–163.

22. The following analysis builds on the preliminary findings reported in Lund, *Preventing Violent Conflicts*, chap. 3, "Lessons from Experience." They are promising hypotheses for more rigorous research based on initial study of several cases and other analyses. The author has begun more rigorous comparisons of such cases to test the validity of these conclusions.

23. A partial exception is *The True Cost of Conflict: Seven Recent Wars and Their Effects on Society*, ed. Michael Cranna (New York: New Press, 1994).

SELECT BIBLIOGRAPHY

Adelman, Howard, and Astri Suhrke. 1995. "Early Warning and Conflict Management: Genocide in Rwanda." Study II of the Evaluation of Emergency Assistance to Rwanda. Bergen, Norway: Chr. Michelson Institute.

Bookman, Milica Z. 1994. "War and Peace: The Divergent Breakups of Yugoslavia and Czechoslovakia." *Journal of Peace Research* 31, no. 2: 175–187.

Boudreau, Thomas. 1991. *Sheathing the Sword: The UN Secretary General and the Prevention of International Conflict.* New York: Greenwood Press.

Boutros-Ghali, Boutros. 1992. *Agenda for Peace: Preventive Diplomacy, Peacemaking, and Peacekeeping.* New York: United Nations.

Boutros-Ghali, Boutros. 1992. *Supplement to an Agenda for Peace: Position Paper of the Secretary General on the Occasion of the Fiftieth Anniversary of the United Nations.* A/47/L.50. New York: United Nations.

Clark, John F. 1994. "Elections, Leadership and Democracy in Congo." *Africa Today* (3rd Quarter): 41–60.

Claude, Inis L., Jr. 1984. *Swords into Plowshares: The Problems and Progress of International Organizations,* 4th ed. New York: Random House.

Craig, Gordon, and Alexander George. 1990. *Force and Statecraft: Diplomatic Problems of Our Time,* 2nd ed. Oxford, U.K.: Oxford University Press.

Drohobycky, Maria, ed. 1995. *Managing Ethnic Tension in the Post-Soviet Space: The Examples of Kazakhstan and Ukraine.* Washington, D.C.: American Association for the Advancement of Science.

Evans, Gareth. 1993. *Cooperating For Peace: The Global Agenda for the '90s and Beyond.* New York: Allen and Unwin.

Fauriol, Georges A., ed. 1995. *Haitian Frustrations: Dilemmas for U.S. Policy.* Washington, D.C.: Center for Strategic and International Studies.

Gagnon, V. P. 1994–1995. "Ethnic Nationalism and International Conflict: The Case of Serbia." *International Security* 19, no. 3 (Winter): 130–166.

Goodby, James. 1995. "The Logic of Peace: Priorities for Preventive Diplomacy in U.S.-European Relations." Washington, D.C.: United States Institute of Peace.

Kolstø, Pål, Andrei Edemsky, and Natalya Kalashnikova. 1993. "The Dniester Conflict: Between Irredentism and Separatism." *Europe-Asia Studies* 45: 973–1000.

Larus, Joel, ed. 1965. *From Collective Security to Preventive Diplomacy: Readings in International Organization and the Maintenance of Peace.* New York: John Wiley and Sons.

Lund, Michael. 1996. *Preventing Violent Conflicts: A Strategy for Preventive Diplomacy.* Washington, D.C.: United States Institute of Peace Press.

Lyons, Terrence, and Ahmed I. Samatar. 1995. *Somalia: State Collapse, Multilateral Intervention, and Strategies for Political Reconstruction.* Washington, D.C.: Brookings Institution.

McCrea, Barbara. 1995. "The Politics of Nationalism in Croatia and Slovakia." Notre Dame, Ind.: University of Notre Dame, Joan B. Kroc Institute for International Peace Studies.

Miall, Hugh. 1992. *The Peacemakers: Peaceful Settlement of Disputes since 1945.* New York: St. Martin's Press.

Munuera, Gabriel. 1994. *Preventing Armed Conflict in Europe: Lessons from Recent Experience.* Chaillot Paper 15/16. Paris: Institute for Security Studies, Western European Union.

Okolicsanyi, Karoly. 1992. "Slovak-Hungarian Tension: Bratislava Diverts the Danube." *RFE/RL Research Report* 1: 49–54.

Peck, Connie. 1993. *Preventive Diplomacy: A Perspective for the 1990s.* Occasional Papers Series No. 13 (February). New York: Ralph Bunche Institute on the United Nations.

Rogers, Katrina S. 1995. "Rivers of Discontent —Rivers of Peace: Environmental Cooperation and Integration Theory." *Policy Note* 20: 10–21.

Rostow, Eugene. 1992. *A Breakfast for Bonaparte: U.S. National Security Interests from the Heights of Abraham to the Nuclear Age.* Washington, D.C.: National Defense University Press.

Sahnoun, Mohamed. 1994. *Somalia: The Missed Opportunities.* Washington, D.C.: United States Institute of Peace Press.

Shabad, Goldie, Sharon A. Shible, and John F. Zurovchak. 1993. "When Push Comes to Shove: Simultaneous Transformations and the Breakup of the Czechoslovak State." Paper presented at the 1993 Annual Meeting of the American Political Science Association, Washington, D.C., September 2–5.

Shorr, David. 1994. "The Citizenship and Alien Law Controversies in Estonia and Latvia." Strengthening Democratic Institutions Project, John F. Kennedy School of Government. Boston, Mass.: Harvard University, April.

Simic, Predrag. 1992. "Civil War in Former Yugoslavia: From Local Conflict to European

Crisis." *The Southeastern European Yearbook.* Athens, Greece: ELIAMEP Institute.

United Nations. 1992. *Handbook on the Peaceful Settlement of Disputes between States.* New York: United Nations.

Woodward, Susan L. 1994. *Balkan Tragedy: Chaos and Dissolution after the Cold War.* Washington, D.C.: Brookings Institution.

Zametica, John. 1992. *The Yugoslav Conflict.* Adelphi Paper 270 (Summer). London: Brassey's.

Zartman, I. William. 1995. *Collapsed States: The Disintegration and Restoration of Legitimate Authority.* Boulder, Colo.: Lynne Rienner.

Zimmermann, Warren. 1995. "The Last Ambassador: A Memoir of the Collapse of Yugoslavia." *Foreign Affairs* 74: 2–20.

CASE STUDY

27

Lessons of Preventive Diplomacy in Yugoslavia

SAADIA TOUVAL

The horrors of the wars in the former Yugoslavia raise an inevitable question: Was this avoidable? The question is particularly intriguing because for many months prior to the outbreak of fighting in June 1991, the European Community (EC) and the United States exerted themselves to prevent the growing crisis from erupting into war.

Numerous factors combined to frustrate western efforts to prevent the war. Chief among these were the West's inability to project an image of a clear and unambiguous stance and its lack of leverage. The failure to prevent the war provides a cautionary lesson about the dilemmas and obstacles that the international community faces when trying to prevent civil wars.[1]

This chapter will open with a brief discussion of western attitudes toward Yugoslavia's internal problems during the Cold War. The next section will outline western policies aimed at preventing the war during the 1990–1991 crisis, explaining their

flaws. These arguments will be corroborated by a historical review demonstrating the ambiguities projected by western policies. Next, the surprising absence of mediation will be discussed and explained. The chapter will close with some reflections about the difficulties surrounding preventive diplomacy.

FOREVER PREVENTING, 1948–1990

Preventive action requires timely warning of a coming conflict. In the case of Yugoslavia, the world has always been aware of the nationalist tensions besetting that country. Western policies toward Yugoslavia have accordingly sought to prevent these tensions from threatening the country's stability. The West supported Tito's firm rule, which kept ethnic tensions under control. But it was common wisdom that after he passed from the scene, nationalist pressures might destabilize the country and might even lead to its disintegration and to civil war. Discussion of this issue was not confined to classified government reports; it was pursued publicly by both journalists and academic analysts.[2]

These predictions proved correct. Soon after Tito's death in 1980, nationalist tensions increased. These were reflected in violent clashes between the Albanians and Serbs in Kosovo, starting in 1981. Events there reverberated in Belgrade and fueled the flame of Serbian nationalism; nationalism became visible in other parts of the country as well. In Bosnia, starting in 1983, some Moslems began asserting an Islamic identity, which in the local context was equivalent to an ethnic identity. In Croatia, there were repeated trials of Croatian nationalists. In 1986, public campaigns by nationalists began in Slovenia. There were also reports of Croatian and Macedonian terrorist organizations operating within Yugoslavia. In the mid-1980s, observers of the Yugoslav scene became increasingly pessimistic about the chances of the country holding together. In the winter of 1989–1990, the approaching disintegration of Yugoslavia was the subject of two editorials in the *New York Times*.[3]

During the Cold War years, western interests in Yugoslavia were clearly defined. The West saw Yugoslavia as a de facto ally, helping to contain Soviet expansion in Europe, and it was thus important that the country's territorial integrity be preserved. Even Germany, which by 1991 had become the main supporter of the secessionist claims of Croatia and Slovenia, shared this view. Chancellor Helmut Kohl expressed this policy during a visit to Yugoslavia in the summer of 1985, when he proclaimed Germany's "great interest in maintaining the internal and external stability of Yugoslavia." He said, "Yugoslavia's stability is an important factor of . . . the political balance of Europe."[4] In view of these clearly defined interests, the Yugoslav government's sup-

pression of democracy and of nationalism did not evoke much criticism from western governments.

As the Cold War was winding down, Yugoslavia lost the geopolitical importance it had for the West. As the strategic lens through which Yugoslavia had been viewed during the Cold War was discarded, Yugoslavia came to be perceived as just another Communist country that needed to be encouraged to democratize and reform its economy.

Warren Zimmermann describes this policy shift in his memoir of his ambassadorship. He relates that when he assumed his post in early 1989, he and Lawrence Eagleburger, who had just been named deputy secretary of state and who was one of the foremost American experts on the Balkans, shared the view "that the traditional American approach to Yugoslavia no longer made sense." By now, "Yugoslavia had been surpassed by both Poland and Hungary in political and economic openness. In addition, human rights had become a major element of U.S. policy, and Yugoslavia's record on that issue was not good—particularly in the province of Kosovo, where an authoritarian Serbian regime was systematically depriving the Albanian majority of its basic civil liberties."[5]

The preservation of the country's unity and territorial integrity, which had been a matter of high priority within the Cold War strategic context, was now subordinate to democratization. Zimmermann was to deliver a new message upon his arrival in Yugoslavia: "I was to reassert the traditional mantra of U.S. support for Yugoslavia's unity, independence, and territorial integrity. But I would add that the United States could only support unity in the context of democracy; it would strongly oppose unity imposed or preserved by force."[6]

Democratization, the standard medicine believed capable of curing most of the world's ills, would also cure Yugoslavia's afflictions: It would redress human rights, alleviate ethnic tensions, and keep the country united. This, too, was seen as preventive action.

Unfortunately, when applied to Yugoslavia between 1989 and 1991, western policies promoting economic reforms, democratization, and respect for human rights did not bring about the expected results. Ironically, they may have even contributed to the aggravation of the country's problems. Western economic assistance to help alleviate the economic and social situation, which had been deteriorating since the early 1980s, became conditional upon reforms. The economic reforms desired by the West required returning powers held by the republics (placed there by Tito's 1974 constitution) to the central government. The change was resisted by Croatia and Slovenia, further stimulating already-strong Croat and Slovene aspirations for independence. While these issues were being debated, economic and social conditions continued to worsen, contributing to the malaise that facilitated the propagation of nationalist hatreds. Pressure on Serbia to cease its repression of Albanian nationalist aspirations was exploited by Serbia's president, Slobodan Milosevic, who sought to strengthen his hold on power by fanning the flames of Serbian nationalism. This, in turn, helped feed Croatian and Slovenian distrust of the Serbs. Democratization produced multiparty elections in the republics, and those politicians who campaigned on extreme nationalist platforms won the widest support.[7]

The election results and an increase in nationalistically inspired violence led observers to conclude by mid-1990 that the country was about to break apart. Experts disagreed, however, as to whether this would lead to war. Some hoped that negotiations among Yugoslav political leaders

about constitutional reforms might produce a formula for a peaceful transition to an "association of independent states." The leak to the media in November 1990 of the CIA report predicting a violent breakup was apparently a symptom of the debate within the U.S. bureaucracy.[8]

The timing was still unclear: When would the breakup take place, and when was war likely to erupt? Soon a date emerged. A referendum held in Slovenia on December 22, 1990, approved a proposal calling for independence within six months, unless agreement was reached prior to that date on turning Yugoslavia into a loose confederation of states. Yugoslavia watchers knew that unless something happened to interrupt the process, Slovenia and Croatia would proclaim their independence and a civil war was likely to erupt at the end of June 1991. Since Western policies aimed at alleviating the country's problems were not producing the expected result, they obviously needed to be adjusted. Instead of pursuing policies aimed at remedying the country's ills over the long term, it became necessary to address the more immediate danger of war.

There is, of course, no recipe that can assure the success of preventive diplomacy. The avoidance of war depends first and foremost on the disputants. The challenge facing the international community is to influence the disputants' behavior, deflecting them from a course that is bound to lead to a violent collision. The intervenors obviously failed to persuade any of the key Yugoslav actors to do so. The question is, why was their persuasion unsuccessful?

FLAWED POLICIES

The most common explanation for the failure is the familiar charge of "too little, too late." This diagnosis, however, is flawed. It implies that the policy pursued was basically sound, only insufficient, and that earlier application of this policy would have prevented the war. However, as I shall show, the problem was the policy and, on a deeper level, the inability of the international community to develop a clear purpose and project credibility.

The approach that emerged in the Fall of 1990 had two components. One was a continuation of the policy adopted in 1989, seeking to alleviate ethnic tensions by encouraging democratization, respect for human rights, and economic reform. Added to this was a strategy of economic deterrence aimed at dissuading the principal Yugoslav actors from taking steps that might ignite a war: dissuading the Croat and Slovene leaders from proclaiming independence and dissuading the federal government and the military from enforcing unity.

Successful deterrence and dissuasion require both the projection of clear goals and credible leverage. But instead of clarity, the West signaled ambiguity, leading the Yugoslav actors to varying interpretations of western attitudes. The ambiguity stemmed from the West's definition of goals in terms of broad values, some of which were contradictory in the context of time and place. The main difficulty was inherent in the simultaneous advocacy of both unity and democracy. Within the context of Yugoslavia in 1990–1991, these two objectives were contradictory, undercutting each other. Attempts to preserve unity were accompanied by repression of nationalist and separatist tendencies and by violations of human rights. Democratization opened the way to the formation of nationalist parties and to the victory in freely held elections in Slovenia and Croatia of leaders calling for the secession of these two republics from Yugoslavia. Thus, attempts to preserve unity were antidemocratic, and the promotion of democracy encouraged disintegration. The contradiction inherent in western goals gave them an air of ambiguity, making it difficult

for Yugoslav leaders to predict how the West might react to their moves.

To induce the Yugoslav parties to follow its advice, the European Community, and to some extent the United States as well, offered economic rewards and punishments. If unity were preserved, democracy extended, human rights respected, and economic reforms implemented, then Yugoslavia would receive financial assistance and trading concessions. But if the country were to disintegrate and if it fell short of meeting the other conditions, then some or all of these benefits would be withheld.

Thus the community committed itself between December 1990 and May 1991 to providing Yugoslavia a total of 3.6 billion ECU (over U.S.$4.5 billion) through a variety of programs. Furthermore, the community promised to open negotiations about an association agreement, providing opportunities for expanding trade and access to further economic benefits if Yugoslavia resolved its internal disagreements and remained a single state. Yugoslavia was warned that these benefits would not be available and that current assistance would be curtailed if Croatia and Slovenia seceded through unilateral acts breaking the country apart or if the suppression of nationalist sentiments were pursued by force and were accompanied by violations of human rights.

The obvious reason the community chose to bolster its admonitions with economic inducements was that these were the only instruments of leverage available to the community at that time. It is also possible that to some extent community officials were misled by the economic justifications that Croat and Slovene leaders cited in support of their quest for independence, claiming that their countries wished to rid themselves of the economic exploitation by Serbia and free-riding southern republics and wished to build market economies to facilitate their admission into the European Community.

Moreover, the main item on the agenda in western dealings with Yugoslavia during the previous few years had been the country's economic problems.

Economic statecraft had the additional advantage of not infringing upon Yugoslavia's sovereignty. Unlike mediation and other direct involvement in domestic bargaining between disputants, economic inducements were a weapon that could be fired from a distance, without blatantly violating the prohibition against interference in the internal affairs of states. Respect for Yugoslavia's sovereignty was important not only for reasons of principle—the European Community wishing to uphold a norm that was a cornerstone of international order—but also for the pragmatic reason of avoiding action that might hasten the breakup. Unfortunately, it was an inappropriate strategy. It may even have been counterproductive to continue the earlier policy of delaying economic assistance, thus contributing to the social tensions that were exploited by the extreme nationalists.

Furthermore, the strategy lacked credibility. The ambiguity of western statements and behavior cast doubt on the credibility of both promises and threats. Moreover, the various Yugoslav parties were aware of the divisions among the EC members on the question of Yugoslavia (discussed below). The Croats and Slovenes were more inclined to listen to their sympathizers, who promised support if they seceded from Yugoslavia, than to those who threatened them with punishment. Moreover, knowing the complexity of intergovernmental decision making, they doubted the ability of the community to deliver on its promises of aid if Yugoslavia stayed united.[9]

Finally, economic punishments (or rewards) were not well attuned to the psychology of the nationalist leaders in the republics, who now were the principal actors in the conflict. Their primary preoccupation at the time was with their nations' physical security and the psychological need to assert their national identity, rather than with economic prosperity. The gap between the intervenors' mind frame and that of the Yugoslavs was reflected in European Commission President Jacques Delors' comments about his meetings in Yugoslavia, expressing disappointment that the presidents of the republics with whom he and Jacques Santer, Luxembourg prime minister and president of the European Council, had met concentrated on their ethnic disputes, not attaching enough importance to economic problems.[10] In these circumstances, placing one's hopes in the potency of economic influence was bound to lead to disappointing results.

AMBIGUITIES

It is generally assumed that the West supported the preservation of a unified Yugoslavia until the summer of 1991. This view rests upon a somewhat narrow and literal interpretation of what was said, not taking into account the nuances: how statements were qualified, what was implied, and how the wording and phrases evolved over time. Nor does this interpretation consider the information available to the contending Yugoslav parties about the attitudes of political elites and the debates in the West about the policies it ought to follow. When these additional aspects of the western messages are taken into consideration, western policies appear far more equivocal. The equivocations undermined the credibility of western positions, as well as of the promises and threats aimed at influencing the behavior of the Yugoslav parties. The uncertainties that western policies created led each of the contending Yugoslav parties to believe that its actions would not be punished, but rather, that after a brief interval of time, they would be accepted and perhaps supported by the western governments.

American Ambiguities

Two principal considerations helped to shape the American response to the growing crisis in Yugoslavia. One was the assessment that events in Yugoslavia no longer affected vital American interests. Second, senior U.S. officials—most notably Lawrence Eagleburger, the deputy secretary of state, and Brent Scowcroft, the president's adviser on national security—doubted America's ability to effectively influence the course of internal developments there. They may also have expected active engagement in the Yugoslav crisis to require military involvement, which public opinion would be unlikely to support.[11]

American reluctance to act was made easier by the West Europeans' claim that the European Community ought to take care of the Yugoslav problem. This seemed logical in view of the economic leverage that was believed to be available to the community: Over 40 percent of Yugoslavia's trade was with the community, and less than 5 percent with the United States.[12]

Although reluctant to become engaged in the problem, the United States could not detach itself completely from it. As a result, its diplomacy alternated between passivity and activism. When active, it was marked by pontification on fundamental values and principles, accompanied by equivocations concerning the immediate issues on the agenda.

The passive disposition was reflected in the absence of high-level contacts between senior American and Yugoslav officials for much of 1990 and until June 1991, when Secretary of State James Baker visited Belgrade one week prior to the date announced by Croatia and Slovenia for their independence to take effect. (The only prior high-level contact was Baker's meeting with Foreign Minister Budimir Loncar at the Conference on Security and Cooperation in

Europe [CSCE] meeting in Paris in November 1990, at which the main topic was the American plea for Yugoslav help in enlisting support among nonaligned states for its policy on the Gulf, not Yugoslavia's internal crisis.) In 1990, when Prime Minister Ante Markovic wanted to visit Washington for talks, he was discouraged from coming, and the administration did not issue the desired invitation.[13]

Moreover, American diplomats in Yugoslavia largely avoided contacts with the Serb, Croat, and Slovene nationalist leaders whose influence was growing daily. Not that the rising nationalist leaders were overlooked; their activities were a cause of increasing concern, and the Embassy maintained contact with Albanian leaders in Kosovo. But for a variety of reasons, contacts with Serb, Croat, and Slovene nationalist leaders were few. Relations with the Serb leader Slobodan Milosevic were strained, because of public American criticism of the repression of Albanians in Kosovo, the virulent nationalist rhetoric in which he engaged, and Milosevic's anger at the Embassy's close relations with the liberal democratic opponents of his policy. As a result, the U.S. ambassador and the Serb leader did not meet for months. The Croat and Slovene nationalist leaders advocating secession were also shunned because of the extreme nature of their rhetoric and perhaps because such contacts could have added to their stature. As a result, Zimmermann met Franjo Tudjman for the first time only in May 1990, on the morning of Tudjman's victory in the Croatian elections. Furthermore, American diplomatic representatives did not maintain any contacts with Serb separatist leaders in Croatia.[14]

This passivity was punctuated by spurts of activism stimulated by a variety of factors. One was congressional criticism of Serb policies in Kosovo; led by Senator Robert Dole, Congress took a much stronger stance on this issue than the administration, culminating in a highly publicized visit by a congressional delegation to the troubled region in August 1990. Other stimulants for activity were events in Yugoslavia: outbreaks of violence, calls for military intervention against separatism, and a political confrontation paralyzing the presidency of the republic.

The U.S. intent to promote democratization in Yugoslavia was demonstrated by its repeated criticisms of repression in Kosovo and by imposition of economic sanctions in an attempt to influence Yugoslav policies on this issue. In November 1990 Congress passed the Nickles Amendment to the foreign aid bill, barring U.S. loans and credits to Yugoslavia, unless directed to a constituent republic "which has held fair and free elections and which is not engaged in systematic abuse of human rights." The sanctions were to take effect in six months, unless the president decided that aid needed to be continued.[15]

Parallel to pressures for democratization, the Bush administration continued to express its support for preserving Yugoslavia's unity. In February 1991, a joint Croat-Slovene announcement that both republics intended to secede unless Yugoslavia became a "community of sovereign republics" (which was a breakup by another name) prompted the administration to reiterate its continued support for unity.[16]

Support for unity was hedged, however, by warnings against enforcing it. On at least two occasions, January 25 and March 13, the United States publicly cautioned the Yugoslav federal authorities not to use military force against those wishing to secede.[17]

While these positions could logically be reconciled, they were perceived as equivocal. The feeling that the United States was uncertain about its policy was further strengthened by the mixed impressions obtained by Croat and Slovene representa-

tatives who came to the United States to lobby for their cause. While executive branch officials urged upon them the need to preserve Yugoslavia's unity, Senator Dole and members of Congress expressed sympathy for their desire to break away from Yugoslavia and become independent.

On May 6, the administration announced that because of continued abuse of human rights, it was imposing the punishment prescribed by the Nickles amendment and cutting off financial assistance to Yugoslavia. Recognizing the futility of sanctions against the federal government—and their counterproductivity, as Milosevic used them to rally Serbian nationalism—the administration soon reversed itself. On May 20, 1991, in a phone call to Markovic, President Bush informed him that aid would be resumed and that the United States continued to support the existence of a unified Yugoslav state.

The resumption of aid was accompanied by a statement outlining American policy. It said that the policy was "based on support for the interrelated objectives of democracy, dialogue, human rights, market reform, and unity." It further said that the United States would oppose the "use of force or intimidation to settle political differences, change external or internal borders, . . . or impose a nondemocratic unity."[18] This was an admirably balanced statement, reflecting American values. But it provided little indication as to what the United States might do in the face of the rapidly escalating crisis.

With the deadline announced by Croatia and Slovenia for their independence approaching, the United States embarked on a last-minute effort to prevent the war. In the middle of June, David Gompert, the director of European affairs at the National Security Council, went to Belgrade. He was followed on June 21, four days before the Croatian and Slovenian independence was scheduled to take effect, by Secretary of State James Baker. This was the first high-level meeting between American and Yugoslav officials in almost two years. The secretary came directly from the CSCE meeting in Berlin where Yugoslavia was discussed. Baker held nine meetings during his one-day visit—with the federal prime minister and foreign minister, the presidents of the six republics, an Albanian leader from Kosovo, and concluding his visit with another meeting with the prime minister. The meetings with the republics' leaders were occasions at which the visitor and the host lectured each other, anxious to recite their points before their time expired.

Aware that the war was imminent, Baker hoped to put it off by trying to persuade the Slovene leader Milan Kucan to postpone proclaiming Slovenia's independence. It was expected that if Slovenia delayed taking this step, Croatia would follow suit, thus allowing more time for the search for a peaceful settlement. Baker thought that Kucan acceded to this request and was reportedly surprised and disappointed when Kucan denied that he had made such a promise.[19]

It has been claimed that Milosevic misinterpreted Baker's reference to unity and democracy as a "green light" to use force to prevent Slovenia and Croatia from seceding.[20] This seems doubtful, because Baker's visit took place against the backdrop of a sharply deteriorated Serbian-American relationship, with the United States rebuking the Serb leadership for violating human rights in Kosovo and charging that Serbia was the main obstacle for a peaceful resolution of the crisis. Baker described his encounter with Milosevic as "the most contentious meeting of the day." Moreover, Baker conveyed a warning to the military leadership not to use force. He also warned Markovic: "If you force us to choose between unity and democracy, we will always choose democracy."[21]

The visit did not help clarify American policies. The reassertion of American opposition to both secession and the enforcement of unity sounded like an equivocation, not a statement of policy. It contributed to the sense that western attitudes toward events in Yugoslavia remained highly ambiguous. It is not surprising that such equivocations were unable to impress the Yugoslav parties of the need to change their policies and avoid a violent confrontation.

European Ambiguities

Western European states were more motivated to act to prevent the war than the United States. Some, like Germany and Italy, were close geographically and thus saw that their security and well-being were likely to be affected by the fighting and the inevitable outpouring of refugees. They, and other members of the European Community, were inspired to act in the hope that joint action through the European Community would provide an impetus to the launching of the new European institutions, including its common foreign and security policy. But they were also aware of the differences in their attitudes to the problem, and each government expected to use the common institutions to restrain the others from pursuing what it regarded as wrongheaded policies. Britain and France wanted to constrain Germany, partly because they were apprehensive about the foreign policy that a reunified Germany might pursue, but also because they perceived Germany's involvement in Yugoslavia as tactless, as the perfect example of the bull in the china shop. Germany, on the other hand, considered Britain and France remote and lacking a sufficient understanding of Balkan nationalist movements.

Their divergent attitudes stemmed largely from cultural-historic preconceptions existing in their respective societies. German and Austrian officials were socialized in a culture that put much of the blame for

Balkan instability during the past 100 years —as well as for World War I and its disastrous consequences for the Austrian and German empires—on Serb nationalism. The establishment of Yugoslavia in 1918 is closely associated with the unjust peace settlements imposed on Austria and Germany at the end of that war. Italian history, too, was not favorable toward the establishment of Yugoslavia. Territorial conflicts with Yugoslavia after both world wars had contributed to an unfavorable image of that country in Italian eyes.

These historical-cultural preconceptions were reinforced by the political and ideological climate prevailing at the time (1989–1991). Engrossed with the process of reunification, which they perceived as an act of self-determination, some German elites accepted the Croat and Slovene argument that these two nations' desire to secede from Yugoslavia was also an act of self-determination, no less justified than the unification of the two German states. Support for Slovene and Croat aspirations was particularly strong among sections of the Catholic public and in parts of the media, especially the *Frankfurter Allgemeine Zeitung.* Support was also strong among left-leaning circles, critical of human rights violations committed by Serbian authorities in Kosovo. The presence of a large number of Croats among "guest laborers" *(gastarbeiter)* in Germany helped to build sympathy for Croat national aspirations.[22]

In Britain and France, attitudes were very different, favoring the preservation of Yugoslavia. Indicative of the French attitude was the official government statement welcoming Prime Minister Markovic to Paris, on May 23, 1991. It was laced with a pro-unity historical allusion, tracing the friendship between the two nations to "the Napoleonic era and the creation of the Illyrian provinces"—suggesting perhaps a link between the legacy of the French administration and nineteenth-century expressions of

South Slav solidarity known as the "Illyrian Movement." The statement further stated that it is up to the Yugoslavs alone, through a process of a political dialogue "shielded from internal provocations and external interventions, to determine the future of their state. It is this unitary state . . . that Europe awaits as a partner."[23] The reference to "external interventions," though ambiguous, was assumed to be directed at German and Austrian supporters of Croat and Slovene self-determination.

Wishing to present a common stance, the European states developed policies that reflected a compromise between their initial attitudes. As a result, the policy statements issued by the Council of Ministers and the European Commission were ambiguous. The ambiguity was reinforced by discrepancies between the collective European policies emanating from the European institutions and the policies of individual states conveyed in bilateral contacts.

A declaration by the European Community–Yugoslavia Cooperation Council, meeting in Brussels on December 18, 1990, welcomed Yugoslavia's progress toward a pluralist, parliamentary democracy and toward a market economy. It expressed the wish that these objectives be pursued with "full respect for human rights and the preservation of the unity and territorial integrity of Yugoslavia."[24] On February 4, 1991, the foreign ministers called on Yugoslav authorities to maintain the unity and territorial integrity of the country and to avoid the use of force. They also expressed the hope that the discussions within the country would lead to a "new Yugoslavia on the bases of freedom and democracy."[25]

Doubts about the community's support for the unity of Yugoslavia were raised ten days later, however, when a meeting took place between the Slovene Prime Minister Alojz Peterle and European Commissioner Abel Matutes.[26] These doubts were deepened when the European Parliament, reflecting political opinion in the member-states, adopted a resolution on March 13 saying "that the constituent republics and autonomous provinces of Yugoslavia must have the right freely to determine their own future."[27]

A visit to Belgrade on April 4 by the Troika representing the presidency of the European Council—Luxembourg's Foreign Minister Jacques Poos, Italian Foreign Minister Gianni De Michelis, and Dutch Foreign Minister Hans van den Broek—tried to allay these doubts and to reaffirm the European Community's support for the preservation of the country's unity. The Troika made its point by meeting only with federal office holders and refraining from direct contact with leaders of the republics.[28] Throughout this period, the twin conditions of the maintenance of Yugoslavia's unity and democratic reform were emphasized as requirements for joining the European integration process.

In May, the community's position was modified. When the current president of the European Council, Luxembourg Prime Minister Jacques Santer, and the president of the European Commission, Jacques Delors, visited Belgrade, they met not only with the federal officials, but also with the presidents of the republics. Moreover, the community no longer explicitly listed the preservation of Yugoslavia's unity among the conditions for opening negotiations on association, though this condition could be seen as implicit in a longer and more detailed list of conditions that was now put forth: respect for the constitution, respect for human rights and minorities, negotiations for new structures, and continued economic reforms. Similar conditions were reiterated in early June at a meeting of the European Community's foreign ministers in Dresden, Germany, and in a letter from Santer to Markovic.[29]

Only in May, as tensions and violent incidents in Yugoslavia increased and as the military authorities threatened to intervene against the secessionists, did the community emphatically express its opposition to the use of force. Balancing its opposition to enforced unity, the community also stated its opposition to secession by unilateral acts, reiterating its support for a mutually agreed solution to the crisis. A final attempt to deter secession by unilateral acts was made on June 23, two days before Croatia and Slovenia proclaimed their independence, with the community's foreign ministers agreeing "not to acknowledge" unilateral declarations of independence and affirming that they would refuse "any contact" with the secessionists. The current chairman of the European Council qualified these statements by adding that "the Twelve do not state that they will never recognize a Yugoslavian Republic wanting to leave the federation but that this decision [to secede] 'must be the result of negotiation and internal agreement.'"[30]

The ambiguities emanating from the collective European institutions were deepened by contradictory signals sent from member states. As already mentioned, important voices in Germany supported Slovene and Croat aspirations for secession and independence. The perception of German support for Croat and Slovene claims was reinforced by a February letter from Kohl to Markovic expressing concern about the crisis; Kohl called for political dialogue and respect for human rights, but made no mention of the need to preserve Yugoslavia's unity.[31] In March, Slovenia's President Milan Kucan held talks in Bonn with German Foreign Minister Hans Dietrich Genscher.[32] In May, the chairman of Germany's Social Democratic Party, Norbert Gansell, proposed that the party call on the European Community to change its policy, suggesting support for Croatian and

Slovene independence and calling on Croatia to grant autonomy to the Serbian minority.[33] Support was also expressed by the Christian Socialist Union party's foreign affairs committee in Munich on June 1. The Croats were also encouraged by the warm reception accorded at the end of May in Italy to visiting President Tudjman by the Italian president and prime minister, as well as by the pope.[34] The strongest support for the opposite view (favoring the preservation of Yugoslav unity) aimed at quashing Croat and Slovene hopes of early association with the community once they became independent, came from French Prime Minister Edith Cresson. Her welcoming remarks to Markovic on May 23, already cited, proclaimed that "Yugoslavia cannot be part of Europe unless she remains united."[35]

THE OMISSION OF MEDIATION

It might occasion some surprise that the western intervenors did not try to mediate among the Yugoslav parties. An opportunity to mediate presented itself in the negotiations about constitutional reform conducted among the republics' leaders. But the western governments held back from any significant involvement in these talks, and, indeed, on several occasions the community rejected responsibility for intervening in the constitutional debate or mediating in the conflict. Only on June 23, 1991, two days before Croatia and Slovenia proclaimed their independence, did the community offer to help the federal government and the republics to draw up a new constitution.[36]

The West avoided mediation because such involvement would have been interpreted by the parties as implicit acceptance of the Croatian and Slovenian republics' desire to be treated as sovereign states, equal in status to the federal government of Yugoslavia. Croat and Slovene leaders had in fact indicated their interest in mediation by the European Community, and one of their principal supporters, Austrian Foreign Minister Alois Mock, advocated it. But the federal government, the Serb leadership, and the military opposed it.[37]

In these circumstances, an attempt to mediate between the parties would have exposed the European Community to criticism that it was violating the normative and legal injunction against interference in the internal affairs of a sovereign state. To be sure, the community had already been engaged for months in efforts to influence the internal politics of Yugoslavia; but it was doing so indirectly, from a distance. Mediation would have required an intensive involvement in the political maneuvering inside the country. The European Community and the United States were reluctant to become involved in this way. Mediation would have drawn the intervenors into a much deeper participation in Yugoslavia's internal politics, leading them into commitments that they were not prepared to assume.

It is, nevertheless, interesting to speculate whether mediation could have succeeded in preventing the war. This seems unlikely. Mediation can be pursued in different styles. A nonintrusive mediation, with the mediator not expressing a preference for any particular solution, and only insisting that the conflict be resolved peacefully through a mutually acceptable agreement, would have been perceived as another indication of western equivocation. It would have indicated the West's indifference to the substantive content of the solution that finally emerged, thus encouraging the Yugoslav parties to stick to their goals, even at the risk of a war.

An attempt to engage in a different style of mediation, "with muscle," also had little chance of success. This approach would have required the mediator to propose a formula for a settlement and induce the parties to accept it through threats and promises. The main obstacle to success would have been lack of credibility. It would have been difficult to persuade the Yugoslav parties that the mediator was both able and willing to fulfill promises and inflict punishment. In view of the budgetary difficulties in the United States, the reluctance to expose troops to danger as demonstrated in the debate about sending troops to the Persian Gulf, and the pursuit of the contradictory policies of supporting both unity and democracy simultaneously, American attempts to exercise leverage would not have appeared credible. European promises and threats would have been even less so. The community lacked a military instrument with which to threaten punishment. Awareness of the community's difficulty in agreeing on major expenditures for economic assistance, coupled with Croat and Slovene expectation that their sympathizers would not allow the European Community to punish them, would have undermined any claim that the community possessed leverage. The lack of credibility that impeded the community's efforts to deter and dissuade the Yugoslav parties from pursuing their confrontational course would have undermined its attempt to apply leverage in mediation as well.

LESSONS

The unsuccessful efforts to prevent the war in Yugoslavia point to several lessons for those seeking to engage in preventive diplomacy.

First, the international community must rank its priorities. As the example of Yugoslavia demonstrates, the focus on the long-term goal of democratization clashed with the short-term goal of preventing ethnic tensions from boiling over. If one is trying to prevent an imminent war, then concentrating on this immediate goal must take precedence over the pursuit of long-term reforms.

Second, intervenors must avoid equivocations and should beware not to create an air of ambiguity about their goals. They are more likely to avoid ambiguity if they refrain from reciting broad values and instead define in concrete terms what they expect from the disputants. This is easier said than done, especially when the preventive efforts are a collective, multilateral endeavor. While sharing the broadly defined objective of preventing a war, each participating state is likely to view the issues somewhat differently; it is easier to develop a common platform by asserting generally accepted norms and principles than it is to agree on specifics. The unfortunate consequence of such a course is equivocation, undermining the intervenors' efforts to influence the disputants' behavior.

Another lesson is that trying to prevent an ethnic conflict through a strategy of economic inducements is unlikely to be effective. While there are precedents of the successful application of economic sticks and carrots to modify governmental policies, it is doubtful that they can influence the behavior of loosely controlled mass movements. This strategy seems to stem from a belief common to both marxism and capitalism, that political behavior is universally determined by people's desire for material gains. But people engulfed in ethnic conflict are dominated by other feelings: fears for their physical safety and security that may be endangered on account of their belonging to a certain ethnic group, the desire for national autonomy—not to be subject to rule by another nation, and an ambition to rectify real or imaginary wrongs inflicted upon their nation in recent history. The economic rewards and punishments proffered by the international community are irrelevant to such concerns and can have little effect, if any, on the calculations and behavior of the multiple parties colliding in such situations.

IMPEDIMENTS TO PREVENTIVE DIPLOMACY

When we probe beyond these lessons, more fundamental impediments to preventive diplomacy become apparent.

One concerns timing. It is believed that wars are easier to prevent than to stop once they have started. Prevention is assumed to be easier, because in the early stages of a conflict the disputants have not yet invested their resources and reputations in the struggle, and they are therefore likely to be less committed to pursuing their goal through confrontation. It is doubtful, however, that this logic applies to conflicts that are inspired by nationalism. Once nationalist ideologies have taken hold, the early stages have already been passed. Nationalist leaders and their aroused followers are already firmly committed to their goals, and it is much more difficult to persuade them to modify their objectives.

In fact, preventive diplomacy aimed at preventing ethnic conflict is likely to be launched at a highly inauspicious moment —after the parties have committed themselves to their goals, but before they have reached a hurting stalemate that might dispose them to rethink their policies and become amenable to outside influence. Worse than that, intervention tends to be launched at a moment when each party has high expectations that it will prevail. It occurs at a moment when each is convinced of the justice of its cause, believing its goals to be consistent with international norms and with the interests of some of the major powers, which sooner or later will come to its assistance.

When we try to uncover the reasons western policies projected an image of equivocation and lack of credibility in the case of Yugoslavia, additional fundamental impediments to preventive diplomacy become apparent. These impediments stem from the inability of governments pursuing preventive diplomacy to demonstrate that their citizens are willing to risk their lives and fortunes in pursuit of such a policy.

It will probably only be on rare occasions that political leaders will feel strongly enough about an impending war in another country to call on their people to sacrifice for the sake of preventing a war. The difficulty of doing so is inherent in the nature of the situation. Citizens are more likely to accept sacrifices when events pose a direct threat to their own society. But efforts to thwart such dangers are not called preventive diplomacy; they address national defense. Preventive diplomacy addresses situations that pose no threat to national security, or only a remote and indirect one. It addresses situations where *other* people *may* become threatened by war. It is usually difficult, if not impossible, for nations to commit themselves to making all the necessary sacrifices to prevent such a war from erupting. But without a credible commitment, their diplomacy may be to no avail.

This is not to argue that preventive efforts will never be effective. There are situations when successful prevention does not require much of a commitment. But in many cases, success will depend on the intervenors demonstrating a strong commitment to the cause. In the absence of such a commitment, preventive diplomacy may not be able to fulfill the hopes placed in it.

NOTES

1. On the need for preventive diplomacy see Boutros Boutros-Ghali, *Agenda for Peace* (New York: United Nations, 1992); and Michael S. Lund, *Preventing Violent Conflicts: A Strategy for Preventive Diplomacy* (Washington, D.C.: United States Institute of Peace Press, 1996). For a critique, see Stephen John Stedman, "Alchemy for a New World Order: Overselling 'Preventive Diplomacy,'" *Foreign Affairs* 74, no. 3 (May–June 1995): 14–20.

2. To cite only two examples of this discussion: Alvin Rabushka and Kenneth A. Shepsle, *Politics in Plural Societies* (Columbus, Ohio: Charles E. Merill, 1972), pp. 91, 183–187, 202, 205–206; and Pedro Ramet, "Yugoslavia and the Threat of Internal and External Discontents," *Orbis* 28, no. 1 (Spring 1984): 103–121, especially pp. 114, 118.

3. On December 29, 1989, and January 31, 1990.

4. Quoted in Sabrina Petra Ramet, "Yugoslavia and the Two Germanys," in *The Germans and Their Neighbors*, ed. Dirk Verheyen and Christian Søe (Boulder, Colo.: Westview Press, 1993), p. 325.

5. Warren Zimmermann, "The Last Ambassador," *Foreign Affairs* 74, no. 2 (March–April 1995): 2.

6. Ibid., p. 3.

7. For a detailed analysis of this process, see Susan L. Woodward, *Balkan Tragedy* (Washington, D.C.: Brookings Institution, 1995), especially chaps. 3, 4, and 5.

8. *New York Times,* November 28, 1990.

9. This is the view of Stipe Mesic, the Croat representative whose election to the rotating office of president of Yugoslavia was blocked by Serbia, in his *Kako Smo Srusili Jugoslaviju* (How We Brought Down Yugoslavia) (Zagreb: Globus, 1992), pp. 32–33.

10. *Europe,* June 5, 1991, p. 4.

11. David Gompert, "How to Defeat Serbia," *Foreign Affairs* 73, no. 4 (July–August 1994): 32–35; and Don Oberdorfer, "A Bloody Failure in the Balkans," *Washington Post,* February 8, 1993.

12. Data for 1990 based on the table "Principal Trading Partners," *The Europa World Yearbook,* vol. II (London: Europa Publications, 1994), p. 3355.

13. Foreign Broadcast Information Service (FBIS), East Europe, December 12, 1990.

14. For American perceptions of Yugoslavia at the time, see Gompert, "How to Defeat Serbia," pp. 33–35; and Zimmermann, "The Last Ambassador," pp. 3–11.

15. *New York Times,* November 28, 1990. See also Jery Laber and Kenneth Anderson, "Why Keep Yugoslavia One Country?" *New York Times,* November 10, 1990, p. 23.

16. FBIS, East Europe, February 13, 1991.

17. Woodward, *Balkan Tragedy,* p. 157 and p. 458, n. 27.

18. "United States Policy Toward Yugoslavia," statement released by State Department spokesperson Margaret Tutwiler, May 24, 1991. *Dispatch,* June 3, 1991, pp. 395–396.

19. Zimmermann, "The Last Ambassador," pp. 11–12; and Gompert, "How to Defeat Serbia," p. 34.

20. John Newhouse, "The Diplomatic Round," *New Yorker,* August 24, 1992, p. 62.

21. James A. Baker III, with Thomas M. DeFrank, *The Politics of Diplomacy* (New York: G. P. Putnam's Sons, 1995), pp. 481, 482. See also Zimmermann, "The Last Ambassador," pp. 11–12; and Mesic, *Kako Smo Srusili Jugoslaviju,* pp. 34–39.

22. Hans Stark, "Dissonances franco-allemandes sur fond de guerre serbo-croate," *Politique étrangère,* no. 2 (1992): pp. 340–341; and Woodward, *Balkan Tragedy,* pp. 148–149, 153.

23. Quoted in Stark, "Dissonances franco-allemandes," pp. 339–340.

24. EC-Yugoslavia Cooperation Council, press release, Brussels, December 18, 1990.

25. *Europe,* February 6, 1991, pp. 4–5.

26. *Europe,* February 16, 1991, pp. 7–8.

27. Quoted by James Gow, "Deconstructing Yugoslavia," *Survival* 33, no. 4 (July–August 1991): 308. For a subsequent statement by the European Parliament reiterating support for Croat and Slovene aspirations for independence, see *Europe,* May 17, 1991.

28. *Europe,* March 28, 1991, p. 5; and April 6, 1991, p. 10.

29. *Europe,* March 8, 1991, pp. 7–8; March 28, 1991, p. 5; April 6, 1991, p. 10; May 31, 1991, p. 3; June 1, 1991, p. 7; June 5, 1991, p. 4; and June 12, 1991, p. 5.

30. *Europe,* June 24/25, 1991, pp. 4–5. See also May 11, 1991.

31. *Europe,* February 14, 1991, p. 4.

32. Woodward, *Balkan Tragedy,* p. 159.

33. *Archiv der Gegenwart* 61, no. 14 (May 1991): 35795–35796.

34. Mesic, *Kako Smo Srusili Jugoslaviju,* pp. 18, 40.

35. Quoted by Pia Christina Wood, "European Political Cooperation: Lessons from the Gulf War and Yugoslavia," in *The State of the European Community,* vol. 2, ed. Alan W. Cafruny and Glenda G. Rosenthal (Boulder, Colo.: Lynne Rienner, 1993), p. 233.

36. The disclaimers are reported in *Europe,* May 13/14, 1991, p. 3; and June 1, 1991, p. 7. For the offer to help in constitutional talks, June 24/25, 1991, p. 4.

37. Gow, "Deconstructing Yugoslavia," p. 304; *Europe,* May 6/7, 1991; and interview, Geneva, May 13–14, 1994.

28

Prenegotiation and Circum-negotiation

Arenas of the Peace Process

HAROLD H. SAUNDERS

Crucial as it is, negotiation around the table is only a later part of a larger political process in which conflicts are resolved by peaceful means. That larger political process is the peace process—a mixture of politics, diplomacy, changing relationships, negotiation, mediation, and dialogue in both official and unofficial arenas. Work apart from negotiation is a significant part of that process because it deals with people, problems, and moments that are not yet ready for formal mediation and negotiation. But that work, like every other act of peacemaking and peace building, must be understood as an intertwined part of an overall peace process.

In many cases, the process in which conflicting groups first contact one another, then talk, and eventually commit to an agreed settlement is even more complicated, time consuming, and difficult than reaching agreement in negotiations. Those who try to resolve conflict peacefully need to consider the context of a larger political process that deals with the obstacles to negotiation as well as the hurdles in negotiation. We call that larger context the peace process, and only in that setting do we understand the fullest meaning of what has been called prenegotiation.[1]

Unless we enlarge our conceptual framework to understand why parties to a conflict will not talk and what might enable them to engage in dialogue, we are not constructing a theory of negotiation or of peacemaking that will give negotiation the greatest possibility of success. We must deal with questions such as these:

- What causes and enables individuals to conclude that they have "had enough"—that a situation hurts their interests so badly that they cannot let it continue?

- Why and how do they arrive at the conclusion that some kind of joint effort with other involved parties is both necessary and possible?

419

- Why is the relationship conflictual?
- What are the obstacles to change and the junctures at which the dynamics of the relationship might be changed?
- Why and how might parties to a conflict reach out to the other side?
- What are the possible ways of seeking a joint solution?

The responses to these questions and others like them shape the tasks that have been called prenegotiation. Approaches to these tasks may call on some of the skills of mediation and negotiation, but they also require the insights and the art of those who think deeply about why human beings fear, hate, kill, and change their relationships. These approaches draw on the varied capacities of the psychoanalyst, the psychologist, the politician, the lawyer, the teacher, the person of God, and the compassionate human being.

This work is done in the political arena, not in the negotiating room or its antechambers. Its challenge in today's world is that no single academic or professional discipline is designed to educate the whole human being to participate in this whole political process. The thinking required will not come from combining existing disciplines; it will emerge only from large new perspectives. It will be "supradisciplinary." The peace process as a human process for peacemaking and peace building may offer such a perspective.

The concept of a full peace process— with the work apart from negotiation woven continuously through its fabric—provides the largest possible framework both for creating opportunities to address these questions and for moving toward peace. Until we work within that large a conceptual context, we will not have adequate theories of conflict prevention, management, resolution, mediation, and negotiation. We need a concept large enough to allow us to draw on the broadest reservoirs of resources and insights from which to choose the most appropriate instrument for a particular problem.

At some moments in that process, participants may decide that negotiation provides a workable framework for their situation; at others, they may decide that a problem is too dangerous to ignore but is not ready for formal approaches. Many of today's deep-rooted human conflicts are not ready for formal mediation or negotiation. Human beings do not negotiate about their identities, fears, suspicions, anger, historic grievances, security, dignity, honor, justice, rejection, or acceptance.

Peace requires a process of building constructive relationships in a civil society— not just negotiating, signing, and ratifying a formal agreement, central as this may be in defining new relationships between groups or countries. That will increasingly be true of conflicts in the twenty-first century. The peace process provides a conceptual context within which to combine the fullest possible range of instruments for moving from violence to peace. The tasks of the peace process apart from negotiation provide an important framework for this movement.

CLARIFYING TERMS: PRENEGOTIATION AND CIRCUM-NEGOTIATION

The term *prenegotiation* can be confusing in at least three respects. Thus it is crucial to define my use of terms.

First, the prefix *pre* suggests a position in time before negotiation. We can more accurately say that this work is accomplished apart from negotiation. It can indeed pave the way for formal mediation and negotiation. But it can also take place during a negotiation, but apart from it, when negotiators are stuck and need a larger perspective, new formulations, or broader political support. It can even take place after one successful negotiation when parties move to tackle the next problem.

Second, the use of the word *negotiation* suggests that the problem is how to start a negotiation. The real problem is how to start a political process that can change relationships and lead to the end of violence, to peace, and to reconciliation. The methods used in that process may or may not include negotiation.

I once asked an academic colleague whether every conflict has a negotiated solution? He replied that he thought so. But as I reflected on my very different experience, I concluded that there must be solutions through means other than negotiation. Having worked for five presidents, I have heard leaders say, "This problem is too tough to negotiate, yet I must do something about it." I want leaders and citizens alike to have as many options for reframing issues or taking steps in the political arena to change conflictual relationships as they have options for getting people to the negotiating table.

Third, some scholars have defined prenegotiation as an exactly limited period of preparation for negotiation. "Prenegotiation begins," writes I. William Zartman, "when one or more parties considers negotiation as a policy option and communicates this intention to other parties. It ends when the parties agree to formal negotiations (an exchange of proposals designed to arrive at a mutually acceptable outcome in a situation of interdependent interests) or when one party abandons the consideration of negotiation as an option."[2] The important work of setting the agenda, staffing the negotiation, defining ground rules, and solving problems of the setting might more accurately be called negotiation preparation. Or perhaps this is the appropriate meaning of prenegotiation.

With these points made, we will now discuss the times and the tasks apart from negotiation that have the purpose of beginning, sustaining, and nourishing a peace process by changing relationships and paving the way for negotiation or other peaceful steps to resolve conflict. For this work, I prefer the term *circum-negotiation*—the work that goes on around negotiation.[3] The peace process embraces prenegotiation, negotiation, and circum-negotiation.

THE PEACE PROCESS IN A CHANGING GLOBAL SETTING

Our changing world demands that we broaden our conceptual framework. For the past 350 years, we have tended to think of conflict in the context of the nation-state system. Attempts to resolve conflict have relied on the traditional instruments of statecraft—force, mediation, negotiation, propaganda, and economic sanctions and incentives. In this power-politics model for analyzing international relations, leaders of nation-states amass economic and military power to pursue objectively defined interests in zero-sum contests of material power against other nation-states.

Our increasing experience of the complex interdependence of today's world causes us to think beyond a system focused mainly on the nation-state. Relationships among countries today are increasingly a political process of continuous interaction among significant elements of whole bodies politic across permeable borders.

As normally defined, the state-centered concepts of the past do not embrace this relationship between whole bodies politic. Citizens outside as well as within government are both instigators and resolvers of conflict. There are some things that only governments can do, such as negotiate binding agreements; there are others that only citizens outside government can do, such as change human relationships. State borders no longer exclude a large range of interactions among citizens, and human beings have many identities—ethnic, racial, linguistic, regional, global, cultural, professional, avocational, religious, ideological, economic—many of them not defined or bounded by the nation-state.

I have settled on the concept of relationship to capture that dynamic political process of continuous interaction between whole bodies politic. Although this term is unfamiliar in international relations, I intend to bring the human dimension into the study, teaching, and conduct of international relationships and into the prevention, management, and resolution of conflict. The term relationship suggests the need to study not only relations between states but the overall relationships among groups of human beings and whole bodies politic.

I focus not only on negotiating a division of material goods to settle a conflict between institutions but also on changing the conflictual relationships that gave rise to the struggle and that therefore must be changed in order to resolve the conflict. That is the work of whole human beings in whole bodies politic—citizens both in and out of government. That is the work of a whole peace process, involving all levels of a body politic.

Formal negotiation may evolve from preparations explicitly devoted to starting negotiation; or negotiations may become possible only after citizens who have no authority to prepare for negotiation decide in dialogue apart from negotiation that it is time to risk trying to live together in peace. In another circumstance, a new phase in negotiation may be blocked until a positive political environment has been created by citizens outside government. As they change relationships through their own interactions, the need for an entire phase in negotiation may be bypassed. The challenge is to understand how work in all of these arenas—including the work apart from negotiation—interacts to initiate and sustain movement from violence toward peace.

THE OVERALL PEACE PROCESS: FOUR ARENAS

Our understanding of the whole peace process has evolved since 1974. We now think of the process as operating in four interactive arenas. The work of prenegotiation can be accomplished in any of them. One is not superior to another; one may simply be more feasible or appropriate in a given situation. The important task is to understand how they can work together in complementary ways.

The Official Process

In the early months of U.S. Secretary of State Henry Kissinger's 1974 shuttle diplomacy in the Middle East, those of us flying with him first used the phrase *negotiating process* to describe our mediation of a series of interim agreements. Soon, however, we realized that the phrase was too narrow, because our stated purpose was for each interim agreement to change the surrounding political environment and make possible a further step. We coined the phrase *peace process* to capture the experience of this series of mediated agreements embedded in a larger political process. It was in that larger political process that relationships changed. Human interactions changed the attitudes in bodies politic that constrained governments or pressed them to move forward. At that time, we were focusing on how governments could reshape the political environment.

In the 1970s the Soviet-U.S. governmental effort called *detente* aimed to "move from confrontation to negotiation" as the heart of the relationship between the nuclear superpowers. A decade after detente foundered, Soviet President Mikhail Gorbachev recognized the need not just to negotiate arms control agreements but to address directly the deep distrust Americans felt toward the

Soviet Union. His address to the United Nations General Assembly in December 1988 was essentially a speech to convince the American people that the Cold War could end and that a new relationship was possible. Again, this was an official act. Similar official processes in El Salvador, Guatemala, South Africa, Northern Ireland, and the former Yugoslavia have yielded agreements that will require years to play out. Official as well as quasi-official and public peace processes are ongoing as of this writing in Tajikistan; Armenia, Azerbaijan, and Nagorno-Karabakh; and Georgia.

The Quasi-Official Process

Unofficial groups closely related to the official process have formed on a number of fronts. Although made up of citizens outside government, these groups consult with officials, feeding them ideas or formulations.

For example, in 1993 a small group of Israelis and Palestinians outside government began meeting with the informal acquiescence of officials; they graduated to talks moderated by the Norwegian foreign minister, with officials informed at each stage, and they finally produced an agreement that was formally adopted by the Israeli government and the Palestine Liberation Organization. As another example, the National Commission for the Consolidation of Peace (COPAZ) was created in El Salvador by the 1992 peace agreement between the government and guerrilla forces. Made up of representatives of all political parties in the Legislative Assembly, its mandate was to oversee implementation of the political aspects of the agreement. This required working out compromises on major legislative acts. Finally, the Soviet-U.S. Dartmouth Conference—the longest continuous bilateral exchange between American and Soviet citizens, started in 1960 at the initiative of President Dwight Eisenhower with the

approval of Chairman Nikita Khrushchev— fell partly into this category because Soviet participants normally spoke under the discipline or instruction of the Soviet Communist Party. Each group was briefed by officials before meetings and reported to them afterwards.

Public Dialogue

In today's world, many of the deep-rooted conflicts that command our attention have resulted from the breakdown of states or seem beyond the reach of governments. Many of these situations are not ready for negotiation; therefore, since the 1960s, citizens outside government have developed approaches built around sustained dialogue. These dialogues address the human causes of conflict. They engage representative citizens from the conflicting parties in designing steps to be taken in the political arena to change perceptions and stereotypes, to create a sense that peace may be possible, and to involve more and more of their compatriots. In 1991, some of us coined the phrase *public peace process* to name this work of citizens outside government.[4]

Israelis and Palestinians outside official bodies met in countless dialogues for almost two decades before official and quasi-official negotiations took place. These dialogues created a critical mass of people in each body politic who recognized the other group as persons with valid human needs and desires to fulfill their own legitimate aspirations. More important, the people decided they could risk trying to live at peace. The dialogues also produced many of the formulations and reassurances that made possible formal negotiations between Israel and the Palestine Liberation Organization.

In Tajikistan, parties to a civil war met in unofficial dialogue for thirteen months before UN-sponsored negotiations between the government and the opposition began.[5]

In the public domain, the opposition created its own organization and put forward a platform that provided a basis for government agreement to negotiations. Two dialogue participants were signatories. The dialogue group wrote an unsolicited "Memorandum on a Negotiating Process for Tajikistan" before negotiators first met in April 1994. Three of those who produced that memorandum became delegates in the formal negotiations as citizens outside government. A year later, when the official negotiations were stalled over a mechanism to oversee a "process of national reconciliation," the dialogue group produced two memos on the subject—one outlining options and a second fleshing out one option when leaders agreed on it. Although the dialogue group has sent memos to negotiators and is known by officials, it is not responsible in any way to official bodies, nor are participants instructed by them.

Civil Society

The fragmentation and reconfiguration of civil society that underlie conflict and its resolution need to be considered when planning peacemaking and peace building. Most thinking about preventing and resolving conflict has focused on the dynamics of conflict itself—its causes, escalation, stalemate, and settlement. A larger framework would include what happens in a civil society as violence breaks it down into warring units and as genuine peace rebuilds and reconnects them. Picture the following sequence of developments:

- First: A functioning society includes many relationships and networks of relationships. Whether in totalitarian societies or democracies, some span the fault lines that divide people and provide spaces where perceptions can change and differences can be handled peacefully.

When a regime collapses, those organizations are dismissed, and the vacuum is often filled by armed groups vying for control.

- Second: As a society fragments, whatever social units survive—tribal, clan, ethnic, or regional groupings, ideological movements, or criminal networks—coagulate into like-minded "alliances." Relationships between unlike groups that pursued shared interests across fault lines are severed. Violence is the medium of exchange.

- Third: Mediators help opposing factions reach agreement on ending the violence. They address tangible issues and interests and the division of power. But the agreements they produce are like skeletons without the necessary ligaments, muscles, sinews, flesh, nerves, or blood vessels. They cannot change human relationships, and they do not normally think of the need to regenerate those groups and political processes that span the divisions in a peaceful civil society.

- Fourth: During a civil conflict, citizens outside government may begin dialogue across the lines of conflict. They create organizations to help refugees return home, restore local water systems, or re-create trading patterns. They begin to generate connections between the coagulations of warring groups forming the sinews of nascent cohesion in a society building peace. Those connections provide the first ingredients of economic recovery.[6]

This picture was drawn from the experience of Tajikistan's first four years of independence, but it could apply to other conflicts. The point is that work critical to implementing agreements is done apart from negotiations in this arena.

The purpose of identifying these four arenas in the overall peace process is not to give primacy to any one, but to underscore the importance of a comprehensive strategy developed around the complementarity in their interactions. The official process can be enabled, constrained, or impelled by work in the other arenas. The process may lead to negotiation, but sometimes, as the dynamics of relationships change in the larger political process, a whole phase in preparation for negotiations may be superseded. Key issues—for example, adversaries accepting each other's identity—can be resolved in the public arena and not come to the negotiators' agenda except as a given. Sometimes, projects in the civil society bring together important elements of a whole body politic and build public support for official agreements—an approach crucial to implementing the Dayton Accords on Bosnia, for example.

These arenas characterize collections of actors in the peace process, but these collections of actors alone are not the peace process. We must add the dimension of time. The peace process embraces the interactions of these collections of actors over time to change relationships. That is why the process is laid out in phases below.

A Brief Word about Third Parties

Although not the main subject of this chapter, it is important to note that both governmental and nongovernmental third parties can work in each of these four arenas of the peace process—the official process, the quasi-official process, the public dialogue, and civil society. Each task in each arena may benefit from a different leadership.

The most creative thinking about third-party involvement focuses not on the role of a single actor but on the process through which a complex of functions is performed. One can identify, for example, the roles of instigator, communicator, persuader, organizer, precipitator, legitimizer, convenor, moderator, manager, funder, teacher, idea formulator—all played by different combinations of actors. The issue is not whether a bilateral initiative or a third-party role is the correct approach, but rather what mix of involvement is most appropriate at a particular time.[7]

When I was explaining the Dartmouth Conference—the bilateral dialogue between Soviet and U.S. citizens that involved no third party—a colleague asked, "But who performs the third-party role?" I replied, "One organization on each side organized and paid for the meetings. Co-moderators chaired meetings, set the agenda, jointly advanced it, and were stewards of the process." After the Cold War ended, the Dartmouth Conference Task Force on Regional Conflicts acted as a third-party team—perhaps the first Russian-U.S. citizens' peacemaking team—to launch the dialogue mentioned above among the factions from the civil war in Tajikistan. The role played depended simply on the needs to be met.

The Peace Process

A peace process operates in different arenas over time—sometimes simultaneously, sometimes in sequence, sometimes in parallel, sometimes overlapping. Its purpose is to reconcile parties in conflict, seeking to understand how the interaction among those arenas over time helps prepare human beings to change conflictual relationships. For the sake of illustration, this chapter examines the interaction between two of these arenas—the official and the public—as parts of the overall peace process.

The remainder of this chapter examines that interaction in each of five phases of the peace process. The stages of both the official peace process, which is normally built around negotiation or mediation, and the public peace process, built around a process of sustained dialogue, have been described elsewhere.[8] I focus here on the interaction of arenas.

Use of the term *phases* in this chapter is simply a convenient way of focusing on who can do what at each point in the evolution of a peace process. Speaking of phases suggests precision and rigidity that do not exist in the real world. In reality, participants move back and forth between stages in a circular rather than linear fashion as they revisit assumptions or tackle new problems. But presenting the process in phases sharpens thought about the tasks that need to be performed at each step, and it adds the dimension of time to the process.

One example of the value of analyzing the peace process in phases comes from the Arab-Israeli experience. From 1974 through 1979 the world came to see the Egyptian-Israeli peace process as a series of negotiated agreements, culminating in the peace treaty of 1979. When the focus shifted to the Israeli-Palestinian front, those two parties did not even recognize each other; the process was back in a period before negotiation where the instruments of negotiation were useless. Attention needed to return to the task of bridging the deep human gulf between two peoples. Much of that work needed to be done by citizens outside government.

PHASE ONE: DEFINING THE PROBLEM AND DECIDING TO ENGAGE

Phase one is a time when those involved in a conflict—citizens both in and out of government—decide whether they can allow a situation to continue as it is or whether to reach out to the other side. Deciding how to act on those decisions is likely to be more complicated and to take longer for those inside than those outside government.

Some individuals both in and out of government are ready to say, "Enough!" and to risk working toward a solution. Policymakers recognize that they cannot get what they want by unilateral action and decide to explore whether negotiation—an effort

with the other side to find a joint solution—might be possible. But their exploration may often have to be made unilaterally, because the symbolism of talking with an enemy may make direct talk taboo. Citizens outside government, on the other hand, have more freedom to talk to people on the other side to get a firsthand feel for what might be possible. Learning what brings people to this conclusion is crucial. Often it is stark recognition that the costs of continuing conflict have already become too high. Or some individuals may be far-sighted enough to recognize that the consequences of continuation will become intolerable at some future point.

Often individuals on the threshold of taking a step are reluctant or even fearful to reach out to the other side, with good reason. Some deny that a problem exists because they are not yet ready to face others' pain. Citizens in some situations risk assassination; governments risk vehement backlash; even in nonconflict situations, individuals are afraid to talk with people who they feel discriminate against them, do not care about them, or even hate or harm them.

Public Dialogue

At this stage, before participants ever come face to face, they need to understand the nature, purpose, and ground rules of the dialogue. Four questions must be addressed: Who will take the initiative? Who will participate? How can resistance to meeting and talking with the adversary be overcome? Under whose auspices and where will the dialogue take place?

An individual or small group in one community may reach out directly to individuals on the other side, or a respected third party may find and communicate to each side that some of the opposition want to talk. Someone on each side or a third party carefully identifies a dialogue group of about a dozen members who reflect thinking in various sectors of each party and who are respected in their communities. Some individuals may need to discuss their fears of meeting with the adversary. Finally, they agree to meet to listen to each other with respect and to speak to each other from the heart. They will meet in a place considered safe by both sides.

The Official Process

Policymakers have a more complex task during phase one. After reaching a personal decision that they must reach out to the other side, they have to pave the way for bringing a government and a body politic along with that decision. Because of the time this will take, those in the public peace process (who can act on their individual decisions) may start talking long before officials are ready to move. In policymaking, how one defines a problem begins to determine what one will do about it. Heated national debate can focus on the definition of a problem. Disagreements can lead factions to kill one another. So the policymakers—probably consulting an ever-widening inner circle—work carefully to frame the issue.

Once a small group of policymakers has defined the problem, they must understand how nearly unified or divided their own side is, how they and the adversary differ, and what barriers must be overcome. As they bridge differences within their own group, they begin forming an internal base in the official and civic arenas. The steps they take become part of the larger political process that eventually surrounds a negotiation.

Where the gap between one party and another seems large, policymakers must consider—still among themselves—how their pictures of the problem can be brought into closer alignment. It is a milestone when one party includes the other's definition of the problem in its own. It is normal for each side to buttress its own position by ignoring the rights, the claims, or the pain of others. One condition for deciding to seek a joint solution is seeing that a problem is at least partly a shared problem and that the hopes, pains, needs, positions, and political base of each party suggest the possibility of mutual responsiveness.

Policymakers may decide not to go beyond this in-house deliberation because of conditions either within their own group or on the other side. One option is for them to suspend their efforts and watch a public process explore possibilities, change relationships, generate options, and build public support. This is what happened in the Israeli-Palestinian and Tajikistani peace processes. Redefining a problem and changing relationships are often tasks for the public arena, and that public experience can contribute to the official assessment of the feasibility of negotiation.

PHASE TWO: MAPPING ISSUES AND RELATIONSHIPS

In this phase, both officials and citizens design an exploration of possibilities on the other side, but each group moves differently. Officials must be able to stop at any time. They need to estimate the chances of success in order to build political support for a commitment to negotiate, but they may have to do this without serious discussion with the other side. Citizens, on the other hand, begin face-to-face dialogue to develop a firsthand picture of how issues and priorities are defined and begin to judge the possibilities of working together.

Public Dialogue

Coming together for the first time, participants "map" or draw a mental picture of the main problems that affect their relationships and identify the significant relationships that are responsible for creating these problems and that would need to be changed to resolve them. The group has a dual agenda: Concrete problems are the starting point, but the purpose is always to probe the dynamics of the relationships that underlie them.

This stage ends when the group identifies and gives priority to a few problems it feels it must address systematically, one at a time. What they learn during this process becomes the essence of an agenda for either negotiation or their own continuing work.

At this point, those in the public peace process are moving ahead of officials. They are hearing directly the positions of people on the other side, as well as the feelings and assumptions that lie behind those positions. They are also gradually learning to see those in their dialogue as human beings. In many cases, officials are still working from their perceptions (or misperceptions) of the other side's positions and motives unless they are in close touch with those in the public arena.

Official Process

Perhaps the most critical period in the official peace process comes when leaders are deciding whether to commit themselves to an attempt at a negotiated settlement. Crystallizing that commitment is a complex part of the official peace process, because it involves interrelated judgments both about constituents' views and about the adversary's. Leaders are engaged in a mapping exercise, but they are mapping both their own political terrain and possibilities and the elements of the relationship with the other side.

Before leaders will openly commit to negotiate, they have to answer four questions: Will a negotiated solution be better than continuing the present situation? Can a fair settlement be fashioned, one that would be politically manageable? Will leaders on the other side accept the settlement and survive politically? Will the balance of forces permit agreeing to such a settlement?

Before taking a new direction, officials have to be more open about testing the waters in their own body politic. Judgments of the highest political and human order— about how much damage or pain a people can suffer—are required. Also required are the courage and foresight to try to persuade others that the current situation cannot continue. Judgments about where a course of action will lead over time will have to be convincing. Astute political judgments must be made about when a constituency is ready to move, and skill is needed to create the catalyst.

It is essential to understand the other side's human and political needs. Officials must estimate the likelihood of success as a basis for deciding whether to commit themselves to try negotiation, but they will often need to explore the other side's views only quietly and indirectly. While citizens outside government can make this determination in dialogue with the adversary, officials are normally constrained by their positions; sometimes, the mere act of shaking hands or meeting casually with an adversary carries symbolic significance. Even if they talk directly, they must be guarded. In such situations, a third party who can talk with both sides may help assure each that enough common ground exists as a basis for beginning negotiation. If policymakers judge that the two sides are close to a mutually acceptable agenda, they will open more formal communication to try to arrange a negotiation.

PHASE THREE: GENERATING THE WILL FOR A JOINT SOLUTION

In this phase, individuals in each arena will probe the main issues more deeply and determine whether there is a will to deal with them. The aim is the same in and out of government, but each group will pursue it differently. If those in the public dialogue decide to work together in a new way, they will move into the work of stage four without having to justify their decision publicly. Officials, on the other hand, will often be meeting directly and intensively to write terms of reference for negotiation. From that experience, they will agree to begin negotiation or suspend the effort; either choice will be a public act for which they will be accountable.

Public Dialogue

Participants probe specific problems to uncover the dynamics of underlying relationships with three aims: to determine how badly present relationships hurt their interests, to begin seeing ways to change those relationships, and to decide whether to try implementing such changes.

The main purpose in this stage is to generate the will to change conflictual relationships in order to deal with the problems that face the group. The tasks are (1) to shift discourse from explanation of positions to real dialogue in which participants begin interacting constructively, (2) to probe the problems that participants have agreed need most work and to use that analysis as a vehicle for illuminating the dynamics of key relationships, and (3) to create conditions in which participants can muster the will to design ways of changing destructive relationships that block change, by asking them to assess where the present relationships are leading.

This stage generates several results: (1) the experience of an increasingly probing dialogue that deepens and begins to change relationships within the group; (2) a new body of insight into the perceptions, feelings, and mind-sets of others; (3) a picture of how relationships between the parties need to change; and (4) above all, a judgment that the costs of continuing the situation and relationships outweigh the costs of trying to change them. The critical product—and stage three cannot end without it—is a will to change. If that will is present, the group will move to a significantly different mode of working together in stage four. Their rationale for moving on could influence a decision by officials to begin negotiation.

Official Process

Once the parties have decided to try to negotiate, the third phase of the official peace process turns to preparing for negotiation, substantively and logistically. Four kinds of issues will have to be addressed.

- Determining the larger strategy and character of the negotiations will require answering several questions. Will the negotiations aim at a series of interim steps or at a comprehensive final settlement? What can be accomplished at each step? Are secret exchanges possible, and, if so, how much should be attempted in secret? Can a third party help?

- A second issue will be the mechanics of the negotiation. Will there be direct or mediated negotiation? Where and when will negotiations take place?

- A third question is whether all needed factions are represented and whether they are represented by the right people.

- Finally, terms of reference must be developed to ascertain that the parties have compatible objectives in the negotiation and that similar principles will guide decisions on the elements of a settlement. Sometimes, terms of reference contain ambiguities that both conceal important differences and reveal common ground.

Officials will end this period with a design for negotiation and will decide whether to begin. A crucial purpose has been to accumulate evidence that the risk of negotiation is justified—that negotiation can succeed, that the outcome could improve the situation, and that failure would be manageable.

PHASE FOUR: SCENARIO BUILDING AND NEGOTIATION

Once parties have decided to work together toward a joint solution, citizens and officials will employ two different approaches. They will also aim at two different but complementary products, each reflecting particular capacities and roles.

Public Dialogue

The vehicle for deepening the group's work requires participants to design a scenario of interacting steps that can be taken in the political arena to change troublesome relationships. As a microcosm of the larger relationships involved, the group learns the process of change by experiencing it and experiences what the relationship would have to become if the desired changes were to be accomplished. Such a group goes through four steps:

- It lists obstacles to changing relationships in the ways needed; the obstacles may be physical or psychological.

- Once the group has developed a full list of obstacles, it develops a parallel list of steps that could help erode or remove those obstacles. Some of these may be official steps; most will be steps to be taken by citizens' groups.

- It lists those groups that can take the steps envisioned.

- To change a relationship, the steps must be arranged in a realistic, interactive sequence—a pattern of action, response, and further response. For instance, party

A may be able to take step 1 only if assured that party B will respond with step 2; party B may agree, but only if party A will respond with step 3.

The critical part of the scenario is not the action list, but the idea of reinforcing interactions. It is important because relationships change in the course of those interactions. This differs sharply from the normal government approach—that one will act and the other will react, usually with little consultation about the political process they should be trying to generate.

Official Process

Negotiation may already have begun in stage three, as the parties worked toward a starting point for negotiation or as a third party sought common ground. But the negotiating process changes character when participants begin trying to reduce what they have only talked about to a written agreement that can withstand the judgment of bodies politic.

The negotiation phase in the official peace process has been described extensively elsewhere, so I will make only two comments. First, there is a sharp difference between working out formal solutions to concrete problems and changing the human relationships that create many of those problems. Governments must tackle the formal solutions, but they cannot decree changes in human relationships. That is the task of citizens outside government. Second, there is an equally sharp difference between agreed-upon steps to solve a problem and the process of new interactions between the parties that could be generated in the implementation. Formal negotiations normally pay little attention to the political processes in which relationships actually change; citizens do. Work in both arenas is complementary.

PHASE FIVE: ACTING TOGETHER TO IMPLEMENT AGREEMENTS

Implementing agreements is often thought of as a series of actions to be taken. It is less often thought of as part of a long-term political process for changing relationships, in which negotiation is but one event. Paradoxically, in a continuing peace process that involves a sequence of negotiated agreements, implementation of one agreement may become part of the prenegotiation for the next, as faithful implementation builds confidence in the process and in the other party. It was particularly true in the Arab-Israeli peace process, for instance; each agreement in the early years was explicitly seen as but one step in a "step-by-step" process in which each agreement's implementation paved the way for the next. The history-making Camp David accords changed nothing on the ground, but they provided a framework for at least five more negotiations, which themselves would become part of the process of implementation by laying down new directions for implementation. These new directions would grow out of both the preparation for new negotiations and the work apart from negotiation that takes place in the public and civic arenas.

Public Dialogue

Participants devise practical ways to put their scenario into action. They need to ask specific questions: Do conditions in the body politic permit implementing this scenario? Does the capacity exist to carry it through? Who needs to take what steps? Whatever their action, it both differs from and supports actions that emerge from negotiation.

Official Process

Governments will carefully watch each other to ensure that agreements reached have been scrupulously carried out. The process of implementation may last a number of years. For the most part, the steps agreed will be limited to changing juridical and physical arrangements; governments can also take steps to change perceptions in each body politic, but changing human relationships will still be primarily citizens' business.

In both arenas, implementation is one more phase in developing a long-term political relationship in a framework that recognizes the peace process as designed to change relationships over time. Plotting a course in which the official and public peace processes —along with work in the quasi-official arena and in civil society—can complement each other can lead to new partnerships between governments and their people, which in themselves offer new potential for preventing and resolving conflict.

PRENEGOTIATION, CIRCUM-NEGOTIATION, AND THE PEACE PROCESS

The work apart from negotiation and in negotiation that paves the way for the peaceful resolution of conflict can be most richly understood when placed in the context of a whole peace process and when each arena of that process is seen in interaction with others over time. Governments must organize both substantively and politically for formal negotiations to produce precise written agreements. The political environment for initiating and implementing those agreements—the changes in relationships essential to peacemaking and peace building—may best be shaped by citizens outside government, often interacting in complementary ways with those inside. Today's deep-rooted human conflicts demand the largest possible framework for marshaling the full array of resources and instruments in the whole body politic. That framework is the peace process. The work we call circum-negotiation is often the critical human part of that process.

NOTES

1. I began to develop these thoughts in a progression of articles soon after leaving government work in 1981: "Getting to Negotiation," a review of Roger Fisher and William Ury's *Getting to Yes: Negotiating Agreement without Giving In* (Boston: Houghton Mifflin, 1981), published in *Harvard Law Review* 95, no. 6 (April 1982); a paper prepared for the Center for the Study of Foreign Affairs, U.S. Department of State, Washington, D.C., in June 1983, published by the center in 1984 as "The Prenegotiation Phase," in *International Negotiation: Art and Science*, ed. Diane B. Bendahmane and John W. McDonald, Jr.; and "We Need a Larger Theory of Negotiation: The Importance of Prenegotiating Phases," *Negotiation Journal* 1, no. 3 (July 1985). This chapter draws on this body of work.

2. I. William Zartman, "Prenegotiation: Phases and Functions," in *Getting to the Table: The Processes of International Prenegotiation*, ed. Janice Gross Stein (Baltimore, Md.: Johns Hopkins University Press, 1989), pp. 1–17.

3. For the term circum-negotiation, I am indebted to Carol E. Saunders.

4. The phrase "public peace process" was first used in 1991 for a paper titled "Framework for a Public Peace Process: Toward a Peaceful Israeli-Palestinian Relationship" that was produced by a dialogue among a group of nonofficial Israelis and Palestinians. Held in July 1991, the dialogue was sponsored by the Beyond War Foundation (renamed Foundation for Global Community) in Palo Alto, California, and was moderated by the author of this chapter.

5. The Tajikistan Dialogue was convened in March 1993 under the auspices of the Dartmouth Conference Regional Task Force, chaired by Gennady I. Chufrin and Harold H. Saunders. The dialogue had met fourteen times by the end of 1995. It is funded by the William and Flora Hewlett and the Charles Stewart Mott Foundations. It is conducted within the framework of the five-stage public peace process of sustained dialogue laid out by Chufrin and Saunders in "A

Public Peace Process," *Negotiation Journal* 9, no. 2 (April 1993): 155–177. The Charles F. Kettering Foundation in the United States and the Russian Center for Strategic Research and International Relations in Moscow organized the process.

6. This section on civil society is drawn from a letter written in January 1996 to Cyrus Vance and David Hamburg, co-chairs of the Carnegie Commission on Preventing Deadly Conflict.

7. An excellent presentation of this thinking may be found in Christopher Mitchell, "The Process and Stages of Mediation," in *Making War and Waging Peace: Foreign Intervention in Africa,* ed. David R. Smock (Washington, D.C.: United States Institute of Peace Press, 1993), especially pp. 139–160.

8. For a study of the official peace process, see Harold H. Saunders, *The Other Walls: The Arab-Israeli Peace Process in a Global Perspective,* rev. ed. (Princeton, N.J.: Princeton University Press, 1991), chap. 2; the description of the official peace process in this chapter draws heavily on that source. Sustained dialogue as part of the public peace process was first laid out in Harold H. Saunders, "Four Phases of Non-Official Diplomacy," *Mind and Human Interaction* 3, no. 1 (July 1991): 30. The global context and the need for such a process—now laid out in five stages—were presented in Chufrin and Saunders, "A Public Peace Process." The process is developed in Randa Slim and Harold H. Saunders, "Dialogue to Change Conflictual Relationships," in *Higher Education Exchange* (Dayton, Ohio: Kettering Foundation, 1994), pp. 43–56. A short version for use in ethnic conflicts in the United States appears in "Sustained Dialogue: A Process for Changing Strained Community Relationships" (Washington, D.C.: Kettering Foundation, 1995). A second Russian edition of the Chufrin-Saunders article was published in Dayton, Ohio, by the Charles F. Kettering Foundation in 1995. The process will be described fully and placed in political and global context in Harold H. Saunders and Randa M. Slim, "A Public Peace Process." An organizer's and moderator's manual for conducting sustained dialogue is available from the Kettering Foundation, 444 N. Capitol Street NW, Suite 434, Washington, D.C. 20001.

29

Nongovernmental Organizations and Peacemaking

PAMELA AALL

Editors' Note: In December 1994, the United States Institute of Peace sponsored a conference on "Managing Chaos: Coping with International Conflict into the Twenty-First Century." This meeting brought together representatives of the United Nations and regional organizations, the U.S. government, and nongovernmental organizations engaged in relief work and advocacy to discuss the changing nature of conflict and humanitarian crises and the capabilities of the international community to respond to these crises. This chapter is based on remarks made by several speakers over the course of the three-day conference.

REFRAMING THE ISSUES

Nongovernmental organizations (NGOs) involved in humanitarian relief missions know all too well the devastating effects of conflict. Fear of violence and retribution produces floods of refugees, who instead fall prey to starvation and disease. Agricultural systems and infrastructures are destroyed, causing grave short-term hardships and vanquishing hopes for long-term economic development. At times, attempts to deliver relief to victims of the conflict inadvertently help their persecutors. The end of violent conflict brings its own challenges, as refugees seek safe passage to their villages and former combatants need help reintegrating into a society that may be vastly different from the one they knew before the conflict.

Although many NGOs have had to deal with these circumstances in the course of their work over the decades, their exposure to violent conflict has increased dramatically in the last several years. While there may be a divergence of opinion on the fundamental causes of conflict in the post–Cold War world, it is clear that the nature of conflict has changed, shifting from confrontations between states to struggles for power and dominance within states. These internal struggles often pit ethnic group against ethnic group, religion against religion, and neighbor against neighbor, with intensified impact on select areas of the country or region. Moreover, refugee crises typically draw neighboring countries into the conflict as well, threatening to turn a subnational conflict into a regional and international conflagration.

Not only do NGOs respond to the humanitarian crises these internal conflicts produce, but as a function of their long-term relief and development work, they are often trapped in the midst of the violence. Furthermore, humanitarian crises are increasingly occurring in failed states or in states with only rudimentary governance. In these situations, the humanitarian relief that NGOs provide is usually a vital supplement to governmental functions, playing a crucial role in the re-establishment of civil society. The changing nature of both conflict and humanitarian relief has led the NGO community and officials of the United Nations and its member governments to examine the roles that NGOs can serve in preventing, managing, and resolving conflict.

This environment has been rendered more complex and chaotic by a fundamental change in the nature of conflict. Speaking from the point of view of a major relief and development NGO, Andrew Natsios noted that racial, religious, ethnic, and tribal rivalries have replaced the Cold War's ideological clashes as the principal sources of current conflicts. These rivalries are often perceived as being rooted in past atrocities and recur from generation to generation, each new conflict building on the last. As such, the nature of post–Cold War conflict has not only resisted traditional diplomatic methods for its resolution, but has also raised many challenging theological and psychological questions that are difficult for NGOs and other international institutions to address. Until these questions are resolved, the cycle of atrocities will continue.

In a session on the new post–Cold War diplomacy, Chester A. Crocker set the stage for examining NGO roles by emphasizing the need both to reconsider the concept of intervention and to widen its definition beyond the sphere of military action. "The choices are many: Intervention can be physical, spiritual, bilateral, or multilateral, involving direct action, skills transfer, or institution building. We should recognize that those who are managing chaos have the potential to manage a full-service bank." The recognition that NGOs are major players in this expanded menu of intervention strategies lies at the heart of the discussion on their role as conflict managers.

A key element of an effective response to these changes lies in the reframing of issues and in the way members of the international community view conflict and conflict resolution. Traditionally, NGOs devoted to humanitarian relief operations have not considered their activities as contributing to the amelioration or aggravation of conflict. Yet it has become apparent that their interventions do indeed influence the course of a conflict, and that in making the decision to aid a country in crisis, NGOs are assuming roles that may go far beyond their original mission.

In addition, massive humanitarian interventions, especially in situations of conflict, entail an entirely new set of complex relations among NGOs, international organizations, and national governments. Phyllis Oakley, assistant secretary of state for population, refugees, and migration, asserted that in these crises the U.S. government and NGOs depend on each other to fulfill their respective functions. Jan Eliasson, Swedish undersecretary of state for foreign affairs and former UN undersecretary general for humanitarian affairs, also pointed out that as the chief response to such crises has expanded beyond the security functions of peacekeeping (once the sole province of military forces) into the realm of peace building—including reconciliation, development, and humanitarian action—NGOs are coming to play an increasingly crucial role.

THE CHANGING NATURE OF NGOS

United by a commitment to improving conditions around the world, NGOs otherwise represent a great diversity of objectives, functions, and organizational structures. They also differ significantly in their attitudes toward governments and international organizations. Some NGOs are comfortable working with official institutions to achieve their ends, while others, dedicated to strengthening the grass-roots level, find working with national and international bureaucracies inimical to their objectives and do their best to avoid it.

Operational NGOs serve in the field, mobilizing resources and technical expertise and working directly with the recipients of humanitarian aid and economic development projects. Some operational NGOs focus on humanitarian relief, some on economic development, and more and more of them are beginning to focus on both of these missions.

NGOs dedicated to humanitarian relief operations have attempted to maintain a policy of strict neutrality in situations of conflict, defining their role as providers of aid to those in need without regard to political, ethnic, or religious affiliation. Even within this group, however, there are growing differences regarding the appropriateness of this stance. Some members of this NGO community are now challenging the neutrality policy, pointing to circumstances in Somalia and Rwanda, in which relief organizations unintentionally aided individuals and groups who were perpetuating the conflict.

NGOs engaged in human rights monitoring and advocacy, on the other hand, achieve their objective of changing condi-

tions in various countries through disseminating information and bringing issues to the attention of both the general public and policymakers. Unlike operational NGOs, they are far from neutral and often adopt adversarial positions with regard to both official institutions and the parties engaged in a conflict.

NGOs that focus specifically on conflict resolution may work with individuals, community groups, or official representatives. Like humanitarian relief NGOs, they avoid taking sides in a dispute in order to pursue their goals of promoting dialogue and establishing common ground between antagonists.

Most of the major humanitarian relief and development NGOs—such as World Vision, Catholic Relief Services, OXFAM, CARE, and Save the Children Fund—were founded decades ago in response to very specific circumstances. These organizations provided the model for the thousands of NGOs that have been established since. The NGO community has witnessed tremendous growth in its resources over the years—CARE USA has an annual budget of $346 million, while World Vision has a budget of over $140 million. The 160 NGOs within Inter*Action* have combined annual revenues of $2.3 billion, five-sixths of which comes from private donations. The sheer growth in the number of NGOs in recent years has also been dramatic. Currently, there are approximately 1,500 NGOs registered as observers with the United Nations; this figure consists primarily of NGOs with international missions and does not reflect the vast growth of indigenous NGOs.

The rapid rise in the number of NGOs has resulted in many more institutions that are able to mobilize resources for humanitarian crises in hitherto inaccessible and neglected parts of the world. Yet it has also complicated relief efforts by creating "an extraordinarily complex system that makes medieval Europe look centralized and ordered by comparison," in the words of Professor John Paul Lederach. A very diffuse system, its diversity makes it difficult to develop a comprehensive strategy, especially during complex emergencies, when there is little time for building consensus.

The exigencies of complex emergencies have made NGOs realize that their relief missions involve both peacemaking and peace-building activities. Accordingly, they are forced to examine closely the issue of whether, under what conditions, and how they will work with international organizations, governments, and military units engaged in humanitarian relief efforts. This realization, however, has not necessarily produced a consensus within individual NGOs on these new priorities. It may be easy for an NGO to fund, for example, a well-digging project in Kenya, since that particular budget item falls easily within its developmental mission and thus will find broad acceptance by the NGO's executive staff. On the other hand, that same staff could easily find itself divided over the issue of the NGO's field workers' managing disputes that might arise over access to the well water, since this is not an activity that easily fits into current NGO funding categories or program priorities.

Yet such conflict resolution and conflict management skills are essential to maintaining peace during complex emergencies, according to Lederach. The change requires a growing awareness on the part of humanitarian NGOs that their work in relief and development affects not only the social and economic well-being of their target groups, but also the larger political situation. The way they carry out their projects influences the propensity for peace in the host country, and this responsibility should encourage NGOs to develop and apply conflict resolution skills in their work.

NEW ROLES FOR NGOs

As a consequence of both their growing numbers and resources and the variety of functions they fulfill, NGOs are fast becoming a vital component of the international response to humanitarian crises, especially in situations of conflict. Operational NGOs are going beyond their traditional relief objectives of providing food, water, sanitation, and emergency health measures, to serving as a substitute for local government, encouraging the growth of civil society, and using mediation and negotiation skills to bring antagonists together as part of a relief mission.

While they cannot be expected to solve all the problems associated with humanitarian interventions, NGOs can assume four fundamental roles during these types of crises:

- the relief and rehabilitation functions normally associated with NGOs,
- a preventive function through early warning,
- human rights monitoring, and
- conflict resolution activities, such as mediation and reconciliation.

These distinct functions require different sets of disciplines and skills, some of which already exist in the NGO community and some of which do not. Andrew Natsios stressed the importance of keeping these functions separate, cautioning that "we shouldn't mix the roles." He added, "In a conflict setting, NGOs that are doing relief and development work should not also engage in human rights monitoring—that's a good way to get your people shot. They need to be separate functions performed by separate organizations." Similarly, organizations involved in advocacy should not attempt mediation and reconciliation, and those engaged in relief work should not be involved in security operations. Making these distinctions and assigning different functions to different organizations is an important component of ensuring effective action in conflict situations.

Of the four roles, the early warning and conflict resolution functions typically generate the most debate. The intense discussions surrounding these two NGO roles reflect not only their relative newness in the repertoire of NGO capabilities, but also the fact that both of these roles subsume many other increasingly important and, some would argue, controversial tasks NGOs must consider in carrying out their primary missions during complex emergencies.

Early Warning

NGOs are often well situated to play a role in early warning and preventive action, alerting the international community to potential breakdowns in a distressed country's governance or in relations among the country's major domestic groups. Since many humanitarian NGOs have deep roots in local communities, their relief and development workers in the field have a unique vantage point to identify deteriorating conditions that might lead to conflict.

Jan Eliasson detailed a number of steps, including fact-finding missions, that NGOs and the international community could undertake in order to provide early warning for looming conflicts. These actions would precede more formal approaches, such as peacekeeping operations and peacemaking. NGOs can play a key role in gathering information, providing early warning, and building peace, and they can help the international community move from simply responding to crises to preventing their occurrence. In Eliasson's metaphor, such activity among NGOs moves the international community from merely extinguishing fires to finding the arsonist before the fire breaks out and to identifying conditions that lead to arson.

Vivian Lowery Derryck, president of the African-American Institute, argued that NGOs should use their early warning capabilities to advocate governmental policies aimed at stemming the outbreak of further violence during complex emergencies. In her view, the executive leadership of operational NGOs should serve as advocates to the U.S. government, since their organizations could combine on-the-ground experience with access to policymakers. In carrying out their primary missions, operational NGOs grapple with difficult issues that give them a unique insight into the dimensions of complex emergencies. These insights can be crucial to policymakers in governments and in other international organizations.

In the case of Rwanda, such an advocacy role for operational NGOs would have meant urging early U.S. involvement and requesting that the military stay long enough to complete the job. It also would have meant giving the U.S. administration their views on issues such as disarmament in the refugee camps and the forcible relocation of Hutu soldiers. In dealing with questions of whether to pull out of the refugee camps in the face of de facto Hutu militia control or to remain and attempt to aid the starving majority, NGOs gathered information that could have determined policy in a way that promoted conflict management more decisively.

Others assert, however, that the lack of early warning is not the central problem in preventive action. The key—and often missing element—in prevention is developing the political will to act on early warning signals. Here, too, NGOs play a central role as advocates for action. Lionel Rosenblatt, president of Refugees International, pointed to the history of the conflict in Bosnia as a tragic example of the international system's failure to act on stark and compelling evidence. Agreeing that early action saves lives and resources, he stressed that the inability to detect a conflict's early warning signals was not the main impediment to preventive measures. In the cases of Bosnia and Rwanda, the challenge was to find the political will and leadership necessary to translate early warning into effective intervention. The failures inherent in those conflicts demonstrate the need to create a new international mechanism that promotes early action—a system involving NGOs, governments, and the United Nations.

To move toward that goal, Rosenblatt identified six policy initiatives that could make a significant difference in marshaling resources for early action in humanitarian crises:

- The international community should focus on the need for early response, restructuring intelligence agencies and diplomatic reporting to meet the contingencies arising in the post–Cold War world.

- Agencies operating closest to potential conflicts should hone their tools of prevention. NGOs should work with the United Nations to build direct, hands-on partnerships that capitalize on opportunities for negotiation training, reconciliation, and the implementation of other conflict resolution techniques.

- The United Nations should be given a mandate to form an international rapid deployment force under its control. The current system of nations providing troops to UN peacekeeping missions causes political problems in donor countries— including public protests over deaths and casualties in the ranks of peacekeeping forces—that have eroded badly public support for peacekeeping. Providing the United Nations with the authority and the forces necessary for quick deployment in areas of crisis would eliminate political wrangling and costly indecision. All too often, waiting for donor nations to provide troops in such situations is

tantamount to waiting for another round of genocide to happen.

- The international community must develop counter terrorism capabilities that seek to minimize the problems of mass violence and assassination of political officials. Serious thought should be devoted to ways in which NGOs, states, and the United Nations could intervene in situations where a distressed country's government is incapable of coping with terrorism.

- The international community must develop an organizational capacity to deal not only with refugees but also with internally displaced people. In many complex emergencies, the internally displaced remain invisible amid waves of refugees and are typically denied the resources necessary for their own survival. Recognizing the needs of internally displaced people would involve new roles for the military, NGOs, and the United Nations.

- The international community needs to develop the capacity to reintegrate people displaced by crisis into their societies, recognizing that successful reintegration means much more than simply returning refugees to their villages. Are their homes intact and unoccupied? Do their jobs or farms remain for them to resume their livelihood?

Conflict Resolution, Relief, and Sustainable Development

Based on both his field experience in conflict situations and his work as a practitioner developing conflict resolution programs to accompany the relief activities sponsored by the Mennonite Central Committee, John Paul Lederach focused on the challenges posed to NGOs by the new types of conflict that have become commonplace in the post–Cold War era. These challenges clarified the need for a more comprehensive framework for conflict resolution and reconciliation activities on the part of NGOs.

In Lederach's view, the NGO community and the international community at large should concentrate on techniques that link crisis management and humanitarian relief activities to the longer-term goals of conflict resolution and sustainable development. However, the context in which these needs emerge almost always involves settings of protracted, divisive, and deep-seated generational conflict. To move beyond managing an immediate crisis, NGOs must change their planning time frames to a long-term perspective. The initial emergency relief response should be linked to a set of activities that leads to the transformation of those conflicts in a way that promotes sustained and comprehensive reconciliation among the warring parties.

Developing an infrastructure that sustains peace building within a given conflict is of paramount importance. In looking at a situation of long-term conflict and war, agencies from outside the country, including NGOs, should recognize that there are many levels of activity, as well as many actors and functions necessary for peace building. Most peace operations tend to rely on a top-down approach to peace building, in which the country's political leaders and high-level officials from international organizations make decisions that are supposed to be implemented throughout the rest of the country. In many cases, however, relying solely on a top-down approach to peace building results in failure and frustration.

As a result of their focus on the middle and grass-roots levels of societies in crisis, NGOs are particularly effective at working with both a country's mid-level officials and the recipients of aid at the community level. Because of their familiarity with the country and its decision makers, NGO representatives have a keen understanding of the real-

ities on the ground, allowing them to reach across their counterparts from other agencies into a web of indigenous officials and resources in order to build and maintain a sustainable infrastructure that has a better chance of ameliorating not just the manifestations, but also the causes, of conflict.

Building such infrastructures, however, will require the international community to develop another set of lenses that allow it to recognize and identify local resources and technologies to be used in the resolution of conflict. Lederach noted that in most crisis situations, relief agencies rely on outside resources and view the people in the midst of such conflict settings simply as recipients of the external donor's goodwill. Within any given society, however, many valuable resources are either overlooked or denied official sanction for use in the peace building effort. Indigenous people should be viewed as primary resources for conflict resolution and encouraged to take up the task of building peace themselves in their own locales. "We have to look for the cultural resources that exist for building peace," Lederach concluded. "This assumes that we see culture as a seedbed and as a resource. It assumes that we see people as a resource and that we are willing to take the time to develop respectful relationships."

An essential component of NGO operations revolves around expanding their constituencies and bringing new actors into their domain of activities. Using the example of women's groups in Africa, Vivian Lowery Derryck noted that in numerous recent conflicts, women served neither as primary decision makers nor as active combatants. Rather, they were interested in participating in the peace process. In one noteworthy example, women in Uganda began forming a peace network with women in Rwanda. In Somalia, women's associations were able to play a vital role in establishing communication between the fighting factions, since women are linked across clans by marriage and are able to move from one subclan back to their clan of origin without fear of retribution. Through their many roles in society, women can be significant agents for conflict management and conflict resolution and can be part of a concerted campaign to develop indigenous resources for peace.

Even as NGOs increase their use of indigenous resources, outside resources (such as food shipments) in peacemaking interventions are often unavoidable and, in many situations, essential. In these cases, according to Andrew Natsios, the international community should realize that putting valuable resources into a conflict setting can have unintended consequences. When, for instance, NGOs respond to humanitarian crises such as the relief effort for Rwandan refugees in Goma, they need adequate security. Without it, the food will be used for purposes it was not intended for—to buy weapons, to control populations, or to buy support from various political factions in a conflict. When resources such as food are introduced into a conflict, the political dynamic is altered, and the presence of these resources could intensify the violence. Too often, it is naively assumed that relief will generate goodwill. The international community should be prepared to deal with the fact that people will fight for control of valuable resources.

THE CHALLENGE OF COORDINATION

With so many actors at different levels of the international system available to intervene in complex emergencies, coordination is essential to avoid overlapping and counterproductive responses that result in wasted resources and inefficient operations. While agreeing that the United Nations, international NGOs, regional organizations, and individual governments have integrated and reinforcing roles to play in response to crises, many observers acknowledge that the effectiveness of these roles was diminished by the disjointed nature of the response.

In a crisis situation, so many different things occur simultaneously that one actor often does not know what the others are doing. People operating at the grass-roots level are often considered unimportant or peripheral by those operating at higher levels. A successful intervention, nonetheless, calls for the ability to understand and connect the different levels of activity.

These new kinds of interventions make it clear that NGOs must find the means for establishing improved working relationships with the military. Traditionally, NGOs and the military have perceived their roles to be distinctly different and separate. NGOs have felt uneasy working with military forces, either from their own countries or from the country receiving assistance, particularly when the latter are employed in the service of dictators with unsavory human rights records. Military leaders, on the other hand, tend to regard NGOs as undisciplined and their operations as uncoordinated and disjointed. The experiences in Somalia and Rwanda showed that closer working relationships between NGOs and the military could successfully meet the goal of delivering humanitarian assistance in situations of conflict.

Clear comprehension of the mission's overall objectives is critical. While they enjoyed a high level of cooperation in the Rwanda and Somalia operations, the military and the NGOs were motivated by different goals. The military's concern with "mission creep" resulted in a desire to go in, provide emergency technical assistance, and get out quickly. Conversely, the NGO perspective during these crises was long term, aimed at nation building and developing education skills. While it is unlikely that these divergent goals will change, appreciating the other's perspective and agreeing on immediate objectives are essential for cooperative action.

In this regard, Lionel Rosenblatt argued that humanitarian operations should form a key part of training for the armed forces. Contrary to the belief that humanitarian work erodes military readiness, "the deployment of troops for peacekeeping and humanitarian work is good for our military," he suggested. "This is far better training in preparedness for post–Cold War realities than training at Fort Bragg."

Once a humanitarian crisis is apparent, food, water, and other life-saving resources need to be introduced efficiently, cheaply, and quickly. In Rosenblatt's opinion, this requires getting away from the administrative routines of governments and militaries and fostering a greater degree of cooperation among the relevant actors. In addition, he recommended that the international community establish a chain of command through which all relevant actors—both peacekeepers and providers of humanitarian aid—report their efforts. Given the current practice of disparate groups involved in crisis management reporting to different leaderships, these complex emergencies desperately demand a single emergency coordinator.

The case of Somalia demonstrated that achieving such coordination would be a difficult task indeed. Andrew Natsios suggested that one problem in Somalia was a kind of role reversal among external actors, with NGOs running security operations, which they were not trained to do, while the military delivered relief and aided in development. Lacking a proper understanding of these unfamiliar roles, both actors were bound to make inappropriate decisions. For example, the U.S. military's decision to send in its own engineers and support troops to rebuild roads and infrastructure came at a time when Somali males desperately needed jobs. The military was not interested in hiring the Somalis because it wanted to build the roads quickly. The military officers in charge believed that if they let untrained "locals" or NGOs do the job, it would take longer than a few months. Thus, the potential for encouraging indigenous development was lost, keeping thousands of Somali males idle and frustrated.

One reason for the lack of coordination is that the actors in humanitarian crises are very different organizations. International organizations and governments deal with crises at the national level; NGOs operate mainly at the local level. Military forces assigned to support humanitarian missions receive their instructions from their governments; NGOs are answerable to their boards and to the thousands of donors who support their efforts. In Julia Taft's words, this difference in organizational character has traditionally relegated NGOs to the status of eccentric relatives whose invitation to the policymaking party never arrived. This situation has changed, however, as NGOs are now included at the policymaking table and are recognized as key actors in the design and delivery of humanitarian relief.

The growing awareness that both public and private organizations are essential to the success of any humanitarian venture, however, has not yet resulted in improved coordination. One call for more cooperative action came from Mohamed Sahnoun, former special representative of the United Nations secretary general in Somalia, and former deputy secretary general of the Organization of African Unity in charge of political affairs and crisis situations. Sahnoun proposed creating a new international institution for conflict management that would coordinate humanitarian action and foster ties between organizations and agencies from the international level down to the local level. Such an institution would make essential contributions to the goal of establishing a global framework for conflict management and peace building by coordinating efforts while simultaneously decentralizing them—creating, in essence, a synergy between the regional and international levels. This proposed institution would mobilize all approaches to conflict resolution and would increase communications and networks among different communities in local conflict areas through the integrated efforts of NGOs and the United Nations.

Accountability and leadership issues. Amid the calls for establishing new means to coordinate international responses to these situations, however, a few voices raised concern over issues of accountability and leadership. John Paul Lederach noted that in crisis situations, NGOs have assumed responsibilities far exceeding their intended missions. Two clear examples are Rwanda and Somalia, where the collapse of central authority resulted in a political vacuum that was immediately filled by chaos and internecine warfare. NGOs moved into these "stateless" situations and took on many of the services typically provided by the failed governments. "In many ways the NGO activity can be seen as replacing the state. This raises a crucial question for us all: To whom are the NGOs accountable?"

The issue of accountability extends to governments that take on a large share of the responsibilities in responding to complex emergencies. In Rosenblatt's view, the U.S. government should reform both the way it deals with the United Nations and the way it responds to humanitarian crises in general, including the integration of humanitarian assistance functions presently scattered throughout its various agencies, including the Agency for International Development, the State Department, and the Department of Defense. He urged the U.S. government to gather all these various divisions of responsibility within a single entity with one senior official in charge. Such reorganization would improve not only the

U.S. response to complex emergencies but also the United Nations' role in them. After all, as Rosenblatt observed, the United States cannot demand a higher level of accountability at the United Nations than it is willing to ensure in its own government.

The issue of which institutions should provide the necessary leadership for a coordinated effort led Andrew Natsios to remark that NGOs could not fulfill the functions of world powers in these situations. "There is no substitute for the influence and resources of the great powers in these conflicts. The NGO community cannot act like the U.S. government. It doesn't mean the United States has to intervene all the time, but there are instances when a power with military forces and large budgets can intervene diplomatically to make people talk who might not want to talk. Unless the great powers have the moral and diplomatic impulse to intervene, we are going to be unsuccessful in dealing with these conflicts."

NGOs AS CONFLICT MANAGERS

While NGOs are fast becoming powerful new actors in complex emergencies, managing conflict and taking on certain functions of imperiled governments, several questions arise: Should NGOs be involved in conflict prevention and resolution? If so, how extensive should their involvement be? Effective responses to post–Cold War humanitarian crises often mean that many NGOs must go beyond their traditional mission of providing food, water, and medical assistance, entering the realm of ensuring political stability and fulfilling governmental functions in failed states. Are such expanded roles appropriate for NGOs?

John Paul Lederach agreed that NGOs could effectively manage conflict, noting that they bring several special qualities to peace building, especially through their particular insights into different cultures, their relationships with local partners, and their understanding of the links between crisis management and long-term sustainable development. He recalled how NGO representatives often talk about their operations as comprising a continuum of relief efforts, rehabilitation, reconstruction, and sustainable development. All of these components are essential for developing both new and more effective paradigms for peace building and appropriate strategies to deal with specific conflicts.

In response to the question of roles, certain conditions emerged, conditions that must be met before NGOs engage in conflict management activities:

- The NGO knows the country and the regional institutions involved in the conflict resolution effort.
- The NGO has indigenous partners.
- The NGO staff has a good knowledge of conflict mediation skills.
- The NGO's field staff members fully understand the personal risks they are assuming.

Equally important is the development of further coordination among the different types of operational NGOs and between the NGO community and other actors involved in complex emergency interventions.

It is more than apparent that NGOs of all varieties are seriously grappling with issues raised by working in situations of conflict. There is widespread recognition that NGOs might unwittingly become a party to conflict in the course of their humanitarian relief work; that their actions could be part of a concerted, coordinated effort involving governments, international and regional organizations, and private groups to avert or resolve conflict; that they have the ability both to provide early warning and to shore up the political will of governments to act; and that they could give guidance to policymakers in their own countries and encourage community building and the development of civil societies in countries decimated by war. In short, the work of NGOs forms an important part of the entire repertoire of intervention strategies for dealing with conflict in the post–Cold War era.

SPEAKERS CITED

Chester A. Crocker, Chairman, Board of Directors, United States Institute of Peace, and Research Professor of Diplomacy, Georgetown University

Jan Eliasson, Undersecretary of State for Foreign Affairs, Sweden, and former undersecretary general for humanitarian affairs, United Nations

John Paul Lederach, Director, International Conciliation Service, Mennonite Central Committee

Vivian Lowery Derryck, President, African-American Institute

Andrew Natsios, Executive Director, World Vision Relief and Development

Phyllis Oakley, Assistant Secretary for Populations, Refugees, and Migration, U.S. Department of State

Lionel Rosenblatt, President, Refugees International

Mohamed Sahnoun, former special representative of the UN secretary general in Somalia

Julia Taft, President, Inter*Action* (American Council for Voluntary International Action)

30

International Mediation in the Post–Cold War Era

I. WILLIAM ZARTMAN AND SAADIA TOUVAL

International conflicts are frequently the subject of third-party mediation. We do not know how common mediation was in earlier history, but studies of modern international relations indicate that it has been a frequent occurrence for at least 200 years. It remains so in the present post–Cold War era. Although the end of the Cold War has brought about many changes in international politics, it has neither reduced the incidence of international conflicts nor the tendency to submit them to mediation.

"Conflict" here refers to politico-security issues. Typically, in international economic or environmental disputes, rival parties are not as forcefully competitive, nor are the means of conducting the dispute as violent as in politico-security conflicts. Conflicts over politico-security issues take place within a context of power politics, which has a major effect on international mediation. This premise provides the conceptual underpinning of our analysis of the participants' motives in mediation, the conditions that affect the performance and roles of mediators, and the keys to effective mediation of international conflicts. The term "international conflict" refers here both to interstate conflicts and to domestic ones that are affected by the involvement of external parties. When external parties provide political, economic, or military assistance or asylum and bases for actors involved in domestic struggles, domestic conflicts inevitably assume an international dimension.

Mediation is a form of third-party intervention in a conflict. It differs from other forms of third-party intervention in conflicts in that it is not based on the direct use of force and it is not aimed at helping one of the participants to win. Its purpose is to bring the conflict to a settlement that is acceptable to both sides. Mediation is a political process with no advance commitment from the parties to accept the mediator's ideas. In this respect, it differs from arbitration, which employs judicial procedure and issues a verdict that the parties have committed themselves beforehand to accept. Mediation is best thought of as a mode of negotiation in which a third party helps the parties find a solution which they cannot find by themselves. To accomplish its purposes, mediation must be made acceptable to the adversaries in the conflict, who must in turn cooperate diplomatically with the intervenor. But mediators often meet initial rejection from the conflicting parties; thus their first diplomatic effort must be to convince the parties of the value of their services before the mediation process can get started.

THE MEDIATOR'S MOTIVES

States use mediation as a foreign policy instrument. Their intervention as mediators is legitimized by the goal of conflict reduction, which they typically proclaim. The desire to make peace, however, is intertwined with other motives best described within the context of power politics. To understand these motives it is most helpful to employ a rational-actor approach, using cost-benefit considerations. Mediators are players in the plot of relations surrounding a conflict, and so they have an interest in its outcome; otherwise, they would not mediate. In view of the considerable investment of political, moral, and material resources that mediation requires and the risks to which mediators expose themselves, motives for mediation must be found as much in domestic and international self-interest as in humanitarian impulses. Mediators are seldom indifferent to the terms being negotiated. Not surprisingly, they try to avoid terms not in accord with their own interests, even though mediators' interests usually allow for a wider range of acceptable outcomes than the interests of the parties. Self-interested motivation holds for superpowers, medium-sized powers, and international organizations.

Mediation by States

Mediating states are likely to seek terms that will increase the prospects of stability, deny their rivals opportunities for intervention, earn them the gratitude of one or both parties, or enable them to continue to have a role in future relations in the region. Both defensive and offensive goals can be promoted through mediation, and they often blend together. (For a further discussion of states' interest in managing conflict, see Udalov 1995 and Zartman 1995.) Mediators act defensively when a continuing conflict between others threatens the mediator's interests. An end to the conflict is therefore important to the mediator because of the conflict's effects on the mediator's relations with the disputing parties. For example, if two of the mediator's allies engage in a conflict, it can disrupt and weaken the alliance or strain the parties' relations with the third-party mediator. A conflict between two states may also upset a regional balance or provide opportunities for a rival power to increase its influence by intervening on one side of the conflict.

In some situations, a conflict may threaten to escalate and draw in additional parties. Actors who fear such escalation and expansion may seek to reduce the conflict to avoid becoming involved in hostilities. Mediation in such cases may involve one intervenor or it may be a collective endeavor by two or more states acting within or outside the framework of an international organization. For example, the efforts to mediate the various conflicts arising out of the dissolution of Yugoslavia involved the European Union, the Organization for Security and Cooperation in Europe, NATO, the United Nations, the informal "Contact Group," Russia, and the United States. Even rival powers, protecting their turf, are known to have cooperated and engaged in joint mediation when they feared that continuation of a particular conflict might endanger their security (for example, U.S.-Soviet cooperation on Laos in 1961–1962 and on the Arab-Israeli war in 1973).

The second self-interested motive for mediation is offensive: the desire to extend and increase influence. In this case, the solution of the conflict has no direct importance for the mediator and is only a vehicle for improving relations with one or both parties. A third party may hope to win the gratitude of one or both parties in a conflict, either by helping them out of the conflict or by aiding one of them to achieve better terms in a solution than would otherwise be obtainable. Although the mediator cannot throw its full weight behind one party, it can increase its influence by making the success of the negotiations depend on its involvement and by making each party depend on it to garner concessions from the other party. Mediators can also increase their presence and influence by becoming guarantors of any agreement, which necessarily includes risks and responsibilities.

A number of historical examples illustrate these interests. U.S. mediation in the Rhodesia/Zimbabwe conflict in 1976–1979 and the Soviet mediation between India and Pakistan in 1966 were inspired by a mixture of defensive and offensive motives. From a defensive vantage, the United States feared the Rhodesian conflict would provide opportunities for the Soviet Union to gain influence by supporting the African nationalists. But because the African groups concerned were already politically close to the Soviet Union and China, the U.S. mediation was also an attempt to improve relations with these groups and thus extend American influence.

Soviet mediation between India and Pakistan was partly inspired by its desire to improve relations with Pakistan, a country which had hitherto been on better terms with the United States and China than with the Soviet Union. It also sought to build its prestige and establish a precedent that would justify future involvement in the affairs of the region. At the same time, there were important defensive motives for its intervention. The Indo-Pakistan conflict provided China an opportunity to extend its influence into Pakistan and thus establish a presence close to the southern borders of the Soviet Union. By reducing the conflict, this expansion would become more difficult for China.

The United States has been the most active mediator of international conflicts since 1945 (Touval 1992). This involvement is consistent with an interest-based explanation of mediators' motives. Because the United States feared that conflicts would provide the Soviet Union with opportunities to intervene and expand its influence, the United States often sought to dampen conflict, and mediation was an appropriate instrument to that end. In addition, without reference to the Soviet Union, U.S. help was sometimes solicited by smaller states engaged in conflict because of the United States' power and prestige. Pressed by its friends for support, and always fearful that support for one side in a local conflict would throw the other side into the Soviet embrace, the United States often found that the least risky course in such situations was to mediate between the disputants.

That Americans were involved in mediation more often than the Soviets during the Cold War can easily be understood if we remember the preeminent status that the United States has enjoyed in international politics for many years, and the unequal extent of the two powers' spheres of influence. The Soviet sphere was at first limited to Eastern Europe and China. Starting in the mid-1950s, it expanded to include a few additional countries that became dependent on Soviet military aid (at the same time, however, China broke away from the Soviet sphere). The remainder of the world, sometimes called the Free World, was considered by the United States as part of its own sphere (notwithstanding that some states in this group proclaimed themselves to be nonaligned). Although actual American influence varied among these Free World states, what they had in common was that the Soviet Union carried less influence there than did the United States. The claim made in 1971 by Andrei Gromyko, then Soviet foreign minister, that Soviet interests extend to every corner of the globe and that "there is no question of any significance that can be decided without the Soviet Union or in opposition to it" reflected ambition rather than reality. Thus, the wider sphere of American influence explains why the United States mediated so many more conflicts than did the Soviets.

The patterns of interest prompting states to mediate have not changed since the end of the Cold War, although the readiness of third parties to become involved and the political geography of mediatory interventions have been modified. The United States seems less willing to mediate than in the past. Its reluctance to engage in mediation can best be explained by its perception that other peoples' conflicts now pose less of a threat to American security than they did during the Cold War. Russia, on the other hand, has become somewhat more active, especially in the Caucasus (Nagorno-Karabakh, Georgia-Ossetia) and other areas of the former Soviet Union, where it believes that its security is endangered. A notable shift has been taking place in Western countries, where humanitarian concerns of public opinion have come to play a more important role in shaping foreign policies than in the past. The need to respond to domestic public opinion has sometimes led a government to intervene in foreign conflicts, including civil wars, even when they are not perceived as impinging on its

security interests. Since mediation carries fewer costs for intervenors than military action, especially if pursued through international organizations, collective mediation seems to be on the increase. Examples of such mediation include the mediations in Afghanistan, Angola, Haiti, Liberia, Mozambique, Rwanda, Somalia, Sudan, and the former Yugoslavia.

Mediation by Small- and Medium-Sized Powers

Mediation by small- and medium-sized powers is also motivated by self-interest, some of which is related to domestic concerns. Such interests include the possibility that a conflict may spill over into the mediator's territory; the fear that the local conflict may expand and draw in powerful external actors (India's mediation in Sri Lanka prior to its military intervention is an example of both these concerns); the reluctance to take sides in a conflict between other nations (Saudi Arabia in many inter-Arab conflicts); and the attempt to promote norms that tend to enhance the mediator's own security (the 1963 Ethiopian mediation between Algeria and Morocco concerning the validity of borders inherited from the colonial period).

Small- and medium-sized powers may also wish to enhance their influence and prestige through mediation. Egypt's and Algeria's mediation between Iran and Iraq in 1975 was motivated by the desire to prove their usefulness to both belligerents, as well as to reduce intra-Islamic conflict. Algerian mediation between the United States and Iran on the issue of American hostages seems to have been inspired by the hope that mediation would generate goodwill from the U.S. public toward Algeria and thus help improve relations between Algeria and the United States. This hope was related to U.S. support for Algeria's adversary, Morocco, in the Western Sahara war against the Algerian-supported Polisario movement. Other cases in which states sought to enhance their international standing through mediation include India's attempt to mediate between the United States and the Soviet Union and China in the 1950s; Ghana's effort to mediate in the Vietnam war in 1965–1966; and Romania's try at an intermediary role in that same conflict, in U.S.-Soviet relations, and in Arab-Israeli relations (notably in helping to arrange Egyptian President Anwar Sadat's visit to Jerusalem in 1977).

Small and medium states have few alternative foreign policy instruments at their disposal, and mediation increases their usefulness and independence in relation to their stronger allies. Moreover, when pressed to take sides in a conflict, they may seek to escape their predicament by assuming the role of a mediator in the conflict. In the post–Cold War era, small and medium states continue to have a role as mediator. Kenya and Zimbabwe attempted to mediate the Mozambique conflict, Zaire the Angolan conflict, South Africa the conflicts in Nigeria and Swaziland, the Association of South East Asian Nations (ASEAN) the conflict in Cambodia, Norway the Palestinian-Israeli conflict, and Saudi Arabia the conflicts in Yemen and Lebanon. Many states—including South Africa, Togo, Tunisia, Algeria, Saudi Arabia, Costa Rica, and Colombia—consider mediation of the conflicts in their regions to be a major element of their foreign policy.

Mediation by International Organizations and NGOs

The motives of international organizations are somewhat more complex than those of states. Peacemaking is the raison d'être of several international organizations and is thus enshrined in their charters. Yet inter-governmental organizations are also subject to the particular policies and interests of their member-states. Accordingly, the United Nations was frequently paralyzed by the Cold War and engaged in peacemaking much less than its charter suggested it should. Some of the mediation efforts that it undertook were often smoke screens to conceal the intensity of American involvement (for example, in the Arab-Israeli conflict). Regional organizations were not hindered by the Cold War to the same extent as the United Nations. However, because mediation requires agreement among the organizations' most influential members, as well as acceptance by the parties directly involved, regional organizations were not as actively engaged in peacemaking as they might have been.

The end of the Cold War freed international organizations from their bipolar constraints, and they rushed into mediation and conflict management. As a result, their reputations and resources became overextended and their efforts were not rewarded with the expected quick success. In as short a time, member-states pulled back, blamed the organizations (which they ran), and greatly reduced their mediation activities. On his own, UN Secretary General Boutros Boutros-Ghali sent special representatives to conflict areas; the Organization of African Unity (OAU) added a section on conflict prevention, management, and resolution to the Secretariat; ASEAN took on new mediation roles; and the Economic Community of West African States (ECOWAS) and the West African Economic Community (CEAO) mediated conflicts in their midst. Thus the post–Cold War era has seen new regional organization activity to fill the slack left by the United Nations, plus a gradual reevaluation of UN potential. The UN experiences in Somalia, Rwanda, and Cambodia have shown both the great possibilities for mediation by the world organization and the difficulty in separating its role from the specific—indeed, narrow—interests and concerns of leading member-states in the Security Council.

Nonstate mediators, whose interests are not as apparent or suspect as the primary players of power politics, nevertheless share motives of self-interest. At the very least nonstate mediators have a role and a reputation to establish or defend and thus an interest in appearing as good and successful mediators. (The concerns of the World Council of Churches and the All-African Council of Churches in launching their mediation of the Sudanese civil war in 1971 is an interesting example [Assefa 1987], as is the highly motivated work of the Vatican in 1978–1984 in mediating the Beagle Channel dispute [Princen 1992] and of the Sant'Egidio community in mediating in Mozambique and Algeria [Johnston and Sampson 1994; Zartman, ed. 1995]). Often this role extends beyond mediation to become an organizational interest in establishing a presence and in keeping the organization clean and ready for other functions. In this regard, nonstate mediators come very close to state mediators in the nature of their interests.

Concern for peace as a value in and of itself, suspicion of interested mediators' motives, and perception of the inherent limitations on states' mediating roles have led a variety of nonstate actors to propose themselves as international mediators. Many of these are interested in a particular outcome, not because it affects them directly, but because they believe in its inherent desirability. Thus, the several private agencies striving for usefulness in the Rhodesian and Liberian civil wars were working to find an acceptable path to Zimbabwean independence and to a new political system in Liberia, respectively, not some other outcome. All nonstate actors have an interest in enhancing their positions as useful third parties, not out of any venal

egotism but because they believe they have something to offer; furthermore, a reinforcement of their standing and reputation helps them do their job.

THE PARTIES' MOTIVES IN ACCEPTING MEDIATION

Opponents in a conflict face two interrelated questions: whether to accept mediation and, if so, whose offer of mediation to accept. Parties accept intervention because they, like mediators, expect it to work in favor of their interests. The most obvious motive is the expectation that mediation will gain an outcome more favorable than the outcome gained by continued conflict—that is, a way out. The parties also hope that mediation will produce a settlement when direct negotiation is not possible or will provide a more favorable settlement than can be achieved by direct negotiation. Although the adversary may not have a similar assessment, it may accept and cooperate with the mediator if it feels that rejection might cause even greater harm—for example, damaging relations with the would-be mediator, decreasing the chances for an acceptable negotiated outcome, or prolonging a costly conflict. Such considerations sometimes help to induce states to accept intervention even in domestic conflicts (for example, Sri Lanka's acceptance of India's mediation, and Angola's acceptance of U.S. mediation). The parties may also accept mediation in the hope that the intermediary will reduce some of the risks entailed in making concessions and the costs incurred in conflict, protecting their image and reputation as they move toward a compromise. They may also believe a mediator's involvement implies a guarantee for the final agreement, thus reducing the danger of violation by the adversary.

The acceptance of mediation by international organizations can also be premised on the ability of these organizations to bestow normative approval, rather than on their capacity to influence the adversary or arrange for a satisfactory compromise. This factor is present in the case of the United Nations but is perhaps clearest in the case of the International Committee of the Red Cross (ICRC). The ICRC's ability to offer an improved image to a fighting or detaining authority can be a powerful incentive for the parties to accept its presence and services and to accede to its proposals.

Partiality and Acceptability

If the acceptance of mediation is based on a cost-benefit calculation, then the assumption that mediators must be perceived as impartial needs to be revised (Touval 1982). The mediator's impartiality is not as important to the adversaries' decision to accept mediation as is their consideration of the consequences of accepting or rejecting mediation: How will their decision affect the prospects of achieving a favorable outcome? And how will it affect their future relations with the would-be mediator?

Initially, third parties are accepted as mediators only to the extent that they are seen as capable of bringing about acceptable outcomes; then, their subsequent meddling is tolerated because they are already part of the relationship. Although there is no necessary relationship between a mediator's past partiality and its future usefulness, good relations between it and one of the adversaries may in fact be an aid to communicating, to developing creative proposals, and to converging the two parties' positions. Closeness to one party implies the possibility of "delivering" it, thereby stimulating the other party's cooperation. Indeed, the implications of closeness can be carried one step further: Since mediators are not likely to be successful (that is, attractive to the other party) if they are perceived as preferring a solution favoring the party to which they are close, a biased mediator's acceptability and success lies in the likelihood of its delivering the party toward which it is biased into an agreement.

Several examples illustrate these points. In the Rhodesia/Zimbabwe mediation, the Africans' belief that British and U.S. sympathies were with the white Rhodesians rendered British and U.S. mediation promising and stimulated African cooperation. In several mediations between Arab parties and Israel, the Arabs' belief that the close American-Israeli ties would enable the United States to deliver Israeli concessions made American mediation attractive to them. In the Tashkent mediation, the Soviet Union was accepted as a mediator by Pakistan, despite its close relationship with India. Pakistan perceived the Soviet Union as concerned enough about Pakistan's growing cooperation with China to want to improve its own relationship with Pakistan and as close enough to India to bring it into an agreement. Algeria was accepted by the United States as a mediator with Iran not because it was considered impartial, but because its ability to gain access to and facilitate the agreement of people close to Khomeini held promise that it might help to release the hostages.

Although they cannot fully side with one party, mediators can allow themselves some latitude in their degree of partiality. This latitude may allow them to express their preference regarding the outcome of the negotiation. In the Zimbabwe and Namibia negotiations, the United States was not indifferent to the nature of the settlement: The outcome had to open the way for majority rule. Although this meant that the United States supported the essence of the African position and, by implication, sought to eliminate the white settlers as a sovereign political actor, the white settlers nevertheless accepted U.S. mediation as a means to get them out of a no-win situation.

An interest in specific outcomes is quite common in the mediations of international organizations. The United Nations, the OAU, the ICRC, and the Organization of American States (OAS) all have some general norms that they wish to uphold beyond the principle of peaceful settlement. They try to promote solutions that can be interpreted as compatible with the standards of the Geneva conventions and of their charters and that protect their image as guardians of these standards. Indeed, they can formally condemn parties for deviating from these standards as a means to enforce them. On the other hand, the OAU was so strongly attached to the principle of successor state inviolability that it was incapable of mediating the Biafran or Namibian conflict, so strongly attached to the principle of *uti possidetis* (legitimacy of inherited boundaries) that it was unable to mediate the Ogaden war, and so strongly attached to the principle of noninterference in internal affairs that it was unable even to constitute a commission to mediate the Sudanese and Rwandan civil wars.

Acceptance of mediation, whether the mediator is a state or an international organization, is not automatic. It depends on the promise of attractive outcomes for the parties. When the OAU establishes an ad hoc commission to mediate a dispute, consultation procedures give the parties an implicit say in the composition of the commission. The result is often a balanced slate rather than an impartial commission, because members are likely to seek to protect the interests of their friends and not to form their views solely on the basis of abstract principles.

Independent nonstate agencies, such as the ICRC or the Sant'Egidio community, do not have partiality or composition problems. Nevertheless, their acceptance as a mediator is still not automatic. Conflicting parties are not concerned whether the ICRC or Sant'Egidio will perform humanitarian functions objectively, but whether the framework of its involvement will further their interests. Thus, states may deny that an armed conflict that would justify an ICRC intervention is occurring or has occurred or that a Sant'Egidio venue for dialogue is appropriate. Yet, the legal framework is sometimes subject to negotiation, and the terms of involvement can be influenced by their perceived effect on the interests of the parties, rather than by the latter's perception of the mediator's impartiality.

Mediators must be perceived as having an interest in achieving an outcome acceptable to both sides and as being not so partial as to preclude such an achievement. Again, the question for the parties is not whether the mediator is objective, but whether it can provide an acceptable outcome.

TIMING OF MEDIATION

Since mediators are motivated by self-interest, they will not intervene automatically, but only when they believe a conflict threatens their interests or when they perceive an opportunity to advance their interests. Such threats and opportunities are unlikely to be noticed when there is a mild disagreement between parties. Usually it is only after the conflict escalates that its implications are perceived. By then, the parties are likely to have become committed to their positions and to a confrontational policy, ever reducing the common grounds on which mediation must proceed. For that mediation to succeed, the parties must be disposed to reevaluate their policies.

Two conditions are especially conducive to such reevaluation: mutually hurting stalemates and crises bounded by a deadline or, to use a metaphor, plateaus and precipices (Zartman 1989). A mutually hurting stalemate begins when one side realizes that it is unable to achieve its aims, resolve the problem, or win the conflict by itself; it is completed when the other side reaches a similar conclusion. Each party must begin to feel uncomfortable in the costly dead end that it has reached. Both sides must see this plateau not as a momentary resting ground, but as a flat, unpleasant terrain stretching into the future, providing no later possibilities for decisive escalation or graceful escape.

Mediation plays upon the parties' perceptions of having reached an intolerable situation. Without this perception, the mediator must depend on persuading the parties that breaking out of their deadlock is impossible. Indeed, the mediator may even be required to make it impossible. Thus, deadlock cannot be seen as a temporary stalemate, to be easily resolved in one's favor by a little effort, a big offensive, a gamble, or foreign assistance. Rather, each party must recognize its opponent's strength and its own inability to overcome that strength, as well as the cost of staying in the stalemate.

For the mediator, this means cultivating each side's perception that its unilateral policy option—to take action without negotiation—is a more expensive, less likely way of achieving an acceptable outcome than the policy of negotiation. A plateau is therefore as much a matter of perception as of reality for the parties and as much a subject of persuasion as of timing for the mediator. Successful exploitation of a plateau shifts both sides from a combative mentality to a conciliatory mentality.

A crisis, or precipice, represents the realization that matters are swiftly becoming worse. It implies impending catastrophe, such as probable military defeat or economic collapse. It may be accompanied by a policy dilemma that involves engaging in a major escalation, the outcome of which is unpredictable, or seeking a desperate compromise that threatens one side as much as the other. It may also be a catastrophe that has already taken place or has been narrowly avoided. Whatever its tense (because parties

are bound to disagree about the inevitability of an impending event), it marks a time limit to the judgment that "things can't go on like this" (Zartman 1987, pp. 285ff).

For the mediator, the crisis as precipice should reinforce the dangers of the plateau, lest the parties become accustomed to their uncomfortable deadlock. Mediators can manipulate stalemates and crises: They can use them and they can make them. If there is a recognized impending danger, mediators can use it as a warning and as an unpleasant alternative to a negotiated settlement. And if they do not agree that a crisis exists, mediators can work to implant a common perception that it or a mutually hurting stalemate does exist. In its most manipulative role, a mediator may have to create a plateau or a precipice, usually citing pressure from a fourth party. That is what the United States did in 1977 to get the Namibia negotiations started, citing irresistible pressure for sanctions if the sides did not start talking. Plateau and precipice are precise but perceptional conditions, and they have governed the timing of successful mediation in most cases. They are not self-implementing: They must be seen and seized. Unfortunately, they depend on conflict and its escalation. It would be preferable if the need for a ripe moment could be combined with the desirability of treating conflict early, as sought in preventive diplomacy. To do this, mediators need to develop a perception of stalemate at a low level of conflict, or to develop a sense of responsibility on the part of a government to head off an impending conflict, or to develop an awareness of an opportunity for a better outcome made available through mediation. There are few examples, as yet, of mediators using such tactics successfully.

MODES OF MEDIATORS

Mediators use three modes to marshal the interests of all the involved parties toward a mutually acceptable solution to the conflict. The mediator uses communication, formulation, and manipulation, in that order. Since mediation is helping the parties to do what they cannot do by themselves, each of these three modes refers to a different level of obstacle to the conduct of direct negotiations.

When conflict has made direct contact between parties impossible, thereby preventing the parties from talking to each other and from making concessions without appearing weak or losing face, the mediator can serve as communicator. In this situation, mediators simply act as a conduit, opening contacts and carrying messages. They may be required to help the parties understand the meaning of messages through the distorting dust thrown up by the conflict or to gather the parties' concessions together into a package, without adding to the content. This role is completely procedural, with no substantive contribution by the mediator, and in its simplest form it is completely passive, only carrying out the parties' orders for the delivery of messages. Tact, wording, and sympathy, mixed in equal doses with accuracy and confidentiality, are necessary character traits of the mediator as communicator.

The second mode of mediation requires the mediator to enter into the substance of the negotiation. Since a conflict may not only impede communications between parties, but be so encompassing that it prevents them from conceiving ways out of the dispute, the parties need a mediator as formulator. Formulas are the key to a negotiated solution to a conflict; they provide a common understanding of the problem and its solution or a shared notion of justice to govern an outcome. Just as the conflict often prevents the parties from finding imaginative ways out, it may also prevent them from seeing the value of the mediator's suggestions at first hearing. Therefore, the mediator as a formulator often needs to persuade the parties, as well as to suggest solutions

to their disputes. Persuasion involves power and therefore requires greater involvement than mere communication. Not only does the mediator get involved in the substance of the issue, but it must also lean on the parties —albeit in the subtlest ways—to adopt its perceptions of a way out. Mediators as successful formulators must be capable of thinking of ways to unblock the thinking of the conflicting parties and to work out imaginative ways to skirt those commitments that constrain the parties.

The third mode requires the mediator to act as a manipulator. Here the mediator assumes the maximum degree of involvement, becoming a party to the solution if not to the dispute. As a manipulator, the mediator uses its power to bring the parties to an agreement, pushing and pulling them away from conflict and into resolution. When the obstacle to agreement is the seemingly paltry size of the outcome, the mediator must persuade the parties of its vision of a solution; it must then take measures to make that solution attractive, enhancing its value by adding benefits to its outcome and presenting it in such a way as to overcome imbalances that may have prevented one of the parties from subscribing to it. The mediator may have to go so far as to improve the absolute attractiveness of the resolution by increasing the unattractiveness of continued conflict, which may mean shoring up one side or condemning another, either of which actions strains the appearance of its own neutrality. This is the role of the "full participant," such as American diplomats played in the 1970s Middle East peace process and in the 1980s Namibian-Angolan negotiations.

Mediation is a triangular relationship. When the mediator operates as a communicator, it operates as a bridge between two contestants, or as a pump on the conduit between them. As a formulator, the mediator assumes a position of greater activity, one from which pressures and messages emanate as well as pass through. As a manipulator, the mediator becomes so active that it calls into question the triangular relationship. It may even unite the two adversaries in opposition to the mediator; for example, in the Yemen civil war (1962–1970) the two sides resolved their differences in order to oppose Egyptian interference, when Egypt was acting more as an intervenor than as a mediator. But the mediator, by throwing its weight around, threatens and is threatened by the possibility of turning the triangle into a dyad. The mediator's threat to side with one party may bring the other party around, for fear that mediation might end and with it any possibilities for a solution. As a threat to the mediator, each party may try to win the mediator over to its own side to increase its chances of winning rather than of having to come to terms. At the same time, of course, each party may regard the mediator with high suspicion as a potential ally of the other side. Although it makes the mediator's job more difficult, suspicion is good because it keeps the mediator honest.

POWER IN MEDIATION

Power—the ability to move a party in an intended direction—is often referred to in mediation as "leverage." Although leverage is the ticket to mediation, mediators tend to remain relatively powerless throughout the exercise. The extent of the mediator's power depends entirely on the parties, whose acceptance of a mediator depends on its likelihood (potential power) of producing an outcome agreeable to both sides. This circular relationship plagues every mediation exercise. Contrary to a common misperception, mediators are rarely "hired" by the parties; instead, they have to sell their services, based on the prospect of their usefulness and success. From the beginning, the mediator's leverage is at the mercy of the contestants.

The parties, whose interest is in winning, view mediation as meddling, unless it produces a favorable outcome. They welcome mediation only to the extent that the mediator has leverage over the other party, and they berate the mediator for trying to exert leverage over them.

A mediator has five sources of leverage: first, persuasion, the ability to portray an alternative future as more favorable than the continuing conflict; second, extraction, the ability to produce an attractive position from each party; third, termination, the ability to withdraw from the mediation; fourth, deprivation, the ability to withhold resources from one side or to shift them to the other; and fifth, gratification, the ability to add resources to the outcome. In every case the effectiveness of the mediator's leverage lies with the parties themselves, a characteristic that makes leverage in mediation difficult to achieve.

The first source of leverage is persuasion. The mediator in any mode must be able to point out the attractiveness of conciliation on available terms and the unattractiveness of continued conflict, a purely communicative exercise independent of any resources. Secretary of State Henry Kissinger, whose country was not devoid of resources or the willingness to use them, nevertheless spent long hours painting verbal pictures of the future with and without an agreement for Egyptian, Syrian, and Israeli audiences. His actions may not have been sufficient in the last rounds of the withdrawal negotiations, but they certainly were necessary. President Jimmy Carter's mediation at Camp David in September 1978 and in Cairo and Jerusalem in March 1979 bear the same characteristics of the power and limitations of persuasion.

Mediation is unwelcome until it can extract a proposal from one party that is viewed as favorable by the other. This second source of leverage is the most problematic, yet it is the basis of all mediation. The crucial moment in mediation comes when the mediator asks a party's permission to try for the other's agreement to a proposal; this exchange is the heart of the formulation mode. But its success depends on the parties' need for a way out of the impasse of conflict—demonstrating the importance of the mutually "hurting stalemate" as an element of the ripe moment. Assistant Secretary of State Chester A. Crocker and his team shuttled back and forth between Angola and South Africa in search of attractive proposals to carry to each side, but that exchange was not forthcoming until the conditions of 1988 made the stalemate intolerable to both sides.

The third source of leverage, termination, lies in the mediator's ability to withdraw and leave the parties to their own devices and their continuing conflict. Again, the impact of withdrawal is entirely in the hands of the disputing parties; they may be happy to see the mediator leave, but if the mutually hurting stalemate is present, they will be sensitive to the threat of leaving. However, if the mediator needs a solution more than the parties, it will be unable to threaten termination credibly. Secretary Kissinger brandished the threat in mediating the Golan Heights withdrawal in 1974 and activated it at the second Sinai withdrawal the following year.

The remaining sources of leverage use the conflict and the proposed solution as their fulcrums, thus making manipulation their primary mode of mediation. Leverage derives from the mediator's ability to tilt toward (gratification) or away from (deprivation) a party and thereby to affect the conditions of a stalemate or of movement out of it. The activity may be verbal, such as a vote of condemnation, or more tangible, such as visits, food aid, or arms shipments. The point of this leverage is to worsen the dilemma of parties rejecting mediation and to keep them in search of a solution.

The mediator might shift weight in order to prevent one party from losing the conflict because the other's victory would produce a less stable and hence less desirable situation. Such activity clearly brings the mediator very close to being a party in the conflict. Arms to Israel and Morocco, down payments on better relations with South Africa, and abstentions on UN votes are examples of U.S. shifts-in-weight during various mediation processes. The Soviet Union threatened to shift weight away from India in the Security Council debate on the Indo-Pakistan war, and Britain threatened to shift weight against the Patriotic Front in Rhodesia. Threats of this kind are effective only to the degree that they are believed.

The last source of the mediator's leverage is the side payment, the subject to which the term "leverage" is usually applied. As weight shifts affect the continuing conflict, side payments may be needed to augment or enhance the outcome to one or more parties. Side payments require considerable resources and engagement from the mediators, thus they are rarely made and certainly not the key to successful mediation. Yet when the outcome is not large enough to provide sufficient benefits for both parties or to outweigh the present or anticipated advantages of continued conflict, some source of additional benefits is needed. Side payments may be attached to the outcomes themselves, such as third-party guarantees of financial aid for accomplishing changes required by the agreement, or they may be unrelated to the outcome itself, simply additional benefits that make agreement more attractive. The graduated aid package attached to the Israeli and Egyptian agreement to disengage in the Sinai and then to sign a peace treaty is an example. Sometimes the demand for side payments by the parties may be as extraneous to agreement as is their supply.

Of all these, the principal element of leverage is persuasion—the ability of the mediator to reorient the parties' perceptions. Like any kind of persuasion, the mediator's ability depends on many different referents that are skillfully employed to make conciliation more attractive and continuing conflict less so. These referents may include matters of domestic welfare and political fortunes, risks and costs, prospects of continuing conflict and of moving out of it, reputations, solidity of allies' support, world opinion, and the verdict of history.

The other basic element in leverage is need—the parties' need—for a solution that they cannot achieve by themselves, for additional support in regional or global relations, and for a larger package of payoffs to make a conciliatory outcome more attractive. Perception of this need can be enhanced by the mediator, but it cannot be created out of nothing. Side payments with no relation to the outcome of the conflict are effective only insofar as they respond to an overriding need that outweighs the deprivation of concessions on the issues of the conflict itself. Parties can be made aware of needs that they did not recognize before, particularly when the chances of assuaging them seem out of reach. The provision of Cuban troop withdrawal from Angola, which met South Africa's need for a countervailing reward, led to the South African troop and administration withdrawal from Namibia, yet this need was not formulated during the 1970s rounds of the mediation. Persuasion often depends on need, but then need often depends on persuasion.

What do these characteristics say about "powerful" and "powerless" mediators? The common distinction between "interested" and "disinterested" mediators is less solid than might appear. All mediators have interests, most mediators are interested in the conflict situation in some way, and "biased" mediators may even have an advantage in access to one or both of the parties. If mediation were only persuasion, or "pure"

persuasion, it would not matter who practiced it, and entry into the practice would be equally open to any silver-tongued orator. But mediation is more than simple persuasion, and the basis of effective persuasion is the ability to fulfill both tangible and intangible needs of the parties. The mediator's leverage is based therefore on the parties' need for the solution it is able to produce and on its ability to produce attractive solutions from each party.

Although official mediators are usually needed to help conclude agreements between disputing parties, unofficial (that is, nonstate) mediators may be effective persuaders and may be useful in helping to reorient the perceptions of the parties' values and opportunities. If the required mode of mediation is low—limited to communication—and the felt need for a solution is high in both parties, informal mediation may be all that is necessary to bring the parties to negotiation. However, the higher the required mode, the lower the felt needs, the more structural interests involving a third party, and the more the conflict involves states rather than nonstate actors, the less likely informal mediation can be an effective substitute for the official attention of states. Statesmen are not necessarily better mediators, but they can provide interest- and need-related services that informal mediators cannot handle.

Unofficial mediation in Africa provides a good illustration. Textbook cases of mediation were effected by the World Council of Churches and the All-African Conference of Churches in the southern Sudanese civil war in 1972, and the Sant'Egidio community in Mozambique in 1990–1992 and Algeria after 1994. The church bodies widened the perceptions of opportunity among the parties and persuaded them to move to resolution. The mediators were not unbiased, having closer ties with the southern Sudanese and Mozambican rebels than with the government, and they were not without means of leverage, being able to threaten a resumption of supplies if the government broke off talks; in Algeria, all they could offer was a venue and encouragement. The stalemates that had been building over the years were reinforced by a mediator-induced perception of an attractive way out for the parties. The nonstate mediator played a major role and deserves credit for the operations; the subsequent collapse of the Sudanese agreement a decade later and the incompleteness of the Algerian démarche were due to other causes, not to a failed mediation. But behind the nonstate mediator in the Sudan stood an international organization—the assistant secretary general of the OAU, Mohamed Sahnoun—and behind him stood a mediator of last resort—the emperor of Ethiopia, Haile Selassie; and around the nonstate mediator in Mozambique stood an array of interested states—the United States, Russia, Italy, Portugal, Kenya, Zimbabwe, and South Africa. At a number of telling points in the operation, state actors were needed because guarantees that only a state could provide were required. The loneliness of the nonstate mediator in Algeria in 1995 goes far to explain its limited success.

Nearly two decades after the Sudanese venture, another private mediation was attempted in 1990 in a related conflict between the Eritrean rebels and the Ethiopian government. The private mediator was a former head of state, Jimmy Carter, who was perceived in the field as carrying official backing. The démarche responded to an appeal elicited from the parties and was carried out with dedication and skill. It failed because there was no mutually hurting stalemate and because the nature of the conflict changed during the mediation. The success of the Tigrean rebellion caused any ripeness in the previous moment to dissipate. The mediator was unable to persuade the parties of their deadlock or of their need to find a way out or to respond to any of the parties' needs for solutions, support, or side payments. Carter was in contact with heads of state in the region and obtained their sympathy and interest, even their benevolent neutrality during the mediation. But only states could have supplied the missing elements of support and side payments, and even then there was no guarantee that they would have been any more successful than Carter was, especially given the absence of a ripe moment.

An example of a private mediation backed by a state was Carter's intervention in Haiti in 1994. When the ruling junta refused to give up power and transfer it to the elected president Aristide as demanded by the United Nations, Carter went to Haiti, persuaded the junta leaders to withdraw, and negotiated the terms of their withdrawal. Carter succeeded this time mainly because his mediation took place hours before the scheduled launch of an American military invasion intended to remove the junta by force and because political credibility was added by the participation of Senator Sam Nunn, chairman of the Senate Armed Services Committee, and General Colin Powell, former chairman of the Joint Chiefs of Staff.

Many other mediations have benefited from a reversal of the roles portrayed in the Horn and in Haiti, that is, from informal support and assistance in a mediation performed by a state actor. In Zimbabwe, and more broadly in the Arab-Israeli dispute, many private efforts have helped strengthen the context and prepare the terrain for official mediation. Although any efforts to improve premediation conditions make a contribution, private efforts actually to mediate in the Northern Irish, Falklands, Cyprus, and current Arab-Israeli conflicts have been notorious failures. Ripe moments and leveraged buy-offs by state mediators are the necessary ingredients, and even they may not be sufficient.

ETHICAL DILEMMAS

Mediators often pursue the double goal of stopping a war and settling the issues in dispute. They will pursue both, trying to end the bloodshed and to devise a settlement that is perceived to be fair by the parties involved, and thus be acceptable and durable.

However, in trying to achieve these goals, mediators are often confronted with the realization that settling the conflict in a manner that is considered fair by the disputants is likely to take a long time. Mediators may therefore face a dilemma of whether or not to give priority to a cease-fire and postpone the settlement of the conflict for later. Viewed somewhat differently, the choice may be seen as one between order and justice; to be sure, the two objectives are closely related. A durable cessation of hostilities requires a peace settlement. Justice requires order, and order, to endure, must be just. But these are long-term historical perspectives. For mediators, the choice is immediate: What should they do next? Should they pursue both objectives simultaneously, or should they give priority to a cease-fire?

The ethical dilemma arises because the issue is not merely one of sequencing. The sequencing has consequences. As we have seen, warring parties are more likely to settle when the continuing confrontation hurts badly and produces grave risks. A cease-fire, ending the bloodshed, is likely to ease the pain and reduce the risks. It will create a tolerable stalemate, a situation that the disputants might find preferable to the alternative of granting the concessions necessary for a compromise settlement. But cease-fires tend to be unstable and are often punctuated by wars and additional bloodshed, for example, the cease-fires between Israel and various Arab parties, between India and Pakistan, between Greeks and Turks in Cyprus, and between the warring parties in the former Yugoslavia.

Unfortunately, it is impossible to predict reliably which course of action will ultimately cost more—an early cease-fire that may collapse and be followed by more fighting because the conflict remains unresolved, or a continuation of a war while the search goes on for a definitive settlement of the conflict. An argument for giving priority to a cease-fire is that predictions of the near term are generally more reliable than those of the more distant future. The mediator can be certain that an ongoing war will produce casualties. The proposition that cease-fires break down, leading to the renewal of war and producing higher casualties over the long-term, is far less certain. Nevertheless, the dilemma exists.

Another dilemma is whether to facilitate an attainable settlement that violates international norms or to hold out for one that is consistent with principles of justice adopted by the international community. One might argue that mediators of international conflicts should pursue terms that are attainable, even if they are attainable mainly because they reflect the balance of power between the adversaries, rather than jointly held notions of justice. There are two important arguments against such a course of action. One is that such a settlement is unlikely to endure. One of the parties (sometimes both) will resent terms that it considers unjust and will seek to overturn them at the earliest opportunity. The other argument concerns the wider ramifications of such settlements for world order. A settlement that is inconsistent with international principles may tend to undermine their validity, creating uncertainties about the norms and thus weakening constraints upon international conduct. In other words, such settlements, while appearing to settle a particular conflict, may cause wider long-term damage by undermining the foundations of international peace and security.

Such a dilemma has been faced by the international community seeking to mediate the conflict in Bosnia. The choice there has been perceived as one between separating the warring parties through a partition, or pursuing a settlement that will preserve the integrity of a multi-ethnic Republic of Bosnia and Herzegovina. Partition has been criticized as tantamount to legitimizing territorial conquests and the consequences of ethnic cleansing, and thus rewarding aggression. Insistence on a settlement respectful of the norm of preserving the integrity of the Bosnian state has been criticized for prolonging the war and thus costing tens of thousands additional casualties (besides the argument that it is inconsistent with the reluctance of the international community to protect the integrity of the pre-1991 multi-ethnic Yugoslav state).

The dilemma facing mediators in such situations is stark. What comes first—striving to protect the norm of respect for the integrity of states, trying to teach members of warring ethnic groups (Serbs, Croats, and Bosnian Muslims; Greeks and Turks in Cyprus; southern and northern Sudanese; Armenians and Azeris in Afghanistan) to coexist in peace, or saving lives by separating the groups and postponing the search for justice until later?

A good answer would require prescience. It is possible that promoting a settlement that is perhaps attainable, but inconsistent with international norms, might cause serious long-term injury to international peace and security. Should mediators work for terms that seem attainable, provided they promise to stabilize a cease-fire, despite their corrosive long-term effects? Viewing norms as merely tentative and conditional propositions is destructive to order. But eschewing settlements that do not conform to established norms, even if doing so allows mutual slaughter to continue, is also destructive to peace and order. Such dilemmas are not new. But these and other ethical issues have become pressing for international mediators in recent years. Guidelines for resolving such dilemmas are not easy to come by.

CONCLUSION

More interest and less leverage is involved in third-party mediation than is commonly assumed. Adversarial parties and potential mediators each make an interest calculation that involves much more than the simple settlement of the dispute. Their calculations include relations among the conflicting parties and third parties and the costs and benefits of all of them in both conflict and conciliation. Leverage comes from harnessing those interests and from the third party's ability to play on perceptions of needs, above all on needs for a solution.

Mediation acts as a catalyst to negotiation. It facilitates the settlement of disputes that parties ought to be able to accomplish on their own, if they were not so absorbed in their conflict. Mediation becomes necessary when the conflict is twice dominant: providing the elements of the dispute and preventing parties from seeking and finding a way out. Even when it is successful, mediation can only cut through some of those layers, providing a means for the parties to live together despite their dispute—it does not provide deep reconciliation or cancel the causes of the conflict. Left again to their own instincts, the parties may well fall out of their mediated settlement, and there are plenty of cases (often unstudied by analysts and practitioners focusing on the moment of mediation) in which the hard-bargained agreement has subsequently fallen apart under changed conditions or revived enmities. For this reason, although the mediator is often tempted to start a process and then slip away as it develops its own momentum, it may in fact be required to be more involved in the regional structure of relations after its mediation than before. Yet it must not be a crutch forever, lest it become a party to the conflict. This is the final challenge and dilemma for mediators: How to disengage from a mediating role without endangering the carefully brokered settlement.

REFERENCES

Assefa, Hizkias. 1987. *Mediation of Civil Wars.* Boulder, Colo.: Westview.

Johnston, Douglas, and Cynthia Sampson. 1994. *Religion: The Missing Dimension of Statecraft.* New York: Oxford University Press.

Princen, Thomas. 1992. *Intermediaries in International Conflict.* Princeton, N.J.: Princeton University Press.

Touval, Saadia. 1982. *The Peace Brokers.* Princeton, N.J.: Princeton University Press.

———. 1992. "The Superpowers as Mediators." In *Mediation in International Relations: Multiple Approaches to Conflict Management*, ed. Jacob Bercovitch and Jeffrey Z. Rubin. New York: Macmillan/St. Martin's Press.

Udalov, Vadim. 1995. "National Interests and Conflict Reduction." In *Cooperative Security: Reducing Third World Wars*, ed. I. William Zartman and Victor Kremenyuk. Syracuse, N.Y.: Syracuse University Press.

Zartman, I. William. 1987. "The Middle East: Ripe Moment?" In *Conflict Management in the Middle East*, ed. G. Ben-Dor and D. Dewitt. Lexington, Mass.: Heath.

———. 1989. *Ripe for Resolution.* 2nd ed. New York: Oxford University Press.

———. 1995. "Systems of World Order and Regional Conflict Reduction." In *Cooperative Security: Reducing Third World Wars*, ed. I. William Zartman and Victor Kremenyuk. Syracuse, N.Y.: Syracuse University Press.

Zartman, I. William, ed. 1995. *Elusive Peace: Negotiating an End to Civil Wars.* Washington, D.C.: Brookings Institution.

31

Mediation in the Middle East

KENNETH W. STEIN AND SAMUEL W. LEWIS

Since World War II, every U.S. administration has had to deal with the Arab-Israeli conflict in the Middle East. Over the past half-century, the conflict has proved to be a rich source of insights into the role of third-party official mediators in a complex, protracted, multiparty negotiation. In 1991, in order to cull these valuable insights, the United States Institute of Peace convened a study group composed of veteran diplomats, policymakers, and scholars to review the history of UN and U.S. mediation efforts and to extract practical lessons, applicable not only to the Middle East but also to other peace processes that include official third-party involvement in the negotiations.

This chapter, which is an amended version of portions of the study group's report, considers the necessary elements of successful mediation in the Arab-Israeli conflict, examining the mediator's role in bringing about and sustaining peace talks, the effect of timing and ripeness on the success of the mediation, the challenges of building a negotiating structure, the essential component of presidential engagement, and the impor-

tance of good intelligence to the mediator's effort. The last part of the chapter contains key observations on the role of mediation throughout the whole negotiating process.

NECESSARY ELEMENTS FOR SUCCESSFUL MEDIATION

The Mediator's Role

A mediator is primarily responsible for finding ways around stalemates and for proposing compromise language to bridge conflicting positions; but a successful mediator of the Arab-Israeli conflict must also be in a position to provide incentives, assurances, and guarantees. The role of a third party is as central to the history of the Arab-Israeli conflict as is the tradition that such a third party has a dual obligation. Both sides have expected and continue to expect a "mediator-umpire" to play an active role in resolving differences.

The history of British mediation during the mandate period was marked by both sides threatening the mediator with

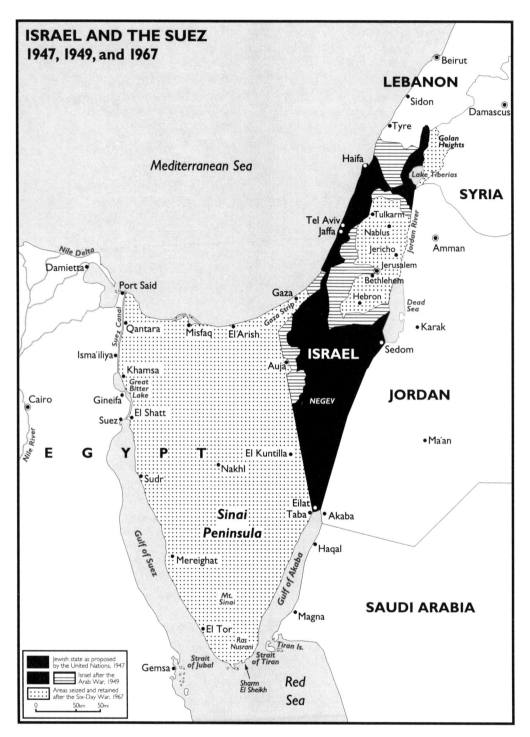

ISRAEL AND THE SUEZ
1947, 1949, and 1967

Mediterranean Sea

LEBANON

●Beirut

● Sidon

Damascus ◎

●Tyre

Golan Heights

Haifa

Lake Tiberias

SYRIA

Tel Aviv
Jaffa

●Tulkarm

●Nablus

Jericho

Jordan River

● Amman

Jerusalem
Bethlehem

Hebron

Dead Sea

● Karak

Gaza

Gaza Strip

Nile Delta

Damietta ●

Port Said ●

Suez Canal

Qantara ●

Misfaq ● El'Arish ●

ISRAEL

Sedom ●

Isma'iliya ●

Auja ●

JORDAN

Khamsa ●

Great Bitter Lake

NEGEV

Cairo ◎

Gineifa ●

Suez ● El Shatt ●

E G Y P T

El Kuntilla ●

●Ma'an

Nile River

Nakhl ●

● Sudr

Sinai Peninsula

Eilat
Taba ●

● Akaba

Gulf of Suez

Mereighat ●

Haqal ●

Gulf of Akaba

Mt. Sinai

SAUDI ARABIA

El Tor ●

Ras Nusrani

Magna ●

Tiran Is.

Strait of Tiran

Gemsa ●

Strait of Jubal

Red Sea

Sharm El Sheikh

■ Jewish state as proposed by the United Nations, 1947
▤ Israel after the Arab War, 1949
⋯ Areas seized and retained after the Six-Day War, 1967

0   50km   50mi

Redrawn from *The Middle East: A History,* 3rd ed., by Sydney Nettleton Fisher (Alfred A. Knopf, New York, 1979). Used by permission of McGraw-Hill Inc.

464

disruptive behavior—such as public protests, boycotts, civilian disturbances, or prolonged violence—if the petitioner's demands were not met. Each side expected the mediator to validate the righteousness and justice of its claims and to force the other side to acknowledge a new status quo. If a decision were not to one side's liking, it felt free to disregard the decision and to circumvent or disregard the decision maker whenever possible. U.S. mediators in the 1970s and 1980s were occasionally confronted with similar obstacles.

Although direct talks between parties symbolize mutual recognition, parity, and legitimacy, they do not ensure progress in the negotiations. Private, unpublicized face-to-face talks between Israeli and Arab officials have sometimes created a climate of better understanding, indicated areas of possible compromise, and even developed mutual trust between the participants. But more typically, direct Arab-Israeli talks without the presence of a mediator have been short and ineffective. A striking example was the disappointing outcome of Prime Minister Menachem Begin's bilateral meeting with President Anwar Sadat at Ismailia a few weeks after Sadat's historic trip to Jerusalem in 1977; the Ismailia meeting produced a significant setback. Even so, Israeli leaders have consistently pressed for direct negotiations. Arab leaders, by contrast, have consistently tried to avoid direct negotiations, judging them too politically costly if they do not remain secret. They risk personal and national isolation from their fellow Arabs for recognizing Israel and its claims "directly." Therefore, Arab leaders have usually judged indirect talks through the United Nations, the United States, or others to be less politically dangerous.

The Oslo Agreement of 1993 between Israel and the Palestine Liberation Organization (PLO) was the first major achievement of Arab-Israel peacemaking reached without a large component of third-party

mediation. The Norwegian "good offices" role was important, but wholly nonsubstantive. Subsequent Israel-Palestinian agreements and the Israel-Jordan peace treaty were then completed with only marginal help from U.S. mediators. However, the U.S. role as third-party mediator was critical in talks between Israel and Syria as well as between Israel and Lebanon.

Missed opportunities for talks between Arabs and Israelis have resulted from either or both sides being unwilling to risk—or unable to risk—domestic political upheaval or political, economic, and communal isolation. A mediator provides the political cover necessary for a leader who wants an understanding but who must defer to domestic politics or to inter-Arab political constraints. Israeli cabinet members also have often relied on U.S. mediators to present certain difficult positions so that the blame for accepting an unpopular compromise can be put on American "pressure," not on their own government.

The history of mediating Arab-Israeli disputes provides a number of lessons about the mediator's role. First, in this conflict, mediators must be prepared to take significant risks, including that of failure. A lot of brinkmanship is involved in successful mediation; mediators must be cautious but not nerveless. They must be ready to go beyond what the parties say the mediator's role should be. Even though the parties (Israel in particular) will often remind the mediators that they are not participants and that their role is merely to bring the conflicting parties together, both sides actually do expect the mediators to play active roles, especially when an impasse develops.

This peculiarity of mediation of the Arab-Israeli conflict may apply more to American mediators than to UN mediators, although the overriding reason that the special representative of the UN secretary general, Gunnar Jarring, failed in his 1971 mediation effort was that he was overly cautious. Jarring might have achieved more had he pressed the Israelis harder and gone beyond simply conveying messages between the parties. He apparently lacked the necessary self-confidence to exceed the letter of his formal brief. Procedurally, his fastidiousness had a negative impact on the parties.

Jarring's lack of success may also have reflected the inherent ambivalence of his position at that time as UN mediator. In contrast, UN Undersecretary General Ralph Bunche's success in the 1949 armistice negotiations reflected U.S. confidence and support for the UN mediation effort and for Bunche personally. It is clear that if the great powers do not actively back the UN mediator's mission, that mediator will achieve little. This is particularly true if the parties to the conflict sense any American hesitancy toward the mission. Moreover, as with any UN activity, the degree to which the United Nations alone can implement and sustain an agreement sets an outer limit to the direct leverage a UN mediator has available to bring parties to agreement. That leverage is likely to be sufficient only with a relatively few small nations; it is wholly inadequate among the Arab-Israeli antagonists. Therefore, it is unrealistic to expect a UN mediator in the Arab-Israeli conflict to go much beyond providing "good offices" on the part of the UN secretary general.

The second lesson is that mediators should facilitate, not dominate, the negotiating process. Mediators should not offer proposals without having consulted carefully with both parties in advance. Jarring violated this rule, as have others. As issues arise throughout the negotiations, mediators should remain approachable and responsive to each side's concerns.

Third, mediators should be extremely wary of threatening to withdraw and leave the parties to their own devices. Understandably, mediators may assume that the parties will pay a price to keep them involved. In fact, however, the parties often have mixed feelings. Even while having to rely on outside mediators, they are never wholly comfortable with having third parties involved. They would sometimes welcome an excuse to end the negotiations rather than be forced to make difficult decisions.

Fourth, mediators cannot rush the parties to a conclusion. Deadlines are dangerous. Rushing governments into accepting a mediator's formula may risk collapsing the talks altogether. Proposing an early deadline can have two disastrous results: the parties' and the mediator's bitter disappointment about unfulfilled expectations, and the mediator's loss of credibility with the parties. Mediators must work patiently and persistently, realizing that their personal stamina alone often sustains the mediation process. Rarely are complex Middle East negotiations concluded quickly.

American representatives on the Palestine Conciliation Commission in 1949 believed that they could have an Arab-Israeli peace treaty signed and the Palestinian refugee problem solved within two months. Similarly, in 1983–1984, Special Middle East Envoy Donald Rumsfeld initially believed that he could quickly arrive at a solution. Such optimism is invariably unrealistic.

A fifth lesson is that mediators should understand and accommodate the particular negotiating styles of different leaders. President Assad might take nine hours of tête-à-tête to make a very few points. A strategist and a tactician, he derives enjoyment from hearing new ideas and debating the issues. Prime Minister Yitzhak Shamir tended to listen rather than talk, and he disliked theoretical argument. Mediators tried to elicit responses from him in private, with his advisers not present. They were well advised to remain patiently attentive through prolonged periods of silence.

Prime Minister Begin often began and frequently punctuated his discussions with emotional references to tragic events in Jewish history. By recognizing that penchant, an informed mediator could use Israel's history to emphasize how vital a lasting peace could be for the Jewish people. President Jimmy Carter drew on this understanding at Camp David by personally inscribing photographs for Begin's grandchildren, a gesture that apparently moved Begin to soften his position on several issues in the waning hours of the negotiations. President Sadat disdained details. He concentrated on broad principles, leaving it first to Secretary of State Henry Kissinger and later to Carter, in effect, to negotiate details on his behalf. Carter, who insisted on acquiring a personal mastery of details, was ideally suited to undertake this role.

Sixth, a mediator must demonstrate a knowledgeable grasp of the history behind the issues. History weighs much more heavily on Arab and Israeli leaders than on Americans. Memories of past injustices, wars, and betrayals crowd and shape today's decisions. All parties fear being pulled by outside forces into a risky negotiating process whose end could be national disaster. Naturally, Middle Eastern leaders have a comprehensive grasp of their history that American mediators lack. They can also draw on better official records of earlier periods and can rely upon more continuity among the officials and diplomats dealing with the issues. Yet if Israeli or Arab leaders are to acquire any real confidence in a third-party mediator, that person will have to demonstrate real understanding not only of the issues, but also of the historical connections, underlying fears, and basic principles that shape the behavior of both sides.

Seventh, a mediator needs to be clear about the limitations on all the parties. The mediator should be able to convey effectively to each party an understanding of the frame of reference within which the other side is operating, plus the objective constraints that place limits on the other party's negotiating flexibility on specific issues. Kissinger, U.S. Secretary of State Cyrus Vance, and Carter all demonstrated this capacity very successfully.

Timing

Arab and Israeli leaders must have strong incentives to justify taking the political risks incurred by entering into negotiations. Moreover, negotiations have only succeeded at moments when the status quo seemed more painful or dangerous than a potential negotiated compromise, at least for some of the parties. A real or anticipated crisis can provide the essential catalyst to get them to the negotiating table. Breaks in the status quo, such as wars and regime changes, provide unique conditions for reviving a stalled negotiation or launching a new initiative.

Timing in launching negotiations is often decisive. The October 1973 war, Sadat's 1977 visit to Jerusalem, Israel's 1982 invasion and expulsion of the PLO from Lebanon, the outbreak of the 1987 *intifadah*, and the 1991 Persian Gulf War all seemed to provide promising openings for American initiatives. Washington used each of those opportunities to position itself in a central role in the negotiations, to prescribe or circumscribe Moscow's role in a future negotiating process, and to pressure both Arab and Israeli leaders to try diplomacy one more time. In fact, however, only some of these situations were truly "ripe." For example, the comprehensive policy initiative launched by President Ronald Reagan on September 1, 1982, was intended to turn regional attention away from Israel's invasion of Lebanon and back to peace negotiations over the West Bank and Gaza. It misfired, in large part because of bad timing: Neither Israel nor Syria would consider a broader agenda while the outcome of the Israeli gamble in Lebanon remained unclear.

In late 1973, Secretary of State Kissinger was able to choreograph the diplomatic process after the war because U.S. diplomacy had played a central role in defining how the war would end. Soon after Egypt and Syria launched their surprise attack on Israel, Sadat began signaling that he wanted contact with Washington. Israel desperately needed U.S. military and political assistance. Kissinger maintained close communication with both sides. When the war ended somewhat inconclusively (under strong pressure from the United States, the Soviet Union, and the UN Security Council), each side was ready to talk and to see Kissinger assume the role of mediator.

Although Sadat's visit to Jerusalem in 1977 surprised Washington and threw Carter's comprehensive peace approach off stride, the Carter administration soon seized the opening presented by Sadat's dramatic initiative and embarked on the mediation efforts that ultimately produced the Camp David Accords and the 1979 Egyptian-Israeli peace treaty.

In 1988, Secretary of State George Shultz tried unsuccessfully to exploit the situation produced by the *intifadah* in the West Bank and Gaza by bringing Israelis and Palestinians together to negotiate the transitional arrangements originally foreseen in the Camp David Accords, with the addition of a tighter time frame. Most recently, the regional repercussions of the Gulf War, combined with a much weakened Moscow anxious to cooperate with Washington's approach, spurred President George Bush and Secretary of State James Baker to pursue energetically their goal of convening a broad-based Middle East peace conference in Madrid.

Attemping to predict the next major status quo shift is a futile exercise. Leadership changes in all the regional protagonists

during this decade are, however, highly probable, and such changes might loosen some uncompromising negotiating positions anchored to historical ideologies. They might also harden them. For example, PLO Chairman Yasser Arafat's replacement would not necessarily have rescinded the PLO Charter. Nonetheless, changes in leadership can offer outside mediators new opportunities. Yitzhak Rabin's election as prime minister of Israel in the summer of 1992 provided such an opportunity. Whether or not Washington is already actively engaged in the region at such moments, U.S. diplomats should be prepared. In this complex negotiating environment, diplomatic timing is crucial.

Principles or Process

Putting together a negotiating process is almost as difficult as trying to negotiate the actual substance of a peace settlement. In this conflict, as in others, the parties see the procedural and substantive issues as fundamentally entwined. While mediators talk about procedure, or negotiating venue, or what the agenda might be, or how to finesse procedural road blocks (such as who will represent the Palestinians), each side is calculating how a particular procedure might affect the eventual substantive outcome. The mediator's objective is to achieve a peace settlement that safeguards the fundamental interests of all and that all parties can eventually accept. No particular process is intrinsically better than any other to achieve this end.

In this regard the United States has long endorsed several general principles that should be reflected in any outcome of Arab-Israeli negotiations. These are expressed in UN Security Council Resolution 242, with added emphases on safeguarding the security of Israel and on finding an acceptable way to provide legitimate national political rights for the Palestinian people. Washington's flexible approach to process should not be mistaken for flexibility in supporting these principles. Yet, in the last analysis, the U.S. interest is in achieving a genuine, durable peace. Whatever formula can be freely accepted by all parties that achieves that goal should satisfy the United States.

U.S. mediators have most successfully managed the dual task of facilitating and guiding negotiations by following a step-by-step approach, working toward a broad, long-term objective. Setting the goal as something broadly desirable for both sides, this approach has avoided putting parties at immediate loggerheads and deadlocking the mediation effort. Attempts by either the United Nations or the United States to resolve all major issues in a single conference or negotiating process have thus far failed.

Presidential Engagement

Vigorous and continuous participation by the United States at the highest government level is essential for progress. Only when the president is active and when his personal involvement is obvious do the parties to the conflict take a U.S. mediation effort seriously. Only then do they seriously begin to consider possible outcomes. The prospect of U.S. mediation at the presidential level forces domestic debate on basic issues.

Presidents have successfully employed special envoys or senior diplomats for exploratory missions and for hammering out implementation arrangements after political agreements have been reached. But for handling the main issues, only the president or a secretary of state who enjoys the president's visible backing will suffice.

Although such an active role can divert a president from other pressing responsibilities, unfortunately no alternative route to success in the Middle East exists. To a certain extent, the culture demands that leaders must negotiate directly. All these regimes,

including Israel's, are highly personalized. Kings and presidents meet often, sending personal emissaries if they have something private to convey. Foreign ministers generally count only as secondary players, though Moshe Dayan was clearly an exception, and professional diplomats are not given much weight. Furthermore, nearly thirty years have passed in which American presidents and secretaries of state have been personally involved in pushing forward sometimes very trivial issues inch by inch. This history cannot be erased. No Israeli, Syrian, Jordanian, or Palestinian leader will believe the United States is serious about a major initiative unless the president himself is visibly involved on a regular basis. Only the secretary of state, if properly anointed (as in the cases of Nixon and Kissinger, Carter and Vance, Bush and Baker, and Clinton and Christopher) and if able to devote the energy and time, can substitute for the president in much of the detailed negotiation.

President Carter's enormous commitment of time and attention during the Camp David process and the treaty negotiation that followed gave rise to expectations about the role of future presidents that may be highly unrealistic; but the expectation is there just the same. Secretary Shultz's effectiveness on overall Arab-Israeli issues was seriously undermined by the perception in the region that Middle East peacemaking was not high among President Reagan's priorities. President Bush's frequent public underscoring of his strong concern about Israel's settlement policies provided clear evidence of his engagement in the substantive issues involved in any Arab-Israeli mediation effort.

Good Intelligence

Timely intelligence can be critical to the mediators' work. Directing U.S. intelligence agencies to provide it often requires White

House or National Security Council staff support for the U.S. mediation team, which underscores the need for an active presidential role. Mediators are at a great disadvantage if they must rely heavily on governments whose interests are directly involved for information about the actual circumstances on the ground. For example, in mediating the lines to which Israeli forces were to withdraw in Sinai, U.S. negotiators had precise data about the location of unexploited oil reserves in the Gulf of the Suez and their relationship to alternate possible withdrawal lines, as well as three-dimensional scale models of the passes and terrain in the Sinai. In fact, U.S. information was more accurate than that available to either Israel or Egypt.

American intelligence was indispensable to the success of Kissinger's shuttle diplomacy during the mid-1970s. Intelligence collection and dissemination during that critical period were effectively geared to the needs of diplomacy. No other period during the history of U.S. mediation has evidenced such superior intelligence targeting and analysis. It enabled Kissinger to avoid what would have been unsustainable agreements. During Carter's pursuit of an Egyptian-Israeli agreement, intelligence products were also very useful, especially in preparing for the Camp David conference and during subsequent negotiations over the peace treaty. But "faulty" intelligence assessments too often characterized the 1980s. For example, during Ambassador Philip Habib's mediation missions in Lebanon, U.S. intelligence assessments were at times so misleading that Habib's team had to stop relying on them to any significant degree. Understandings based on inaccurate intelligence can quickly fall apart, leading to charges of bad faith.

Sometimes American intelligence has been led astray by misinformation deliberately provided by foreign intelligence agencies or, conversely, has been forced to rely excessively on foreign sources for dependable information because of the lack of reliable U.S. intelligence sources in the region. U.S. mediators have been embarrassed to discover in the middle of negotiations that they lacked a vital piece of information. A 1968 UN mission headed by U.S. Ambassador to the United Nations George Ball was made especially difficult because of a lack of reliable information from the parties involved. The UN group was seeking agreement from a number of Arab states and Israel on the interpretation of UN Security Council Resolution 242. U.S. negotiators who accompanied Ball on the mission knew that King Hussein and Israeli officials had been meeting directly, but the Israelis refused to acknowledge the meetings. The Americans were therefore forced to rely solely on Jordanian information about those meetings. Moreover, any message the U.S. negotiators might bring from the Israelis would be compared by the king to what he was hearing directly from the Israelis. This situation became untenable when the king displayed skepticism over a pledge the Israeli foreign minister expressly gave Ball to carry to the king because Hussein had already heard or understood it differently from the Israelis.

Although exchanging intelligence is a common practice among the intelligence agencies of friendly or allied nations, independently obtained and properly assessed raw intelligence is critical to a U.S. mediator's effectiveness.

GENERAL OBSERVATIONS

The study group report also contained a number of observations on the larger context of peacemaking in the Middle East. These conclusions, although drawn from the Arab-Israeli experience, offer valuable lessons for U.S. mediation in other conflicts.

Context

- Success in Arab-Israeli negotiations has come only at moments when the status quo was riskier or more painful than potential compromise, at least to one side. A real or anticipated crisis has usually provided the essential catalyst for the parties to come together. The timing of an initiative can determine its outcome.

- Direct talks between Arabs and Israelis are important symbols of acceptance and normalcy and are well worth pursuing. However, because of the wide historical and psychological gap between the parties, direct talks have not produced agreement unless a vigorous, creative, and persistent third-party mediator was involved.

- All comprehensive approaches to mediating this conflict have ultimately failed. Starting in the direction of a comprehensive settlement, however, has sometimes provoked serious bilateral negotiating. Success has come only in bilateral negotiation, and then only with a very active third-party mediator.

- Since 1967, the United States has been that essential third party, the only mediator able to provide credible incentives, assurances, and guarantees—the necessary complementary elements outside the parameters of the negotiating agenda.

- Successful mediation requires tedious, prolonged prenegotiation to achieve three goals. The first goal is to narrow the agenda, removing insolvable issues from the negotiating table, at least temporarily, thereby reducing the political risks for the parties taking part. When the agenda has not been narrowed in advance, negotiations have invariably failed. Second, narrow the list of active participants to those parties most driven to achieve some agreement. Finally, informally identify the general outlines of an eventual agree-ment, should formal negotiations succeed. Both sides must believe that they can produce an acceptable agreement; if they do not, entering into formal negotiations may pose unacceptable political risks.

Mediation Guidelines

- Involve the U.S. president directly. Only when the president is active and only when his personal involvement is obvious do the parties take a U.S. mediation effort seriously. Only the secretary of state or a high-level presidential emissary can be an effective surrogate for the president —and then only if the president's hand remains clearly visible on the throttle.

- Concentrate on private meetings with top Middle East leaders. Each of these regimes is highly personalized, and foreign ministers do not make the final decisions, although they and senior aides can do important groundwork in exploring possible compromises.

- Choose a venue for negotiations that is conducive to unpressured, informal discussions among participants when they are not in formal negotiating sessions. The setting should be sufficiently isolated to prevent unfettered media access to the negotiators.

- Try to base the mediating process on already accepted negotiating guidelines —for example, Security Council resolutions 242 and 338 and the Camp David agreement. Avoid creating broad new frameworks with untested or unfamiliar elements or terminology.

- Discuss concepts with top leaders until the shape of possible areas of agreement emerges. Tentative understandings may, nevertheless, evaporate. Verbal compromises made to bridge intrinsically irreconcilable positions are inherently fragile and subject to much renegotiation when committed to writing.

- Understand that no party will give up a hard-core principle, especially in advance of a real "end game." It may, however, agree to negotiate about how that "right" or principle might be exercised or applied.

- Consult privately with top leaders of all parties before introducing any significant new U.S. proposal. Public surprises will produce rejection and defiance, not flexibility.

- Avoid public rejection of U.S. ideas or proposals; such a rejection could preclude reintroducing any of these ideas in a different context. Yesterday's rejected idea can be, and often has been, part of tomorrow's accepted plan.

- Try to maintain maximum confidentiality while possible compromises are in play. If leaders want the mediator to succeed, they will protect the confidentiality of sensitive details, at least temporarily. Fewer premature leaks will occur if fewer key people are privy to the details.

- Avoid offering American interpretations for positions taken by other parties. The only reliable interpretations are those of the parties themselves. Above all, avoid giving private U.S. assurances to either side about anticipated outcomes.

- Refrain from characterizing any proposal as a formal "U.S. plan." It will immediately become a political target on which to vent frustrations or be used as an excuse for putting off difficult choices.

- Keep in mind that leverage or "pressure" is of little or no value until the negotiating process is well advanced and parties can "smell" agreement. Only when they fear losing a good deal that is within reach can the mediator's careful use of pressure facilitate the "end game." Pressure tactics are of no use and are likely to be self-defeating in the prenegotiation phase.

- Persevere, once a serious mediation effort has been launched. Tenacity and persistence are crucial to success, as is continuity. Don't pause long between mediation rounds; small openings will freeze over and unpredictable upheavals in the region will divert leaders' attention. Between top-level mediating missions, keep the ball in play through a trusted deputy negotiator.

- Keep Congress well informed about the progress of negotiations. Executive branch consultations with key members of Congress should take place before, during, and after watershed moments in negotiations. These consultations can test the boundaries of congressional support and minimize congressional interference in the administration's diplomatic strategy.

Dealing with Particular Parties

- Refrain from relying on any Arab leader to "deliver" another's support for a process or a position. Too often, such assurances cannot be carried out. However, general endorsements of a U.S. negotiating initiative by major Arab governments not directly involved can be very helpful.

- Do not become involved in internal Israeli politics, regardless of how tempting the prospect might appear. Deal straightforwardly with the government in office and focus on the prime minister as the ultimate source of decision making.

- Russia's primary interest (as was the Soviet Union's) is to be seen as playing a diplomatic role commensurate with superpower status. This may be even truer today, when actual Russian influence in the region is at an all-time low.

- Russian or Western European leaders can only marginally influence the negotiating positions of either Arabs or Israelis—but they can substantially complicate matters if they are not included in consultations throughout the negotiation process.

THE FUTURE

As for the future of the Arab-Israeli negotiating process, history suggests that the United States will have to play multiple roles as catalyst, confidant, choreographer, and certifier for each party, regardless of the number of other mediators or sponsors involved in the process. Success will come in discrete, largely bilateral agreements, probably sequential rather than simultaneous. In this series of prolonged, multiple negotiations, the U.S. role will be demanding and crucial. Most of all, it will require a continuing commitment to diplomatic resources and presidential attention that will stretch over several years.

CASE STUDY

32

Successful Mediation

Lord Carrington and the Rhodesian Settlement

DONALD ROTHCHILD

With Rhodesia's internal war increasing in intensity during the 1970s, and with no sign of a mutually hurting stalemate in sight, only two scenarios seemed likely to end the fighting. First, the insurgent forces, which were in a position to carry the war to its enemy for the foreseeable future, could continue the fighting in hopes of a military victory. Such a "victory" promised to be very costly in terms of human life and economic growth and development. Moreover, to achieve a stable transition, the new government would have to make concessions to ensure the support of the white-led army and civil service during an interim period. In the second scenario, a third party could mediate between the insurgents and the government, enabling them to negotiate a peaceful change of regimes and helping to enforce the agreement by getting the parties to deliver on their commitments. Under this strategy, the negotiated settlement would benefit all groups minimally, saving lives and preserving the economic gains of the

past, but leaving open the possibility of serious instability in the future should any of the main rivals seek to alter the economic or social balance of power in a significant way.

In Rhodesia (renamed Zimbabwe with the approach of independence), the warring parties took the second route, although Zimbabwe African National Union (ZANU) leader Robert Mugabe, correctly assessing his forces' military advantage, did so reluctantly. The resulting negotiations were greatly aided by the diplomatic intervention of British officials, in coalition with the African frontline states and the United States. To the surprise of many, the negotiated settlement held up and terminated the bitter civil war, with its overtones of racial hostility.

Although Britain, which was still recognized by the international community as the colonial power, was the logical and (with Commonwealth support) legitimate mediator, it nonetheless lacked significant leverage over the contending parties. It had failed to use coercive power to bring Rhodesia's prime minister, Ian Douglas Smith, in line following his 1965 proclamation of a Unilateral Declaration of Independence (UDI), and by the late 1970s Britain could exert only limited influence over the calculations of the various local parties. How, then, could a partially disengaged, external actor emerge as a powerful intermediary at the Lancaster House Conference in 1979? And how was Great Britain's foreign secretary, Lord Carrington, able to combine pressures and incentives so effectively that warring parties reconsidered their options and committed themselves to a peaceful solution? In answering these questions, we will offer some insight on the strategies for successfully mediating intense conflicts.

THE PLAYERS AND ISSUES

Although the Rhodesian white community was a tiny five percent of the total population, it exercised commanding influence over agricultural and industrial activities and exerted considerable control over state institutions. Such a privileged position contributed to a sense of political insecurity, particularly as most members of Rhodesia's black community lacked land, education, or opportunity in terms of modern-sector employment. A spiral of conflict became evident over time, as the minority white Rhodesians sought greater autonomy from Britain and the majority black Rhodesians' collective disadvantage led to political opposition, hit-and-run attacks, and—after the 1974 military coup in Portugal, with its enormous implications for regime change in Mozambique—an escalation to full guerrilla warfare.

The internal war pitted a modern, well-equipped government army and air force against the main insurgent forces of ZANU and ZAPU (Zimbabwe African People's Union), led by Mugabe and veteran political leader Joshua Nkomo, respectively. Despite

ethnic and ideological dissimilarities, these movements did manage to paper over their differences and unite into a loose Patriotic Front (PF) at the time of the 1976 Geneva conference. Then, as Smith negotiated an internal settlement with moderate black nationalists in 1978, and universal adult suffrage enabled the moderate black Rhodesians to win a majority of seats in parliament, a new coalition emerged between the black members of parliament (MPs) and the white officials controlling the civil and security services, along with some Smith holdovers. By the time the independence negotiators assembled at Lancaster House, the white Rhodesians had no delegation of their own, but were included in delegations led by Mugabe and Nkomo of the PF or by Bishop Abel Muzorewa, the head of the Rhodesian government delegation. Behind the scenes, however, another Rhodesian white, Lieutenant-General Peter Walls, did play a critical role in assuring Muzorewa about the holding of new elections and the transfer of power.[1]

THE NEGOTIATIONS PRECEDING LANCASTER HOUSE

The negotiations between the government and insurgents that preceded Lancaster House were important in clarifying the issues and narrowing the differences. The issues themselves changed little with each successive bargaining encounter, only the willingness of the parties to accommodate their adversaries on critical points and to commit themselves to an agreement changed. The problem of commitment was central to their dilemma. Until a strong mediator emerged and was prepared to offer credible guarantees that all of the main parties would fulfill the terms of the contract, no enduring negotiated outcome was possible.[2]

At the time that Smith came to power in 1964 and threatened to rebel against any remaining British restrictions on his freedom of action and in the period immediately after his proclamation of a UDI in 1965, various British governments held a series of direct talks with Rhodesian authorities to work out a compromise. The British, having little leverage over Rhodesia's white leadership, responded to Smith's demands by offering to concede greater autonomy to white minority control, proposals that were spurned by hardline elements in the cabinet who feared that the governor's right to appoint broad-based cabinets would open the way to future majority rule. In brushing aside British government concessions following talks aboard the *H.M.S. Tiger* in 1966 and aboard the *H.M.S. Fearless* in 1968, the leaders of the Rhodesian Front (the predominantly white party led by Smith) squandered a major opportunity to end the civil war on terms favorable to their interests. Later, in 1970, another set of Anglo-Rhodesian talks did produce an agreement that included Smith's acceptance of the principle of majority rule—hedged by provisions to put the transition off for 50 years or more. A commission, chaired by Lord Pearce, was set up to determine whether this compromise was acceptable to all communities and concluded in 1972 that the majority of black Rhodesians rejected the proposals as a basis for independence. This outcome revealed the limitations of making concessions to only one side in a deeply polarized situation.

It was time now to bring the black Rhodesian majority into the negotiations and to try third-party mediation. With guerrilla forces penetrating the rural areas and mobilizing wider local support for their cause, the war increasingly spilled over into the southern African region. President Kenneth Kaunda of Zambia and Prime Minister John Vorster of South Africa, concerned over the growing costs of the war, prevailed over their respective Rhodesian allies to

meet at the Victoria Falls bridge in 1975. Although Kaunda and Vorster did manage to establish a possible framework for a settlement and to press the black Rhodesian nationalists and the Smith regime to negotiate at Victoria Falls, they failed to maintain sufficient pressure once the deliberations began. As a consequence, the discussions collapsed soon after such substantive issues as majority rule and amnesty were placed on the table.

The following year, with the internal war intensifying, U.S. Secretary of State Henry Kissinger seized the initiative. Kissinger was determined to prevent a repeat of the Angolan crisis, where the Soviets and Cubans had intervened in the confrontation; he also sought to show that disputes in deeply divided societies could be managed through negotiation. In an important speech in Lusaka in April 1976, he outlined a series of measures intended to advance the goal of a peaceful settlement in Rhodesia, and he followed this up by holding discussions with Kaunda, Vorster, and Tanzanian President Julius Nyerere. Upon receiving their encouragement for a new American initiative to broker a peace in Rhodesia, Kissinger flew to South Africa to meet with Smith.

The meetings with Smith took place in Pretoria on September 19 under reasonably favorable circumstances, for Kissinger was well positioned to use both noncoercive and coercive incentives to influence Smith's calculations. Kissinger discussed, in vague terms, a $1.5-billion plan to reassure whites, in case it became necessary for them to leave the country; meanwhile, he secured strong support from Vorster, who softened Smith with threats to shut down locomotive traffic from South Africa to Rhodesia unless Smith agreed to the Kissinger proposals. Hence, when Kissinger confronted Smith with bleak intelligence reports regarding his military situation, a bewildered Smith, feeling extremely vulnerable and with little prospect of a Western rescue in the event of a collapse, "surrendered" to the go-betweens and accepted the majority rule principle.[3] Ultimately, the Kissinger-orchestrated package deal fell apart over misunderstandings regarding the importance of the Council of State (with its disproportionate representation of white interests) and Smith's right to appoint whites to head the ministries of law and order and of defense during the transition period.

With both Smith and the PF leaders showing a declining commitment to the Kissinger bargain, the package unraveled once the parties assembled at Geneva in October 1976 for negotiations. It is significant, in terms of what was to follow during the decisive negotiations at Lancaster House, that the mediator (Great Britain's ambassador to the United Nations, Ivor Richards) was not in a position to control the conference agenda or to use pressures and incentives to bring the adversaries to an agreement. After the conference adjourned in December 1976, Richards engaged in a last-ditch attempt to gain acceptance of alternative proposals before the conference reconvened in January. When Smith rejected his proposal for a transitional government that included a large black Rhodesian majority and was headed by a British-appointed interim commissioner, it became clear that Richards lacked the leverage to push the parties back to the bargaining table, and the Geneva conference never reconvened.

Following the collapse of the Geneva conference, the United States and Great Britain undertook new efforts to initiate talks leading to a peaceful settlement. U.S. President Jimmy Carter and British Prime Minister James Callaghan, meeting in Washington in early 1977, agreed to undertake a joint effort to overcome the impasse and to build support for a transition to majority rule. The resulting Anglo-American initiative responded to local demands, offered mate-

rial incentives, and used implicit pressures. After two diplomats, J. A. N. Graham and Stephen Low, consulted with the various Rhodesian leaders, the British-American coalition partners launched a comprehensive plan. This plan called for a peaceful transition to independence in 1978, free elections on the basis of universal adult suffrage, the reservation of 20 of the 100 seats in the National Assembly for the minority communities for at least eight years, and a $1–1.5-billion development fund to revive the economy. Other recommendations included the appointment by the British government of a resident commissioner to administer the country during the transition and an international peacekeeping force to supervise the cease-fire.

Although the proposals incorporated in the Anglo-American plan appeared logical, they ran up against grave difficulties in terms of implementation. Smith, now supported by Vorster, preferred an internal settlement and indicated reservations over the plan's suggestions of a unified army and international peacekeepers. He now responded to international pressures by engaging in a new effort to negotiate an internal settlement with the moderate black Rhodesian nationalist leaders. These endeavors came to fruition in March 1978, with the signing of an agreement providing for majority rule on the basis of universal adult suffrage, the reservation of 28 seats in the 100-member legislative assembly for whites, an interim government, the drafting of a constitution, and the holding of general elections. Although the PF leaders firmly rejected this internal settlement as illegal and unacceptable, important elements in the political spectrums of the United States and the United Kingdom found it to be a credible basis for a transitional arrangement. Later, during the Lancaster House negotiations, British Prime Minister Margaret Thatcher's and Lord Carrington's credibility in threatening a "second-class solution" (recognition of the internal settlement) depended in part on their view of it as a possible alternative solution to the problem of governance in Rhodesia. An impasse had been reached: The British and American governments lacked sufficient pressure to convince the adversaries to change their preferences regarding the Anglo-American initiative, and the negotiation of an internal settlement stalled the Western bid to orchestrate a change toward peace.

LANCASTER HOUSE

By late 1978, it had become apparent that the world community would not give the internal settlement any legitimacy and that the cost of the war would remain high for both the Smith/Muzorewa government and the insurgents. The new Conservative government in London recognized the need for decisive action. Although it wavered over the campaign pledges of some of its leaders to end sanctions and recognize the internal settlement, it nonetheless placed these promises on hold while it attended the Lusaka Commonwealth Conference of August 1979. Upon arrival in Lusaka, a confrontation seemed likely between Prime Minister Thatcher, who inclined toward recognizing the Muzorewa government, and the militant frontline presidents and their supporters, who backed the PF as the sole, legitimate authority in Rhodesia.

However, once the meetings began, a spirit of conciliation became evident. Nyerere did not rule out concessions on reserved seats for minorities, and Thatcher, in response, criticized the white MPs' ability to block legislation. She also affirmed her country's responsibility for bringing about an internationally acceptable solution in Rhodesia. The conferees went from there to agree on the principles of "genuine" majority rule and the inclusion of appropriate safeguards for minorities in the constitution. In addition, the conferees lent international legitimacy to the British mediation effort by recognizing Britain's responsibility to hold a constitutional conference, supervise free and fair elections (monitored by Commonwealth observers), and grant independence on the basis of majority rule. These prenegotiations proved critical to the success of the negotiation and implementation processes that followed.

British authorities, in accord with the agreement to undertake a new effort to mediate between the warring parties, invited Muzorewa and the PF leaders to bring their delegations to London for a constitutional conference at Lancaster House on September 10, 1979. Some key lessons from past failures had been learned. In contrast to the Geneva conference, the foreign secretary, Lord Carrington, presided over the deliberations. Not only was he a shrewd and confident negotiator, but he surrounded himself with a high-powered team of foreign office personnel who were determined to resolve the Rhodesian question once and for all. He could also rely on important support from the African frontline states and the United States at critical junctures. From the outset, Carrington combined a coherent strategy with considerable leverage, making effective use of various pressures and incentives to induce an agreement.

Carrington's firmness of purpose was unmistakable, even before the deliberations began. At the time that the invitations were extended, Carrington attached proposals addressing several of the most contentious issues. In particular, the British government recommended giving the Rhodesian prime minister greater flexibility in making top-level appointments; easing the advance of black Rhodesians into the senior ranks of the police, military, and civil service; and eliminating the ability of white MPs to block bills in the legislature.

Then, laying out the strategy it planned to follow at the conference, the British government went on to indicate that it would cope with the more basic issues of majority rule and the main constitutional issues before turning to the more intricate ones of the cease-fire, the transition period, and the elections. This phased strategy marked a sharp shift away from the comprehensive approach of the Anglo-American plan and, in Carrington's eyes, had the advantage of increasing momentum and "reducing the maneuvering space of the participants."[4]

Not everyone present at Lancaster House was as positive about the step-by-step approach, though. At the opening session, Nkomo expressed a fear that this strategy would place the PF in danger: Great Britain and Rhodesia could take advantage of the situation if the constitution was accepted and control of the armed forces was left unresolved. The PF leaders, however, facing solid opposition from both Carrington and the frontline presidents, decided not to press the issue further.

Carrington's determination to dominate the conference was recognizable from the beginning. He pressured the delegations by writing draft proposals on the major issues, controlling the agenda, making effective use of deadlines, threatening the PF delegation with British recognition of the internal settlement, and establishing implicit alliances, for tactical purposes, with the frontline presidents, South Africa, and the United States. To be sure, Great Britain, as the colonial power, was an interested mediator—anxious to see Rhodesia achieve internationally accepted independence and ready to go on to other issues. Yet, because of the legitimacy Great Britain derived from the Lusaka Commonwealth Conference endorsement, the African countries tended to regard the presence of British interests as a secondary concern. More important, from their standpoint, was the need for a strong intermediary able to override obstructions to an agreement and able to implement the contract fairly.

Phase I: Constitutional Matters

Carrington, having prevailed over his PF challengers on procedural questions, now focused on constitutional issues. He presented draft proposals that were in line with his original conference proposals calling for the following: a democratic and parliamentary system, an extensive list of fundamental rights (including freedom from deprivation of property), a two-house legislature with 20 out of 100 lower-house seats reserved for whites (elected on a communal roll for at least seven years), liberal provisions on citizenship, and safeguards for pension rights. Muzorewa approved the British proposals. This brought sharp criticism from Ian Smith, who contended that white interests could only be protected by the inclusion of a blocking mechanism in the legislature, accompanied by control of the public service commissions. When the matter was put to a vote in the delegation, the members—white and black—overwhelmingly endorsed the Muzorewa position.

PF delegates, however, criticized several features in the Carrington recommendations, including the reserved seats for whites, the extension of citizenship to people who arrived in the country after UDI, the weakness of presidential power, and the restrictions on land redistribution. In response to heavy frontline pressure to get on with the negotiations, Nkomo quickly backed down on the issue of reserved seats during an interim period.

Much more serious was PF opposition to the fundamental rights recommendations regarding land redistribution. Grievances over the availability of land were at the heart of the struggle during the Rhodesian war, and no nationalist movement could afford to be perceived as too conciliatory on this issue. Consequently, despite Carrington's hints of accepting an internal settlement, PF leaders were not prepared to act on the question by the time of Carrington's first deadline.

In the face of this impasse, Carrington did extend the deadline, but he refused to alter his step-by-step strategy by leaving the land redistribution matter on the table for the time being and going on to the issues of the transition. To keep the conference from collapsing, President Samora Machel of Mozambique interceded and urged Mugabe not to break up the conference over the issue of compensating white farmers (although the black Rhodesians felt dispossesed and the lands had been acquired at extraordinarily low cost).

In an effort to save the PF leaders' "face," frontline leaders encouraged the British and Americans to offer financial aid to purchase land from white farmers for resettlement purposes. British diplomats in London responded positively, but with limited funds at their disposal they looked to the United States to support their efforts. President Jimmy Carter also responded favorably to the idea of supplying aid for resettlement and agricultural development (but not for a buyout of white farmers per se), and he authorized American diplomats in London to make a nonspecific commitment, conditional upon successful conclusion of the conference. With the Anglo-American pledges in hand, Patriotic Front leaders could safely drop their main reservations about the draft constitution. As Nkomo and Mugabe stated, these assurances of assistance for land resettlement, agriculture, and economic development went "a long way in allaying the great concern we have over the whole land question."[5] As a result, the delegates completed their deliberations on constitutional matters and proceeded to the transitional arrangements.

Phase II: Transition Issues

The transition process inevitably became a highly contentious subject at the conference, because of its critical importance in determining who would come to power in the future. Great Britain's ineffective control over the army and police made intense conflict virtually certain over such issues as the cease-fire and the resumption of direct British rule during the transition. Carrington's proposal that the British government appoint a governor with broad powers for a two-month period to rule the country and create the conditions for free and fair elections drew criticism from both sides. Muzorewa, uncomfortable that his acceptance of the British proposals for new elections would be interpreted as weakness, expressed general reservations; in the end, however, he accepted Carrington's proposals, still hoping that a collapse of the conference would lead to British recognition.

Mugabe and Nkomo's suspicions of British intentions ran deeper. They raised doubts about the impartiality of a British-appointed governor who would rely entirely upon the Rhodesian government's security forces and bureaucracy during the transition period. In addition, the PF leaders criticized the extensive powers invested in the governor, the short length of the transition, and the lack of provision for a UN election observer mission. The gap between the British and PF positions was wide, and with the issues at stake very intense, there was the real possibility the conference would collapse.

Tensions increased further when the British threatened to accept the second-class solution to the Rhodesian problem, a threat that was credible because of the Thatcher government's readiness to deliver on it.[6] Signaling an intent to consider other options, the British government introduced a bill that allowed it to let part of the sanctions legislation lapse. The PF leaders were put on notice that the British were contemplating the possibility of recognizing Muzorewa. Mugabe and Nkomo responded to this pressure by failing to appear for a scheduled session at Lancaster House.

At this point in the crisis, international action again emerged as a critical factor. The Commonwealth and frontline leaders, effectively in alliance with the British mediators, feared a breakdown of the conference and pressed for the adoption of an accommodating formula. Although some of the Commonwealth leaders had doubts of their own regarding Carrington's proposal to have the governor rule on the basis of the existing civil service and security forces during the interim period, at a meeting of the Commonwealth Committee on Southern Africa, they carefully refrained from condemning Britain's leadership of the all-party conference.

Then, while meeting with Thatcher and Carrington in London, Kaunda called for concessions from Great Britain on the timing of the elections and on the deployment of a Commonwealth military force. Lord Carrington, still preferring a first-class solution (that is, an agreement that included the PF), softened his stance somewhat to allow the creation of a small Commonwealth monitoring force. As further negotiations took place with Kaunda, a major breakthrough was achieved. Carrington conceded many of the points of greatest concern to the PF leadership. These included extending the pre-election period, providing equal status to all parties on the election council, and furnishing food and housing for PF forces at the assembly points. Agreeing to make the military commanders on both sides equally responsible for maintaining the cease-fire was also highly symbolic, because it implied equal status for the rival armies. The PF forces were no longer guerrillas, but legitimate participants in the implementation process. When, at Mugabe's

insistence, a reference to the PF forces' role in implementing the peace agreement was included in the British draft proposals, he was able to agree formally with the mediator on the transition process and to turn to the difficult questions involved in a cease-fire accord.

Phase III: Cease-Fire Issues

Cease-fires between hostile antagonists backed by separate armies inevitably provoke grave insecurities on all sides. They are difficult both to arrange and to implement because they make the rivals, who already mistrust each other's intentions, highly vulnerable during the transition period. Political leaders on both sides of the divide fear that deceitful commanders may be able to shift the balance of power in their favor at the time the cease-fire is implemented. The possible emergence of a hegemonic party leads to acute uncertainty and a possible war (or return to war), as the weaker factions seek to prevent a situation where they will be exposed to the will of another.[7] This final hurdle was the most exacting.

Carrington, recognizing that he needed to address this issue most carefully, designed his cease-fire proposals in a way that made the military commanders an integral part of the process. His general proposals made the military commanders responsible to the governor for the observance of the cease-fire. A cease-fire commission, composed of representatives of the two military forces, was set up and charged with the responsibility of investigating actual or threatened breaches of the cease-fire agreement. The British also proposed establishing a cease-fire monitoring group and invited several Commonwealth governments to contribute forces.

The PF leaders were uncertain about their survival once the two armed forces (government and insurgent) were separated.

They were also concerned that the Commonwealth monitoring force was of insufficient numbers to ensure security during the transition period. Therefore, they proposed an alternative plan to address these uncertainties; Carrington rejected their plan and submitted detailed proposals of his own. The monitoring force was now to deploy both to the fifteen assembly points set up for PF troops and to the existing bases for government troops. The cease-fire commission was to be put into effect on the day of the cease-fire, and the assemblage process itself was to be accomplished seven days after the cease-fire took effect.

Although the Muzorewa delegation expressed reservations about Carrington's cease-fire proposals (particularly about monitoring the government forces and locating the assembly points inside the country), it did voice satisfaction with the general thrust of the plan. The PF leaders, however, strongly objected to some of its features. Fearing that government units might take advantage of the PF forces' containment in the designated assembly areas to launch a preemptive attack following an election defeat, the PF leaders criticized both the vulnerable locations of the assembly points and the small size of the Commonwealth monitoring force.

The African frontline and Commonwealth states again played a critical intermediary role. In public, they supported Mugabe and Nkomo's calls for changing the size and composition of the monitoring force and for removing government forces from the areas along the borders; privately, however, they lobbied the British for effective monitoring of the Rhodesian air force and other key units and encouraged the PF leaders toward accommodation. Having reached the final phase at Lancaster House, the frontline and Commonwealth states did not want the conference to collapse. To underline his concern, Mozambique's President Machel, whose country provided a staging base for Mugabe's insurgents, warned the PF not to count on continued support for ZANU's army if the war resumed.

Carrington, lacking forceful control over events at this stage, bowed to the forces around him and acted in a more conciliatory manner. In particular, he allowed real negotiations to take place, not only with the conferees but between the military commanders from the two sides. As Stephen Stedman observed, "this was the only time when Carrington's emphasis on arbitration had to yield to a softer approach."[8] The upshot was an effort to respond to the main PF demands, including changes in the size and composition of the monitoring force, greater efforts to provide security and improve accommodations at the assembly points, and a key role for the monitors in preventing breaches against the cease-fire. Mugabe accepted these proposals conditionally, but he continued to resist the proposed number and location of assembly points.

Again, the coalition of mediators acted to push the proposed agreement to a conclusion. The British government, in a risky move, sent a governor-designate, Lord Soames, to Salisbury to take over the institutions of state, even though he had no forces at his disposal. Meanwhile, the frontline presidents increased their mediatory efforts, pressing Mugabe to stay in London and negotiate and warning him of the high costs of renewing the war. After securing further concessions from Carrington regarding a sixteenth assembly point and an extension of the deadline for assembling PF troops, Mugabe pulled back from his adversarial stance and agreed to the peace accord. Significantly, the two sides remained committed to the bargain throughout the period leading up to the general elections of February 1980.

CONCLUSION

Carrington's successful mediation effort in Rhodesia/Zimbabwe took place at a propitious time. Government forces had no prospect of a military victory and were fatigued with the war and the sense of isolation that resulted from the international sanctions. PF leaders, who could foresee the likelihood of a military victory sometime in the future, nonetheless recognized that the military and economic costs of such a conquest would be high. As for the mediator, Britain's role was legitimized by the 1979 Lusaka Commonwealth Conference, and Carrington was able to exercise great influence over the conference proceedings. Carrington, moreover, profited greatly from the third-party negotiation initiatives and benefited from the development of a supporting coalition of African frontline and Commonwealth states and the United States. This coalition of allies possessed leverage because it was prepared to use its influence and resources at critical junctures to keep the conference from collapsing. Under these circumstances, it was possible for a partially disengaged, external actor to offer strong leadership at Lancaster House.

As this Rhodesia case study shows, a third party can play a critical role in intense internal conflicts, encouraging the adversaries to commit themselves to a peaceful outcome. Distrust between Smith (and then Muzorewa) and the PF leaders was too great for them to negotiate a direct settlement on their own. They required an influential mediator or coalition of mediators, capable of encouraging them to rethink their preferences and, above all, of enforcing an agreement during the precarious transitional period. This meant that Great Britain's preparedness to ensure that an adequate monitoring force was present during the assembling of forces, integrating of armies, and the holding of elections was critical in promoting the commitment of all the parties to the terms of the agreement.

When intervening in an intense civil war situation such as Rhodesia's, an external intervenor (or intervenors) needs appropriate timing, resources to influence the preferences of warring parties, and determination to achieve the intervention objectives. But the intervenor must also display great skill in combining pressures and incentives, manipulating carrots and sticks to prompt the local parties to reexamine their priorities and preferences, thereby influencing the course of negotiations. In this respect, Carrington and his team brought an active dimension to the diplomacy of peacemaking.

By the time of Carrington's initiative, the importance of external pressures in Rhodesia's mediation process was already apparent. When the mediator's own leverage was circumscribed (as in the direct Anglo-Rhodesian talks), or when the mediator's influence was limited by South Africa's unwillingness to pressure Smith to yield (as in Ivor Richard's mediation effort following the Geneva conference or the Anglo-American plan), the mediator lacked leverage and was unable to encourage the disputing parties to shift their preferences. By contrast, Kaunda and Vorster at the 1975 Victoria Falls conference and Kissinger in his negotiations with Smith in South Africa were able to push the adversaries to the bargaining table, although they both were unable to gain a credible commitment from the main rivals.

At the Lancaster House conference talks, Carrington and his coalition of supporters succeeded in maintaining pressure on the Rhodesian delegations both throughout the negotiation stage and during the implementation stage that followed. The British team gained the support of the Muzorewa delegation at each critical juncture in the negotiations, because in the event that the PF refused to cooperate and the conference fell apart, the British offered the Muzorewa team the hope of recognition as the legitimate government and the possibility of ending sanctions as a reward.

Influencing the PF's preferences was more of a challenge. However, even here the mediators could encourage consideration of alternatives by direct and indirect means. At the conference itself, Carrington was in a position to use the power of the chair to control the agenda, issue draft proposals, place deadlines, and threaten a second-class solution. When these measures failed to sway the PF leaders, he received invaluable support from the Commonwealth and frontline state leaders (as well as from the United States) who took the initiative at critical points both to warn the PF of the consequences of allowing the conference to disintegrate and to provide face-saving side payments. The pressure of a coalition of international mediators was also able to gain PF consent to the agreement and the implementation of the provisions leading up to the general elections. The possible loss of frontline support for the war effort made defection too costly an alternative, especially as Mugabe's chances of winning political power through the election process seemed reasonably high.

During the extended negotiating process, the mediators used various incentives to promote a reconsideration of preferences. Kissinger shrewdly combined rewards (in the form of side payments) with punishments (the threat of South Africa's closure of its borders). These incentives had an impact on Smith's stance toward the establishment of a provisional government and a new constitution. However, as it became clear that the black Rhodesian nationalists would not be willing to allow the two security ministries to remain under white control, Smith recoiled and allowed the agreement to lapse. In this case, the incentives had been effective in moving a peace agree-

ment ahead, but they were not sufficient to overcome the competing claims of the rivals at the Geneva conference.

At Lancaster House, the two delegations, both headed by black Rhodesians, had different sets of interests than before; consequently, incentive patterns had to shift considerably to remain relevant to these new leaders. As noted earlier, Muzorewa's concessions on the constitution and the holding of new elections were predicated on his hopes for British recognition and the end of sanctions. Most of the whites within his delegation did not expect to maintain political hegemony on their own, and they now sought to secure their position in a postwar Zimbabwe. Not surprisingly, they found the "sunset clauses" in the interim constitution establishing twenty communally elected seats in parliament and making assurances regarding their positions in the civil service and military to be as much as they could anticipate under the changed circumstances of the country.

The PF leaders, who were in a strong bargaining position at Lancaster House because of their prospects for military success, had the least incentive to change course at this juncture. They recognized that an extended military struggle would entail heavy human and economic costs, but, for Mugabe at least, the prize was an opportunity to restructure what he considered to be a colonial and racist society. Nevertheless, as the conference gained momentum and held out prospects of an honorable and beneficial end to the war, it became increasingly difficult for Mugabe to call on his supporters for heavy sacrifices. PF leaders, especially Nkomo, recognized that they would lose local support if they returned from the conference empty-handed. Moreover, as British pressure increased and the Commonwealth and frontline states became more inclined to use their leverage to bring about a peaceful settlement, the PF leaders were left with less and less room to maneuver. Hence, coercive incentives became linked with the timely use of financial incentives and led Nkomo and Mugabe to reconsider their commitment to a military victory.

Finally, the role of the British and the Commonwealth monitoring force in implementing the settlement proved critical in addressing the rivals' great fear that their opponent would launch a preemptive strike at a time of great vulnerability. Third-party enforcement is an incentive to settle a civil war because it restrains opponents from taking the military initiative while their troops are assembling and being demobilized. But the third party must make a credible commitment to carry out its responsibilities fully during the transition period. If the local adversaries have any reason to suspect that the mediator is not fully committed to the pact, then they may come to see defection as in their interests and return to the field. Recognizing the importance of third-party commitment, the great powers are wise to invest heavily in implementing the pacts they mediate; the alternative is a loss of credibility that leaves everyone worse off than before the negotiations began.

NOTES

1. Jeffrey Davidow, *A Peace in Southern Africa* (Boulder, Colo.: Westview, 1984), pp. 69–70.

2. James D. Fearon, "Commitment Problems and the Spread of Ethnic Conflict" (paper presented to the University of California Institute of Global Conflict and Cooperation Workshop on the International Spread and Management of Ethnic Conflict, Davis, Calif., March 10–11, 1995), p. 3.

3. Colin Legum, *Southern Africa: The Year of the Whirlwind* (New York: Africana Publishing, 1977), p. 39.

4. M. Tamarkin, *The Making of Zimbabwe* (London: Frank Cass, 1990), p. 261.

5. Bridget Bloom and Michael Holman, "Constitution Agreed as Patriotic Front Makes Concession," *Financial Times* (London), October 19, 1979, p. 1.

6. Stephen John Stedman, "Mediation in Civil War," in *The International Dimensions of Internal Conflict*, ed. Michael E. Brown (Cambridge, Mass.: MIT Press, 1996).

7. Robert Harrison Wagner, "The Causes of Peace," in *Stopping the Killing: How Civil Wars End*, ed. Roy Licklider (New York: NYU Press, 1993), pp. 250–251.

8. Stephen John Stedman, *Peacemaking in Civil War* (Boulder, Colo.: Lynne Rienner, 1991), p. 199.

33

Negotiating Across Cultures

RAYMOND COHEN

It should be admitted from the outset that it is hard to gauge the precise influence of cultural factors on international negotiation. Negotiators tend to be more conscious of the impact of culture when talks fail than when they succeed (Hendriks 1991). A variety of factors clearly impinge on any negotiation, including system of government, individual psychology and belief, ideology, public opinion, and misperception. Thus, the decisive influence on the course and outcome of events in any single case is likely to be open to dispute. Moreover, the student of diplomatic negotiations cannot contrive the conditions of a laboratory experiment, in which different variables are modified in turn while the others are held constant. One can, however, observe phenomena that recur over time, even though the circumstances, cast of actors, and subject matter may change.

In autobiographical literature, American diplomats frequently allude to the marked differences between American and "nonwestern" (for want of a better term) approaches to negotiation and the impact of those differences on their work (for example, Lewis 1989; Moser 1986; Quandt 1987; Solomon 1987). That this is not simply an American problem is confirmed by French, British, and Swedish experience, among others (Elgström 1990; Plantey 1982; Yahuda 1993).

Cross-cultural conundrums have been exemplified in recent years in such key diplomatic episodes as the Iran-Contra affair, the failures of diplomacy that preceded the Falklands and Persian Gulf wars, the debacle over renewing China's most-favored-nation status, the intervention in Somalia, and the ongoing saga of trade talks with Japan. Australian Prime Minister Keating's contretemps with Malaysian leader Mahathir (Cohen forthcoming), British Governor of Hong Kong Chris Patten's botched talks over Hong Kong with Beijing (Yahuda 1993), and the long stalemate in Syrian-Israeli negotiations (Cohen 1994) are other cases in point.

There are many possible definitions of culture. Lately, culture has come to be seen as more about software than hardware, about the operating instructions for group life and not simply about behavior or material artifacts. According to this view, culture is made up of meanings, conventions, and presuppositions, that is, the grammar that governs the creation and use of symbols and signs. It can also be thought of as the shared "common sense" or "local knowledge" underpinning a group's construction of reality (Geertz 1983). Indeed, culture molds the community, because without it communication, coordinated activity, and social life itself would be impossible.

Cross-cultural differences have been demonstrated to affect many kinds of human relationships and activities (for example, Samovar and Porter 1994). If unencumbered discourse rests on harmonious expectations, then the encounter of incongruent conventions of meaning is likely to lead to confusion. International negotiators are no more immune to the projection of culturally inappropriate assumptions onto members of unfamiliar societies than are business people, exchange students, and tourists. Disputing this position, Zartman and Berman (1982) argue that "negotiation is a universal process . . . and that cultural differences are simply differences in style and language" (p. 226). However, birth, life, and death are also universal experiences, yet this has not prevented humankind, in its great cultural diversity, from evolving profoundly discrepant understandings of their significance.

LINGUISTIC DISSONANCE

One suggestive approach to intercultural dissonance rests on the perception of culture as a store of shared meanings. The body of implicit, received truth held by the group is reflected most revealingly in language. Every society can be observed to possess a specialized negotiating vocabulary loaded with affective and metaphorical connotations. When negotiation takes place across cultures, the ostensible point at issue may be complicated by semantic and procedural discontinuities. Culturally grounded assumptions about negotiation (and about the subject in contention) can be uncovered, in the first instance, by lexical analysis. Comparison of the meaning (and also, as important, usage) of relevant terms across cultures reveals potential sources of both dissonance and reconciliation, which can then be checked against behavior.

Most theoretical writing on international negotiation presupposes the existence of a fixed linguistic and behavioral framework permitting the drawing of conclusions valid for all nations. Key concepts and categories of analysis such as "opening proposal," "concession," "compromise," "contract," and so on are taken to have the same weight and function across cultures. But reliance on a single language with its built-in cultural viewpoint imposes a misleadingly uniform structure and excludes deviant possibilities. For example, if modern English has no use for terms associated with group conciliation in a situation of endemic feuding or bargaining distinctions at different hierarchical levels, then the observer restricted to English may overlook relevant non-Anglo-Saxon dimensions of negotiating behavior. Negotiation possesses both universal and particular features reflecting local traditions and needs. Specific understanding of and approaches to it are embedded within given cultural settings. Imagine trying to describe the American approach to law and governance in the language of a society unfamiliar with individual rights and the adversarial system —without once resorting to the English language. Just as such complex social phenomena as conflict resolution and human relationships are conceived differently across cultures, so too is negotiation.

Studies of Chinese negotiating style, for example, indicate the central role of *guanxi* (very loosely, personal connections) in the process of negotiation (Pye 1982; Solomon 1987). Lee Kuan Yew of Singapore goes so far as to explicitly offer the services of his country to outsiders as a privileged intermediary with the People's Republic of China because of Singapore's *guanxi* (Foreign Broadcast Information Service, March 1, 1994). But it would be restrictive to think of *guanxi* simply as a "bargaining chip," though it is easiest for westerners to understand it this way. Rather, it should be seen as a way of doing business completely different from that customary in the West.

If long-term relationships and not the one-time "negotiation" are of the essence, then categories of analysis expressed by such English terms as "opening proposal" or "final agreement" lose the well-defined (and for native English speakers self-evident) significance that they possess in an American context. Cultivating friendship may be the first task to be performed when doing business with the Chinese, but it is not an opening proposal or even move. Within a relationship-oriented rather than a deal-oriented context, informal contacts, tacit hints, and the reciprocal sensitivity of partners to each other's needs are of paramount importance. (Compare a successful marriage with a "brief encounter.") In these circumstances, there may be no formal "opening bid" at the "negotiating table" at all.

Study of Japanese negotiating style suggests a similar caveat. The English term "contract," for instance, the official document containing the authoritative and legally binding text of the mutual obligations agreed upon by the signatories, is usually translated into Japanese by the word *keiyaku*.

> Yet *keiyaku* has a narrower meaning than the word contract as it is used in the United States as a legal term. While contract is used in the United States to mean a legally enforceable promise or a set of promises with accompanying duties and rights, *keiyaku* implies just part of the process of negotiation, namely, the promissory stage, in which two parties agree to work together to create a mutually advantageous relationship. The implications of a transaction created by a *keiyaku* [are] unclear to Americans because much of the negotiation and most of the details of the transaction are intended to be filled in later [Zhang and Kuroda 1989, p. 206].

Negotiation, then, is more than a set of behavior patterns, though this may be what we first observe. Form is simply the outward expression of meaning. Societies have certain profound cultural needs and themes that language and behavior serve and reflect. *Musyawarah* is a Malay word meaning consensual decision making through discussion and consultation, in which elaborate and prolonged efforts are made to reach an agreed position while saving everyone's face and ensuring group harmony. The term and the activity are central to the politics of the Association of Southeast Asian Nations, because open disagreement and controversy are abhorred in the acutely face-salient cultures of Southeast Asia (Thambipillai and Saravanamuttu 1985). To decipher a society's mode of operation, one must penetrate the surface of behavior to reach the underlying stratum of culturally grounded meanings as revealed in the language.

Thus, linguistic analysis provides a good point of entry to the study of negotiation across cultures. The appearance of predicted semantic antinomies—contradictions of basic principles—in the form of incongruent behavior at the negotiating table can then be observed empirically. Although the examples given so far have related to procedure, an identical analysis can also be applied to issues of substance. In Israeli-Arab negotiations in recent years, for instance, much has hung on sometimes profound differences in the meaning and resonance of the equivalent Hebrew and Arabic terms for such concepts as "normalization," "withdrawal," "land," "water," and "peace."

HIGH-CONTEXT VERSUS LOW-CONTEXT COMMUNICATION

Along with the detailed lexical comparisons required to identify possible cross-cultural dissonance, another more general distinction found to be both descriptively and prescriptively useful is that between high-context and low-context cultures (Hall 1976; Ting-Toomey 1985). High-context communication is associated with key elements in the ethos of collectivistic societies: the requirements of maintaining face and group harmony. The high-context culture communicates allusively rather than directly. As important as the explicit content of a message is the context in which it occurs, that is, the surrounding nonverbal cues and nuances of meaning. People in cultures that put the group before the individual are acutely concerned about how they will appear in the eyes of others. Speech is therefore more about preserving and promoting social interests than transmitting information. High-context speakers must weigh their words carefully, for whatever they say will be scrutinized and taken to heart. Face-to-face conversations contain many emollient expressions of respect and courtesy. Directness and contradiction are greatly disliked. Speakers in this kind of culture feel acutely uncomfortable about delivering a blunt "no." They want to please others and prefer inaccuracy and evasion to painful precision: The substantive element of a message, though elliptical and encoded, will be unmistakable to insiders.

It is hard for members of a collectivistic culture to deal with a stranger from outside their circle, and a personal relationship must be established before a frank exchange becomes possible. Timing is also important. Much probing and small talk will precede a request, because a rebuff causes great embarrassment. To the outsider, the high-context individual may appear insincere, suspicious, and devious, but these traits are simply part of the veneer of courtesy and indirection essential to preserve social harmony. Nor is mistrust a deviant characteristic, but the manifestation of an ingrained caution required for dealing with members of other groups. Collectivistic individuals, in their own society, are justifiably receptive to hidden meanings, always on the watch for subtle hints known from experience to be potentially present in the tone of a conversation and the accompanying facial expressions and gestures—body language—of interlocutors.

The low-context culture, exemplified by the United States, reserves a quite different role for language. Very little meaning is implicit in the context of an articulation. On the contrary, what has to be said is stated explicitly. Indirect language is strongly disliked; "straight-from-the-shoulder" talk is admired. "Get to the point" is the heartfelt reaction to small talk and evasive formulations. One has little time or patience for "beating around the bush," but wishes to get down to business and move on to another problem. Why waste time on social irrelevancies? Doing business should not require interlocutors to be bosom friends. Clearly, this propensity is associated with an individualistic freedom from group constraints and niceties, an ability to distinguish between professional and social role playing.

Language performs, then, an informational rather than socially lubricative function in low-context cultures. Accuracy and truthfulness are great virtues. Politeness does not dictate contrived formulas and verbal embellishments. Contradiction is not deemed offensive; indeed, society flourishes on debate, persuasion, and the hard sell. Subtlety and allusiveness in speech, if grasped at all, serve little purpose. Nor does face possess the crucial importance it has for the high-context culture. There is less sensitivity to what others say. Allusion and gesture are secondary to verbal content.

The depiction presented here of high- and low-context cultures is generalized and over-simplified; many outstanding American negotiators have departed markedly from the low-context model. No culture ever possessed precisely the features depicted by the two paradigms, which represent simplified ideal types. What is important for the purpose of this brief survey, however, is not the particular traits of a culture in isolation, but the chemistry that occurs when negotiators representing mutually discordant traditions come into contact. It is the relative gap between the protagonists that counts, not their respective idiosyncratic features. Should a cross-cultural divide exist, certain typical patterns of miscomprehension can be observed to recur. A final proviso to be noted is the effect of power. For example, in Israeli-Palestinian talks cultural dissonances have been marked, but given the power discrepancy, the Palestinians have had to take, in the final analysis, what has been offered.

DIPLOMATIC MISREADINGS

The contrasting uses of language by Americans and their high-context negotiating partners have provided fertile grounds for misunderstanding. The first lesson to learn in Egypt, one former ambassador remarked, is that "Egyptians hate to turn you down; they never say no." And again: "They don't say no, . . . but nothing happens" (Veliotes 1988). Another U.S. diplomat with long service in Mexico City notes that the Mexican habit was "not to say no, just never to say yes," which means that a negotiation might continue indefinitely and indeterminately (Wilcox 1989). How then is one to know whether consent is genuine or feigned? If one's antennae are sufficiently

attuned to accompanying verbal and nonverbal signals, it may be possible to read between the lines. Otherwise, the true message becomes clear only in retrospect. If nothing happens, one has been the victim of the "social affirmative."

Since persistence, not taking "no" for an answer, is a familiar trait of American diplomacy, the Mexican and Egyptian reluctance to disappoint their interlocutor may set the scene for mutual bafflement and frustration. William Quandt (1987), who participated in the Camp David negotiations, argues that drawn-out negotiations may be a "sign that the Egyptian side is not ready for a deal but does not want to bear the onus for breaking off negotiations" (p. 119).

This inconclusive pattern of behavior has repeated itself on several occasions in recent years, often in negotiations involving the U.S. Department of Defense. One negotiation that dragged on for almost a decade concerned the passage of nuclear-powered warships (NPWs) of the U.S. Sixth Fleet through the Suez Canal. There is no doubt that the Egyptian government was genuinely sensitive to the environmental risks, real or imagined, of nuclear power and of its possible effect on navigation through the canal. U.S. Ambassador Hermann Eilts first raised the issue in the mid-1970s with President Sadat, who passed him on to Defense Minister Gamasy. The latter noted in turn that his authority did not extend to running the waterway and shuffled Eilts off onto the bureaucracy (Eilts 1988). Egyptian procrastination continued for an extended period without the U.S. Defense Department grasping that the Egyptians wished to let the matter drop. Eventually, some years later, President Mubarak was persuaded to agree, and in 1984 an NPW went through for the first time. But it was a pyrrhic victory; when news of the ship's passage was tactlessly leaked by Deputy National Security Adviser John Poindexter, the agreement, entered into by the Egyptian government reluctantly and against its better judgment, was immediately called off by the embarrassed Egyptians (Veliotes 1988).

High-context individuals always find it easier to agree than to disagree. Confronted by a persistent and undesirable request, the "social affirmative" is simply the line of least resistance in order to escape from an uncomfortable situation. The fault is not theirs, but that of their unobservant interlocutor, who has failed to draw the correct conclusions from the hesitancy and unenthusiastic nature of the reply. Not even the sophisticated and cosmopolitan John Kenneth Galbraith, President Kennedy's appointee as ambassador to India, was immune from this lapse. During the first days of the 1962 Sino-Indian border war, the State Department (looking ahead to the postwar period and a possible resolution of the Indo-Pakistani Kashmir dispute) decided that it would be helpful for Prime Minister Nehru to request, through U.S. good offices, Pakistani assurances of nonintervention. Galbraith (1969) describes in painful detail his insensitive importuning of the Indian leader.

Galbraith first asked Nehru if the United States could inform Ayub Khan, the Pakistani president, that India would welcome Pakistani assurances. Nehru replied, lukewarmly, that "he would have no objection to our saying so." This was not good enough for the ambassador. Galbraith then "moved in very hard." Would Nehru say that he would *"warmly accept"* such assurances? Looking "a little stunned"—as well he might—Nehru consented, adding that such a gesture might be helpful for the future. Galbraith resolved to press home his advantage. Could Nehru *"assure"* him that he would respond to such assurances? Yes, "on some appropriate occasion he would," Nehru responded with telltale discomfort. Galbraith moved in for the kill. "This was a time for generosity, and he should be

immediately forthcoming." Pressed to the wall, Nehru agreed (p. 385, emphasis added). It was another ultimately counterproductive success. Nehru, under extreme duress, his army being pushed back by seemingly irresistible Chinese pressure, had no choice but to give his unwilling consent. But to beg a favor of Pakistan, a sectarian state that in Indian eyes stands for the antithesis of everything secular India represents, was humiliating. In the end, the mediation failed and the United States squandered most of the credit it had gained by helping India in its hour of need (Coon 1989).

To the dislike of confrontation and contradiction, high-context cultures add a related and characteristic propensity for indirect and understated formulations. The motive in both cases is the same: the wish to avoid an abrupt and abrasive presentation, to maintain harmony, and to save the face of the interlocutor. Meaning is imparted by hints and nuances. Set against the American preference for "straight talk," subtlety and opacity may be taken for evasiveness and insincerity. However, this is to judge the habit from a culture-bound perspective. Protecting the feelings of one's interlocutor is very far from deliberate falsehood. Despite their professional skills, American diplomats have often fallen into this pattern of error.

Nehru's "habit of understatement," posed, in its time, a conundrum for U.S. diplomats. A classic failure of understanding occurred in February 1954. In what was to be a watershed in U.S.-Indian relations, the Eisenhower administration had decided to grant military aid to Pakistan. This was a bitter moment for Nehru and the Indian government and marked the failure of a diplomatic campaign. In the Indian world view, Pakistan was seen as the "enemy of the race," and its arming by the United States was a most alarming development. Before the public announcement of the deal, U.S. Ambassador Allen had been instructed to deliver a personal letter from President Eisenhower and to make clear that the American decision was not directed against India and that it was hoped that friendly relations between the two countries would in no way be impaired. If the aid were misused for aggression against India, the United States would take action both within and without the United Nations to thwart it. An Indian request for military aid would also be sympathetically considered.

Nehru carefully read through the letter and the text of the forthcoming announcement. When he had finished "he smiled, studied his cigarette for a few moments, then said in a pleasant and almost confidential tone, 'I have never at any moment, since the subject arose two or three months ago, had any thought whatsoever that the U.S. government, and least of all President Eisenhower, wished to do any damage to India.'" After expressing appreciation for the letter, Nehru proceeded to a judicious and calm explanation of his concerns. "What disturbed him was not American motives but the possible consequences of this action." He spoke of "small groups of extremists among the Indian Muslims who did not conceal their pleasure over Pakistan aid because they hoped it might lead to a renewal of Muslim domination of India." Communal violence in India and increased tension throughout India and Pakistan might follow. Moreover, although the present government of Mohammed Ali in Pakistan was moderate, its political organization was weak, and some successor might depart on a reckless adventure.

For all the dignity and restraint of his manner, Nehru was, in fact, revealing his innermost fears. The American decision was a nightmare come true. Nehru had publicly expressed his opposition to military aid for Pakistan and the government of India had officially protested such a move. But Allen completely missed the true

meaning of Nehru's words. The ambassador commented on how "surprisingly pleasant" the conversation had been and how Nehru had "made a conscious effort to be agreeable." In an extraordinary misjudgment, both of Nehru's reaction and of Nehru's policy of nonalignment, Allen concluded that Nehru "showed no adverse reaction to the President's offer to consider sympathetically any Indian request for military aid, and it is possible that he was rather pleased." The ambassador hoped that discussion on this subject would diminish after a few days. "I do not anticipate serious public demonstrations" *(Foreign Relations of the United States* 1985, pp. 1738–1739).

In fact, the subsequent Indian reaction was vehement: demonstrations, official protests, and an extended period of strained relations. Particularly offensive to the government of India were the cynical offer of military aid and the patronizing assurances that the deal was in no way directed against India, but that if necessary the U.S. would thwart any aggression. As one historian of U.S.-Indian relations concludes, to this day Indians complain about the 1954 episode: "It may have done more to complicate Indo-American relations than any other single development" (Palmer 1984, p. 24).

TEMPORAL DISCONTINUITIES

Besides linguistic dissonance, disparate concepts of time can also have an important impact on negotiations across cultures. In any negotiation, participants are obliged to make judgments on three key issues in which culturally grounded assumptions about the negotiating posture of the opposing side are of the essence: the relationship between its opening bid and the minimal outcome it will ultimately settle for; the most favorable timing of concessions, if any; and the optimal point at which to make a truly final offer. There are various ways in which low- and high-context expectations of bargaining could be contrasted. For instance, the U.S. propensity to view negotiation generally as an instrumental exercise in problem solving stands in marked contrast to the tendency of collectivistic cultures to distinguish between "normal" distributive bargaining and negotiation that entails a challenge to identity or test of honor. In the latter cases, special techniques of reconciliation and face saving may be more appropriate than "carpet trading" (see Quandt 1987, p. 120).

Contrasting high- and low-context assumptions about tempo and timing are particularly salient in negotiations across cultures. Not all high-context concepts of time can be condensed into a single ideal type, but the American view of the linear, sequential, and compartmentalized nature of time is sufficiently distinctive to be meaningfully juxtaposed against other variants.

Beliefs about the meaning and structure of history, the importance of the future, and the organization of the present are fundamental to a society's construction of reality (Hall 1973). From the point of view of negotiation, American temporal rigidity can be contrasted with high-context flexibility. In the context of the American "can do" work ethic, time is viewed as a quantifiable, linear commodity that extends from the present into the future at an unchanging rate and is to be precisely divided up and allotted in advance. Planning is supposed to enable individuals and organizations to use their resources efficiently, while reducing the element of future uncertainty to a minimum. Schedules are rigid, and tight deadlines are fixed so as to maintain work discipline and retain the sequential ordering of tasks. As E. T. Hall (1973) points out, "once set, the schedule is almost sacred, so that not only is it wrong, according to the formal dictates of our culture, to be late, but it is a violation of the informal patterns to keep changing

schedules or appointments or to deviate from the agenda" (p. 157). Individuals are expected to accommodate themselves and their work to the time previously allotted, rather than the reverse.

The tight scheduling of American industrial culture has little meaning for societies closer to the rhythms of traditional rural life. Caught up in the cycle of the seasons and their timely tasks, the village dweller is indifferent to the arbitrary divisions of the clock. Every task has its due time; steadiness, not haste, is the cardinal virtue. The day is punctuated by concrete activities—prayer, food, work—but there is no sense of a uniform progression of time divided up into equal bits (Eickelman 1977). Furthermore, in "face-to-face" societies, in which relationships have priority over objects, the subjugation of man to calendar violates fundamental proprieties.

The competition between rigid and flexible concepts of time is unequal, for patience and perseverance stand the negotiator in better stead than habits of urgency. It is hard enough negotiating the issues; bargaining against an inner clock compounds the difficulty. Worse, American negotiators join an instinctive impatience to an overwhelming obligation to succeed; American culture—in the form of public opinion, career dictates, and governmental expectations—does not take kindly to inconclusive outcomes. In the contest of wills, as their opposite numbers are well aware, Americans are at a disadvantage. Whereas Americans must bring matters to a prompt conclusion, their opponents can sit them out or, if necessary, credibly threaten to walk away from the bargaining table altogether. These are valuable tactical advantages.

The tendency of American negotiators to give ground in the face of an obdurate rival was commented on years ago by the U.S. delegate to the Panmunjom armistice talks for ending the Korean War (see Young

1968). A similar asymmetrical propensity to concession emerged in the 1955 talks for the release of American citizens kept in the People's Republic of China (PRC) against their will. The United States displayed a pattern of early, unreciprocated concession. At the second session of the negotiations, on August 2, Chinese delegate Wang seized the initiative and put forward a series of demands. Among other things, he called on the United States to supply a list of names of Chinese who had been issued exit visas. At the next session two days later, U.S. Ambassador Johnson spent the whole time responding to the Chinese position and handed Wang the requested list of seventy-six names. Far from thanking him, Wang "expressed dissatisfaction" and demanded a complete list of Chinese nationals in the United States. Other unreciprocated U.S. concessions followed in subsequent sessions.

By August 23, the negotiations had stuck on the Chinese refusal to agree to release all the Americans at the same time. Ambassador Johnson was reduced to appealing to Wang's sense of fair play by pointing out the "successive concessions" made by the American side. Not even a "definite promise" had been made in return. But the Chinese delegate tenaciously declined to accept either an explicit commitment or a deadline. By August 31 Johnson concluded that the Chinese position was intractable. Wang "showed no great sense of urgency." In its instructions of September 2, the State Department accepted Johnson's judgment that the immediate release of half the Americans was "as good as can be expected." The final agreement left many Americans in Chinese hands, where they were to languish for years *(Foreign Relations of the United States* 1986, pp. 9, 14, 42, 52, 59, 62, 64, 73–74, 75, 85, 86).

It might be thought that the American position was inherently weaker than that of China, in that American nationals were being held under duress, while any Chinese resident in the United States was free to leave at any time. Actually, the United States had a very strong card to play, had its patience extended beyond the five weeks that marked the apparent limit of its endurance. The agenda of the talks, agreed to on August 1, contained two items. The first was the civilian repatriation issue; the second was "other practical matters at issue between the two sides," implying the U.S. economic blockade of China and the confrontation over Taiwan. The Chinese were really interested in this latter item, not the handful of unfortunate American civilians. Item one was simply the entry price for item two. However, Wang, with great poise, never revealed his interest in any other issue by the merest hint and simply ignored Johnson's threat not to proceed to anything else until the first item was settled.

The dysfunctional American propensity for self-induced deadlines was also evident in the 1978 normalization talks with the PRC (Bernstein 1988). It is now clear that the haste with which these negotiations were pursued by the Carter administration was particularly inappropriate because time was really working against Peking. There were some tactical, but mostly scheduling, reasons that the United States wanted an agreement by the end of 1978—the forthcoming Senate debate over ratification of the Panama canal treaties, the Strategic Arms Limitation Treaty (SALT) talks with the USSR, and ongoing involvement in the Egyptian-Israeli peace process—but none of these were insurmountable. China's need for a normalization of relations was, in fact, far more pressing. The establishment of full diplomatic relations between the two countries was the condition for a visit to the United States by Deng Xiaoping. This visit was vital to Deng to obtain the appearance of U.S. complicity in the February 17, 1979, People's Liberation Army attack on Vietnam as a deterrent to feared Soviet intervention.

At a meeting of top U.S. officials on June 20, 1978, it was first decided to aim for completion of the normalization negotiations by December 15. Clearly, the Chinese were not supposed to be informed of this target date. Secretary of State Vance argued that this deadline "would allow us to proceed with Peking at a reasonable pace and would have some negotiating advantages over a stretched-out process." However, National Security Adviser Brzezinski (1983) had already told Deng that President Carter was prepared to move as quickly as possible, and in September Carter himself openly stressed to the head of the PRC liaison office in Washington the desirability of a quick normalization. While the Chinese remained firm on their insistence that the United States terminate its arms relationship with Taiwan, Brzezinski made little attempt to conceal his own sense of urgency. He "told the Chinese ambassador that if we missed this opportunity, we would have to delay normalization until far into 1979. The congressional schedule would be overloaded and we would have to move ahead on SALT and a possible meeting with Brezhnev" (p. 229).

The negotiating advantages to the Chinese of this artificially induced sense of urgency are obvious. It was made to appear, with no basis in the objective situation, that the United States was more eager than China for agreement. As might be anticipated, there was a price to be paid for American impatience. Washington had early on reconciled itself to the Chinese refusal to renounce officially its right to use force to reunify Taiwan with the mainland. In lieu of an explicit Chinese concession, it was decided to settle for an American statement of "interest in the peaceful resolution of the Taiwan issue," which would not be contradicted by a simultaneous Chinese statement. But on December 15, 1978, U.S.

desires notwithstanding, Peking went ahead with a statement that did reject the American position. The manner in which Taiwan would be brought "back to the embrace of the motherland," the PRC declared, "is entirely China's internal affair." It was a ringing slap in the face for Carter. To add insult to injury, in 1982 fresh negotiations on the problem of Taiwan produced a new agreement. In return for a remarkable U.S. commitment not to exceed past qualitative and quantitative levels of arms sales to Taiwan, China now pledged to seek a peaceful solution to unification. It had succeeded in selling the same horse twice.

INTERCULTURAL COMMUNICATION IN THE NEW GLOBAL DIPLOMACY

Classic diplomacy, as it evolved over centuries in the European states system, came to reflect the values and assumptions of an "international diplomatic culture." Coming from similar social backgrounds, grounded in common civilizational canons, educated to the same convictions, diplomats constituted something like a medieval guild. Formidable immunities and privileges protected their exclusive position. Thus, they could be assured of dealing with colleagues who had a shared loyalty to the profession and "spoke the same language" as they did. Like other guilds, the diplomatic corps possessed a proprietary claim over its specialty, the conduct of negotiations. This meant not only that international negotiations rested on a common stock of technical procedures and terms, but also that understanding prevailed at a deeper, common-sense level about what the activity was all about. Martin Wight (1977) correctly pointed to the possession of a common culture as the prerequisite for the emergence of states systems, from the time of the ancient Greeks onward.

Over the course of the last half century, this situation has radically changed. For the first time in history a universal, inclusive diplomatic system has come into existence, in which almost all states maintain relations with almost all other states. In the new dispensation, the West still enjoys certain marked advantages: the continuing preeminence of the United States, the centrality of western cities, especially New York and Washington, and the dominance of the English language. But as the international system has accepted new members, the balance has gradually shifted toward other civilizations and economies. "The order that is now emerging," Henry Kissinger (1995) observes, "will have to be built by statesmen who represent vastly different cultures" (p. 27).

Only a generation ago cross-cultural dissonance was of little concern to a still exclusive, self-centered western diplomacy. Treating Nasser like a supplicant in the 1956 Aswan Dam talks, U.S. Secretary of State Dulles made little effort to broadcast on the same wavelength as the emerging Third World nations. Today, reflecting the altered agenda and makeup of the international community, the West necessarily conducts a greatly increased proportion of its business outside the former charmed circle. In the past, leaders like Galtieri (Argentine junta leader), Saddam Hussein, and the Ayatollah Khomeini would not have qualified as interlocutors; today, they negotiate as equals.

Cultural differences might remain marginal if professional diplomats still enjoyed an exclusive position at the negotiating table, but today they are no longer the only actors in international negotiations. In an age of "Concorde diplomacy," politicians, officials from domestic agencies, and figures from the private sector are just as likely to be involved in international negotiation. Ease of travel has particularly reduced the role of the resident embassy (Henderson 1994). Multilateral negotiation at international conferences is another feature of the shifting professional scene. As nondiplomats

play an increasing role, narrow, culture-bound attitudes and habits, usually unmodified by diplomatic training, knowledge of languages, or experience of service abroad, risk overshadowing shared specialist skills.

What conclusions are to be drawn from the potential for discord suggested above? The first conclusion is linguistic: Where possible, the problem of cultural-linguistic dissonance can be alleviated by using a common language, a *lingua franca*, almost inevitably English. In Israeli-Palestinian talks, English saved the day: "Redeployment" sounds much more neutral and technical than its Hebrew and Arabic equivalents. Unfortunately, this solution is not always available to negotiators for prestige or technical reasons, and officials and leaders may be unwilling or unable to use English.

Nor should it be thought that reliance on English obviates all misunderstanding, as State Department interpreter Edmund Glenn argued (1966). Not everyone who speaks in English, thinks in English; disguised dissonances remain. It was essential that basic United Nations texts be published in French and other languages, one UN official explained, "because they translate lines of thought and outlooks different from an Anglo-Saxon vision and perspective" (*Ha'aretz,* January 7, 1996). Expertise in the language and culture of one's interlocutor is still needed. This lesson was dramatically brought home by the fall of the shah of Iran. In 1979 the United States possessed few officers in Tehran who knew Farsi. This not only inhibited its capacity to gather intelligence, but also meant that officials from the two cultures often unwittingly talked past each other (Sick 1985). Foreign language is not just a medium of communication but is also a means of penetrating beneath the surface of a society.

A second conclusion relates to the acquisition of professional skills. In comparison to the situation of only a few years ago, there has been an expansion in negotiation training, both for diplomats and executives in the private sector. Here, though, the position is less favorable than it appears. Many of the courses in negotiation—often based on a culture-bound, can-do philosophy of "getting to yes"—pay insufficient attention to cross-cultural variation. This tendency can be readily observed in the work of Roger Fisher, an influential author and educator and founder of the Program on Negotiation at Harvard Law School. His practical recommendations for international negotiators invariably underestimate cultural differences. In the 1990–1991 Persian Gulf crisis, for example, Fisher repeatedly called for fair and sympathetic consideration of Saddam Hussein's legitimate needs and concerns. This "you win, I win" approach, doubtless appropriate to a domestic American market, was strikingly unsuited to the requirements of compelling the Iraqi leader to withdraw his army of occupation from Kuwait; it merely repeated the initial error of assuming that Saddam Hussein was a reasonable statesman who would prefer a peaceful, compromise outcome to war (Baram 1994; Fisher 1990). Negotiation training, then, has to incorporate both a general sensitivity to cross-cultural differences and detailed coaching in individual national styles.

If my arguments in this chapter are accepted, a third, more general conclusion can be drawn about the role of diplomacy. In a situation of increasing globalization it follows that a culturally informed diplomacy is peculiarly suited to act on the boundary between societies as an interpretive and conjunctive mechanism, facilitating comprehension and the smooth conduct of negotiation. Within governments, foreign ministries are uniquely well equipped not just to coordinate international delegations, but also to provide an authoritative cultural interpretation of the interlocutor and advice on negotiating strategies. In this vital area of expertise, this evolutionary niche, diplomats have an evident comparative advantage. No other agency, private or official, is in a better position to cultivate cross-cultural skills and foreign languages (and the long-term relationships that underpin business in high-context societies). Linguistic proficiency—the key to cross-cultural insight—and local knowledge have been valued attributes of the skilled diplomat since time immemorial (for example, Henderson 1994). These traditional assets are more appropriate today than ever. By laying special emphasis on the attributes of cross-cultural negotiating competence, diplomats will be well placed to help their societies meet the challenges of globalization in the years ahead.

REFERENCES

Baram, A. 1994. "The Iraqi Invasion of Kuwait: Decision Making in Baghdad." In *Iraq's Road to War*, ed. A. Baram. New York: St. Martin's Press, pp. 5–36.

Bernstein, T. P. 1988. *The Negotiations to Normalize U.S.-China Relations.* Pew Case Studies No. 426. Pittsburgh, Pa.: University of Pittsburgh, Graduate School of Public and International Affairs.

Brzezinski, Z. 1983. *Power and Principle: Memoirs of the National Security Adviser, 1977–1981.* London: Weidenfeld and Nicolson.

Cohen, R. 1994. "Culture Gets in the Way." *Middle East Quarterly* 1: 45–53.

———. Forthcoming. "Conflict Resolution Across Cultures: Bridging the Gap." In *Culture in World Politics*, ed. D. Jacquin, A. Oros, and M. Verweij. London: Macmillan.

Coon, C. 1989. Interview of former ambassador to Nepal by author.

Eickelman, D. F. 1977. "Time in a Complex Society: A Moroccan Example." *Ethnology* 16: 39–55.

Eilts, H. 1988. Interview of former ambassador to Egypt by author.

Elgström, O. 1990. "Norms, Culture, and Cognitive Patterns in Foreign Aid Negotiations." *Negotiation Journal* 6: 147–159.

Fisher, R. 1990. "Getting to 'Yes' with Saddam: How Words Can Win." *Washington Post*, December 9, 1990.

Foreign Broadcast Information Service (FBIS), Southeast Asia, March 1, 1994, pp. 50–51.

Foreign Relations of the United States. 1985. Vol. 11, 1952–1954. Washington, D.C.: U.S. Government Printing Office.

Foreign Relations of the United States. 1986. Vol. 3, 1955–1957. Washington, D.C.: U.S. Government Printing Office.

Galbraith, J. K. 1969. *Ambassador's Journal: A Personal Account of the Kennedy Years.* Boston: Houghton Mifflin.

Geertz, C. 1983. *Local Knowledge.* New York: Basic Books.

Glenn, E. S. 1966. "Meaning and Behavior: Communication and Culture." *Journal of Communication* 16: 248–272.

Hall, E. T. 1973. *The Silent Language.* New York: Anchor Press.

———. 1976. *Beyond Culture.* New York: Anchor Press.

Henderson, N. 1994. *Mandarin.* London: Weidenfeld and Nicolson.

Hendriks, E. C. 1991. "Research on International Business Negotiations: An Introduction." In *Business Communication in Multilingual Europe: Supply and Demand*, ed. C. Braecke and H. Cuyckens. Antwerp: ENCoDe/UFSIA, pp. 169–186.

Kissinger, H. A. 1995. *Diplomacy.* New York: Simon and Schuster.

Lewis, S. W. 1989. Interview in the *San Diego Union*, May 8.

Moser, L. J. 1986. "Negotiating Style: Americans and Japanese." In *Toward A Better Understanding: U.S.-Japanese Relations*, ed. D. B. Bendahmane and L. J. Moser. Washington, D.C.: U.S. Department of State, Foreign Service Institute, pp. 43–51.

Palmer, N. D. 1984. *The United States and India: The Dimensions of Influence.* New York: Praeger.

Plantey, A. 1982. "A Cultural Approach to International Negotiation." *International Social Science Journal* 93: 535–544.

Pye, L. 1982. *Chinese Commercial Negotiating Style.* Cambridge, Mass.: Oelgeschlager, Gunn, and Hain.

Quandt, W. B. 1987. "Egypt: A Strong Sense of National Identity." In *National Negotiating Styles*, ed. H. Binnendijk. Washington, D.C.: U.S. Department of State, Foreign Service Institute, pp. 105–124.

Samovar, L. A., and R. E. Porter. 1994. *Intercultural Communication: A Reader.* 7th ed. Belmont, Calif.: Wadsworth.

Sick, G. 1985. *All Fall Down: America's Fateful Encounter with Iran.* London: I. B. Tauris.

Solomon, R. H. 1987. "China: Friendship and Obligation in Chinese Negotiating Style." In *National Negotiating Styles*, ed. H. Binnendijk. Washington, D.C.: U.S. Department of State, Foreign Service Institute, pp. 1–16.

Thambipillai, P., and J. Saravanamuttu. 1985. *ASEAN Negotiations: Two Insights.* Singapore: Institute of Southeast Asian Studies.

Ting-Toomey, S. 1985. "Toward a Theory of Conflict and Culture." *International and Intercultural Communication Annual* 9: 71–86.

Veliotes, N. 1988. Interview of former U.S. ambassador to Egypt by author.

Wight, M. 1977. *Systems of States.* Leicester, U.K.: Leicester University Press.

Wilcox, R. 1989. Interview of former U.S. official in Mexico City by author.

Yahuda, M. 1993. "Hong Kong's Future: Sino-British Negotiations, Perceptions, Organization, and Political Culture." *International Affairs* 69: 245–266.

Young, K. T. 1968. *Negotiating with the Chinese Communists: The United States Experience, 1953–1967.* New York: McGraw-Hill.

Zartman, I. W., and M. R. Berman. 1982. *The Practical Negotiator.* New Haven, Conn.: Yale University Press.

Zhang, D., and K. Kuroda. 1989. "Beware of Japanese Negotiation Style: How to Negotiate with Japanese Companies." *Northwest Journal of International Law and Business* 10: 195–212.

34

The Interactive Problem-Solving Approach

HERBERT C. KELMAN

Interactive problem solving is an unofficial, academically based, third-party approach to the analysis and resolution of international and ethnic conflicts, anchored in social-psychological principles. The approach is derived from the seminal work of John Burton (see Burton 1969, 1979, 1984; Kelman 1972). My colleagues and I have been developing and applying this approach for more than two decades, working within a scholar-practitioner mode. Our practice is informed by theoretical analysis and empirical research on international conflict, social influence, and group interaction. The experience gained in practice, in turn, contributes to developing our theoretical framework and to evaluating and refining our intervention model. Thus, the work represents an integration and continuing interaction between practice, research, and theory building.

The fullest—in a sense, the paradigmatic—application of the approach is represented by problem-solving workshops, which bring together politically influential members of conflicting parties in a private, confidential setting for direct, nonbinding communication. Workshops are designed to enable the parties to explore each other's perspective and, through a joint process of creative problem solving, to generate new ideas for mutually satisfactory solutions to their conflict. The ultimate goal is to transfer the insights and ideas gained from these interactions into the political debate and decision-making processes in the two communities. (See Kelman 1979, 1986, 1990, 1992; Kelman and Cohen 1986; Rouhana and Kelman 1994. For a review of other work within this general framework, see Ronald Fisher 1989.)

Problem-solving workshops are not negotiating sessions and they are not intended either to simulate or to substitute for official negotiations. Their unofficial, nonbinding character clearly distinguishes them from formal negotiations, which can only be carried out by officials authorized to conclude binding agreements. At the same time, such workshops and similar mechanisms for interactive problem solving are closely linked to negotiations and play an important complementary role at all stages of the negotiation process. In the prenegotiation phase, they can help create a political atmosphere conducive to movement to the table; in the active negotiation phase, they can help to overcome obstacles to productive negotiations and to frame issues that are not yet on the table; and in the postnegotiation phase, they can contribute to implementation of the negotiated agreement and to long-term peace building. It is precisely the nonbinding character of workshops that allows their unique contribution to the larger negotiation process: They provide an opportunity for sharing perspectives, exploring options, and joint thinking—an opportunity not readily available at the official negotiating table (Kelman 1996).

AN ACTION RESEARCH PROGRAM ON THE ISRAELI-PALESTINIAN CONFLICT

I have long been interested in applying the interactive problem-solving approach to the Middle East. Our first effort in this direction was a pilot workshop on the Israeli-Palestinian conflict organized in 1971 (see Cohen et al. 1977). Since 1974, my colleagues and I have been intensively engaged in an action research program on the resolution of international and intercommunal conflicts, with special emphasis on the Arab-Israeli conflict—and particularly the Israeli-Palestinian component of it.[1]

A major part of the program has involved developing our intervention methodology and the theoretical, social-psychological base of interactive problem solving, as well as training a new generation of scholar-practitioners in this emerging field. This approach is applicable to a wide variety of conflicts; indeed, its relevance is becoming increasingly evident with the proliferation of ethnic conflicts in the post–Cold War

era. Personally, I have continued some involvement in the Cyprus conflict and have remained in touch with several other protracted identity conflicts around the world through the work of my students and associates and through exchange and occasional collaboration within the growing network of practitioners in this field. Still, both because of my special interest in the Arab-Israeli conflict, and because this work—at least in my particular style of practice—calls for almost complete immersion in the region and its problems and for a sustained effort over a number of years, I have concentrated on the Middle East. Our work there is based, of course, on applying general principles to this specific setting, and it must be informed by a comparative perspective. However, close familiarity with the region and a long-term commitment to it contribute significantly to our credibility and effectiveness.

In the remainder of this chapter, I will (1) highlight some of the assumptions derived from a social-psychological framework that we bring to our intervention efforts, (2) briefly describe our intervention methodology and its application to the Israeli-Palestinian conflict, and (3) indicate how I believe our work can contribute, and indeed has contributed, to the search for a peaceful resolution of that conflict. Regarding the last point, I do not propose that interactive problem solving—or any other form of unofficial diplomacy—can substitute for official diplomacy or that it can operate independent of the constellation of historical forces and national interests that are themselves shaped by domestic and international political processes. I am convinced, however, that this approach can make a significant contribution to conflict resolution and that it should be seen as an integral part of a larger diplomatic process, rather than as a sideshow to the real work of diplomacy.

In the current context of an active Israeli-Palestinian peace process, the greatest strength of this approach is its potential contribution to transforming the relationship between the conflicting parties. Our work is based on the proposition that in conflicts like that between Palestinians and Israelis—conflicts about national identity and national existence between two peoples who are destined to live together in the same small space—conflict resolution must ultimately aim toward establishing a new cooperative and mutually enhancing relationship and must involve a process that paves the way to such a relationship. At one level, this may be an idealistic aspiration, but it is actually the most realistic approach to resolving such a conflict. Nothing less will work in the long run; and, even in the short run, only a process embodying the principle of reciprocity that is at the center of a new relationship is likely to succeed.

SOCIAL-PSYCHOLOGICAL ASSUMPTIONS

The practice of interactive problem solving is informed by a set of assumptions about the nature of international or intercommunal conflict and conflict resolution, derived from a social-psychological analysis. These assumptions enter into the formulation of the structure, the process, and the content of problem-solving workshops. I shall mention five general assumptions that are central to our approach.

First, although war and peace, and international relations as a whole, are societal and intersocietal processes, which cannot be reduced to the level of individual behavior, there are many aspects of international conflict and conflict resolution for which the individual represents the most appropriate unit of analysis. Most important, the satisfaction of the needs of both parties—the needs of human individuals as articulated through their core identity groups—is the ultimate criterion for a mutually satisfactory resolution of their conflict (Burton 1990;

Kelman 1990). Unfulfilled needs, especially for identity and security, and existential fears—fears based on threats to national existence—typically drive the conflict and create barriers to its resolution. By probing beneath the parties' incompatible positions and exploring the identity and security concerns that underlie them, it often becomes possible to develop mutually satisfactory solutions, since conflicts about identity, security, and other psychological needs are not inherently zero-sum.

Both in our theoretical work and in our practice, we need to determine the relevant points of entry for psychological analysis—those points in the theoretical model or in the diplomatic process at which the cognitions, emotions, and intentions of individuals and the interactions between individuals can play a specific role in determining outcomes. Thus, we can identify certain processes central to conflict resolution (such as empathy, insight, creative problem solving, and learning) that must take place at the level of individuals and interaction between individuals. Problem-solving workshops provide a setting in which these processes can occur. Changes at the level of individuals—in the form of new insights and ideas—resulting from the micro-level process of the workshop can then be fed back into the political debate and the decision making in the two communities, thus becoming vehicles for change at the macro level.

Second, international conflict must be viewed not merely as an intergovernmental or interstate phenomenon, but also as an intersocietal phenomenon. Insofar as the conflict is between two societies, it becomes important to examine what happens within each society. In particular, the intersocietal view of conflict alerts us to the role of internal divisions within each society in international conflicts—that is, the crucial relationship between intragroup and intergroup conflict. Internal divisions create serious constraints on decision makers in their pursuit of peaceful solutions, yet they also provide opportunities and levers for change: They challenge the monolithic image of the enemy that parties in conflict tend to hold, enabling them to deal with each other in a more differentiated way. Conflict resolution efforts that are sensitive to the role of intra- and intersocietal processes require analysis of both the dynamics of public opinion on both sides and the requirements for consensus building within and coalition forming across the conflicting societies (Kelman 1993).

An important implication of the intersocietal view of conflict is that negotiations and third-party efforts should ideally be directed not merely toward settling the conflict in the form of a brokered political agreement, but toward resolving it. Conflict resolution in this deeper and more lasting sense implies arrangements and accommodations that emerge out of the interaction between representatives of the parties themselves, that address the basic needs of both parties, and to which the parties are committed. Only this kind of solution is capable of transforming the relationship between societies locked into a protracted conflict that engages their collective identities and existential concerns. There is no presumption, of course, that conflicts can ever be totally or permanently resolved; conflict resolution is a gradual process conducive to structural and attitude change, to reconciliation, to the development of a new relationship mindful of the interdependence of the two societies and open to cooperative functional arrangements between them. The real test of conflict resolution in deep-rooted conflicts is how much the process by which agreements are constructed and the nature of the resultant agreements contribute to transforming the relationship between the parties.

The conception of international conflict as an intersocietal phenomenon also suggests a broader view of diplomacy as a complex mix of official and unofficial processes. The peaceful termination or management of conflict requires binding agreements that can only be achieved at the official level. Unofficial, noncommittal interactions, however, can play a constructive complementary role by exploring ways of overcoming obstacles to conflict resolution and by helping to create a political environment conducive to negotiations and other diplomatic initiatives (Saunders 1988).

Third, conflict is an interactive process with an escalatory, self-perpetuating dynamic. The needs and fears of parties involved in an intense conflict relationship impose perceptual and cognitive constraints on their processing of new information. A major effect of these constraints is that the parties systematically underestimate the occurrence and possibility of change and therefore avoid negotiations, even in the face of changing interests that would make negotiations desirable for both. Images of the enemy are particularly resistant to contradictory information. The combination of demonic enemy images and virtuous self-images on both sides leads to the formation of mirror images, which contribute to the escalatory dynamic of conflict interaction and to resistance to change in a conflict relationship (Bronfenbrenner 1961; White 1965). Moreover, interaction between conflicting parties is governed by a set of "conflict norms" that encourage each party to adopt a militant, uncompromising, threatening posture, thus reinforcing the enemy's hostile image and creating self-fulfilling prophecies. The conflict dynamics tend to entrench the parties in their own perspectives on history and justice; dehumanization of the enemy makes it even more difficult to acknowledge and access the perspective of the other.

Conflict resolution efforts require promoting a different kind of interaction, one capable of reversing the escalatory and self-perpetuating dynamics of conflict: an interaction conducive to sharing perspectives, differentiating the enemy image, and gaining insight into the processes that contribute to escalation. At the micro level—in problem-solving workshops or similar forums—such interaction can contribute to the development of de-escalatory language, of ideas for mutually reassuring gestures and actions, of commitment to reciprocity, and of proposals for win-win solutions. At the macro level, such products can translate into new discourse among conflicting parties, characterized by a shift in emphasis from power politics to mutual responsiveness, reciprocity in process and solutions, and invitation to a new relationship.

Fourth, conflict resolution requires a wider range of influence processes than those typically employed in international conflict relationships. It is necessary to move beyond influence strategies based on threats and to expand and refine strategies based on promises and positive incentives. Conflict resolution efforts, by searching for solutions that satisfy the needs of both parties, create opportunities for mutual influence by way of responsiveness to each other's needs. They can demonstrate the possibility of influencing the other through one's own actions. A key element in this process is mutual reassurance. In existential conflicts in particular, parties can encourage each other to negotiate seriously by reducing both sides' fears—not just, as more traditional strategic analysts often suggest, by increasing their pain. At the macro level, this broader understanding of influence processes calls for shifting emphasis from deterrence and coercion to mutual reassurance. The use of influence processes based on responding to the other's needs and fears and searching for ways of benefiting the other can do more than affect specific behaviors of the other. It can contribute to a creative redefinition of the conflict, to joint discovery of win-win solutions, and to transformation of the relationship between the parties.

Fifth, and finally, the present expanded conception of influence processes that can be brought to bear in a conflict relationship is itself based on the assumption that international conflict is a dynamic phenomenon, marked by the occurrence and possibility of change. Conflict resolution efforts are geared, therefore, to discovering possibilities for change, identifying conditions for change, and overcoming resistance to change. Such an approach favors an attitude of strategic optimism (Kelman 1978, 1979)—not because of an unrealistic denial of malignant trends, but as part of a deliberate strategy to promote change by actively searching for and accentuating whatever realistic possibilities for peaceful resolution of the conflict might be on the horizon.

PROBLEM-SOLVING WORKSHOPS

The assumptions summarized in the preceding section are reflected in our intervention methodology. In describing this methodology, I will focus on problem-solving workshops, which represent the fullest, though not the sole, expression of interactive problem solving (see Kelman 1979, 1986, 1992).[2]

Problem-solving workshops are intensive meetings between politically involved and often politically influential (but unofficial) representatives of conflicting parties—for example, Israelis and Palestinians, or Greek and Turkish Cypriots—drawn from the mainstream of their respective communities. Thus, in our Israeli-Palestinian work, participants have included parliamentarians, leading figures in political parties or movements, former military officers or government officials, journalists or editors specializing in the Middle East, and academic scholars who are major analysts of the conflict for their societies and some of whom have served in advisory, official, or diplomatic positions.

The number of participants has varied; our workshops generally include three to six members of each party, as well as a third party of two to eight members. The third party consists of a panel of social scientists knowledgeable about international conflict, group process, and the Middle East region. The third party's skills and knowledge in these areas and its academic status serve as the basis of its credibility. The credibility and effectiveness of the third party are also enhanced by the ethnic balance of the panel. In the last few years, for example, I have worked closely with Nadim Rouhana, whose Palestinian background provides a helpful balance to my own Jewish background. The third party in our model does not offer solutions, but assumes a strictly facilitative role.

Recruiting participants is one of the most important tasks of the third party. Effective recruitment requires intimate familiarity with the two communities and their political elites, establishing links to various networks within these communities, and maintaining both parties' trust in our evenhandedness, integrity, and knowledge of the region. Depending on the occasion and the political level of the participants, we may discuss our plans for a workshop with relevant elements of the political leadership on both sides in order to keep them informed, gain their support, and solicit their advice on participants and agenda. Many potential workshop participants consider approval or encouragement from their political leadership a necessary condition for their involvement. Recruitment, however, is generally done on an individual basis and participants are invited to come as individuals, rather than as formal representatives. Invitees, of course, may consult with their leadership or with one another before agreeing to come. Whenever possible, we start the recruitment process with one key person on each side; we then consult with that person and with each successive invitee in selecting the rest of the

team. At times, the composition of a team may be negotiated within the particular community that we approach, but the final invitation is always issued by the third party to each individual participant. An essential part of the recruitment process is a personal discussion with each participant of the purposes, procedures, and ground rules of the workshop before obtaining his or her final commitment to the enterprise.

Participants' motives for accepting our invitation have varied, depending on the nature of their political involvement and on the stage of the conflict. In earlier years, when there were virtually no forums for Israelis and Palestinians to meet as equals and discuss political issues, many participants saw the workshops as opportunities to learn about the other side's thinking, to inform the other side about their own thinking, and to see if they could find any common ground. More recently, with increasing Israeli-Palestinian contacts and, particularly, with the onset of negotiations, motives for participation are often more specific. Participants want to know about the political divisions and the state of public opinion on the other side, about the reasons for the other's actions or failures to act, and about the prospects for movement. They also want to inform the other side about their own thinking and reactions to events, about their own political divisions and public opinion, and about their priorities, limits, and frustrations. In addition, they want to present some of their own ideas and proposals and test the other side's reactions, and they want to explore possibilities for resolving difficult issues in mutually satisfactory ways. Over the years, workshop participants have been motivated by an interest in finding a negotiated solution to the conflict, or at least in testing, in a safe environment, whether the possibility for such a solution exists at all. They have also been interested in demonstrating to the other side and to the third party that they are committed to the quest for peace.

A typical workshop consists of a preliminary session of four to five hours for each of the parties and joint meetings for two and one-half days. The workshops take place in an academic setting: Most of our workshops have been carried out under the auspices of the Harvard Center for International Affairs. The university has the advantage of providing an unofficial, nonbinding context, with its own set of norms to support a type of interaction that departs from the norms that generally govern interactions between conflicting parties.

The discussions are completely private and confidential. There is no audience, no publicity, and no record, and the central ground rules specify that statements made in the course of a workshop cannot be cited for attribution outside of the workshop setting. These and other features of the workshop are designed to enable and encourage workshop participants to engage in a type of communication that is usually not available to parties involved in an intense conflict relationship. The third party creates an atmosphere, establishes norms, and makes occasional interventions—workshop features that are all conducive to free and open discussion, in which the parties address each other, rather than third parties or their own constituencies, and in which they listen to each other in order to understand their differing perspectives. They are encouraged to deal with the conflict analytically rather than polemically—to explore the ways in which their interaction helps to exacerbate and perpetuate the conflict, rather than to assign blame to the other side while justifying their own. This analytic discussion helps the parties penetrate each other's perspective and understand each other's concerns, needs, fears, priorities, and constraints.

Once both sets of concerns are on the table and have been understood and ac-knowledged, the parties are encouraged to engage in a process of joint problem solving. They are asked to work together in developing new ideas for resolving the conflict in ways that would satisfy the fundamental needs and allay the existential fears of both parties. They are then asked to explore the political and psychological constraints that stand in the way of such integrative, win-win solutions and that, in fact, have prevented the parties from moving to (or staying at) the negotiating table or from negotiating productively. Again, they are asked to engage in a process of joint problem solving, designed to generate ideas for "getting from here to there." A central feature of this process is the identification of steps of mutual reassurance —in the form of acknowledgments, symbolic gestures, or confidence-building measures—that would help reduce the parties' fear of entering into negotiations when the outcome is uncertain and risky. Problem-solving workshops also contribute to mutual reassurance by helping the parties develop —again, through collaborative effort—a non-threatening, de-escalatory language and a shared vision of a desirable future.

The workshops have a dual purpose. First, they are designed to produce changes in the workshop participants themselves—changes in the form of more differentiated images of the enemy (see Kelman 1987), greater insight into the dynamics of the conflict, and new ideas for resolving the conflict and for overcoming the barriers to a negotiated solution. These changes at the level of individual participants are not ends in themselves, but vehicles for promoting change at the policy level. Thus, a second purpose of workshops is to maximize the likelihood that the new insights, ideas, and proposals developed in the course of the workshop are fed back into the political debate and the decision-making process within each community. One central task of the third party is to structure the workshop in such a way that new insights and ideas are likely to be both generated and transferred effectively to the policy process.

The composition of the workshop is crucial in this context: Great care must be taken to select participants who, on the one hand, have the interest and ability to engage in the kind of learning process that workshops provide and, on the other hand, have the positions and credibility within their own communities that enable them to influence the thinking of political leaders, political constituencies, or the general public. As noted above, the third party's role, though essential to the success of problem-solving workshops, is strictly facilitative. The critical work of generating ideas and infusing them into the political process must be done by the participants themselves. A basic assumption of our approach is that solutions emerging out of the interaction between the conflicting parties are most likely to be responsive to their needs and to engender their commitment.

Although the workshops are governed by the principle that ideas for conflict resolution must emerge out of the interaction between the parties, the facilitative role of the third party is essential—at least at certain stages in the conflict—to making that interaction possible and fruitful. The third party provides the context in which representatives of parties engaged in an intense conflict are able to come together. It selects, briefs, and convenes the participants. It serves as a repository of trust for both parties, enabling them to proceed with the assurance that their confidentiality will be respected and their interests protected even though (by definition) they cannot trust each other. It establishes and enforces the norms and ground rules that facilitate analytic discussion and a problem-solving orientation. It proposes a broad agenda that encourages the parties to move from exploring each other's concerns and constraints to

generating ideas for win-win solutions and for implementing such solutions.

Furthermore, although the third party tries to stay in the background as much as possible once it has set the stage, it is prepared to intervene in order to keep the discussion moving in a productive, constructive direction. Thus, if the discussion goes too far afield, becomes repetitive, or systematically avoids the issues, the third party—usually with the help of some of the participants—will try to bring it back to the broad agenda. At times, we also make substantive interventions in the form of suggestions for potentially useful conceptual handles or observations about the content and process of the interaction. Content observations are designed to summarize, interpret, integrate, clarify, or sharpen what is being said in the group. Process observations, which suggest how interactions between the parties "here and now" may reflect the dynamics of the conflict between their communities, are among the unique features of problem-solving workshops. They generally focus on incidents in which one party's words or actions clearly have a strong emotional impact on the other—leading to expressions of anger and dismay, of relief and reassurance, of understanding and acceptance, or of reciprocation. The third party can use such incidents, which are part of the participants' shared immediate experience, as a springboard for exploring some of the issues and concerns that define the conflict between their societies. Through such exploration, each side can gain some insight into the preoccupations of the other, and the way these are affected by its own actions. Process observations must be introduced sparingly and make special demands on the third party's skill and sense of timing. It is particularly important that such interventions be pitched at the intergroup level, rather than the interpersonal level. Analysis of "here and now" interactions is not concerned with the personal characteristics of the participants or their personal relations with one another, but only with what these interactions can tell us about the relationship between their national groups.

I have already stated that these workshops are not negotiating sessions. Unlike official negotiations, they are not binding, but it is precisely this nonbinding character that is the source of their potential contributions, that makes it possible for new understandings and new ideas to emerge out of the interaction between the parties. While the workshops are clearly separate from negotiations, they are intended to contribute to the negotiation process. The nature of their potential contribution depends on the status of the negotiations—on whether, for example, the parties are engaged in a prenegotiation phase, in early negotiations, in advanced negotiations, or in an implementation phase. Whatever phase the negotiations are in, however, maximizing the political impact is a central consideration in defining the purpose of a particular workshop, in shaping its agenda, in steering the discussion, and in selecting workshop participants.

Most of our work over the years on the Israeli-Palestinian conflict (that is, all of our workshops before the fall of 1991) took place during the prenegotiation phase. The primary function of this work was to help create a political environment conducive to negotiations: a set of conditions that would enable the parties to overcome the obstacles to negotiation and to move to the table. Participants in the workshops that we have conducted over the years, as well as many analysts of the Arab-Israeli conflict, seem to agree that our program has indeed contributed, in a small but significant way, to paving the way to the negotiating table. Workshops have enabled the parties to enter each other's perspective and thus gain insight into the other's concerns, priorities, and constraints. They have contributed, within each community, to a more differentiated image of the other side, to a greater awareness of the changes that have been taking place, to the discovery of potential negotiating partners, and thus to the sense that there is both someone to talk to on the other side and something to talk about. More concretely, the workshops have contributed to the development of cadres of individuals with experience in productive communication with the other side and with the conviction that such communication can be fruitful. Thus, representatives in the various Israeli-Palestinian negotiating sessions that have been conducted since the fall of 1991 have included a considerable number of individuals who have taken part in our workshops and other unofficial Israeli-Palestinian meetings over the years. In particular, many members of a continuing workshop that met periodically between 1990 and 1993 (see Rouhana and Kelman 1994) have been actively involved in the official peace process as negotiators or advisers. "Alumni" of our workshops can now be found in the Israeli cabinet, Knesset, and foreign ministry, as well as in leading positions in various official Palestinian agencies.

These workshops have also contributed to creating a political environment conducive to negotiations through the development of a deescalatory language, based on sensitivity to words that frighten or humiliate and words that reassure the other party. Anecdotal evidence for this effect is provided by the changes in the tone of the political discourse among Palestinians and Israelis in recent years, changes that can at least in part be traced to participation in workshops and similar experiences. Moreover, workshops have helped identify mutually reassuring actions and symbolic gestures; these often take the form of acknowledgments of the other's humanity, national identity, ties to the land, history of victimization, sense of injustice, genuine fears, and conciliatory moves. They have contributed to the development of shared visions of a desirable future, helping to reduce the parties' fear of negotiations as a step into an unknown, dangerous realm. They have generated ideas about the shape of a solution to the conflict that meets the basic needs of both parties, as well as ideas about how to get from here to there—that is, about a framework and set of principles for getting negotiations started. Perhaps the greatest value of these workshops is that, for the short run, they helped to keep alive a sense of possibility—a belief that a negotiated solution remains within the parties' reach—and, for the long run, they helped to begin the process of transforming the relationship between former enemies.

RECENT ACTIVITIES AND THEIR POLITICAL CONTEXT

Since 1990, our program has moved in two important new directions: First, as already indicated, we initiated our first continuing workshop in the fall of 1990 (Rouhana and Kelman 1994). Second, with the start of official negotiations in the fall of 1991, and the subsequent signing of the Oslo agreement in September 1993, we have adapted the structure and functions of our work to the new requirements of the evolving negotiation phase.

Until the fall of 1990, the workshops and related opportunities for interaction that we organized were all self-contained, one-time events, even though there was continuity in our earlier efforts. A number of individuals participated in two or more of our workshops. Alumni of the workshops also continued to be involved in a variety of other efforts at Israeli-Palestinian communication and collaboration, in which they drew on their earlier interactions. Moreover, our workshops had a cumulative effect in helping to create a political environment conducive to negotiations. Because of logistical

and financial constraints, however, and because of a certain lack of political readiness, we had not attempted before 1990 to organize a workshop in which the same group of participants would meet regularly over an extended period of time.

A continuing workshop can make several unique contributions to the larger political process. It represents a sustained effort to address concrete issues, enabling the participants to push the process of conflict analysis and interactive problem solving further and to apply it more systematically than they can in one-time workshops. The longer time period and the continuing nature of the enterprise make it possible to go beyond sharing perspectives to jointly producing creative ideas. Moreover, the periodic reconvening of a continuing workshop allows for an iterative and cumulative process, based on feedback and correction. The participants have an opportunity to take the ideas developed in the course of a workshop back to their own communities, to gather reactions, and to return to the next meeting with proposals for strengthening, expanding, or modifying the original ideas. It is also possible for participants, within or across parties, to meet or otherwise communicate with one another between workshop sessions in order to work out some of the ideas more fully and bring the results of their efforts back to the next session. Finally, a continuing workshop provides better opportunities to address the question of how to disseminate ideas and proposals developed at the workshop most effectively and appropriately.

We succeeded in convening such a continuing workshop in the fall of 1990, when a group of high-level, politically influential Israelis and Palestinians agreed to take part in a series of three meetings over the course of one year.[3] The participants in these meetings were all individuals with broad experience and high credibility in their respective communities, close to the center of the political mainstream, and occupying positions—in political organizations, academic institutions, think tanks, or the media —that enabled them to have a major impact on the framing of the issues and the perception of available options by decision makers, political elites, and the general public. The first session of this continuing workshop took place in November 1990, in the midst of the Persian Gulf crisis, when the level of mutual distrust was at its height. The second session took place in June 1991, after the Gulf War, when a great deal of repair work on the Israeli-Palestinian relationship had to be undertaken. By the time of our third session, in Bellagio, Italy, in August 1991, the participants were ready to engage in a constructive effort of joint thinking and to begin to formulate mutually acceptable approaches to some of the more difficult issues. At the end of this meeting the group committed itself to continuing the workshop.

Shortly after our August meeting, however, the political situation changed dramatically with the initiation of Arab-Israeli peace talks. Four of the six Palestinian participants in the continuing workshop were appointed to the official negotiating teams. We thus had to reassess the functions of the continuing workshop in the context of ongoing official negotiations and to consider how the overlap in participants between the official process and our unofficial process affected our future work. After exploring these questions in a series of bilateral consultations (in May 1992) with Israeli and Palestinian participants, we organized a fourth meeting of the continuing workshop in Leuven, Belgium, in July 1992. By that time, the political situation had changed even more as a result of the Labor Party's victory in the Israeli elections. With the formation of a new government, the Israeli participants in the continuing workshop became increasingly influential in the policy process within their own society. Thus, par-

ticipants on both sides felt that they were speaking to counterparts who were consequential and well-informed about the current situation. The political relevance of the continuing workshop was clearly enhanced by these developments, since Israelis and Palestinians who had productively interacted with one another in a series of unofficial meetings were now actively engaged in the negotiating process.

But this convergence and overlap between the official and unofficial processes also created some new dilemmas. It became inevitable that some ambiguities and role conflicts would arise if official negotiators also met with representatives of the other side separately, in an unofficial context—despite the fact that these unofficial meetings had begun well before the official negotiations and were clearly independent of the official process. We were not able to resolve these issues at the Leuven meeting. On the one hand, the participants found the discussions in Leuven extremely useful; it was clear that they greatly valued the continuing workshop and were very eager to continue the group and to capitalize on the working trust and the effective working relationship that they had developed over the preceding two years. At the same time, they realized that it might be necessary to reconstitute the group in view of the involvement of so many of its members in the official negotiations, in order to safeguard the integrity of both the official and the unofficial processes. In the end, it was decided to maintain the group, while continuing to explore the questions of whether and how the group should be reconstituted, and how to promote a productive interplay between the official and unofficial processes, one that could make best use of the excellent working relationship that the two sides had developed within the continuing workshop.

There was general consensus in our deliberations before, during, and after the

Leuven meeting about the new functions of the continuing workshop. We agreed that there was a continuing need for an unofficial forum, but that its functions would have to be redefined with the onset of official negotiations. We wanted to be very clear that our process was separate from and independent of the official negotiations and that it was not designed to serve as a forum for back-channel negotiations. Workshop participants —whatever their official positions—do not come with instructions, nor are they expected to make commitments on behalf of their leaderships. However, while our process is completely independent of the official process, it is designed to contribute directly to the success of that process by exploring obstacles to and constraints on the negotiations and ways of overcoming them; by helping to formulate shared principles on which the negotiations can proceed; by addressing long-term issues that are implicitly on the agenda and will eventually have to be addressed explicitly; and by beginning the process of building peace and transforming the relationship between the parties that must accompany and follow the process of peacemaking. The composition of our continuing workshop enabled us to link our work to the official process in both directions. The participants were well informed about what was happening in the negotiations themselves, as well as in the decision-making circles and the general public in their own societies; and they were also in a position to feed back what they learned in the course of a workshop into the negotiations and into the decision-making process and public opinion in their respective communities.

With these functions and special advantages in mind, we convened a fifth meeting of the continuing workshop in Salzburg, Austria, in August 1993. Several members of the continuing workshop were unable to attend this meeting, either because they found it in conflict with their official roles or because of competing obligations. We therefore invited other participants to replace them, which produced a significant change in the group's composition: A large minority of the participants in the Salzburg meeting were new to the group and had to be integrated in it. A good part of the discussion was devoted to some of the issues relating to the interim arrangements on which the negotiating teams in Washington had been unable to reach agreement. The participants found these discussions, as always, useful and instructive, but there was some sentiment that in future meetings it would be best to focus more systematically on specific issues, with advance preparation and with a commitment to working on a concrete written product. The events that unfolded within days after the Salzburg meeting ended reinforced this sentiment.

The first rumors of a major breakthrough in the Israeli-Palestinian negotiations reached us on the last day of the Salzburg meeting. On September 22, 1993—nine days after the signing of the Israeli-Palestinian accord —we arranged a consultation in Jerusalem with seven members of the continuing workshop who were within commuting distance of the city. At this meeting, and in subsequent consultations, there was general consensus that our work needed to continue and that we had a special contribution to make in this new phase of the peace process. However, it was clear that the latest developments had created a new political situation in which our efforts—though no less significant than our earlier work— would require a change in their structure and functions. Our work, like the peace process itself, now had to enter a new phase.

Accordingly, we decided in the late fall of 1993 that the time had come to close the continuing workshop in the form that it had taken over the preceding three years and to build a new project directly and immediately on the experience and achievements of that effort. The new project takes the form of a joint working group on Israeli-Palestinian relations, with an initial emphasis on systematically exploring the difficult political issues that are expected to be on the table in mid-1996, when negotiations of a final agreement are scheduled to begin.[4]

The working group, consisting of politically active and highly influential Israelis and Palestinians, held its first meeting in May 1994. The new project has drawn extensively on the members of the continuing workshop to provide advice, access to the official process, and the nucleus of the new working group itself. However, there are important differences—in structure, format, and participants—between the current working group and the earlier continuing workshop. Much of the work of the new project is done in smaller groups that meet more frequently and for longer periods of time than in the past. The focus is more specific and the work more product-oriented. Moreover, we have been recruiting new participants with the particular expertise and experience required by the issues to which the working group addresses itself. We hope that this new phase of our work will contribute significantly to the negotiation of the final Israeli-Palestinian agreement as well as to the further refinement of third-party mechanisms for creating unofficial inputs into ongoing official negotiations. At the present stage, there are three types of contributions that an unofficial working group like ours can make to the peace process.

At the level of the most immediate concern, the group can address the difficult issues that have arisen and will inevitably continue to arise in implementing the interim agreement. Unless these issues are resolved, the entire process may collapse or be sidetracked for a long time. As in our past activities, the purpose of such discus-

sions is to explore the state of public opinion on each side, the obstacles that have arisen, and ways of providing mutual reassurance (in the form of symbolic gestures, reciprocal acknowledgments, or confidence-building measures) that will improve the political atmosphere for implementing interim agreements and keeping the process on track. The kind of relationship that is established on the ground during the interim phase has an important bearing on whether the interim agreement will be successfully implemented and on the quality of the final agreement that will emerge from the interim stage.

At an intermediate level, the group can focus on the major political issues that will be on the table for the final-status negotiations. The issues to be addressed by such discussions include the status of Jerusalem, Palestinian refugees and the right of return, the future of Israeli settlements in the occupied territories, the final borders of the Palestinian polity, the nature of Palestinian self-determination, and the future relationship among the states in the region. The purpose is not to produce blueprints or draft agreements, but to develop a range of options, general approaches to each issue, and ideas for reframing each issue so that it becomes more amenable to negotiation. This is the kind of process that cannot readily take place, even under the best of circumstances, in the official context, where participants come with instructions, must check back with decision makers, and are charged with producing agreements to which the parties are officially committed. Unofficial interlocutors can engage in a joint exploratory process, which can provide the needed inputs into the official negotiations. In particular, our framework allows these issues to be discussed and formulated in a way that avoids the shortcomings of power bargaining and mechanical compromise by taking account of the needs and constraints of both parties and of the requirements for building a new long-term relationship between them.

At the level of long-range concerns, the group can focus on the requirements for developing a new relationship between the two communities during and beyond the interim period, exploring the role of the media, of education, of economic ties, and of institutional links in contributing to the peace-building process that must accompany and follow successful peacemaking. An unofficial joint forum for exploring issues in the relationship between the two communities, such as our new working group, is in itself an institutional mechanism that can help build a civil society across the political borders. In other words, the working group can serve, not only as a means for promoting a new relationship between the parties, but also as a manifestation and model of that new relationship.

We have placed the main emphasis of our Israeli-Palestinian working group, at least initially, at the intermediate level. Advance consideration of the difficult political issues that will have to be tackled in the negotiations for the final agreement is essential if these negotiations are to be productive. This kind of consideration, however, is not taking place at the official level, where the focus is almost entirely on immediate concerns. Indeed, consideration of these issues was deferred to the next stage of the negotiations precisely because of their difficulty, and even when that stage is reached, they cannot be adequately addressed within the bargaining framework of official negotiations.

Systematic exploration of these specific issues and preparation of joint concept papers—papers that can be submitted to decision makers and official negotiators as relevant background for their deliberations and disseminated more widely to help identify and frame the issues for the general

public as well—are the most relevant and unique contributions that we can make at this stage of the process. The unofficial context makes it possible for knowledgeable and credible Israelis and Palestinians to engage in a process of joint thinking and exploration, which can help to frame the issues in a way that is conducive to productive negotiations and to agreements that can form the basis of a mutually beneficial relationship.

Although the initial emphasis of the working group is at the intermediate level, we do not ignore either the immediate or the long-range issues. In fact, framing the issues for the final-status negotiations on which we are now concentrating has considerable relevance for the interim phase and for the long-term relationship between the two societies. Thus, for example, implementation of the interim agreement requires some provisional decisions regarding Jerusalem and the Israeli settlements. The sensitivity of these issues can easily create obstacles to implementation of the interim agreement; by the same token, any progress that our working group makes in framing and developing an approach to the issues of Jerusalem and the settlements may prove useful in overcoming obstacles at the interim stage. Similarly, as we work on specific issues to be addressed in the final-status negotiations, we begin to develop a broader framework for the future relationship between the two states. The formula for sharing Jerusalem, for example, may serve as a prototype for the way the country will ultimately be shared by the two peoples and the two states; discussions of the approach to the problems of Palestinian refugees or Israeli settlers may serve as a starting point for exploring the long-term question of the status of ethnic minorities in the two states after the conclusion of a final peace agreement.

THE CONTRIBUTIONS OF
UNOFFICIAL EFFORTS

The Israeli-Palestinian agreement of September 1993 represents a fundamental breakthrough in the long-standing Arab-Israeli conflict. The crucial element of this breakthrough is the mutual recognition between Israel and the PLO, expressed in the exchange of letters between the late Prime Minister Rabin and Chairman Arafat and in the opening of formal negotiations between the two sides. Israel's recognition of the PLO constitutes acceptance of Palestinian nationhood and it signals—to Palestinians, to Israelis, and to the rest of the world—that the most likely eventual outcome of the negotiations, after a peaceful transition period, will be a Palestinian state (perhaps in confederation with Jordan). PLO recognition of Israel constitutes a formal acknowledgment of the legitimacy of the State of Israel within its pre-1967 borders, and opens the door to the recognition of Israel by the Arab states and acceptance of its rightful place in the region.

The significance of this act of mutual recognition becomes apparent in light of the history of the Israeli-Palestinian conflict, which was marked by mutual denial of the other's nationhood and systematic efforts by each side to delegitimize the other. The conflict had been perceived by the two parties as a zero-sum conflict around national identity and national existence, in that each saw acknowledgment of the other's national rights and even the other's existence as a nation to be antagonistic to its own national rights and existence. The September 1993 agreement thus represented a conceptual breakthrough. To be sure, the process that it set into motion is not irreversible: Any political process is potentially subject to change. But the fact that what has been unthinkable for the entire history of this conflict has now not only been thought, but actually spoken and acted upon at the highest level of each community and in the international arena, has created a new historical reality that cannot be undone. Moreover, the political costs of reversing the process that has been set into motion with the peace agreement would be extremely high for the leadership on both sides. There is no doubt that Rabin and Arafat made a strategic decision to bring an end to the conflict through a historic compromise and that each staked his political future and his standing in history on the achievement of this goal. In doing so, they responded to a widespread, though far from unanimous, sense within each community that continuing the conflict does not serve its fundamental needs and long-term interests.

I believe that our workshops and related activities over the past two decades have made a modest, but not insignificant, contribution to this recent breakthrough in the Israeli-Palestinian conflict (Kelman 1995). They have done so by developing cadres of individuals prepared to carry out productive negotiations, by sharing information and formulating new ideas that provided important substantive input into the negotiations, and by fostering a political atmosphere that made the parties open to a new relationship.[5] The continuing workshop of 1990–1993 greatly enhanced these contributions and strengthened the political relevance of our work, both because it represented a sustained effort of joint Israeli-Palestinian exploration of key issues and because of the high level of the participants in terms of their political influence and their intellectual power. With the onset of the negotiations, we found ourselves at an important new turning point. Unofficial communication, far from being irrelevant under the new circumstances, became a potentially important vehicle for helping to create the momentum that was still lacking in the negotiation process and to develop ideas to sustain the process and improve its outcome. The participants in the continuing workshop, given their roles in the negotiations and their increasing political influence in their respective communities, were particularly well situated to make such contributions.

Despite the historic breakthrough of September 1993, there is a continuing need for the potential contributions of unofficial diplomacy. The Israeli-Palestinian negotiations are by no means complete and enormous obstacles have yet to be overcome. Implementing the interim agreement and concluding a final agreement will inevitably be a long and arduous process, and there is no assurance that it will succeed within the five-year period stipulated in the peace accord. The difficulties are exacerbated by sharp divisions within each society. Ideological opponents of the peace process, who want to hold out for sole possession of the entire land—although they represent only a minority on each side—are strengthened by the existential fears and profound distrust of the other side that pervade both communities. Under these circumstances, the peace process is particularly threatened by acts of violence—such as the Hebron massacre of Palestinians in February 1994 and the series of suicide bomb attacks on Israeli civilians starting in February 1996—that heighten the public's sense of vulnerability and its dread that the leadership has embarked on an uncertain and dangerous course. On both sides, such acts of violence deepen the sense of doubt and disillusionment created by the difficulties in implementing the interim agreements: Among Palestinians, they reinforce the feeling that the peace process is not producing the hoped-for changes in their daily existence; among Israelis, they erode the belief that the process can succeed in transforming the status quo into a state of peaceful coexistence.

Delays and difficulties in negotiating details of the agreement and in implementing it are inevitable in a conflict with such a long history of bitterness and distrust. Indeed, they arise from the very nature of the Declaration of Principles (DOP) for negotiating interim and final agreements that was signed in Washington on September 13, 1993. The DOP was a compromise document, designed to give Palestinians the hope and expectation that in the end they would have an independent state and to give Israelis the assurance that they were not committing themselves irrevocably to a dangerous set of arrangements. These two requirements contain some inherent contradictions, since interim arrangements must be seen by Palestinians as first steps toward the anticipated future state and by Israelis as gradual, limited steps that leave the future open to further negotiation. Thus, provisions intended to offer reassurance to one side may create disappointment and anxiety for the other. It was precisely in order to straddle these contradictory requirements that the DOP postponed discussion of some of the most contentious political issues—including the status of Jerusalem, refugees, settlements, security arrangements, and borders—to the permanent-status negotiations, scheduled to begin in the third year of the five-year interim period. For the interim process itself, these contradictions have created ambiguities and delays in implementation. Moreover, they have led the leadership on both sides to make statements and use rhetoric that are designed to reassure their own public, but that arouse suspicion and fear on the other side.

Thus, a great deal of effort and skill are still required in the arenas of diplomacy, political decision making, and public education if the major breakthrough of September 1993 is to be fulfilled through implementation of a viable interim agreement, passage of a peaceful transition period, conclusion of a mutually satisfactory final agreement, and establishment of a new relationship between the two nations. Accomplishing these tasks requires a systematic process of mutual reassurance that is responsive to both sides' existential fears, and creative reframing of the final-status issues so that they become amenable to negotiation. Unofficial efforts, such as those that my colleagues and I are engaged in, can make useful contributions at this stage, particularly by facilitating a joint Israeli-Palestinian forum for addressing the obstacles and constraints that impede implementation of the interim agreement and negotiation of the final agreement, for developing principles and options for resolving the difficult political issues left to the negotiations over the final agreement, and for exploring the requirements for building a new relationship between the two communities.

CONCLUSION

Let me return to my conceptual analysis to summarize the two ways in which interactive problem solving can potentially make such contributions to peacemaking in the Middle East and elsewhere.

First, it provides a micro process that can generate new insights into the conflict and new ideas for advancing negotiation and shaping mutually satisfactory solutions, and can infuse these insights and ideas into the political debate and the decision-making processes in the two communities. The special value of these ideas is that they emerge from a process of joint thinking and interactive problem solving by politically influential, mainstream members of the parties themselves.

Second, interactive problem solving contributes to the development of new approaches to conceptualizing and conducting the macro process of conflict resolution and international relations in general. The central features of this reconceptualization are

(1) a view of conflict resolution as an attempt to change the relationship between the conflicting parties, which, in turn, implies the principle of reciprocity in the process and the product of conflict resolution; (2) a new kind of political discourse in international relations—one that involves a shift in emphasis from power politics to joint problem solving; and (3) a new view of the influence processes employed in international relations—one that involves a shift in emphasis from deterrence and coercion to mutual reassurance.

NOTES

1. The action research program discussed in the chapter has been supported by grants from the Nathan Cummings Foundation, the John D. and Catherine T. MacArthur Foundation, the William and Flora Hewlett Foundation, the Ford Foundation, the United States Institute of Peace, and Rockefeller Family and Associates. I am grateful to these organizations for making this work possible and to the Harvard Center for International Affairs for providing the institutional base for it.

2. At several points in this section, I draw on my chapter, "Informal Mediation by the Scholar/Practitioner," in the Bercovitch and Rubin volume on *Mediation in International Relations* (Kelman 1992).

3. The continuing workshop was initiated and organized in partnership with Nadim Rouhana of Boston College, and we chaired the program throughout its three-year duration. We were joined on the third-party panel of facilitators by Harold Saunders of the Kettering Foundation and C. R. Mitchell of the Institute for Conflict Analysis and Resolution at George Mason University. We are very grateful to them, as well as to the members of our third-party staff, which included Cynthia Chataway, Rose Kelman, Susan Korper, Kate Rouhana, and William Weisberg.

4. This project, like the continuing workshop, is chaired by Nadim Rouhana and myself. It is carried out under the auspices of the

Program on International Conflict Analysis and Resolution, which was established at the Harvard Center for International Affairs in 1993 with a grant from the William and Flora Hewlett Foundation. Until May 1995, Eileen Babbitt administered the project and was a member of the third-party facilitation team. Donna Hicks now performs these roles. Kate Rouhana serves as the project's editor and coordinator, and Rose Kelman rounds out the third-party staff. We are grateful to the Nathan Cummings Foundation, the CRB (Charles R. Bronfman) Foundation, and the U.S. Information Agency for their financial support of this work.

5. Assessment of the contributions of our work is based largely on anecdotal evidence. The "hardest" part of that evidence relates to the number of Israeli and Palestinian participants in our various workshop projects who have been involved in the official negotiations and who now hold key positions in the foreign service, in ministries, and in other government agencies, as well as in research centers, think tanks, and the media on both sides. We can thus say with some certainty that there is considerable opportunity for the ideas developed in problem-solving workshops to be transferred to the policy process. For various reasons—ethical and methodological considerations, as well as the need to set personal priorities—I have not actively pursued formal evaluation of our intervention efforts. I do consider such evaluation essential, however, and my students and associates have been engaged in a variety of evaluation studies. These have included intensive follow-up interviews, analyses of workshop transcripts, laboratory simulations, and empirical tests of some of the underlying assumptions of interactive problem solving.

REFERENCES

Bronfenbrenner, U. 1961. "The Mirror-Image in Soviet-American Relations." *Journal of Social Issues* 17(3): 45–56.

Burton, J. W. 1969. *Conflict and Communication: The Use of Controlled Communication in International Relations.* London: Macmillan.

———. 1979. *Deviance, Terrorism, and War: The Process of Solving Unsolved Social and Political Problems.* New York: St. Martin's Press.

———. 1984. *Global Conflict.* Brighton, U.K.: Wheatsheaf.

———, ed. 1990. *Conflict: Human Needs Theory.* New York: St. Martin's Press.

Cohen, S. P., H. C. Kelman, F. D. Miller, and B. L. Smith. 1977. "Evolving Intergroup Techniques for Conflict Resolution: An Israeli-Palestinian Pilot Workshop." *Journal of Social Issues* 33(1): 165–189.

Fisher, R. J. 1989. "Prenegotiation Problem-Solving Discussions: Enhancing the Potential for Successful Negotiations." In *Getting to the Table: The Processes of International Prenegotiation*, ed. J. G. Stein. Baltimore, Md.: Johns Hopkins University Press, pp. 206–238.

Kelman, H. C. 1972. "The Problem-Solving Workshop in Conflict Resolution." In *Communication in International Politics*, ed. R. L. Merritt. Urbana: University of Illinois Press, pp. 168–204.

———. 1978. "Israelis and Palestinians: Psychological Prerequisites for Mutual Acceptance." *International Security* 3: 162–186.

———. 1979. "An Interactional Approach to Conflict Resolution and Its Application to Israeli-Palestinian Relations." *International Interactions* 6: 99–122.

———. 1986. "Interactive Problem Solving: A Social-Psychological Approach to Conflict Resolution." In *Dialogue Toward Interfaith Understanding*, ed. W. Klassen. Tantur/Jerusalem: Ecumenical Institute for Theological Research, pp. 293–314.

———. 1987. The Political Psychology of the Israeli-Palestinian Conflict: How Can We Overcome the Barriers to a Negotiated Solution? *Political Psychology* 8: 347–363.

———. 1990. "Applying a Human Needs Perspective to the Practice of Conflict Resolution: The Israeli-Palestinian Case." In *Conflict: Human Needs Theory*, ed. J. Burton. New York: St. Martin's Press, pp. 283–297.

———. 1992. "Informal Mediation by the Scholar/Practitioner." In *Mediation in International Relations: Multiple Approaches to Conflict Management,* ed. J. Bercovitch and J. Rubin. New York: St. Martin's Press, pp. 64–96.

———. 1993. "Coalitions Across Conflict Lines: The Interplay of Conflicts Within and Between the Israeli and Palestinian Communities." In *Conflict Between People and Groups,* ed. S. Worchel and J. Simpson. Chicago: Nelson-Hall, pp. 236–258.

———. 1995. "Contributions of an Unofficial Conflict Resolution Effort to the Israeli-Palestinian Breakthrough." *Negotiation Journal* 11: 19–27.

———. 1996. "Negotiation as Interactive Problem Solving." *International Negotiation: A Journal of Theory and Practice* 1(1): 99–123.

Kelman, H. C., and S. P. Cohen. 1986. "Resolution of International Conflict: An Interactional Approach." In *Psychology of Intergroup Relations,* ed. S. Worchel and W. G. Austin. 2nd ed. Chicago: Nelson-Hall, pp. 323–342.

Rouhana, N. N., and H. C. Kelman. 1994. "Promoting Joint Thinking in International Conflicts: An Israeli-Palestinian Continuing Workshop." *Journal of Social Issues* 50(1): 157–178.

Saunders, H. H. 1988. "The Arab-Israeli Conflict in a Global Perspective." In *Restructuring American Foreign Policy,* ed. J. D. Steinbruner. Washington: Brookings Institution, pp. 221–251.

White, R. K. 1965. "Images in the Context of International Conflict: Soviet Perceptions of the U.S. and the U.S.S.R." In *International Behavior: A Social-Psychological Analysis,* ed. H. C. Kelman. New York: Holt, Rinehart and Winston, pp. 238–276.

35

An Israeli-Palestinian Women's Workshop

Application of the Interactive Problem-Solving Approach

EILEEN F. BABBITT AND TAMRA PEARSON D'ESTRÉE

Interactive problem-solving workshops bring together unofficial representatives of the parties to a conflict for informal, off-the-record meetings to analyze the conflict as a shared problem and to generate new approaches to its resolution. These workshops are not intended as a substitute for official diplomacy, but as a complement; they typically take place in the background and, if successful, can feed new ideas into official negotiations. A third party, someone acceptable to the conflicting parties, sponsors the workshop, acting as the convener and facilitator.

Over the years, Herbert Kelman and his colleagues, under the auspices of the Center for International Affairs at Harvard University, have sponsored many interactive problem-solving workshops. In 1987, this group sponsored the first such workshop exclusively for politically active women in the Israeli and Palestinian communities. In

1991, the planning began for a follow-up to this initial effort. The description and analysis below present both the possibilities and the complexities of an unofficial third-party approach to conflict resolution, illustrating themes raised in earlier chapters. The workshop's agenda is included at the end of this chapter for those who would like a better sense of the kinds of activities involved.

The workshop was held in December 1992, before the historic Oslo Accords in which the Israeli-Palestinian relationship was irrevocably changed by the unprecedented acknowledgment of each nation by the other. These accords were arguably made possible by the cumulative results of similar workshops carried out over a period of years.

Our operating assumption was that a stable peace required a transformation in the relationship between the communities in conflict. They did not have to like one another, but they did have to develop a "working trust" to make it possible for existing and emerging problems to be dealt with in a constructive way. Our second assumption was that unofficial processes of conflict analysis and resolution could be beneficial, even while official negotiations were proceeding.

DEVELOPMENT OF THE WORKSHOP

To investigate these issues, a faciliation team led by the authors designed an interactive problem-solving process that brought together five Israeli and five Palestinian women for a four-day workshop. On the Israeli side, participants included high-ranking women from the Labor, National Religious, and Meretz parties and an active spokeswoman from the Russian Jewish community. A woman from Likud had accepted our invitation but was unable to attend because of a family emergency. (To our knowledge, this was the first workshop that had issued invitations to members of the more right-wing political parties and had received acceptances.)

On the Palestinian side, there were members of the Palestinian diaspora community as well as women from the West Bank, and women with centrist as well as left-wing affiliations. They were also politically influential, as some had been advisers to the peace talks initiated in Madrid after the Persian Gulf War.

Many of the women had participated in some kind of dialogue with members of the other community. Some were quite experienced, having attended the first Israeli-Palestinian women's workshop at Harvard and several other meetings since that time. Four, however, had never been in a dialogue like this before, a situation that illustrated the continued polarization of the two communities, even as official peace talks were

being conducted. These four women were politically active and influential members of their communities, and yet their contacts with women from the other side had been very limited or nonexistent.

The facilitation team, which consisted of six women, met several times to plan and prepare for the workshop. The high level of sophistication of the participants, as well as their varied levels of experience with interactive problem solving, posed some unique challenges for the facilitators. We felt that some adjustment to the previously used workshop format was in order now that formal negotiations were in progress. For example, we added a section in both the preworkshop and workshop agendas for the participants to talk about their views of the current negotiations, as we knew this would be on everyone's mind. We also made provision for the groups to meet separately in caucuses in the middle of the workshop, to give each community the chance to talk frankly among themselves about the proceedings and to assess the extent to which the information they had hoped to gain from the discussion had actually been covered. In the actual workshop, we abandoned this caucus idea, since the women themselves expressed a strong preference to stay together. They felt they had enough opportunity during the "social" time to confer with their own community members and didn't want to take valuable workshop time for this purpose. There was a sense of urgency in the group, that the opportunity to talk *together* so freely was unique and should not be wasted.

Two preparatory sessions were held before the workshop, one with the Palestinian women and the other with the Israelis. Not all of the women on each side knew one another, and these sessions enabled each group to establish some connection internally before meeting with the other side. They also allowed the facilitators to review the workshop agenda with those who had not previously participated and to get a sense of the dynamics within each group before bringing the two groups together. In addition, the facilitators asked the participants to describe their goals for the workshop and what they hoped to learn from the other side in the course of the discussions. As mentioned above, we wanted to integrate specific concerns of the participants into the agenda as much as possible.

Some notable differences within each group emerged during these advance sessions, differences which would later have an impact on the workshop itself. Discussions within the Palestinian group revealed a difference in perspective on the peace process between the Palestinians living in the Occupied Territories and those living abroad. Within the Israeli group, differences reflected the left and center-right political perspectives, as well as variation in cultural background, with the introduction of the Russian Jewish experience into the mix. A difference that emerged in both groups was between those women who had previously participated in problem-solving workshops with the other side and those who were new to such dialogue.

The workshop itself began with a dinner and formal introductions. As we had learned in the first women's workshop, the introductions were extremely important, as they set the tone for the workshop itself. We encouraged people to take some time in talking about themselves, not only in terms of their professional work but also to share (if they felt comfortable) some personal statement about why they had come to participate in such a meeting. These personal statements opened up some channels for connection across the two groups, and even within each group, by putting a human face on the political issues. They also modeled the personal self-disclosure necessary for the building of relationships. The group

shared lunch all three days of the workshop, as well as a closing dinner. These social times provided rich opportunities for the participants to get to know one another as individuals, and to begin to develop relationships that could potentially last beyond the actual meeting.

Interviews with participants were conducted seven months after the workshop, to determine if and how it influenced subsequent thinking and behavior.

WHAT WERE OUR OBJECTIVES AND WHAT DID WE ACCOMPLISH?

The project set out to investigate four principal questions: What constitutes "transformation of a relationship"? What characterizes the successful transfer of learning from a workshop setting to the political arena? How can an unofficial problem-solving workshop make a contribution when official negotiations are also occurring? Is there a unique role for politically influential women in building a stable peace?

These questions flowed from our conceptions of what contributes to the construction of a stable peace. First, stability is not just a function of finding the right substantive formulation. In the process of constructing a formulation, opinion leaders from the communities in conflict must meet together, repeatedly and under constructive circumstances, in order to dispel the myths and misconceptions that each has of the other. This can help to diffuse the stereotypes that abound in each community, especially during crisis moments, which can hinder recognition of change in the other side. For example, the inclusion in this workshop of a Jewish Israeli woman from a right-wing religious party was instructive, both to the Palestinians and to the Israelis. Many commented on the value of hearing a "reasonable" voice from that end of the political spectrum—and unexpectedly coming from someone who was quite senior in her party and well respected among her colleagues. We observed that she challenged many existing stereotypes that both the Palestinians and the more left-wing Israelis hold of members of her political party.

Second, communities in conflict must develop the capacity to solve continuing problems. Every conflictual issue that is resolved will undoubtedly produce several more, hopefully of decreasing intensity. Complete absence of conflict will be impossible to achieve. Therefore, the communities must learn ways to work together when problems arise. Rather than allowing each new problem to dredge up old wounds and old stereotypes, the communities must establish a new working relationship, so that actual problem solving occurs, rather than blaming and escalation.

A discussion of each of our four questions follows, with examples drawn from the post-workshop evaluation and the follow-up interviews.

What constitutes "transformation of a relationship"? Transformation involves changing the underlying assumptions that each party in a conflict holds of the other. In a conflict such as the one between the Israelis and Palestinians, where the identity and security of each community are at stake, many of the operating assumptions are about the physical and psychological harm that the other community intends. These include the beliefs that the other community's goal is to destroy you and that there is no one on the other side whom you can trust enough to enter into any meaningful agreements.

In this context, transformation of the relationship is seen as occurring in three stages. The first involves increasing the willingness to explore the underlying assumptions, rather than taking them as immutable. The second entails changing the assumptions, based on supporting evidence, in a direction more conducive to negotiating and

problem solving. The third concentrates on sustaining the changes in assumptions, based on continuing interaction and confirmation that the changes are a true reflection of the other side's intent.

In our workshop, we saw evidence of the first stage both in the willingness of participants to come to such a meeting and in their actual dialogue during the workshop process. Each person, even those who regularly interacted with the other community, came to this workshop with questions she wanted to ask of the other side. The workshop provided the setting and the safety to bring up such questions, and the answers provided the basis for reexamining assumptions.

For example, in the preparatory session, the Palestinian women expressed several questions they had for the Israelis. Why didn't they accept the Palestinian definition of who was Palestinian? Why wouldn't they define Israel's borders? What did the Palestinians have to prove in order to get the Israelis to withdraw from the Territories? How could Israeli women say they support the peace process and still allow their children to serve in the military in the Occupied Territories?

Likewise, the Israeli women had questions. Was there a readiness for peace on the Palestinian side? How did they really feel about Yasser Arafat? Did he represent the Palestinian perspective? How did they "see" the Israeli community? What did they think of the Israelis? Could the two groups find a common ground as women?

The purpose of asking such questions and of engaging in our workshops was to develop a "working trust" of the other side. This development of a working trust is the second stage of transformation, in which it is possible to change some of the underlying assumptions that threaten each community's sense of physical and psychological security. The most effective means for changing such assumptions is through opportunities to experience new behavior in the other. The new assumptions in turn make it possible to pursue negotiations with the expectation that some kind of acceptable agreement will emerge. This means believing that the other side, as a whole and as a policy, is not out to destroy your community and that there are people in the other community whose integrity and sincerity can be trusted.

There were many signs during the workshop that this second stage of a working trust was developing. One of the Israeli participants reported in a follow-up interview that our workshop was the first time she had heard the Palestinian participants willing to admit to internal differences among their own group. She felt this showed a level of trust, both in the process and in the Israeli participants, that she had not witnessed before.

Similarly, a Palestinian participant discussed the importance of continuing contact with the same Israeli women participants, over the course of many workshops and meetings. She felt that each encounter reinforced the others, allowing her to observe whether people were consistent in their words and actions. It helped her to develop, over time, the sense that she could "trust" these individuals, in that they had demonstrated their integrity. Another Palestinian participant discussed how important it was for her to understand the limits that her Israeli counterparts are operating under. Understanding these constraints helped explain behavior that could otherwise be interpreted as inconsistent and therefore suspect.

What characterizes the successful transfer of learning from a workshop setting to the political arena? The most consistent criticism of the value of unofficial processes is that they have no proven impact on the real political issues that divide communities in conflict. Data that provide evidence of such impact

are hard to generate, primarily because so many other variables influence the behavior of political actors and it is difficult to isolate which specific inputs produce specific outcomes.

In our follow-up interviews, we asked participants to discuss the ways the workshop experience had affected their thinking or their political activity. From their responses, we have identified two possible ways to assess "transfer of learning."

The first has to do with the development of networks. In the political arena, it is often said that who you know is as important as what you know. This is because who you know can often determine what information is made available to you and therefore what you know. This is especially true in conflict conditions, which are characterized by a notable lack of information, especially about what is really happening in the other community. The most common hallmark of intense conflict is the severing of official communication channels as a strong demonstration of displeasure with something the other side has said or done.

It is therefore important for unofficial linkages between communities in conflict to be created, so that accurate information can be exchanged that can counteract escalatory behavior. This process, described by Herbert Kelman as building coalitions across conflict lines, is extremely important and difficult to sustain. It requires walking a fine line between the pursuit of a transformed relationship with the other community, as described above, and maintaining the trust of one's own community. Without such efforts, however, stereotypes persist and the more radical groups that strive to disrupt a peace process can attract more support because of fears in their own community that go unaddressed.

After the workshop, there was evidence that such coalition building and networking had occurred among group members. The most significant example emerged in the weeks following the workshop. The day the women arrived back in the Middle East at the conclusion of the workshop, over fifty Hamas followers were expelled from Israel in response to a terrorist attack for which Hamas had claimed responsibility. Relations between the two communities, which had been on a gradual upswing, soured considerably. Two of our participants, an Israeli and a Palestinian, were in close contact with each other throughout the political debates within each community, discussing how to respond to the deportations. Both reported that it was extremely important to them to have people on the other side whom they could consult during this period, to understand the thinking on the other side, rather than to make assumptions based on their own group's worst fears.

A second way of assessing the transfer of learning concerns the extent to which options generated within each community are responsive to the needs of the other community. This is not the same as an exchange of "interests," in which trade-offs are fashioned that give one side something in exchange for getting something. It is, instead, a search for solutions based on a reciprocal understanding and acknowledgment of what the other community believes to be its basic needs. As stated above in the discussion of transformation, it begins with a shift in operating assumptions about the motivations and integrity of the other side. It is also evident in how individuals report their personal experience of political events and behaviors. For example, one of our Palestinian participants reported that when discussing political issues with other Palestinians, she was much more aware of the Israeli people and of how to construct and present ideas in a way that was acceptable and palatable to them, as well as to the Palestinian public. The most striking example was the ability of the group to talk about

the issue of Jerusalem. Many participants thought it was a very important step to see the issue discussed in a constructive way, with people representing very diverse views within each community. Because the purpose of the discussion was to improve the understanding of each group's point of view by the other, and because many of the participants had ties to Jerusalem, there was a willingness to listen to each other that few had experienced before. No one could give an example of how this had affected behavior in a specific way after the workshop, especially because of the immediate crisis of the expulsions. But one Israeli participant later said that even though she couldn't give specific examples, she was consciously aware of the workshop discussion when she engaged in subsequent political activities.

How can an unofficial problem-solving workshop make a contribution while official negotiations are also occurring? This question is based on the belief that unofficial processes are only useful in bringing parties to the table. However, our experience with this and other workshops shows that this belief is mistaken. All the contributions mentioned above—examining assumptions, establishing a working trust, building coalitions across conflict lines, and seeking solutions that meet the needs of the other community as well as one's own—are just as valuable when negotiations are proceeding as they are before negotiations begin.

However, differences may exist in the relative emphasis given to one or more of these themes and to who is invited to participate. The "new" participants (that is, those for whom this was the first workshop), placed importance on examining assumptions and developing a working trust. The more experienced participants emphasized building coalitions and generating mutually beneficial options.

Many participants in both communities mentioned that the surfacing of internal differences within the Palestinian community was very significant. It demonstrated a degree of comfort and trust in the group that had not occurred before. And it also presaged the disagreements that were to occur later, and with more vehemence, in the real negotiations. If this had been an explicit agenda item for a subsequent workshop, possibly one within the Palestinian community rather than with Israelis, it might have allowed clarification of the growing tension between internal factions, which could only help in the negotiations across the table with Israel.

Is there a unique role for politically influential women in these unofficial processes? The women in our workshop did not feel that their role was unique. They did stress in their follow-up interviews, as they did at the workshop itself, that they appreciated coming together as women and that they thought that the discussion was more constructive than it would have been in a mixed group. This was, in their view, because they could listen more attentively to one another and because there were some experiences, such as child rearing, that bound them together as women.

However, as high-level political actors, they did not feel that, as women, they contributed uniquely. They saw themselves as coalition builders and networkers, but noted that men were also accomplished in these activities. They suggested that perhaps the most significant difference was in their ability to develop empathy for the other side. This study did not permit us to make any comparative statements about mixed workshops, because we have not systematically gathered data on women-only versus mixed-gender groups. But observation suggests that in the all-women sessions, participants could understand one another's point of view more clearly than in a mixed group. In turn, this could lead to the increased likelihood of the other conditions discussed

above—working trust, coalition formation, and the ability to construct mutually beneficial options.

EVALUATING THE EXPERIENCE

After the workshop was over, the facilitation team identified important achievements of the workshop and some problematic issues for further analysis. One notable success included the enthusiasm and important contribution to the dialogue made by the woman from a center-right political party in Israel, whose views were different than many participants had expected. A second success was the ability of this group of women to productively discuss the very divisive topic of the fate of Jerusalem. On the other hand, it was evident that future workshops would have to address more effectively the very painful divisions that emerged within the Palestinian group, as well as the different expectations and types of participation in this process exhibited by the experienced and inexperienced participants.

Another notable theme that developed was the tension between conducting an intervention and conducting research on the same intervention. The facilitators made it clear to the participants at the preparatory sessions that, as a secondary goal of the workshop, we would be evaluating its effectiveness by looking at interactions both during and after the meeting itself. Most participants were comfortable with this. But one or two voiced concern at the final session, saying that at some points in the process they felt a bit like "laboratory animals." This was possibly because of the extensive note-taking and the relatively large number of facilitators.

We also left time at the end of the workshop for an evaluation by the participants. The Palestinian women appreciated meeting someone from the Israeli religious community and seeing that they could communicate with her and even share some of her points of view. Many of the "experienced" workshop participants (that is, women who had participated in many dialogues and at least one previous problem-solving workshop) felt that the structure should be loosened to allow for more discussion of political events and options. The new participants, however, appreciated the discussion of concerns and fears and felt that they learned an enormous amount, both from the other community and from members of their own group.

CONCLUSION

Transformation of the relationship between communities in conflict is a long, slow process, one that proceeds "step by step," as one of our participants noted. It involves the questioning and changing of underlying assumptions about the other side as well as your own side, and the building of a working trust that allows productive negotiation to begin and continue.

In the case of the Israeli-Palestinian relationship, that working trust has been building over many years, resulting in the Oslo agreement and an ongoing peace process that is continuing even in the face of periods of heightened violence. The women who participated in our workshops are part of that trust-building process. Like their male counterparts, they are interested in working constructively with members of the other community to find workable solutions to their conflicts. Their additional contribution may be their empathy for the other side, and their interest in building personal relationships that span the conflict divide.

The events in the Middle East over the last few months have severely tested that empathy. To their credit, these women are continuing to work for peace. It is our belief that the workshop experiences have made their efforts more possible and effective.

WORKSHOP AGENDA

Pre-Workshop Sessions (4 hours)

(To be held separately with the Israeli and Palestinian groups)

1. Introductions: Who are you? What are your reasons for coming?

2. Facilitator explains the composition of the group, presents the agenda, and reviews the ground rules. Questions from the group.

3. Solicit individual responses to the following questions: What is your previous experience with dialogue? What are your hopes and expectations for this workshop? What are your concerns about this workshop?

4. Focusing on the Israeli-Palestinian conflict relationship, what are your key concerns for your own community? For the other community? Are there any positive shifts in this relationship? Any promising directions for solutions?

5. How are the current negotiations addressing or not addressing the concerns that you have raised?

6. What are the reactions to the negotiations in your community? How do you place yourself in relation to these reactions?

7. Are there areas in which you find it hard to comprehend the other side? What would you most like to ask the other side in order to understand them better as a group?

8. How has your being women affected the discussion tonight, both in process and in content?

Workshop Sessions (3 days)

(Joint sessions with both Israeli and Palestinian women present, except for one separate session on the second day)

1. Introductions: What brings you here and what do you hope to come away with (that is, your experience, interests, hopes)?

2. Review background and context of this workshop, agenda, ground rules; discuss questions on any of the above.

3. What are the current views in your community regarding the relationship with the other side?

4. What are the concerns, needs, and fears in your community (for the purpose of being sure the other side understands these concerns, not for the purpose of debate or criticism)?

5. Are there ways in which being a woman affects your concerns, needs, and fears?

6. Can you see solutions that are responsive to these concerns? What would be the nature of an alternative relationship between the two communities that would be responsive to these concerns (not worrying for the moment about how to get there)?

7. Do you see any recent movement in this direction? Anything giving hope and reassurance?

8. What are the constraints to movement?

9. From the point of view of your community, what other steps need to be taken to move in this direction?

10. How can women, in particular, contribute to moving forward? What are special constraints for women? How can women overcome these constraints?

11. (In separate sessions) In the preparatory sessions, we discussed areas in which you find it hard to comprehend the other side and questions you would most like to ask the other side to understand them better as a group. Did you learn anything more about those areas during the joint session, and were those questions answered to your satisfaction?

12. (In joint session) Are there questions that did not yet come up in the earlier discussion that you would like to ask of the other group?

13. What future activities would this group like to initiate or participate in that would address the constraints that were identified?

14. Evaluation: Have you learned anything new (insights, understandings, information)? About your own community? About the other community? Have you come away with new ideas about things that should be done in your own community? In the negotiations? In the relationship with the other community? What were the most difficult moments in the workshop? The highlights or most important moments? How has the existence of the ongoing negotiations affected your workshop experience, if at all?

PART IV

CONSOLIDATING THE PEACE
New Challenges and Dilemmas

36

Why Orphaned Peace Settlements Are More Prone to Failure

FEN OSLER HAMPSON

The failure of humanitarian interventions and various international mediation efforts in Rwanda, Somalia, and, until quite recently, Bosnia-Herzegovina have tarnished the reputation of the United Nations and jeopardized public support for peacekeeping and third-party involvement in the settlement of intrastate disputes. If there is "new" conventional wisdom in some circles, it is that outside third parties have little to contribute to the peaceful settlement and resolution of such disputes, and that intervention is only desirable when a conflict has reached a "hurting stalemate" and the parties themselves are exhausted and sufficiently wearied by war to begin searching for alternatives to the use of force.[1]

Consider the following admonition by *New York Times* columnist Thomas L. Friedman: "There is no such thing as a peacekeeper or neutral force in an ethnic conflict. The very meaning of an ethnic conflict is that a society has been torn asunder, every community has grabbed a slice and there is

no neutral ground left." Friedman says that "to try to extinguish one of these ethnic conflicts when it is raging at full force is futile. . . . No amount of rational argument can tone it down, and if you try to smother it with your own body or army it will burn a hole right through you."[2]

The same pessimistic outlook is echoed by historian and foreign policy analyst Benjamin Schwarz in the pages of the *Atlantic Monthly*. Schwarz writes that "stability within divided societies is normally based on some form of domination, and once internal differences become violent, usually only the logic of force can lay them to rest." He believes that the United States has only two real options in dealing with ethnic, nationalist, and separatist conflicts: "Adopting a passive role once violence has erupted in a failed state, Washington can await the time when mutual exhaustion or the triumph of one group over another will create an opening for intervention in a purely peacekeeping capacity. Alternatively, the United States can effectively intervene, not only by building civil societies or pacifying such conflicts but by helping one side impose its will on the other, as Turkey did in Cyprus."[3]

This refrain, which has become all too familiar, construes the options and potential role of outside third parties in the peaceful settlement of civil disputes too narrowly. There are other options beyond "doing nothing" or, at the other extreme, intervening with large-scale military force. Not all civil conflicts have to end with a victor and a vanquished. It is possible to construct power-sharing arrangements between dissatisfied minorities and intransigent majorities through third-party assisted negotiations. By sustaining a process of mediation, negotiation, and assistance with the subsequent implementation of the peace settlement in question, third parties can help bring an end to military conflict and lay the basis for a durable settlement that advances the process of national reconciliation in divided societies. The challenge is to cultivate the right conditions that will bring warring parties to the negotiating table and sustain the peace process once a settlement is in place.

This chapter argues that third parties have a critical role to play in nurturing peace and helping implement peace settlements. Who are these third parties? Typically they include international organizations like the United Nations and its associated relief and development agencies, nongovernmental organizations (NGOs), regional organizations, great powers, regional powers, and even groupings of smaller states. By acting independently or in unison, these third parties can help sustain the commitment and cooperation of the disputing parties in the overall peacemaking and peace-building process.[4] This chapter discusses the potential contribution of these third parties to the peace process, not only in "cultivating ripeness" but also in helping establish the conditions that can move the peace process forward.

CULTIVATING "RIPENESS"

In addressing the role of third parties in postconflict peace building, it should be recognized that conflict resolution and settlement processes may well depend upon factors that are intrinsic to the conflict itself, so that the contributions of outside third parties are marginal, at best, to the achievement of a durable and lasting peace settlement. It is axiomatic in much of the burgeoning literature on international mediation and negotiation that many conflicts have a self-sustaining dynamic of their own. In order for third-party interventions to be effective, it is often argued, the conflict has to reach a plateau, the level of a hurting stalemate, so that the parties no longer think they can use force to gain a unilateral advantage and they become willing to consider other options. At this point, the conflict is, to use William Zartman's phrase, "ripe for resolution"; that is, the parties perceive the costs and prospects of continued confrontation to be more burdensome than the costs and prospects of a settlement.[5]

In low-intensity conflict situations, however, the ability and willingness of the parties to sustain an ongoing campaign of violence are formidable, even after a negotiated settlement has been reached. Moreover, the fact that absolute victory is unattainable does not mean that the parties will be willing to lay down their arms. Rather, the protagonists may view the existence of a military stalemate as a strong reason to keep on fighting. Not only does this make it difficult to negotiate a settlement, but it also means that the settlement itself is precarious. Paradoxically, the negotiation process can set in motion a search for military gains that tends to drive the parties further apart instead of narrowing their political differences.

It should come as no surprise that most civil wars in the twentieth century have ended, as Stephen Stedman notes, "in elimination or capitulation." In the period from 1900 to 1989, out of a total of sixty-five cases, only fifteen percent were resolved through negotiation, and "of these eleven cases of negotiated settlement, six were terminated through international mediation." The figure is somewhat higher (twenty out of sixty-five cases) if one includes "colonial wars, cases formalized by one-sided agreements, and cases that ended in the negotiated partition of the country."[6] There is also strong evidence that negotiated settlements of civil conflicts are more likely to collapse than those in which one side is victorious on the battlefield. According to Roy Licklider, only "one-third of the negotiated settlements of identity civil wars that last for five years 'stick.'" And of those conflicts that end in military victory, "military victories may be more likely to result in genocide or politicide after the war."[7]

Given that negotiated settlements are difficult to achieve, and obviously somewhat of a rarity, the question of what determines success in bringing about a restoration of domestic order and an end to civil violence is a critical one. The recent history of international relations is marked by some notable successes and some conspicuous failures in postconflict peace building efforts directed at ending civil conflict. While some peace settlements have proven durable and have succeeded in bringing an end to military hostilities and violence, others have failed to prevent a relapse into armed confrontation and violence or, to transform a cease-fire into a genuine political settlement.

Outside interventions are typically more effective when third parties entrench and institutionalize their role in the peacemaking and peace-building process, that is, when they cultivate ripeness. A successful peace process depends upon a lot of outside help and assistance, not only with the negotiation of a peace agreement, but also with its implementation. By being involved in the implementation phase of a peace settlement, third parties can help restore confidence, build trust, and change the perceptions and behavior of disputing parties. Their involvement can include technical activities ranging from peacekeeping and monitoring cease-fires, which help reduce the likelihood of armed confrontation and "accidental" encounters,[8] to assisting with the establishment of participatory political institutions (for example, externally supervised and monitored elections) that channel the frustrations and aspirations of the politically mobilized elements of society, thus reducing the prospects of armed violence.[9] As Brian Mandell notes, confidence-building measures are especially crucial in the early stages of a peace settlement because they can forestall a resort to the use of force by the disputants, generate additional confidence-building measures beyond those initially implemented, heighten the cost of returning to the status quo, and create additional incentives for collaboration.[10] Mediation, conciliation, and arbitration by third parties can also help resolve outstanding or unanticipated issues that emerge during the postconflict peace-building phase and threaten to derail the peace process.

This means that third parties must have enough resources and resolve to remain fully engaged in the negotiations leading up to the settlement and through the subsequent peace-building process. Settlements that fail have generally been "orphaned," because third parties either failed to remain fully engaged in implementing the settlement or were unable to muster the requisite level of resources, both economic and political, to build the foundations for a secure settlement.

In negotiations leading up to the Angola-Namibia peace accords of 1988, for example, the conflict was beginning to approach the conditions of ripeness in 1987. South African Defense Forces (SADF) were unable to bring the South West African People's Organization (SWAPO) to a decisive conventional battle, nor could they eradicate the effects of a continuing bush war without a major commitment of additional forces and an escalation of the war that the South African government was unwilling to undertake. Similarly, Cuban and Angolan defense forces were having limited success in conducting offensive operations against SADF and UNITA (National Union for the Total Independence of Angola). Although both sides were in the midst of negotiations, the buildup of Cuban forces in Angola in 1987 raised serious questions in Pretoria and Washington about the depth of Cuba's commitment to a negotiated settlement. It was only the active intervention of the U.S. mediator, who realized that Castro wanted a settlement with a face-saving formula for Cuban troop withdrawal, that kept the negotiations on track. This enabled the theoretical "ripe moment" to be exploited successfully. Once a negotiated settlement was reached, however, implementation was threatened by a renewed outbreak of fighting when SWAPO launched a surprise military offensive against South African security forces on April 1, 1989. Although the situation may have been ripe for resolution, the risks of resumed violence and armed confrontation were very real in the post-settlement phase, and it took active intervention by third parties, particularly the United States, to ensure that the settlement remained on track.

In Angola, the fact that the military situation was ostensibly at a stalemate during the negotiation of the 1991 Bicesse Accords did little to advance the peace process and enhance the possibilities of achieving a durable settlement. In the period 1988 to 1991, the military situation had remained relatively balanced; neither side had been able to gain a sufficient strategic advantage despite repeated offensives by the Popular Movement for the Liberation of Angola (MPLA) and UNITA. Military and civilian casualties were enormous and the war had exacted a huge toll on the country's economy. One would have thought that the stalemate would have enhanced the prospects of achieving a durable settlement; in fact, it had quite the opposite effect. Almost immediately after a settlement was reached, each side took advantage of the weak monitoring provisions in the accords to cheat on its commitment to demobilize its forces. Few of UNITA's troops were disarmed and very few were actually demobilized. There was also poor government attendance in the assembly and demobilization areas. Cease-fires were recklessly broken by both UNITA and the MPLA. When UNITA's Jonas Savimbi lost the election, he had little incentive to accept the results, because he believed that there were widespread irregularities and felt that the MPLA-dominated government had little interest in seeking a *modus vivendi* with its political rivals. In this case, the absence of an effective third-party presence to monitor implementation of the accords hurt the prospects of achieving a workable peace settlement.

In Cambodia at the time of the signing of the Paris Peace Accords in 1991, there was a hurting stalemate in the sense that the different Cambodian factions had lost their principal external sources of support in a civil war that had exacted an enormous price from the Cambodian people. The Vietnamese were pulling out, leaving the government without its principal backer. China and the Soviet Union were ending military assistance to their proxies, as was the United States. The Khmer Rouge was unable to establish permanent control of its territories and was suffering from desertions. Once the Paris Peace Accords were signed, however, it became clear that this stalemate was not sufficient to lay the foundations for a durable settlement. The Khmer Rouge refused to cooperate with the United Nations Transitional Authority in Cambodia (UNTAC) in implementing the provisions regarding cantonment, disarmament, and demobilization, and it repeatedly violated the cease-fire. It also refused to participate in the elections. There were also other disputes between Cambodia's different factions, which helped to undermine the military elements of the peace process and eventually led to the suspension of UNTAC's peacekeeping component. While there may have been enough ripeness to pursue negotiations and reach a political settlement, there clearly was not enough ripeness to keep the Khmer Rouge from defecting from the peace process and resuming its armed struggle against the government afterwards.

Although the government of El Salvador and the Farabundo Marti Liberation Front (FMLN) were deadlocked for years in a costly confrontation that had all the features of hurting stalemate, the stalemate was not sufficient to get the parties to engage in serious peace negotiations. There were various efforts to initiate negotiations between the government of El Salvador and the FMLN in 1984, 1986, and 1987, all of which failed. When UN-mediated negotiations began in 1989, the fighting still had not stopped. The reduction of U.S. aid to the Salvadoran military lent new momentum to the peace process, as did the election of Alfredo Cristiani, a moderate conservative, to the Salvadoran presidency. Still, the fact that the government and the FMLN brought fundamentally conflicting objectives to the negotiating table meant that a settlement was not foreordained. Even when a formal agreement was reached, the high levels of mistrust and suspicion that characterized relations between the two parties meant that the potential for violence and resumed military hostilities remained elevated.

These illustrations suggest that successful peacekeeping cannot take place without a successful peace process. Peacekeeping and peace-building activities cannot exist in a va-

cuum; they are adjuncts to a process of negotiation during which the parties to the conflict redefine their interests and develop a real commitment to a political settlement. Third-party assisted negotiations play a critical role in helping the parties realize that there are options other than a continued campaign of military violence and bitter civil conflict.

Another major lesson is that it takes strong support and unified political direction from outside actors to help conflicting parties realize their desire for peace. Third parties can play a critical role in nurturing the conditions that lead to a negotiated settlement and in advancing the peace process once a settlement has been reached so that it can take root. In some instances, the third-party role is confined to a limited, intermediary role during the negotiation phase of the peace settlement. In others, third-party involvement is far more extensive, involving not only the mediation of a negotiated agreement between warring parties, but also assistance with a wide range of functions during implementation of the settlement. These tasks go beyond peacekeeping to include verifying and assisting with the demobilization of forces, assisting refugees, monitoring and observing elections, promoting human rights, and assisting with a broad range of political, social, and economic reforms. When there is unified and sustained third-party involvement in both the negotiation and implementation of a peace agreement, settlements are more likely to endure than when third-party intervention is sporadic or limited to a few poorly defined roles.

TERMS OF SETTLEMENT

How do the design and terms of a peace settlement affect the prospects of achieving peace, and what role can third parties play in assisting with its implementation? The design of an agreement, particularly with regard to its provisions for reconstituting political authority in a country that has been wracked by civil war, can significantly affect the prospects of achieving a viable peace process and a durable settlement. A solid document is a key element for peacekeeping operations and the establishment of a viable political settlement. Without it there are high costs, delays, and a real risk that the settlement will fail.

What are the specific requirements for a successful settlement? First, it is absolutely essential that all of the warring parties be represented at the negotiating table and involved in discussions about the new constitutional and political order that will be created after the fighting stops. A "good" agreement is one that has been crafted by all parties to the conflict. Parties that are excluded from these negotiations, or whose interests are not represented at the bargaining table, will have a much stronger incentive to defect from the peace process and resort to violence to achieve their aims. For instance, the 1960 constitutional settlement in Cyprus was seen as being imposed on the parties—the Greek and Turkish Cypriot communities—by the British and other outside powers. This contributed to the agreement's failure during the implementation phase. Parties that decide to defect from the political process later on, as did the Khmer Rouge in Cambodia after they had signed onto the Paris Peace Accords, find their legitimacy undermined because they are breaking commitments to which they had previously agreed. It is difficult for a party to garner outside allies and build domestic political support if it defects from a process which it earlier endorsed.

Second, a good agreement is one that contains power-sharing provisions for winners and losers in the aftermath of elections. The context in which elections take place is crucial to the peace process. There need to be positions for both winners and losers in a new government. "Winner-take-all" elec-

tions are seen as zero-sum contests: Unless there is some form of compensation, the loser will have strong incentives to take up arms and return to a renewed campaign of violence in pursuit of political objectives. A lack of power-sharing arrangements is one reason the 1991–1992 Bicesse agreements in Angola fell apart. In contrast, the elections that followed the peace settlement in Cambodia resulted in a coalition government between the ruling Cambodian People's Party and the National Front for an Independent, Neutral, Prosperous, and Cooperative Cambodia (FUNCINPEC), which had won the popular vote. This happened because the parties recognized that a coalition government was necessary to appease rival factions and advance the process of national reconciliation. This followed a pattern of power sharing that had been established during the Paris peace negotiations with the formation of the Supreme National Council in 1989. Electoral mechanisms, such as proportional representation, may also be required so that minorities feel they have adequate representation in parliament.

In the absence of power-sharing mechanisms or provisions for developing inclusive coalitions, a settlement must establish a level playing field and allow equal and fair access to the political process by formerly excluded groups. All must have a sense that they can participate and that political life is not zero-sum. The new rules about political competition must also be seen as fair and just. In the Salvadoran case, the FMLN was less interested in power sharing than in securing free elections and the right to form a political party. The FMLN was also eager for wholesale reform of the military, police, and judicial institutions of the country, which were seen as corrupt and subversive of the democratic process. The peace settlement allowed the FMLN to compete alongside the National Republican Alliance (ARENA) in national elections for the presidency, Legislative Assembly, and municipal-level positions.

Another important element is that peace agreements must contain provisions for re-negotiation and third-party mediation during the implementation phase of the settlement process. A settlement is an imperfect road map to the future: Key provisions of any settlement often have to be renegotiated because they are ambiguous or unimplementable in their current form. New problems can emerge, which must be accommodated within the framework of the settlement. There are frequently major unresolved issues at the time an agreement is reached; these issues remain the subject of ongoing negotiation and discussion. Poorly negotiated and badly designed agreements are a sure prescription for disaster. However, this does not mean that the converse is true. A well-negotiated, well-crafted agreement is no guarantee of success because—as experience shows—there are always ambiguities, differences of interpretation about key provisions, and major unresolved issues (or new ones) that can scuttle the peace process even after an agreement has been signed.

The Angolan-Namibian peace accords were successful because of strong third-party involvement in implementing the agreement. A number of problems—some minor, some more serious—surfaced during the implementation of the agreements. One set of issues concerned the ratification process for the new constitution, whether the Constituent Assembly would be legally bound to new constitutional principles, and how the new government would be chosen. Mechanisms for demobilizing and disbanding local forces also proved to be a source of contention after the agreement was signed. The status of Walvis Bay, an issue that could not be resolved during the negotiations, was deferred to future talks. Furthermore, there were continuing disputes over electoral laws and how elections would be run during the

implementation of the agreement. None of these issues derailed the peace process because institutional mechanisms had been created beforehand to allow continuing consultation and negotiations among the parties. In particular, the Joint Commission was a critical dispute resolution mechanism, as in the key role it played in defusing tensions following the SWAPO incursion into Namibia after the agreements were signed.

The Chapultepec accords, which ended the civil war in El Salvador, were also well crafted, but they nonetheless suffered from some ambiguities and problems of omission. The land-for-arms exchange to ex-combatants in the agreement was hastily negotiated and became the most contentious issue during the implementation of the accords. The resulting impasse threatened to bring a halt to the demobilization of the FMLN and government reform of the armed forces. It was only when the United Nations intervened with a new proposal for an agreement on land transfers that the peace process was salvaged. The overly ambitious schedule in the accords for demobilizing forces and reforming the military also had to be renegotiated—again with UN assistance —in order to secure the commitment of the parties to the peace process.

Major unanticipated problems arose during the implementation of the Paris Peace Accords in Cambodia. These included verifying the complete withdrawal of Vietnamese troops along the Vietnam-Cambodian border; handling the large numbers of Vietnamese immigrants who had come into Cambodia in search of jobs; establishing a massive demining program; and working within the confines of an inadequate infrastructure to support the cantonment, disarmament, and demobilization provisions in the accords. Most of these problems were addressed on an ad hoc basis and with varying degrees of success by the United Nations. The most serious problem, however, was the

Khmer Rouge's refusal to comply with its commitments under the accords. This problem had less to do with the structure of the agreement and more with the Khmer Rouge's own defection from the peace process.

The experience of Angola in the early 1990s underscores the proposition that badly designed agreements are prone to failure. But it also suggests that hasty, ill-conceived peace proposals offered by third parties may actually be counterproductive if they contribute to feelings of bad faith and make it more difficult to resume negotiations later on. The Gbadolite accords did just that. They quickly broke down because there was no formal written accord and the substance of the agreement was left to the individual interpretation of the parties. Ambiguities in the agreement were immediately contested by the parties and tensions mounted. The residue of bad faith and mistrust made it difficult to resume negotiations and discredited any future regional role in the peace process. In contrast, the Bicesse accords, which were negotiated under Portuguese-U.S. auspices, were a much better set of agreements. The agreement provided for a staged cease-fire, a phased schedule for demobilization of forces, passage of enabling electoral laws, and other provisions that would culminate in national elections for a new government. However, the Achilles' heel of the agreement was the lack of an adequate and effective third-party presence and monitoring mechanism to supervise and assist with implementation. In some respects, the accords were far too elaborate for the implementation mechanism, so cheating and discrediting were inevitable. As a consequence, disputes over the assembly points and demobilization procedures outlined in the agreement, the electoral timetable, and other issues were not properly addressed and contributed to an escalation of tensions and resumption of interfactional fighting.

If ambiguity is one potential source of error in the design of a peace agreement so, too, are a lack of flexibility and overly restrictive provisions. Early efforts to establish a bicommunal structure for the government of Cyprus, which came from the London-Zurich accords of 1959–1960, failed because the settlement was too rigid and led to a set of constitutional arrangements that was unacceptable to the island's Greek community. The constitution contained 196 articles and six annexes. It mandated specific ratios between Greek and Turkish Cypriots for jobs in the public service, the legislature, and the courts. The cumbersome and politically unwieldy nature of the constitution, rather than bringing the two communities together, quickly drove them apart as efforts to implement it proved unworkable. Successive constitutional crises paralyzed the government and eventually spilled over into intercommunal fighting.

Since the Turkish intervention of 1974, there have been numerous efforts to negotiate a new federal, bicommunal structure for Cyprus with the assistance of third parties. None have succeeded, because agreement between the parties over the actual details of a new set of constitutional arrangements has proven elusive in spite of the fact they have been able to agree on general principles. The constitutional ghost of 1960 still haunts the process, as both parties continue to point to various elements in the constitution that they consider fundamental to any future settlement.

All peace agreements are prone to failure, regardless of how well structured and designed they appear at first blush. Parties will exploit ambiguity in an agreement to advance their interests. Unresolved issues can easily become bitter points of contention later on. If the parties fail to abide by rigidly established timetables for demobilizing their forces, the peace process can quickly become unhinged. Badly designed agreements clearly need some other force—namely a third-party presence during implementation —to sustain the peace process and keep it on track. But so do well-designed, properly structured agreements. A peace settlement requires effective conflict-resolving measures that "include procedures and institutions for identifying, monitoring, managing, and resolving major conflicts."[11] The successful implementation of the peace accords in Namibia and El Salvador, in particular, illustrates the use of such mechanisms.

WHY THIRD PARTIES MATTER

Negotiated peace agreements are little more than a road map to the peace process. A settlement indicates the direction the parties must move if they are to consolidate the peace, but it usually does not tell them how to get there except in very general terms. There is usually plenty of ambiguity in an agreement, because "ambiguity is the mother of compromise." Intractable issues that are left out of the agreement for subsequent negotiation can quickly come back to haunt those elements of the peace process on which there is widespread agreement. Although there may be a will for peace when the accords are signed, this does not mean that the parties necessarily wish to fulfill all of their commitments under the agreement. Furthermore, the act of signing an agreement does not mean the parties will immediately lay down their arms, stop fighting, and return to civilian life. Although most settlements typically include a timetable for a cease-fire and the subsequent demobilization of armed combatants, the details usually have to be worked out as the agreement is implemented. This is fertile ground for misunderstandings and delays, as each side jockeys for advantage in the tense political atmosphere that follows the signing of a

peace settlement. The risk of sliding back into armed confrontation is therefore high in the early stages of the peace process. Even after a modicum of trust is built up between the parties, it can be undermined by perceived violations and failures of compliance. Thus, one of the key functions of third parties is to foster trust between warring factions by monitoring compliance and holding them accountable to their negotiated commitments.

Third parties can provide much-needed political status and legitimacy to the interests of warring factions by creating instruments that allow the parties to work as equal partners during both the negotiation and implementation of an agreement. In the Salvadoran case, for example, the New York agreements led to the creation of a National Commission for the Consolidation of Peace (COPAZ), which was comprised of two government representatives and two FMLN members, as well as one representative from each party in the Legislative Assembly. The commission was responsible for overseeing the implementation of the accords and discussing both the progress and problems of the peace process. Although COPAZ did not function terribly well and lacked proper compliance and enforcement mechanisms, it accorded the FMLN political status and the opportunity to be seen as an equal and legitimate partner in the peace process.

However, the role of third parties in nurturing and sustaining the peace process goes well beyond the legitimizing and monitoring functions envisioned in traditional notions about peacekeeping. Some of their activities represent a continuation of functions carried out during the negotiations that led to the agreement, such as mediation. Others represent new contributions to the peace process, such as the promotion of new norms and what might be termed proxy governance functions.

PEACEKEEPING AND DEMOBILIZATION

Another third-party role is peacekeeping, which is defined by Gareth Evans as "the deployment of military or police, and frequently civilian, personnel to assist in the implementation of agreements reached between governments or parties who have been engaged in conflict." He goes on to note that "peacekeeping presumes cooperation, and its methods are inherently peaceful: The use of military force, other than in self-defense, is incompatible with the concept."[12] Useful as this definition is, it is important to note that the actual form and functions of peacekeeping vary considerably from one operation to another. Cyprus is generally viewed as the classical model of a peacekeeping operation. The United Nations Force in Cyprus (UNFICYP) forces are deployed in a neutral buffer zone that separates the island's two communities. Through its presence, UNFICYP has helped deter major military operations and has promoted an uneasy truce between the two communities. Maintenance of the buffer zone has been an important confidence-building measure and has prevented accidental confrontations from escalating to greater levels of conflict. However, UNFICYP has also been involved in activities that go beyond "traditional" peacekeeping, including assisting with food distribution, providing transportation, and restoring basic government services.

Although monitoring cease-fire provisions is a key element in any peacekeeping operation, another function—just as important—is assisting with the demobilization of forces. Demobilization is defined as "the process by which the armed forces (government and/or opposition factional forces such as guerrilla armies) either downsize or completely disband." A restructuring of the armed forces, to include "an ethnically and/or politically balanced 'national army,'" may also accompany demobilization.[13] Demobilization, disarmament, and restructuring of armed forces are politically sensitive and challenging tasks. If forces are demobilized and the state's security institutions are restructured within the general time frame allotted by an agreement, the peace process has a much greater chance of succeeding than if there are major delays and commitments are poorly kept. Outside monitors can facilitate the demobilization process if they are seen as neutral by the parties and if they have sufficiently broad mandates and adequate resources (financial and human) to do the job.[14]

The experiences in Namibia and El Salvador bear this out. In Namibia, the peace plan (UN Resolution 435) called for the complete demobilization of forces prior to the holding of free elections. The United Nations Transition Assistance Group (UN-TAG) was responsible for monitoring the cease-fire; confining South African and SWAPO forces to their bases; assisting in the withdrawal of South African forces; confining the remaining South African forces until elections were completed; and monitoring the disbandment of citizen forces, commandos, and relevant command structures. Although there were some delays in meeting the demobilization schedule, demobilization was completed in time for the UN-supervised elections.

Similarly, in El Salvador, demobilizing the FMLN and reducing and restructuring the armed forces were also concluded before elections were held. To be sure, there were delays in implementing the original schedule, which had to be renegotiated several times. There were also violations: The FMLN failed to provide a complete inventory of the weapons it had in its possession, and the government failed to completely demobilize its forces in the countryside. These violations were investigated by the United Nations Observer Mission in El Salvador (ONUSAL), but they were not serious enough to upset the peace process or undermine the elections.

In Angola, the United Nations Angola Verification Mission (UNAVEM) assisted with the partial demobilization of government/MPLA and UNITA forces, as called for in the Bicesse agreements; this work was hampered by a lack of resources and personnel to carry out effective monitoring operations on the scale that was necessary for such a large country. In Namibia, UNTAG enjoyed a contingency of over 4,600 personnel; however, the UNAVEM operation was comprised of only 425 military and police observers, who were overwhelmed by the size of their task. The demobilization of the two forces in Angola fell far behind schedule. "By the election date, 40,000 troops had yet to be demobilized, the two opposition forces were nearly intact, and the new, integrated army barely forged. When the UNITA leader, Savimbi, was dissatisfied with the election results, the continued existence of the two armies contributed to a rapid resurgence of the conflict."[15] Without doubt, the unrealistic timetable and the lack of cooperation by both parties contributed to the failure of demobilization efforts in Angola, but UNAVEM's lack of resources also affected the poor result.

Under the terms of the Paris peace treaty for Cambodia, the United Nations was to demobilize and disarm 70 percent of each of the four factional armies and to supervise the activities of the remainder prior to elections for a new constituent assembly. To help with this task, UNTAC deployed nearly 16,000 military personnel. However, the Khmer Rouge's refusal to participate in the peace process and its repeated delays in meeting cantonment, demobilization, and disarmament schedules led to the eventual suspension of the second phase of the demobilization program, leaving more than a half-million Cambodians still armed. Although legitimate national elections were held in an atmosphere that was generally free of violence and intimidation, the inability to complete the demobilization plan mandated in the Paris agreements has plagued the restoration of civilian rule in Cambodia ever since.

Demobilization of forces is a key element in any political settlement, and experience suggests that demobilization plans, even if they are only partial, need to be carried out before elections are held; otherwise, there is a strong likelihood that fighting will resume afterward if various parties are unhappy with the election results. Successful settlements in El Salvador, Namibia, and Mozambique were achieved by demobilizing military forces and integrating guerrilla forces into a new reformed military. Where settlements fail or are only partially successful, such as in Cambodia or in Angola following the 1991–1992 accords, the suspension of demobilization plans allows fighting to resume when parties become dissatisfied with the political process. Thus, third parties have an important role to play in assisting with demobilization efforts, and the success of peace processes partly hinges on how well they are able to perform this task. In Namibia, Mozambique, and El Salvador, they did the job well; in Angola and Cambodia, if for different reasons, they did not, and the result had a negative impact on the peace process.

It is also important to link demobilization plans to a realistic timetable. As the experience in El Salvador and Cambodia suggests, an unrealistic timetable can weaken the ability of parties to achieve the political objectives of the accord. Synchronizing political tasks with refugee resettlement, economic reconstruction, military and security provisions, and the advancement of human rights is a daunting task. As deadlines are threatened by foot-dragging and broken promises, third parties must use whatever pressure is necessary to sustain the linkage between political and military benchmarks, regain the political momentum, and recalibrate timetables as appropriate. It is critical to develop a coordinated rhythm to the peace process so that elections can be held in an environment that is free of violence and intimidation.

THE ROLE OF FORCE

When should third parties use force to stabilize the political process and bring those elements that are intent on wrecking the peace process into line? There is no easy answer to this question. As illustrated by a number of recent cases, for each case when third-party force failed to achieve political aims (for example, Somalia), one can also point to instances where, arguably, if force had been used early in the conflict and in a decisive fashion, tragedy might have been prevented (Rwanda).

The dilemmas were just as stark in Cambodia: UN officials faced the difficult decision of whether or not to use force against the Khmer Rouge and rout them from their guerrilla hideouts once the Khmer Rouge decided it was going to fight with guns rather than for votes. The United Nations decided not to use force, fearing military action would jeopardize its neutrality and tie down UN forces in a costly counterinsurgency campaign they were ill-equipped to handle. Such action would have delayed the elections and the implementation of the peace plan. Critics charge that the United Nations' failure to take more decisive action against the Khmer Rouge created serious problems later on. But they fail to address the prior question of whether a preventive use of force by the United Nations would have worked anyway, since UN forces were neither equipped nor trained to carry out peace enforcement operations.

Timely military intervention can make a difference and help bring parties to the negotiating table, as we have seen in the case of the NATO airstrikes in Bosnia. However, much depends upon who that third party is and whether it has the requisite forces available to it. Unlike NATO, the United Nations is not an effective instrument of coercive diplomacy; it is handicapped by its inability to deploy forces quickly to arenas of conflict. The United Nations is also hampered by domestic opposition to enforcement actions where peacekeeping forces are put in the direct line of fire; thus, enforcement is therefore best left to others. The United Nations is most successful when it confines itself to peacekeeping, policing, and peace-building functions that are carried out under a carefully defined mandate, with clear strategies for both entry and exit.

Effective mediation, however, is possible without resorting to force. In Namibia and El Salvador, third-party mediators were able to get warring sides to the negotiating table and to persuade them that the benefits of a political settlement outweighed the continued costs of confrontation, without making military threats. The most successful agreements are those which are self-enforcing and where the parties have come to recognize the benefits of the peace process for themselves. Where such recognition and commitment are lacking, enforcement operations are likely to be ineffective at best and counterproductive and self-defeating at worst. It is better to lay the political groundwork before committing forces to a peacekeeping operation. Reversing this sequence is a prescription for failure. Nonetheless, there is a real dilemma of responding to defections (as opposed to minor infractions or violations) from the terms of the settlement after a peace agreement has been signed and the peace process has been set in motion. There is no simple answer to this problem. One approach, tried in Cambodia, is to isolate the defectors through the political process so that the peace process does not lose its momentum. The government of Cambodia was undeniably in a stronger position to deal with the Khmer Rouge after elections than it was before. The Khmer Rouge was not eliminated, but it was a thorn, not a sword, in the side of government.

MEDIATION AND RENEGOTIATION

Once an agreement is reached, the demand for mediators does not end, because negotiations between the parties typically do not end. As discussed above, the terms of a settlement are constantly being renegotiated during its implementation, and problems can emerge that have the potential, if left unresolved, to jeopardize the peace process. If the parties are unable to resolve these problems on their own through direct negotiations, they may be forced to turn to outside mediators for assistance. Thus ongoing dispute resolution is needed throughout the duration of the peace process and implementation of a settlement.

In the case of the Angola-Namibia peace accords, negotiations were assisted first by the western Contact Group and then by the Reagan administration, which played a key role in sustaining the negotiation process and ripening the possibilities of an agreement by defining the critical elements of a settlement package. In El Salvador, UN mediators played a similar role. Although the conflict had reached a stalemate, fighting had not stopped. A political settlement was by no means inevitable, because the parties brought competing political objectives to the negotiating table. As mediator, the United Nations played a key role as a constant source of new ideas that narrowed differences and moved the parties toward a negotiated settlement. The five permanent members of the Security Council likewise sustained the negotiation process among the different factions that were fighting to seize control over Cambodia, and the

final settlement package could not have been reached without the active intervention of France and the United States in the negotiations.

Viewed this way, the negotiation and implementation phases of the peace process are overlapping, intertwined, and interdependent. Furthermore, there is an obvious need for continuing third-party mediation during all phases of the peace process, including implementation. It is therefore more accurate to view ripeness as a *cultivated* condition, which has to be sustained even after a settlement has been reached in order to prevent the peace process from sliding back into violence.

ESTABLISHING NEW NORMS

Third parties also have a key role to play in promoting new norms and codes of conduct, particularly in the area of human rights. One unfortunate characteristic of civil war is that atrocities and violations of human rights are all too common. The security institutions of the state—that is, the armed forces and police—are usually suspect because they are seen as instruments of coercion by the state against its people. Reforming these institutions is usually fundamental to the peace process and the consolidation of democratic reforms, but dismantling or reforming them can lead to increased anarchy and violence in a society that is unaccustomed to the rule of law. Similar problems accompany reform of the judiciary and legal system, which are seen as instruments of repression and state-sponsored violence and whose overhaul is essential. Yet, if a new social order based on the rule of law and accepted principles of justice is to be fashioned, respect for human rights and due process must be nurtured.

In El Salvador, the deployment of ONUSAL's human rights monitoring team before the fighting had ended and the final accords had been signed helped instill a sense of confidence in the nascent peace process among Salvador's warring parties. ONUSAL investigated cases and situations involving human rights violations and pursued these investigations with relevant bodies in the government. It also developed regional and local contacts with the main political, judicial, and military authorities and maintained an ongoing contact with FMLN leaders inside the country. Working closely with local human rights organizations, ONUSAL was also able to design a human rights program for the armed forces, a group responsible for some of the worst human rights abuses in the country. The El Salvador experience illustrates that the early promotion of human rights can also serve as an important confidence-building measure before a formal negotiated settlement is reached. By putting all parties on notice that certain actions and behaviors will not be tolerated and that human rights violators will be dealt with accordingly, third parties can help advance the cause of justice.

There is obvious tension between conflict resolution and the promotion of human rights, judicial reform, and the development of legal systems governed by due process. Peace and justice do not always work in tandem. The need to establish power-sharing structures that accommodate rival factions and interests may clash with the desire to root out the perpetrators of human rights abuses. Similarly, the need to reform the security institutions of the state, including the police and military, may be at odds with the practical need of bringing those groups who wield power and have a monopoly on the instruments of coercion in a society into the peace process. Without peace there can be no justice; without justice, democratic institutions, and the development of the rule of law, the peace itself will not last. But the political requirements for reaching a peace settlement may well clash with the desire to

lay the foundations for long-term democratic stability. Which model works best when and where: the conflict manager's power-sharing model or the democratizer's political justice model? Evidence suggests that a concern for justice must be tempered by the realities of negotiation and the parties' interests in reaching a political settlement.

In Cambodia, for example, implementation of the human rights provisions in the Paris Peace Accords was weak not only because of the practical difficulties of implementation, but also because "more vigorous pursuit of human rights goals ran the risk of upsetting the delicate political balance that was necessary for elections to take place." Moreover, in "a country with a history of human rights abuses that approached genocide, it was going to be an uphill task to educate the population, to develop indigenous human rights organizations, and most important, to develop mechanisms that would truly protect the peoples from human rights abuses."[16] By opting out of the elections, the Khmer Rouge, which was guilty of the worst human rights abuses in Cambodia, isolated itself and, ironically, facilitated the task of developing democratic institutions and the rule of law because it does not have the power or political legitimacy to block judicial and democratic reform.

At the outset of the peace process in El Salvador, all parties were sensitive to the need to address human rights problems. The success of the peace process is largely attributable to the fact that political reform was linked to the promotion of human rights and the principle of accountability for those who were guilty of the worst human rights abuses. However, given the volatile conditions in El Salvador and the fact that the local efforts to investigate human rights abuses were infeasible and not credible, the disputants relied on international authorities to evaluate and assess the evidence assembled by local interests. The Truth

Commission helped develop greater confidence in the peace process and efforts to reform the judicial system and the security institutions of the state, even though not all of its recommendations were implemented. The slow pace of judicial reform reflects the fact that significant obstacles to such reforms remain.

In Namibia, all parties recognized the need to develop strong democratic institutions based on the rule of law that simultaneously entrenched minority rights in the constitution. In El Salvador human rights problems were initially addressed through the Truth Commission, which identified perpetrators of the most egregious human rights abuses. In contrast, all three recent political agreements in Angola have focused on the need for sharing power, while displaying little regard for justice, moral accountability, or the need to address past human rights abuses. In Cambodia, the question of accountability and prosecution of those responsible for war crimes under the Pol Pot regime remains a difficult and controversial one. It is not clear whether an attempt to put Khmer Rouge leaders on trial for war crimes, genocide, and crimes against humanity would advance the process of national reconciliation or would further radicalize the Khmer Rouge and jeopardize political stability.[17]

The problem in any settlement is not how to resolve the theoretical tension between human rights, democracy, and power sharing, but how to work with the parties themselves, who may be reluctant to push the frontiers of human rights too far. The challenges for third parties are to advance the cause of human rights without undermining the settlement itself and to foster institutional mechanisms that will advance human rights and democratic development once the political situation has stabilized. Third parties can play a critical role in investigating human rights abuses and other war crimes and evaluating evidence assembled by local authorities before arrests are made. In the fragile political climate that exists following a settlement, the temptation for retribution and revenge is considerable. International commissions and tribunals bring the impartiality that is required to restore faith in the judicial process and the rule of law. It is both unwise and unreasonable to expect parties to be able to reestablish the rule of law and due process on their own.

PROXY GOVERNANCE

Proxy governance is another potential area for third-party involvement in the peace process. Civil conflicts usually take a severe toll on the administrative and fiscal capacity of state institutions. Not only do such institutions lack political legitimacy in the form of trust and support from the people, but they often have difficulty performing key administrative tasks such as the provision of basic services. By taking over some of these administrative functions until local authorities are able to perform them themselves, third parties (including NGOs and other bodies) can help with the administration and governance of the state, thus contributing to the development of a more stable social, political, and economic order. Third parties can also play a critical role in observing and monitoring elections to ensure that they are free and fair and that the results are accepted by the electorate and parties who previously have been at war with each other. The term "proxy" describes these various governance functions, because third parties are temporary stand-ins for local authorities who are unable or unwilling to perform these activities themselves. The assumption is that within a relatively short period of time, third parties will turn over full responsibility and authority for these activities to local officials.

In Cambodia, the proxy governance functions undertaken by UNTAC were extensive. The elections for a new Cambodian government were organized by UNTAC. UNTAC's civil administration unit also took over those government bodies or agencies perceived to be vulnerable to outside manipulation and, therefore, able to influence the election process; these units included foreign affairs, national defense, finance, information, and public security. UNTAC relinquished its control over these bodies once the new government had been formed. In Namibia, the UN special representative had extensive review powers over the activities of the local South African administrator-general and helped draft electoral laws and plans for a Constituent Assembly. ONUSAL's involvement in the reform of the judiciary, political institutions, armed forces, and police in El Salvador was also quite extensive, going well beyond its initial mandate. Various UN agencies such as the United Nations Development Program, the Food and Agriculture Organization, and the United Nations High Commissioner for Refugees also played key roles in helping El Salvador with its social, political, and economic reforms.

As the difficulties that were experienced by UNTAC's civil administration component in Cambodia suggest, proxy governance is a difficult undertaking and successful implementation can be hindered by delays in deployment; by a third party's lack of familiarity with local conditions, culture, and forms of government; and by the lack of a cease-fire, which can upset timetables and thwart cooperation among the parties at other levels. There is also the danger that if a third party becomes too involved it will leave itself open to charges of neocolonialism by local critics; the situation in El Salvador illustrates some of these risks. Furthermore, if third parties become too intrusive, they may actually weaken local author-ities and rehabilitation elements, rather than strengthen them. It is important to set clear and realistic peacekeeping mandates that are sensitive to local conditions and to limit external intervention to functional areas where the need is compelling and mandates can be properly executed. Otherwise third-party efforts to develop local governance structures will be counterproductive and, ultimately, self-defeating.

WHY THIRD PARTIES NEED OTHER THIRD PARTIES

In those instances where a workable settlement was reached, such as El Salvador and Namibia, third parties made a critical contribution to the peace process by helping not only with the negotiations but also with the implementation of the agreements. On the other hand, in those instances where the peace process clearly failed, failure was associated with a lack of adequate third-party support and involvement during the peace process.

Third parties need other third parties if they are to work efficiently and effectively in nurturing the conditions for peace. No single third party has the resources or leverage to make the peace process work. Great powers need the local support of a country's neighbors. Regional actors and groups need the assistance of subregional groups. Governments and international organizations also require the active assistance and involvement of nongovernmental organizations and agencies, particularly during the implementation of the agreement.

In El Salvador, for example, UN mediation efforts were assisted by the "Four Friends" (Mexico, Colombia, Venezuela, Spain) and the United States, which played a key behind-the-scenes role during negotiations. Earlier, neighboring states had played a key role in drawing up a general proposal for a regional peace plan, paving the way for the initiation of the peace process in El Salvador. Once the agreement was in place, ONUSAL's efforts were complemented by other UN agencies and NGOs that helped with development assistance, repatriation of refugees, electoral monitoring and observation, and a host of other activities. Similarly, although the five permanent members of the Security Council were the key players in bringing the different Cambodian factions to the peace table (with the United States and France as central figures), they received crucial support from the Association of South East Asian Nations and individual states in the region, including Australia and Indonesia. The United States was obviously the key player in the negotiation of the Angola-Namibia peace accords, but much of the groundwork was laid by the western Contact Group, which had earlier defined some of the key elements for a settlement. Once the United Nations assumed direct responsibility for managing the implementation of the peace settlement in Namibia, it had to work closely with the U.S. mediator to make sure that the peace process was not scuttled by SWAPO's incursion into Namibia in direct violation of the accords. NGOs also worked closely with the United Nations in helping with voter registration and electoral observation and monitoring in the time preceding the elections. In Portugal's efforts to mediate an end to the civil war in Angola, the American and Soviet presences were keenly evident in negotiations. Although the 1992 agreement failed, that failure had more to do with the lack of adequate third-party involvement in implementing the accords than the lack of third-party support for the negotiations themselves.

Peacemaking and peace building are nurturing processes. Past agreements provide strong evidence that negotiated agreements cannot be put on autopilot; they require skillful, committed people at the controls.

Peace settlements, no matter how precise, are not refined road maps providing specific (let alone wise) answers to the hundreds of questions that arise each week. Rather, they set forth the expectations, goals, and compromises that the parties and mediators identified at a given point in time. The implementation of peace accords is thus full-time work for those placed in charge. By entrenching their roles and remaining fully engaged, outside implementing agents can help settlements take root.

NOTES

1. As David C. Unger writes about the United Nations, for example, "Historically it has done best by intervening only after contending parties reach a mutually acknowledged stalemate. It can then play the role of neutral peacekeeper, monitoring agreements the parties have already reached" ("U.N. Troops Cannot Stop Genocide: Pretending They Can Invites Failures," *New York Times,* July 31, 1994, p. E14).

2. Thomas L. Friedman, "Lift, Lift, Contain," *New York Times,* June 4, 1995, p. E15.

3. Benjamin Schwarz, "The Diversity Myth: America's Leading Export," *Atlantic Monthly,* May 1995, pp. 66, 67.

4. See Jacob Bercovitch, "Third Parties in Conflict Management: The Structure and the Conditions of Effective Mediation in International Relations," *International Journal* 37, no. 4 (Autumn 1985): 736–752; Loraleigh Keashly and Ronald J. Fisher, "Towards a Contingency Approach to Third-Party Intervention in Regional Conflict: A Cyprus Illustration," *International Journal* 45, no. 2 (Spring 1990): 424–453; and Fen Osler Hampson, "Building a Stable Peace: Opportunities and Limits to Security Cooperation in Third World Regional Conflicts," *International Journal* 45, no. 2 (Spring 1990): 454–489.

5. See I. William Zartman, *Ripe for Resolution: Conflict and Intervention in Africa* (Oxford, U.K.: Oxford University Press, 1985).

6. Stephen John Stedman, *Peacemaking in Civil War: International Mediation in Zimbabwe,*

1974–1980 (Boulder, Colo.: Lynne Rienner, 1988), p. 9.

7. Roy Licklider, "The Consequences of Negotiated Settlements in Civil Wars, 1945– 1993," *American Political Science Review* 89, no. 3 (September 1995): 685–687.

8. See, for example, Husch Hanning, ed., *Peacekeeping and Confidence-Building Measures in the Third World* (New York: International Peace Academy, 1985); Louis Kriesberg, "Transforming Conflicts in the Middle East and Central Europe," in *Intractable Conflicts and Their Transformation*, ed. Louis Kriesberg, Terrell A. Northrup, and Stuart J. Thorson (Syracuse, N.Y.: Syracuse University Press, 1989), pp. 109–131; and Brian S. Mandell, *The Sinai Experience: Lessons in Multimethod Arms Control, Verification, and Risk Management*, Arms Control and Verification Studies No. 3 (Ottawa, Canada: Arms Control and Disarmament Division, Department of External Affairs, 1987).

9. See, for example, *Nation Building: The United Nations and Namibia* (Washington, D.C.: National Democratic Institute for International Affairs, 1990).

10. Brian S. Mandell, "Anatomy of a Confidence-Building Regime: Egyptian-Israeli Security Cooperation," *International Journal* 45, no. 2 (Spring 1990): 202–223.

11. Kalevi J. Holsti, *Peace and War: Armed Conflicts and International Order, 1648–1989* (Cambridge, U.K.: Cambridge University Press, 1991), p. 338.

12. Gareth Evans, *Cooperating for Peace: The Global Agenda for the 1990s and Beyond* (London: Allen and Unwin, 1993), p. 11.

13. *Demobilization and Reintegration of Military Personnel in Africa: The Evidence from Seven Country Case Studies*, Report No. IDP-130 (Washington, D.C.: World Bank, October 1993), p. vi.

14. Ibid., p. viii.

15. Ibid., p. 26.

16. Janet E. Heininger, *Peacekeeping Transition: The United Nations in Cambodia* (New York: Twentieth Century Fund Press, 1994), p. 39.

17. United States Institute of Peace, "Accounting for War Crimes in Cambodia," *Peace Watch*, October 1995, p. 2.

CASE STUDY

37

The Regional Peacekeeping Role of the Organization of American States

Nicaragua, 1990–1993

CAESAR SERESERES

The peacekeeping role of the Organization of American States (OAS) in Nicaragua was a unique experience for this regional organization. Fifteen years (1975–1990) of periodic and often intense warfare in Nicaragua, ten years of regional peace efforts by the United Nations, the OAS, the Central American presidents, Mexico, Venezuela, Colombia, and over a half-dozen peace plans and treaties brought the OAS into its first-ever peace implementation effort.[1] That effort, organized as the International Commission for Support and Verification (CIAV), was a milestone for the OAS. The CIAV first worked with the United Nations to demobilize 22,000 combatants during the April–June 1990 period. The CIAV assumed sole responsibility for the reintegration, socioeconomic support, and protection of the resistance combatants and over 100,000 of their family members.

While unique in the history of the OAS, the peacekeeping mission in Nicaragua offers insights and lessons concerning the comparative advantage that regional organizations may have over a global organization such as the United Nations. However, the lessons of the Nicaraguan peace process also suggest the weaknesses of regional organizations. This chapter seeks to provide an assessment of (1) the conditions and politics that drew the OAS into the unfamiliar role of peacemaker and verifier of a peace agreement, (2) the organizational development of the CIAV peacekeeping mission, (3) CIAV strategies to carry out the peace settlement mandate of the Central American presidents, (4) the successes and failures of the CIAV during the first three years of its mandate, and (5) the lessons that can be drawn from the case of the OAS in Nicaragua.

THE CONTEXT OF THE INTERNAL WAR IN NICARAGUA

Nicaraguans have been at war with themselves since the early 1960s when the Frente Sandinista (FSLN) was established for the purpose of engaging in a guerrilla war with President Somoza and his National Guard. The Somozas—a father and two sons—had governed Nicaragua since the early 1930s. Controlling elections, dominating the economy, and dealing harshly with any form of political opposition, the Somoza "dynasty" eventually fell to a broadly based revolution.[2] In 1979, after over fifteen years of prolonged insurgency—with significant financial, military, and political assistance from outside actors, including the United States—Somoza was driven from the presidency and the National Guard defeated on the battlefield. The war cost thousands of lives and led to the establishment of a Sandinista government that by 1980 had allied itself with Cuba and the Soviet Union.[3]

Within less than a year, Sandinista government policies, especially programs that affected traditional rural and agricultural communities, created conditions that pushed landed peasants and cattle ranchers (primarily from northern and central Nicaragua) and Miskito Indians (from the Atlantic coast) to rebel against the authority of the Marxist-oriented revolutionary government of the Sandinista Front. The initial rebellion took place in the northern rural town of Quilali in late 1980. Additional uprisings took place along the Atlantic Coast towns of Puerto Cabezas and Bluefields; later, Miskito villages along the Rio Coco took up the rebellion. Cold War politics soon followed. By early 1982, the survivors of the Nicaraguan National Guard living in Honduras were joined by the various rebelling groups that had been driven out of Nicaragua by the Sandinista military and security forces.

By the mid-1980s the Contras, or Nicaraguan Resistance as they came to be known, had established a full-fledged insurgency that threatened the economic and political security of the Sandinista regime. The Resistance operated with the full and open support of the United States government.[4] The war reached its high point in 1987, largely driven by a $100 million assistance package provided by the U.S. government. However, in February 1988, the U.S. Congress voted against continued lethal aid to the Contras. On March 23, 1988, the Nicaraguan Resistance and the Sandinista government signed the Sapoa Agreement, which called for implementation of a cease-fire. However, sporadic fighting continued through early 1990, stopping only a few months before elections. The February 25, 1990, elections represented the symbolic end to the near decade-long anti-Sandinista insurgency that began as an indigenous rural rebellion in 1980.[5]

The war between the Sandinista government and the Resistance had taken its toll on Nicaraguan society, a population of approximately 3.5 million in the late 1980s. Between 8,000 and 12,000 members of the Resistance were killed—mostly rural peasants who fought with organized units or who provided active support to the anti-Sandinista insurgents. Thousands more were permanently disabled—wounded on the battlefield and the casualties of land mines. Over 10,000 Sandinista soldiers, militiamen, and internal state security personnel died. And, like the Resistance soldiers, several thousand left the war with serious disabilities as amputees. Sixty percent of the central government budget was allocated for fighting the war and supporting the Sandinista army. By some estimates, the economy was suffering an annual inflation rate of over 1,000 percent. The underemployment/ unemployment rate was as high as 30 percent. The standard of living for the average Nicaraguan by 1990, measured in terms of

San Pedro Sula

La Mosquitia

Puerto
Lempira

HONDURAS

★ **Tegucigalpa**   Yamales

**EL
SALVADOR**

San Miguel

*Golfo de
Fonseca*

Rio Coco

Rio Coco

Puerto
Cabezas

NUEVA SEGOVIA

MADRIZ   ● Quilalí

ZELAYA

Estelí   Jinotega

Chinandega   ● Matagalpa

NICARAGUA

Corinto   León

*Lago de
Managua*   ● Boaco

*North
Pacific Ocean*

Managua ★   Masaya

CHONTALES

● San Pedro de Lóvago

Granada

CARAZO

Bluefields

RIO
SAN JUAN

*Caribbean
Sea*

Rivas

*Lago de
Nicaragua*

Rio San Juan

Liberia

COSTA RICA

International boundary
Departamento boundary
★ National capital
◉ Departmento capital
*Departmentos have the same name
as their capitals except where noted.*
0   50km   50mi

553

per capita income and quality of life, had fallen to 1950 standards. Over 500,000 Nicaraguan citizens had fled their country during the 1980s. Another 300,000 to 400,000 had been driven from their rural villages and ranches by the Sandinistas in order to deprive the Resistance of its support base. Thus, the election defeat of the Sandinistas had as much to do with economic and social conditions as government policies and Sandinista party ideology.[6]

The elections were held in February 1990, in exchange for the internationally supervised disarming and demobilization of the Contras. While the Arias Peace Plan (Esquipulas II) of August 7, 1987, set the broad parameters for a regional peace process, the actual end of the war was set in motion by the Tesoro Beach (El Salvador) Accord signed by the five Central American presidents on February 14, 1989. The implementing agreement—called the Tela Declaration—called for the United Nations and the OAS to supervise the Contras' demobilization. It was signed by the Central American presidents at Tela, Honduras, on August 7, 1989.

Thus, the last major step to end the war came about through an internationally supervised and monitored national election and demobilization process. The elections became the first point of entry for the OAS; previous participation of the OAS in the Nicaraguan peace process had actually been in the persona of Secretary General João Clemente Baena Soares—not the OAS as a regional organization. From its role as election supervisor and monitor emerged the verification commission of the OAS for both disarming and demobilizing the Resistance and supporting and verifying their reintegration into Nicaraguan society. The basis of the CIAV mandate came from the Central American presidents, not from the OAS General Assembly. From the beginning, the CIAV mission in Nicaragua is best

described as largely unplanned, often spontaneous, and based on the intelligent and creative intuition of a dozen individuals— none of whom had any formal training in the peacekeeping mission they were asked to carry out and only one of whom was a professional OAS bureaucrat.

THE CIAV MISSION

The CIAV functioned under its parent institution, the OAS. This was the first time in its history as a regional political organization that the OAS undertook such a mission. The experiences of the CIAV provide helpful information on the possible advantages and disadvantages of regional organizations involved in peacekeeping missions and on the particular organizational strategies used by the peacekeepers on the ground. It is important to point out that much of the character and style of the CIAV in Nicaragua emanated from one individual: Santiago Murray, an Argentine economist who had served in the OAS headquarters in Washington, D.C. Santiago Murray was appointed general coordinator of the CIAV at its inception in late 1989. At times, it is difficult to separate the character, style, and successes of the CIAV from the personalities of its staff. If one had to point to one factor to explain the success of the CIAV from 1990 to 1993, it was the personnel of the CIAV and its general coordinator. The institutional character and prestige of the OAS was secondary.

The story of the CIAV in Nicaragua is one of constant improvisation and willingness to be flexible, unconstrained by the bureaucratic culture of the OAS. To its credit, the OAS senior staff—including Secretary General Baena Soares and his chief of staff, Hugo de Zela—seldom intervened or dictated operational procedures to the CIAV in Managua.

Aside from learning how the CIAV

functioned and succeeded within its established mandate, it is also possible to draw useful lessons for both the OAS—should it repeat a proactive peacekeeping role elsewhere in the Western Hemisphere—and other regional organizations facing the challenge of ending civil wars and monitoring the peace. Much of what happened in Nicaragua with the CIAV could be labeled unique; however, beyond the recognizable uniqueness of the Nicaraguan case—which includes the nature of the Resistance insurgency, the surprising electoral defeat of the governing Sandinista party, the central role played by the U.S. government, and the origin of the mandate given by the Central American presidents—there are concrete lessons to draw and apply to other regional organizations, peacekeeping missions, and regions of the world.

THE TONCONTIN AGREEMENT AND THE CIAV

One month after the unexpected electoral victory of Violeta Chamorro, neither a definitive cease-fire nor a peace agreement had been arranged with the Nicaraguan Resistance. By mid-March 1990, the Resistance general staff, headquartered in Honduras in the Yamales Valley along the Nicaraguan border, was developing a strategy to infiltrate into Nicaragua most of the combatants remaining in Honduran territory. The general staff resisted pressures from the U.S. government and the Honduran president to immediately disarm in Honduras and to cease sending heavily armed troops back into Nicaragua. Both Washington and Tegucigalpa feared that the Sandinista leadership, having suffered a devastating electoral defeat on February 25, could use the return of thousands of armed Resistance combatants as a pretext for staying in power. Despite the elections, all it would take to renew the war, many observers believed,

would be a small incident between a Sandinista military unit and a Resistance task force in northern Nicaragua.

Such fears were eventually dispelled. The Sandinista army suffered massive desertions within days of the election; some military positions were completely abandoned without orders from the Sandinista Army staff. The desire to challenge the incoming Resistance units was virtually absent among Sandinista units in the field. For their part, the Resistance leadership, now firmly controlled by the combatants, primarily peasant field commanders who had endured close to ten years of combat, no longer trusted the United States. A decision was made to negotiate with the new Chamorro government, but from a position of strength. The best position to bargain from would be with 20,000 fully armed combatants inside Nicaragua, rather than disarmed combatants in Honduras.

The U.S. government could do nothing to stop the exodus of Resistance troops from Honduras, and the Hondurans wanted the combatants and family members out of their territory. Thus, beginning in mid-March 1990, an average of 300 combatants per day began the strategic return to Nicaragua, joining some 7,000 to 8,000 Resistance fighters who had maintained a presence through the February 1990 elections. When a second round of negotiations began between the Chamorro government and the Resistance, the three organized military fronts could point to over 20,000 combatants located inside Nicaragua, in an area stretching from the Honduran to Costa Rican borders. Most were located in regions that had voted three to one or four to one in favor of the political coalition that had elected President Chamorro. Neither the new Chamorro government nor what was left of the Sandinista army was prepared to ignore or play down the urgency of serious negotiations with the Resistance leadership, negotiations that had been frustrated since the signing of the March 23, 1988, Sapoa agreement.

Talks were needed between the newly established peasant leadership of the Resistance and representatives of the newly elected government. This first meeting took place at the Officers' Club of the Honduran Air Force, at Toncontin International Airport in Tegucigalpa, Honduras, on March 23, 1990—two years to the day after the signing of the Sapoa agreement. The decision by the Resistance general staff to negotiate with the new government with its fully armed cadre inside Nicaragua decidedly changed the magnitude of the role of the CIAV. The representatives (as well as the conventional wisdom) of the United Nations and the OAS who negotiated the respective roles and missions of each organization in carrying out the Tesoro Beach and Tela Accords had made two assumptions: The Sandinistas would win the February elections, and the disarming and demobilization of the three military fronts of the Resistance would take place outside Nicaragua. Because these assumptions proved incorrect the CIAV had to assume a role and responsibility not contemplated by the Central American presidents, the United Nations, the OAS, the Chamorro government, and (least of all) the CIAV staff. The latter was hired on a two-month contract (May–June 1990), not realizing that most would stay for three years!

The first meeting between the Resistance and President-Elect Chamorro's representatives took place one month before the coalition government took office. Representing the president-elect were her son-in-law, Antonio Lacayo, and her long-time confidant Emilio Alvarez Montalban. The Resistance delegation was headed by Commander "Ruben" (Oscar Solbalvarro) and Aristides Sanchez, the last active member of the Nicaraguan Resistance Directorate trusted by the commanders. Cardinal Miguel Obando y Bravo acted as an intermediary and as a guarantor and signatory of the Toncontin Agreement.

The essence of the Toncontin Agreement, which was largely drafted by Emilio Montalban during the half-day session in the Officers' Club, dealt with a general understanding between the new government and the Resistance combatants. For its part, the Resistance agreed to (1) observe a cease-fire verified by the United Nations, the OAS, and Cardinal Obando y Bravo; (2) move its forces currently inside Nicaragua into security zones for the purpose of beginning the demobilization to be carried out by the United Nations and the OAS; and (3) begin a process of general demobilization of all forces in Honduras by April 20.

For their part, the Chamorro representatives pledged that the newly elected government would (1) recognize the willingness of the Nicaraguan Resistance to accept a cease-fire, terminate all military actions, and begin the process of demobilization; (2) do all that was necessary to protect the wounded, orphans, and widows of the war through programs of rehabilitation and re-adaptation, including monthly stipends; (3) establish a special transition commission made up of members of the Chamorro government and representatives of the Resistance to carry out the Toncontin Agreement; and (4) seek assistance from other governments to provide the needed humanitarian aid for members of the Resistance and their families, as well as the medical treatment of the wounded and disabled throughout the demobilization process.

The Toncontin agreement marked the first time in nearly ten years of civil war that there had been a face-to-face meeting between Resistance commanders (rather than the political leadership that had lived in exile in Miami, Tegucigalpa, and San Jose, Costa Rica) and individuals who had remained in Nicaragua during the 1980s in opposition to the Sandinista government.

However, implementing the agreement was to prove a real challenge. The Resistance had misrepresented the actual number of combatants both in Yamales and inside Nicaragua. The unstated assumption of the Chamorro representatives was that only a few thousand Resistance combatants remained inside Nicaragua, and that a few thousand more (perhaps up to 8,000–10,000) would be demobilized in Yamales; in the Mosquitia, where the YATAMA (United Nations of Yapti Tasba—The Sacred Motherland) Indian combatants were headquartered; and along the Rio San Juan in Costa Rica, where Southern Front combatants preferred to be disarmed. In fact, only a few thousand Northern Front, YATAMA, and Southern Front combatants actually demobilized outside Nicaragua. These were mostly older veterans, wounded combatants, and some female combatants, all of whom turned in antiquated and largely unusable weapons to UN officials. Beginning with Toncontin, the actual role of the CIAV changed dramatically, forcing it to redefine its mandate and "understanding" with the United Nations over the division of labor.

It would take three months to bring about the complete disarming and demobilization of over 22,000 Resistance combatants. The last day of significant demobilization was on June 27 in the small rural, pro-Contra town of San Pedro de Lovago, in the province of Chontales. The entire general staff and special operations commandos of the Northern Front presented their weapons to President Violeta Chamorro.

Between Toncontin and San Pedro de Lovago, the CIAV negotiated with the Chamorro government to establish its diplomatic credentials and authority to investigate violations of the peace agreements. The CIAV also facilitated and mediated several more negotiations between the government and the Resistance on April 18–19, on

May 4, and again on May 30 to ensure that demobilization took place. In each case, the CIAV provided the needed security environment for the Resistance negotiators and also acted as guarantor of the signed agreements. The CIAV, usually represented by Director General Santiago Murray, was present at all of the negotiations. His role was to provide whatever support the negotiating teams needed. The CIAV took it upon itself to encourage and facilitate negotiations among the government, the Sandinista security organizations, and the Resistance. Also, as the CIAV would find out throughout the 1990–1993 period, promises made by the government would more than likely fall upon the CIAV to actually carry out.

Throughout the tense months between Toncontin and San Pedro de Lovago, the CIAV provided the glue that kept the government, the Sandinistas, and the Resistance talking. It is important to note that at this time the United Nations Observer Mission in Central America (ONUCA), the military arm of the UN/OAS peacekeeping operation in Nicaragua, kept its distance from many of the political aspects of the negotiations. The senior Spanish military officers in charge of disarming the Resistance dealt mostly with senior Sandinista military officers and provided the CIAV and the government with the necessary transportation to and from the negotiations. It was CIAV personnel, under the title *oficiales de protección* (protection officials), who provided security to Resistance commanders and their civilian advisers.

Within days of the San Pedro de Lovago demobilization, Spanish military officers and Venezuelan troops that carried out the disarming of the Resistance began to leave Nicaragua. San Pedro marked the beginning of a new period for the CIAV. It now inherited sole responsibility for supporting the social and economic reintegration of Resistance combatants, family members, and Nicaraguans repatriated from Honduras and Costa Rica. The CIAV was ultimately responsible for over 120,000 individuals, and it had to make organizational and personnel adjustments to meet its unexpected responsibilities. Santiago Murray and his deputy, Roberto Menendez, therefore took steps toward developing a strategy to carry out the mandate of the Central American presidents—a mandate that had not anticipated a Chamorro electoral victory, had not expected over 120,000 beneficiaries, had not expected demobilization to take place inside Nicaragua, and had not planned for the difficulties arising from a divided government (the civilian side was under the authority of President Chamorro, and the military, police, and intelligence side under the control of Sandinistas). Improvisation became the cornerstone feature of the CIAV after San Pedro de Lovago.

CIAV OPERATIONS

The life of the CIAV began on April 18, 1990, with a promise from the chief of the OAS Mission to Nicaragua, Mario Gonzalez, to feed all armed and unarmed combatants placing themselves in the designated security zones. Settling combatants into the security zones was the first step toward disarming and demobilization. CIAV's promise was made to the Resistance commanders in order to finalize the negotiations on the definitive cease-fire and the demobilization calendar. On April 18, Santiago Murray made his first major decision as the newly named director general—one that would reflect the style and personality of the CIAV. Knowing that the CIAV "had neither one cent in its budget nor one bean in its warehouse," he nodded in agreement that the CIAV was willing and able to feed the expected 10,000–12,000 combatants who would demobilize. As Murray later recalled, "It was the only way to ensure an agreement

that would begin demobilization. Audacity and improvisation would mark the operational style of CIAV."[7]

The peace verification officers, or protection officials, who by mid-1992 numbered fewer than ten, lived by their word. They often spoke in terms of having an historic mission to carry out and of having an internationally recognized agreement and mandate to fulfill. At times they were accused of being religious zealots about keeping the peace. Their critics saw CIAV peacekeepers as foreigners. They were welcomed by some and detested by others, and they created both uncertainty and hope in the minds of most Nicaraguans. But regardless of how the CIAV was perceived they were known and recognized throughout Nicaragua, especially in the rural regions where the war had taken place.

There was a constructive distancing and estrangement between OAS headquarters in Washington, D.C. (primarily the office of Secretary General Baena Soares) and the CIAV mission in Managua. On balance, it worked in favor of verification, reintegration programs, and mediation operations in Nicaragua. However, there were moments when the strong voice or the physical presence of the OAS secretary general would have made life easier for the CIAV and boosted the morale of the staff.

The CIAV leadership and staff eventually learned to depend primarily on their own political acumen, professional skills, and individual intuition and to act on the basis of how they interpreted the peacekeeping mandate, the real-world needs of the population they were to protect, and the national reconciliation process they were to support. They sustained this view for nearly three years in spite of the hostility of Sandinista security forces that were beyond the control of the Chamorro government and in spite of the indecisiveness and lack of interest displayed by the government itself.

The CIAV was, as described by one veteran verification officer, "little more than a buffer, a kind of fireman, for the government."[8]

The ultimate danger, and the unfortunate reality, was that the work of the CIAV could, at any moment, be washed away by the inability of the Chamorro administration to govern. A transition protocol signed in April 1990 between the outgoing Sandinista regime and the incoming Chamorro administration left all the military, police, security, and intelligence services in the hands of Sandinista officers. Thus, the CIAV faced a security apparatus that functioned with virtual autonomy from the government. The CIAV often found itself documenting and reporting on abuses of the Sandinista security forces and judicial system, creating new problems for the Chamorro government.

More than once, senior CIAV personnel, including the director general, were threatened with expulsion by Nicaraguan authorities. In one difficult period in early 1992, Santiago Murray was dismissed by OAS Secretary General Baena Soares at the request of President Chamorro.[9] The CIAV's leadership also survived repeated efforts to remove personnel, restrict its operations in the field, and place limits on its investigations and reporting on the treatment of the Resistance and their families.

Unencumbered by institutional traditions, formalized operational practices, or the watchful presence of Washington-based senior officials of the OAS, the CIAV could be creative, innovative, and experimental. Much can be learned from the process of improvisation that led to a particular decision-making process and "operational code," as well as from the programs initiated by the CIAV in support of the verification mission. The employment of several hundred demobilized guerrilla commanders and combatants helped win their confidence even though Nicaraguan government officials were taken aback and the Sandinista political and military leadership dismayed by this decision.

Land and homes were essential for reintegrating the combatants into society. More important for the CIAV was the stability land and homes brought to the mandate-protected population. Without them, the population would have been in constant movement and easily agitated to seek stability and security—even if it meant taking up arms again. For the CIAV, a geographically stable population was one that could be easily monitored and protected.

THE LESSONS FOR THE OAS

Nicaragua was a milestone for the OAS. Did the OAS electoral and verification missions to Nicaragua change the institution in any significant manner? Is it now a "new" institution? Has the OAS (or even its member-states) come to see similar peacekeeping activities as more probable? While the CIAV mission was successful given its mandate, how should the OAS institutionally adapt to the experience of an unarmed international group that incorporated a human rights and development dimension into its peace-building responsibilities? Recent OAS activities in Haiti and Peru and a possible role in Guatemala suggest that the OAS as an institution needs to address and incorporate the experiences of the CIAV sooner, rather than later. The OAS remains, at its heart, a nineteenth-century institution with a highly formal and orthodox culture dominating its thinking and actions.

Old and new Western Hemisphere security issues are now blending together. Verification missions, while still an option for elections and peacekeeping, will most likely be needed in such areas as antidrug programs, environmental regulation, weapons production and acquisition, and human rights practices.[10] The CIAV experience in

Nicaragua has applications beyond peace-keeping.

Lessons drawn from situations influenced by unique political, historical, and institutional factors are limited. Nevertheless, it is worth mentioning the lessons of commission and omission during the three years of CIAV peacekeeping operations in Nicaragua. These lessons are fairly simple and straightforward:

- The peacekeeping mission's leadership should have the autonomy to take the necessary initiatives for effective action in the field.

- A sufficient budget is not the key to success, but flexibility in using the funds is necessary.

- A mission's operational style should develop from the circumstances of the environment, not from a standard manual on peacekeeping designed and implemented by bureaucrats headquartered away from the field of operation.

- Excessive reliance on career professionals and "professional" peacekeepers from international organizations may be a liability if they are risk-averse, whereas youthful and energetic recruits from universities, government ministries, and private practice may be more willing to take risks and improvise in the field.

- Social and development programs must be integrated with verification and mediation missions in order to stabilize the population, gain needed "reconnaissance" skills and information, and maintain a proactive operational style for personnel to position themselves for potential peace process conflicts.

- Social programs managed by the verification mission (especially health and food distribution) should focus on geographical areas of conflict and areas where beneficiaries are concentrated, not limiting assistance to mandated beneficiaries.

- A computerized database should be established at the beginning of the demobilization process in order to create a baseline of relevant socioeconomic, demographic, and personal data for reintegration and monitoring programs.

- Peacekeeping mission staff must develop their own intelligence and support network throughout their areas of operation and must not rely on the government or its security forces.

- A public information strategy should be developed to keep the government, media, beneficiaries, and interested observers informed of verification mission activities.

- An exit or transition strategy to disengage the peacekeeping mission in an orderly and institutionalized manner should be established by the day of arrival.

Many of these "lessons" are difficult to carry out without leadership on the ground, an enlightened staffing policy, and an operational code that allows the mission to work in an audacious and proactive style.

CONCLUSION

As of mid-1996, the CIAV remains in Nicaragua. Between 1993 and 1996 it endured an internal OAS audit for allegations of improper management of funds and improper hiring of personnel; although no wrongdoing was found, some personnel changes were made. It has suffered cuts in budget and personnel and the closing of numerous field offices. The CIAV continues to bear the brunt of Chamorro government and Sandinista military and police criticism. The Sandinista critics have accused the CIAV of trafficking in arms and contraband, conducting inappropriate investigations into the deaths of Resistance combatants and family members, and unjustly attacking the Sandinista military and police institutions.

The Chamorro government requested that the OAS establish an electoral observation mission in Nicaragua for the September 1996 presidential elections. By early May, the first OAS observers arrived to establish an office and to monitor ad hoc voter registration in the conflictive northern communities, where over 300,000 eligible voters remained disenfranchised because the electoral tribunal had been unwilling to register voters in the region. The justification given was the lack of security, including periodic acts of violence, in the areas largely populated by former Resistance combatants, family members, and supporters who had returned from exile, refugee camps, or internal displacement programs under the Sandinista government.

Despite strong pressures from officials within the Chamorro government, senior Sandinista military and police leadership, and OAS staff in Washington to remove the CIAV from Nicaragua by June 30, the Chamorro government (under strong pressure from the U.S. government) requested that the presence of the CIAV be extended until December 31, 1996. The CIAV will continue its peacekeeping and related verification responsibilities but will not have a direct role in election monitoring and verification.

Thus, what was originally planned to be a two-year peacekeeping mission has turned into a six-year effort to keep Nicaraguan society at peace with itself and to act as a buffer between former combatants (including ex-Sandinista soldiers) and a weak, resource-poor government whose priority has been to activate an economy that was seriously damaged by fifteen years of war, including ten years of Sandinista rule.

Some observers argue that the 1990–1993 CIAV mission period was the high point of the OAS peacekeeping endeavor. Since 1993, the OAS has played virtually no role in the El Salvador peace process and has remained on the margins of the Guatemala peace process. The OAS did play an important electoral observation role in Peru, but its valiant attempt to play a role in Haiti was hampered by the lack of international support. All indications suggest that the OAS is more comfortable with passive roles than with proactive and politically involved peacekeeping missions like that of the CIAV in Nicaragua. The irony is that the OAS has refused to take the credit for a highly successful peacekeeping mission that functioned under the most difficult of conditions. From beginning to end, the CIAV has been treated as a diplomatic orphan or a mischievous stepchild by the OAS.

The CIAV mission in Nicaragua could have been a turning point for the OAS as a proactive, modern regional organization in the Western Hemisphere. In the words of one senior diplomat in Washington, the CIAV experience in Nicaragua gave much-needed "credentials to the Organization of American States."[11] The CIAV demonstrated that the OAS can operate a peacekeeping mission and sustain a presence in a post–civil war society undergoing a healing process. It is incumbent on the leadership of the OAS to draw on this legacy when future peacekeeping challenges present themselves.

NOTES

This chapter is based on work performed by Caesar Sereseres, University of California at Irvine, and Jennie K. Lincoln, Georgia Institute of Technology, under a grant awarded by the United States Institute of Peace

1. For a concise chronology and analysis of the Central American peace process and an assessment of the role of the OAS in Nicaragua, see Jack Child, *The Central American Peace Process, 1983–1991: Sheathing Swords, Building Confidence* (Boulder, Colo.: Lynne Rienner, 1992).

2. The most detailed picture of the Somoza dynasty is portrayed by Richard Millett, *Guardians of the Dynasty* (New York: Maryknoll Press, 1977).

3. For an excellent discussion of the long history of U.S.-Nicaraguan relations, particularly the era of Somoza, the Sandinistas, and the Contras, see Robert Kagan, *A Twilight Struggle: American Power and Nicaragua, 1977–1990* (New York: Free Press, 1996).

4. Cynthia J. Aronson provides a regional overview of U.S. policy in Central America and points out the role of the Contras in the U.S.-Nicaragua confrontation. See *Cross-Roads: Congress, the Reagan Administration, and Central America* (New York: Pantheon Books, 1989). A global, U.S.-USSR context to the politico-military issues raised by Washington is found in Gordon McCormick, Edward Gonzalez, Brian Jenkins, and David Ronfeldt, *Nicaraguan Security Policy: Trends and Projections* (Santa Monica, Calif.: RAND Corporation, 1988).

5. Several studies provide a detailed examination of the origins and evolution of the Nicaraguan Resistance. See Christopher Dickey, *With the Contras* (New York: Simon and Schuster, 1985); Stephen Kinzer, *Blood of Brothers: Life and War in Nicaragua* (New York: G. P. Putnam's Sons, 1991); and Glenn Garvin, *Everybody Had His Own Gringo: The CIA and the Contras* (New York: Brassey's, 1992).

6. Assessments of the war years in Nicaragua can be found in Shirley Christian, *Nicaragua: Revolution in the Family* (New York: Random House, 1986); Lawrence Pezzullo and Ralph Pezzullo, *At the Fall of Somoza* (Pittsburgh, Pa.:

University of Pittsburgh Press, 1993); and Robert Pastor, *Condemned to Repetition: The United States and Nicaragua* (Princeton, N.J.: Princeton University Press, 1987).

7. Interviews by the author with CIAV officials, 1993.

8. Interviews by the author with CIAV officials, 1993.

9. The decision was rescinded when the Department of State threatened to withhold funding for the OAS to support CIAV operations in Nicaragua. Since 98 percent of the CIAV budget came from the U.S. foreign aid budget, the Nicaraguan government and the OAS secretary general faced the possibility of removing the CIAV director general and, in the process, losing not only the entire CIAV budget of millions of dollars but also the presence of CIAV in Nicaragua.

10. For a discussion of the evolving OAS agenda for the twenty-first century, see *The Future of the Organization of American States and Hemispheric Security,* Woodrow Wilson International Center for Scholars and Organization of American States, Washington, D.C., April 1991; and Luigi R. Einaudi, "The United States and the OAS," U.S. Department of State, Current Policy No. 1279, Bureau of Public Affairs, Washington, D.C., May 1990.

11. Interview by the author, Washington, D.C., 1993.

38

Conflict Resolution Versus Democratic Governance

Divergent Paths to Peace?

PAULINE H. BAKER

Contrary to the public impression that "small wars" do not significantly threaten American interests, internal conflicts based on ethnic, religious, or linguistic identities constitute one of the biggest dangers to world peace since the end of the Cold War.[1] While the perils of nuclear nonproliferation are real and there is a compelling need for the United States to retain the military capabilities to fight two regional wars simultaneously—as current military strategy envisions—actual military engagements of American forces since the collapse of the Soviet Union have primarily occurred in response to internal conflicts.

None of the thirty-one instances of active hostilities around the world in 1994, for example, were "classical" interstate wars.[2] Yet, in the five years following Operation Desert Storm, the U.S. military was involved in twenty-seven overseas operations, ranging in scope from a noncombat evacu-

ation in Sierra Leone in May 1992 to Operation Restore Democracy in Haiti in September 1994.[3]

The political consequences of these conflicts have also been greatly underestimated. Ethnic conflicts and internal wars have endangered emerging democracies from Mexico to Russia, led to the worst atrocities since World War II, shaken public confidence in multilateral organizations, and strained bilateral relations with some of our closest allies. There have also been some positive responses to these conflicts: Effective short-term strategies to relieve human suffering have been developed; progress has been made in mediating long-simmering conflicts, such as the Middle East and Ireland; and the U.S. military is developing new peacekeeping capabilities.

But the international community is no closer to reaching a political consensus about peacekeeping than it was when the

U.S. Marines landed on the beaches of Somalia in December 1992, the first post–Cold War peace enforcement intervention. As Assistant Secretary of State Richard Holbrooke observed with respect to Bosnia, peace is being invented as we go along, often with uncertain domestic and international support.

After the Somalia experience, many Americans vowed never to get involved in such crises again. But other crises inevitably followed, with varying responses. When Rwanda erupted in an orgy of ethnic blood-letting shortly after the misadventure in Somalia, the Canadian commander of the UN peacekeeping force in that country argued that he could stem the violence. But the United Nations, backed by the United States, ordered UN troops to withdraw after some Belgian peacekeepers were killed. What followed was the worst genocidal violence since the Nazi era, with 500,000 people slaughtered in four months of unrelenting butchery. In other crises, the reluctance of the United States to get involved similarly led to deteriorating circumstances. For example, it was only after refugees fled to American shores in droves and domestic pressure for action mounted that Washington responded to the crisis in Haiti. Likewise, U.S. leadership in Bosnia occurred only after Serbian forces overran UN safe havens and held UN peacekeepers hostage, and the conflict threatened to split NATO. Dire circumstances, not preventive diplomacy, are driving the United States to respond in those instances. By the time circumstances demand a response, however, massive military intervention is often unavoidable.

The failure of the international community to address the problems posed by small wars at an earlier stage has made matters worse. Ethnic crises do not rapidly burn themselves out, at least not without enormous human and material damage. Nor does a reluctance to intervene necessarily

relieve the international community of the burden of involvement. Often, it makes intervention more costly, more difficult, and more dangerous. Better predictive capabilities and a wider range of preventive measures must be developed so that full-scale catastrophic explosions can be avoided and nonmilitary options explored.

In confronting the problem, however, the United States faces a dilemma. It is not so much a question of whether the United States should engage in nation building, but rather of how it should get involved—specifically, how it can reconcile the two imperatives of peace: conflict resolution, on the one hand, and democracy and human rights, on the other.

Should peace be sought at any price to end the bloodshed, even if power-sharing arrangements fail to uphold basic human rights and democratic principles? Or should the objective be a democratic peace that respects human rights, a goal that might prolong the fighting and risk more atrocities in the time that it takes to reach a negotiated solution?

The need to create power-sharing arrangements with rival factions and to include all major groups in a peace process often clashes with the need to bring human rights abusers to justice, establish political legitimacy, establish the rule of law, and build new state structures that can earn the confidence and trust of the people. This dilemma is at the heart of the current debate about how best to pursue peace in the twenty-first century.

A NEW TERRAIN OF CONFLICT

It is not surprising that difficulties arise in crafting policies toward peacemaking. Indeed, this has become a central issue in the debate between isolationists and internationalists. However, adding to the complexity of the problem is a nascent rift within the internationalist community itself. In one camp are those who stress conflict resolution to end destructive wars as soon as possible; in the other are those who believe that democracy and human rights must be the overriding objective of peace efforts.

Theoretically, isolationists should largely be out of this debate, because they oppose international involvement on all but the most narrow criteria. But they nevertheless cast their shadow because they set limits, particularly in the U.S. Congress, on the resources available for meaningful action. Hence, peacemakers may tilt toward the most expedient resolution of conflict not because they necessarily believe in that approach, but because they need to dampen domestic opposition, silence critics, and minimize American culpability if anything goes wrong. The architects of peace have to assuage combatants at home as much as they have to assuage combatants abroad.

Putting these political considerations aside, however, the two types of peacemakers diverge in substantive ways as well. What are these groups and what, precisely, are their differences?

For the purposes of this discussion, they will be described as "conflict managers" and "democratizers." The term "conflict managers" is used to denote those who are involved in a range of activities, from preventive diplomacy and mediation to dispute resolution of various sorts (including efforts that go under various other names such as conflict or dispute regulation, control, or mitigation). The "democratizers" include those who advocate human rights, democratic institutions, the rule of law, and the prosecution of those who commit war crimes and atrocities.

In practice, these groups often overlap and share many perspectives, especially on the larger questions of U.S. engagement and leadership. For this reason, it may not always be easy to separate them. But in con-

crete cases, from Rwanda to the former Yugoslavia, conflict managers and democratizers have emphasized different values, goals, and strategies. At times, their differences may appear to be partisan in nature or to echo the Cold War rivalry between realists and idealists. But however much such factors may be present, this is largely a nonpartisan dialogue between people who share a common concern to end conflict, but favor different strategies for achieving it.

That there is an emerging problem is evident not only in the controversies that have surrounded the various wars that have preoccupied peacemakers since the late 1980s, but also in the political evolution of one of the world's leading mediators, former President Jimmy Carter.

President Carter's thematic emphasis on human rights was the cornerstone of his presidency. As a result of his advocacy, Congress began to attach human rights conditions to various foreign policies, an Office of Humanitarian Affairs and a Bureau of Human Rights were created in the State Department, and nongovernmental organizations—among them Freedom House, Human Rights Watch, and Amnesty International—issued public reports on the human rights records of other countries. The United Nations unanimously adopted the Universal Declaration of Human Rights. More than any other president, Carter placed human rights on the agenda of American foreign policy.

After he left office, Carter became a skilled conflict resolution mediator, building on his Camp David experience. He defused a looming crisis between the United States and North Korea, mounted an eleventh-hour successful diplomatic mediation in Haiti, and initiated a confidence-building effort in Central Africa to hasten the return of two million refugees displaced by the genocide in Rwanda. Yet, in doing so, Carter began to be criticized for unnecessarily offering deals, making concessions, or offering legitimacy to oppressive leaders. Despite the pivotal role he played in facilitating a peaceful transition in Haiti, for example, Carter was castigated by the Haitian people for granting too many concessions to the deposed military dictator, Raoul Cedras, who was allowed to go into exile with his family and live comfortably off his property without being held accountable for his crimes.

The fact that Jimmy Carter could be attacked on human rights grounds is a mark of how far the wheel of history has turned in the new international environment. Unlike during the Cold War, peace is no longer acceptable on any terms; it is intimately linked with the notion of justice. Conflict resolution is not measured simply by the absence of bloodshed; it is assessed by the moral quality of the outcome. And while pragmatism and flexibility continue to be admired, they are not seen as virtues in their own right, but as skills whose value is determined by the ends to which they are applied.

The need to ensure public accountability and entrench basic human and political rights is not only a luxury of the rich and stable; it is a demand being made by victims of oppression in societies around the world. Indeed, hard choices between the imperatives of peace and the demands for justice are being made in countries as far apart as Ethiopia, Honduras, and the Philippines. These demands are reflected in amnesties, judicial commissions, and Nuremberg-like tribunals in Latin America, Eastern Europe, Asia, and Africa.

For the United States, the tensions emanating from these opposing objectives have perhaps been drawn most dramatically in the former Yugoslavia, which history may see as a critical test of American diplomacy in the post–Cold War era. "Some people are concerned that pursuing peace in Bosnia and prosecuting war criminals are incompatible goals," stated President Clinton. "But

I believe they are wrong. There must be peace for justice to prevail, but there must be justice when peace prevails."[4]

Several observers believe that these goals are, in fact, not compatible in the former Yugoslavia, at least not in the long term. As of this writing, Bosnian Serb leaders have been indicted by the International War Crimes Tribunal in The Hague, but they represent only a fraction of the parties who might stand condemned for atrocities. Moreover, the Dayton agreement recognized borders defined by ethnic cleansing and converted those who were seen as warmongers into latter-day peacemakers, with little or no accountability for their past actions.

Not long ago, American leaders were singing a different tune. In 1992, former Secretary of State Lawrence S. Eagleburger stated that Serbian President Slobodan Milosevic should be tried for crimes against humanity, and the former U.S. ambassador to Belgrade, Warren Zimmermann, called the Serb leader "the slickest con man in the Balkans."[5] U.S. policymakers now argue that pragmatism requires putting aside those sentiments. "If you want to end the conflict, you have to deal with Milosevic," observed one diplomat.[6] Thus, in merely three years, the politician most closely associated with starting the war and initiating ethnic cleansing had turned condemnation into praise. Richard Holbrooke, who engineered the Bosnian accords, singled out Milosevic for the breakthrough he brokered with Bosnian Serb leaders indicted by the UN tribunal to negotiate on their behalf. By clearing the way for talks to proceed, Milosevic became a pivotal figure on whom the success of American diplomacy and the peace settlement depended.[7]

"Should we not be pursuing some measure of principled or agreed consistency?" mused Stephen Rosenfeld in his assessment of this diplomatic ploy, which obviously raised eyebrows. Not necessarily, he

Table 38.1. Peacemaker Profiles.

Conflict Managers	Democratizers
Inclusive approach	Exclusive approach
Goal is reconciliation	Goal is justice
Pragmatic focus	Principled focus
Emphasis on the process	Emphasis on the outcome
Particular norms and cultures of the societies in conflict	Universal norms endorsed by the international community
Assume moral equivalence	Insist on moral accountability
Conflict resolution is negotiable	Justice is not negotiable
Outside actors should be politically neutral	Outside actors cannot be morally neutral

concluded. "If this is what 'peace' takes, then pragmatism needs no defending," even if it "may be the enemy of the multiethnic ideal that appeals deeply to many Americans" and violates our sense of justice.[8] General Charles G. Boyd, the former deputy commander in chief, U.S. European Command, who served in Bosnia, argued that there is no room for justice in the Balkans because there are no clean hands. Balkan diplomacy, as he put it, meant "making peace with the guilty."[9] "A heartbreaking outcome," concurred columnist Jim Hoagland, "but the lesser of competing evils."[10]

PEACE OR JUSTICE?

In some respects, this conclusion is reminiscent of the traditional debate between realists and idealists, in which the former argued for pragmatism over too rigid adherence to morality. But that would be rendering the contemporary debate too simplistically. Although there are parallels, this is not simply a replay of the usual tensions in foreign policy, such as the trade-offs that often must be made between human rights and resource dependence (for example, Saudi Arabia) or human rights and trade (for example, China).[11] In these cases, the dilemma boils down to defining which conflicting interest should take precedence. The debate over peace strategies, by contrast, arises in areas

in which the United States often has few strategic or economic interests, except peace itself. It is precisely on this issue—how best to pursue peace—that the differences arise.

The major traits of the two types of peacemakers are presented in table 38.1. This list is not intended to be exhaustive and, in specific instances, there may be agreement between the two types. In fact, during negotiations, diplomats may employ elements of both sets of approaches.[12]

- Conflict managers tend to be inclusive, to neutralize those who might obstruct negotiations. Democratizers tend to be exclusive, to punish or purge human rights offenders. Simply put, conflict managers want to keep an eye on the "bad guys" while making them part of power-sharing arrangements; democratizers want to sideline the "bad guys," holding them accountable for their crimes and excluding them from power.

- Conflict managers stress reconciliation as the primary goal of peace; democratizers stress justice as the primary objective of peace.

- Conflict managers focus on pragmatic, confidence-building steps to build trust among the leaders personally; democratizers focus on principles that institutionalize the rule of law to build trust in the system.

- Conflict managers are preoccupied with the process, emphasizing negotiating skills to facilitate dialogue and end the violence; democratizers are preoccupied with the outcome, emphasizing constitutionalism and the legal protection of political and civil rights.
- Conflict managers call attention to the importance of the particular cultural values of the societies in conflict; democratizers call attention to the importance of the universal values and standards of the international community.
- Conflict managers assume the moral equivalence of the belligerents and do not attribute blame; democratizers identify human rights offenders and hold them morally accountable.
- Conflict managers argue that conflict resolution is negotiable; democratizers argue that justice is nonnegotiable.
- Conflict managers insist on the political neutrality of outside actors as a necessary condition of effective mediation; democratizers insist that outside mediators cannot be morally neutral and must take sides, supporting those who stand for democracy and human rights.

In summary, conflict managers tend to concentrate on short-term solutions that address the precipitous events that sparked the conflict; above all, they seek a swift and expedient end to the violence. Democratizers tend to concentrate on longer-term solutions that address the root causes of the conflict; they search for enduring democratic stability. The former see peace as a precondition for democracy; the latter see democracy as a precondition for peace.

In reality, these approaches rarely appear in a "pure" form, but usually tilt in favor of one direction or the other. Illustrations of conflict resolution that tilted toward the conflict managers' model are Cambodia, Mozambique, and Angola. Elections were held as part of the peace agreement but there has been, to date, no accountability for war crimes committed by the Khmer Rouge, RENAMO, or UNITA, respectively, even though all three rebel groups were accused of atrocities. Basically, settlements in these countries represent power-sharing arrangements with weak democratic foundations. While they ended brutal wars, they are unfinished agreements that are inherently fragile. The duration of the settlements rests primarily on the continued goodwill of the parties, not on the legal authority of the agreements they signed or the representative institutions they created.

Examples of conflicts settled along the lines of the democratizers' model are South Africa, Namibia, and El Salvador, where real political change included measures to ensure moral accountability and justice in the long term. Indeed, in these conflicts, recognition that the crises were basically human rights struggles, rather than mere power grabs by disgruntled interests, enabled real power sharing to go forward.

In some cases, the outcome tilts too far in one direction, leaving many issues unresolved. In Chile, for example, which returned to democracy in 1990, the military was included as a powerful partner in the government despite accusations of widespread human rights abuses by the security forces. As a result, Chile experienced two near-rebellions by Pinochet, who was allowed to serve as commander of the army until 1998. Moreover, only one military commander has been jailed for actions taken during seventeen years of military rule: Manuel Contreras, the former head of the secret police who ordered the 1976 assassination of ex-foreign minister Orlando Letelier in Washington. Fundamental issues of civilian-military relations and moral accountability for past crimes remain unresolved. The "protected democracy" (as the junta defined it) or "imperfect democracy" (as President Eduardo Frei described it) failed to address human rights abuses committed during military rule. This omission casts a long shadow on Chile's ability to complete its transition to a full democracy.

In the immediate post–Cold War era, there appears to be an inclination toward solutions that favor the conflict managers' model. In Liberia, for example, Charles Taylor, who started the civil war, was part of the 1995 settlement, a feature that was widely regarded as enhancing the chances for peace. Previous cease-fires and negotiations collapsed, it was believed, largely because he had been left out. (Unfortunately, the 1995 agreement also collapsed.) In Ethiopia, where a battlefield solution created another power-sharing experiment based on ethnic lines, a Tigrey-dominated government staged Nuremberg-type trials for members of the previous regime. But Ethiopia may not be stable either, because it has not succeeded in building confidence among all the major communal groups, particularly the Oromos, the country's largest ethnic group, which largely boycotted the last elections.

Each conflict must be looked at on its own terms, and the solutions adopted must meet its particular needs. However, settlements built on solid democratic foundations have a far better chance of achieving sustainable security. While South Africa and Cambodia are considered "successes," for example, having made the historic transition from civil strife to peace through elections, their long-term prospects for a sustainable democratic peace are quite different.

South Africa adopted a power-sharing arrangement in conjunction with a new constitution negotiated by the internal parties themselves. Political violence diminished substantially following the first election held on the basis of universal suffrage, although fighting continued in KwaZulu-Natal, much of it tied to local issues. Nevertheless, the country moved forward, particularly on the question of balancing justice with reconciliation. On the justice side of the ledger, for example, former Defense Minister General Magnus Malan and ten other retired senior officials were arrested in connection with 1987 murders, and a Truth and Reconciliation Commission was launched with the power to offer amnesty (including to Malan and the others arrested) in exchange for disclosure of crimes. On the reconciliation side of the ledger, local elections that included proportional representation for minorities were successfully held only eighteen months after the general election, and racial reconciliation has become a hallmark of the government of national unity. Clearly, democracy is taking root and is likely to endure beyond Mandela's term (which expires in 1999), in large part because South Africa is actively dealing with both justice and reconciliation.

Cambodia's settlement, by contrast, may be troubled after King Sihanouk leaves the scene. Its power-sharing arrangement was largely forged by external parties and it has failed to address the issue of accountability. As one observer noted after the agreement was reached, "the current leadership of the Khmer Rouge is identical, to a man, to that which produced the killing fields."[13] Though the threat from the Khmer Rouge diminished after the settlement, none of its leaders have been prosecuted, its violence has not ceased, and it maintains an army of 8,000 to 10,000 troops, a large stockpile of weapons, and tens of millions of dollars safely deposited in banks in Thailand.[14]

CONCLUSION

The tensions between justice and reconciliation are confronted not only by local players, but also by external parties who want to contain the costs of war. Diplomats, soldiers, relief workers, international organizations, nongovernmental organizations, and concerned private citizens each in their own way face common problems in today's internal wars: How do we deal with the guilty and achieve justice while advancing peace? Should diplomats rehabilitate warmongers? Should military assistance and training be given to professionalize militias that perpetrated human rights violations? Should relief workers feed refugees who committed atrocities? Should international organizations assume the moral equivalence of belligerents known to be responsible for war crimes? Should individuals involved in "track-two diplomacy" (unofficial mediation or good offices provided by nongovernmental groups or individuals) legitimize leaders associated with violence in the name of healing? These are not easy questions, and they will not be answered soon.

Nonetheless, it is important to underscore that justice and democracy need not be antithetical. Democracy may be reached in stages, so long as the transition is credible, has the support of the majority of the people, and aims for the same end. The sequence and timing of power-sharing arrangements and judicial inquiries can also be incremental, allowing cooling-off periods. Precisely how and when the twin goals of conflict resolution and democracy are reconciled, and which will take precedence under what circumstances, are issues that should be resolved on a case-by-case basis. However, experience thus far should serve as a cautionary tale. The pursuit of peace in the post–Cold War period will be an infinitely more complex and morally ambiguous process than anyone ever imagined it would be.

NOTES

1. The term "small wars" denotes internal disputes (within states) that do not affect geostrategic interests of the major powers or risk interstate warfare. However, the death rate in such conflicts often exceeds that of conventional wars. The term is therefore a misnomer, since the costs in human life are enormous. For more on this subject, see William J. Olson, special ed., "Small Wars," September 1995 issue of *Annals of the American Academy of Political and Social Science*.

2. *SIPRI Yearbook 1995* (Oxford, U.K.: Oxford University Press, 1995), p. 1.

3. *Strategic Assessment 1995: U.S. Security Challenges in Transition* (Washington, D.C.: Institute for National Strategic Studies, National Defense University, 1995), pp. 14–15. The inventory of overseas military operations covered the period from March 1991 to October 1994.

4. President Bill Clinton in a speech at the University of Connecticut. "Clinton Pushes for U.N. War Crimes Tribunal," *Washington Post*, October 16, 1995, p. A4.

5. "Milosevic Transformed into Peace Talks Partner," *Washington Post*, September 24, 1995, p. A31.

6. Ibid.

7. See "Peace in the Balkans Now Relies on Man Who Fanned Its Wars," *New York Times*, October 31, 1995, p. A1.

8. Stephen S. Rosenfeld, "Ethnic Diplomacy," *Washington Post*, September 29, 1995, p. A27.

9. See Charles G. Boyd, "Making Peace with the Guilty," *Foreign Affairs* 74, no. 5 (September–October 1995): 22–38.

10. Jim Hoagland, "Bosnia: The Ego Factor," *Washington Post*, October 15, 1995, p. C7.

11. See the discussion on the tension between trade and human rights in "U.S. Shifts Goals in Markets of Asia," *Washington Post*, August 9, 1995, p. A14.

12. An example of using parallel tracks occurred in the Bosnia negotiations in Dayton, Ohio, when American diplomats proposed to the three Bosnia presidents that suspected war criminals should be constitutionally barred from running for office in any part of the future Bosnian state. This demonstrated a U.S. commitment to prosecuting the Bosnian Serb leaders who had already been indicted. However, the proposal seemed to conflict with complaints

made by the chief prosecutor of the tribunal, Judge Richard Goldstone, that the United States had not been forthcoming in handing over open-source intelligence information that could be used to build criminal cases against those suspected of atrocities. Moreover, while the proposed prohibition would prevent Bosnian Serb leaders Radovan Karadzic and General Ratko Mladic from running for office, it could also eventually apply to the Balkan leaders at the table if it were determined that any of them had command responsibility for massacres and killings. Then they, too, could be indicted as war criminals, as members of the Bush administration had originally recommended. But if the United States protected some Balkan leaders while indicting others, it would represent unequal jus-tice, a clear decision of the mediators to take sides in the dispute and a factor that could inflame passions in Bosnia itself. See "War Crimes Prosecutor Says U.S. Information Insufficient," *Washington Post,* November 7, 1995, p. A19; and "U.S. Says It Is Withholding Data From War Crimes Panel," *New York Times,* November 8, 1995, p. A10.

13. Marvin C. Ott, as quoted in Janet E. Heininger, *Peacekeeping in Transition* (New York: Twentieth Century Fund, 1994), p. 2. For a further discussion of this issue, see United States Institute of Peace, "Accounting for War Crimes in Cambodia," *Peace Watch,* October 1995, pp. 1–3.

14. Ibid., p. 3.

39

Promoting Peace Through Democracy

JOSHUA MURAVCHIK

The greatest impetus for world peace is the spread of democracy.[1] In a famous article and subsequent book Francis Fukuyama argued that democracy's extension was leading to "the end of history." By this he meant the conclusion of the human quest for the right social order, but he also meant the "diminution of the likelihood of large-scale conflict between states."[2] Fukuyama's phrase was intentionally provocative, perhaps even tongue-in-cheek, but he was pointing to two historical facts: Democracies are more peaceful than other kinds of government, and the world is growing more democratic. In this essay, I will endeavor to demonstrate the importance of democracy both to peace among states and to the resolution of internecine conflicts. I will then assay the spread of democracy in modern history and its prospects for further spread, describing some of the actions that can be taken to encourage it. Finally, I will consider the obstacles to democratization that are presented by civil conflicts and will consider some of the things that can be done to overcome them.

It is now widely recognized that in some sense democracies are more peaceful. Only a few decades ago, the distinguished observer of international relations George Kennan made a quite contrary claim, and few demurred. Democracies, he claimed, were slow to anger, but once aroused "a democracy . . . fights in anger . . . to the bitter end."[3] Kennan's view was strongly influenced by the policy of "unconditional surrender" pursued in World War II, but subsequent experience, such as the negotiated settlements America sought in Korea and Vietnam proved him wrong. Democracies are not only slow to anger but also quick to compromise and to forgive. Notwithstanding the insistence on unconditional surrender, America treated Japan and the part of Germany that it occupied with extraordinary generosity.

In recent years, a burgeoning literature has discussed the pacific nature of democracies.[4] Indeed, the proposition that democracies do not go to war with one another has been described by one political scientist as being "as close as anything we have to an empirical law in international relations."[5] Some of those who find enthusiasm for democracy off-putting have challenged this proposition, but their challenges have only served as empirical tests that have confirmed its robustness. For example, the academic Paul Gottfried and the columnist-turned-politician Patrick J. Buchanan have both cited democratic England's declaration of war against democratic Finland during World War II.[6] In fact, after much procrastination, England did accede to the pressure of its Soviet ally to declare war against Finland, which was allied with Germany. But the declaration was purely formal: No fighting ensued between England and Finland. Surely this is an exception that proves the rule.

A somewhat clearer exception is the war between the nascent state of Israel and the Arabs in 1948. Israel was an embryonic democracy and Lebanon, one of the Arab belligerents, was also democratic within the confines of its peculiar confessional division of power. But Lebanon was a reluctant party to the fight. Within the councils of the Arab League, it opposed the war but went along with its larger confreres when they opted to attack. Even so, Lebanon did little fighting and soon sued for peace. Thus, in the case of Lebanon against Israel and in the case of England against Finland, democracies went to war against democracies only nominally and only when they were dragged into conflicts by authoritarian allies.

As the number of democracies continues to grow, and as this camp encompasses increasing numbers of poor, young, less stable states, it would scarcely be surprising if we encounter some more meaningful exceptions to the rule of peace among democracies. The political scientist Bruce Russett, who has plumbed the democratic peace with various statistical tests, has found that "the more democratic [two states are] the less likely is conflict between them."[7] It follows that as the world fills with young polities that are democratic, but weakly so, conflict between them grows more likely. Even several conflicts, however, would not change the point that war among democracies is rare.

Russett, however, offers a different challenge to the notion that democracies are more peaceful: "That democracies are *in general,* in dealing with all kinds of states, more peaceful than are authoritarian or other nondemocratically constituted states . . . is a much more controversial proposition than 'merely' that democracies are peaceful in their dealings with each other, and one for which there is little systematic evidence."[8] Russett invokes statistical studies showing that while democracies rarely fight one another, they often fight against others.

The trouble with such studies, however, is that they rarely examine the question of who started or caused a war. To reduce the data to a form that is quantitatively measurable, it is easier to determine whether two states were fighting than whose fault it was. But the latter question is important. Democracies may often go to war against dictatorships because the dictators see them as prey or underestimate their resolve. Indeed, such examples abound. Germany might have behaved more cautiously in the summer of 1914 had it realized that England would fight to vindicate Belgian neutrality and to support France. Later, Hitler was emboldened by his notorious contempt for the flabbiness of the democracies. North Korea almost surely discounted the likelihood of an American military response to an invasion of the South after Secretary of State Dean Acheson publicly defined America's defense perimeter to exclude the Korean peninsula (a declaration which merely confirmed existing U.S. policy). In 1990, Saddam Hussein's decision to swallow Kuwait was probably encouraged by the inference he must have taken from the statements and actions of American officials that Washington would offer no forceful resistance.

Russett says that those who claim democracies are in general more peaceful "would have us believe that the United States was regularly on the defensive, rarely on the offensive, during the Cold War."[9] But that is not quite accurate: The word "regularly" distorts the issue. A victim can sometimes turn the tables on an aggressor, but that does not make the victim equally bellicose. None would dispute that Napoleon was responsible for the Napoleonic wars or Hitler for World War II in Europe, but after a time their victims seized the offensive. The United States may have initiated some skirmishes during the Cold War (although in fact it rarely did), but the struggle as a whole was driven by one side. The Soviet policy was "class warfare"; the American policy was "containment." The so-called revisionist historians have argued that America bore an equal or larger share of responsibility for the conflict. But Mikhail Gorbachev made nonsense of their theories when, in the name of glasnost and perestroika, he turned the Soviet Union away from its historic course. The Cold War ended almost instantly—as he no doubt knew it would. "We would have been able to avoid many … difficulties if the democratic process had developed normally in our country," he wrote.[10]

To render judgment about the relative pacificness of states or systems, we must ask not only who started a war but why. In particular, we should consider what the Catholic just-war doctrine calls "right intention," which means roughly, what did the disputants hope to get out of it? In the few cases in recent times in which wars were initiated by democracies, there were often motives other than aggrandizement, for example, when America invaded Grenada. To be sure, Washington was impelled more by

self-interest than by altruism, primarily its concern for the well-being of American nationals and its desire to remove a chip, however tiny, from the Soviet gameboard. But America had no designs upon Grenada, and the invaders were greeted with joy by the Grenadan citizenry. After organizing an election, America pulled out. In other cases, democracies have resorted to war in the face of provocation, such as Israel's invasion of Lebanon in 1982 to root out an enemy sworn to its destruction or Turkey's invasion of Cyprus to rebuff a grab for power by Greek nationalists. In contrast, the wars launched by dictators—such as Iraq's invasion of Kuwait, North Korea's of South Korea, and the Soviet Union's of Hungary and Afghanistan—have often aimed at conquest or subjugation.

The big exception to this rule is colonialism. The European powers conquered most of Africa and Asia and continued to hold their prizes as Europe democratized. No doubt many of the instances of democracies at war that enter into the statistical calculations of researchers like Russett stem from this history. But colonialism was a legacy of Europe's predemocratic times, and it was abandoned after World War II. Since then, I know of no case where a democracy has initiated warfare without significant provocation or for reasons of sheer aggrandizement, but there are several cases where dictators have done so.

The proposition that democracies are more peaceful in general was first put forth by eighteenth-century German philosopher Immanuel Kant, who observed, or forecast, the pacific nature of democracies. Kant reasoned that "citizens . . . will have a great hesitation in … calling down on themselves all the miseries of war."[11] But this insight, though valid, is incomplete: It suggests a deeper reason for democratic pacificness. Democracy is not just a mechanism; it entails a spirit of compromise and self-restraint. At bottom, democracy is the willingness to resolve civil disputes without recourse to violence. Nations that embrace this ethos in the conduct of their domestic affairs are naturally more predisposed to embrace it in their dealings with other nations.

In trying to explain why democracies are more peaceful toward one another, Russett constructed two models. One model hypothesized that the cause lay in the mechanics of democratic decision making (the "structural/institutional model"), the other that it lay in the democratic ethos (the "cultural/normative model"). His statistical assessments led him to conclude that "almost always the cultural/normative model shows a consistent effect on conflict occurrence and war." However, "the structural/institutional model . . . often does not."[12]

If it is the ethos that makes democratic states more peaceful toward one another, would not that ethos also make them more peaceful in general? Russett implies that the answer is no, arguing that a critical element in the peaceful behavior of democracies toward other democracies is their anticipation of a conciliatory attitude by their counterpart. But this is too simple. The attitude of live-and-let-live cannot be turned on and off like a spigot. The citizens and officials of democracies recognize that other states, however governed, have legitimate interests, and they are disposed to try to accommodate those interests except when the other party's behavior seems threatening or outrageous.

A different kind of challenge to the thesis that democracies are more peaceful has recently been raised by the political scientists Edward G. Mansfield and Jack Snyder. They claim statistical support for the proposition that while fully fledged democracies may be pacific, "in th[e] transitional phase of democratization, countries become more aggressive and war-prone, not less."[13] However, like others, they measure a state's likelihood of becoming involved in a war but do not report attempting to determine the cause or fault. Moreover, they acknowledge that their research revealed not only an increased likelihood for a state to become involved in a war when it was growing more democratic, but an almost equal increase for states growing less democratic. This raises the possibility that the effects they were observing were caused simply by political change per se, rather than by democratization.

Finally, they implicitly acknowledge that the relationship of democratization and peacefulness may change over historical periods. There is no reason to suppose that any such relationship is governed by an immutable law. Since their empirical base reaches back to 1811, any effect they report, even if accurately interpreted, may not hold in the contemporary world. They note that "in [some] recent cases, in contrast to some of our historical results, the rule seems to be: go fully democratic, or don't go at all."[14] But according to Freedom House, some 61 percent of extant governments were chosen in legitimate elections.[15] (This is a much larger proportion than are adjudged by Freedom House to be "free states," a more demanding criterion, and it includes many weakly democratic states.) Of the remaining 39 percent, a large number are experiencing some degree of democratization or heavy pressure in that direction. So the choice "don't go at all" is rarely realistic in the contemporary world.

Not only is democracy conducive to peace among states, but it can be the key to resolving bloody battles within them. The end of the Cold War set the stage for the resolution of a host of local broils in places like Central America and southern Africa. During the Cold War, commentators debated whether such conflicts were driven more by local antagonisms or by superpower intervention. Both elements were essential. In the end, the withdrawal of outside instigation—or rather the transformation of the role of the superpowers from sponsors of strife to promoters of reconciliation—paved the way to settlements. (It remains, however, uncertain whether peace will endure in these once-fractured societies.)

The United States and the Soviet Union ceased their material support to combatants, but the more important effect of the end of the Cold War was psychological. No groups stopped fighting because they ran out of ammunition; rather they ran out of rationale. No longer could they see themselves as part of a historic world drama. The utopian model that had roused Communist guerrillas to action was repudiated by its exemplars. In a place like El Salvador, with military victory nowhere in sight and with the mystique of historical right and inevitability shattered, why not settle for a compromise? Conversely, the shriveling of Communism changed the equation for those who fought on the other side. White South Africans feared rule by the black majority, but such fears had been magnified by the specter of a takeover by forces allied with the South African Communist Party, which could be expected to confiscate white-owned property and to liquidate thousands of "enemies of the people" or send them to "reeducation" camps. When that specter evaporated, when the official Communist line became a counsel of moderation, majority rule lost much of its terror.

But if removal of the overlay of Cold War made peace thinkable, and if the pressure of the outside world now weighed on the side of accommodation rather than conflict, local antagonisms and issues still remained. How could these be resolved? In El Salvador, Nicaragua, Namibia, South Africa, Cambodia, and Angola, free elections and the promise of democratization offered neutral ground to which former antagonists could repair. In Angola, the election results led to renewed warfare, initiated by Jonas Savimbi's National Union for the Total Independence of Angola (UNITA), the faction disappointed in the outcome. In the other cases, the democratic transition to peace has, as of this writing, worked successfully, although the political stability of Cambodia seems to hang by a thread and it should not be considered fully secure in any of the other nations.

It is not self-evident that democracy was the path to peace. Conceivably, insurgents could have given up their battle in exchange for economic or other policy concessions. But in these countries, none were willing to forego a chance to gain or share political power—that was the essence of what they were fighting for. In South Africa and Namibia, where political strife turned on racial and ethnic cleavage, perhaps a political settlement could have been based on dividing the land into separate nation-states. Indeed, this demand was put forward by some white extremist groups, but it drew remarkably little support. For most citizens of all races, the unity of their country was not an issue.

More plausibly, power-sharing arrangements could have been sought. Such a formula had been the basis of the formal resolution of the civil war in Laos in the 1950s, but it proved only a fig leaf over continued strife. A variant on this was attempted as a solution to the civil war in Afghanistan, albeit just among the factions that had collaborated to oust the Communist regime, but this arrangement collapsed in anarchy.

Temporary power sharing in the interim preceding elections is a different matter. Such an arrangement was integral to the peace formula in Cambodia: A new national authority was created, the Supreme National Council, half composed of representatives of the incumbent regime and half of representatives of the three guerrilla factions that had fought against it. The Council in turn shared its power with the United Nations Transitional Authority in Cambodia. In

South Africa, on the other hand, the peace settlement included a commitment to a degree of power sharing following elections. According to the agreement, every party that received at least five percent of the vote was assured representation in the cabinet. This system was to hold for five years. In Cambodia and Nicaragua, although it was not prearranged, some degree of power sharing followed the elections, at least insofar as representatives of the electoral losers were included in post-election cabinets. In these forms, power sharing was not an alternative to democratic governance, but an adjunct to it, although perhaps a deleterious one.

While having in common the democratic method of conflict resolution, these cases were quite diverse in procedures. For example, in South Africa the electoral plans and all other aspects of the peace agreement were worked out entirely among the domestic factions. In contrast, in neighboring Namibia, not only did outside parties organize the negotiations that led to the election, but the United Nations largely superseded the nominal local authorities in conducting the elections. "UN police and election monitors were in the country for the eight months preceding the elections," write Jennifer McCoy and colleagues, and they even "negotiated critical changes in the election law."[16]

In Nicaragua the settlement revolved entirely around free elections, all other issues being secondary. In contrast, elections in El Salvador constituted just one part of a peace package and would not have been agreed to without the other parts, which were the creation of a "truth commission" to investigate and redress human rights violations, demilitarization, reconstruction of the national police force, overhaul of the judicial system, and land reform.

For all the differences in detail, the essential common element was that the combatants recognized that democracy (as

opposed to power sharing by fiat) was their best prospect for securing "half a loaf," or at least for securing a continuing voice in the political process. It offered some assurance that relinquishing one's own quest for total power was not tantamount to delivering oneself to the mercy of one's opponents. In some cases, such as that of the Sandinista government in Nicaragua, miscalculation may have played a critical part. Believing themselves to represent "the people," the Sandinistas plainly thought that they would carry the election that they actually lost. In a few cases, leaders seemed to exhibit real democratic conviction, notably South Africa's F. W. de Klerk and Nelson Mandela. In others, the circumstances seemed more to support Giuseppe Di Palma's claim: "Genuine democrats need not precede democracy. . . . Ultimately, the viability of a new democracy can rest on making the transfer appealing, convenient, or compelling. Ultimately, it can rest on its attractiveness relative to its alternatives."[17]

In addition, however, to the "convenience" of democracy as a method of compromise or political transition, a second factor that seems to encourage these settlements is the unparalleled prestige of democracy. The fall of Communism not only ended the Cold War; it also ended the only universalist ideological challenge to democracy. Because democracy now enjoys an unrivaled legitimating power, 61 percent of the world's states have come to be ruled by freely elected governments, according to the most recent survey by Freedom House, although democratic institutions in many of these states are flawed or fragile.[18] Radical Islam may still offer an alternative to democracy in parts of the world, but it appeals by definition only to Muslims and has not even won the assent of a majority of these. Communists no longer muddy the waters by claiming to embody a different, even a truer, form of democracy. Gorbachev ended that subterfuge when he wrote in *Pravda* in 1989: "We oppose the rejection . . . of the formal principles of democracy."[19] Not only regimes need legitimacy; so do insurgencies. In the face of the growing global consensus for democracy, it became hard for either party to these conflicts to resist a settlement based on democratization.

Democracy's power to legitimate derives not just from its prestige in the world of intellectual discourse, but also from its proven appeal to the imagination of common people worldwide. During the great democratic upheavals of 1989, mass clamor for democracy arose in such unforeseen venues as Ulan Bator and Katmandu, as well as in Beijing and scores of other cities in China. Skeptics pointed out that the demonstrators might not possess a clear understanding of democracy and that some did not even behave democratically themselves; however, that notions of democracy may be inchoate does not render the demand for it meaningless. People surely have some idea of what they mean when they say they want democracy, as has been demonstrated in countries enjoying their first free elections, where time and again voters have turned out in large numbers, tolerated long lines, and demonstrated independence in their choices. For example, in Cambodia in May 1993, despite a boycott backed by death threats by the Khmer Rouge and preelection campaign violence and intimidation on the part of the incumbent pro-Vietnamese Communist regime, 90 percent of the voters turned out, and they gave the majority of their votes to the parties of the non-Communist opposition.

Freedom House counted 117 freely elected governments at the end of 1995, pointing to a vast transformation in human governance within the span of roughly three lifetimes.[20] In 1775, 220 years ago, the number of democracies was zero. In 1776, the birth of the United States of America brought the total to one. Since then, democracy has spread at

an accelerating pace, most of the growth having occurred within the twentieth century; the greatest momentum has occurred since 1974. This momentum has slackened somewhat since its pinnacle in 1989, destined to be remembered as one of the most revolutionary years in all history.

So many peoples were swept up in the democratic tide that it was inevitable that there would be subsequent backsliding. Indeed, most countries' democratic evolution has included some forward-and-back movement, rather than a smooth progression. The backsliding has created the impression that the democratic upsurge was ephemeral. This is wrong, however, because the historical global trend of democratization has been quite strong, even though for the world as a whole, just as for individual countries, the line of progress has not been smooth.

The temptation to overestimate the significance of the backsliding may have been encouraged by Samuel Huntington's fine book *The Third Wave: Democratization in the Late Twentieth Century*. Huntington sees the democratization trend that began in the mid-1970s in Portugal, Greece, and Spain as the third such episode. The first "wave" of democratization began with the American revolution and lasted through the aftermath of World War I, coming to an end in the interwar years, when much of Europe regressed to fascist or military dictatorship. The second wave, in this telling, followed World War II, when wholesale decolonization gave rise to a raft of new democracies. Most of these, notably in Africa, collapsed into dictatorship by the 1960s, bringing the second wave to its end. Those who follow Huntington's argument may take the failure of democracy in several of the former Soviet republics and some other instances of backsliding since 1989 to signal the end of the third wave.

Such an impression, however, would be misleading. One unsatisfying aspect of

Huntington's "waves" is their unevenness. The first lasted about 150 years, the second about 20. How long should we expect the third to endure? If it is like the second, it will ebb any day now, but if it is like the first, it will run until the around the year 2125. And by then—who knows?—perhaps humanity will have incinerated itself, moved to another planet, or even devised a better political system.

Furthermore, Huntington's metaphor implies a lack of overall progress or direction. Waves rise and fall. But each of the reverses that followed Huntington's two waves was brief, and each new wave raised the number of democracies higher than before. Huntington does, however, present a statistic that seems to weigh heavily against any unidirectional interpretation of democratic progress. The proportion of states that were democratic in 1990 (45 percent), he says, was identical to the proportion in 1922.[21] There are two explanations of this phenomenon. In 1922, there were only 64 states; by 1990 there were 165. This was not due to a dramatic growth in the number of nationalities. The difference was that in 1922, most peoples were colonial subjects; their homelands were colonies, not states. The 64 states of that time were mostly the advanced countries. Of those, two-thirds had become democratic by 1990, which was a significant gain. The additional 101 states counted in 1990 were mostly former colonies. Only a minority, albeit a substantial one, were democratic in 1990, but since virtually none of those territories were democratic in 1922, that was also a significant gain. In short, there was progress all around, but this was obscured by asking what percentage of *states* was democratic. Asking the question this way means that a people who were subjected to a domestic dictator counted as a non-democracy, but a people who were subjected to a foreign dictator did not count at all.

Moreover, while the criteria for judging

a state democratic vary, the statistic that 45 percent of states were democratic in 1990 corresponds with Freedom House's count of "democratic" polities (as opposed to its smaller count of "free" countries, a more demanding criterion). However, by this same count, Freedom House now says that the proportion of democracies has grown beyond 60 percent. In other words, the "third wave" has not abated.

What can be done to extend it? Short of conquest, states cannot control what happens in other states. In particular, democracy, meaning self-rule by a people, would seem to be something that each people must achieve for itself. In fact, however, states have often deeply influenced the politics of others; in particular the United States, the first modern democracy, has done much to spur democratization elsewhere.[22] Because America today is as influential as any state has ever been, even such simple tools as rhetoric and diplomacy make an impact. To the extent that the words and actions of American representatives attach a high value to democracy, foreign publics and leaders will feel this pressure.

In recent years, our foreign aid programs have placed greater emphasis on "political development," which means democratization. For example, we underwrite the costs and provide some of the training necessary to construct functioning judicial systems and legislatures in countries where all power has traditionally rested with the ruler. We are helping to overhaul educational systems—including the production of new texts and the training of teachers—so that they may rear a citizenry attuned to democratic rights and responsibilities. In Russia and other former Communist countries, we have furnished technical expertise and material support for the privatization of industries by disbursing instruments of ownership to millions of individuals. In various authoritarian countries, we have underwritten local NGOs (nongovernmental organizations), thereby inducing a modicum of pluralism. Our military training programs work to inculcate the principles of civilian control as an element of an officer's code of honor. Similarly, the United States undertook the training of a new national police force for El Salvador, which, as part of that country's peace settlement, replaced the old force that was notorious for its abuses. We have done something similar in Haiti. Of course we use our aid as a carrot, bestowing it most generously on those countries where political evolution adheres most faithfully to democratic principles.

Another instrument for fostering democratization is overseas exchange. In particular, when emerging leaders from the newly democratic or semidemocratic countries come to the United States to study politics, law, local government, journalism, business, and other fields—observing or even working as apprentices in appropriate American institutions—they receive a kind of training that they cannot get at home.

One of the most effective tools we have to try to bring democracy to countries that are not yet democratic is foreign broadcasting. When the "iron curtain" fell, testimonials poured forth from leaders like Lech Walesa and Vaclav Havel and from innumerable ordinary citizens about how important Voice of America and Radio Free Europe (RFE) had been to the subjects of the Soviet empire. In 1992, the Commission on Broadcasting to the People's Republic of China, appointed jointly by Congress and the president, recommended the creation of an Asian analogue to RFE designed to broadcast to China, Indochina, North Korea, and Burma. The estimated cost was about thirty million dollars annually. Although this project has been endorsed by leaders of both parties, implementation has proceeded at a snail's pace.

Support for international radio broadcasting has weakened in some quarters, on

the the grounds that radio is being superseded by television. Why bother supporting Voice of America or Radio Free Asia when people around the world can watch all the news on CNN? However, while western businessmen can view satellite television in Beijing hotel rooms, it will be a while before television can replace radio as a means of conveying uncensored news and political ideas to people still languishing under dictatorships. In countries like China, most people do not own televisions, and most of those who do, do not speak English. Moreover, the government of China, like its authoritarian cousin in Iran, has banned the private ownership of satellite dishes to forestall people from watching programs of their own choice. Beijing also prevailed upon Star Television, the independent commercial cable network broadcasting to Asia from Hong Kong, to remove CNN from its lineup. In time, as technological advances render satellite dishes smaller and cheaper, thereby lowering both the economic and political obstacles to their proliferation, the United States should develop direct television broadcasting capable of reaching the citizens of closed societies in the manner that shortwave radio broadcasting does today.

The National Endowment for Democracy and its four cognate institutes, sponsored by labor and business and the two political parties, give vital aid to individuals and groups struggling to foment democracy in the nondemocratic world and to consolidate it in the recently democratic world. Through small grants, they encourage the circulation of democratic ideas and spur the growth of independent groups that make up "civil society," the critical counterpoise to state power.

It is not necessarily true that the existence of civil society is a prerequisite to a democratic transition. In Poland, the independent trade union Solidarity, the Catholic church, and a rich array of underground publications were the engines of political transformation. In Czechoslovakia, in contrast, a more draconian regime had succeeded in repressing almost all independent forces after 1968. Yet when a shift in tone and policy in Moscow opened new prospects for change, Czechs and Slovaks rallied to the banner of the "velvet revolution," effecting a rapid transition to democracy. Czechoslovakia had the benefit of a successful democratic tradition on which to draw: It alone among the states of Central Europe had maintained democracy throughout the interwar years. It also was blessed in the moment of transition with extraordinarily able leadership in the persons of Vaclav Havel and Vaclav Klaus. Effective leadership is crucial to the success of democratization, and civil society, in addition to other valuable functions, generally provides a setting for the development of leadership. A key reason for South Africa's surprisingly smooth transition has been effective leadership. It was in independent organizations like the African National Congress (ANC) and the Confederation of South African Trade Unions that men like Nelson Mandela and Cyril Ramaphosa developed their followings and honed their leadership skills.

Whatever may be true for the process of transition, it is hard to doubt that the development of civil society—as well as what Freedom House President Adrian Karatnycky calls "civil information" (a free press) and "civil economy" (the private sector)—is essential to the survival and success of democracy. "Power tends to corrupt," as Lord Acton famously told us, and whether or not it corrupts, it tends to aggrandize itself. The most effective check on governmental power is the power of organizations and resources outside of government. Furthermore, every society witnesses the occasional emergence of political leaders whose ambitions are unbounded, and every society experiences periodic stress from economic

downturns or ethnic quarrels that may lead some part of the citizenry to seek a savior in a strong leader. Part of the ballast that keeps the democratic ship upright in such stormy seas is the existence of multiple organized constituencies, whose interests vary from one another's as well as from the government's and who will fight to maintain their freedom and independence.

In countries where internecine conflicts are being resolved through a transition to democracy, outside mediation is often essential. While South Africa achieved such a settlement through its own efforts, in most other cases outsiders have played a large role. The Cambodian settlement was suggested by Australian Foreign Minister Gareth Evans and was agreed to at an international conference in Paris. The Salvadoran settlement was largely brokered by the United Nations, which even helped to draft forty-seven amendments to the Salvadoran constitution that were integral to the agreement.

In these countries and others with fledgling democratic procedures, election monitoring is crucial. Monitoring has been undertaken by international organizations, governments, and nongovernmental organizations. In the Philippines, monitoring was done by a domestic group, the National Citizens Movement for Free Elections, which received financial support from the U.S. Agency for International Development. Monitoring activities can range from simple observation, as, for example, was undertaken in much of Eastern Europe and Latin America, to actual administration of the elections, as in Namibia and Cambodia. Monitors can discourage cheating, encourage voter turnout by creating a sense of security, and expose fraud.

While democracy can be a mechanism for resolving internecine conflict, such conflict —or its legacy—makes it difficult to build democracy. The reasons are as simple as hatred, grievance, and distrust. Even parties that are sincerely willing to turn to democratic procedures and to play by the rules may not trust their adversaries to do so, and they may therefore be tempted to seek their own advantage. Bridging the gap of trust is a critical role for outsiders. Even in South Africa, where the terms of peace were established without outside help, foreign election observers were still required to reassure all sides against procedural irregularities. In other cases, the role of outsiders has been much more decisive, administering elections, helping to formulate the rules, and sometimes persuading losers to live by the outcome, as a team of election observers led by Jimmy Carter did in Nicaragua when the Sandinistas lost the 1990 election. The less formal role of foreign diplomats and aid personnel in encouraging cooperation among formerly warring factions can also be important.

Outsiders can play a critical role as human rights observers. In El Salvador, an essential element of the peace settlement was agreement on the creation of a "Truth Commission" to investigate the most egregious human rights violations that had occurred during the years of conflict. This commission was to consist not of Salvadorans—who would have been divided along partisan lines—but of outsiders under the authority of the secretary general of the United Nations. The secretary general appointed three commissioners: a Colombian, a Venezuelan, and an American. The commission issued a devastating report, allocating responsibility for political killings to the military and security forces, to private death squads, and (in far lesser numbers) to the guerrillas. Where it could, it named perpetrators, and it called for various sanctions against them.

The Salvadoran Truth Commission was a mechanism for dealing with an inescapable problem facing states riven by conflict and others coming out from under authoritarian rule: the abiding sense of grievance on the part of people who were injured physically or materially, who lost loved ones in the conflict, or who suffered wrongfully at the hands of old authorities. The national healing that is essential to strengthen democratic fabric requires that people achieve some feeling of closure of their wounds, and yet a full settling of accounts either may be impossible or may be a prescription for renewed strife.

This issue is painful, however handled. After World War II, in addition to the prosecution of top German and Japanese officials for war crimes, vast purges were undertaken against lower-level officials and activists of the Nazi and militarist regimes. These purges helped open the way for the emergence of new democratic-minded elites, but they also gave rise to myriad complaints about the unevenness of justice meted out on such a vast scale. After the fall of Communism, Czechoslovakia passed a "lustration" law, barring former Communist officials and secret police collaborators from certain offices for a period of time. The law was widely criticized on the grounds that it constituted collective punishment. President Havel himself criticized the lustration law for being too harsh, but explained the motivation behind it: "Try to picture the case of one of my friends . . . who was persecuted for 20 years. . . . Today he has a pension of 1,000 Czech crowns because he could not be promoted and his salary was always low. Meanwhile the person who persecuted him and prevented him from having a normal job today has a pension of 5,000 Czech crowns."[23]

In Bosnia, the UN Security Council created an international tribunal—the first of its kind since the Nuremberg and Tokyo trials—to prosecute war crimes, and the Bosnian peace settlement takes this into account by barring those under indictment from holding office in Bosnia. Still, it is unlikely that any action will be taken against Serbian President Slobodan Milosevic, under whose authority and inspiration most of the war criminals were acting.

For many countries, the best of the various unsatisfactory solutions may be the model of Chile and Argentina, two countries with a widespread yearning to come to account with grievous human rights abuses committed mostly by their military forces, but where the continuing power of that military precluded free-handed prosecution of the perpetrators. Both countries resorted to truth commissions. Unlike the Salvadoran commission, these were made up of nationals, not outsiders. They could not punish the guilty, but they did bring to light many of the details of "disappearances" and other abuses, thus providing the victims or their heirs with a sense of vindication, if not of justice. South Africa, too, has created such a body and given it the power to grant amnesty to those who confess to illegal acts.

In Bosnia, human rights adjudication has been entirely external, an action the UN Security Council initiated at a time when no meaningful peace process was at hand. Ordinarily, however, a reckoning of human rights abuses would be carried out internally. In these cases it will rarely be a first item on the agenda of transition. Although it is important, it is also potentially disruptive and may have to wait until several steps have been taken to solidify the new order.

Perhaps the most difficult obstacles to knitting a democratic fabric arise in societies that have been riven along racial or ethnic lines; even longstanding divisions of an ideological variety can sow hatred and distrust. For this reason, among others, the victors in some elections in states in transition have included members of the losing parties in their governments. The issue is far more severe when divisions are ethnic. Although the ANC was adamant in its insistence on a nonracial political system in South Africa, it agreed to guaranteed representation within the government of political

minorities for a period of five years, a step calculated to reassure whites and other racial minorities. The ANC also "agreed that residents of existing white, colored, and Indian areas would elect at least 30 percent of councillors in the first nonracial elections for local authorities, a concession that was harshly condemned by many white liberals as well as blacks."[24]

It is ironic that the transitional experience of South Africa, the country that so long symbolized racial division, has been so positive, while in many other places around the world, ethnic strife has worsened. Who can explain why South Africans can live together while Yugoslavs, Czechoslovaks, and Canadians cannot?

Ever since the French revolution, democracy and nationalism have been twinned. The revolutions of 1848 were driven by both democratic and nationalist yearnings, as were the revolutions of 1989. The yearning for self-rule naturally includes the wish to be free from foreign rule. But since virtually every state on earth includes citizens of more than one nationality, democracy necessarily means granting some degree of political power to those who are ethnically different. If this is intolerable, as in recent times the Serbs have so fiercely found it to be, then we will have no end of divisive conflict in pursuit of the arid and chimerical goal of ethnically pure states. This creates a grave threat that the hopeful prospects for world peace engendered by the growth of democracy will be vitiated by the efflorescence of nationalism, its natural concomitant. Defining and propounding reasonable limits to nationalism, therefore, constitutes an urgent agenda of peacemaking for the twenty-first century.

Notes

1. "Democracy" is one of the most freely, one might say wantonly, used terms in the polit-

ical lexicon. I define it to consist of three elements: principal government officials are chosen in elections that are free, open, and relatively fair, and in which all competent adults are eligible to take part; freedom of expression; and rule of law. These elements may take many institutional forms (parliamentary or presidential, unitary or federal, etc.) but they are essential: A one-party state or a state that prohibits private news media cannot be a democracy.

2. Francis Fukuyama, "The End of History?" *National Interest* 16 (Summer 1989): 18.

3. George F. Kennan, *American Diplomacy, 1900–1950* (New York: Mentor Books, 1952), p. 59.

4. See, for example, R. J. Rummel, "The Freedom Factor," *Reason* 15 (July 1983): 32–38; Michael W. Doyle, "Liberalism and World Politics," *American Political Science Review* 80, no. 4 (December 1986): 1151–1169; and Bruce Russett, *Grasping the Democratic Peace: Principles for a Post–Cold War World* (Princeton, N.J.: Princeton University Press, 1993).

5. Jack F. Levy, "Domestic Politics and War," *Journal of Interdisciplinary History* 18 (Spring 1988): 662.

6. Paul Gottfried, "At Sea with the Global Democrats," *Wall Street Journal,* January 19, 1989; and Patrick J. Buchanan, "America First—and Second, and Third," *National Interest* 19 (Spring 1990): 81.

7. Russett, *Grasping the Democratic Peace,* p. 86.

8. Ibid., p. 11.

9. Ibid., p. 30.

10. Mikhail Gorbachev, *Perestroika: New Thinking for Our Country and the World* (New York: Harper and Row, 1987), p. 32.

11. Cited in Doyle, "Liberalism and World Politics," p. 1160.

12. Russett, *Grasping the Democratic Peace,* p. 92.

13. Edward D. Mansfield and Jack Snyder, "Democratization and War," *Foreign Affairs* 74, no. 3 (May–June 1995): 79.

14. Ibid., p. 95.

15. Adrian Karatnycky, "Democracy and Despotism: Bipolarism Renewed?" *Freedom Review* 27, no. 1 (January–February 1996): 5.

16. Jennifer McCoy, Larry Garber, and Robert Pastor, "Pollwatching and Peacemaking," *Journal of Democracy* 2, no. 4 (Fall 1991): 106.

17. Giuseppe Di Palma, *To Craft Democracies: An Essay on Democratic Transitions* (Berkeley: University of California Press, 1990), p. 30.

18. Karatnycky, "Democracy and Despotism," p. 5.

19. Mikhail Gorbachev, "Face of Socialism," *Pravda,* November 26, 1989.

20. Karatnycky, "Democracy and Despotism," p. 5.

21. Samuel P. Huntington, *The Third Wave: Democratization in the Late Twentieth Century* (Norman: University of Oklahoma Press, 1991), p. 26.

22. For a detailed description, see Joshua Muravchik, *Exporting Democracy: Fulfilling America's Destiny* (Washington, D.C.: American Enterprise Institute Press, 1991).

23. Adam Michnik and Vaclav Havel, "Justice or Revenge?" *Journal of Democracy* 4, no. 1 (January 1993): 27.

24. Jeffrey Herbst, "Creating a New South Africa," *Foreign Policy* 94 (Spring 1994): 129.

40

The Rule of Law in the Postconflict Phase

Building a Stable Peace

NEIL J. KRITZ

The changed nature of war at the end of the twentieth century requires a fresh perspective on the methods of managing conflict on the one hand and of making and maintaining peace on the other. Today, the overwhelming majority of wars around the world are intranational, rather than international. Wars fought between the military forces of two sovereign countries are increasingly the exception to the norm. In their stead, ethnic and religious conflicts, disputes over self-determination or secession, and violent power struggles between opposing domestic political factions account for 96 percent of the major armed conflicts recorded in recent years worldwide.[1] This statistic has profound ramifications for the processes of conflict prevention, conflict resolution, and postconflict peace building. Tools and techniques that may be appropriate for resolving "classical" wars between state actors are often inadequate for achieving a meaningful ac-commodation and reconciliation between domestic adversaries, who together must build a durable national union. One element that assumes far greater importance in this changed context of war is the development of the rule of law.

It is essential at the outset to distinguish between the rule of law and simply rule *by* law. Broad concepts like democracy and the rule of law can easily be distorted. Even totalitarian regimes frequently use law as a tool in their arsenal of mechanisms for social control. The Nazis clothed much of their atrocities with a veneer of legality. The Soviet constitution of 1936 reads like a litany of legal entitlements, yet it served Stalin well with its wide loopholes for contortion.[2] During its final weeks in power, the Ceaucescu regime in Romania invoked the law even while killing its citizens. These were each examples of rule *by* law, in which courts, statutes, and regulations are manipulated in the service of tyranny. In contrast, the rule of law does not simply provide yet one more vehicle by which government can wield and abuse its awesome power; to the contrary, it establishes principles that constrain the power of government, oblige it to conduct itself according to a series of prescribed and publicly known rules, and, in the postconflict setting, enable wary former adversaries all to play a vital role in keeping the new order honest and trustworthy.

Adherence to the rule of law entails far more than the mechanical application of static legal technicalities; it involves an evolutionary search for those institutions and processes that will best facilitate authentic stability through justice. Beyond its focus on limited government, the rule of law protects the rights of all members of society. It establishes rules and procedures that constrain the power of all parties, hold all parties accountable for their actions, and prohibit the accumulation of autocratic or oligarchic power. It also provides a variety of means for the nonviolent resolution of disputes between private individuals, between groups, or between these actors and the government. In this way, it is integrally related to the attempt to secure a stable peace. At a historic meeting in Copenhagen in 1990, the thirty-five nations then comprising the Conference on Security and Cooperation in Europe (CSCE) affirmed this linkage, declaring that "societies based on . . . the rule of law are prerequisites for . . . the lasting order of peace, security, justice, and cooperation."[3]

The shift from international to intranational conflict engages the rule of law in two significant ways. First, international law is tracking and adapting to these new circumstances through evolutionary changes in the rules of warfare. There is now a growing consensus that many of the normative standards that had previously governed only wars between states, proscribing a variety of wartime abuses as violations of international law, are increasingly applicable to intrastate conflicts as well.[4] A half-century ago, when the world held individuals to account for war crimes and crimes against humanity at Nuremberg, those crimes were generally understood in international law as engendering liability only when perpetrated in the context of battles between states. By November 1994, when the United Nations Security Council established an international criminal tribunal to prosecute the recent genocide in Rwanda, that understanding had changed. As approved by the Security Council, the charter of the Rwanda tribunal severs any nexus requirement between the international prosecution and punishment of crimes against humanity, on the one hand, and the international or non-international character of the conflict in which they were committed, on the other, applying these international prohibitions to purely domestic conflict.[5]

The second sense in which law is pertinent to the changed nature of war—and the principal focus of the present essay—is the central role played by the rule of law in establishing stability and a durable peace following an intranational conflict. It is completely plausible—and often the case—that a classical war between two independent states can be resolved and a durable peace developed without any modification to the internal rules, structures, or institutions of either party to the conflict. The 1980–1988 war between Iran and Iraq, the border conflict between Peru and Ecuador, and the India-Pakistan war all demonstrate this proposition. In none of these six combatant countries did conclusion of the conflict entail any significant degree of internal reorganization. On the other hand, resolving violent conflicts between groups within a state and preventing their recurrence require the nurturing of societal structures and institutions to assure each combatant group that their interests will be protected through nonviolent means. This is rarely, if ever, possible without attention to the establishment of the rule of law. As stated by United Nations Secretary General Boutros Boutros-Ghali in his description of peace building, "Peacemaking and peacekeeping operations, to be truly successful, must come to include comprehensive efforts to identify and support structures which will tend to consolidate peace and advance a sense of confidence and well-being among people. . . . There is an obvious connection between . . . the rule of law and . . . the achievement of true peace and security in any new and stable political order."[6]

EMERGING INTERNATIONAL STANDARDS

In recent years, international standards have evolved to define the meaning of the rule of law with ever-greater detail, providing an increasingly nuanced road map for those engaged in peace-building efforts. This articulation of explicit standards results primarily from the convergence of trends in two areas—democracy and human rights—each of which is closely related to, but distinct from, the rule of law.

During the past few decades, one school of thought focused on democratic systems as the best guarantor not only of freedom, but also of peace. (This school was largely, but not exclusively, the domain of western political conservatives who advocated democracy in a Cold War context.) Extensive research demonstrated what was to some an obvious postulate: Democracies are less likely to go to war with one another than are totalitarian or authoritarian regimes.[7] But promoting democracy as a paradigm for the organization of society invites further inquiry. How does one create and ensure a democratic polity? Answering this question requires a shift from democracy as a macro concept to an examination of those specific institutional structures and mechanisms that are essential to democracy and that distinguish it from a nondemocratic system. The result is a recognition and articulation of the basic elements of the rule of law, which is the ultimate guarantor of democracy.

The human rights stimulus followed an opposite path of analysis, moving from the specific to the general. Prompted in part by the atrocities of the Second World War, international law, as defined by the United Nations and various regional organizations, provided guarantees for an ever-widening catalogue of human rights. Over time, however, the international human rights movement (dominated to some degree by more liberal perspectives) increasingly recognized a basic fact: While an international campaign could often free a political prisoner from detention, he or she could quickly be replaced by many new victims unless the system and structures that permitted their abuse was changed. Stated differently, fundamental guarantees of individual human rights, already provided in international law, could most effectively be secured by more detailed guidelines on the institutions and procedures through which these rights should be enforced. The result once again was a greater sophistication, a recognition of the need to elaborate on the meaning of the rule of law.

As a consequence, a growing corpus of UN conventions, resolutions, declarations, and reports today elaborates standards on the rule of law, addressing such subjects as criminal procedure, free elections, independence of judges and lawyers, and compensation of victims of abuse. A variety of UN agencies and programs help countries emerging from conflict implement the rule of law.

Much of the recent international effort to guide and assist countries in implementing the rule of law has occurred within various regional organizations. The Organization for Security and Cooperation in Europe (OSCE)[8] has produced a detailed definition of the institutional and procedural elements of the rule of law—the most comprehensive catalogue of this sort ever adopted by an international organization—which serves as a standard for its fifty-three member-states. These requirements include the following:

- a representative government in which the executive is accountable to the elected legislature or to the electorate,
- the duty of the government to act in compliance with the constitution and the law,
- a clear separation between the state and political parties,
- accountability of the military and the police to civilian authorities,
- consideration and adoption of legislation by public procedure,
- publication of administrative regulations as the condition for their validity,
- effective means of redress against administrative decisions and provision of information to the person affected on the remedies available,
- an independent judiciary,
- protection of the independence of legal practitioners, and
- detailed guarantees in the area of criminal procedure.

OSCE policy with respect to the rule of law also commits the participating states to a list of particulars on periodic and genuine free elections and political organizing, including the right of any citizen to seek public office, nondiscriminatory access to media for all participants in the political process, and an endorsement of the role of international election observers. They reiterate and expand on traditional human rights commitments, including freedoms of association, religion, expression, and movement, and protection against torture. In light of the

transition from Communism in a majority of the member states, they also recognize the right to property. Finally, noting that "questions relating to national minorities can only be satisfactorily resolved in a democratic political framework based on the rule of law, with a functioning independent judiciary," OSCE documents elaborate on the rights and protection of minorities.[9]

The Council of Europe has also developed a sophisticated series of standards, requiring adherence to the rule of law as a requisite of membership in the organization. With respect to some aspects of the rule of law, the council's standards are, in fact, elaborated in far more detail than their OSCE counterpart provisions.

Beyond the articulation of standards, these regional organizations conduct a variety of programs to facilitate their implementation, including training, consultation, and observer and advisory missions. The same is true of the Organization of American States (OAS), which recently created a Democracy Unit to pursue a variety of technical assistance activities to bolster the institutions and processes necessary for the rule of law in member-states. The OAS and the Council of Europe each enforce their rule of law standards principally through a regional commission and a regional court on human rights. In accordance with the 1995 agreements to end the war in the former Yugoslavia, the OSCE and the Council of Europe will both play influential roles in helping to develop the rule of law as an essential element in the consolidation of peace there.

The evolution of increasingly detailed international standards with respect to the rule of law has not gone wholly unchallenged. In the past few years, voices have been heard periodically in parts of Asia, Africa, and the Arab world to make the case for cultural relativism. They suggest that the international standards developed over the past fifty years are in fact not universal but simply reflect a western approach, alien to their own respective cultures. It is certainly true that regional activity on these issues is found almost exclusively in the organizations of Europe and the Americas. It is important to note, however, that these standards of the rule of law are not American or western but universal in their applicability. Ironically, many of the key principles have been promulgated or endorsed by the same United Nations organs that are often viewed by the West as Third World dominated. Thus, disagreement between regional blocs is likely to continue in the near term.

SOME MAJOR STRUCTURAL AND PROCEDURAL ELEMENTS

The rule of law incorporates many of the elements necessary to ease tension and lessen the likelihood of further conflict. While a comprehensive review of all aspects of the rule of law is far beyond the scope of this essay, an examination of some of the major elements is warranted to understand their vital role in postconflict peace building.

An Independent Judiciary

A primary requisite for the functioning of the rule of law, of course, is an independent judiciary. At the most fundamental level, the principal purpose of the courts in virtually any system is to serve as a forum for the peaceful resolution of disputes. Conflict and disagreement are inevitable in any human system; it would be foolhardy to construct an idyllic model that did not assume disagreements between individuals and between groups. To forge a durable peace, it is necessary to channel those conflicts into a routinized and accepted mode of amelioration before they become violent and less tractable.

In any country emerging from armed conflict, numerous claims and grievances

will remain. These may include demands for punishing the perpetrators of war crimes and other atrocities. Wars frequently displace large numbers of people; the return of refugees or prisoners will often result in competing claims to property. In the postconflict context, courts are also often called upon to resolve disputes regarding the use of minority languages or the eligibility of various factions to participate in elections. Each of these is a highly volatile issue; an independent judiciary provides a peaceful and trustworthy means of addressing them. The judiciary also addresses, of course, the normal, everyday disputes between people, hopefully contributing to an overall culture that resolves its conflicts through such nonviolent means.

It is important to note that not every dispute is amenable to judicial resolution. Some points of conflict are purely political, not addressed by any law which the courts might apply. To make the courts the arbiter of such disputes—particularly if the judiciary is still a fragile institution—risks politicizing the very institution that must be blind to politics, undermining the credibility and independence of the judicial system. Several analysts have suggested that this sort of politicization characterized the Russian constitutional court in the early 1990s, rendering it a more high-profile but less effective institution for easing the often-turbulent Russian transition.

Law Enforcement and Criminal Justice

The rule of law requires a system of criminal justice that deters and punishes banditry and acts of violence, allowing the citizenry to live with a sense of security. At the same time, the criminal justice system must be immune from abuse for political purposes and must adhere to a lengthy list of internationally recognized rights of criminal procedure.[10] In other words, if societal tensions and the likelihood of further conflict are to be minimized, people must become confident that they will not be abused either by private sector criminals or by the authorities.

An additional problem confronting many countries emerging from war or from a repressive regime to a democracy is the hiatus in enforcement capabilities. A transitional period unfolds during which the old police and security forces (as well as the system of authority in general) are eliminated or weakened, but the new order has yet to take hold. Retaining the old police and judiciary, many of whom were part of the problem rather than of the solution, undercuts the credibility of the new order and could threaten the ability of the new government to manage the transition. It takes a couple of years or more to train new personnel, establish new lines of command, and build a new and credible criminal justice system. In Russia, Georgia, South Africa, and El Salvador, to cite a few examples, this time lag has resulted in a security vacuum readily capitalized upon by criminal elements. In each of these four countries, the transition has produced a soaring crime rate; the same trend occurs in numerous states in the postconflict phase. In El Salvador, for example, an official inquiry determined that the death squads that killed thousands of leftists and moderates during the war transformed themselves into new criminal bands, unchecked and undaunted by an ineffective criminal justice system. While people's daily fear of being caught in the cross fire of war or of being viciously repressed by the authorities because of their political views has dramatically receded, it has been partially replaced by a new fear of the thieves, gangs, and mafias that operate with relative impunity in the interim period. In some cases, these new criminals are demobilized combatants and officers of the conflict just ended, still possessing their weapons but no new livelihood. Uncontrolled, this dramatic

rise in crime poses a very real threat to the stability of the new peace.

To address this problem, postconflict reconstruction has to move quickly to establish courts that are above corruption and intimidation by criminal elements; police forces need to be supported, and individual officers must be held accountable for violations of the rule of law; and training and cleansing of the law enforcement and criminal justice systems need to begin promptly following the conflict. The Bosnia accords, for example, attempt to integrate this lesson, addressing each of these points explicitly in the terms for the postconflict phase.[11]

Representative Government Freely Elected

Beginning from the basic principle of free elections, detailed international standards have evolved.[12] The first two or three elections in the postconflict phase may be a source of great tension, as they constitute one of the first real tests of the extent to which all parties can play an authentic role in determining the direction of the country.

The international role in elections can be extremely important in such countries. International activities include providing education and training in advance of elections, helping to draft election laws, and sending delegations to observe the elections to ensure their fairness. Between October 1992 and October 1993, the United Nations responded to requests for electoral assistance from thirty-five countries, many of them with fragile political conditions.[13]

The rule of law requires a freely elected democratic legislature, which can provide a forum for airing and managing numerous disputes between factions within the country. It requires that this representative body be more than a debating club; it must have authentic and meaningful power in the government, enabling these factions to have a stake and a role in determining the country's direction.

Transparency and Predictability

It is accepted and proven that transparency and predictability of action by adversaries reduces the likelihood of international conflict. In recent years, confidence-building measures have been instituted to reduce tensions in a variety of regions. Under these arrangements, certain actions that might agitate the other party (troop movements or missile testing, for instance) can only be taken according to prescribed procedures that facilitate communication and reduce suspicion.

Traditionally, diplomats and those involved in conflict resolution and conflict prevention have applied this principle primarily to conflicts between states. As conflicts have become increasingly intranational, however, the principle is equally valid. Confidence and trust will be increased —and the potential for suspicion, surprise, and tension reduced—when parties are required to conduct their activities in the open. The rule of law requires that governments adhere to principles of transparency and predictability, and it establishes several mechanisms to ensure that this is so. These include requirements that laws be adopted through an open and public process by a representative body, all regulations be published, no rules be applied retroactively, government agencies conduct their affairs according to prescribed rules, and the whole system be subject to judicial scrutiny to ensure compliance with these rules. As articulated by the conservative Austrian economist Friedrich Von Hayek,

> Nothing distinguishes more clearly conditions in a free country from those in a country under arbitrary government than observance in the former of the great principles known as the Rule of Law.

Stripped of all its technicalities, this means that government in all its actions is bound by rules fixed and announced beforehand—rules which make it possible to foresee with fair certainty how the authority will use its coercive powers in given circumstances and to plan one's individual affairs on the basis of this knowledge.[14]

Controlling the Bureaucracy

Even when the relationship between securing the rule of law and avoiding further conflict is recognized, attention and foreign assistance tend to focus fairly exclusively on the courts and the legislature. These may be the primary institutions, but as technology advances and as society becomes more complex, parliaments are able to address a decreasing proportion of the issues with which governments must deal. Legislative bodies can generally only paint with broad brushstrokes, leaving more and more of the details, as well as the implementation, to be provided by the administrative bureaucracy of the modern state.

In many countries, the average citizen will most frequently experience the presence or absence of the rule of law (and will accordingly feel less or more alienated from the system) not through any interaction with the legislative or judicial process, not through any involvement in broad constitutional questions, but through encounters with the administrative state. Resolving a problem with their social security benefits, obtaining a license to fish and support their family, getting a permit to build a house or a church or register a political party, obtaining state certification and funding for an ethnic language school—these are the sorts of events that bring most people into contact with the state, and they are not generally in the purview of the legislative branch. Unless the rule of law is extended to administrative decision making, these interactions are unlikely to be subject to public scrutiny and thus are open to corruption, manipulation, and discrimination. For most nationals and foreign advisers engaged in reconstructing war-torn societies, administrative procedure is hardly as glamorous as constitution writing or elections, but they are ill-advised to neglect it, for it is in this realm that, unnoticed, the seeds of grievance and confrontation may quietly, even unwittingly, be sown.

In Peru, where some correlation is believed to exist between the level of public confidence in the government on the one hand and the effectiveness of the violent opposition on the other, economist Hernando de Soto examined why most Peruvians avoided any transactions entailing contact with government personnel—clearly a measure of public confidence. De Soto's 1984 study found that for the average Peruvian to obtain the necessary licenses to open a small industrial business, it took ten months, ten requests for bribes to different bureaucrats, and fees totaling thirty-two times the monthly minimum wage.[15] Peru had a functioning democratic legislature, with laws adopted and published following public debate; to the casual observer, the system adhered to the rule of law. Despite this appearance, de Soto and his team learned that 99 percent of the rules governing daily life in the country never went through the legislative process. They were, instead, the result of regulations issued by executive branch agencies, a process that was not subject to public participation, procedural controls, or any oversight.[16] At the end of the twentieth century, this kind of situation is not unique to Peru. Insofar as the power of these administrative bureaucracies continues unchecked in the postconflict period, it makes it more likely that individuals and groups will feel disenfranchised from the system, individual and national economic growth will be hampered, and administrative regulations or decisions may discriminate on the basis of

political affiliation, ethnicity, religion, race, or geography. As a result of de Soto's work and extensive foreign consultation, Peru has now adopted a number of rules governing the administrative process.[17]

In implementing these principles of the rule of law, those involved in postconflict peace building will often need to focus on two challenges of particular urgency for the process of reconciliation. These are discussed in the next two sections.

RECKONING WITH WAR CRIMES AND OTHER PAST ABUSES

A basic question confronting many societies in the postconflict phase is whether to prosecute those on each side of the conflict for the abuses they inflicted upon the nation. The worst of these offenses are those classified by international law as war crimes, crimes against humanity, and genocide. In addition, however, nations need to come to terms with the question of accountability for those abuses that, while not constituting such international crimes, still give rise to deeply felt resentment and antagonism in the postconflict phase. Some abuses may have been perpetrated in the context of the conflict; others may have taken place earlier, fanning the resentments that led to the conflict.

Criminal Accountability

Some argue that trial and punishment of these offenses is not only essential to achieve some degree of justice, but that a public airing and condemnation of their crimes is the best way to draw a line between times past and present, lest the public perceive the new order as simply more of the same. Others claim that these are simply show trials unbefitting a search for peace and democracy, that a public review of wartime atrocities will inflame passions rather than calm them, and that the best way to rebuild and reconcile the nation is to leave the past behind by forgiving and forgetting the sins of all parties to the conflict.

The debate occurs time and again. Following the death of Francisco Franco, the relatively peaceful Spanish transition was marked by a mutual amnesty of former combatants. In newly democratic Argentina and Chile, the prospect of trials for the gross violations of human rights perpetrated under the old regime provoked bald threats of military intervention and a return to the terror of the past. In postapartheid South Africa, disagreements at the end of 1994 regarding amnesty reportedly threatened the stability of the new coalition government. That said, in each of the three latter countries, finding a way to reckon with past abuses strengthened the foundation for a more stable, durable democratic peace to follow.

In many countries, prosecutions for abuses committed during the conflict can serve several functions. They provide victims with a sense of justice and catharsis—a sense that their grievances have been addressed and can more easily be put to rest, rather than smoldering in anticipation of the next round of conflict. In addition, they can establish a new dynamic in society, an understanding that aggressors and those who attempt to abuse the rights of others will be held accountable.

Because these trials tend to receive much attention from both the local population and foreign observers, they often provide an important focus for rebuilding the judiciary and the criminal justice system in accordance with rule of law principles. Perhaps most important for purposes of long-term reconciliation, this approach underscores that specific individuals—not entire ethnic or religious or political groups—committed atrocities for which they need to be held accountable. In so doing, it rejects the dangerous culture of collective guilt and retri-

bution which too often produces further cycles of resentment and violence.

When prosecutions are undertaken, how widely should the net be cast in imposing sanctions on those who committed war crimes or similar abuses? How high up the chain of command should superiors be responsible for wrongs committed by their underlings? Conversely, how far down the chain should soldiers or bureaucrats be held liable for following the orders of their superiors in facilitating these abuses?

International legal standards are evolving that help address these questions; there is a growing consensus that, at least for the most heinous violations of human rights and international humanitarian law, a sweeping amnesty is impermissible.[18] On the other hand, it is less certain that international law demands the prosecution of every individual implicated in the atrocities. A symbolic or representative number of prosecutions of those most culpable may satisfy international obligations, especially if an overly extensive trial program would threaten the stability of the country. Argentina, Ethiopia, and some of the countries of Central and Eastern Europe, for example, have adopted this approach in dealing with the legacy of massive human rights abuses by their ousted regimes.

In several cases—ranging from Nuremberg to Ethiopia to Rwanda—given the large number of potential defendants and the risk of further destabilization involved in attempting to detain and prosecute them all, an effort has been made to distinguish three categories of culpability and to design different approaches for each. Roughly, these classifications break down into (1) the leaders, those who gave the orders to commit war crimes, and those who actually carried out the worst offenses (inevitably the smallest category numerically); (2) those who perpetrated abuses not rising to the first category; and (3) those whose offenses were minimal. The severity of treatment then follows accordingly. The Dayton accords concluding the war in the former Yugoslavia more or less adopt this approach. In the first category, the warring parties commit themselves to providing full cooperation and assistance to the international criminal tribunal established to prosecute those on each side of the conflict who perpetrated the most heinous offenses (that is, genocide, war crimes, and crimes against humanity). The accords also prohibit any individuals indicted by the tribunal from holding public office. In the second tier of culpability, the agreement characterizes as a confidence-building measure the obligation to immediately undertake "the prosecution, dismissal, or transfer, as appropriate, of persons in military, paramilitary, and police forces, and other public servants responsible for serious violations of the basic rights of persons belonging to ethnic or minority groups."[19] Finally, all returning refugees and displaced persons charged with any crime related to the conflict "other than a serious violation of international humanitarian law" are guaranteed amnesty for their offenses.[20] While the early postwar period has exhibited some of the challenges of implementing these provisions, the basic framework is sound.

The Rwandan case demonstrates the need for pragmatism to temper an absolutist approach to prosecution. In Rwanda and neighboring Burundi, cycles of violence and counterviolence resulted in the killing of between 300,000 and 600,000 people before 1994. For decades, elites maneuvering for power manipulated ethnic rivalries between Hutu majorities and Tutsi minorities for political ends, without any fear of being called to account for their actions. This culminated in 1994 in one of the most horrific genocidal massacres in recent memory, as 500,000 to 1,000,000 Tutsis and moderate Hutus were brutally slaughtered in just fourteen weeks.

To break this cycle of violence, the new Rwandan government has insisted—correctly—that it is necessary to replace the endemic culture of impunity with a sense of accountability. To achieve this, many senior members of the new government insisted throughout their first year in office that every person who participated in the atrocities should be prosecuted and punished. This approach, however, would put more than 100,000 Rwandans in the dock, a situation that would be wholly unmanageable and would certainly destabilize the transition. As of April 1996, roughly 70,000 Rwandans stood accused of involvement in the genocide and were crowded into prisons built to house a small fraction of that number. To compound the problem, the criminal justice system of Rwanda was decimated during the genocide, with most lawyers and judges either killed, in exile, or in prison. At the time of this writing, not one person has yet been brought to trial. It is clear that the absence of a functioning and fair legal system to process these cases has meant frustration and calls for justice or revenge on the part of the victims. It has also meant uncertainty and fear on the part of nearly two million Hutu refugees, deterring them from returning to their country. Peace and reconciliation in Rwanda will only be achievable through a creative approach that reckons with the genocide and establishes accountability while factoring in the staggeringly large number of potential cases and the overwhelmingly small number of available personnel to process them.[21]

With rare exceptions, it is arguable that capital punishment should not be available in these transitional trials. Given the high emotion and political pressures inherent in these trials, the death penalty may further aggravate tensions the society faces in the immediate postconflict phase.

In Georgia, the two-year civil war which began in 1992 in the secessionist territory of

Abkhazia produced 200,000 refugees, primarily ethnic Georgians ousted from their homes in Abkhazia. It also entailed the commission of numerous war crimes and crimes against humanity, perpetrated by both sides to the conflict.[22] Although no steps have yet been taken in this regard, holding accountable those who committed these crimes will likely be important to the goals of justice and the long-term durability of a still-fragile end to the hostilities. In Cambodia, the issue of legal accountability for atrocities perpetrated by the Khmer Rouge regime of Pol Pot continues to be a volatile point twenty years after the acts in question.

The issue of accountability versus impunity is not only relevant to the resolution of conflict within a war-torn country. It may also have grave consequences for future, seemingly unrelated conflicts in other parts of the world. In explaining his confidence that he could proceed with his diabolical campaign of genocide without fear of retribution by the international community, Adolph Hitler infamously scoffed, "Who remembers the Armenians?"—referring to the victims of a genocide twenty-five years earlier for which no one had been brought to account. Recent evidence suggests that the Bosnian Serb leadership, in pursuing a campaign of ethnic cleansing and genocide in the 1990s, was emboldened by the fact that the Khmer Rouge leadership has never been prosecuted or punished for the atrocities it committed in Cambodia in the 1970s.[23]

Cleansing the Structures of Government

Holding individuals accountable may entail more than criminal trials. In many countries, limitations may be placed on participation in the public sector by those associated with past abuses. A durable peace requires the establishment of public confidence in the institutions of the new order. That confidence can be seriously undercut if these institutions are staffed by the same personnel who gave rise to old resentments. Those who kept the engine of a now-ousted government running may be perceived as of uncertain loyalty. Even though they are not liable in a criminal sense, those who facilitated past abuses should not be permitted to infect or represent the new governmental structures. On the other hand, whether at the level of senior minister or lower-level bureaucrat, it may be argued that in the immediate postconflict phase some of these people are vital to national reconstruction, that their knowledge and experience are indispensable to making the new order function.

In addition, administrative purges do not, as a rule, provide the same level of due process protection as does a criminal proceeding. Because they involve a large number of people, purges tend to be conducted in summary fashion. In stressing the importance of individual responsibility and accountability, the rule of law rejects any notion of collective guilt. When large numbers of people are removed from their places of employment solely because they had worked there during the conflict or because of their membership in a particular political party, without any demonstration of individual wrongdoing, they may legitimately cry foul and question the democratic underpinnings of the new government. Rather than contributing to reconciliation and rebuilding, such purges may create a substantial ostracized opposition that threatens the stability of the new system. In some cases, the dislocational effects of such a measure have been tempered by limiting any ban on public service by implicated individuals to a cooling-off period of a few years, permitting their re-entry only after the initial postconflict phase and after stable and trustworthy public institutions are in place. This problem requires a careful balancing of interests.

Establishing a Historical Record

In the transitional period after an intranational conflict, history is always controversial. Each side will still have its defenders, who will deny that the abuses of which it is accused ever took place, will claim that they were actually perpetrated by others, or will suggest that they were justified by exigent circumstances. Left uncontested, these competing claims may undermine the new order and the effort at peace building; they may also add insult to the injury already inflicted on the victims, deeply sowing seeds of resentment which can result in a new round of violence. The Bosnian war demonstrated unresolved issues of history and resentment dating back some seven centuries.

As a consequence, in addition to the focus on individual perpetrators, establishing an official overall accounting of the past is often an important element to a successful transition, providing a sense of national justice, reckoning, and catharsis. Fairly conducted criminal trials are one way to establish the facts and figures of past abuses; the formation of a "truth commission" is another. While the two processes can complement each other, a truth commission may be all the more useful for healing and reconciliation if the country is not equipped to conduct fair and credible trials. Long-term reconciliation requires a careful examination of the mix that will best fit the society in question.

In El Salvador, the twelve-year civil war between the government and the Farabundo Marti National Liberation Front (FMLN) left some 75,000 people dead. "As the peace negotiations advanced, the charges and countercharges relating to [atrocities committed by each side] threatened to become serious obstacles to any peaceful resolution of the conflict. It was soon recognized, therefore, that the hate and mistrust built up over the years required . . . some mechanism permitting an honest accounting of these terrible deeds."[24] At the war's conclusion in 1992, the judiciary was intact, but it was accurately perceived as a highly politicized, corrupt, and nonindependent entity, a tool of the right wing, incapable of or unwilling to address the difficult issues of accountability for war crimes or egregious violations of human rights in an objective manner. How, then, could a sense of justice and accountability be achieved without a credible judiciary? A major part of the solution was the three-member United Nations Commission on the Truth, established by the peace agreements between the warring parties.[25]

Although not a court, the commission—like similar entities that have been created in several countries facing a legacy of abuses on a mass scale—investigated and reported on abuses that had been committed by both sides during the war, giving both victims and perpetrators an opportunity to make their testimony part of the official record. The tension between justice and reconciliation on the one hand and the impossibility of obtaining either in the Salvadoran courts on the other "confront[ed] the Commission with a serious dilemma. The question is not whether the guilty should be punished but whether justice can be done. Public morality demands that those responsible for the crimes described here be punished. However, El Salvador has no system for the administration of justice which meets the minimum requirements of objectivity and impartiality so that justice can be rendered reliably."[26]

As a consequence, the commission felt obliged to render certain judgments in its 1993 report that would otherwise have been left to the Salvadoran judiciary.[27] (The appointment of a new and independent Supreme Court, which assumed office in January 1995, was an important step in the consolidation of peace in El Salvador; the high court then began to reform the rest of the judiciary.) In its report, the commission analyzed the ways in which the militarization of Salvadoran society had eviscerated all three branches of government; it also made recommendations to enhance the prospects for each of these institutions and the military to function in accord with the precepts of the rule of law.

In Guatemala, the civil war has raged for thirty-five years and cost over 100,000 lives. In providing for the establishment of a truth commission, the tentative peace agreement to end that conflict stresses the importance of establishing the "whole truth" about past abuses by all parties, presenting this as part of a process that "will help lay the basis for a peaceful coexistence" and that "will eliminate all forms of retaliation or revenge as a prerequisite for a firm and lasting peace."[28]

Compensation, Restitution, and Rehabilitation

Finally, from the perspective of the rule of law, a reckoning with past abuses must focus not only on the perpetrators, but also on the victims. Notwithstanding the competing demands for limited resources, which is always an aspect of the war-torn economy, issues of compensation and rehabilitation of victims should be incorporated into most plans for postconflict reconstruction. Compensation serves at least three functions in the process of national reconciliation. First, it helps the victims to manage the material aspect of their loss. Second, it constitutes an official acknowledgment of their pain by the nation. Both of these facilitate the societal reintegration of people who may have long suffered in silence. Third, it may deter the state from future abuses, by imposing a financial cost to such misdeeds. There is a growing consensus in international law that the state is obligated to provide compensation to victims of egregious human

rights abuses perpetrated by the government; if the regime that committed the acts in question does not provide compensation, the obligation carries over to the successor government.

In a few countries, new legal entities are established to deal with this complex aspect of justice in the postconflict phase. In the aftermath of the war in the former Yugoslavia, the peace accords provide for the establishment of a commission to restore land to those displaced by the war, resolve countless disputes over property, and provide compensation to dislocated victims of the conflict. In Rwanda, there are thousands of competing claims to property made by several groups: returning Tutsi exiles who departed the country over a thirty-five-year period, those displaced during the genocide, Hutu refugees who left in 1994, and, before long, returning detainees. In both Rwanda and the former Yugoslavia, the rule of law requires equitable restitution or compensation, which are also essential for the construction of a durable peace. Depending on the situation, compensation may range from return of lost property or educational benefits to pensions for survivors of those killed or funds for minority group cultural activities.[29]

THE CONSTITUTION-MAKING PROCESS

In many countries in transition from civil war to a new government, one of the first important tasks is drafting a new constitution. The constitution is, of course, the foundational legal document from which the entire national system of rules will derive; it is the cornerstone for the rule of law. In addition, insofar as the constitution enshrines the vision of a new society, articulates the fundamental principles by which the political system will be reorganized, and redistributes power within the country, both its substantive provisions and the process by which it is created can play an important role in the consolidation of peace.

When a constitution is drafted and imposed by a small group of elites from the victorious party, a foundation may result that is not only less democratic but also less stable. Alternatively, given the nature of this document, constitution-making can involve a process of national dialogue, allowing competing perspectives and claims within the postwar society to be aired and incorporated, thus facilitating reconciliation among these groups. It can also be a process of national education with respect to concepts of government, the problems and concerns of different groups within the country, the development of civil society and citizen responsibility, and international norms of human rights, nondiscrimination, and tolerance that have been incorporated into recent constitutions. In short, the process of constitution-making can contribute to peace and stability.

In Eritrea, following a thirty-year war for independence, the constitution-making process has intentionally been structured to facilitate the consolidation of peace. The program for drafting a constitution is expected to last two years and has been proclaimed "a historic process of a coming together of Eritreans for a creative national discourse."[30] The Constitutional Commission includes a variety of religious, ethnic, and regional constituencies. Offices were established in five regions of the country; an additional office is responsible for involving the estimated 750,000 Eritreans living abroad in the process. The Constitutional Commission is pursuing a strategy "which involves the widest possible public consultation, a strategy which eschews the top-down approach."[31] Discussions were initiated through an extensive series of civic education seminars, debates, and town and village meetings reaching over 100,000 people. Pamphlets, newspapers, television, and radio are all used to facilitate public education and dialogue. Articulation of basic principles and of a draft constitution will be subject to further public debate and input.

In Cambodia, although not accompanied by the same wide-scale public consultation, the drafting and adoption of a new constitution after the Paris Peace Accords also entailed a process of national dialogue, with rival factions all shaping the distribution of power and rights within Cambodian society. Constitution-making in South Africa provides a further example of the usefulness of this approach. During one session in the spring of 1995, for instance, the Constitutional Assembly spent hours deliberating over provisions in the new draft constitution concerning the security forces in the new South Africa, hardly a minor or noncontroversial topic for opponents emerging from years of conflict. A variety of sensitive issues —such as emergency powers and their limits, the authorization of soldiers to disobey orders that violate international law, and civilian control of the security forces—were all respectfully discussed and debated by former enemies now in Parliament, ranging from Pan-Africanist Congress members on one end of the political spectrum to those of the Freedom Front on the other. Several participants subsequently acknowledged that as little as a year earlier, such a discussion would have been inconceivable.[32] In the context of the transition, however, the lengthy Constitutional Assembly process is providing an important avenue for previously violent adversaries to negotiate and collaborate in constructing each piece of their new order.

Developing a constitution through this process of national dialogue also has certain limitations. It is far less efficient than the common method, in which the terms of this crucial social compact are determined by a small group behind relatively closed doors and handed down to the people like contemporary tablets from Mount Sinai.

Enabling a broad spectrum of society to participate in shaping the compact means that the process will take significantly longer to complete, entail higher administrative costs and greater debate, and possibly result in some compromises that might otherwise be avoided. On the other hand, it may also produce a constitutional system that is more widely understood and accepted, more stable, and more supportive of peace.

There are limits to this approach, and decisions regarding the process will necessarily be affected by the nature of the particular conflict and the circumstances of its resolution. A drawn-out process of constitution-making could be destabilizing, for example, if it means a lengthy transition governed by no basic rules or a transition still governed by an old constitutional system that had exacerbated the conflict. In such situations, interim arrangements may first be needed for the consolidation of peace. Such was the case in South Africa, where a negotiated interim constitution established the basis for transition, and a lengthier process then followed to develop the final document. In addition, it is essential to recognize that not all of society's problems can be resolved through the constitution. As was suggested earlier with respect to the courts, viewing constitution-making as a means of redressing all group grievances may force onto the plate issues that are not appropriate to this process. This can result either in rejection of the process by disgruntled factions or inclusion of promises in the new document that cannot be fulfilled, either of which would damage the credibility of the process and of the new constitution.

HOW LARGE A FOREIGN ROLE?

As noted above, while the challenge of demonstrating a new beginning founded on justice and the rule of law will likely present itself very early in the postconflict phase, constructing new institutions and training new lawyers, judges, police, and other personnel can take years. This a recurring quandary.

In some instances, the solution has been to pursue justice and reconciliation through the medium of an international entity. In El Salvador, for example, the country's relatively small population was far too polarized to achieve any consensus on the abuses committed during the conflict. As a consequence, the members and staff of the UN truth commission were comprised entirely of non-Salvadorans in order to achieve a degree of neutrality, objectivity, and acceptability that could not be garnered by any domestic body at that early stage in the transition from war. Similarly, the parties to the Guatemalan civil war have agreed to create a three-member commission of inquiry, under UN auspices but with joint international and Guatemalan membership. The mission of this body is "to clarify, with full objectiveness, equity, and impartiality, human rights violations and incidents of violence related to the armed confrontation that have caused suffering to the Guatemalan population."[33]

The United Nations Security Council created two international criminal tribunals to respond to civil war and genocide in Rwanda and the former Yugoslavia—the first such bodies established since the Nuremberg tribunal a half-century earlier. Several factors militated in favor of internationalizing the response in these cases:

- The crimes were so horrific and so great a challenge to basic precepts of international law.
- The need for justice as an essential ingredient in achieving reconciliation and breaking the cycle of violence was so apparent.
- The domestic justice systems (particularly in Rwanda) were so thoroughly decimated.

In addition, an international tribunal was better positioned than a domestic court to (1) convey a clear message that the international community will not tolerate such atrocities, deterring future carnage of this sort, not only in Rwanda and Bosnia but worldwide; (2) be staffed by experts able to apply and interpret evolving international law standards; (3) be more likely to have the necessary human and material resources at its disposal; (4) function—and be perceived as functioning—on the basis of independence and impartiality rather than retribution; (5) advance the development and enforcement of international criminal norms; and (6) obtain jurisdiction over many of the worst perpetrators who were no longer in the country.

In rare circumstances such as these, creating an international entity to provide a sense of justice is vital. In the vast majority of instances, however, this should only be the second choice. Even in cases such as Rwanda and Bosnia, where the establishment of international criminal tribunals was appropriate, durable peace requires that the states themselves undertake domestic efforts at justice and reconciliation.

Whether accountability and justice are achieved through a court or through a truth commission, they are generally best achieved through a domestic process managed by the country in question. If it can be conducted in accord with the protections afforded by the rule of law, prosecution before domestic courts can enhance the legitimacy of the new postconflict government and of the judiciary, be more sensitive than outsiders to nuances of the local community, emphasize that the nation will henceforth hold all individuals accountable for their crimes, and stress a viable alternative to vigilante justice. In addition, the state and the body politic will generally be most likely to integrate these lessons of justice, accountability, and reconciliation following a cathartic *domestic*

process that includes representatives of all parties. This internalization is extremely important to building peace. Conversely, if the state is relieved of the need to face these issues, leaving them to be handled and concluded by outsiders (and therefore easily disowned by local leaders if that becomes politically expedient), then the experience may contribute less to a durable peace and the entrenchment of the rule of law.

A UN Commission of Experts that preceded creation of the Rwanda tribunal acknowledged this point, noting that domestic courts could be more sensitive to individual cases and that resulting decisions "could be of greater and more immediate symbolic force, because verdicts would be rendered by courts familiar to the local community."[34] Negotiations are currently under way in the United Nations to create a permanent international criminal court, with jurisdiction over crimes such as genocide, war crimes, and crimes against humanity. Establishment of this court—likely in the next few years—will eliminate the need for the appointment of special ad hoc tribunals such as those set up for Rwanda and Bosnia. Appropriately, the draft statute for the permanent body states that the court "is intended to be complementary to national criminal justice systems in cases where such trial procedures may not be available or may be ineffective."[35]

Conclusion

New challenges to peace require new tools. As war in all parts of the globe changes its complexion, becoming preponderantly intranational, establishing the rule of law plays an increasingly critical role, particularly in the immediate postconflict construction of peace. A two-year study currently under way on rebuilding war-torn societies correctly identifies among the requisite elements for successful reconstruction both the eminently political tasks of reaching agreement among different social and political forces which emerge from the conflict on how to distribute power, of institutionalizing this agreement in a political system and giving it constitutional form, and more [the] "technical" task of building a functioning administrative and legal infrastructure for government. . . . Reconciliation must be based on a minimal degree of equity and justice and on agreement on minimal rules of governance and state authority. . . . This implies that relations between state authority and civil society will have to be defined anew and that appropriate mechanisms of accountability be established.[36]

Each of these elements requires careful attention to the rule of law.

There are those who, even today, imply that emphasis on the establishment of the rule of law is irrelevant, or at best tangential, to the real work of conflict resolution and postconflict peace building—an exercise naively engaged in by those who believe that the simple imposition of legal regulations and institutions will promptly erase deep-seated resentments, hatreds, and power struggles. Nothing could be less accurate. The rule of law has at its core a hard-nosed and not particularly optimistic assessment of human nature and the prospects for conflict. It assumes that pacific pledges and conciliatory rhetoric are obviously important to peace building but can be too tenuous. In the worst case, the rule of law imposes a network of institutions, mechanisms, and procedures that check sources of tension at an early phase, constrain the ability of any party to engage in violent or abusive action, and force an open process and a relatively level playing field. In the best case, when diligently nurtured, this system of accountability, conflict resolution, limits on power, and the airing and processing of opposing views—all undertaken through nonviolent

channels—becomes habit forming, reducing the likelihood of another civil war.

NOTES

1. Ramses Amer, Birger Heldt, Signe Landgren, Kjell Magnusson, Erik Melander, Kjell-Ake Nordquist, Thomas Ohlson, and Peter Wallensteen, "Major Armed Conflicts," in *SIPRI Yearbook 1993* (Oxford, U.K.: Oxford University Press, 1993), p. 81. This study by the Stockholm International Peace Research Institute defines a major armed conflict as a "prolonged combat between the military forces of two or more governments or of one government and at least one organized armed group, and incurring the battle-related deaths of at least 1,000 persons during the entire conflict." This figure is based on 1992 data. Comparable surveys for the subsequent two years found that not one of the conflicts meeting this definition in 1993 or 1994 was of the classical interstate variety.

2. "The proclamation of this constitution . . . not only did not stop lawless and arbitrary rule, but also served to camouflage it, allowing the torture and killing of innocent people while praising Stalin's law for all the people." Aleksandr Iakovlev, "Constitutional Socialist Democracy: Dream or Reality," *Columbia Journal of Transnational Law* 28 (1990): 117.

3. "Concluding Document of the CSCE Copenhagen Conference on the Human Dimension," June 29, 1990. The CSCE member-states explained that "the rule of law does not mean merely a formal legality which assumes regularity and consistency in the achievement and enforcement of democratic order, but justice based on the recognition and full acceptance of the supreme value of the human personality and guaranteed by institutions providing a framework for its fullest expression." *International Legal Materials* 29 (1990): 1305, 1306.

4. See, for example, Theodor Meron, "International Criminalization of Internal Atrocities," *American Journal of International Law* 89 (1995): 554.

5. "Statute of the International Tribunal for the Prosecution of Persons Responsible for Genocide and Other Serious Violations of

International Humanitarian Law Committed in the Territory of Rwanda and Rwandan Citizens Responsible for Genocide and Other Such Violations Committed in the Territory of Neighboring States, between 1 January 1994 and 31 December 1994," UN Doc. S/RES/955, annex, 1994. Even though the war in the former Yugoslavia was treated as international in nature, the international criminal tribunal created to address the abuses of that conflict stated its conviction that its jurisdiction also extends to crimes perpetrated in both internal and international conflicts. Annual Report, UN Doc. A/49/342-S/1994/1007, para. 19, 1994.

6. Boutros Boutros-Ghali, *An Agenda for Peace* (New York: United Nations, 1992), pp. 32–34.

7. See, for example, Melvin Small and J. David Singer, "The War-proneness of Democratic Regimes," *Jerusalem Journal of International Relations* 1, no. 4 (Summer 1976): 50–69; Rudolph J. Rummel, *War, Power, Peace*, vol. 4 of *Understanding Conflict and War* (Newbury Park, Calif.: Sage Publications, 1979); Rudolph J. Rummel, "Libertarianism and International Violence," *Journal of Conflict Resolution* 27, no. 1 (March 1983): 27–71; Bruce Russett, *Grasping the Democratic Peace: Principles for a Post–Cold War World* (Princeton, N.J.: Princeton University Press, 1993); Zeev Maoz and Nasrin Abdolali, "Regime Types and International Conflict, 1815–1976," *Journal of Conflict Resolution* 3 (1989): 3–35; and William J. Dixon, "Democracy and the Peaceful Settlement of International Conflict," *American Political Science Review* 88, no. 1 (March 1994): 14–32. Much of the research on the "democratic peace" finds its roots in the theory propounded nearly two hundred years ago by Immanuel Kant. But see, for example, Edward D. Mansfield and Jack Snyder, "Democratization and War," *Foreign Affairs* 74, no. 3 (May–June 1995): 79–97, suggesting that although fully democratized nations are less likely to go to war with one another, the process of transition to democracy exacerbates instability and thereby enhances the possibility of entry into conflict in the short term.

8. In 1994, to reflect a series of structural changes as the Helsinki process moved from a series of periodic meetings to a permanent organization with several institutional components and full-time staff, the name of the Conference on Security and Cooperation in Europe was formally changed to the Organization for Security and Cooperation in Europe.

9. "Concluding Document of the CSCE Copenhagen Conference on the Human Dimension."

10. For a comprehensive review of this category of rights, see Stanislav Chernichenko and William Treat, *The Administration of Justice and the Human Rights of Detainees: The Right to a Fair Trial—Current Recognition and Measures Necessary for Its Strengthening*, UN Doc. No. E/CN.4/Sub.2/1994/24, June 3, 1994; and William M. Cohen, "Principles for Establishment of a Rule of Law Criminal Justice System," *Georgia Journal of International and Comparative Law* 23 (Summer 1993): 269–287.

11. "General Framework Agreement for Peace in Bosnia and Herzegovina," annex 7, art. I, para. 3, and annex 11, November 21, 1995 (hereafter "Dayton Agreement").

12. For a comprehensive review of these standards, see *Human Rights and Elections: A Handbook on the Legal, Technical and Human Rights Aspects of Elections*, UN Doc. No. HR/P/PT/2, 1994.

13. *Human Rights Questions, Including Alternative Approaches for Improving the Effective Enjoyment of Human Rights and Fundamental Freedoms: Enhancing the Effectiveness of the Principle of Periodic and Genuine Elections—Report of the Secretary General*, UN Doc. No. A/48/590, November 18, 1993, pp. 23–35.

14. F. A. Hayek, *The Road to Serfdom* (Chicago: University of Chicago Press, 1944), p. 72.

15. Hernando de Soto, *The Other Path: The Invisible Revolution in the Third World* (Harper and Row, 1989), pp. 133–134.

16. Ibid., p. 253.

17. The author participated in a project undertaken by the Administrative Conference of the United States (a federal agency) to provide proposed draft legislation in this area to de Soto and his colleagues.

18. See, for example, Diane F. Orentlicher, "Settling Accounts: The Duty to Prosecute Human Rights Violations of a Prior Regime," *Yale Law Journal* 100 (June 1991): 2537–2615.

19. Dayton Agreement (see note 11 above), annex 7, art. I, para. 3(e).

20. Ibid., annex 7, art. VI.

21. At the time of this writing, the Rwandan government is considering a detailed proposal to address these issues.

22. *Human Rights and Democratization in Georgia* (hearing before the Commission on Security and Cooperation in Europe, Washington, D.C., March 28, 1995), p. 10 (testimony of Erika Dailey).

23. The Vietnamese-installed People's Revolutionary Council of Kampuchea did create a "revolutionary tribunal" which tried the two top leaders of the Khmer Rouge for genocide in absentia in 1979, but most observers characterized this as a show trial lacking in credibility. In interviews during the conflict in the former Yugoslavia, Bosnian Serb leaders quickly dismissed any possibility of their being brought to account for war crimes or genocide by pointing to the absence of any trials or punishment in these earlier cases.

24. Thomas Buergenthal, "The United Nations Truth Commission for El Salvador," *Vanderbilt Journal of Transnational Law* 27, no. 3 (October 1994): 503.

25. As Thomas Buergenthal, one of the three members of the commission, has noted, the "establishment of the Truth Commission marks the first time that the parties to an internal armed conflict, in negotiating a peace agreement, conferred on a commission composed of foreign nationals designated by the United Nations the power to investigate human rights violations committed during the conflict and to make binding recommendations. . . . National reconciliation is often difficult to achieve in countries trying to overcome the consequences of a bloody, internal armed conflict or an especially repressive regime without an appropriate accounting for or acknowledgment of past human rights violations. To the extent that the Truth Commission as an institution met the demands of the Sal-vadoran peace process, it has become a model the international community is likely to draw upon in the years to come." Ibid., pp. 501–502. In his article, Professor Buergenthal provides an insightful firsthand description and analysis of the Truth Commission and its relationship to the peace process.

26. *Report of the Commission on the Truth for El Salvador: From Madness to Hope*, UN Doc. S/25500, annex, 1993, p. 178.

27. A prime example of this was the commission's decision to publicly name those individuals it determined were guilty of particularly egregious abuses, even though the commission process had not afforded these individuals all the due process protections to which they would be entitled in a judicial proceeding. Had a credible Salvadoran criminal justice system been functioning, the commission might have kept all such names confidential in its report and instead turned them over to the authorities for prosecution. Ibid., p. 25; and Buergenthal, "United Nations Truth Commission," p. 522.

28. "Agreement between the Government of Guatemala and the Guatemalan National Revolutionary Unity on the Establishment of the Commission for Historical Clarification," June 23, 1994. Although the ultimate conclusion of the peace negotiations has yet to occur as of the present writing, the parties have already provided for the creation of this commission as one of the elements of the final agreement.

29. For a comprehensive overview of this issue, see Theo van Boven, *Study Concerning the Right to Restitution, Compensation, and Rehabilitation for Victims of Gross Violations of Human Rights and Fundamental Freedoms: Final Report*, UN Doc. No. E/CN.4/Sub.2/1993, July 8, 1993.

30. Government of Eritrea, Proclamation No. 55/1994, March 15, 1994.

31. Bereket Habte Selassie, "Constitution Making as a Historic Moment" (keynote speech to the International Symposium on the Making of the Eritrean Constitution, Asmara, Eritrea, January 7, 1995).

32. Interviews conducted by the author.

33. "Agreement Between the Government of Guatemala and the Guatemalan National

Revolutionary Unity on the Establishment of the Commission for Historical Clarification."

34. "Preliminary Report of the Independent Commission of Experts Established in Accordance with Security Council Resolution 935," 1994, p. 31.

35. "Draft Statute for an International Criminal Court, in Report of the International Law Commission on the Work of its Forty-Sixth Session," UN Doc. No. A/49/355, 1994, pp. 3–31. A UN-sponsored study currently under way on postconflict reconstruction proceeds from the same premise: "Wartorn societies inevitably depend to a large degree on external assistance for reconstruction. . . . The question of the relative role, responsibility and authority of external donors and actors, as opposed to local ones, in bringing about and maintaining peace and in rebuilding the country is one of the most important and most delicate questions. . . . External assistance, rather than being subsidiary to local efforts, tends to become a substitute, and worse, destroys local coping and resistance mechanisms and controls emerging local institutions and solutions. A large-scale foreign presence . . . is obviously not sustainable in the long term, neither politically for the local actors nor financially for the external ones. A policy of 'betting on the local' may in the short term be more laborious, less spectacular, and take more time, but in the long term may be the only realistic option." "Rebuilding Wartorn Societies: Problems of International Assistance in Conflict and Postconflict Situations," United Nations Research Institute for Social Development and the Programme for Strategic and International Security Studies of the Geneva Graduate Institute of International Studies (Geneva, August 1994), p. 17.

36. Ibid., p. 11.

41

The Challenge of Rebuilding War-Torn Societies

NICOLE BALL

In the fifty years since World War II, some 45 million people have perished as a result of armed conflict. The cost of these wars in terms of missed developmental opportunities is substantial. Although development may not come to a halt during conflict, what is possible to accomplish under conditions of war tends to be both very limited and constantly under threat of reversal.

Armed conflict not only retards the development process, but it also erodes a country's developmental foundation—as people are killed, abandon their homes and their livelihoods, or flee their countries; as infrastructure is damaged or destroyed; and as resources are diverted from routine maintenance of existing social and economic infrastructure. It has been estimated, for example, that Nicaragua sustained $5 billion in physical damages during the war between the government and the U.S.-supported Contras during the 1980s.[1] Fundamental requirements for economic growth—such as a state capable of furnishing public goods, of impartially protecting property rights, and of pro-viding a predictable, equitable legal framework for investment—are often beyond the capacity of postconflict governments.[2]

Beyond the physical destruction, armed conflict that arises out of internal power imbalances gravely complicates efforts to create an environment conducive to sustainable development. Some of the 150 post–World War II wars resulted from protracted decolonization struggles or external aggression. But in most cases, the wars fought since 1945 have had their roots in local conditions: political and economic inequality, ethnic and religious rivalry, and struggles to control the levers of power.

With the decline of the East-West military competition that fed many of these conflicts, some success—albeit often tenuous—has been recorded during the 1990s in efforts to halt prolonged civil wars: Angola, Bosnia-Herzegovina, Cambodia, El Salvador, Ethiopia and Eritrea, Haiti, Mozambique, Namibia, Nicaragua, and the West Bank and Gaza Strip. These societies are now facing the difficult challenge of making the transition from war-weakened econo-mies and highly polarized political and social relations to rejuvenated economies capable of providing the basic needs of all citizens and political systems that offer all social groups meaningful participation in the deci-sions shaping their future. Since the early 1990s, therefore, the international develop-ment community has faced a burgeoning number of requests from formerly warring parties for assistance in laying the founda-tion for renewed development in their coun-tries by helping to overcome the political, economic, and social ravages of war.[3]

This chapter examines a number of key issues that must be addressed both by gov-ernments of war-torn countries and by the members of the international development community as they confront the task of post-conflict rebuilding. It begins by describing the characteristics of postconflict countries. Then, since different responses are required of donors at different points along the road from war to peace, the phases of the peace process are mapped out. The third section describes the roles of donors, suggesting a new model for donor coordination in post-conflict environments; summarizes the pri-ority tasks for consolidating security and promoting economic and social revitaliza-tion; and discusses the critical importance of strengthening government capacity and sup-porting national reconciliation.[4] The chap-ter concludes by proposing several steps that donors and other members of the inter-national community might take to improve the quality of the assistance provided to war-torn societies.

CHARACTERISTICS OF POSTCONFLICT COUNTRIES

Civil wars occur in countries at different lev-els of political and economic development, with diverse political and social systems, and with varying physical and human resource endowments, cultures, and historical expe-riences. The paths these countries follow along the road from war to peace will diverge in many important respects, and the assis-tance provided by the donor community should reflect individual circumstances. At the same time, the experience of prolonged internal strife produces important similari-ties in the nature and function of civilian in-stitutions, the economy, and the security sec-tor in postconflict environments.

Institutional Characteristics

In countries emerging from prolonged civil war, the state is the dominant actor in virtu-ally all sectors, giving it the appearance of substantial capacity. In reality, however, the political institutions are weak and ill suited to the needs of participatory political sys-tems. Efforts to strengthen and restructure the state apparatus so that governments can fulfill roles critical to social and economic well-being are severely hampered by the postconflict political environment, which is characterized by a vigorous competition for power, often at the expense of any serious consideration of how that power can be used to resolve the critical issues confronting the country. It is also distinguished by limited legitimacy of political leaders, extreme po-larization, and a lack of consensus on the direction the country should follow.

The mechanisms that would mediate this acute struggle for power are either very weak or nonexistent. Politics becomes the means through which the parties hope to resolve the unfinished business of war. This situa-tion is further complicated by the low regard in which the state and political leaders are held, partly because of past policies and be-havior and partly because political parties are a mechanism for gaining control of the government in order to extract the economic benefits and privileges that have traditionally accrued to rulers.

The absence of a consensus on the direction the country should follow is especially acute when conflict ends without a clear winner. At best, the peace agreement signifies acceptance that armed combat must end. It rarely represents a common position on the appropriate strategies for the future. The normal realignment of parties that can be expected as authoritarian regimes and wartime coalitions disintegrate further distracts politicians from the business of governing. This failure to focus on substance and the tendency to view events through the lens of power politics impede the process of developing a national consensus on goals and on prioritizing those goals.

Addressing these problems—which is a prerequisite for lasting peace—is a lengthy process. Even when reforms are mandated by peace accords, their implementation is far from certain, since few willingly cede power and authority, particularly when they retain control over the instruments of violence. Civil-society institutions, which in democratic societies serve as one means of applying pressure to governments, are for the most part poorly developed in war-torn countries. Those that exist are often both inexperienced and highly politicized, seriously undermining their effectiveness.

Economic and Social Characteristics

Prolonged civil wars have significant economic repercussions. On the macro level, economic and social infrastructures—such as the systems for transport and communication, banking, health care, education, and agricultural research and extension—suffer extensive damage as a result of fighting or lack of maintenance. Indebtedness typically reaches very high levels, and unsustainably large military budgets constitute an additional drain on resources.

Since much of the fighting in civil wars occurs in the countryside, rural economies tend to be very hard hit. At the same time, the share of manufacturing, construction, transport, and commerce in gross domestic product declines during lengthy conflicts, while that of subsistence agriculture rises.[5] Consequently, wartime economies tend to contract significantly and trade declines, reducing the economy's capacity to generate the substantial investments required to restart production.

On the micro level, conflicts generate a variety of serious problems associated with human capital, land, and the environment. Human resource shortages are particularly severe in war-torn societies. Individuals with professional training such as doctors, lawyers, teachers, and government officials are often targeted during civil wars. In addition, educational opportunities decrease during wartime, as schools are closed or students opt to participate in the conflict rather than complete their studies. A second war-induced human resource problem is related to the gender imbalance that often results from prolonged civil wars. In Cambodia and Rwanda, for example, women account for more than two-thirds of the population.

Access to land can be limited by the effects of conflict. First, the increasingly widespread use of land mines renders considerable territory unusable until they are removed, often at great cost. Second, conflicts frequently result in multiple claims to land and other assets, which have the potential for long-term economic, social, and political dislocation. In the highly contentious political environment that characterizes war-torn societies, multiple claims are not easily resolved. Yet failure to address these problems adequately can discourage investors from making significant commitments to the economy, thereby slowing the economic recovery vital to the consolidation of peace and generating new conflicts.

Fragile ecosystems, notably hill and coastal regions, are often abused by war-related population movements, the overexploitation of natural resources to finance the war, and the destruction of physical infrastructure.[6] The effects of such war-induced environmental degradation are felt particularly strongly in the rural sector, especially by small producers.

Just as prolonged civil war undermines economic and institutional capacity, it also severely weakens the social fabric of a country, by destroying communities, engendering a culture of violence, creating a sense of impermanence and mistrust that makes collaboration on long-term efforts difficult to achieve, impoverishing the culture, and wreaking psychological trauma. An influx of returnees—refugees, the internally displaced, and former combatants—can create additional disruptions in local society.

The social indicators in many countries that have experienced lengthy civil wars were very poor prior to the armed conflict, and war-induced destruction and poverty cause even further decline. Thus, many postconflict countries record abysmal rates of infant mortality, illiteracy, malnutrition, access to clean water and sanitation facilities, school enrollment, and so on. A substantial number of the countries in the bottom 40 percent of the human development index of the United Nations Development Program (UNDP) owe their ranking in no small measure to the effects of war and conflict.

Security Characteristics

War-torn countries are characterized by bloated security establishments that can no longer be supported by peacetime budgets, by an armed opposition and paramilitary forces that need to be disbanded, and by an overabundance of small arms.[7] Depend-

ing on the terms of the peace agreement, new, peacetime armed forces may need to be created.

The mission of armed forces also needs to be redefined. The armed forces have been primarily concerned with internal security and have often controlled the police. As a result, the security forces are often professionally quite weak. The police are incapable of guaranteeing law and order, and the armed forces cannot adequately protect the country against external aggression. Creating a professional, apolitical police force is a particularly urgent and challenging task given the uncertain political and economic environment.

In addition, these countries lack a tradition of transparency in security affairs, and their militaries are unaccustomed to being held accountable by civilian institutions. Security forces often have a long history of human rights abuses, are among the dominant political institutions in society, and may be major players in the economic sphere as well.

Contextual Characteristics

Several additional characteristics of a post–civil war environment define the context in which war-to-peace transformations occur, and they can have an important influence on donor-host country interactions: the effects of war-induced isolation, the influence of peace treaties on the scope and pace of change, and the magnitude and urgency of the problems confronting postconflict countries.

Civil wars engender isolation at a variety of levels within society. The first is the isolation of the combatant, who is both ill-equipped for civilian life and has unrealistic expectations about life after discharge. A second form of isolation is manifest in the separation between the areas in which fighting occurred and the rest of the country. The people who make decisions that affect the former conflict zones or who are expected to implement peace-related programs in those areas often resided outside the conflict zones during the war and may be quite unfamiliar with conditions there. Finally, many countries are relatively isolated from the international system during civil war and, to varying degrees, face a learning curve for dealing with donors and other international institutions. The impact of each of these forms of isolation can be intensified by the monopoly that the parties to the conflict have over information, a monopoly that enables them to create and maintain significant distortions of the truth during the conflict, even into the postsettlement period.

In countries where conflicts have ended through negotiated peace agreements, the scope and pace of peace building are heavily determined by the provisions of the peace accords and the timetables established for implementing them. Institutional changes that might, under different circumstances, take considerably longer to implement—such as developing an electoral system, restructuring the security forces, and reforming the judicial branch of government—must occur on a specific timetable within a period of a year or two following the cessation of hostilities.

Finally, postconflict countries face a particularly large and complex set of issues that must be addressed rapidly. Resolving the myriad of economic, social, institutional, and political problems confronting war-torn countries takes on a heightened urgency because many of these problems were related to the conflict. Since the capacity to respond to these critical needs may be quite limited, it is difficult to address them as rapidly as the political situation requires. Failing to respond in a timely fashion may create the conditions for a return to organized violence.

PHASES OF THE PEACE PROCESS

Civil wars end either with the victory of one party or through negotiated settlement. Figure 41.1 shows the four phases that the peace process moves through in situations with no outright victor.[8] The length of each phase varies according to the situation in each country. Movement from one phase to the next is not automatic, as the numerous false starts toward peace in countries such as Angola, Liberia, and Rwanda so clearly underscore.

The first stage—conflict resolution—aims at reaching agreement on key issues so that fighting can be halted and social and economic reconstruction can begin. This stage has two components: negotiation and the formal cessation of hostilities.

The peace-building stage consists of two phases: transition and consolidation. Priorities during these two phases center on strengthening political institutions, consolidating internal and external security, and revitalizing the economy and the society. The major objectives of the transition phase are to establish a government with a sufficient degree of legitimacy to operate effectively and to implement key reforms mandated by the peace accords.

The first major objective of the consolidation phase is to continue the reform process. Many peace accords—such as those in Cambodia, El Salvador, and Mozambique —establish transition periods that last between one and two years and conclude with general elections.[9] It is becoming increasingly evident, however, that this time frame is too short for significant progress to be recorded on implementing even the reforms prescribed by the peace accords, let alone those that are necessary to consolidate the peace but are not mandated by the accords. Furthermore, the balance of forces within society can influence outcomes in ways that may be contrary to the terms or intent of

Stages	Conflict Resolution		Peace Building	
Phases	Negotiations	Cessation of hostilities	Transition	Consolidation
Main Objectives	Agreeing on key issues to enable fighting to stop	Signing peace accords Establishing cease-fire Separating forces	Establishing a government with adequate legitimacy to enable it to rule effectively Implementing reforms to build political institutions and establish security Inaugurating economic and social revitalization efforts	Continuing and deepening reform process Continuing economic and social recovery programs

Figure 41.1. The Peace Process in Countries with Negotiated Peace Settlements.

peace agreements.[10] Thus, implementing peace accords is often not completed when the transition phase formally ends and the peacekeeping mission is withdrawn.

In addition, while one might expect peace agreements to address the root causes of conflicts, the compromises necessary to produce a document acceptable to all parties generally leave many of the key issues wholly or partly unresolved. Thus, although the provisions of the peace accord may constitute necessary steps toward consolidating peace, they frequently neither deal adequately with the problems that led to the war nor create an environment conducive to resolving future conflicts peacefully. In consequence, the reform process must also be deepened during the consolidation phase to enable fundamental economic and social grievances to be addressed, whether they are enshrined in the peace agreement or not.

PEACE-BUILDING TASKS

The international community has come to recognize that warring parties not only require assistance in negotiating peace agreements, but they also urgently require assistance in consolidating the peace. As the catalogue of characteristics of war-torn societies suggests, peace building requires action on a wide variety of fronts. The parties' capacity to meet these demands is, however, severely constrained by institutional weaknesses, limited human and financial resources, and economic fragility; thus they have increasingly turned to the international community for technical assistance, financial advice, and political support, particularly during the transition phase.

Because of the profound mistrust and animosity generated by civil wars, the extreme institutional weaknesses characteristic of postconflict countries, and the destruction visited upon society and the economy by armed conflict, repairing the ravages of war is an arduous, complex, and lengthy process. It is therefore crucial that the international community provide sustained assistance throughout the peace process. There has been a tendency to assume that diplomatic and military efforts should be concentrated in the negotiation, cessation of hostilities, and transition phases, while financial and technical assistance should be concentrated in the transition phase.[11] In fact, the entire international community has a role to play throughout the peace process.

Donor Roles and Responsibilities

The degree and nature of donor involvement required varies from phase to phase. During the negotiation phase, a relatively modest amount of resources should be devoted to planning and to building collaborative relationships with the parties to the conflict. The speed with which events occur once peace agreements are signed argues very strongly in favor of donor involvement at the earliest possible moment in the peace process. In addition, institutions that do not maintain a presence in the country during the war should nonetheless maintain a watching brief so that their knowledge base is as up-to-date as possible once the peace process gets underway.

There are several reasons for donors to play a larger role during the negotiation process than they have previously. First, their involvement may encourage the parties to address relevant economic issues in a realistic manner. Second, it will facilitate the process of developing mechanisms for solving crucial economic issues that are likely to become politicized or ignored once the peace agreement is signed. Third, early donor involvement may help avoid raising unrealistic expectations about the amount and nature of assistance that will be forth-

coming from the donors to support the peace process. Managing expectations has become increasingly important as donor fatigue has intensified during the 1990s.

Fourth, early involvement will encourage the donors to engage in advance planning. Fifth, the donors may be able to provide encouragement to the parties in the form of tangible benefits deliverable upon signature of the accords. Finally, donors need to begin early on to build close working relationships with the parties to the conflict and other groups in society to facilitate complete compliance with the peace accords.

During the cessation of hostilities phase, donors can begin adjusting planning assumptions to reality and finalizing programs that need to begin early in the transition phase. Donors involved in demobilization efforts may need to begin providing assistance at this point to equip troop assembly areas. The focus during the transition phase is on helping the parties to the conflict comply with the terms of the peace agreements. It is in this phase that the heaviest demands on donor resources are made. During the consolidation phase, postconflict countries need assistance in maintaining the gains achieved during the transition phase and in deepening reforms in political institutions and the security sector. While the level of assistance will inevitably decrease at the end of the transition phase, a significant decline will reduce donor leverage.

Donor coordination. The need to act rapidly to take advantage of the relatively short-lived opportunities that the end of war creates for fundamental restructuring places a premium on aid coordination in postconflict situations. Coordinating aid is notoriously difficult, even in countries that are not moving from war to peace. In postconflict countries, both the need and the constraints are magnified. Also, political considerations that can hinder coordination efforts are more important in the aftermath of protracted civil wars.

The expansion of donor involvement in postwar environments has underscored the serious conflicts of interest that exist within development cooperation agencies and between these agencies and other members of the international community. Many officials in both bilateral and multilateral development cooperation institutions view peace building as a diversion of resources from "true" development objectives, rather than as a crucial foundation for sustainable development. Military establishments are often loath to see their resources applied to economic revitalization objectives. These and other turf battles that characterize the international community's involvement in postconflict situations are magnified by shrinking aid budgets.

The most critical point for donor coordination comes during the transition phase of the peace process, which is characterized by tight timetables, the need to incorporate new actors (such as the former armed opposition and a multilateral peacekeeping force), and a substantial increase in the size of the donor and NGO communities. The arrival of the multifunctional peacekeeping operation (PKO), which is intended to facilitate coordination, ironically often complicates the process. When PKOs operate under the auspices of the United Nations, there is an expectation that the head of the PKO, the special representative of the secretary general, will coordinate all UN activities.[12] In reality, the UN special representative tends to be more than fully occupied by the political and military aspects of the peace process and thus has little time to oversee its humanitarian aspects.

Different peacekeeping operations have had different relations with the donor community. The United Nations Operation in Mozambique was one of the first peacekeeping missions that attempted to maintain direct control over the coordination of humanitarian assistance by asking the UN Department of Humanitarian Affairs to establish a special unit—the UN Office of Humanitarian Assistance Coordination (UNOHAC)—within the peacekeeping mission. In doing so, it earned the resentment of the United Nations Development Program (UNDP), which thought that UNOHAC had usurped the mandate of its resident representative (who was also the UN resident coordinator), and of much of the bilateral donor community, which viewed UNOHAC as an unnecessary additional layer of bureaucracy. The noncollaborative working style of the first UNOHAC director only added to this resentment. Consequently, relations between many members of the local donor community and UNOHAC deteriorated sharply during 1993. The special representative's capacity to influence this situation was limited, in large part because he simply lacked the time to devote much attention to anything not directly related to creating an environment in which elections could occur.

The international community urgently needs to consider how much responsibility should be placed on the shoulders of the special representative or any individual with a similar assignment, and whether a person who is well suited to shepherd parties through a politically charged atmosphere to comply with the political and security provisions of the peace accords has either the time or the expertise to oversee the broader peace-building efforts. In countries that have a sufficiently large resident donor community when the conflict ends, it might be preferable to constitute a coordinating committee from among the resident donor missions, chaired by the UN resident coordinator (generally the UNDP resident representative) or another senior member of the donor community, such as the World Bank resident representative. For this model to function, all relevant institutions would have to give it strong and consistent support at the highest level.

A local coordinating committee could create a formal mechanism through which the institutions financing the peace accords could participate in shaping peace-building programs from the outset. Such a mechanism could significantly enhance cooperation during the very critical first phase of peace building. It could also facilitate the transition to the consolidation phase of the peace process. When UN peacekeeping operations have complete or significant authority over peace-building activities during the first phase of peace building, problems have arisen regarding the transfer of the PKO's responsibilities at the end of its mandate. Under the local coordinating committee model, the organizations responsible for peace-building activities would be the same during both the transition phase and the consolidation phase.

Whatever model is employed, it is imperative that the ability to coordinate on a sustained basis be enhanced. At present, donors are able to coordinate on issues of particular importance to them, such as assisting the electoral process in Mozambique, or when crises occur, such as the emergency program for provisioning Farabundo Marti Liberation Front (FMLN) combatants in assembly areas in El Salvador. These isolated instances of coordination generally do not extend to all peace-building activities. Failure to work collaboratively both undermines the effective use of increasingly limited resources and has considerable potential for damaging a war-torn society's prospects for long-term recovery.

Security Concerns and Social and Economic Needs

Peace-building activities can be divided into three broad categories:

- strengthening the institutional base,
- consolidating internal and external security, and

- promoting economic and social revitalization.

Since other chapters in this volume discuss many of the key components of building political institutions—democratization, human rights, and the rule of law, for example—the discussion in this chapter will focus on the international development community's support for consolidating security and revitalizing society and the economy. The most critical tasks confronting war-torn societies in these two areas are summarized below.

Reform of the security sector. Peace and security are necessary conditions for sustainable development. The termination of conflict offers a unique opportunity to address fundamental imbalances in the relationship between security forces and the rest of society, imbalances that contribute to conflict and insecurity and make sustainable development more difficult to achieve. In order to successfully consolidate internal and external security after the cessation of hostilities, it is necessary to:

- disband opposition forces, demobilize government troops, and disband paramilitary forces;
- redefine the doctrine and missions of the security forces, including clearly separating internal and external security functions, accepting the primacy of civilian control, and, where necessary, creating a civilian police force;
- evaluate officers from former security forces (including armed opposition) prior to inducting them into the postconflict armed forces or police force;
- institutionalize mechanisms to conduct formal assessments of security needs;
- restructure the security forces based on the new doctrines, missions, and budget realities, in all likelihood leading to additional downsizing;

- increase the transparency and accountability on security-related issues within the security forces, the executive branch, and the legislature;
- train civilian security analysts, both to staff government posts and to fulfill watchdog functions;
- reform military and police education systems to stress the goals of democratic societies; and
- terminate extralegal forms of recruitment to the security forces.

Assistance to meet these objectives has been provided by development cooperation agencies, foreign and defense ministries, and civilian law enforcement agencies.

Social and economic needs. Countries that have suffered prolonged civil wars face enormous economic and social deficits. Donors have been asked to help:

- assess the damage to economic and social infrastructure;
- offer technical assistance to plan and implement rehabilitation and reconstruction efforts;
- rehabilitate the basic infrastructure (health and education services, water and sanitation systems, banking system, roads, bridges, telecommunications facilities, marketplaces, irrigation systems);
- resettle the groups most affected by the war (refugees, internally displaced persons, soldiers and their dependents, female-headed households, orphans, and individuals suffering the physical and psychological wounds of war);
- revitalize communities, including strengthening local capacity to resolve problems through nonviolent means;
- reactivate the smallholder agricultural sector;
- rehabilitate export agriculture, key industries, and housing;

- generate employment (through credits, vocational training, management training, apprenticeships, microenterprise assistance);
- settle disputes over land and other assets;
- demine key areas; and
- implement environmental awareness and protection programs (soil conservation, flood control, reforestation, and wildlife management).

It is clearly not possible to address all the security and socioeconomic problems simultaneously. It is also not possible to develop a hard-and-fast priority list of peace-building activities, given the variations that exist among countries. Nonetheless, the experience of recent peace processes suggests that, in addition to the tasks specified in the peace accords (such as demobilizing excess troops or holding national elections), the activities summarized below should receive attention as early in the peace-building stage as possible. Although many of the priority peace-building tasks are familiar to development practitioners—strengthening household economies, infrastructure projects, and community development programs, for example—it is extremely important to underscore the fact that the context in which these activities are undertaken is very different from the context in which "normal" development proceeds. For example, aid personnel seeking to establish community development programs in Cambodia in the early 1990s often found that it took a year or two to reestablish a sufficient level of trust among community members to enable collaborative projects to be implemented. Additionally, some high-priority tasks such as consolidating civilian security are not usually part of the "development" mandate.

Early action is typically needed to help:

- provide a sufficient level of civilian security to enable economic activity to recover, to encourage refugees and internally displaced persons to return to reestablish themselves, and to persuade the business community to invest in the country;

- strengthen the government's capacity to carry out key tasks;
- assist the return of refugees and internally displaced persons;
- support the rejuvenation of household economies, especially by strengthening the smallholder agricultural sector;
- assist community recovery, in part through projects that rehabilitate the social and economic infrastructure;
- rehabilitate the infrastructure that is crucial to economic revival, such as major roads, bridges, marketplaces, and power generation facilities;
- remove land mines from major transport arteries, fields in heavily populated areas, and other critical sites;
- stabilize the national currency and rehabilitate financial institutions;
- promote national reconciliation; and
- give priority to social groups and geographic areas that are most affected by the conflict.

Because of the toll exacted by war on human and institutional resources, it can be extremely difficult to make rapid headway in war-torn countries. The benchmarks used to measure progress may need to be qualitatively different than those applied to "normal" development programs. For example, the resources invested in ex-combatant reintegration programs have often not been intended primarily to guarantee the beneficiaries' long-term livelihood. Rather, they are intended to provide former soldiers with a breathing space to adjust to civilian life and examine their longer-term options and to give them an incentive not to return to war.

Similarly, the performance targets for postconflict countries may need to be less demanding than for countries that have not experienced prolonged civil wars. In late 1995, virtually all of Mozambique's major donors—including the World Bank—took issue with the International Monetary Fund's demand that the Mozambique government make additional budget cuts in order to meet structural adjustment targets. In the view of the donors, the government had made a serious effort to comply with the terms of its agreement with the IMF and further belt-tightening could very well damage Mozambique's development prospects. The donors thus acquiesced to a government decision to increase the minimum wage by nearly 40 percent and called for significantly increased investment to stimulate the economy and generate employment opportunities.[13]

Restarting Government

One priority area that has generally not received the attention it deserves is that of strengthening governmental capacity. When wars end, governments are typically seriously overextended and unable to fulfill key functions and deliver critical services. The opposition—which retains control of its weapons through a portion of the transition phase—remains highly wary of the government. Opposition leaders frequently believe that the government will fail to deliver benefits in an equitable fashion and may seek to limit the government's role in peace-building activities in areas formerly controlled by the armed opposition. At the same time, there is significant pressure to implement peace-building programs rapidly to keep the peace process on track.

These conditions present donors with a dilemma. In order to implement peace-building activities, resources can either be channeled through the government or through nongovernmental bodies and international organizations. The sitting government is simultaneously the government and one of the factions contesting for political power in the period prior to the election. It aspires to fulfill all functions of government, but lacks adequate capacity and may have ceded certain responsibilities to a peacekeeping mission under the terms of the peace agreement. Consequently, donors may view bypassing the government as the desirable course to follow in the name of efficiency and impartiality.

This short-term strategy may, however, create significant problems in the medium- to long-term. If the donors postpone substantially strengthening institutions and building human-resource capacity until a new government is elected, and if they turn to nongovernmental bodies to design and execute peace-building programs, there is a strong probability that the postelection government will be no more prepared to carry out key tasks than was the preelection government. Indeed, since the transition phase generally lasts between eighteen and twenty-four months, governments may well reach the consolidation phase with their capacity for independent action severely weakened. Cambodia offers an excellent example of the hazards of this approach. Yet, as El Salvador demonstrates, the result of making the government the main vehicle of peace-building assistance can be equally problematic. The dangers are great that assistance will be used to gain electoral advantage at the expense of the groups most affected by the war, fostering a political environment inimical to reconciliation.

What is necessary—although extremely difficult to achieve in practice—is a nuanced approach that progressively strengthens the central government's capacity to carry out key activities while minimizing its ability to use resources for partisan political purposes.

As a first step, a donor-government forum could be created to generate dialogue on several central issues. First, it is important

to develop a policy framework within which peace-building activities will occur. Second, the key tasks for government, a priority ranking of these tasks, and the appropriate level of government to assume responsibility for each task must be identified. Third, methods of incorporating input both from the former armed opposition and, more broadly, from civil society must be developed. Dealing solely with the government will not foster political reconciliation. Nor will it support the development of responsible civil-society institutions. Finally, the specific roles that different donor agencies will play in helping to implement peace-building programs, during both the transition and consolidation phases of peace building, should be defined. Where appropriate, government agencies or public sector entities could be given the responsibility for implementing programs under close financial monitoring by donor agencies.

Where donors are already supporting activities designed to increase human-resource capacity, to strengthen public and private sector institutions, and to decentralize government, peace-building objectives should be incorporated to the greatest extent possible. An additional option—which would also support these objectives—would be to constitute local committees composed of government representatives, community leaders, local nongovernmental organization (NGO) leaders, business leaders, and other local citizens to provide input on a range of issues pertaining to designing and implementing specific peace-building projects.

There are, of course, problems associated with such local committees. They frequently require assistance in identifying priorities, and someone has to set the process in motion. Identifying committee members, ensuring that committees are reasonably representative, and helping members to prioritize community needs is undeniably time consuming. Nonetheless, in postconflict countries where this has been attempted, such as Cambodia, community groups have shown themselves to be capable of assuming full responsibility for managing community rehabilitation projects, including financial management. It may therefore be worth establishing one or two committees in different regions to test the concept's feasibility.

Governments should not be expected to meet all of society's needs, and donors should collaborate with NGOs and other representatives of civil society and with private enterprise. Strengthening NGOs can help build civil society, enhance opportunities for participation, and foster political reconciliation. Similarly, involving private enterprise in rehabilitation and reconstruction can augment its capacity to generate employment and provide goods and services at affordable rates. Therefore, identifying the areas in which private sector actors have an appropriate role to play is critical. At the same time, bypassing government simply because it is inefficient may further undermine its ability to fulfill the functions that governments must provide. The challenge, therefore, is to find the appropriate blend of actors and to determine what role each of them is best suited to play in the peace-building process.

National Reconciliation

Donors also need to give special attention to promoting national reconciliation. Signing a peace agreement engenders enormous expectations in war-torn countries. It is often assumed that reaching an agreement signals the successful resolution of all the outstanding issues between the parties and that society will be transformed once the terms of the accords have been fulfilled. In reality, peace agreements provide a framework for ending hostilities and a guide to the initial stages of postconflict reform. They do not create conditions under which the deep cleavages that produced the war are automatically surmounted. Successfully ending the divisions that lead to war, healing the social wounds created by war, and creating a society where the differences among social groups are resolved through compromise rather than violent conflict requires that conflict resolution and consensus building shape all interactions among citizens and between citizens and the state.

Collaborative modes of behavior need to be fostered, and donors have an important contribution to make in this respect. First, projects can be designed so that different groups are given an incentive to cooperate. Second, the parties should be encouraged to focus on solving specific problems, rather than using peace-building programs to continue their efforts to dominate each other.

Third, the way in which language is used can bring the parties together or keep them apart. For example, Salvadoran NGOs that had been FMLN supporters in wartime complained during the transition phase that the U.S. Agency for International Development (AID) still referred to "FMLN NGOs," while no one would think to label NGOs associated with the ruling Arena party or the moderate Christian Democratic Party (PDC) as "Arena NGOs" or "PDC NGOs." An external evaluation of AID's peace process programs recommended that NGOs should be classified according to area of expertise, geographic location, or administrative and financial management capacity, but "not by the politics of its board of directors."[14]

Collaboration can also be cultivated by guaranteeing all relevant groups a seat at the table—from the local level to the national level—when issues of importance to them are discussed. During the transition phase, the parties to a conflict are often consumed by the political in-fighting attendant upon the dissolution of wartime coalitions and are consequently unable to represent adequately the interests of ordinary citizens, particularly those who have been most affected by the war.[15] Supporting the empowerment of civil society can help mitigate the detrimental effects of this behavior by offering citizens the means to make their voices heard, especially at the local level.

An increasingly popular mechanism for helping societies overcome the trauma of many years of systematic violence is the truth commission. Although some postconflict governments have argued that linking individuals with specific acts of violence would impede reconciliation, others have decided that it is vital to know the truth about abuses on both sides of the conflict to avoid repeating the past and to promote national reconciliation. While the truth commission can be a useful mechanism for raising sensitive issues and helping society as a whole come to terms with past abuses, a number of conditions need to be met if it is to promote national healing.

First, the process needs to be internally generated and supported, as in South Africa. Second, the role of external actors must be carefully circumscribed. They can provide information on different models and their strengths and weaknesses; they can also offer material support, such as lending office space or office equipment. External actors should not, however, drive the process or play a major role in the process, as in El Salvador. Finally, admissions of guilt and involvement in illegal practices many years after formal inquiries in Argentina and Chile suggest that truth commissions may be only the first step in a multiyear, multistep process. Governments need to be prepared to see the process through to its conclusion, and the donors should strongly encourage them to do so.

NEXT STEPS

While the international community has gained valuable experience since the beginning of the 1990s in addressing the needs of postconflict countries, a number of steps still need to be taken, particularly by the development cooperation agencies, to improve the effectiveness of assistance to support economic and social revitalization and consolidate security. These policy recommendations include the following measures.

- First, senior managers of development cooperation agencies should transmit two messages to their staff. An immediate return to traditional development activities in postconflict environments is neither possible nor desirable. It is important to recognize that peace building is not a distraction from development efforts, but a critical condition for development in postconflict environments.

- Second, donors should take steps to lengthen the time frame for postconflict peace-building activities. The current two- to three-year planning cycle is insufficient to foster the adoption of policies and patterns of behavior that will minimize disparities among social groups and maximize the opportunities for the peaceful resolution of disputes.

- Third, in order to maximize the effectiveness of the external resources invested in peace building, a division of labor urgently needs to be established, both between the international development organizations and other members of the international community and among development cooperation agencies. Institutional turf battles, which continue to prevail over collaboration in many instances, undermine the effectiveness of resources invested in peace building and damage the long-term recovery prospects of war-torn societies. Mechanisms must be developed to reinforce the preference for institutional collaboration, a message that senior managers need to deliver consistently and forcefully.

- Fourth, donors should use informal policy dialogue and formal performance criteria to press the parties to the conflict to comply fully with the obligations they have assumed under the terms of the peace agreement. This pressure should be exerted, however, in a manner consistent with the peace accords, rather than to the partisan advantage of the donors themselves.

- Finally, donors should make every effort to ensure that peace-building activities enhance national reconciliation. Two key objectives in this regard are to create conditions in which the parties to the conflict focus on solving specific problems, rather than using peace-building programs to continue their efforts to dominate each other, and to increase the opportunities for participation by civil society.

In view of the institutional weaknesses of postconflict societies, donors need to give top priority to building institutional capacity in both the public and civil sectors as early as possible. In the public sector, the objectives should be to identify key tasks of government, to set priorities for those tasks —establishing time frames and assigning responsibility to the appropriate government agency—and to determine the assistance the government will need to carry out these tasks independently and in an apolitical manner. Objectives in the civil sector should be to enhance the ability of relevant organizations to evaluate policy and to develop and implement programs in their respective spheres of activity.

Postconflict reconstruction has captured the attention of the international development community. As the international community begins to translate its growing experience into operational guidelines, it must not lose sight of the fact that the responsibility for moving from war to peace rests ultimately with the people and the govern-

ments of the countries in conflict. Donor strategies need, therefore, to give particular emphasis to creating an environment in which reconstruction and reconciliation can take root and to building the capacity of both the public and private sectors of wartorn countries to take advantage of a climate favorable to the consolidation of peace.

NOTES

1. Alejandro Martínez Cuenca, *El Comportamiento Inversionista en Nicaragua* (Investment behavior in Nicaragua), No. 13 (Managua: FIDEG–Friedrich Ebert Stiftung, February 1994), p. 8. An earlier study estimated that some $1.4 billion in production and property losses occurred in Nicaragua between 1980 and 1988 as a result of the war. Benjamin L. Crosby, "Central America," in *After the Wars: Reconstruction in Afghanistan, Indochina, Central America, South Africa, and the Horn of Africa*, ed. Anthony Lake, Overseas Development Council U.S.–Third World Policy Perspectives No. 16 (New Brunswick, N.J.: Transaction Publishers, 1990), p. 111.

2. Of course many postconflict governments were unable to fulfill these functions satisfactorily prior to the conflict, but it is nonetheless clear that their capacity is further eroded by lengthy wars.

3. The international development community consists of bilateral and multilateral development assistance agencies (such as the United States Agency for International Development and the United Nations Development Program), international financial institutions (such as the International Monetary Fund and the World Bank), and development-oriented nongovernmental organizations. The word "donors" is used interchangeably with the terms "international development community," "development assistance agencies," and "development cooperation agencies."

4. Some of the key components of peace building are "demilitarization, the control of small arms, institutional reform, improved police and judicial systems, the monitoring of human rights, electoral reform, and social and economic

development." *Supplement to an Agenda for Peace: Position Paper of the Secretary General on the Occasion of the Fiftieth Anniversary of the United Nations*, A/50/60*, S/1995/1*, January 25, 1995, para. 47.

5. Paul Collier, "Introduction," in *Some Economic Consequences of the Transition from Civil War to Peace*, ed. Jean-Paul Azam, David Bevan, Paul Collier, Stefan Dercon, Jan Gunning, and Sanjay Pradhan, Policy Research Working Paper 1392 (Washington, D.C.: World Bank, December 1994), pp. 4–5.

6. See, for example, Republic of El Salvador, Ministry of Planning and Coordination of Economic and Social Development, *National Reconstruction Plan: Executive Summary* (San Salvador, February 1992), p. 3.

7. The security establishment consists of the armed forces (army, navy, air force), intelligence forces, police, and paramilitary forces.

8. These phases do not apply to countries where civil wars end with the victory of one party. However, the problems confronted by the government and society in these countries are very similar to those faced by countries where wars end with negotiated settlements.

9. The Dayton Accords, which govern the peace process in Bosnia-Herzegovina, envisioned elections occurring within six to nine months of the signing of the agreement in December 1995.

10. For example, in mid-1993, a former El Salvador Army officer was appointed to head the National Civilian Police, which was expressly forbidden by the peace treaty.

11. Development assistance agencies are by no means the sole source of financial and technical assistance. Ministries of finance, foreign ministries, and private enterprise also have a role to play.

12. *An Agenda for Development: Recommendations—Report of the Secretary General*, A/49/665 (New York: United Nations, November 11, 1994), p. 15, para. 89. In Bosnia-Herzegovina, a somewhat different model was employed. The terms of the Dayton Accords required that the NATO-led peacekeeping operation collaborate with a civilian entity headed by a high representative who was responsible for coordinating political, social, and economic reconstruction efforts, but who was not a representative of any organization and thus had limited institutional support.

13. "The IMF in Africa: Affray," *Economist*, October 28, 1995, p. 46.

14. Development Associates, *Final Report: Evaluation of the Peace and National Recovery Project, El Salvador* (Arlington, Va.: Development Associates, January 1994), pp. V-10, V-11, VII-8.

15. It might also be argued that the parties to a conflict do not represent the interests of many noncombatants during the conflict.

Conclusion

CHESTER A. CROCKER AND FEN OSLER HAMPSON WITH PAMELA AALL

It is our careless modern assumption that as trade borders fall and systems of communication advance, the countries of the world will be brought closer together. Nothing could be further from the truth. The end of the Cold War has seen such a loosening of bonds and allegiances, and such a dying of forbearance on the part of the oppressed, that the old and new worlds are fragmenting as never before.

John Le Carré, "The Shame of the West"

The end of the Cold War has shattered several myths and foreign policy shibboleths. One was that much of the conflict in the world had its origins in the U.S.-Soviet rivalry and that with the end of that rivalry, the prospects of international peace and security would improve as international trade and global interdependence grew and former communist states embraced democracy and capitalism. As the quotation from John Le Carré indicates, it is not working out that way. Some commentators also believed that international organizations would play a new role in international relations and that the United Nations, in particular, would finally come to fulfill the original vision of its founders. These hopes were set back in Somalia, Bosnia, and Rwanda, where the United Nations was caught between tepid, even ambiguous, support from its key members and "mission impossible" demands for humanitarian relief that could neither provide adequate comfort to victims nor end a succession of brutal, genocidal civil wars. Still others feared that the United States would either retreat into isolationism or become the world's global supercop. Neither has occurred. The United States remains the world's only superpower, but it has exercised its power and leadership erratically, unsteadily, and seemingly with scant regard for the unique opportunity of this current moment of systemic transition.

623

But is Le Carré right in suggesting that events after the end of the Cold War have crushed the hope that cooperation or concerted action by the international community in response to conflict is possible? Is the present characterized by constantly shifting patterns of action that lead only to a random pattern of reaction? Or is some kind of formal or informal understanding emerging that will help international organizations, states, and nonstate actors respond to the forces of chaos threatening Le Carré's old and new worlds? While the answers to these questions remain unclear, this volume identifies many ways to respond constructively to conflicts of different types. It singles out the unique capabilities of many actors, including the United States, great powers, the United Nations, regional organizations, coalitions of the willing, private conflict resolution groups, and nongovernmental organizations (NGOs) engaged in humanitarian work. It isolates the successes and failures among a variety of intervention attempts and methods and suggests broad policy prescriptions that might increase the likelihood of successful action. All the discussions of possible responses, however, reflect an underlying assumption that effective choices about the nature and timing of the response are based on an informed understanding about the sources of conflict.

CHANGING SOURCES OF INTERNATIONAL CONFLICT

International relations in the post–Cold War world are exhibiting many different trends and tendencies. Although the forces of ethnonationalism and religion are on the rise, great-power politics and rivalries over spheres of influence have not ended; on the contrary, they are coming back in strength. Witness China's flexing of military muscle over Taiwan and Russia's efforts to assert its influence in the "near abroad." Power politics and traditional forms of coercion in international relations continue to exist alongside centrifugal forces that threaten domestic stability in an increasing number of states.

This book does not make the claim that international conflict is shifting downward from the international or systemic level to the domestic as some suggest.[1] Rather, it argues that there are new forces operating alongside more familiar conflict sources at both the domestic and the international levels, forces that are increasing the potential for conflict at both the intrastate and interstate levels in ways that almost certainly will have long-term, systemic implications. What are some of these factors, and what are their consequences for international peace and security?

The first factor is the proliferation, on a global scale, of weak, internally divided states. Mohammed Ayoob documents the problem of the "failed state" in his chapter. He points out that in much of Asia, the Middle East, and Africa, internally divided states (often lacking political legitimacy) are unable to provide basic services and security for their citizenry, let alone adhere to democratic principles and the rule of law. As these weak states fragment, the potential for local conflict increases as different ethnic and social groups become involved in conflicts over territory or as small states fall prey to more powerful neighbors seeking to expand their influence and power in the region. State weakness is compounded when governments fail to keep up with the demands placed upon them by the international system, local constituencies, and burgeoning younger generations.

These factors have both structural and nonstructural roots. The breakup of the Soviet empire (discussed by Mark Katz in his chapter) has changed the structure of the international system, not only by ending bipolarity but also by creating a multiplicity of new states in Central Europe and Central Asia. Many of these new states suffer from serious internal ethnic or religious divisions and are weak political entities as a result of years of communist and Russian rule. In addition, the Soviet collapse brought with it the demise of a global system that had supported the status quo in areas previously decolonized by the Europeans. At the same time, poor economic performance, rapid population growth rates, and a lack of social cohesion are sources of state failure in these and other regions of the globe.

A second factor, related to the first, is the growing importance of the politics of identity in international relations. The recent changes in the structure of the international system (resulting from the collapse of the Soviet Union) have made identity more, not less, salient in international politics, as has the end of communist ideology and rule in some countries, like the former Yugoslavia. These changes have weakened social and political cohesion and undermined the artificial unity of the old order. The concept of national self-determination based on ethnicity, language, and culture also appears to have acquired greater saliency, as evidenced by the growing strength of separatist movements in Europe, North America, Asia, and Africa. Janice Gross Stein and Ted Robert Gurr discuss the nature and causes of ethnopolitical conflict in their respective chapters. They caution about the dangers of viewing ethnicity in overly reified terms. Both underscore the fact that the origins and dynamics of ethnopolitical conflict are highly complex, subjective, and situationally dependent, and they both stress the role of political elites in manipulating ethnic tensions and creating the conditions that lead to conflict.

A third factor is religious and cultural militancy, which is often a direct response to growing levels of economic interdependence and contact with western society. Although cultural assertiveness does not necessarily lead to militancy, religious militancy is present in many societies. Sometimes this militancy takes on a nationalistic form, as David Little argues in his chapter; sometimes it is transnational and aimed at promoting violence both at home and abroad. Violent, intolerant movements appear to be on the rise in all religions and regions of the globe, even though efforts to tie religious identity to violence, in Little's words, ultimately may be "ineffective and self-contradictory."

A fourth factor is the impact of environmental degradation as a result of population pressure on scarce resources and large-scale population movements across borders. Research in this area is new and the linkages between population growth and displacement, resource use and scarcity, and migration and acute conflict are complex and poorly understood. Astri Suhrke examines the claim in the literature on security and the environment that pressures on the environment are new sources of conflict in international relations. Her conclusions suggest that environmentally induced migrations have not always led to conflict and that distress migrations induced by environmental degradation have been gradual rather than sudden. However, situations of acute displacement may occur in coastal and ecologically vulnerable regions where there are large concentrations of people, particularly if global warming becomes a reality.

A fifth factor is the growing potential of scarce resources—renewable and nonrenewable—to contribute to conflict in international relations. Richard Bissell argues that resources have been central to international conflict throughout history, even though they have often been in the background. He asserts that resources (renewable or nonrenewable) are rarely the principal cause of conflict in international relations; rather, they emerge as an adjunct to other issues, such as national pride and other political and economic considerations. However, the balance of strategic value of certain resources, like oil and natural gas, can sometimes shift quite rapidly and unexpectedly, thus contributing to conflict. Also, so-called renewable resources—like fish, clean air, and fresh water—may lead to conflict in international affairs as stocks dwindle or are polluted and states try to assert property and ownership rights. Interest in the concept of "sustainabilty" is partly based on the desire to avoid social and political conflict.

A sixth factor affecting international security is the globalization of the world economy and the rapid increase in the transborder flows of goods, services, capital, and technology, the subject of Ted Moran's chapter. Moran challenges the traditional assumption that countries linked by trade and other economic ties are more likely to have peaceful relations than those that pursue mercantilist policies by erecting barriers to trade and investment. Globalization, Moran argues, is imposing adjustment costs on firms and workers and sharpening the debate over disparities in wealth and income as a result of external competition. As their economies adjust, great powers may be less willing to accept the burdens and costs of leadership. Major industrial states may also be less willing to offer their support for trade liberalization, preferring instead to erect preferential regional trade barriers. Although the commitment to look for multilateral solutions to common economic problems remains strong, there is still the risk that domestic political pressures will push elites to favor "beggar-thy-neighbor" trade policies that would have profound long-term consequences for political stability and international security.

A seventh factor is the impact of new military technology on regional security as discussed by Geoffrey Kemp. Longer missile and aircraft ranges, together with the acquisition of technologies to build weapons of mass destruction, now allow regional powers to project their capabilities on an increasingly wide, even global, scale. Accurate lethal weapons, better reconnaissance, and a wide range of information-based military systems are revolutionizing conventional warfare, dramatically changing target structures and raising the risks of preemptive attacks in a crisis. Megaterrorism—efforts to take hostage or kill thousands of people—could be on the rise, and there are also concerns about "cyberterrorism," involving attacks on electronic systems that could wreak havoc on financial markets and modern military communications systems. Kemp argues that although the prospects of a nuclear holocaust involving superpowers have greatly diminished with the end of the Cold War, the probability that nuclear warheads and other weapons of mass destruction might be used in regional conflicts or terrorist acts rises as more groups gain access to these technologies. He notes that these developments are changing the character of warfare and changing the way various actors think about the use of force in international relations

Viewed together, these seven factors point to a world that is becoming increasingly fragmented and less orderly. The number of conflicts in the world has not declined with the end of the Cold War and remains steady (at about fifty). Although many of today's conflicts are national in nature and origin, they tend to engulf their neighbors and expand in scope. Revolutionary changes in global communications and technology, coupled with the transnational movement of ideas and people, also mean that few conflicts are local or even regional anymore.

These factors and trends are not intended as an exhaustive list of "new" conflict sources, still less as a full catalogue of all major sources. Jack Levy's opening chapter reminds us of the humbling variety of explanatory theories identifying sources at all levels of political interaction. But these seven "new" factors represent—by themselves—a full agenda of issues and challenges; more will surely be added. An early candidate to join the seven as we near the twenty-first century is the proliferation of international criminal enterprises and trading mafias. Such organizations represent a direct challenge to local, regional, and global order. By dealing in everything from drugs and stolen automobiles to illegal migrants, protected species, and illicitly plundered natural resources, they subvert weakened states and live off war. In the fragile context of peace negotiations and postsettlement peace building, they can often be found prolonging the agony. This is becoming an important frontier for conflict research.[2]

What is particularly striking about the new and long-standing sources of conflict is the way they interact at the systemic, state, and substate levels of analysis, often in ironic and perverse ways. Instability at the substate level has the potential to spill across borders, as transnational alliances form between warlords and international arms dealers and social and religious movements intent on exploiting the situation for their own special purposes. Neighboring regional powers can be drawn into a conflict if it is seen as a threat to regional stability or internal domestic stability (or both). The international media and NGOs also have the capacity to catapult the plight of refugees and victims of war crimes onto the agenda of policymakers and the public, turning a hitherto "domestic" problem into an international one.

The immediate end of the Cold War and the successful resolution of a number of key disputes in the early 1990s led many to conclude that any problem, no matter how distant, was amenable to positive intervention by the United Nations and other international peacemakers. The world subsequently witnessed the effects of overreaching by the Permanent Members of the UN Security Council, which placed too much on the United Nations' platter: too many assignments, too many loosely defined military tasks, and a too-ambitious concept of military capability. Then, the inevitable consequence of the overload became clear and the pendulum began to swing sharply the other way. As a form of global triage takes hold, political actors around the world are learning that "their" conflict will just not make the cut, now that western officials and policy analysts are preoccupied with the dilemmas of "mission creep" and "exit strategy." That trend is reinforced by growing concerns about the direction of events in Russia and the stability of the East Asian balance.

What effect will this apparent lack of response from external sources have on local actors in scores of conflict-torn places like Tajikistan, Kashmir, Iraq, and Sudan? Should the world resign itself to the fact that global enmity and chaos will be around for a long time? The essays in Parts II through IV in this volume argue that it should not. In particular, people should look for opportunities to prevent and avoid conflict and should examine opportunities for intervention when timely action has a chance of defusing hostilities and de-escalating conflict. As Stanley Hoffmann argues elsewhere, "Even a small number of successful cases of restoration of internal peace or of radical healing may help contain or even roll back chaos and anomie, and build into the new and volatile world system we now face a capacity for collective management it desperately needs."[3]

INTERVENTION AND INTERNATIONAL ORDER

To many, the term intervention implies the pursuit of national objectives. The changes, however, in the nature of global conflict and a growing sense of moral urgency, partly driven by modern communications, have added humanitarian emergencies and protection of human rights as well as peacekeeping and enforcement missions to the list of objectives for which international military intervention is a distinct option.

More important, intervention can take many forms other than coercive action. Diplomatic and unofficial intervention offer many avenues for preventing, managing, and resolving conflict, including preemptive actions, such as well-planned demobilization efforts, official mediation, private track-two activities, economic incentives, and development work. If they are to contribute to international order and to reducing the level of chaos in the world, all effective interventions require committed and sustained leadership, careful definition of mission, adequate support (both political and material), coordination among strategies and players, and flexibility. Chester Crocker's chapter provides an overview of the strategic and operational issues involved in intervention and highlights the relationship and continuity between military and nonmilitary approaches covered by Parts II and III of this volume, respectively. Taken together, these two sections show that there is a growing interchange and cross-fertilization between traditional security analysts and those in the fields of peace studies and conflict analysis.

Military power is crucial to international order. However, we must also recognize that governments no longer have a monopoly on the use of force and instruments of violence. The only effective response to the growing range of actors who have the capacity to threaten the security of nation-states and international order is to strengthen governmental and intergovernmental capacity and structures to deal with the various threats described above, both military and nonmilitary.

The chapters by Richard Haass, Alexander George, Eliot Cohen, and James Goodby discuss the appropriate roles of force, coercive diplomacy, and collective security in contributing to international order. Haass, George, and Cohen argue that force remains a key instrument of diplomacy and order in international relations. Some interventions will be military, even though the type and range of instruments will vary enormously depending upon the situation involved. Some forces will be needed for deterrence purposes, whereas others will be used for coercion, peacekeeping, war fighting, interdiction, and humanitarian and rescue missions. The role of the military in many operations, however, is changing insofar as the military is being used to support other groups and is facing new rules of engagement that do not sit comfortably with traditional military doctrine. Noticeable particularly in humanitarian crises, this change in the role of the military is as new a trend as is peace enforcement.

When should the United States intervene and how should force be used? George places this continuing dilemma for U.S. policy in a historical context, showing that the recent debate in the United States about when and how to use force in Bosnia and elsewhere is not new. George argues that "efforts to deter adversaries from serious encroachments on one's interests and those of friendly states often require the ability to make threats that are sufficiently credible and potent enough to dissuade the adversary. This is especially true when sanctions and other nonviolent measures are expected to be or prove to be an ineffective backup to diplomacy." Low-level conflicts pose unique challenges. The problem is not so much a lack of credible military capabilities, but how and whether to escalate the use of violence (or to make credible threats to do so) to achieve political aims. George discusses the ingredients that go into an effective military strategy (short of outright war) and the essential tools of coercive diplomacy.

Nonetheless, at a time when military budgets are shrinking, as Eliot Cohen argues, the choices about when to use force are becoming harder. Advances in technology of the kind discussed above are also changing the way force is likely to be used. Haass advances the provocative thesis that any kind of military intervention by U.S. forces must pass four general tests: (1) the intervention must be achievable, (2) the benefits of intervention must outweigh the costs, (3) the ratio of costs and benefits must compare favorably with that of other options, and (4) military intervention must advance identifiable interests, whether they are tangible or matters of principle (for example, the sanctity of borders). In discussing different scenarios for military intervention, it is important not to lose sight, in Cohen's words, of the fact that "American military power will serve as the indispensable security partner of particular states, the leader of coalitions seeking to thwart or contain particularly aggressive powers, and as the guarantor of the stability of the international system itself."

Although the United States will sometimes be required to use force unilaterally, collective interventions that share risks and burdens among "coalitions of the like-minded" are more likely to gather public and international support. James Goodby argues that collective security should be redefined to make it useful to policymakers considering the use of force. Collective security need not be at the global level, nor should it be dedicated solely to preserving the status quo. Goodby believes that collective security has a better chance of working in a regional setting among like-minded nations than at a global level. The Organization for Security and Cooperation in Europe (OSCE) is positioned to conduct long-term conflict resolution in Europe, as is the North Atlantic Treaty Organization (NATO). In the case of the Yugoslav crisis, Goodby notes that there was collective action early on, but he concludes that the great powers did too little, too late, thereby discrediting for many people the principle of collective security. But even though the concept of collective security is flawed, Goodby argues, it is better to base international security on shared principles and rules about enforcement and collective action than to leave the task of maintaining order to the prerogative of great powers that may seek to reestablish spheres of influence and revert to old-style, balance-of-power politics.

Jack Maresca's case study of the conflict over Nagarno-Karabakh and Ruth Wedgwood's chapter on regional and subregional organizations together highlight the different strengths and weaknesses of regional entities in international conflict management. They underscore Goodby's more general proposition that regional security response mechanisms are an attractive political option in conflict management, particular in the areas of early warning and crisis prevention. Not all regional entities are similarly effective, however. A lack of resources, weak organizational capacity, and ineffective leadership are problems for some.

HUMANITARIAN INTERVENTIONS AND PEACEKEEPING

As a result of problems experienced in Somalia and the Balkans, there has been a sharp curtailment of UN peacekeeping operations. This curtailment begs the question of when force should be exercised in peacekeeping and humanitarian interventions. Barry Blechman, Adam Roberts, and Denis McLean address this issue. Blechman describes the post–Cold War circumstances that persuaded governments to overload the UN agenda in order to be seen as "doing something." As the results of this habit became clear, we have seen a new "realism" in U.S. approaches to peacekeeping that is based, in Blechman's words, on "mustering pragmatism as the first line of defense against the political impulse to intervene." Roberts places the UN peacekeeping debate in its historical context, discussing central concepts such as consensual versus hostile environments, impartiality versus peace enforcement, and military rules of engagement. McLean, a veteran peacekeeper, builds on this foundation by underscoring the modest, but not insignificant, place of peacekeeping in the policy arsenal of smaller powers as well as medium and major powers. He suggests that participants in the U.S. debate might profit from closer familiarity with the record and a cost-benefit analysis of how peace operations play into the national interests.

Debates about national interests in our age take place in the context of modern communications and mass media. In fulfilling their legitimate role, the media have played a key part in dramatizing humanitarian disasters and, consequently, in shaping public support for or against intervention. But, as Ted Koppel and Warren Strobel note, they are not alone in manipulating tragedy for public consumption. NGOs and government officials often use the media to dramatize the human costs of bitter civil strife in regions like the Balkans and the Horn of Africa. These dramatizations can fire up public support, but there is often little attempt to educate the public about what it will take in blood and treasure to end these wars. The influence of the media increases dramatically when there is a policy vacuum and an absence of leadership.

Humanitarian relief workers have traditionally maintained a policy of neutrality in their dealings with societies in conflict. Richard Betts, however, relates humanitarianism to political and diplomatic strategy, asserting that no intervention is impartial, since every intervention has an effect on the local balance of forces. There is no such thing as a "pure" or neutral humanitarian peace operation. This argument parallels Crocker's thesis that all forms of intervention should be part of broader political strategies for conflict management, settlement, or resolution. This theme is sustained and elaborated in Hampson's discussion of the postsettlement implementation phase and his discussion of the ingredients of successful postconflict peace-building enterprises.

In terms of institutional capacities, there are ongoing efforts to establish a clearer division of effort and responsibility between the United Nations and other actors and organizations for peacekeeping and humanitarian relief efforts. There is now more focus, as noted above, on strengthening regional capacities in peacemaking and peace building and on not throwing an overstretched, much criticized, slowly changing United Nations at every problem that arises. NATO's role through the Implementation Force (IFOR) in Bosnia is part of this general effort to create a better division of labor among international organizations.

Nongovernmental organizations responding to humanitarian catastrophes are also becoming more sensitive to the impact of their activities on conflict situations. Mary Anderson discusses the opportunities for NGO intervention in civil wars and the mechanisms through which NGO interventions can exacerbate conflict through the misuse and misallocation of resources. There are interesting parallels between Anderson and Betts in this regard, since both argue that no intervention—whether by a governmental or nongovernmental actor—can be politically neutral in terms of its impact on the relationship between warring parties.

Pamela Aall argues that the effect of NGO exposure to violent conflict has changed the role that they play in fragile or warring societies. At times, NGOs have responded to humanitarian crises generated by civil and regional conflicts by serving as a vital supplement to government functions. They have also learned to work in coordination with a large group of key players, including international organizations and international military coalitions dedicated to supporting humanitarian responses. Finally, the changing nature of conflict and the challenges of humanitarian relief have sparked a recognition of NGOs' roles and functions, not only in inadvertently exacerbating conflict, but also in preventing, managing, and resolving conflict.

NONCOERCIVE OFFICIAL AND UNOFFICIAL INTERVENTIONS

Reflecting contemporary ideas about effective policy options, discussions during the Cold War revolved around the use of force and military instruments. Post–Cold War thinking has moved far afield from these narrow responses. The recognition that the use of force is so costly—and that even low-threshold military interventions like peacekeeping have had a decidedly mixed record of success—has led to growing attention to noncoercive approaches to conflict management, prevention, and resolution. Part III of this volume focuses on these instruments, not only identifying various diplomatic, political, economic, and social approaches, but also discussing the appropriate relationship between action and actors in order to prevent and manage international conflict. Many of the chapters in this section of the volume identify and delineate new strategies and tools of conflict management. Together, they authoritatively define and demarcate a wide array of potential response strategies and tactics that are available to policymakers (inside and outside of government) engaged in conflict management and prevention. At the same time, the contributors in this section are careful not to oversell a particular

method or technique of intervention. Some of the approaches and concepts are problematic; others are theoretically attractive, but they have yet to prove themselves as successful techniques of conflict management.

It is now generally recognized that most conflicts have a life cycle of their own, characterized by various phases or stages (see the chapters by Lund and by Zartman and Touval). These include a period of rising tension between or among the parties, followed by confrontation, the outbreak of violence, and the escalation of military hostilities. In the postagreement or postsettlement phase, a conflict may go through several de-escalatory phases as well, such as a cease-fire, followed by a formal settlement, rapprochement, and eventual reconciliation. There is an important psychological element to these various phases or stages. Perceptions among different factions or warring sides typically harden during the escalatory phase of the conflict. As elites whip up public sentiment to build political support for violence and military action, perceptions are less amenable to contradictory information about the other side's intentions. Worst-case assumptions about enemy motivations and beliefs are prevalent. The possibilities for peacemaking in conflicts that are escalating decline correspondingly. However, once a conflict has reached a military plateau (or what some have called a "hurting stalemate"), new windows of opportunity may emerge as the parties becoming increasingly disenchanted with their military options and begin to consider other ways out of the conflict, such as negotiations and a political settlement.

At the low end of the conflict spectrum, parties may be more able and willing to handle disputes on their own or to consider interventions by local entities or nonstate actors—what are sometimes referred to as second-track or multi-track diplomatic initiatives and interventions. There may also be a strong desire to keep international organizations and great powers out of the conflict, because intervention by these actors may further complicate the issues and raise the stakes in ways that further polarize attitudes. This is not to say that great-power intervention is undesirable or should be avoided at lower rungs on the escalatory ladder; sometimes, a dramatic intervention is just what is needed to bring the parties to their senses and avert violent conflict. At the upper end of the conflict ladder, however, official first-track diplomacy and intervention by great powers is generally required to bring the parties to the negotiating table—what is sometimes referred to as "mediation with muscle." This is because nonstate actors and other bodies often lack the requisite resources and leverage to change the cost-benefit calculus of warring parties in favor of a negotiated settlement.

That being said, it is important to recognize that effective third-party intervention depends upon the capabilities, leverage, and linkage of third parties to the conflict and the extent to which they see themselves as stakeholders. Third parties that are not stakeholders and have limited resources may have greater difficulty exercising leverage than those that have the capacity to bring something to the table. Moreover, the availability of entry points to the conflict may well be a function of where the conflict stands on the rungs of the escalatory/de-escalatory ladder. Peacemakers and intervenors must recognize that different techniques and tools are appropriate to different levels of violence or escalation to the conflict. Some tools may work better than others, depending upon the nature of the particular conflict and the number of parties and issues in the dispute.

Which tools work best, when, and where are subject to continuing debate among conflict analysts. Given the obvious difficulties of intervention at high levels of vio-

lence, increasing attention is now being paid to preemptive actions that can avert violent conflict. The concept of preventive diplomacy, in particular, has received an extraordinary amount of attention over the past several years. In spite of this attention, the concept remains vague and poorly understood. Michael Lund's chapter on the tools of conflict prevention clears away much of this underbrush, providing a systematic assessment of this concept and its policy implications. Lund argues that preventive diplomacy—under whatever name—has a long and distinguished record in international relations and that critiques of the concept are misplaced if they assert that effective conflict prevention is not possible. Lund argues that preventive diplomacy can work in situations of ethnopolitical conflict, democratizing "transition" conflicts, and "new democracy" conflicts. However, leadership is required not only from those officials at the top levels of government and international agencies, but also those at lower levels in the field who have both the ability to watch for and the authority to respond to budding crises in time to keep them from escalating.

International conflicts are also the subject of third-party mediation, as occurred most recently in the U.S. role in bringing about the Dayton Accords in Bosnia. Mediator functions in a conflict typically do not involve the use of force; the purpose of mediation is to bring the warring sides to the table through political means. Mediation is often viewed as third-party assisted negotiation, a process in which the mediator becomes the third part of a negotiating triad. Mediation can be undertaken by great powers, small powers, international organizations, regional organizations, and even nonstate actors. William Zartman and Saadia Touval explore how mediation can serve as a catalyst to negotiation in their essay, assessing the strengths and weaknesses that different mediators bring to this task. Their discussion of this important subject is complemented by substantial case studies of mediation in the Middle East and Africa in the chapters by Kenneth Stein and Samuel Lewis and by Donald Rothchild, respectively. In many cases, there is simply no substitute for competent and sustained official mediation.

There is a growing body of empirical evidence showing that international negotiation processes are affected, in varying degrees, by cross-cultural differences. The success of a negotiation may well depend on the sensitivity different parties show to the cultural background of their negotiating partners. Raymond Cohen discusses the problems of "cross-cultural dissonance" in negotiation and offers a number of recommendations on how to avoid some of the cross-cultural pitfalls into which diplomacy can sometimes stumble.

Official mediation efforts tend to dominate headlines and capture public attention, but many successful peacemaking programs have taken place among private citizens and groups. These unofficial, nongovernmental activities increase contact and mutual understanding between hostile communities; allow moderates in societies in conflict to meet in neutral circumstances that do not compromise their standing with their own groups; and encourage grassroots support for peacemaking and peace-building efforts. In his chapter, Harold Saunders discusses how small groups of Israelis and Palestinians outside of government laid the ground for talks that were moderated by the Norwegian foreign minister, the late Jorgen Johann Holst, and led to the formal agreement between the Israeli government and the Palestine Liberation Organization. He also describes a similar initiative in Tajikistan to help end the civil war in that country. Saunders makes the important point that the political environment for initiating

and implementing peace agreements can be "shaped by citizens outside government, often interacting in complementary ways with those inside" and that the unofficial efforts can support the official process. This complementary role is also the subject of chapters by Herbert Kelman and by Eileen Babbitt and Tamra Pearson d'Estrée, who discuss how scholar-practitioners can bring together politically influential parties in what Kelman calls interactive problem-solving workshops, the goal of which is "to transfer the insights and ideas gained from these interactions into the political debate and decision-making processes in the two communities." The interactive problem-solving approach has provided important new insights into the broader processes of conflict resolution in international relations. Kelman's pioneering work in this area demonstrates the importance of reciprocity in conflict resolution and identifies the strategies and tactics that third parties can employ to change relations between warring sides to one based on mutual reassurance.

CONSOLIDATING THE PEACE

Those who take the view that humanitarian intervention and multilateral peace operations in ethnic, nationalistic, and separatist conflicts are likely to be ineffective (at best) and counterproductive (at worst) should consider the fact that many successful interventions have helped end violent conflict. In places as diverse as Namibia, Mozambique, El Salvador, Cambodia, and Nicaragua, the international community has played a crucial role in ending military hostilities, defusing tensions, and laying the groundwork for peace. The final section of this volume examines the problems of rebuilding war-torn societies and the kinds of intervention strategies that are appropriate to consolidating the peace. The chapters by Fen Hampson and Caesar Sereseres underscore the point that "success" in the context of peacemaking and peace building is inherently relative and is usually tied to the availability of viable third-party implementation mechanisms—governmental as well as nongovernmental. The settlements that seem to work are those nurtured by continuous and sustained third-party leadership, mediation, problem solving, and peace building.

The tension between conflict resolution and democratic governance is the subject of Pauline Baker's chapter. She argues that "the need to create power-sharing arrangements with rival factions and to include all major groups in a peace process often clashes with the need to bring human rights abusers to justice, establish political legitimacy, establish the rule of law, and build new state structures that can earn the confidence and trust of the people." The dilemma is as old as Thomas Hobbes' efforts to grapple with this problem in *Leviathan*. But whereas Hobbes came down firmly on the side of order and the preservation of peace and security, some contemporary peace-building initiatives have attempted to institutionalize the search for justice and human rights alongside basic security and order. In both Bosnia and Rwanda, the peace settlements were accompanied by the establishment of internationally mandated war crimes tribunals; in El Salvador and South Africa, truth commissions were established by the locally legislated authority to investigate and publicize the most flagrant violations of human rights. Neil Kritz discusses how the rule of law can be advanced in war-torn societies to advance the cause of justice and lay the foundations for a more peaceful, democratic order based on the principles of human liberty and "due process."

The bigger challenge of laying the foundations for democracy is the subject of Joshua Muravchik's chapter. Much recent scholarship on the relationship between civil society and democratic institutions suggests that there is a vital link between sturdy civic institutions, including the norms and networks of civic engagement, and the performance of representative government.[4] Not only is civil society important to democracy, but it also has a vital role to play in consolidating the peace process in societies making the transition from war to peace. Muravchik discusses the importance of engaging civil society in building peace and the need to lay democratic foundations early on in the peace process.

In the final chapter of this volume, Nicole Ball examines the role of the international development community in the task of post-conflict rebuilding. Her chapter begins by describing the economic and social conditions that exist in postconflict countries; she then identifies the responses that are required of donors at different points along the road from war to peace. In discussing the priorities for donors in postwar reconstruction efforts, Ball argues that coordination of donor efforts is fundamental to success, even though it is difficult to achieve because of turf battles among competing donor agencies. Like other authors in this volume, Ball highlights the importance of political leadership in social and economic reconstruction efforts and the need to channel scarce resources into those areas of activity where they can have the greatest impact.

CONVERGING FIELDS

This volume of essays is intended to serve as a bridge between the fields of security studies and conflict and peace studies. At the same time, it seeks to capture the dynamic interaction between them. The contributors include those who would consider themselves hard-headed realists and those who would not. As editors, we have been struck by evidence of cross-fertilization and even convergence among what were previously warring schools of thought. That is a reassuring impression, supporting the conclusion that practitioners and theorists across the spectrum have much to learn from one another.

The collective experience reflected in this volume shows that the challenge of global chaos requires a concerted and vigilant approach. By this, we mean that there are no grounds for complacency about the future of violent conflict. Globalization and interdependence mean that the "butterflies of chaos" are increasingly being felt on a worldwide scale. Some delicate equations can be affected by conflict in places of modest strategic importance, while major power shifts appear to fuel change dynamics that often lead to fresh or renewed conflict along the fault lines and shifting plates of an even more complex international system.

The evidence, in other words, suggests that the world will not become more peaceful if leaders permit old systems of security and order to fall away and be replaced by nothing. By the same token, the world will get neither security nor peace unless people learn how to analyze international conflict. Each set of concerns is becoming the context for creative thinking about the others, and each contains the seeds for fresh thinking about how to use most effectively the tools and strategies for preempting, responding to, managing, settling, and eventually resolving pieces of chaos.

This volume is not intended to serve as a veiled apologia for "interventionism" or still less for a post–Cold War "triumphalism" that imagines the omniscience of a few strong nations. Nor do we view the challenge of responding to various forms of chaos as an easy one. Rather, this volume is

intended as an antidote to those arguments that view many contemporary conflict phenomena as essentially intractable and, at the same time, conveniently peripheral, so that the leading nations of the global system no longer need to exercise leadership. Those arguments will almost certainly compound the chaos by encouraging its promoters and by fostering a "Look, Ma, no hands" line of thinking in major world capitals. Such arguments encourage passivity, defeatism, and just plain sloppy foreign policy. A sober grasp of the range of problems and conflict sources, as well as of tools and strategies of response, is needed for the coming period. We hope this volume contributes to that endeavor.

NOTES

1. See, for example, John A. Vazquez, James Turner Johnson, Sanford Jaffe, and Linda Stamato, eds., *Beyond Confrontation: Learning Conflict Resolution in the Post–Cold War Era* (Ann Arbor: University of Michigan Press, 1995).

2. See Jonathan M. Winer, "International Crime in the New Geopolitics: A Core Threat to Democracy," in *Crime and Law Enforcement in the Global Village*, ed. William F. McDonald (Cincinnati, Ohio: Anderson Publishers, forthcoming).

3. Stanley Hoffmann, "The Politics and Ethics of Military Intervention," *Survival* 37, no. 4 (Winter 1995–96): 49.

4. See, for example, Robert D. Putnam, *Making Democracy Work: Civil Traditions in Modern Italy* (Princeton, N.J.: Princeton University Press, 1993); and Robert D. Putnam, "Bowling Alone: Declining Social Capital," *Journal of Democracy* 6, no. 1 (January 1995): 65–78.

Abbreviations

AID	Agency for International Development [U.S.]	DOP	Declaration of Principles [Israeli-Palestinian agreement]
ANC	African National Congress [South Africa]	EC	European Community
APEC	Asia-Pacific Economic Cooperation [group]	ECOWAS	Economic Community of West African States
ASEAN	Association of South East Asian Nations	EU	European Union
AWACS	airborne warning and control system	FBIS	Foreign Broadcast Information Service [U.S.]
CBN	chemical, biological, and nuclear [weapons]	FMLN	Farabundo Marti Liberation Front [El Salvador]
C3I	command, control, communications, and intelligence	FSLN	Frente Sandinista [Nicaragua]
		FUNCINPEC	National Front for an Independent, Neutral, Prosperous, and Cooperative Cambodia
CEAO	West African Economic Community	GATT	General Agreement on Tariffs and Trade
CIAV	International Commission for Support and Verification [Nicaragua]	GCC	Gulf Cooperation Council [Persian Gulf]
CIS	Commonwealth of Independent States	GDP	gross domestic product
CND	Campaign for Nuclear Disarmament	GRIT	graduated reduction in international tension
CNN	Cable News Network	ICJ	International Court of Justice
COPAZ	National Commission for the Consolidation of Peace [El Salvador]	ICRC	International Committee of the Red Cross
		IFOR	Implementation Force [Bosnia]
CSCE	Conference on Security and Cooperation in Europe [now OSCE]	IGO	international governmental organization

INF	intermediate-range nuclear forces	R&D	research and development
IPCC	International Panel on Climate Change	RENAMO	National Mozambican Resistance
JSTARS	Joint Surveillance and Attack Radar System	RFE	Radio Free Europe [U.S.]
MFO	Multilateral Force and Observers [Sinai]	RMO	regional multilateral organization
MPLA	Popular Movement for the Liberation of Angola	SADF	South African Defense Forces
NAC	North Atlantic Council	SEATO	Southeast Asia Treaty Organization
NACC	North Atlantic Cooperation Council	SIPRI	Stockholm International Peace Research Institute
NAFTA	North American Free Trade Agreement	START	Strategic Arms Reduction Talks
NATO	North Atlantic Treaty Organization	SWAPO	South West African People's Organization [Namibia]
NGO	nongovernmental organization	UNAVEM	United Nations Angola Verification Mission
OAS	Organization of American States	UNDOF	United Nations Disengagement Observer Force [Golan Heights]
OAU	Organization of African Unity		
ODC	Overseas Development Council	UNDP	United Nations Development Program
OECD	Organization for Economic Cooperation and Development	UNEF	United Nations Emergency Force [Sinai]
OIC	Organization of the Islamic Conference	UNFICYP	United Nations Force in Cyprus
ONUC	United Nations Operation in the Congo	UNHCR	United Nations High Commissioner for Refugees
ONUCA	United Nations Observer Mission in Central America	UNICEF	United Nations Children's Fund
ONUMOZ	United Nations Operation in Mozambique	UNIFIL	United Nations Interim Force in Lebanon
ONUSAL	United Nations Observer Mission in El Salvador	UNITA	National Union for the Total Independence of Angola
OSCE	Organization for Security and Cooperation in Europe (formerly CSCE)	UNITAF	Unified (later changed to United) Task Force [Somalia]
PDD	Presidential Decision Directive [U.S.]	UNIKOM	United Nations Observation and Monitoring Force in Kuwait
PF	Patriotic Front [Rhodesia/Zimbabwe]	UNOHAC	United Nations Office of Humanitarian Assistance Coordination
PFP	Partnership for Peace		
PKO	peacekeeping operation	UNOMIG	United Nations Observer Mission in Georgia
PLO	Palestine Liberation Organization		
PRC	People's Republic of China	UNOSOM	United Nations Operation in Somalia

UNPA	United Nations protected area	UNTSO	United Nations Truce Supervision Organization [along Israeli borders]
UNPREDEP	United Nations Preventive Deployment Force [Macedonia]	USAID	United States Agency for International Development
UNPROFOR	United Nations Protection Force [in the former Yugoslavia]	WEU	Western European Union
		WTO	World Trade Organization *or* Warsaw Treaty Organization
UNTAC	United Nations Transitional Authority in Cambodia	YATAMA	United Nations of Yapti Tasba—The Sacred Motherland [Nicaragua]
UNTAG	United Nations Transition Assistance Group [Namibia]	ZANU	Zimbabwe African National Union
		ZAPU	Zimbabwe African People's Union

Credits

The following publishers have generously given permission to reprint or adapt previously published work. The numbers refer to chapters in this book.

3. Adapted from the author's chapter in *Between Development and Destruction: An Enquiry into the Causes of Conflict in Post–Colonial States,* ed. Rupesinghe, Sciarone, and van de Goor (London: Macmillan, 1996).

11. Reprinted by permission of Simon and Schuster, Inc., from *Diplomacy,* pp. 17–28. Copyright © 1994 by Henry A. Kissinger.

12. Adapted from an earlier version presented at the Aspen Institute's conference on "Managing Conflict in the Post–Cold War World" on August 3, 1995, in Aspen, Colorado.

13. Parts of this chapter first appeared in *Intervention: The Use of American Military Force in the Post–Cold War World* (Washington, D.C.: Carnegie Endowment for International Peace, 1994). They appear here with the permission of the Carnegie Endowment for International Peace.

14. From Gordon A. Craig and Alexander L. George, *Force and Statecraft: Diplomatic Problems of Our Time,* 2nd ed. (Oxford, U.K.: Oxford University Press, 1990). Copyright © 1990 by Oxford University Press, Inc. Reprinted by permission.

17. This essay was prepared as a report to the Carnegie Commission on Preventing Deadly Conflict, Washington, D.C., and appears here with the permission of the commission. The views expressed are the author's and do not necessarily reflect those of the commission.

19. Adapted from "The Intervention Dilemma," *Washington Quarterly* 18 (Summer 1995): 63–73.

20. Adapted from *Survival* 36, no. 3 (Autumn 1994): 93–120, with permission from Oxford University Press.

21. Adapted from *Peace Operations and Common Sense,* Peaceworks No. 9 (Washington, D.C.: United States Institute of Peace, 1996).

22. Adapted from *Foreign Affairs* 73, no. 6 (November–December 1994): 21–33. Copyright © 1994 by the Council on Foreign Relations. Used by permission.

24. Reprinted from the *New York Times,* July 1, 1994.

29. Adapted from *NGOs and Conflict Management,* Peaceworks No. 5 (Washington, D.C.: United States Institute of Peace, 1996).

30. Adapted from "Mediation: The Role of Third-Party Diplomacy and Informal Peacemaking," in *Resolving Third World Conflict,* ed. Sheryl J. Brown and Kimber M. Schraub (United States Institute of Peace Press, 1992), pp. 239–261. It draws on the authors' previous work, especially their chapter in *Mediation Research,* ed. Kenneth Kressel, Dean G. Pruitt, and Associates (San Francisco: Jossey-Bass, 1989).

31. Adapted from *Making Peace Among Arabs and Israelis: Lessons from Fifty Years of Negotiating Experience* (Washington, D.C.: United States Institute of Peace, 1991).

34. Adapted from "Social-Psychological Contributions to Peacemaking and Peacebuilding in the Middle East," *Applied Psychology: An International Review* (forthcoming).

United States Institute of Peace

The United States Institute of Peace is an independent, nonpartisan federal institution created by Congress to promote research, education, and training on the peaceful resolution of international conflicts. Established in 1984, the Institute meets its congressional mandate through an array of programs, including research grants, fellowships, professional training programs, conferences and workshops, library services, publications, and other educational activities. The Institute's Board of Directors is appointed by the President of the United States and confirmed by the Senate.

Chairman of the Board: Chester A. Crocker
Vice Chairman: Max M. Kampelman
President: Richard H. Solomon
Executive Vice President: Harriet Hentges

Board of Directors

Chester A. Crocker (Chairman), Research Professor of Diplomacy, School of Foreign Service, Georgetown University

Max M. Kampelman, Esq. (Vice Chairman), Fried, Frank, Harris, Shriver and Jacobson, Washington, D.C.

Dennis L. Bark, Senior Fellow, Hoover Institution on War, Revolution and Peace, Stanford University

Theodore M. Hesburgh, President Emeritus, University of Notre Dame

Seymour Martin Lipset, Hazel Professor of Public Policy, George Mason University

Christopher H. Phillips, former U.S. ambassador to Brunei

Mary Louise Smith, civic activist; former chairman, Republican National Committee

W. Scott Thompson, Professor of International Politics, Fletcher School of Law and Diplomacy, Tufts University

Allen Weinstein, President, Center for Democracy, Washington, D.C.

Harriet Zimmerman, Vice President, American Israel Public Affairs Committee, Washington, D.C.

Members ex officio

Ralph Earle II, Deputy Director, U.S. Arms Control and Disarmament Agency

Toby Trister Gati, Assistant Secretary of State for Intelligence and Research

Ervin J. Rokke, Lieutenant General, U.S. Air Force; President, National Defense University

Walter B. Slocombe, Under Secretary of Defense for Policy

Richard H. Solomon, President, United States Institute of Peace (nonvoting)

MANAGING GLOBAL CHAOS

The text of this book is set in Caslon; the display type is Gil Sans. Hasten Design Studio designed the cover, and Joan Engelhardt and Day W. Dosch designed the interior. Helene Y. Redmond of HYR Graphics did the page makeup, and Kenneth Allen was in charge of computer cartography. The book was printed by Port City Press of Baltimore.